A *Backwoods Home* Anthology:

The Twenty-second Year

Published by
Backwoods Home Magazine
P.O. Box 712
Gold Beach, OR 97444

ISBN: 978-1-62440-083-4

Editor: Dave Duffy

Senior Editor: John Silveira

Art Director: Don Childers

Contributors: *Dorothy Ainsworth, Massad Ayoob, Jared Bedke, Richard Blunt, Jackie Clay-Atkinson, Kim Dieter, Dave Duffy, Ilene Duffy, David Eddings, Carolyn Evans-Dean, Michael D. Faw, Doug Fluckiger, Winston Foster, Linda Gabris, Enola Gay, Sylvia Gist, Cynthia Hummel, Tony Jakacky, Tanya Kelley, Tom Kovach, David Lee, Patrice Lewis, Vernon Lewis, Joyce Lindsey O'Keefe, O. E. MacDougal, Mary Marvin, Ed Mashburn, Ian McCollum, Len McDougall, Margaret Mills, Kai Moessle, Tim Murphy, Cindi Myers, Melissa Nelson, Robin Nessel, Raymond Nones, Dani Payne, Rose Peck, Dale Petry, Connie Rabun, AJ Reissig, Habeeb Salloum, Charles Sanders, Leon Shernoff, John Silveira, Tim Thorstenson, Howard Tuckey, Jim Van Camp, Jim Van Sant, Claire Wolfe, Jeff Yago, Alice Yeager*

Cover Art: Don Childers

Layout Design and Proofreading: Lisa Nourse, Rhoda Denning, Jessie Denning, Ilene Duffy

Contents —

Issue Number 127

Issue Number 128

Issue Number 129

Issue Number 130

Issue Number 131

Issue Number 132

Backwoods Home magazine

practical ideas for self-reliant living

Jan/Feb 2011
Issue #127
$5.95 US
$7.50 CAN

Sitting pretty as the economy tanks

Canned bacon
Chicken tractor
Meatless meals
Gun semantics
Eric's house, part 4

www.backwoodshome.com

D. CHILDERS

My view

California conservatives missed a chance to speak up for "all" constitutional rights

As much as the results of the November elections gave me some hope for the future, the most important voter initiative, California's Proposition 19 which would have legalized marijuana in that state, went down to defeat. It was a missed opportunity for conservatives to join with liberals, independents, and Tea Party activists to pass a measure that could have had a major impact on rolling back federal government power, especially its power to assert its will over states and individual constitutional rights.

Passage of Proposition 19 would have forced a legal showdown between the nation's most populous state and the feds, since President Obama's attorney general, Eric Holder, had vowed to enforce federal drug laws even if the measure passed. But conservatives were scared off by unfounded and exaggerated fears about the evils of marijuana, proving once again that conservatives are no better than liberals when it comes to protecting "all" constitutional rights, but prefer instead to protect only the ones they cherish.

Marijuana legalization, even legalization of all drugs, is no longer just a liberal cause to make it legal to get high. If you're going to be for the *U.S. Constitution*, you have to be for all the rights it contains, and that includes the right to do with your body as you want. There is no prohibition in the *Constitution* about drugs and there is no power in it that grants the government the power to ban anything, whether it be guns or drugs. You may feel drugs are the worst evil, but that's how some liberals feel about guns. It makes no sense to make a "constitutional exception" for either.

This issue is bound to come up again, and soon, because the tide in the country is clearly in favor of legalizing marijuana, and maybe even some other drugs made illegal by the government's War on Drugs, if only to eliminate the violence and taxpayer expense that attend the drug war. It's a cause that conservatives need to embrace. And it's a cause, I think, that has the power to bring an out-of-control federal government to its knees.

Let's take a look at what marijuana illegalization, and the rest of the War on Drugs, has cost us.

It is because of the police and court excesses allowed under the federal government's War on Drugs that the police can now stop us on the street or in our vehicle without probable cause, seize our property without ever charging us with a crime, and imprison our children if they dare do what youths in every age have done, namely, experiment with mind-altering substances such as drinking a beer or smoking a joint. It is a rite of passage that has been taking place for thousands of years, and no law will change this aspect of human nature.

Dave Duffy

If you are against drugs, that's fine. I am too! After experimenting with marijuana in my youth, I realized that drugs are by and large a handicap that destroys people's lives when overused, just like alcohol is. But the War on Drugs, just like alcohol Prohibition of the 1920s and 30s, has undermined our individual freedoms to a level that borders on the destruction of the *U.S. Constitution*. It's time to do with drugs what we wisely did in 1933 with alcohol's Prohibition — take them out of the criminal arena and put them into the health arena where they can be monitored and where people with problems can get help. It works with alcohol and cigarettes, although there are those among us who want a return to alcohol prohibition and want to outlaw cigarettes. I suppose they'll go after saturated fat next, another substance that is bad for people if overused.

As a result of the federal government's War on Drugs, corruption among our police and public officials is nearing the levels seen in the Prohibition era of the 1920s and 30s. Not only that, our prisons are overflowing with our youth, the very people the feds said the War on Drugs was meant to protect. And violence on an unprecedented scale has been unleashed on our southern border as Mexican gangs vie for control of the drug trade with the United States.

Notice I used the phrase "drug trade." It might as well be an illicit trade because the importation of drugs into America is almost as profitable for America's criminal justice system as it is for international drug gangs and dealers. It keeps them employed! If drugs are legalized, the big losers will be both the drug cartels and the American criminal justice system. There will be significant layoffs among government bureaucrats when America's prisons are emptied of our youth, when attorneys no longer have easy drug cases involving teenagers smoking pot, and when the cops will be restricted to going after real criminals whose belongings they won't be able to seize and sell to add to their own coffers.

The damage caused to our Constitutional freedoms thanks to the War on Drugs is appalling. To understand why we as a formerly free people have allowed this to happen, it helps to go back through the history of alcohol and drug prohibition.

The War on Drugs is pretty much a rerun of alcohol's Prohibition Era, which held its reign of terror in the United States from 1921 to 1933. Both had their beginnings in the minds of moralists and those would-be do-gooders in society who are determined to change people to fit their view of how people should behave.

Women provided the muscle to ban alcohol in 1921. With the help of suffrage which empowered them to vote, they were the main supporters of the Anti-Saloon League, the most powerful political pressure group ever in American history. In an effort to reform their men and free them from the evils of booze, the moralists and their army of suffragettes succeeded in 1921 in passing the Eighteenth Amendment, which outlawed alcohol. It unleashed a wave of criminal violence unlike anything in the nation's history and caused the suspension of major freedoms in the *U.S. Constitution* to enforce it. It took the wholesale corruption of the nation's police forces, judges, and politicians, along with an out-of-control gangster war to control the illicit alcohol trade (gangster income exceeded U.S. Government income) to convince the public, in 1933, that Prohibition didn't change a man's determination to have a drink. It was a catastrophic lesson for the thousands imprisoned, left dead, or poisoned by bathtub gin. The end of Prohibition calmed American society like the passage of a great storm, but much of the erosion of freedoms remained permanent.

America's War on Drugs is the sequel to Prohibition, only modern day do-gooders didn't go to the trouble to pass a Constitutional amendment. Drug banning initially began in 1914 when religious missionaries who had been to China's opium dens got Congress to pass the Harrison Act, which outlawed opiates. But it wasn't until the 1960s that government got serious. I was in my 20s then and everyone my age experimented with drinking beer and smoking pot. Others who admit they at least experimented with marijuana during their younger years include former presidents Bush and Clinton, current President Obama, and notables such as Sarah Palin, Newt Gingrich, and Al Gore.

Just like in the 1920s, the moralists went to work. No one was willing to redo Prohibition, so instead they went after drugs, especially marijuana, the demon weed that was turning our kids into crazed and violent dope addicts. Nothing could have been further from the truth, according to testimony from former New York narcotics officer Joe McNamara, who has testified and written extensively on the subject and states, "There is no record of anyone dying from marijuana or committing a murder under its effects."

But the government crackdown began, and it gradually built up until, in 1972, President Nixon declared a War on Drugs. The price for an ounce of marijuana increased tenfold almost overnight, drugs went underground, and police arrests, incarcerations, and the corruption of officials began its dramatic rise just like in Prohibition days. At a 1999 Cato Institute Conference on Drugs, McNamara said, "... in hundreds of thousands of cases, police officers violated their oath to uphold the *Constitution* and often committed perjury so that the evidence would be admitted. The practice is so prevalent that the term 'testilying' is often substituted in police jargon for 'testifying.'"

The main difference from Prohibition is that drugs became the choice of youth. Alcohol still provided the high for the older generations, but marijuana was an irresistible lure for youth. The more government cracked down, the more young people lit up. It became a rite of passage.

It has now been 38 years since Nixon declared the War on Drugs. Government statistics show there were 850,000 arrests for marijuana last year, yet usage by young adults increased 9 percent during that time. Surveys repeatedly show that at least half of all high school kids say they have smoked marijuana.

The government has now spent more than a trillion dollars of taxpayer money on the War on Drugs, with last year's government expenditure topping more than $40 billion. Approximately half of our prison population, which is the highest in the world, contains young people doing time for minor drug offenses. After tens of thousands of our youths have had their lives ruined due to imprisonment, many being labeled felons unable even to vote, surveys now show more than 75% of Americans acknowledge the drug war has failed.

The money that keeps the war alive

Unfortunately the drug war will not die easily. It now represents a $400 billion industry to international drug cartels and a $40 billion annual taxpayer-funded payday for the giant federal and state bureaucracies responsible for arresting, prosecuting, and imprisoning their fellow Americans who use drugs. Not only are prisons that hold nonviolent drug offenders the main source of income for many towns in America, but policing agencies have gotten themselves hooked on both the annual billions of taxpayer dollars, plus the billions they seize from innocent bystanders through the use of civil asset forfeiture laws.

Civil asset forfeiture laws are one of the most sinister aspects of the drug war. It is a direct government assault on one of the cornerstone's of America's *Constitution* — private property. Federal forfeiture laws were used on a widescale basis during alcohol Prohibition in the 1920s and 30s, and in 1970 they were reintroduced to American society with the Racketeer Influenced and Corrupt Organizations (RICO) Act, then were greatly expanded in 1984 with the Comprehensive Crime Control Act. Originally designed to seize the assets of drug lords, they are now used regularly by cops to seize the assets of ordinary people. The laws became so lucrative for the feds that all 50 states now have their own civil asset forfeiture laws.

As opposed to criminal asset forfeiture where prosecutors must prove someone has committed a crime to seize their property, civil asset forfeiture allows police to seize property that police "suspect" was involved in a drug crime. The property's owner doesn't have to be charged with a crime, and in more than 80 percent of cases, according to a major study done by the Institute for Justice, a libertarian civil liberties law firm, they are not.

The typical scenario is this: you get stopped by the cops for any reason and they discover you have $10,000 in cash on you. The only reason someone would have that much money on their person is because it's payment for drugs, the cops reason, so they seize it. That money is confiscated, and the burden of proof and the expense is on the hapless victim who must go to court to try and get it back. Most instances of civil asset forfeiture are never challenged in court, according to the Cato Institute, because the cost of going to court to prove the property was not involved in a drug crime typically exceeds the cost of the property. In addition, the cops often threaten to bring drug charges against the victim if they don't relinquish their property willingly.

Abuse of asset forfeiture laws has been rampant for years, as *BHM* writer John Silveira has pointed out in several past articles (contained in his book, *The Coming American Dictatorship*). The forfeiture fund controlled by the federal government's Justice Department contained more than $3 billion as of 2008, but it's difficult to ascertain how many millions or billions are in state asset forfeiture funds because there is no strict accounting required; it is tantamount to a slush fund divvied up among the cops.

The Institute for Justice study found that "Civil forfeiture laws at the federal level and in 42 states dangerously shift law enforcement priorities toward the pursuit of property and profit." Disturbingly, it also found that when states try to reform their own forfeiture laws, police circumvent the reforms by turning over seized property to the feds who then return some of the seized loot back to the state under their own more law enforcement-friendly forfeiture laws. In my own state of Oregon, voters in 2000 passed an initiative curtailing some of the worst abuses of our state's civil asset forfeiture laws. The cops challenged the initiative, tied it up in court until 2006 when the law was upheld. So the cops merely agitated for a new law, passed in 2008, which circumvented many of the reforms of the 2000 voter initiative. At least Oregon cops get to keep only 63% of the assets seized, while in other states' cops often keep 100%.

The study ranked states by how onerous their forfeiture laws were. States that got an "F" were Massachusetts, South Carolina, Montana, Alaska, Wyoming, and Delaware. But by using a combination of factors, including how aggressive the cops are when going after assets, and how willing they are to circumvent their own laws to nail you, you are most at risk if you live in West Virginia, Virginia, Texas, Michigan, and Georgia. Only Maine, North Dakota, and Vermont got an overall grade of "B" or higher. The entire report is available online at www.ij.org.

If this type of behavior were happening in non-government segments of society, someone would be arrested for robbery, extortion, racketeering, and other crimes, but thanks to the War on Drugs, it's "just business" for America's criminal justice system.

The toll on our youth

And let's not forget the human cost of the War on Drugs. At least half of our prison population consists of nonviolent youthful drug offenders. Their lives are ruined, their families devastated. I was lodged among some of them for two days between issues of this magazine when I was convicted of drunk driving, a first offense of any kind for me. Although I vehemently asserted my innocence at trial, I quickly realized my brief incarceration was a godsend. For years my senior editor, John Silveira, and I had written about the abuses of our prison system and the fact it mainly houses nonviolent offenders. Now I was incarcerated (and how easy it was to go to jail) among 19 and 20-year-old kids whose only offense was possessing small amounts of drugs, either marijuana or meth.

These kids were hapless and clueless, represented by overwhelmed public defenders who had to do battle with a state armed with unlimited resources. Most of them had been picked up on probation violations. One was 19 years old, the same age as my son, Jake, who is in his first year of college. It occurred to me that Jake too could be busted and put in jail if he experiments with marijuana in college, like most college students do. Three of my fellow inmates, in their 20s, had lost their jobs when they were jailed for probation violations involving charges like "being in the presence of a known drug user" and "having an unopened case of beer in a car in which he was a passenger."

These kids were part of a revolving-door local jail system that kept the cops, prosecutors, judges, and jailers employed at an average salary, according to county records, of more than $70,000 a year. They simply represented paychecks for the bureaucracy charged with arresting, incarcerating, releasing, following, then rearresting them for minor probation violations. I interviewed the kids extensively and wrote about some of them in my online blog at the *BHM* website, www. backwoodshome.com. None had committed violent crimes. These kids needed counseling and help, not jailing in a dungeon-like cell with nothing to do and no job prospects when they got back out.

America is a police state

America has become a de facto police state thanks to the War on Drugs. Many Americans can't see what has happened to their country because they have become the frogs in the slowly heated pot of water. They don't yet realize they have been boiled and their freedoms evaporated away. We let our government violate our rights, seize our property, and imprison our youth because we have been conditioned to believe that drugs are the ultimate evil in society — so evil that it is worth giving up freedom to eradicate them.

We hear a lot of talk from politicians about how Mexico is on the verge of becoming a failed state due to its ongoing drug violence. I would argue that America is already a failed state in terms of it having thrown out its own *Constitution* and given our police nearly unlimited power over us in the name of winning the War on Drugs. For God's sake, the percent of our population in jail is the highest in the world, nearly eight times higher than Europe's.

But how do we repeal the War on Drugs? By 1933, Americans had had enough of alcohol Prohibition and demanded its repeal. But by that time police had a vested interest in maintaining the huge bureaucracies it had built to battle illegal alcohol and in the huge amounts of assets the government was seizing from ordinary people, including the cars of those who had alcohol on board. With the Depression in full swing, it had become a money and employment issue for government, and some people thought Prohibition would never be repealed because of that fact. But it did get repealed, although the freedoms lost during that era were never fully restored.

We are in the same position today, with a steep recession and huge bureaucracies dependent on all those billions they get to fight the War on Drugs. Government wants to keep drugs illegal, and they'll wage a campaign of lies and threats every time voters have a chance to change things.

And what about all those terrible predictions about how legalized marijuana will unleash hordes of marijuana-addicted criminals among us who will be driving and going to work under its influence? Portugal has been the testing laboratory for this theory since 2001, when it decriminalized (next best thing to legalizing) all drugs, including even heroine and cocaine. In those intervening nine years, Portugal's drug usage rates have not increased, and Portugal has gone from one of the worst drug-abusing nations in the European Union to one of the least abusing, especially when compared to European countries that have increased their crackdown on drug use. According to the Portugal experiment, government crackdowns make drug usage worse, while a government backoff, which takes drug abuse out of the criminal arena and puts it into the medical arena, does not increase usage rates.

The next time a measure like Proposition 19 comes up for a vote, conservatives need to get beyond the government lies, understand that it is a freedom issue and not just a drug issue, and vote to support the *U.S. Constitution*.

— Dave Duffy

Sitting pretty
as the economy tanks

By Jackie Clay

I'm not a "doom and gloom" crier, but I have studied history and I can look around me. Prices on everything have gone up tremendously. I'm talking about increases of more than $1.50 in one week for a bag of chopped corn and oats for the steers. I'm talking about groceries in the store increasing by a quarter or more in a few days. I'm talking about the cost of gasoline and heating fuel rising for no reason overnight.

And how many people's income has risen enough to stand these rising costs? Folks on Social Security were recently denied a "cost of living

If you live fairly remotely and have stocked your pantry, planted your garden, have a few animals, and gathered a few other necessities like things to barter and a generator, you'll have few problems if the infrastructure of society breaks down.

If you live in an apartment in the city, you are going to be in bad shape. There's no soft peddling this type of scenario.

increase" for the second year in a row. So a lot of people, especially the elderly, are facing a bleak winter.

Do I think there's a magic formula that the government will surprise us with, coming to our rescue, like the Lone Ranger and Tonto? Hardly!

This economic slide has been coming for years. The wise people who have also seen it have been making preparations. Becoming more self-reliant is no longer just for extremist "nutcases." Churches, local government, gardening clubs, and mainstream magazines are all promoting such things as growing and preserving a large garden, raising small livestock such as chickens and dairy goats, debt reduction, establishing a long-term food storage pantry, and even reducing your energy consumption by installing an alternative energy production source.

We readers of *BHM* have been on the path to greater self-reliance for years. The "Y2K scare" got a lot of folks thinking about their delicate position should the country's economic structure collapse. Y2K was a great "dry run," so to speak. Many people took a close look at what it would take to become self-reliant if society's infrastructure were to break down. Those people gained knowledge as a result of the experience. But what about the others?

What about the millions of people who brush off self-reliance, preparedness, and concern for the economy's future? What *if* society's infrastructure collapses quite quickly? What can they do? What would they do?

Here's a scenario for you, and before you stop and think, "this will never happen," go back and read your history books — scenes like this aren't such a distant memory in our country's past.

Companies face bankruptcy and close, laying off workers who thought they had "stable" jobs. Food prices skyrocket because of the cost of producing and shipping; those same shipping costs limit how much food makes it to market, and soon there's not much available — at any cost. At this point, food is rationed by the government as it was during World War I and World War II. Gasoline rises to more than $5 a gallon, and to top it off, gasoline is rationed and the cost of heating fuel shoots through the roof. Folks are being evicted from apartments and even homes that they've lived in for years, for lack of money to make their payments. There are significantly more people, even

It will only take a few days for most stores to close as their shelves empty. Businesses that sell food use a "just in time" inventory system.

This kale soup, made by BHM Senior Editor John Silveira, will be canned and will store for years. When food cannot be bought from the store, it will become a nourishing, delicious meal.

families with children, living on the streets, selling anything they can to eat tomorrow. Break-ins are on the rise, as is violent crime, due to growing frustration and anger. In a nutshell, it's a royal mess! What are folks to do?

Big-city high-rise apartment dwellers

I'm sorry to say it, but if you live in an apartment in the city, you are going to be in bad shape. Yes, it's nice to grow a couple of container tomatoes on the balcony, but they won't feed your hungry family if food becomes scarce. You have no room to store up a goodly amount of food for just such a situation. You might have your savings — if the bank doesn't fail — but if the situation doesn't right itself soon, your savings will soon be gone in rent, utility bills, and food costs. If you've lost your job or had your hours severely cut, there isn't much you can do. You're completely at the mercy of the local infrastructure. I'll bet you look at those homeless people with different eyes now.

If you're lucky, you might be able to go to rural relatives for refuge, until the economy straightens out. But if you consider this, be absolutely sure you'll be welcomed and be prepared to work hard to earn your keep. There is no room on a farm or homestead for freeloaders.

What you should do now

I understand that some people's choice of careers and living preference cause them to gravitate toward the big city. That's fine. I know that many people would simply *die* if they "had" to live way out in the woods in the north, like we do. I would die in the big city. We're all different.

But *all* people should build a safety net around themselves and their family, just in case — city apartment dwellers, included.

You should reduce your debt. Credit cards are never a good thing. Not only do they cost a lot to use (unless you pay them off every month, which few users do), but a missed payment or two snowballs to eat up your financial security. You do *not* know if you will lose your job, have your hours cut, or be injured and unable to work for

Jackie Clay's pantry. It has every imaginable food staple.

BHM Managing Editor Annie Tuttle plants elephant garlic along the fence of her family's ¼-acre lot in town. All you need is a small plot of garden space to grow many vegetables.

awhile. It's easy to make your payments when everything is rosy, but hard to do when things get tougher — and it doesn't need to be much tougher, either. Late fees on top of late fees eat up your cash fast. Cut back on spending and work extra hours now to significantly reduce and eliminate your credit card debt before things get out of hand.

Keep a stash of ready cash at home. The banks could fail or restrict your withdrawals.

Purchase a small, cheap acreage with some sort of dwelling on it. It should have a well or other dependable water source, a few acres of timber to cut and use for heat, and maybe a garden site with a few established trees and plants like apples, rhubarb, and berries. It doesn't have to look like much, but it would beat living on the filthy, crime-ridden city streets. At least you would have a small home, fresh air, food from the garden, wood to heat by, a bathroom (even if it's an outhouse), and fresh water to drink.

Take an occasional vacation to this little plot of serenity to renovate the cabin and make it livable. Don't spend a ton of money, it doesn't have to be sleek and beautiful. Fence off and clear a garden site and make other simple improvements.

Homeowners with a large lot in the city

If you own a home on a nice lot in the city, you are in a much better place than are the high-rise apartment dwellers in big cities. You are still in a bad situation, but have a chance of coming through it by careful planning, economizing, and work.

During the Great Depression, many city-dwelling families survived by tightening their belts, using what basic foods they had on hand and digging up their backyard to make a large garden. Remember hearing about Victory Gardens during World War II? My own grandmother and parents had a huge garden, complete with fruit trees, berry bushes, a grape arbor, and plenty of vegetables, right in Detroit, Michigan. Of course, in those days, people already knew survival skills, such as cooking and baking on a shoestring, practicing frugal living, gardening, and preserving foods. Some of my first memories are

Annie plants an apple tree to supplement her other fruit-bearing trees. Fruit trees look just as beautiful as ornamental trees, but they're more valuable in hard times.

BHM Publisher Dave Duffy chops kindling. The more trees you have nearby, the more independent you'll be when it comes to keeping your family warm.

of "helping" Grandma and Mom spade the garden, harvesting and canning peaches, and adding lawn trimmings from the old push lawnmower to the compost heap.

Of course, many lawn-loving city dwellers have lost these survival skills, and most have no idea what to plant or how to care for a garden, let alone how to preserve any food from it.

With a house, instead of an apartment with limited storage, you at least have the capacity to store a modest amount of food.

What you should do now

Plant fruit trees around your yard instead of ornamental trees such as blue spruce, maple, or oak. An apple or cherry tree looks just as good — even better, when you're hungry! Grape vines and berry bushes can replace a hedge between the neighbors' house and yours. Start your garden. It sometimes takes a couple of years to get a garden "up and going," taking into consideration building fertile soil, weed control, and gaining experience. Gardening is not hard to learn, but it is somewhat of an art.

For additional garden space where there is none, try growing in containers. Friends of ours, Bill and Carolyn, grow dozens and dozens of tomatoes and peppers in five-gallon buckets and large black nursery containers right on their cement garage pad and driveway.

Reduce and eliminate your debt. Make extra payments on the principal of your mortgage so you can get your house paid off much sooner, and avoid foreclosure. Even paying an extra $50 a month on the principal can often make *years* of difference in the projected pay-off time and the actual pay-off date.

If your house payments are too large, downsize. Sell the 5-bedroom, 3-bath home in the "perfect" neighborhood and buy a 2-bedroom, 1-bath home a few miles further out. Young children will get used to sharing a room. The big yard and a paid-off home will more than make up for lack of space when things get tough.

Stock up on food, especially things you can't raise, such as wheat and flour, cornmeal, sugar, canned meat, etc.

Install a wood-burning stove or fireplace, where legal. Even in the city, one can usually find sources of wood to burn in the winter. Demolished buildings, storm-fallen trees, pallets, old fencing, tree prunings, and scraps

You may not use a woodstove all the time, but having one in your home is good insurance against going cold if the fuel deliveries stop.

One of Jackie Clay's gardens. Yours doesn't have to be this big, but even a small one will be worth its weight in gold if the grocery stores run out of food.

from the lumberyard can all provide heat for the family at no cost. Stock a cord or two of firewood in the unused part of your garage, as well.

Raising livestock in the city is already taking an upward swing. Thanks to city homesteaders, a lot of zoning boards have re-thought their prohibitions regarding city chickens and rabbits. Often a family is (or could be, with a little work) allowed to have a few chickens (but usually no rooster) or rabbits (often considered pets), housed in the garage or other discrete place in the yard. Out of sight, out of mind usually works. With six hens or four doe rabbits and a buck, you suddenly would *not* be without eggs and meat. With your large garden, fruit, and stored food, this "livestock" would make a huge difference.

Little money savers, such as replacing all lights in the house with compact fluorescent bulbs, adding insulation to the walls and attic, replacing old windows with more efficient (and warmer) double pane ones, caulking and weather stripping around all doors and windows, and adding an insulated jacket to the water heater all can make a terrific difference in home comfort and home utility expenses. Likewise, adding gutters and rain barrels can cut your water bill, and provide plenty of water for the garden.

Getting by for less

In tough times, the first order is to spend less — for everything. We grew up with Dad always telling us to "turn off the lights." Mom and Dad had grown up during the Depression, and carried thrift into all of their future years. Even with compact fluorescent light bulbs, leaving lights on with no one in the room will run up your electric bill — something to be feared when money is tight.

Close off all unused rooms during the winter. There's no sense heating a room when no one is using it. For some rooms, such as a sewing room, take the equipment and supplies out as you need them, then close the door. Mom used to sew in the living room during the winter. An unused upstairs? Close the door to the stairwell during the winter. It'll still get enough rising heat from below to prevent freezing, but stay way cooler than the heated part of the house. Close all registers to rooms you plan on leaving unused during the winter, then lay a rug over them.

If an apple a day keeps the doctor away, imagine what several bushels on the branch can do.

A small garden will provide you with lots of veggies to enhance meals. BHM Business Manager Ilene Duffy regularly harvests her garden for dinner.

I used to cut one-inch-thick panels of foam insulation board to fit tightly in the upper part of our windows during the winter. It was an old farm house and you could feel cold seeping in through the old single-pane glass. It really helped keep the living room and bedrooms warmer. Having heavy drapes and closing them during the night and during storms also helps a lot.

Learn to eat more frugally. This means making old-time meals, such as big pots of beans, spaghetti, roasts with vegetables (heavy on the vegetables), lots of rice, noodles, and other pasta. A big loaf of homemade bread fills up the family at mealtime and tastes great, too. Breakfasts of hot oatmeal with fruit, coffee cakes, pancakes, and waffles keep you going all day and take away that hungry feeling. We always had one big meal a day. Breakfast was usually hot cereal and toasted homemade bread, lunch was a hearty sandwich and salad, and supper was the big hearty family meal.

Consider renting out a spare bedroom and bath. Grandma did that, renting the upstairs to two sisters who had good jobs and needed cheap rent. They split the rent, giving them economical lodging, and Grandma had extra income for utilities and house payments.

As jobs are skinny to non-existent, get creative to earn needed cash. There have always been jobs in the odd-job category, such as digging a ditch, sawing downed trees, tilling up a garden, light carpentry (repairing steps, a roof, or putting in a window), even farmwork in nearby rural areas (sometimes having a bonus as fresh milk, vegetables, wheat to grind, or pork for the table). The pay won't be much, but if you suck it up, you won't need too much, either. *Any* money is better than *no* money.

Yes, you may have a college degree and were earning $50 an hour, with a hefty benefit package. But now, be happy with whatever you can earn until something better can be found. Again, *any* money is better than *no* money. Don't waste time being proud. If you have to shovel manure, spit on your hands and learn to shovel!

The small acreage holder

Even if you have a few acres in the country, you're still not immune to the woes of a crappy economy. You may have lost your job, but at least you probably have a garden and some small livestock to help the family situation. You still have land payments and taxes to meet, as well as utility bills. Maybe you have no savings and no cash on hand. Suddenly, you can't afford gas for the truck, home heating fuel, or groceries. Credit card companies are demanding full payment, as are the local merchants who extended credit at the beginning of the collapse. You can't grow sugar or sufficient wheat to grind for flour. You could have bought a couple of milk goats and chickens, but never got around to it.

Maybe you haven't gotten too serious about a garden, growing mostly summer and salad crops and are just learning to can your harvest. Feeling it was foolish, you didn't store up food in the basement and pantry, as you could always go buy it at the store.

You do have a woodstove with enough wood for a storm or extended cold spell, but you haven't cut and split enough dry wood to last a month, let alone the winter.

Chickens are easy to keep…

What you should do now

Like everyone else, first reduce and eliminate your debt. Yes, it's hard, but by developing a goal, a family can do nearly anything. Work at paying off the credit card with the highest interest rate first, then move on to the next one. It's amazing how quickly it can be done. To get "extra" money for this, severely limit eating out, entertainment, vacations, or buying "toys." (Do you really *need* an MP3 player, a new 42-inch flat screen TV, a llama, a state-of-the-art deer stand, or a bigger truck?) All of us have wants, which are not necessarily needs. We need shelter, clothing, water, and food. We don't need toys. By saving up to buy something (as opposed to buying on credit), you are forced to really consider whether you need it or not — usually *not*. And if you do buy it, it is paid for, free and clear, not costing even more as the interest on your credit card compounds.

Pay extra on your mortgage every month. Sometimes extra money for this can come from your land itself. While most people can't make a living on a small homestead, they often can round up a little extra cash every month from such things as selling extra fruit and vegetables, crafts or soaps, extra eggs, kid goats, corn stalks (and other country decorations), tilling nearby gardens, etc. This money could be put back into the homestead to pay it off earlier so it could never be taken away through foreclosure.

Keep a modest supply of cash on hand.

Even though you may have only a few acres, take homesteading seriously. Learn to garden effectively and how to put up your harvest for the future. Not only are you learning a valuable skill, but you are also collecting supplies and equipment you need, such as a pressure canner, canning jars, rings and lids, a tiller for the garden, and livestock fencing and supplies.

If you build a small chicken coop and yard, you can stock them with a modest flock of chickens and maybe even a pair of heritage breed turkeys (the heritage breeds can reproduce and raise babies on their own). You would not only have plentiful eggs, but also a steady supply of meat from setting hens and young turkeys from time to time.

…and a small flock will provide you with plenty of colorful eggs.

If you build a small goat barn and milking room you could also have a pair of dairy goats, supplying you with year-round milk and meat from the surplus wethered male kids. You can make yogurt, cheese, and ice cream from this sweet, flavorful milk, and even trade some of the milk or other dairy products for other things of value with your neighbors.

You have room to stock up a year's worth of food or more, making this time of trials much easier.

Install a small solar array or wind charger and battery bank, because eventually you'll run out of fuel for your generator, and the power grid may be unreliable.

The self-reliant homesteader

Yes, things are tight. There is not sufficient gas for the tractor, you can't go to town for groceries or "fun," and you've cut your cell phone minutes down to bare bones, limiting calls to checking on the family and emergencies. You've had to cut back on the grain you feed to your livestock, and it seems like everyone you ever knew has called, asking if you have room for them to come and live.

Of course, in your small, home-built cabin there really isn't any extra space, but you've made room already for your daughter and her family, your sister, and an elderly friend.

There's more work now, for you and your extended family, as nearly everything is homemade, provided for by your land and livestock.

You had the foresight to prepare for any future emergency or upheaval, whether financial, a terrorist attack, or just a period of "bad luck." So your pantry is stocked with two years' worth of basic staple food, such as flours, cornmeal, baking powder, yeast, sugar, brown sugar, confectioners' sugar, wheat, popcorn (to eat or grind for fresh cornmeal), masa harina (corn flour from dried hominy), rolled oats, baking soda, dry beans of all kinds, white rice, brown rice, salt, spices, lye to make soap, and a whole lot more.

You've been gardening for a few years and putting up all of your bounty. There are rows and rows of jewel-colored, shining jars in your basement, lined up like soldiers in the war against hunger. Just about every food anyone could imagine is waiting there: spaghetti, pizza, and taco sauce, beets, corn, carrots, green beans, pinto beans, black beans, venison, beef, pork, chicken, broth of all kinds, cabbage, tomatoes, salsas, pickles of every kind and description, jams, jellies, preserves, cherries, apples, apricots, blueberries, chili, meatballs, soups, stews, nuts, and so much more.

In one end of your basement pantry is a shelf full of plump cheeses, aging to sharpen them to full flavor.

Then there are shelves of dehydrated food, too: broccoli, squash, potatoes, carrots, green beans, corn, fruits, and berries of all kinds.

And the root cellar bins are brimful of solid garden and orchard produce: potatoes, carrots, rutabagas, turnips, parsnips, onions, apples, cabbages, and even some grapes and plums for short-term storage.

Upstairs in the warm closet are squash and pumpkins and even a basket of nuts, waiting to be shelled and canned.

Outdoors, you've built a moderate-sized poultry house for your 25 hens and their hatched and growing clutches of chicks, along with your half dozen heritage breed turkeys and their own hatched-out and growing poults. You've been butchering the extra cockerels to eat and can, as well as the fattening young turkeys. The extra pullets can be saved to expand the

If you have a larger piece of land, goats provide milk and meat, and they are easy to take care of.

flock or traded to friends for other needs. Of course eggs are plentiful, even during the winter, as the coop is insulated, well ventilated, and has lighting from a small solar panel on the roof.

Years ago, you built a goat barn, complete with a snug milking room, which now houses your six does and their young. The buck lives up the hill, in his own "cottage" with three wethers that you are growing up to butcher. As the does all give a gallon of milk a day, you have plenty for their offspring and to use for the house. Of course, you have all the fresh milk, yogurt, cottage cheese, cream cheese, and cheeses that you can use. In fact, you can even trade some off to friends. As the goats have a large, wooded pasture and you have an extra brushy pasture to rotate them in, you don't have to buy any feed during the summer. Luckily, you had cleared and developed a small five-acre hay field and can cut their hay, a little at a time, and put it up in the barn for winter.

You can't rely on wild game for food, but remote areas have more than in the city and suburbs, like this wild turkey that hangs out in the yard of BHM's editor.

Over on the hill is the steer pasture. The land is rolling and not much good for agricultural purposes, but it does grow grass and brush, and two steers a year to butcher for household meat and trading or cash.

Below that is the pig yard, with a snug hut in the nearby end of a large,

Items to have when the economy tanks

After reading this article by Jackie, *BHM's* editors came up with a few of their own ideas about items to have on hand if society's structure breaks down.

Personal protection items in all scenarios, including **hunting weapons** if you are in a rural setting. In a world gone sour, when police are laid off, personal protection may be very important. Common calibers are best because they not only serve as great tools, but they and their **ammunition** make great barter items.

Bicycles. Used but reliable bikes can be had for a song now at thrift shops and yard sales. They'll be priceless if gasoline is either unavailable, super-expensive, or rationed.

Basic medicines for when you can't find or afford a doctor. Lay in a first aid kit. (See Jackie's Medical kits for self-reliant families in the *Tenth Year Anthology*.)

Basic fishing equipment that is appropriate for the area you're living in or where you may flee to. Fishing gear will not only put food on the table, but it's good recreation in a world that might have very little entertainment.

Comfort items include general and personal. General comfort items could be alcohol, candy, canned fruit, tobacco for smokers, seasoning (especially hot sauces), toys and sports equipment, paper and pencils, puzzles, board games, and a decks of cards. Figure out what you couldn't stand to live without: it's knitting needles for *BHM* Editor Annie Tuttle.

Hygienic items including female necessities, lots of toilet paper, and soap.

Brewing supplies to make alcoholic beverages including beer and wine, whether you drink them or trade them. You can go expensive, if you want, but remember that humans were brewing alcohol before there were hydrometers, carboys, or even an alphabet.

Barter items. All the items listed above, and the comfort items in particular, would work as barter items when either there's no money to be had or, because of inflation, money becomes worthless.

Junk silver. I'm not so sure that now is the time to be buying junk silver, but if you have some, stow it away because it and gold may become the only currencies people will accept.

If you do live remote, shooting a deer can keep your family in food for a long time. Of course, you will have to remember to have a few guns and extra ammo (great also as a barter item) on hand.

fenced pasture. In it are a young sow and her litter of piglets. In the other end is a smaller enclosure, housing a young boar. Two half-grown pigs wait at the gate for extra garden produce. They are being raised to butcher this fall.

Below the cabin is the barn. The milk cow and her heifer calf live in it during the winter, along with the horses that are used both for farm work such as plowing and haying and for riding, too.

Near the cabin is the ¾-acre garden, fenced against plentiful deer. Not only can you grow all the fresh food eaten by your family, but also enough to put up for winter, as well as a small plot of wheat to grind into flour.

The small orchard is nearby, with the berry patch next to it, both fenced against deer. The poultry get the run of the orchard, so they rustle much of their own feed during the summer, while keeping down the clover and bugs. The orchard provides fruit for the family, canning, and preserves, food for the animals in the form of extra and damaged fruit, and trade or cash from sales.

There are 40 acres of woods, so cutting the winter's wood is simple, although still plenty of work. Luckily, although gasoline *is* very expensive, a few gallons' worth of gas cuts the winter's wood.

A wind generator and solar array sit in the open, on the hill next to the cabin, providing electricity to run the modest household needs. The well has its own solar panels and provides water to the house and animals.

During the winter, your family makes soap and laundry soap from the fat you saved when you butchered pigs, steers, and deer. You also have time to read from your large library of old Western novels, old *Mother Earth News*, *Countryside*, *Rural Heritage*, and, of course, *Backwoods Home Magazine* (your favorite!). Canning continues all winter, making easy-to-fix meals-in-a-jar, but it's a more leisurely canning than when harvest is under full swing. The sauerkraut is ready to can, turkey broth with meat and noodles can be made from the Thanksgiving leftover turkey, and so on. And there's plenty of time to sit in front of the glowing, warm woodstove and visit with your loved ones around you.

What these folks could have done differently

Not a darned thing!

Of course, this has all been sort of make believe. But if it made you think, even a little, as it did me, that's great. Preparedness is *always* a good idea. No wonder my favorite childhood fable was *The Ant and the Grasshopper*. Wouldn't today be a good time to check on your own family's state of preparedness? Just in case the make believe becomes reality? Δ

Woodstove cooking

By Cindi Myers

If you have a woodstove for heat, take advantage of the fire to cook your dinner for no extra cost and very little effort. The heat of a woodstove can cook yummy baked potatoes and apples, savory soups and stews, roast chicken or beef, and many other dishes.

Though you can adapt almost any pots and pans to woodstove cooking, you'll save yourself trouble and ensure better results if you invest in a cast iron Dutch oven with a lid and a cast iron trivet. The Dutch oven heats evenly and stays hot for a long time, which is perfect for roasting meat or stewing moist dishes. The trivet allows you to regulate the amount of heat the Dutch oven receives. Aluminum foil, a wooden spoon, a set of tongs, a fireplace shovel, and some potholders will round out your woodstove cooking supplies.

Cooking inside the firebox

Start a fire in your stove and let it burn for an hour or more before you begin cooking. This allows the stove to heat up and creates a good bed of coals if you're going to be cooking in the stove. Once the stove is hot, you only need to keep a low, steady fire going to cook almost anything.

Bake white potatoes, sweet potatoes, onions, or apples inside the stove. Wrap each fruit or vegetable individually in two layers of aluminum foil. This helps to keep the food from burning. Push the fire to one side of the stove box and lay the food on the coals. Use the fireplace shovel to pile more coals on top. Close the stove door and bake for half an hour, then use the tongs to turn each foil packet over and cook for another 30 minutes. If one part of the firebox feels hotter than the other, you can switch the packets around to different positions.

Deluxe baked apples:

4 apples (Braeburn, Granny Smith, or other baking apples work best)
¼ cup butter, softened
¼ cup brown sugar
¼ cup raisins
¼ cup chopped walnuts
½ tsp. cinnamon

Wash and core the apples. Cream the butter and brown sugar together. Stir in the raisins, walnuts, and cinnamon. Set each cored apple on a sheet of aluminum foil. Stuff the center of each apple with the filling mixture. Fold the foil up around the apple and pinch closed. Wrap with a second sheet of foil and bake in oven or woodstove one hour.

Stove top cooking

The Dutch oven acts like a slow cooker on top of the stove to cook soups, stews, casseroles, and roasts. The tight-fitting lid keeps juices in and ensures moist, flavorful meat. The trivet allows you to regulate the heat so the bottom of the pot doesn't burn.

Start by putting all your ingredients in the Dutch oven. Place the oven, uncovered, on top of the hot woodstove.

In ten minutes or less, the ingredients should start to bubble. Set the trivet on the stove and move the oven onto the trivet. Put the lid on the oven and allow to cook as you would a slow cooker. You can leave soups and stews all day. A roast with vegetables takes three to four hours. Check the food every hour or so to make sure nothing is sticking, and that the food is still hot. If your fire dies down and the food in the Dutch oven starts to cool, set the pot back on the stove top and build up the fire again. Move the Dutch oven to the trivet when everything heats up again.

Roast chicken and vegetables:

- 1 frying chicken
- 1 onion
- 3 potatoes, peeled and cut into chunks
- 2 carrots, peeled and cut into chunks
- 1 clove garlic, peeled and chopped
- salt and pepper
- rosemary
- 1 cup water

Wash the chicken and remove any innards and discard. Quarter the onion and stuff this into the cavity of the bird. Arrange the chicken, breast side up, on a meat rack in the bottom of the Dutch oven. (If you don't own a meat rack, arrange three metal canning jar rings in the bottom of the pot and set the chicken on these.)

Arrange the vegetables and garlic around the chicken. Sprinkle the bird with rosemary, salt, and pepper. Pour the water over the vegetables. Put the lid on the pot and cook on the woodstove or in the oven for three to four hours.

Potatoes and sausage:

- 4 large baking potatoes
- 1 onion
- 2 links Polish sausage, Kielbasa, chorizo, or other sausage
- ½ cup grated cheddar cheese
- ½ cup milk
- salt and pepper

Peel the potatoes and cut into ¼-inch-thick slices. Dice the onion. Slice the sausage into 1-inch chunks. Grease the inside of the Dutch oven. Layer the potatoes, onions, and sausage. Sprinkle on the cheese. Pour in the milk. Season with salt and pepper. Place the lid on the pot and cook on the stove for three to four hours. If the potatoes start to stick, add a quarter cup of water.

Chicken noodle soup:

- leftover chicken carcass and meat from roast chicken
- 2 stalks celery, chopped
- ½ onion, diced
- 2 carrots, peeled and chopped
- salt
- pepper
- rosemary
- 1 pound egg noodles
- 1 cup frozen peas
- water

Place the chicken carcass in the Dutch oven and cover with water. Boil on top of the woodstove for one hour. You'll want to have the oven directly on the stove top the whole time. Remove the Dutch oven from the stove. Fish out the chicken carcass and add the leftover chicken meat, celery, onion, carrots, salt, pepper, and rosemary. Return the Dutch oven to the woodstove and allow the soup to simmer until ½ hour before you're ready to eat. Add the egg noodles, frozen peas, and more water, if necessary, to cover. Allow to simmer for 30 minutes.

You can adapt almost any slow cooker recipe to woodstove cooking, since the combination of Dutch oven and trivet produces slow, even heat. You can also reheat liquids such as soup or stew, or boil water for tea or coffee by placing the pot directly on top of the hot stove. Master the art of woodstove cooking and you may find your kitchen stove sits idle most of the winter. Δ

the gee-whiz! page: brains

By O. E. MacDougal

In many science fiction stories and comic books, people in the future evolve larger brains than we modern humans have. But is that likely? In an article in the September 2010 issue of *Discover Magazine* the author, Kathleen McAuliffe, writes that over the last 20,000 years human's brains have actually shrunk. That is, our "primitive" ancestors had larger brains than we do, and no one knows why we're losing our minds. In fact, the brains of Neanderthals, an extinct branch of the human race who we consider primitive, were considerably larger than our own.

Some researchers think our smaller brains are because our ancestors and the Neanderthals had bodies more muscular than our own, and much of the brain is simply for regulating and controlling the various organs and muscles. Larger bodies need more grey matter to control them. For this reason, women's brains are usually smaller than men's because they themselves are smaller, not because they're dumber. Elephants, on the other hand, have larger brains than we do, and most of theirs is dedicated to controlling the muscles in their enormous bodies. So, our brains may have shrunk because we're less muscular than our ancestors. And it should be pointed out that even after size is taken into account, the human brain is still about three times the size of that of other mammals. And that size differential is mainly in the frontal lobes where most of our abstract reasoning takes place. Compared to other animals, ours are enormous; it is the most conspicuous part of our anatomy that separates us from other animals.

In trying to account for our shrinking brains, it should also be noted that all the animals we've domesticated (dogs, cats, cattle, pigs, etc.) have smaller brains than their wild ancestors. Wild animals need more brains to survive while our domesticated pets and farm animals can do with less since they're "taken care of." Consequently, some researchers think our brains have shrunk because, to become civilized, we've "domesticated" ourselves.

Others theorize "brainy" people developed civilization which allowed the not-so-bright to survive and they've come along for a free ride which has allowed them to pass their not-so-brainy genes on to posterity.

Last, at least one researcher claims our brains are smaller because they're now more efficient. In other words, our ancestors had these big clunky brains while we, their descendents, have these classy sports models. But I don't think that's likely because I think we'd see it in other species, and we haven't.

Whatever the reason, the fact remains our brains are shrinking and we may be getting more and more like Homer Simpson.

Vision uses more of your brain than anything else. About 30% of your cerebral cortex is used solely to process what you see, while only 8% is used for touch and a mere 3% goes for hearing.

The adage that we use only 10% of our brains is an old wives' tale. Every part of your brain is used.

Your brain has about 100,000 miles of blood vessels, enough to go around the world at the equator four times. It also has about 100 billion neurons — roughly the same as the number of stars in our galaxy.

To feel pain anywhere else in your body, the nerve signals must be sent to your brain. Your brain, however, has no pain receptors of its own and cannot feel anything. Brain surgery needs no anesthesia other than that required to make the incision in your scalp to get to it.

Your brain is expensive. Though it's a mere 2% of your body's weight, it consumes about 20% of your calories. That's about 400-500 calories a day for a man's brain, 350-400 for a woman's. Put another way, overall your body burns energy at the rate of about 100 watts, so your brain uses as much energy as a 20-watt light bulb.

Now, here's something: A child's brain is more active than an adult's because they're learning at a prodigious rate, and the metabolic energy consumption of their brains is more than twice that of an adult's. In other words, kid's brains burn more energy than the brains of both their parents combined.

Your brain is processing information from outside your body even when you're asleep. It's the reason a mother can sleep through a thunderstorm but instantly wake up when her baby whimpers.

Canned bacon — roll your own!

By Enola Gay

I have to admit, I am somewhat of an extreme canner. I love to can unusual things—canned foods you just don't find on everyone's shelves. My latest canning adventures have included everything from canned cheese to canned butter to canned bacon.

When I was a young woman, my grandparents would occasionally pack up a huge box full of wonderful treasures and present it to me as a care package. It was so much fun to go through each item and wonder where they could have possibly found such a unique cache of canned delights such as Ethiopian chicken chunks or Hungarian canned bacon. The canned bacon was a special treat because I couldn't afford such extravagances on my meager salary. I did, however, learn to rinse the bacon quite well, or it was completely inedible due to the outrageously high sodium content.

To can bacon all you need are quart jars, 12-inch-wide masking paper, pressure canner, and bacon.

Years went by, and I forgot all about Hungarian canned bacon, until my husband came across a group buy of canned bacon on a website he frequents. Eager to see if canned bacon was as good as I remembered, we ordered a case.

Our bacon arrived, and it was everything we had hoped for. We loved the fact that it was shelf stable, because, being off the grid, we have very limited refrigerator and freezer space. It was incredibly convenient, as it took only minutes to fry up for breakfast. And, because it was pre-cooked and canned, it was perfect for our long-term food storage goals. There were a few drawbacks, however. First, it was expensive. One case of 12 cans was roughly $120. It was in no way affordable for our large family. Secondly, the bacon, although tasty, was very thin, therefore extreme care had to be taken when removing it from the can and laying it on the griddle to cook. More often than not, we ended up with bacon chunks versus bacon strips.

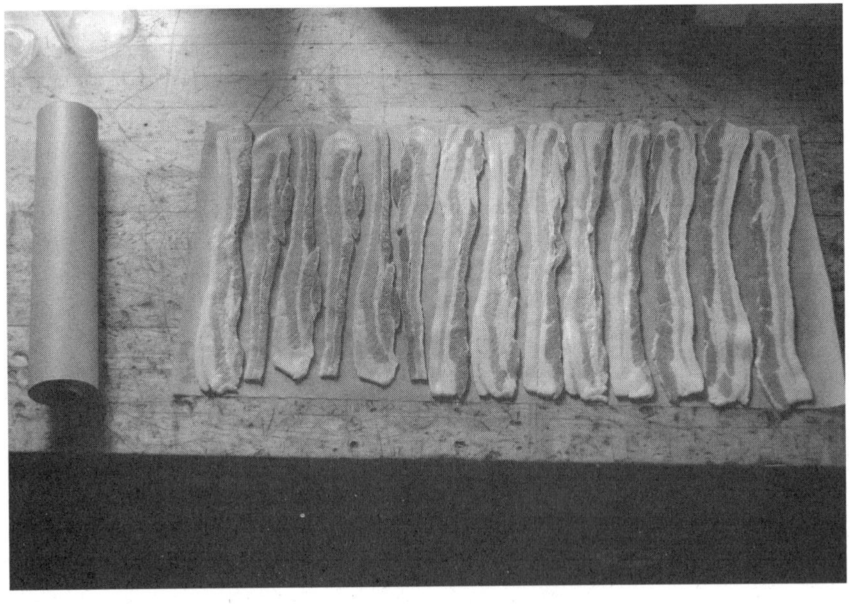

Cut a piece of masking paper 18 inches long and lay your bacon out in a single layer.

Armed with the knowledge that it was possible to can bacon and the desire to have a stock of canned bacon lining our shelves, I decided to delve into the process of canning bacon at home. After researching canned bacon through Internet sources and looking in every canning book I owned, to no avail, I decided to pioneer my own method.

Talking to numerous friends who had tried to can their own bacon, only to feed the horrible, greasy, wadded up mess to the dogs, I looked to the cans of bacon I had bought, and liked, to give me a clue how to home can bacon. The main difference between the home canned bacon and the commercially canned bacon seemed to be the paper used to package the bacon and the lack of water added to the can.

Lay another piece of masking paper over the top of the bacon then fold it in half.

My first attempt to can bacon met with measurable success. I laid the raw bacon slices out on a large piece of brown paper, folded the bacon in half and rolled the bacon, paper and all, into a large roll that slid right into my wide-mouthed canning jar. I put a sterilized lid and ring on the jar, processed for 90 minutes in my pressure canner and out came beautiful jars of home-canned bacon. The real test came the next morning, when we opened a jar for breakfast.

The jar of bacon had about 1½ inches of juice at the bottom and another inch of grease that had collected on top of that. I opened the jar, tugged at the paper slightly, and the roll of bacon slid right out. It unrolled well, but when I attempted to unfold the paper, the bacon stuck to itself where it had been folded. We had thick half-strips of bacon rather than long, thinner strips of bacon. Although short, they cooked up wonderfully and tasted just like crisp, fresh cooked bacon. Other than the bacon sticking to itself, the experiment had been very successful. Now I knew why the commercially canned bacon had a layer of paper on the bottom of the bacon and another on the top. The top layer of paper keeps the bacon from cooking together while it is canning.

Tightly roll up the bacon and paper and slide it into the jar.

Originally, I had opened up a paper lunch sack and used that to lay the bacon on for canning. Knowing that would not be practical for canning large quantities of bacon, as you had to overlap two bags and then open another two to cover the bacon, my oldest daughter began looking for an alternative. She came up with 12-inch masking paper that you can buy in the hardware store. It comes in a large roll and costs less than $5. It is very convenient to roll out the amount you need. You can also use parchment paper, purchased at a large grocery or specialty store.

A sale on bacon at our local restaurant supply store was the incentive to give canning bacon another try. This time I was even more prepared with experience and the proper supplies.

I cut a piece of masking paper about 18 inches long and began laying raw bacon on it, side by side. I have found that thick cut bacon holds together much better during the canning and cooking process. After putting between 12 and 14 pieces of bacon on the paper (averaging 1.2 to 1.4 pounds of bacon) I cut another 18-inch piece of masking paper and laid it on the top of the bacon. I then folded the bacon in half and rolled it tightly into a large roll.

Once rolled, I slid the bacon into a jar, capped it off, and processed it for 90 minutes at 10 pounds of pressure in my pressure canner. Again, it came out beautifully, but the test would still be taking it out of the jar and cooking it up.

The canned bacon, after processing for 90 minutes at 10 pounds pressure

Breakfast again, and time for the great bacon test. This time, success—it unfolded perfectly with no bacon sticking to itself. I then took the top layer of paper off the bacon. It peeled off nicely. As I began carefully lifting the bacon off the bottom layer of paper, I noticed that it wanted to tear where it had been folded, but most of the bacon stayed together quite nicely. Three minutes later, we had beautiful, crisp, tasty slices of bacon ready to eat.

We now have canned bacon lining our shelves. It is the epitome of a convenience food—ready whenever we need a quick meal. No longer do I have to try to finagle freezer space every time bacon goes on sale or thaw it in time for an evening meal. I have it ready at my fingertips. Forget about that expensive canned bacon—roll your own! Δ

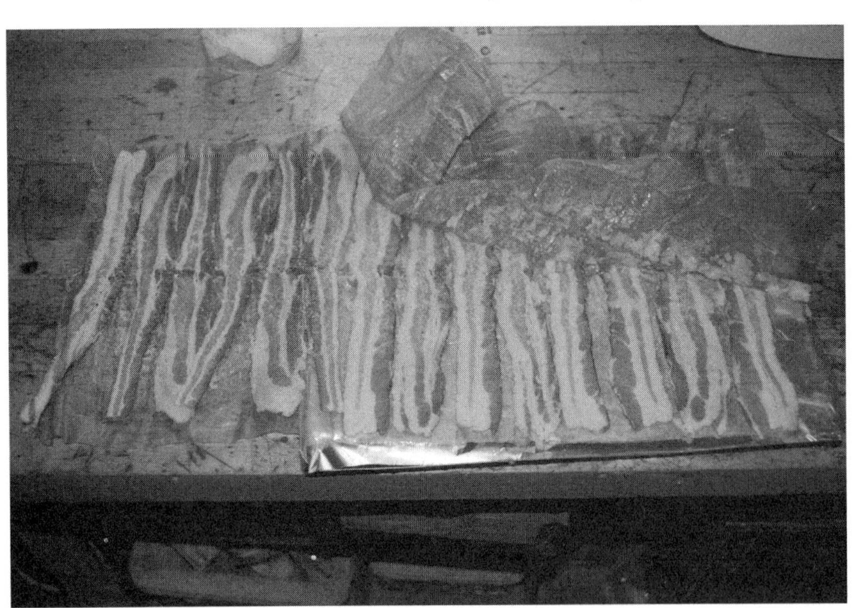

Removing the masking paper reveals delicious bacon that fries up quickly and tastes just like fresh bacon.

Healthy, hearty, meatless meals

By Linda Gabris

Sometimes getting a good old-fashioned "hungry man's" meat-based supper on the table can be quite the hassle, especially if you—the cook—forget to take a package of something out of the freezer in the morning to thaw for supper.

Other times, the freezer might simply be running low on meat. Then again, maybe your family doctor advised that you or one of your loved ones should cut back a little on the "red" stuff for the sake of better health. Various studies have indicated that too much meat in one's diet—namely red meat—may increase the risk of certain cancers. One way to help safeguard your family is to trim down the size of red meat portions, or better yet, whip up some meatless creations like the ones below that are guaranteed to satisfy the appetites of even those who are hungry enough to "eat a bear."

If you're like me, you don't need any reason at all for going "meatless" once in awhile. In fact, after introducing your family to some of these delightfully good meatless meals that are fast to make and easy on the budget, meat in your house might become more of a treat than a daily eat.

When going "meatless" you want to choose recipes that dish up good sources of protein and iron which are two of the biggest health benefits of eating meats, especially red ones. Many vegetables alone may not provide enough protein, so other sources of these needed nutrients should be included when planning meatless meals.

Dairy products and eggs are number one substitutes for meat, as are beans, lentils, nuts, seeds, whole grains (barley, wheat berries, rye berries), rice, and flours which are enriched with iron—essential, according to my grandma's old hand-written doctoring journals, for "building strong blood..."

Vegetable-rich pizza

If you are watching your fat intake, low-fat or soy cheeses can be used in any of the following recipes calling for other types of cheeses. From a budget standpoint, cheese may appear to be expensive, but I find that it goes a long way at earning its weight on the grocery bill. And cooking with cheese is a great way to use up all of the old tidbits in the fridge.

To save money, I buy Parmesan cheese in bulk instead of prepackaged shaker-style Parmesan cheese. I always watch for reasonably priced cheese ends and marked-down packages of cheese that are about to expire their prime shelf life in the store. Good buys such as these are worth cashing in on as cheese can be frozen when intended for cooking use. (It tends to turn a little "rubbery" after being frozen but can still be eaten out of hand, too.) A quick thaw and it is easy to grate.

Another way to save money, especially when buying cheeses for cooking purposes, is to buy no-name or store-brand cheese instead of higher priced name brand cheeses, saving the latter ones especially for platters and nibbling.

Here are some of my favorite meatless recipes that always earn big raves at my table. Even when meat is on the

Potato gnocchi

menu, these favorites are welcome as a side dish or as company fare when unexpected drop-ins show up around suppertime and a meat-based meal has to be stretched a great deal.

Meatless meals freeze exceptionally well, so when time permits and I have the fixings on hand, I often double or triple a batch of whatever I am making and stick the excess in the freezer for those times when I need to put a good hearty supper on the table in no time flat.

Vegetable-rich pizza

If your family loves pizza, here's a hearty homemade pizza that commercial pizzas just can't hold a candle to. It is so much more economical to make your own pizza at home than to buy it ready-made from the supermarket or to order in. There are no measurements given for the vegetables or cheeses as you can adjust them to suit your family's taste.

Crustless quiche

Crust:

1½ cups warm water
1 Tbsp. sugar
pinch salt
1 Tbsp. bulk yeast (or 1 envelope)
¼ cup olive oil
3 cups—more or less—of flour (you can "grain-up" your family's diet by using whole wheat flour)

Toppings:

tomato sauce as needed
dried crushed basil and oregano or Italian seasoning to suit taste
any or all of the following thinly sliced vegetables: onions, tomatoes, sweet peppers, chili peppers (for those who like it hot), mushrooms, zucchini, black pitted olives, cauliflower, asparagus tips…
grated Parmesan cheese and grated mozzarella or other cheese or a mixture of grated or crumbled cheeses in amounts to suit your own taste
dried crushed chilies on the side for individual shaking

To make crust: put warm water into a large bowl, add sugar, salt, and sprinkle with yeast. Let stand until yeast is foamy. Stir in olive oil and beat in two cups of flour with wooden spoon. Add enough remaining flour to make workable bread-like dough. Knead until smooth and elastic. Place in oiled bowl, cover, and let rise in warm place 20 to 30 minutes until risen.

This makes one large thicker crust pizza or two or three medium to small thinner crust pizzas. Oil the pizza pan(s), punch down dough, and press the dough out with your hands to desired thickness, working up an edge around the crust. Spread sauce evenly over top and sprinkle with herbs. Scatter vegetables and olives over sauce and top with the cheeses. Bake in preheated 375° F oven for 15 to 20 minutes. A tossed green salad on the side is all you need for the full meal deal. Serves six.

Variation: if you have tidbits of pepperoni or salami or cooked leftover meats such as browned ground meat, meatballs, meatloaf, roast chicken, or ham, they can be chopped and scattered over the vegetables for the "meat-lover's" special.

Potato gnocchi

Like pizza, gnocchi is of Italian origin. I learned to make gnocchi from Grandmother who, although she was not Italian, made the best gnocchi ever. This is a well-suited recipe to make a double or triple batch on a lazy Sunday afternoon. Divvy them up into needed portions and pop them into the freezer and they're ready for any hurry-up weeknight supper. You can serve gnocchi with so many different types of toppings that your family will never tire of it. Gnocchi can simply be sprinkled with fresh minced parsley and served. Or try these light, fluffy dumplings tossed with olive oil and chopped garlic or pesto or other pasta sauce. Sprinkle them with grated or crumbled cheese, chopped nuts, toasted seeds, or bacon crumbs. Or try Grandma's favorite way of serving them, mixed into a bowl of fried cabbage and onions, sprinkled with dried chili flakes, and served with a dollop of sour cream on top.

2 pounds scrubbed potatoes
½ tsp. salt
1½ cups flour (more if needed)
1 egg

Cook the whole unpeeled potatoes in boiling salted water until tender but not falling apart. When cool enough to handle, scrape off the peelings and grate or run through a potato ricer or large-holed sieve. Add salt, flour, and egg and work the mixture with your hands until smooth, adding more flour if too sticky to handle. Divide dough into four balls and, working on a floured surface, roll each ball into a 1-inch thick rope and cut into 1-inch slices. If you have the time, prick the gnocchi with a fork or roll them one by one over the grater to form a professional-looking pattern. When I was a kid, I loved helping grandmother put imprints on the little dumplings. To cook, drop into a large kettle of boiling lightly-salted water and cook until they rise to the surface. Remove with a slotted spoon. Top and serve. This makes enough for eight hefty servings. Leftovers can be stored in the fridge for up to five days or frozen for safekeeping.

Variation: if you prefer a smaller dumpling, ropes can be rolled out longer and cut into smaller portions to suit your taste. Smaller gnocchi are especially well-suited for adding to the soup pot to take the place of traditional soup noodles.

Lentil, chickpea, and vegetable stew

Peppery pea balls

Refried beans in tortillas

Crustless quiche

This recipe is always my number one pick when time is running short and supper's running late. It also makes a delightful company breakfast or brunch dish and is easy to double when needed. Grease a 9-inch round by 2-inch deep casserole dish with butter. Cover the bottom of the dish generously with grated cheese of choice. Break six large eggs into a bowl, add ¼ cup grated Parmesan cheese, ½ cup each of minced onion and minced sweet pepper, salt, pepper, and dried basil to taste. Beat and then pour over the cheese in the dish. Sprinkle top with additional ¼ cup of grated cheese and bake in preheated 350° F oven until a toothpick inserted in the center comes out clean, about 20 minutes. Let stand five minutes to ensure easy slicing. Slice into wedges and serve. My crew enjoys salsa (warmed first in the microwave) drizzled over the top. Makes six slices.

Variation: if you have leftover cooked bacon, ham, or sausage in the fridge, it can be minced and added to the egg mixture in which case you can cut down on the egg count if you wish.

Lentil, chickpea, and vegetable stew

This warm, filling stew only takes about 15 minutes to cook, barely enough time for everyone to wash up while you set the table.

2 chopped onions
4 cloves minced garlic
3 Tbsp. olive oil
1 diced sweet pepper
1 stalk finely diced celery
1 cup shredded cabbage
1 cup thinly sliced carrots
1 cup diced turnip and/or potatoes
1 tsp. each of ground cumin and ground coriander
¼ tsp. ground cardamom
¼ tsp. black pepper
4 cups water (use the liquid off the chickpeas as part of the measure)
1 cup red lentils
3 cups cooked or canned chickpeas
salt to taste
slivered almonds or other chopped nuts or toasted sesame seeds for garnish

In a Dutch oven or heavy-bottomed pot, heat olive oil and sauté onion and garlic until soft. Add remaining vegetables and spices and cook until spices are absorbed. Add water and lentils. Cover and simmer until lentils are tender, about 10 minutes. If using yellow or green split peas in place of red lentils, cook about 30 minutes or until tender. Add chickpeas and salt and heat through. If stew is too thick, add more water during cooking. If too thin, thicken with flour and water mixture at the end of cooking time. Garnish each bowl of stew with a scattering of slivered almonds upon serving. Serve with crusty bread for dipping into the stew. This makes six servings. Leftover stew can be pureed in the blender along with a spoon or two of lemon juice and served in the same manner as hummus (chickpea dip). It goes great with whole wheat crackers for a nutritious snack and keeps for up to a week in the fridge.

Peppery pea balls

When my kids were little, they'd giggle at the silly name of these tasty, economical, meatless "meatballs." They can be served with homemade tomato sauce over cooked pasta or over rice. This recipe makes a big batch, about 45 to 50 balls, depending on size. Don't fret about having leftovers, as they make delicious snacks, lunch box fare, or appetizers for tomorrow night's supper. Simply insert a toothpick into each leftover ball and serve with sweet chili or other dipping sauce, hot or cold. They can be frozen, too.

2 cups dried split yellow or green peas
(Cook peas the night before and let them stand in the fridge until evening. If you find that the cooked peas are not smooth enough, you can puree them.)
1 Tbsp. vegetable oil
1 minced onion
½ cup minced red or green pepper
3 cloves minced garlic
¼ tsp. dried basil
salt and pepper to taste
1 beaten egg
2 cups soda cracker crumbs (more or less as needed)
flour
additional vegetable oil for frying

Heat 1 tablespoon vegetable oil in skillet and sauté onion, pepper, and garlic until soft. Mix into the pea puree and add seasonings. Add enough crumbs to render the mixture

Sam's spinach, zucchini, and pasta wok supper

the same consistency as ground meat. Since some types of split peas retain more liquid than others, the amount of crumbs may vary. Let stand until crumbs have completely absorbed all of the moisture, adding more crumbs as needed. With floured hands, form the mixture into traditional meatball-sized balls and lay on surface that has been sprinkled with flour. When all balls are formed, sprinkle generously with flour to coat. Heat a frying depth of oil in skillet and cook balls until golden on all sides, shaking pan gently to evenly brown. Or you can brown the balls in the broiler instead of frying.

Refried beans in tortillas

This is fast, it's good, and so easy even your kids can make it when you're running late and they can't wait!

2 Tbsp. vegetable oil
3 cloves minced garlic
2 cans (14 oz.) baked beans (or left-over home-baked beans, kidney beans, or other dark-bodied cooked or canned beans)
1 tsp. oregano
1 tsp. ground cumin
1 tsp. ground coriander
¼ tsp. crushed chili peppers (optional)
1½ cups grated cheddar cheese

Heat the oil in skillet and sauté garlic until soft. Add remaining ingredients, except cheese, and cook for five minutes. Remove from heat and mash with a fork until smooth. If using home-baked beans you can puree them in the blender if they are too hard to mash. Stir in the cheese and heat, stirring until cheese is melted. Divvy the refried beans up onto tortillas, pile on some fresh spinach or chopped lettuce, diced ripe tomato, a dot of sour cream, and anything else you fancy. Roll up and devour.

Tip: If you don't have homemade or store-bought tortillas on hand, you can serve the refried beans spread on crisp toast, in taco shells, or simply in a bowl surrounded with sturdy corn chips or nachos for scooping. The latter makes a tasty, quick appetizer when unexpected company drops in and you need something super quick to whet their appetites. Makes enough filling for six to eight tortillas.

Sam's spinach, zucchini, and pasta wok supper

My husband, Sam, created this dish a number of years ago and it has been a family favorite ever since. It is simple, yet elegant, and is one dish in our house that never leaves a lick of left-overs.

3 Tbsp. olive oil
1 sliced onion
3 cloves sliced garlic
1 sliced red pepper
1 finely sliced chili pepper
1 medium sliced zucchini
salt and freshly ground black pepper to taste
4 cups fresh spinach (or other available greens such as Swiss chard, beet tops, or dandelion leaves)
1 cup grated mozzarella cheese
¼ cup grated Parmesan cheese
2 Tbsp. crumbled blue cheese (if your family is not a blue cheese fan, this can be omitted but it gives the dish a rich, zingy flavor)
½ cup cherry or grape tomatoes sliced in half
4 cups pasta bows, cooked *al dente*

Cook the pasta bows in boiling water until *al dente*. Drain, toss with 1 tablespoon of the olive oil, and hold hot. Heat the remaining oil in a wok and sauté onion, garlic, peppers, and zucchini until soft. Lower heat and place spinach on top of the sautéed vegetables. Sprinkle with salt and pepper and spread the cooked bows over the spinach layer. Sprinkle with the cheeses and the cherry tomatoes. Cover the wok and cook over very low heat until cheese is melted, spinach is slightly wilted (not fully cooked), and tomatoes are heated through. Serves six. Δ

Building Eric's house

By Dorothy Ainsworth

My curmudgeonly father used to grumble in jest: "Nothing's so bad that it can't get worse." And now I know what he meant. That's exactly how I felt about installing fiberglass insulation and then hanging sheetrock. As soon as the itchy twitchy fiberglass job was done, it was time to hurry and cover the walls with sheetrock so we could install the electrical outlets and all the light fixtures. The *final* electrical inspection deadline was coming up fast!

(Note: "Building Eric's House, Part 3" article left off with passing the *rough* electrical inspection.)

The sheetrock

We both knew *how* to do the job, but we'd be slow—painfully slow. The prospect of hanging 100 heavy 4x12 sheets of ½-inch sheetrock on the walls and 50 sheets of even heavier 4x12x5/8 inch on the vaulted ceilings made me sigh and groan. Considering our regular job schedules, I figured it would take us four months to hang, tape, and texture if we averaged two sheets a day. With the county's mandatory inspection time frame, that was unacceptable, so I grabbed the phone and called a highly recommended drywall guy named Larry Anderson. I asked if he would come up and give us an estimate for the entire job including taping and texturing (two more groan-jobs).

He's a busy man but he rushed up after work and took measurements and made his calculations on the spot, all the while being incredibly cheerful and accommodating. (I don't think I've ever met a more likable contractor; he could get rich selling his attitude!)

He charged the local going rate which is calculated by multiplying the square footage of the house by a factor of 3.5, but was willing to work with us to keep the price down by letting us do the clean-up work for a $200 deduction. He threw in some extras like using green board on the wrap-around window sills (for moisture resistance) and rounded bullnose on all the edges, as well as wrapping the ridge beam and the kitchen archway. His estimate also included covering the basement ceiling with soundproofing board hung from the joists on JC channel and sheetrock over that. This extra step was Eric's request so the basement can be used for piano recordings.

He said the whole job would only take five days. It sounded too good to be true, but it was an offer we couldn't refuse. Eric agreed that this purchase would be the wisest use of a credit card he ever made in his life. For $5700, his house and basement ceiling would be ready to paint within a week. We were ecstatic.

If you want to do it yourself, the best website I found for a quick description of how to hang drywall and the basic tools to do it is at www.hometime.com. (Note: "drywall" and "sheetrock" are synonymous.) My experience in hanging and taping drywall was with 4x8 sheets that I could handle just fine by working with another helper of average strength. There is more waste and there are more seams created using 4x8 sheets rather than 4x12s but

Larry Anderson's sheetrock team works on scaffolding to install 4x12 sheets of drywall on the vaulted living room ceiling. Stovepipe is already installed and ready for the woodstove that will eventually heat the house.

smaller sheets are more doable for a non-professional.

Anybody can do it, but it takes a *lot* of doing to get really good at it. Fortunately, a novice can cover mistakes with extra mud (sheetrock joint compound), and the savings on labor costs is always huge.

Sheetrock is cheap (about $10/sheet) and so is the tape and mud. The basic tools aren't expensive either. If the county wasn't breathing down our necks for mandatory timely inspections, we would have done it ourselves and saved $4,000.

Basement first

Before the soundboard and sheetrock could go on the basement ceiling, we installed 12-inch thick R-38 insulation in the rafters for extra soundproofing. While we were at it we installed R-21 insulation in the walls, then covered the walls with ½-inch OSB (oriented strand board) at $7/sheet and a coat of paint. To completely finish the basement job first, I installed all the electrical GFI outlets as were required down there, and four 8-foot fluorescent light fixtures on the ceiling joists.

The basement has no windows so it's now lit with warm spectrum bulbs. It was fun punching new holes in the metal fixtures using a set of specialized electrician's hole punchers I bought at a garage sale for only $5 (nobody knew what they were, much less what they were worth). I cut the new holes so the fixture wiring would line up with the electrical boxes already installed on the ceiling joists.

The insulation

After the rough electrical inspection, we proceeded to install rolls and rolls of faced fiberglass insulation batts using a battery-powered stapler. We put the vapor barrier side facing the warm (inside) of the room and overlapped the tabs over the stud surface to make a continuous sealed barrier against air infiltration. We were careful to gently part and tuck the insulation around the wires so there were no air gaps.

Green board is used in areas of the house where moisture might be a problem, like around windowsills. The bullnose trim finishes off corners neatly.

In southern Oregon, 2x6 16 inches OC (on center) framing is required in the walls which in turn takes 6-inch thick R-21 insulation. We put 10-inch thick R-30 between the 2x12 roof rafters. 12-inch thick R-38 would have been optimal but is a lot more expensive. The cost of insulation in the entire 2020 square foot house and basement totaled $2000, averaging about $1/square foot.

Important step

Before the insulation could go in and be in the way, I had to make sure there was a nailing surface provided for the sheetrock where the intersection of the ceiling met the gabled walls on the front and back of the house. This should have been done during the framing of the house, but was overlooked.

I screwed 2x4 furring strips to the top of the gable-angled top plates and let one inch protrude out for the necessary nailing surface. If I had forgotten this step, the ceiling-sheetrock would have no substantial support except for the wall-sheetrock to hold it up.

Mechanical work

After passing the insulation inspection with flying squirrels (yay!) I got ready for the mechanical inspection. It required a stovepipe installation through the roof, a bathroom ceiling fan vented through the roof, and an overhead range hood vented through the roof. I was nervous about cutting holes in the roof, but had to grit my teeth and just do it. My main concern was measuring carefully enough to cut the holes in exactly the right spots. There is a catch when cutting a hole in an angled roof. The circle is not flat to the roof; the pipe or ducting has to go through the slanted roof but remain *plumb* (straight up). Therefore the hole cut in the roof will actually be an oval. I held the pipe/duct up to the ceiling and traced around it with a black marking pen, then I drilled up through the roof (from the inside) with a long skinny drill bit held plumb to make a series of holes around the perimeter of the circle. I then cut through the tiny holes with a jigsaw and presto! Daylight.

The stovepipe installation through the vaulted ceiling required some extra framing between the 24-inch spaced rafters, in order to attach a 14-inch square metal four-sided box that went through the roof as part of the mounting kit. The insulated Metalbestos stovepipe needed two inches of cool air clearance all around it where it went through the roof. The box provided that, but it was a challenge building that frame while atop a 12-foot ladder! We could have done it when we installed the rafters, but we weren't sure exactly where the woodstove would go and where the stovepipe would end up exiting through the roof, and we didn't have the mounting kit yet. So after the fact, we located the center of the opening to be cut in the ceiling by hanging a plumb bob down from the ceiling to exactly where it would hit the stove's exit hole, 18 inches out from the wall. (Note: Each woodstove has its own wall clearance requirement, but 18 inches is usually a safe bet.)

We passed the rough mechanical inspection and at the same time, the gas line air-pressure test inspection. That was months ago and the gauge is still holding. I don't think it has lost a molecule of air, which means it won't leak any propane either when the time comes. (Note: The gas line pipe was stubbed out when the plumbing was done.)

The windows

During the harsh winter and spring of 2010 when we were working inside the house, we left the window openings covered with the OSB house-sheathing because of high winds and rainy weather that didn't calm down until the very end of June.

Eric had already bought all his Jeld-Wen vinyl-flanged double-paned Low-E glass windows and had them stored in the house. Home Depot gave him a contractor's discount for buying all nine windows at once, for a total of $1000.

The kitchen archway under construction

As soon as we could, we cut out the openings with a Sawzall in July, and after we applied the recommended sticky sill-seal tape, we installed the windows according to the Jeld-Wen instructions. They pressed into their prepared openings and fit perfectly. They are all rectangular horizontal sliders with screens, except for the fixed pane 5x3.5-foot picture window in the living room.

From the outside it looks like very modest fenestration, but from the inside the amount of light streaming in is plenty and the views are incredible. Eric, who likes cozy more than exposed, is very pleased with the window sizes and their placement. Being a pianist, he's more of an auditory than a visual person, and more of a cave dweller than a light seeker. He loves the basement room even with *no* windows and sometimes practices his piano in the dark. That's the real beauty of building your own home… you can do it *your* way!

The archway

Last winter I built an archway to add some curvy beauty to the big rectangular entranceway into the kitchen. It was a satisfying rainy day project that required some creative engineering to make it strong and perfect, but it turned out to be a pleasing addition to the design of the interior.

Final electrical inspection

Larry completed the sheetrock work exactly as promised—and it looked snowy white and beautiful. But it didn't end there: one of Larry's texturing specialists was also a house painter and he offered to spray paint the whole interior with a primer coat and the satin "Antique White" Eric wanted, for a few hundred bucks—and have it done in two days—so Eric sprung for that too. Now he was in debt, but happily ahead of schedule. When it comes to building a house, sometimes you can't have one without the other.

The kitchen is taped and sanded

When it was all said and done, we finally unveiled the attractive laminated beam that spans the living room (it was wrapped for protection) and we were pleased with the colorful and varied laminations of Douglas Fir wood grain in contrast to the soft white walls.

I floated from room to room for a few heavenly minutes, marveling at how a simple wall covering like ½-inch gypsum board could artistically transform all that went before into such clean and defined living spaces. Millions of houses are sheet-rocked, but when it's your own and you know all too well the work that went into the anatomy inside those walls, it seems miraculous. But being a practical taskmaster, I quickly came back to earth and proceeded to install the 60 outlets, 16 lights, and 2 ceiling fans. Eric bought all brushed-nickel fixtures for a slightly industrial look which he likes, and they are handsome indeed.

I established a routine when hooking up each set of wires so I wouldn't accidentally overlook a step, and treated the wires as if the voltage was on even though it wasn't yet. I connected the ground wire first, then the white wire, and then the hot wire (black and/or red). When working with electricity, it's critical to have impeccable work habits or one strike and *your* lights are out!

After an intense week of fiddling with wires and fixtures, I called for the *final* electrical inspection—and the only shock I got was passing it without a hitch.

Piano move

Eric moved his 9-foot grand piano into the now finished 24x30-foot basement so it would be easy to keep at a constant temperature and humidity through all the seasons—to stay in tune. Not only that, the acoustics bouncing off the smooth concrete floor sound like a concert hall! But I must say that even with all the sound-proofing we did, Beethoven is still loud and clear upstairs, and the reverse will be true when the piano is upstairs someday. The sound-proofing board was no more effective than putting a little cream rinse on Beethoven's hair.

Future final inspections

The next inspection will be the *final* mechanical, which requires the propane cooking range and range hood to be in. Gas ranges cost big bucks, so that'll be a while.

Then there's the *final* plumbing inspection which requires kitchen and bathroom sinks and toilets and the shower to be in, which requires the floors to be done first. We already have two toilets (free donations) and the vintage enameled cast iron sinks I

The kitchen, after paint and light fixtures

The metal hole cutter I found at a garage sale for $5, used to cut new holes in electrical boxes and fixtures.

bought for $1 each at the dump back in the 80s and kept stored. Our contractor friend, Vadim, gave us enough of his leftover tile to do the shower, so now we just need to put in the labor. Eric's dad, Ron, gave him an electric water heater, so he'll use that until he can afford a propane one (gas water heaters are three to four times the cost of electric).

So the next job to tackle will be installing the kitchen and bathroom floors. Eric will probably use some kind of attractive but reasonably priced linoleum tile for those three rooms. He'd love *all* hardwood floors, but his budget dictates some compromises. Maybe someday...

Another *final* is the fire safety and woodstove inspection. The woodstove purchase will have to wait, but at least the stovepipe is already in and ready to hook up.

The interior doors will be easy, and the built-in countertops and cupboards will all be hand-built by Eric. Someday he will install a metal roof over the existing rolled roofing, but for now he's good and dry.

The exterior siding will have to wait until we have the money, then we'll install it ourselves, no matter what it is. Eric is contemplating painted metal (industrial fireproof look) or board and battens (barn style look). We estimate it'll cost $2000 in materials.

House wrap

We wrapped the house with Tyvek in the fall of 2010 to withstand the winter of 2011, and then waterproofed around each window with 6-inch wide sticky tape called "Protecto Wrap," a butyl-hybrid window and door sealing tape made for that purpose. The nine window perimeters and two door perimeters took four 50-foot rolls at $17 each.

Tyvek is just one brand of a breathable membrane house-wrap required by code. Eric bought two 9-foot wide rolls (1500 sq. ft. each) to the tune of $300 and stapled it on.

He then taped all the Tyvek seams with 2-inch-wide Tyvek tape. It took six 164-foot rolls at $13 each. All totalled it was $450 well spent to waterproof the entire house.

Summary of our progress

We're almost home free compared to five years ago when we broke ground for the foundation pad. The *final* building inspection and occupancy permit will optimistically happen by 2012. Maybe I'll hit the lottery before then, but I'm more likely to be hit by an asteroid. Now I sound like my father...Δ

Eric staples on Tyvek housewrap with a hammer tacker.

LED LIGHTING

a breakthrough for independent living and emergency preparedness

PART 1: LED technology essentials

By Tim Thorstenson

LEDs—short for Light Emitting Diodes—offer significant advantages for certain types of lighting, such as flashlights and lanterns for camping, chores, and emergencies, or in bulbs and fixtures for the cabin or off-the-grid home.

However, LED technology is advancing rapidly, which means there are plenty of products on the market that use older and less efficient LEDs. There are also situations where other lighting alternatives may be a better choice. Purchasing LED lights without the proper background information could lead to an expensive investment in stuff that is not nearly as bright and efficient as it could be.

With this in mind, let's examine the things we should know when evaluating and selecting LED-based products. Our main emphasis will be on general principles rather than on details related to specific products. Such details can become outdated pretty rapidly, but a solid background on the technology itself is something that will remain useful even as the products continue to improve.

Our exploration will consist of three parts. In the first, we will focus on the LEDs themselves. In the second, we will examine different categories of LED-based products: flashlights, headlamps, portable lanterns, work lights, and, bulbs and fixtures for area lighting. The things to watch out for can vary quite a bit from one product category to the next. Finally, we'll explore the option of building your own LED-based lights and we'll also consider the important topic of *delivering* light efficiently. Making your own lights does not need to be complicated, and it can allow you to build the most efficient LEDs into finished lights that will work well for your specific needs.

Small LEDs like this can offer a huge efficiency advantage when compared to incandescent bulbs. But it is important to understand the details of this new technology.

LEDs vs. incandescent lights—efficiency is the key

Note: The reader who pursues more information on lighting will find that the term "efficacy" (rather than "efficiency") is often used to describe the performance of light sources. I elected to stick with a more familiar term for our visits.

Efficiency—making as much light as possible from a given amount of power—is critical for anyone interested in independent living or emergency preparedness. Flashlights and lanterns of practical size only have so much room for batteries and we want them to be able to run for a good long time without having to have a huge reserve of batteries on hand. An off-the-grid home will have access to a lot more juice than tiny flashlight batteries, but the power is still sharply restricted in comparison to that available in a conventional home. Some folks take a lead-acid battery to the cabin and then lug it back home for recharging. In this last case, efficient power use is a particularly weighty issue.

Compact, efficient, and flexible: The LED flashlight at center can produce several times more light than the 2-D-cell incandescent at left. But it can also be turned down to roughly the brightness of the incandescent mini-light at right.

In all of these situations, the superior efficiency of LEDs can provide amazing benefits relative to incandescent light bulbs. With respect to flashlights and lanterns, LEDs can accomplish the "impossible" by allowing for products that are small, bright, *and* long running. In the cabin or home, LEDs can offer a choice of benefits. Depending on your goals, they can provide brighter lighting or a reduced power demand or some combination of the two. But to see the benefits and to decide whether the improvement is worth the effort, we need to first examine efficiency in more detail.

Understanding LEDs and comparing efficiency

It is their superior efficiency that makes LEDs worth considering, but what's so hot about them? Well, the answer is quite literally that they are "cool." Conventional incandescent bulbs use the brute force of electrical energy to heat a metal filament until it glows white hot. As a result, most of the electricity actually goes into making heat (invisible infrared radiation) rather than light. In contrast, the process used by LEDs generates a lot less heat. The conversion from electricity to light is still not 100%, but it is dramatically more efficient than the incandescent method.

To see the difference, we need to compare LED and incandescent light sources. To do that, we first need to consider how light is measured. You are probably familiar with the "candlepower" ratings found on things like spotlights, but candlepower measurements are dependent on how the light is focused. This means that the same light bulb can have either a high candlepower value (if placed in a reflector that focuses the light tightly) or a low one (if placed in a lantern that is designed to spread the light uniformly over a large area). The "lumen" is far more useful because it represents the *total* amount of light produced by a source and it is independent of how the light is focused.

In stores, you will find that many light bulbs—and even some flashlights and lanterns—have lumen ratings on the packages. You probably know what a 60-watt incandescent bulb can light up in practical terms. So if you file away the fact that this same bulb produces about 840 lumens of light, you have a mental reference point that can be used to estimate what other light sources will be able to do based on their lumen ratings.

To evaluate *efficiency*, we need to consider the power used as well as the light produced and we already have the numbers we need for our 60 watt incandescent light bulb: if we divide the 840 lumens of light produced by the 60 watts of power consumed, we get 14 (rounded off), which is the number of lumens produced for *each* watt of power used. If we now look at a very different incandescent bulb, we find something rather interesting. A 2-D-cell flashlight with a standard bulb and fresh batteries will produce much less light (about 20 lumens) and it also uses much less power (around 1.5 watts). But if we divide the lumens by the watts, we get a very similar efficiency, about 13 lumens per watt. This may seem surprising at first, but it actually makes sense because there is a fundamental limit to incandescent efficiency which isn't greatly influenced by the brightness of the bulb. To be fair, we should understand that this can be improved somewhat: "halogen," "xenon," and "krypton" bulbs include chemicals that allow the filament to be run at higher temperatures without burning out quickly. With these strategies, incandescent efficiency can be increased to about 20 lumens per watt or a little better.

Now that we have a baseline for what ordinary light bulbs can do, let's consider the LEDs. A readily available LED that is widely used in flashlights can produce up to 230 lumens of light while using about 3.7 watts of power. Dividing this out gives us an efficiency of a little over 60 lumens per watt. This is about *three times* more efficient than the best incandescent bulbs and it illustrates the potential value of LEDs. But consider this: the same LED maker has just released a newer LED that can produce more light (about 340 lumens) while using *less* power (only about 3.3 watts). That calculates out to around 100 lumens per watt and it represents a huge increase in efficiency relative to the older LED. Buying a couple of flashlights without knowing this would probably not be the end of the world, but equipping an entire off-the-grid home with LED bulbs before discovering that newer and better LEDs are available could be pretty darned irritating. Depending on your preferences, the newer technology could allow for a lot brighter lighting or a significant reduction in the size (and expense) of your charger and battery system.

Raw efficiency *is* very important, but there are also several other essential things to consider. In the rest of this article, we'll look at efficiency in more detail, but we'll also identify and examine other important variables.

Other benefits of LEDs

In addition to efficiency, there are some other potential benefits to LEDs that should be mentioned up front. First, they can be very durable and long-running. In a properly designed flashlight or lamp, they can operate for tens of thousands of hours while being very resistant to impact, vibrations, and other stresses that can easily break the filament in an incandescent bulb. LEDs can also be "dimmed" quite easily. You can also dim incandescent bulbs, but the light will change from white to yellow or even orange as the power is reduced. In contrast, LEDs can be run at reduced lumen outputs while still producing white light. This allows you to easily tailor the brightness of the lighting to the needs at hand. Perhaps more importantly, LEDs actually become *more* efficient as the power input is reduced, so they can provide for effective energy management in the event of an emergency or if the wind and sun are not cooperating with a charging system.

The nuts and bolts details

Now that you have a general idea about LEDs and their potential advantages, let's consider a number of technical details.

Not all LEDs are created equal.

The process of forming the little "chip" of light-emitting material in an LED is rather touchy. This means that *individual* LEDs can vary considerably in efficiency from one to the next within the *same* product line. If you ran into handgun ammo that varied in velocity by 20% from cartridge to cartridge, I bet you'd find a different supplier. But with LEDs, this is simply the way it is. Fortunately, the LED manufacturers don't make their customers play roulette. Rather, the LEDs are tested and sorted into different "bins" based on their efficiency. As an example, a company called Cree makes a line of LEDs called the "XR-E." This is a high quality LED that is suitable for a number of purposes and, until recently, it was about as efficient as you could get. Now the best readily available bin of the XR-E (which is labeled "Q5") can boast an efficiency of 92 lumens per watt when run at low power. But the lowest bin of this same LED (called the P4) has a notably lower efficiency—only about 70 lumens per watt. Not surprisingly, the best bins command a premium price while the less efficient ones are cheaper.

A company making LED-based bulbs or flashlights could honestly state that it uses a certain brand of LED that is known for good efficiency. But the maximum possible efficiency of that specific product will depend on exactly which "bin" of the LED is being used. Makers of certain better-quality products will tell you exactly which bin they are using, but

Efficiently adjustable brightness is a major benefit of LEDs. These beams are from identical flashlights, but the beam at left is the lowest of three available outputs, while the one at right is the highest. Runtime ranges from 45 minutes to dozens of hours.

most consumer quality products will not. In most cases, consumer products will use less efficient bins to keep the production costs down. Such products are not necessarily a bad deal (and there is nothing wrong with lower bin LEDs in terms of their mechanical quality or reliability), but this is certainly a good thing to understand before making a purchase.

There is a law of diminishing returns.

The brightness (lumen output) of an LED can be varied over a wide range by adjusting the power input. Thus, the same compact flashlight that can belt out a couple hundred lumens for security or for checking cattle can be dialed down to a couple dozen lumens for routine tasks or even down to just a few lumens to provide electric candlelight for camping or a long-duration emergency. Fixed lighting in a cabin or home could be adjusted in a similar fashion to accommodate different lighting requirements and to conserve power when needed.

LED makers specify the maximum power that their products are designed to handle. But they often measure performance at a lower power input and the difference in efficiency at these two points can be considerable. For instance, a Cree XR-E LED from the Q5 bin will produce around 230 lumens at maximum power with an efficiency of about 62 lumens per watt. At the lower power level used during testing (which is about 1/3 of maximum), only about 107 lumens of light is produced, but efficiency climbs to about 92 lumens per watt. In other words, one must roughly triple the power input in order to double the light output. The numbers will vary with different LEDs, but the general principle is the same—efficiency decreases as the power input is increased.

With flashlights, it is nice to be able to crank the LED up to a high power level because, in some situations, you can use all the light you can get. But the ability to reduce the brightness is not only useful for preventing glare and temporary blindness during close-range work, it is also extremely valuable for battery conservation during emergencies. With a properly designed LED flashlight, a disproportionate power savings can be gained as the brightness is reduced. As an example, a company called Fenix is well regarded for making good quality LED flashlights and their "LD20" model will produce 180 lumens for up to two hours from a pair of rechargeable AA batteries. But if the light is switched to its lowest output of 9 lumens (about the brightness of a good penlight), runtime stretches to 71 hours. Here, the light output is being reduced by a factor of 20. But in exchange, the runtime is extended by a factor of 35. Proper electronics are essential to actually getting this sort of performance, so careful flashlight selection is essential.

Somewhat different (but related) considerations apply to bulbs and fixtures. The *cheapest* way to make a bulb of a given brightness would be to select a suitable LED and run it at maximum power. But a much more efficient approach would be to use two or three of the same LEDs and run them at a more conservative power level. It is certainly reasonable to suspect that bargain basement products will use the cheap approach rather than the efficient one. As we will see, the "cheap" strategy can have other serious drawbacks in addition to reduced efficiency.

Beware of rosy numbers.

The lumen outputs and efficiencies are values for the LEDs themselves. But the overall efficiency of an actual bulb or fixture will always be somewhat lower, for a number of reasons. First, electronic controllers are usually used in LED-based lights and these consume some power, too. Second, any real-life lighting product requires "optical" components like reflectors, lenses, and diffusers, and even the best of these will scatter and absorb some light and keep it from getting to where it is needed. Third, virtually all real life products will run the LEDs at temperatures which are somewhat

Cool white LEDs (left) are more efficient. But a warm white output (right) can be more pleasant and provide better color perception.

Electronic controllers (or drivers) are usually used to power LEDs and they provide several benefits. Drivers can be purchased as separate components by those interested in building LED-based lights.

higher than ideal and this causes output and efficiency to decline somewhat. As a result of these factors, even a carefully designed product will generally have an overall efficiency that is no more than about 75% of the published efficiency of the LED itself. With inexpensive, mass-produced products, it is reasonable to expect even a little lower performance. But a poorly designed product could have an overall efficiency that is much lower yet.

The raw lumen and efficiency values provided by LED makers such as Cree are invaluable for comparing different LEDs to each other. But when it comes to comparing products, we need to have honest lumen measurements and efficiency ratings for the *final product*. This is generally not a big deal with things like flashlights and camp lanterns, but it is critical if you will be buying a number of (potentially expensive) bulbs or fixtures for lighting up a cabin or off-the-grid home. It is also useful to understand that this same concern applies to other lighting technologies, too. For instance, currently available "compact fluorescent" (CFL) bulbs are capable of certain efficiencies, but this is not a guarantee that any given CFL bulb will actually provide this level of performance.

Regardless of the type of product or the technology being considered, the most reliable way of dealing with this issue is by getting reliable numbers from a reputable manufacturer. But it should be noted that the required testing can be prohibitively expensive for a small company. For instance, there are several makers of some pretty decent quality flashlights that use excellent electronics and top-grade LEDs, but they do not conduct actual lumen output measurements because the required equipment is touchy and expensive. I mention this for an important reason: as LED technology continues to improve, the big companies will likely focus on bulbs and fixtures designed for use with 120 volts AC. But a smaller company can focus on specialty applications and quickly incorporate the newest and most efficient LEDs. Thus, small manufacturers may offer some very good products for off-grid applications, but they may not be able to provide the sort of testing and "independent certification" that we would expect from an outfit like G.E. or Sylvania. A good understanding of the technology can help with a sensible evaluation of products like these.

Heat is a concern.

There is a diminishing return with LEDs—as power input is increased, efficiency will decrease. But a higher power input will also cause the LED to produce more heat. If this heat is not removed, it will cause the LED to operate at a higher temperature with a couple of negative consequences. First, the efficiency and lumen output of the LED will decrease as the operating temperature increases. Second, LEDs usually fail by slowly deteriorating rather than "burning out" quickly like an incandescent light bulb. This process happens more quickly at a higher temperature, so an increased operating temperature will result in a shorter service life. Because good quality LEDs are rather expensive, getting a long service life is important.

For these reasons, LEDs must be mounted to a metal surface that will conduct the heat away from the LED. For things like flashlights, the metal mass of the light itself is often an adequate "heat sink." But bulbs used for area lighting are often operated for extended periods, so sheer metal bulk may not do the job. If the heat is not transferred to the surrounding air, it will build up in the metal and the temperature of the LED will increase over time. Here, surface area is more important than sheer bulk and "cooling fins" are the key. These are occasionally used in flashlights, but they are especially critical with area lights. For making your own lights, aluminum "heat sinks" can be purchased for a reasonable price and these provide heat removal that is far superior to what can be had from a simple block or chunk of metal. "Active cooling" (using a small fan) can provide extremely effective heat

A multi-die LED provides a greater lumen output by packing several light-emitting chips into a single LED housing. The one shown here contains four chips.

removal, but it is often impractical for lighting applications.

When it comes to buying products, it can be difficult to determine whether the design includes good "heat management" just by looking at the product. This heat issue also reveals that there are some situations where LEDs can be less than ideal. "Recessed cans" and other enclosed fixtures may prevent good cooling and result in higher operating temperatures and shorter service lives. Many flashlights are designed with the assumption that the product will not routinely get used for long, uninterrupted periods. If you intend to habitually use a flashlight as an "electric candle" it would be a good idea to select one with adjustable brightness settings and dial it back somewhat during such use.

One note: This discussion of heat may make it sound like these LEDs are veritable blast furnaces. While this heat is an important technical issue so far as good LED performance is concerned, it is only a fraction of what is generated by an incandescent light of equivalent lumen output.

Service life

LEDs often claim a lifetime of many thousand hours, but it is important to understand what is meant by the claim. The numbers will vary from one manufacturer to the next, but here's an example. The Cree XR-E LEDs mentioned earlier claim a service life of 50,000 hours. But LEDs do fade in brightness with use and 50,000 hours is the point at which lumen output will have fallen to 70% of its original value. Very importantly, this lifespan assumes that the LED is being operated at a specified temperature, so service life in the real world can vary considerably. With a combination of a conservative power input and good heat removal, the LED will operate at a much lower temperature and tens of thousands of hours of operation is possible with little or no deterioration in brightness. On the other hand, conditions that lead to a higher operating temperature can reduce service life and accelerate the deterioration of the LED by quite a bit.

For items like flashlights and headlamps, service life is generally not a major issue because such products rarely get tens of thousands of hours of use. But when it comes to bulbs or fixtures for a well-used room in the home, it doesn't take too long to pile up a lot of hours. A fixture or bulb maker can parrot the service life claims of an LED manufacturer like Cree. But unless the product is properly designed, its real operating life can be much shorter. It can be virtually impossible to assess whether a given product is well designed just by looking at it. Thus, reputable manufacturers are an important consideration because it is often necessary to rely on their claims.

Maximum efficiency isn't everything.

"White" LEDs are actually available in different color tints, ranging from "cool white" to "neutral white" to "warm white" and many LED-based products are available in color tints. It turns out that cool white LEDs are generally best in terms of raw efficiency and things go downhill from there. For instance, the 92 lumen per watt efficiency quoted earlier for the Cree XR-E LED was for the best bin in *cool* white. But in neutral white, the best available efficiency is only 81 lumens per watt. In warm white, it drops even further to 70 lumens per watt.

It can be very tempting to select cool white products for efficiency's sake. With flashlights or portable lanterns that will be used for things like maintenance, security, and emergencies, this may be a sensible strategy. But many users state that the neutral or warm LEDs provide better color perception and they are equally or more effective in the field, even though their lumen outputs may be lower. And when it comes to area lighting in a cabin or home (or even a tent), a lot of folks will find the harsh moonlight color of cool white to be ghostly, sterile, and perhaps even a little unnerving. On the other hand, "warmer" tints are found to be more pleasant and this may be worth the tradeoff in some settings. Neutral white may be a good compromise in certain situations and, in some LED product lines, the efficiency of cool and neutral white are very similar or even identical. The ideal approach would be to try out the different color tints before purchasing a large number of LEDs or bulbs.

Electronics

To control the power flowing to an LED, electronic regulators (often called "drivers") are usually used. Commercial products will incorporate the driver right into the product, but they can also be purchased as separate components for making your own LED-based lights.

Most LED manufacturers specify operation in terms of electrical current. This is the actual flow of electrons through the LED and it is usually measured in "milliamps" (mA). The published efficiencies and lumen outputs of many small LEDs are reported when the electrical current is 350 mA, but most of them can handle higher inputs of 700 or 1,000 mA. If we think in terms of water, the electrical current (milliamps) flowing through the LED would be equivalent to a water flow measured in something like "gallons per minute." Voltage is the pressure behind the electricity and pushing more current through an LED will require more voltage. As an example, it takes about 3.3 volts to run a Cree XR-E LED at 350 mA. But if we want to operate it at maximum (1,000 mA for cool white XR-Es), the voltage (pressure) must be increased to around 3.7 volts. As you may expect, the required voltage will vary from one brand of LEDs to the next. But it will also vary a bit with individual LEDs from the same product line due to the afore-mentioned touchiness involved in the chip-forming process. Because of this variation and because a small difference in voltage can produce a large change in current flow, trying to power LEDs by adjusting the supply voltage to some measured value is not the best approach.

This is where the driver comes in. Most drivers are designed to prevent problems by maintaining a fixed flow of electrical *current* under varying voltage conditions. There are two general classes of drivers: "boost" drivers take a voltage which is too low and increase it to push the needed current. "Buck" drivers, on the other hand, can take a voltage which is too high and reduce it to keep the current flow at a specified level. Some very cheap flashlights and other products use a simple resistor to restrict the flow of current to the LED, but this inexpensive strategy will not compensate for a changing source voltage and it may not be very efficient. In contrast, a driver can control things on the fly and the benefits are well worth the expense in most cases. The electrical current delivered by many drivers can be manually adjusted by the user, so the driver can also serve as the means of adjusting brightness when that capability is desired.

A common annoyance with incandescent flashlights is that their brightness fades as the batteries discharge. But an LED flashlight that uses a well-designed driver can maintain almost full brightness until the batteries are nearly dead. In addition, the right driver design can allow a flashlight to use several different battery options that provide different voltages. Proper drivers can offer a similar benefit in a home or cabin equipped with storage batteries and a wind or solar charger. The driver will not only maintain full brightness as voltage drops during battery discharge, it will also protect the LEDs from excessive current when the charger is running and voltage increases. An important precaution here is to make sure that the drivers can handle the maximum voltage produced by the charger (this can be up to several volts higher than

LEDs are ideal for use in weapon-mounted lights like the Streamlight "TLR-1" at left. Safariland's "Rapid Light System" (RLS), at right, can be had with an included flashlight, but the handy RLS mounting bracket can also be ordered alone and mated with a number or readily available "tactical" flashlights.

There is a dizzying array of LED-based flashlights available. Selecting the right ones can be a challenge, so we'll explore the details in our next visit. For size comparison, a 2-D-cell incandescent flashlight is shown at the far right.

the "nominal" 12 or 24 volts at which the system is rated). If you are thinking about making your own, you can get drivers with pre-connected wiring harnesses and versions that allow the brightness of the LEDs to be adjusted simply by turning a knob.

Drivers do consume power and this can have a significant impact on the overall efficiency of a real life flashlight, fixture, or bulb. A good driver can be very efficient (90% or better) but a poor design can greatly reduce the overall efficiency of an LED-based product. An honest and accurate efficiency value from a reputable manufacturer will include the power used by the driver.

Some real-life LEDs

There are a few distinctly different types of LEDs and each has different benefits and drawbacks. As the technology continues to advance, the specific LEDs cited here (along with the efficiencies and lumen outputs) will become outdated, but the general principles will remain useful. Most manufacturers specify some "tolerance" (such as +/- 5%) when it comes to the performance of individual LEDs within a given bin, so the numbers presented here are subject to some variation. If you want an idea of what real life products are capable of offering, you can generally deduct about 25% from the raw lumen outputs and efficiencies that I cite to allow for various sources of efficiency loss.

Pin type LEDs: These little LEDs look like small plastic bulbs or bubbles and they are usually connected via a couple of small metal wires (i.e. pins) that stick out of the bottom of their plastic housings. While some of them can be fairly efficient, they are not very bright. Typically, anywhere from a few to several dozen of these LEDs are ganged together to produce a reasonable amount of light output. These little guys DO have their uses, but they are definitely not in the same class as the high-power, high-efficiency LEDs that are our primary interest. The nature of their design prevents good heat-sinking and this can lead to problems when they are used in applications that involve extended operation.

"Single die" LEDs: I will refer to the small LEDs suitable for applications like flashlights as "single die" LEDs. The Cree XR-E LED that we have used as a working example is an LED of this type and, until recently, it represented about the best efficiency you could find. Once again, a best bin Cree XR-E LED in "cool white" (the Q5 bin) can produce about 107 lumens with an efficiency of 92 lumens per watt at low power. Run at maximum power, an output of about 230 lumens is possible, but efficiency falls to around 62 lumens per watt.

Similar LEDs are also available from other companies, including Phillips (maker of the "Luxeon" brand) and Seoul Semiconductor Corporation (or SSC). But Cree blew everyone's doors off recently (including their own) with the release of the XP-G LED. At low power, the best version (the R5 bin) can generate 140 lumens with an efficiency of 130 lumens per watt. At maximum power, it can produce 340 lumens while retaining an efficiency of about 100 lumens per watt. Right now, it is available only in "cool white," but it is likely that warmer color tints (along with even more efficient cool white bins) will become available with time. Several flashlight makers have already incorporated the XP-G LEDs into at least some of their products. Unfortunately, the gears are turning more slowly when it comes to bulbs and fixtures for *area* lighting.

"Multi-die" LEDs: If more light is needed than one "single die" LED can provide, a viable strategy is to simply use two or more such LEDs. For area lighting, this is often the best approach because it allows both the light and the heat to be spread out over a larger area. But this can also be impractical in some situations, especially when space is limited. Because of this, another option called the "multi-die" LED is also available. We can understand both the name and the operation of this LED by simply imagining several (usually four) individual chips of light-emitting material packed into a single LED housing.

Example LEDs in this category include the "MC-E" from Cree and the "P-7" from Seoul Semiconductor Corporation (SSC). The best bin P7s are a little brighter, but the MC-E provides a little more flexibility with respect to how it can be connected and powered. Fed at low power, best bin versions of these LEDs can produce 400 to 500 lumens with efficiencies of around 90 lumens per watt. At maximum power, around 700 to 900 lumens is possible with efficiencies of 70 lumens per watt or better. Although the total lumen outputs are higher, the efficiencies here are quite similar to those of single-die LEDs like the Cree XR-E. This reflects the fact that multi-die LEDs use basically the same technology. Sticking several light-emitting chips into one package can provide more lumens, but it will not increase efficiency. Of course, advances in single-die LEDs could certainly be incorporated into multi-die units.

Multi-die LEDs are a viable alternative for brighter area lights, but heat management becomes especially important because they produce a comparatively large amount of heat which is concentrated in a small area. These LEDs are also used to make bright portable flashlights.

Different design strategies can be used to turn a given LED into very different final products. Even if you are not specifically interested in flashlights, this is a useful lesson that applies to other LED-based products as well:

First, a flashlight capable of running these LEDs at maximum power for any significant period of time will need to be somewhat bigger than the compact alternatives which use single-die LEDs. Even so, such products can still be smaller and lighter weight than a metal 2-D-cell incandescent flashlight, while belting out as much light as a small plug-in spotlight and running for an hour or more on self-contained batteries.

A second strategy is to put a multi-die LED into a more modest-sized package and run it at low to medium power. Initially, this may seem like a waste of the LED's potential, but it can actually be a very sensible approach that makes use of the relationship between power and efficiency: a multi-die LED at *low* power can produce more light than a single-die LED at *high* power, but the power demand and heat production remain modest enough to allow for a reasonably small package.

Finally, the multi-die LED is again built into a fairly compact flashlight, but the electronics now allow operation at maximum (or close to maximum) power. The caveat here is that full-power operation is restricted to only a few minutes at a time—either by the electronics or by the user. A perfect application for this design is self-defense (armed or otherwise): the flashlight is small enough to allow convenient on-person carry, but its ability to belt out 700 lumens or more for a few minutes can be very useful in an encounter with a weirdo. Lower output settings can be included in such a design to allow extended operation for other uses.

Bigger single-die LEDs: Multi-die LEDs present some technical limitations. Most notably, they can be difficult to focus tightly and uniformly when placed in a flashlight reflector. But there are also LEDs becoming

LED technology update

One of the main points of this series is that LED technology is continuing to advance. When these articles first came to mind, the Cree XR-E LED ruled the roost in terms of efficiency. By the time the articles became finalized, the newer XP-G was widely available, both in flashlights and as a separate component for the home-brewer. But as the first article actually goes to press, the even newer Cree XM LED is becoming readily available.

The XM provides a low power efficiency of 160 lumens per watt (as opposed to 139 lumens per watt for the XP-G and 92 lumens per watt for the older XR-E). The efficiency jump this time isn't as dramatic, but the XM also boasts some other huge benefits. First, it can handle a whopping 2 amps (or 2,000 milliamps) of electrical current. At this power level, the XM will generate about 750 lumens, so it will almost equal the output of a 60 watt incandescent bulb while only using around 7 watts of power. Just as importantly for some uses, it will be more efficient at transferring heat. When it comes to applications like area lights, we saw that it is usually prudent to run LEDs at well below maximum power to keep them reasonably cool during extended use. But the XM's ability to dump its heat efficiently means that it will be possible to push it harder while retaining an excellent service life (an adequate "heat sink" will still be needed – the benefit is that the XM will essentially be able to make better use of it). The combination of a high power limit and efficient heat transfer means that a lot fewer LEDs will be needed in order to produce a given amount of light. Finally, these benefits are compounded by the fact that this will be a small single-die LED, as opposed to one of the fancier options like the multi-die LEDs and the Luminus "SST-50." It will come close to these in terms of maximum light output, but it should be a lot less expensive. This is good news for both those interested in pre-made products (part two) and those who would like to take a shot at building their own LED lights (part three).

available that use a single, larger chip of light-emitting material to produce multi-die levels of output (and more) without the need for multiple chips of emitting material. A very new and good example is the "PhlatLED" LEDs produced by a company called Luminus. Their "SST-50" LED is pretty comparable to the multi-die alternatives in terms of raw performance (lumen output and efficiency), but it can produce a tighter and/or more uniform beam in flashlight applications. Thus, the SST-50 could be especially useful in any of the flashlight design strategies that were just discussed in the multi-die category. The SST-50 has already been incorporated into a few flashlights.

Luminus also makes a bigger "PhlatLED" LED (the SST-90) and this is a good example of what is becoming possible in area lighting for the home. Its efficiency at low power is close to 100 lumens per watt (in cool and neutral white). Now this is not remarkable in and of itself, but the ability of the SST-90 to maintain this efficiency while providing a big lumen output is definitely noteworthy: at *low* power, the SST-90 can produce about 1,000 lumens. LEDs like this make bright fixtures and bulbs feasible without the need for a multiple number of LEDs and the potential applications for the cabin and home are pretty self-explanatory. At this writing, these LEDs are still quite expensive and I am not aware of any commercial bulbs or fixtures that have incorporated them. That, however, is likely to change with time. By the way, the SST-90 can produce about 2200 lumens when run up to maximum power. Efficiency here drops to about 70 lumens per watt and considerable heat-sinking is needed, but it could prove very useful in applications like car- or battery-powered spotlights and emergency work lights. At least one better-quality flashlight maker is already offering a product that uses this LED to its full effect.

A bit of philosophy

For those who would like to light up a cabin or an off-the-grid home from batteries and a solar or wind charger, LEDs are a very promising technology. For anyone who just wants a flashlight that is super-bright, very-long-running, and/or extremely compact, the darned things are also pretty neat.

But the rapid and continuing advance in technology can also be rather frustrating and—potentially—disappointing. This advance will not continue forever because there is a scientific upper limit on how many lumens can be produced from a watt of power, but LEDs are likely to continue to improve in both brightness and efficiency in the foreseeable future. In addition, it takes some time for the newest LEDs to get incorporated into actual products. This process happens pretty quickly with things like flashlights, but it has been slower when it comes to products like bulbs and fixtures for area lighting. These factors lead to an obvious problem: even if you are armed with all the facts and do the best possible research, it is still likely that products you purchase will be outclassed by ones that become available in the future.

To avoid irritation, confusion, and bad purchases, here's a practical way of looking at it: when it comes to things like flashlights and headlamps, the LED-based choices which are already available can kick the pants off of incandescents in terms of efficiency, so they are an excellent choice for many needs. It still might be best to ease yourself into them instead of immediately outfitting the whole family, all the cars, and all the survival kits. Something "better" is almost guaranteed to turn up in the months following your purchase. A related problem with flashlights is that there are a *lot* of good options available (along with some junk!), so weeding through the choices to fit the products to your needs can be a challenge.

When shopping for fixed area lights for the cabin or home, things are a lit-

Common LED suppliers

Cree: www.cree.com
Luminus: www.luminus.com
Seoul SemiConductor Corporation: www.seoulsemicon.com

General information

www.light-reviews.com is a review site that contains reviews of a large number of LED-based flashlights.

www.candlepowerforums.com is a web forum that contains a lot of information on LED technology and products.

I am familiar with these product sources and confident in their reliability:
4Sevens (Fenix Lights): 678-608-0308 / www.4sevens.com
FlashlightConnection: www.FlashlightConnection.com
FlashlightZ: 866-764-9900 / www.flashlightz.com
LED Supply: 802-728-6031 / www.ledsupply.com
Lighthound: 713-436-2609 / www.lighthound.com
MagnaLight: 800-369-6671 / www.magnalight.com
Malkoff Devices: 334-393-3717 / www.malkoffdevices.com
Pacific Tactical Solutions: 509-214-0302 / www.pts-flashlights.com
Streamlight: 800-523-7488 / www.streamlight.com

tle different and much more caution is required. Because space, weight, and durability are not critical limitations as they are with flashlights, other technologies are practical and these include fluorescent, "metal halide" and, in a few applications, yellow "sodium vapor." Until recently, these alternatives have been able to beat the efficiency of LEDs and this has likely slowed the development of LED-based fixtures and bulbs. The newest LEDs will be able to equal or exceed these other choices with regard to efficiency, but most of the LED bulbs and fixtures available at this writing do not use these newest LEDs. Even once they do, there is always the possibility of even more efficient LEDs (or other technologies) coming down the pipe.

In addition, we also need to consider factors like cost. If things like microwaves, cellular phones, and televisions are any indication, it is quite likely that LED-based fixtures and bulbs will start out very expensive and become much cheaper after they have been around for a while. When considering fixed area lighting, it is important to look at all the options and compare not only efficiency, but also things like total lumen output, purchase price, and service life. The "best" choice will depend on individual needs and it will also change with time as the technologies evolve. Unfortunately, there is no perfect answer here, but we'll try to get a better handle on the issue in our next visit.

The author welcomes comments and feedback. You can reach him at timthorstenson@yahoo.com Δ

COOKING WITH A CAST IRON STOVE

By Cynthia Hummel

The work involved in maintaining our century-old cast iron cook stove never seemed like much of a chore. A 30-percent electric rate hike and several major snowstorms made shaking down the coals and shoveling ashes nearly enjoyable this winter.

A Prizer Regal cook stove came with our mid-1800s farmhouse when we purchased it 15 years ago. It was the former owner's sole cooking and heating source November through April. Although we knew little about old ranges, we decided to keep it running with help from some more knowledgeable folks.

Eighty-five-year-old Suzanna Eberlie of Ephrata, Pennsylvania, along with her 90-year-old sister Annie Huber, cooked on nothing but cast iron ranges until they switched to a modern version in recent years. They share our enthusiasm. "The kitchen range is hard to beat," Suzanna said.

A Prizer Regal cast iron cook stove

Our then-octogenarian great aunt Ida Hummel of Lititz, Pennsylvania, clearly recalled how to begin. "You build a fire until coals get good and hot," Ida said. "Then you add thin layers of coal, until the firebox is nearly full."

The firebox, normally located on the left side, is the heart of the range. Minnie Aker of Ephrata, Pennsylvania, has a two-century-old cast iron stove with a lever to open the entire stove top to add fuel or stoke the fire. Our stove requires us to remove one of the round plates, also known as "eyes" or "lids" on top with a lifter to maneuver wood through openings.

A common first mistake with a cast iron range is not opening the damper on the stove pipe, forcing the smoke into the room. Our stove also has a vertical check lever that can send room-temperature air into a too-hot firebox. The end of the firebox has a top sliding vent that opens down, serving as a broiler when a long-handled wire basket is carefully inserted into the opening. A second vertical check lever below the broiler controls airflow to the fire.

Antique stove restorer Barry Rhoades of Quarryville, Pennsylvania, explained another important mechanism, a lever, that when pulled up, forces hot air to circulate around the oven.

Barry said he can bring water to a boil in his Queen Bee stove within 15 minutes. He places loosely crumpled newspaper below kindling in the firebox and more at the opening to the stove pipe. The suction creates a quick draft.

Suzanna explained that you can cook things over the front of the firebox and move them to the back burner, or further away from the heat as needed.

"If they (the men working outside) didn't come to dinner on time," she recalled, "then you can move it around and the meal will still be warm."

For a quicker heat, remove an eye and place a heavy pan directly over the opening. We use this method with a cast iron griddle when making pancakes each Christmas morning.

Unless you grew up with a coal stove, learning to bake successfully takes practice with opening and closing dampers. Oven door thermometers serve only as a guide. Older stoves and cookbooks sometimes list baking temperatures only as slow (300 degrees), moderate (350 degrees), and hot (425 degrees). Preheating your oven, rotating foods, and mastering dampers helps foods bake more evenly.

A range reservoir provides a constant supply of hot water. Some models even have a spigot at the bottom.

This view through an "eye" shows the start of a wood fire.

A grate at the bottom of the stove should be occasionally shaken, or "riddled," using a cast iron arm until you see light of the hot coals. Antique stoves, which are less airtight, burn less efficiently and need to be emptied more often. Our stove's ash pan is located below a shelf at the left end of the stove.

A broiler door opens up to insert a long-handled metal basket.

Barry explained that cleaning a coal stove is vital to its function. He uses a Shop-Vac® to remove ash and soot from below the ash pan and around the oven through the top of the stove. A soot door, which gives access to an area below the oven, is hidden on our stove by a nickel "skirt" decoration.

The outside of the stove can be cleaned with stove polish, or as Minnie prefers, handmade soap.

The uses of a cook stove are limitless. It can serve as a humidifier by putting a pan of water on the top. We dehydrate fruits, roast garlic, make yogurt, and warm foods. Minnie dries corn on the cob in her oven, then grinds it for cornmeal.

The stove also provides a heat source that continues when the electricity goes out and lowers our utility bills all year long.

As Mary D. Chambers wrote in her 1925 book, *How to Cook on a Wood Cook Stove: The Secret of Better Baking*, "No other article in the home means so much to the entire family as the kitchen range. Health and comfort are dependent upon it." Δ

Build a chicken tractor

By Connie Rabun

In the beginning we had chickens...and no coop! Any homesteader knows that the number one rule is to always have your animal housing prepared before you invest in the animal. We knew the rule but we ignored it! We are still forging our way into mistakes and ignoring smart advice, and I reckon that is how we got started with our chickens. All of a sudden (or so it seemed) we had 30 layer chicks and no permanent place to put them. By the time they outgrew their box in the house, we knew we had to do something. I can't stand to see an animal in a pen with no "natural" browse—just mud and yuck—so I had a pretty good idea of what I wanted in the way of a moveable coop for my chickens. Wonderful hubby and I set about in the scrap lumber pile on the farm and created a moveable brooder pen that could grow with the chicks until they were ready for a big pen. We were instantly "chicken-tractor" fans.

Closeup of spot welds attaching cattle panel to purlin

That was 10 years ago on 10 acres in Texas. We have now updated our homestead to an 80-acre farm here in the beautiful Missouri Ozarks and we are still chicken owners (among the milk cows, hogs, rabbits, wildlife, and seven children). However, we have never built the ideal chicken tractor until my homestead hubby said he would come up with something. I reminded him that it had to be where our ladies were free to browse, yet contained. They had to be protected from ground varmints and from flying predators. It would be nice if it had an egg checking door and was easy enough to move that the children could handle it and after "the look" that says "I love you" (he always gives me that look when I am trying to tell him how to do something) I left the planning up to him. What resulted is the first chicken tractor that we are really happy with.

The "people" end of the pen during construction—nest boxes are in place.

We built our prototype coop a little smaller than the one we planned for the layers with the intention of using it for the broilers we raise in the spring and fall. After using it for a year, we decided to build the real thing. We made the second version larger to permanently accommodate our laying flock of 30 chickens along with all the amenities. First we had to see what materials we had on hand to build it out of. Since my husband has a race engine/metal fabrication shop, metal scraps are plentiful. We like to build with metal for its strength and durability (never mind that Mr. Wonderful is a welder—not a carpenter).

The frame

We started our pen with two 25-foot purlins as the base to make it easy to attach the cattle panels to. The purlins have the added benefit of having some "flex" for those not so perfectly flat spots like we have here in the Missouri Ozarks. He cut and bent the purlin to make the ends 11 feet long and the sides 14 feet long. Next, we spot-welded cattle panels to the purlin, arching them to make the Quonset hut style. Because we wanted this coop to be cheap, and because cattle panels are expensive, we gave up the idea of making the coop tall enough to stand in easily, and just used the arched cattle panels. This makes the middle height (which is the highest) approximately five feet. We overlapped edges of the cattle panels for added strength. On the ends of the pen, we had to cut the panels to fit the arch, which incurred a little waste. All together we used six cattle panels—four down the length and one on each end. After he had the cattle panels secured, we wrapped the sides of the pen in 48-inch chicken wire on top of the panels, then we made one wrap up and over the far end of the coop (where it would not be covered with the tarp) to prevent anything crawling in and deciding to have lunch. We attached the chicken wire to the cattle panels with small pieces of safety wire.

Nest box door for easy access to eggs without entering the pen (note the cattle panel still in place)

Wheel on bolt axle

The door end

Next we had to make the "people" end of the coop. This end of the coop would be enclosed in order to give the coop three closed sides and one open. We cut the door out of the cattle panel end and built the door frame out of some scrap rebar. We framed the door from rebar also, then attached the cut out piece of cattle panel to it. We hung the nest boxes (picked up on the side of the road for $20) to the right of the door on the inside of the coop. We decided to leave the cattle panel in place behind the nest boxes, since hands will easily fit through the squares to gather eggs, and framed up a door out of rebar. We opted to cover the "people" end of the coop with old barn tin, adding even more character and beauty to our designer chicken tractor (besides, the tin has been piled beside the barn for years). We cut the tin to match the shape of the hoop, and also covered the door to make it even more predator proof. Mr. Wonderful made a door latch by welding a nut to the rebar door frame and a matching nut to the coop that would align when the door was closed. He welded a pin on a chain to the coop (so it wouldn't get lost). Now when we close the door, we simply drop the pin into the nuts and it is latched. He made the hinges for the door by screwing a nut onto a bolt, then welding the bolts to the door and the nuts to the coop. It works wonderful. Every time the door opens, it just turns in its little nut. We built the door for the eggs the same way, except that it is just covered with the old tin, no cattle panel since we left it on the coop. Once we had the human end of the coop done, it was time to install some roost poles. We installed them in about the middle of what was going to be the tarped area, that way they are out of the rain. We went into our woods and cut some long skinny trees, which we notched on each end to make them fit over the cattle panel wire, and then wedged them into place. We safety-wired the ends to the panel also to prevent a collapse, and placed two safety wire supports in the middle for added stability. The installation of the tarp cover was next. We used a tarp for the top cover, which we secured with tie wraps onto the coop to keep the wind from whipping it around. It covers the entire top of the coop except for the final three feet, which we had wrapped in chicken wire to be able to keep it open for more sun exposure. We have found that a regular tarp will last about one year in the elements, but if you can get your hands on used billboard tarps, they will last two to three years.

Closeup of "trailer hitch" with dolly lifting the frame

The moving mechanisms

After having the coop mostly complete, all we lacked was a way to move it. We wanted it to be easy to move so that the children could handle it themselves. This was mostly accomplished with the light weight of the metal, but we needed wheels and a pull/push system. We opted to buy a set of solid lawn mower wheels which cost about $8 each. On one end of the coop we welded a bolt onto each corner to mount each tire. We also welded a bolt on the top of the frame on each corner as a place to store the wheel when not in use, since we remove the wheels every day to keep out any digging critters. With the wheels stored right on the coop it is easier for the children to keep track of them. We wanted to be able to make very sharp turns with the coop, so that we could maneuver the chickens through the orchard. The Chief Engineer came up with an idea to make the tongue like a ball and hitch on a trailer, which would allow the sharp turns. He took a very heavy duty 5/8-inch washer and welded a nut on each side of it. He then started a bolt on each nut and welded the head of each bolt (in essence welding the whole thing) to the inside of a 4-inch piece of "C" purlin. This allows the washer nuts to pivot in the

Closeup of homemade door hinge

Roosts are notched and attached to cattle panel with wire

bolts attached to the piece of purlin. Then, he welded the purlin "hitch" to the coop.

We then took a moving dolly, cut off the base, and welded a bolt onto that spot (making it the "ball" of our hitch) where it would be able to fit into the hitch on our coop. With this setup, you can pivot the coop completely in a circle. It really does work nice for making sharp turns.

To us, this coop is exemplary of the ingenuity we homesteaders can come up with. We all learn to use what we have available and make it work. This saves us money up front, allowing us to continue in our humble, quiet life on our farms. In the end, it saves us time also. Together as a family we built it and when I have my coffee on the porch in the mornings, and look out at designs like this, I sometimes wonder at it all. We have no complaints about our new chicken tractor, and that in itself is a miracle! This pen has given us two years of service now and we wouldn't change anything. We have ease of movement, safety, pasture, and not a lot of cost involved. Chalk it up as another successful homestead venture. Now I wonder if Mr. Wonderful would be interested in working on a rabbit hutch next? Δ

Final wrap with used billboard tarp purchased for $20

Do you remember when...

(This new column will look back in time at previous ads, articles, and events that make up the history of *Backwoods Home Magazine*. — Editor)

Office on the mountain

One Friday, in 1993, I quit a job I hated in the defense industry and the following Monday morning I was on a mountain 800 miles away putting in my first day as a full-time employee of *Backwoods Home Magazine*. Though I'd written for *BHM* since it started four years earlier, I'd never been in on its daily operation. Now, I was about to become intimately acquainted with the stuff readers don't see, like how the magazine gets churned out every two months come hell or high water. More importantly, I was also about to see people who truly lived a self-reliant lifestyle out of both choice and, often, necessity.

The original cabin Dave built, which was the inspiration behind launching Backwoods Home Magazine

Dave Duffy, the publisher, started the magazine on a shoestring in a garage conversion in Ventura, California, in 1989. As the magazine prospered, he moved the office several times in those early years before settling where it is today, in Gold Beach, Oregon. But, of all the offices from which it was published, my favorite was the one I went to in 1993.

It was located some 31 miles up in the mountains, east of Ashland, Oregon, the last eight miles of which were then, and are still, unpaved. Dave first built a cabin, then remodeled it into a two-story house/office that had all the comforts of home. For the next two years it was my home away from home when I commuted 10 times a year from my home 800 miles away in southern California.

It was isolated. We were eight miles off the grid, and the magazine's prime power was two huge photovoltaic arrays coupled with 16 deep-cycle batteries. When we were deep in deadline and the sky clouded up, we drained the batteries faster than the panels could recharge them and Dave fired up a China Diesel generator. There was a stream within 50 feet of the front door that actually had fish, and although the cabin had a small, old Servel propane refrigerator, my refrigerator was the stream, which kept an ample supply of milk, beer, and butter at a cold 40 degrees. Dave claimed the delicious water in the creek, which originated from a spring a mile or so away, was 10,000 years old because that's how long it took to percolate through the ground from its source near the Arctic Circle.

After the staff went home at night (Dave's actual home was about 10 miles away), and on many a weekend, I had the whole place to myself. There were three upstairs bedrooms and a decent-sized kitchen and living room downstairs along with the large area where the staff worked. It had all the luxuries I needed: wood heat, a refrigerator/creek, and not far from the back door a cozy little outhouse that on winter nights rarely got colder than 10 degrees.

It was on the mountain that I saw my first real cattle roundup and discovered a new friend, Pat Ward, who was a *real* cowgirl who could outride most men. Driving toward the lake one afternoon, I had to pull over as a herd of cattle languidly made their way up the dirt road toward the ranch, trailed by three mounted drovers, each in his 20s and each looking like a Marlboro man. But careening through the woods on a horse that flew over the deadfalls like a bird was Pat. Already approaching 70 years old and somewhat overweight, she drove strays out of the trees and onto the road for the "men," then rode off into the woods to get another one. I thought she was going to kill herself.

That night I asked why the young guys didn't do that job. She smiled and said. "They're *city* boys. They don't really know how to ride."

"Then why don't you show them?"

She laughed. "They don't want to learn stuff like that from a fat old broad."

It was on the mountain that Annie, today grown and the managing editor of *BHM*, had her own horse, Buddy, that she later used alongside Pat to round up strays from the woods. One day I watched from afar as she put her arms against Buddy's chest and pushed him back. She was 12 and weighed all of 105 pounds, while Buddy tipped the scales at about 1400. She was showing him who was boss and he backed down. Dave confidently predicted back then that Annie would one day run the magazine.

Over the years, Dave added on to accommodate the growing office.

I also learned something about "work ethic" on the mountain. Buddy, two of the neighbor's horses, and a donkey named Donna Quixote had the run of the magazine's grounds and they produced a lot of the stuff horses and donkeys make from hay. Eventually, it became a hazard. Dave offered to pay several people to clean it up (all recent transplants from the city) but no one wanted the job. So Dave and I spent a day shoveling horse crap as we made decisions about which articles to put in the next issue. It taught me something about what it actually took to publish a magazine, or to run any business. I eventually came to realize that Dave was also willing to empty the trash cans in the office and sweep the floors.

There were a lot of stories like these, and I'll relate more in future columns. Δ

— John Silveira

From left, Pat Ward, Stevie Odom, and Annie (Duffy) Tuttle

Growing onions

By Sylvia Gist

I used to think an onion was an onion, but I've come to learn that there are many shades of onion flavor provided by different varieties of onions and their gourmet brothers, leeks and shallots. To produce your own onions, you can start in spring with seeds, sets, or plants, or in the fall with bulbs (or seeds in southern regions). With a little luck you can find a flavor and method that fits your tastes and needs.

Sulfur compounds give onions their characteristic flavor and odor. The soil you grow them in is instrumental in providing this, so we may not be able to grow a Walla Walla onion here in northwest Montana and get the same sweetness that they can around Walla Walla, Washington.

Onions, of the genus *Allium*, are bulbous herbs. The category includes onions, leeks, shallots, garlic, and chives. Onions come in a range of flavors from mild to strong, while leeks are mild. Shallots have a unique flavor, a sort of mix between onion and garlic. While we generally think of onions as a single year crop, some are interesting perennials which perpetuate themselves from year to year without much intervention.

Prisma shallots

All the *alliums* have a reputation for being a great addition to cooking—it is difficult to think of cooking without them—but they are also considered a very healthy, disease-fighting food.

With regular globe onions, there are types that grow in the south and types that grow in the north. The difference involves day length. A line is generally drawn at about 36 degrees latitude or along the Oklahoma-Kansas line. North of this line, long day onions will grow.

Long day types need to grow enough tops to enable them to start growing bulbs, which are part of their stems, when the days are longest (June 21). The green stems have to have enough layers that will fatten into layers of onion. Up north, we plant sets or plants out in the garden about May 1st to get decent-sized onions.

South of the 36 degree line, sets and plants of short day varieties would be put out in the fall to grow during cool fall and spring days.

A basket of leeks offered by Ploughshare Farm at our local farmers' market

Growing from sets

The easiest way to get onions is to start with sets, tiny dry onions available in the spring from local farm stores, nurseries, and seed catalogs. This is a quick solution to a last minute need for onions to plant; it also saves a lot of time and requires no seed starting equipment. Buying sets locally is a good idea as the sets should be appropriate for that region. Generally, these are a storage type, but, unless they are marked (a rarity), you have no idea what variety they are. These have been grown somewhere until they are tiny onions and then dried.

Planting: Sets can be planted early, and if you plant them close together they can serve as scallions. You could thin some of the onions to use as scallions and let the others grow large. If you want large onions, you have to give them space to grow. Planting depth should be about an inch which adequately covers the marble-sized bulbs. When choosing bulbs, if you have the opportunity to pick them out of a bin, choose bulbs that are marble sized; bigger is not necessarily better.

You can get yellow, red, and white sets. This year I planted some yellow ones and some red ones. The yellows turned out to be a flat type, but grew well. The red ones had a mold problem. One drawback with sets is that they tend to go to seed more than plants you start — an onion that sends up seeds won't store well.

As with all onions, consistent watering is beneficial. If allowed to be dry too long, the outer layers can start drying up, and when watered again, those layers burst as the onion grows which makes them unsuitable for storage.

Harvesting: All onions are harvested the same way. In late summer, when the onions have quit growing, stop watering and let them dry down. The tops fall over. I don't break them over, because water can get in the top and cause it to rot. It is fine to pull them and leave them to lie in the garden in the sun. If the weather is rainy, I put them in the garage or other outbuilding to let the stems dry. Good storage onions will have a couple of sturdy dry layers of skin on the outside.

Sometimes I've had to pull onions in late August even though the tops are still green. Then I have to leave them in the garage until they are dry before storing them in baskets or mesh bags. Since they don't like moist storage, I hang them with the canned goods where it is cool.

In *BHM* issue #120 (November/ December 2009), page 56, Jackie Clay tells how to grow your own onion sets, which requires sowing the seed the summer before, drying and keeping the sets until spring.

Starting with plants

Another way to get onions is to plant already started plants, available from many seed catalogs. Plants will be sent to you at planting time. Some catalogs have a nice selection, which may include leek plants. No matter where you order them from, they were likely grown in Texas or somewhere in the south. Instead of growing them indoors to transplant size, onion growers are able to grow them in fields. They are then dug and bundled for shipment. Dixondale Farms is one such grower.

In my area, one greenhouse generally has some plants they have started in fiber flats in their greenhouse. I prefer these since I can transfer them directly from their pot into my garden. Choice is limited though, since they usually grow a sweet variety, for which there is more demand. However, the price is more reasonable than the mail order plants.

While I have had good luck with purchased leek plants, I have had problems with some mail-order onions plants. Once, the plants were so wispy that most of them died. Another time, the plants were so robust that they must have sensed they were in their second year and sent up seed stalks.

Starting from seed

Generally seeds will give you the most choice of varieties. If you want to start from seed, you can grow regular onions (sometimes referred to as globe onions), leeks, shallots, or scallions (what I have always called green onions).

Globe onions: In my opinion, the way to grow the best onions, especially storage onions, is to start with seed. In Montana, this means getting started early. The seeds need to be sown in flats indoors in February. My goal is to have plants to transplant into the garden in late April. Seed should be started 8 to 10 weeks before transplant.

Selection: Since I live north of 36 degrees latitude, I choose a long day type. Some long day storage varieties I have been pleased with are Copra (which I especially liked), Prince, Mars (a red one), and Redwing (also red). Walla Walla is the most popular large sweet onion here.

If you live south of "the line," choose a short day type. There are a number of large sweet onions of the short day types, from what I can find. There are also some that are intermediate for near the line and some that are day-neutral which will grow anywhere. Super Star (a hybrid), for example, is day-neutral.

You also have to decide whether you want a storage onion or a sweet onion, which typically doesn't store so well. Storage onions generally are more pungent, containing the ingredient that keeps them solid. I try to grow some of both. We eat the sweet ones first and then enjoy the storage onions in the winter. Also I prefer making relishes with the storage onions as they hold their shape better in canning than the more delicate sweet ones.

Egyptian walking onions

Starting seed: For starting, I use one of those half-gallon waxy milk or juice containers which I cut one side out of. I fill it half full of seed starting mix and place the seeds about ½-inch apart and cover with ¼-inch of mix. I choose seed starting mix rather than regular potting soil, because when it comes to transplanting, the onion roots separate much better in the loose mix.

As soon as the seedlings are an inch high, I put them under a regular fluorescent light to keep them from getting spindly. When seedlings are a week or so old, I begin a regimen of fertilizing, following the directions of the chosen fertilizer. I prefer fish fertilizer, which is high in nitrogen.

When the tops get so high they are floppy, you can give them a haircut. I trim the tops to about 4-5 inches. When the weather cooperates, I set them outside to harden off, because the more acclimated they are, the better they will transplant.

Pests: One pest I have had to deal with is thrips, which can wipe out baby onion seedlings. If you see any seedling wilt, look carefully (I have to use a magnifying glass) for tiny (1/50-inch to 1/25-inch) fast-moving yellowish to brownish or blackish insects on the lower part. After the seedlings have been trimmed, thrips can do even more damage. The best product I have found is insecticidal soap used according to directions. Onions are pretty delicate at this age, so I'd be careful about homemade products.

Transplanting: Onions should be transplanted into fairly rich soil (pH of 6 or 7) in shallow trenches at four to six-inch intervals. I trim the roots to 1 inch or a tad bit more at this point. I put them in deep enough that they will stand upright and I press the soil down and around them. I have the rows a foot or so apart and sometimes put down compost between them.

Onions do not like weeds, so keep the plot clean. Grass clippings can be put down between the rows to help weed control and provide a source of nitrogen. They also like sun, so don't hide them under the cabbages.

Leeks and shallots: Leek plants are available or you can start your own. They are started the same as onions but differ when it comes to planting. They should be put out after the last frost and can even be sown directly in the garden in spring. Since they do not bulb, day length is not important. Seed sown leeks won't get as big since they won't have as long to grow.

If you want leeks with long white stems, you will need to make a trench and plant the leeks in the trench, and fill it in as the leek grows tall enough to accommodate deeper soil. Otherwise they are pretty much the same, with the exception that you have to dig leeks with a shovel; due to a lot of roots, they cannot be pulled out. They can be harvested after frost or even in winter if they are protected against freeze. Some leek varieties are more winter hardy than others. Leeks are used fresh, so we don't go through the drying process with them.

There are also many varieties of shallots which can be grown from

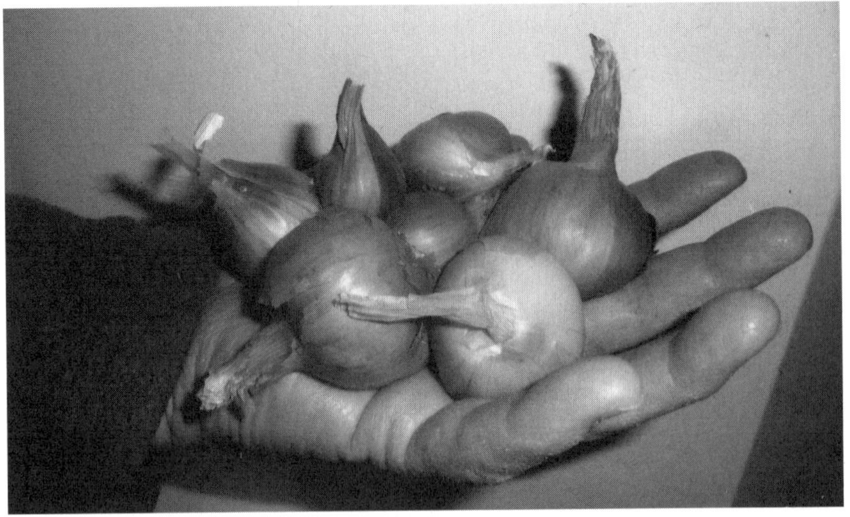

A handful of yellow potato onions, a multiplier onion.

seed. Nicole Jarvis of Ploughshare Farm here in Montana (see "Making a living" in Issue #122, March/April 2010) grows Prisma, a large red shallot, for the co-op she supplies. She starts them from seed in late February in her greenhouse and treats them like her storage onions. Many shallot varieties are day length sensitive (choose the right one for your latitude) and are good for storage.

Nicole tends to use shallots when a recipe calls for a combination of garlic and onions. These shallots, she reports, will make you cry, but cook up mild. Other catalogs offering shallot seeds are Pinetree Garden Seeds (www.superseeds.com), Territorial Seed Company (www.territorialseed.com), and Johnny's Seeds (www.johnnyseeds.com).

Scallions: While immature onions that haven't bulbed can be used as scallions, regular scallions are started from seed. In some catalogs, they are called bunching onions or onions for bunching. This seed is sown in spring directly in the garden. There are quite a few varieties available, including some red ones. These onions are sown right into the garden in spring for harvesting in summer in shorter seasons, but can be sown on a different schedule in longer seasons. Some varieties will not bulb, but others eventually will.

One variety, Evergreen Hardy White, according to seed catalog description, is very hardy, can be sown in spring or fall, *and* can be handled like a perennial, if you like. You just divide the clump to produce a second crop. Evidently they will spread and make a solid patch.

Perennial onions: I have saved the best for last: perennial onions. No seed saving or buying. This category includes walking onions, potato onions/multiplier onions, and shallots.

I grew up with what we call "winter onions." They grew under the eave of the garage and gave us green onions in the spring. They are also known as top-set and Egyptian walking onions. The easiest—and cheapest—way to get started with these is to get a cluster of tiny onions from a friend and put it in the ground. Territorial Seed Company (www.territorialseed.com) in Oregon and Park Seed Co. (www.parkseed.com) in South Carolina are among the few who offer them. The little onions can be planted individually, but I've had better luck putting in the whole cluster.

Storage onions hanging in baskets in my pantry

In the spring, you can dig the clump and clean off the gunk to have scallions. With dry weather or heat, they can get really strong. Always be sure to leave some clumps to make top-set onions to 'walk' and make new clumps. You may have to replant some of those top clusters to assure more the next year. The clump, if not dug up, will multiply itself again the next year and produce a lot more stalks.

The top-set onions (also called bulbils), ranging in size from ¼ inch to ¾ inch, depending on how much water they get, can also be used as onions—if you want to go to the work of peeling the tiny things. Once started, these onions are quite hardy. Park Seed lists them as hardy in Zones 3-10.

When I got my multiplier onions, they were called yellow potato onions, but now the catalogs call them multiplier onions. Another company refers to them as heirloom potato onions. These were quite popular years ago because they kept well in storage and provided their own replacement. I have yellow ones but Southern Exposure Seed Exchange in Virginia offers red and white ones also. Other seed companies offering at least one potato/multiplier onion are Territorial Seed Company and Fedco Seeds.

To grow these, I take an individual bulb and plant it just so the top tip is at the top of the soil, spacing the bulbs at least six inches apart. This I do in the fall and cover the bed with a few inches of mulch. However, I have planted them in spring here and had satisfactory results, just a later harvest. And forgotten bulbs from one year have popped up the next year. In colder winters, that might not happen, so I would rely on mulch.

With ample watering and some fertilizer, the single bulb will "multiply" into several, perhaps up to a dozen, and make quite a clump. Snap off any seed heads that form. Generally they dry down on their own, but final drying should be done out of the sun. These bulbs are hard, pungent, and store extremely well. Select some nice large ones to replant for the next crop.

Another use for multiplier onions is to grow green onions indoors in winter. This "experiment" is on my list for the winter.

Shallots are actually in the same category—*Allium cepa*, Aggregatum group—as multiplier onions. They produce clumps of bulbs from a single bulb. Some catalogs ship the bulbs or sets in the fall, while others ship in the spring. Sometimes they are sold by the pound, sometimes by the pint. I notice that some catalogs offer shallots, but don't list a variety. If you check various places, you can find different colors and shapes, each with their own attributes.

I don't have any experience with growing them from sets, so I would have to follow catalog instructions and experiment a bit. The set grown varieties aren't hybrids while the seed varieties are. The advantage of the sets would be that new sets would not have to be bought each year.

Since shallots can be day length sensitive, it is important to note the description given by the catalog. Don't rely on the location of the catalog. It is always wise to carefully read the information given for each variety.

There are so many choices when it comes to getting your onion flavor. For mild or unique flavors, choose leeks or shallots. For stronger flavor, choose scallions and sweet globe onions. For the strongest flavor—and storage ability, choose storage onions or multiplier onions. One of these should fit your needs. Δ

Lenie in the kitchen

Cheesy fish chowder

By Ilene Duffy

If you've been reading this magazine for a while, you probably already know that my husband, Dave, and I met while he was fishing on the Ventura, California pier. Fishing continues to be one of our favorite family activities. I love the fresh sea air and the feeling of being on wide open waters. We love the challenge of finding the right spot, rigging up our lines, and the anticipation of luring the big ones to bite.

One day about a month ago, the Pacific Ocean lay down flat, there was just a hint of breeze, and the sun shone through our winter clouds. We donned caps and warm layers of clothing and gathered up supplies — ice, bait, the fish cooler, fishing poles, and snacks — and launched the *Olga* out of the south-facing, wind-protected harbor at Brookings, Oregon.

A productive day on the ocean means fish for supper.

Within just a few minutes of lowering our lines, Sammy caught a small black rock fish...and in that same short amount of time I was already busy trying to unsnag my line from debris on the ocean floor. Bummer! After Dave motored the boat a few feet, my line loosened and I was able to reel up without losing the rig. I lowered it again until the weight hit bottom, then quickly reeled in about five feet so it wouldn't snag again. Suddenly, Sammy caught another fish and I got a big bite. Sammy got the net ready but instead of one huge rock fish, I had caught two good-sized ones — one on each hook of my rig! Hurrah! Thank heavens Sammy had the net under those two big guys since my line broke as I brought them into the boat.

We got the fish off the hooks and Dave took his sharp knife and cut through the gills and neck to "bleed out" the fish. This is an important step since the fish is a lot more flavorful this way. Soon, Dave caught a couple of blacks as well.

After a while we decided to head home where Robby filleted our catch. That night I breaded the fish in seasoned cracker crumbs and fried it in hot olive oil. There was so much left over, I needed to think of a good way to use up that fish. When it's breaded and fried, the fish isn't as good the second day since the coating gets a bit soggy, so I got the notion to make a hearty fish chowder using the leftovers. I took the breading off, which my chickens thought was delightful.

I found a recipe online and modified it to my liking. I wanted a lot more vegetables than the original recipe and I also incorporated a can of cream-style corn. I made this soup again just the other day in our magazine office for our staff and this time I added a big can of chopped green chilies. The chowder got a "thumbs up" from everyone.

And if by some chance we get skunked on our future fishing trips, I might still make this hearty soup vegetarian-style.

Cheesy fish chowder

2 Tbsp. butter
2 Tbsp. olive oil
1 medium onion, chopped
¾ cup celery, chopped
1 carrot, chopped
½ cup green bell pepper, chopped
½ cup red pepper, chopped
1 small yellow squash, chopped
10 small mushrooms, chopped
1 pint chicken broth
2 cups water
2 tsp. chicken flavored bouillon
3 medium potatoes, peeled and cubed
4 cups milk, divided
½ cup flour

½ tsp. salt
½ tsp. onion salt
½ tsp. black pepper
1 Tbsp. parsley flakes
1 tsp. no salt seasoning blend
1 15-oz. can cream-style corn
1 7-oz. can chopped green chilies
1 Tbsp. butter
1 Tbsp. olive oil
1½ lbs. rock fish fillets
2 cups cheddar cheese, shredded
shredded cheddar cheese, optional

Preparations:

In a large skillet, heat 2 Tbsp. butter and 2 Tbsp. olive oil. Add onion, celery, carrot, peppers, squash, and mushrooms. Cook over medium heat until just tender. In a large stock pot, heat chicken broth, water, and bouillon. Add potatoes and simmer about 5 minutes. Add heated vegetables. Simmer another 5-10 minutes.

In a mixing bowl add 2 cups of the milk and the flour. Whisk until the flour is thoroughly incorporated. Slowly stir in the flour and milk mixture. Add the rest of the milk. Then add the salt, onion salt, pepper, parsley flakes, and no salt seasoning blend. Stir occasionally and cook over very low heat for about 30 minutes until potatoes are tender. Add the cans of corn and green chilies. If the soup looks too thin, you can mix a tablespoon or two of flour with about ¼ cup of milk in a small bowl and slowly add to the soup pot and stir in well.

In a small fry pan, heat remaining butter and olive oil. Wash fish fillets. Check and discard any small bones that might be left in fillets. Gently fry on medium heat on both sides about 2 minutes. Use a spatula to cut the fish into large chunks and add to the soup pot.

Cook over very low heat about 15 minutes more, stirring frequently. About 5 minutes before serving, add cheddar cheese and gently stir well. Serve with more grated cheddar cheese, if desired.

Some nice fresh dinner rolls will make this meal complete. I love trying new recipes for homebaked bread and rolls. I found the following recipe in my favorite bread machine book, *Better Homes and Gardens Bread Machine Bounty*. I modified the recipe slightly since their version calls for toasted wheat germ. I didn't have any, so I substituted it with wheat bran. I also added a teaspoon of dried oregano since I thought the herbed bread rolls would go nicely with the soup.

It's hard to beat warm, fresh dinner rolls.

Sour cream wheat dinner rolls

⅔ cup milk
½ cup sour cream
2 Tbsp. honey
2 tsp. butter
1 egg
1½ cups whole wheat flour
1½ cups bread flour
⅓ cup wheat bran
¾ tsp. salt
1 tsp. dried oregano leaves
1½ tsp. yeast

Preparations:

In a bowl add milk, sour cream, honey, and butter. Gently warm in microwave. Stir to mix all ingredients. Add the egg and gently mix.

In a separate bowl, add whole wheat flour, bread flour, salt, wheat bran, and dried oregano. Mix until blended.

Add warmed liquid ingredients to the bottom of the bread machine pan, then add the dry ingredients. Make a small well in the flour. Spoon the yeast into the well. Place pan in bread machine and set to the dough cycle.

When the dough cycle is done, take the dough out on a lightly floured board and gently expel the air. Grease and flour two muffin pans. Cut the dough in half. Set aside one of the halves. Cut one of the halves into 12 equal pieces. Grease hands with a bit of olive or canola oil. Roll each dough segment to form a ball and place in muffin pan. Repeat with the second half of the dough. Cover with a damp towel and let rise in a warm place for about an hour. Bake in a preheated 350° F oven for 12 to 15 minutes. Makes two dozen small dinner rolls. Δ

Ayoob on Firearms

Gun semantics

By Massad Ayoob

Every discipline has its own arcane terminology. This Luddite is still trying to figure out computers. You computer-literate people refer to "the cloud," and we dumb-butts assume that there actually *is* a cloud up there that stores all your bits and bytes. That's really kinda cruel…

In my corner of the *Backwoods Home* world, I feel your pain. I grew up with the terminology of the gun, and I understand how many terms came from different angles that were clear to those who created them, but those pioneers didn't realize that, generations after, their words would confuse the hell out of people who were "coming in late" to both the world of firearms and its distinctive, eclectic language.

Let's see if we can't sort some of that out, in the "3,000 words or less" which I am allotted by the editor.

What we shoot

Look at high-powered rifle cartridges that are popular in rural America. Two of the most widely used are the .30-06 and the .30-30. It sounds like the latter has more oomph to it, right? A bigger number and all?

However, the opposite is true. ".30-06" denotes a bullet diameter that is thirty caliber, specifically 308/1000ths of an inch in diameter, adopted by the United States as its standard military cartridge in the year 1906. "Thirty-ought-six" thus denotes ".30 caliber, adopted in ought-six." .30-30, however, describes a bullet of the same diameter, with thirty grains of first-generation smokeless gunpowder. The most popular .30-06 load is a bullet that weighs 180 grains and leaves the muzzle at 2770 feet per second, generating 3068 foot-pounds of energy, while the most commonly used .30-30 cartridge comprises a 170 grain bullet at 2200 feet per second delivering only 1830 foot-pounds of energy. The .30-06 *sounds* smaller than the .30-30 when you just read the numbers that designate the caliber and cartridge, but it drives a bigger bullet faster and makes it hit harder, outgunning the .30-30 in every respect.

Backwoods Home's most popular writer, Jackie Clay, brings home her annual venison supply with her Winchester Model 94 rifle, caliber .30-30. If I can find time to hunt deer this season, and use a rifle instead of the handgun I usually hunt with, I'll probably choose my Ruger Model 77 rifle, caliber .30-06.

You know what? If we each shoot the deer in the same spot at the same angle from the same distance, Jackie and I will both have meat in the freezer, and neither deer will know the difference.

Massad Ayoob

How many *rounds* will Jackie and I have to fire to hit those deer? How many *shots*? It's amazing how many people don't realize that the same question has just been asked twice. When you discharge a firearm once, everyone in the world seems to understand that a single gunshot has been fired. But if you substitute the word "rounds" for "shots," confusion ensues. The English language being what it is, people unfamiliar with

.30-06 Springfield, left, sounds less powerful than .30-30 Winchester, right, but in fact the reverse is true.

We're supposed to call it "semiautomatic," but the maker of this iconic pistol stamps it "automatic."

guns hear "round" and think of "a round of drinks" (several) or a "round of applause" (never only a single hand clap). Many people hear or read the term "round of ammunition" and perceive it to mean a whole gun-load. Nope. Among people who know guns, a "round of ammunition" is one single cartridge, and when it is discharged, a round is one single shot fired.

Each of us will have shot our deer with a *rifle*. Some would say we had shot our deer with *guns*. There are those who insist that "gun" is too generic a term. I know a Navy man who insists that battleships have "guns," but when an American ship disgorges armed Marines ashore, they only have "rifles." And we won't even get into the whole mantra of "this is my rifle, this is my gun, one is for fighting and one is for fun..."

Jackie's gun/rifle/arm/sporting equipment is a "lever action" in design. Mine is a "bolt action." They operate differently to accomplish the same task. Action mechanisms, at least, seem to be pretty clear and distinct, right?

Well...

How does it work, exactly?

Terminology can get awfully confusing in the firearms world. As I write this I have a revolver in my pocket and a semiautomatic pistol on my hip.

The revolver is a Smith & Wesson Model 340 Military & Police, and if you check the manufacturer's website at www.smith-wesson.com, you'll see that it is chambered for the .357 Magnum cartridge. However, it is loaded with shorter, milder, but same diameter .38 Special +P ammunition. You see, it's a very light gun—and the lighter the gun is, the harder it "kicks"—and because I won't carry anything I can't shoot fast and straight, I tend to "download" it. The website will show that this gun will fire both .38 Special and .357 Magnum ammunition. So...is it a .357 Magnum, because that is what it CAN fire, or is it a .38, because that's what it's loaded with?

If you are one of the lucky few who owns a classic Oldsmobile "442" muscle car with a big-for-the-car's size, powerful V8 engine, would you still be driving a 442 if its power plant had been replaced with a more sedate six-cylinder or even four-cylinder engine? Yeah, the car still *says* "442" on it, but "442" is *supposed* to denote "400 cubic inch engine, with two four-barrel carburetors."

Is a small-engine in a "442" body really a 442? Is a .357 Magnum really a Magnum so long as it is only loaded with .38 Special ammunition?

I dunno. You tell me. Personally, I think I've got a .38 in my pocket, because that's all the power I can put out from that particular machine on demand unless I swap out the ammo. But if I had to defend myself with it tonight, the police report would see it logged into evidence as a .357 Magnum revolver. Go figure...

The pistol on my hip is what I would describe, if you asked me, as a "Colt .45 automatic." It is a pistol that the Colt factory has produced for, oh, a hundred years or so. If you look on the pistol's slide, you'll be able to see that when it left the factory its manufacturer stamped it ".45 Automatic." It is loaded with Winchester Ranger-T brand 230 grain jacketed hollow point ammunition from a box produced just this past year and marked, ".45 AUTOMATIC." (The manufacturer's caps, not mine.)

However, there are those on the Internet gun forums who will consider you a semi-literate troglodyte if you say "automatic" instead of "semiautomatic."

If you are talking about how the gun *fires*, the Colt pistol in question is indeed a "semiautomatic." That is, it fires only one shot per pull of the trigger. To fire a follow-up shot, you have to let the trigger come forward to reset the sear mechanism, and then pull the trigger again. That is also true of semiautomatic rifles and semiautomatic shotguns.

Does that mean it is semantically incorrect to call it what the gun's manufacturer *and* the ammunition manufacturer call it, an "automatic?" Not necessarily. While the fire control mechanism may be semiautomatic as described above, the firearm's method of feeding cartridges into the firing chamber is indeed "automatic" — if the gun is working properly, that feeding function occurs *automatically*. That's why everyone considers it semantically correct to call them "autoloaders."

Let's take this argument into the world of rifles. John M. Browning himself designed the BAR, the Browning Automatic Rifle, which used a 20-round .30-06 magazine to fire full automatic as a machine gun. It hit the trenches too late in WWI to make an impact there, but it won a legion of fans in WWII, and in Korea. It was a true machine gun: it would fire "full automatic," capable of hosing out bullets in a burst for as long as the trigger was held back. The BAR was even manufactured giving a speed-of-automatic-fire choice. At high speed, it was hard to control, but at lower speed, its rate of fully automatic fire was closer to the sedate early 20th Century BREN gun beloved by the Brits, than the high rounds-per-minute count of a modern American M4 combat rifle.

In the second half of the 20th century, another firearm bore the name Browning Automatic Rifle. You can still buy one in a sporting goods store or gun shop today, and in the same .30-06 caliber as the WWI era combat weapon, or .300 Magnum or .338 Magnum for hunting larger game. This one, designed decades after John Browning's death, is an upscale semiautomatic hunting rifle, and it can *only* be had in semiautomatic—one shot per pull of the trigger—mode.

Thus far, we've talked about handguns, rifles, and machine guns.

This ammo encompasses half a century or more of manufacture. From yesteryear to now, ammo-makers have said "automatic," not "semiautomatic."

12 gauge (left) sounds like less than 20 gauge (right), but in fact it is distinctly more.

Shotguns have not been immune to terminology confusion, either.

Rifles and pistols have their ammunition designated by "caliber," determined by the diameter of their bullets as per metric (9mm, 10mm, etc.) or decimal (.38, .45, etc) measurement. Shotguns are for the most part (with one exception, which we'll get to momentarily) categorized by "gauge."

It would seem to the uninitiated that a 20 gauge would be more powerful than a 12 gauge, and a ten gauge less powerful yet, while a 410 gauge would seem absolutely monstrous by comparison. Yet, as shotgunners well know, the reverse is true. "Gauge" is determined by how many projectiles the size of the bore (inside barrel diameter) it would take to reach a given weight. Thus, the *smaller* the gauge, the *more* lead the shotgun in question can spit when fired.

Assuming standard pressure ammunition, my Ithaca MAG-10 shotgun will be exactly twice as powerful as any of my 12 gauge shotguns: its 10 gauge Magnum shell expels 18 .33-caliber double-ought buckshot pellets per pull of the trigger, compared to 9 of the same projectiles at roughly the same velocity from one of my 12 gauge shotguns.

Why isn't ".410" more powerful than "20," "12", or even "10 gauge" shotgun ammunition? Well, it's because ".410" isn't a "gauge," it's a "caliber," which is why it appears with a decimal point when properly written. The .410 refers to bore diameter, and it's an "apples and oranges" kind of thing. The .410 bore shotgun vis-à-vis the 12 bore shotgun is the difference between something you would use for squirrels at relatively close range (.410), and what you would use to shoot big, heavy geese at a distance nearly half a football field away (12 gauge), if you expected clean, quick kills on each.

"Combat semantics" in court

As they say on the Internet forums, "words mean things." If you are an armed citizen, the good news is that if someone tries to break into your home and murder you, you have the wherewithal to fight back and survive. The bad news is, when you shoot a human being in this society, you call out politically-motivated prosecutors

Clip on the left (stripper type, for 7.62X39) and magazine on the right (Wilson EDM for 1911 .45).

(possibly) and money-hungry plaintiffs' lawyers (highly likely). What you have to watch out for when you get into court is an attorney who is smart enough to make more use of Webster's Dictionary (Of the English Language) than Black's Dictionary (Of Legal Terminology).

A classic example is the question, "Did you shoot to kill?" Beware this trap! At any given time, you will find Internet forums where people who haven't had to actually deal with this situation in real life in American society will say, "Aw, I don't need Political Correctness, and that's what the 'shoot to stop' mantra is all about! Anybody messes with me or my family, well, I'm gonna shoot to kill!"

You've just heard the sound of someone talking their way into prison. Allowing the benefit of the doubt, I would like to think that the person who uttered those words realized that cops, soldiers, and anyone else who might ever have to shoot another person in self-defense was taught to shoot for center of mass (center of chest) on a human antagonist. This recommendation came from long institutional memory in the criminal justice system of shootings in which "trying to hit the bad guy in the leg" or "trying to shoot the gun out of the bad guy's hand" proved to be hopeless strategies. "Aim for the center" also came from the hard-learned realization that marksmanship degrades under stress, and in real life we're doing well to hit our opponent anywhere at all in a gunfight.

If you are ever charged in criminal court, you'll have to deal with a little thing—actually a very big thing—called *mens rea.* The term, from the Latin, means "the guilty mind." The prosecutor has to establish *mens rea* by showing that you either had intent to commit a crime, or acted with a level of negligence so high that it rose to a guilt-producing "culpable standard." Because this is a very heavy burden to prove, the courts have traditionally given prosecutors considerable latitude in which to prove it.

If you have in any way, shape, or form, indicated that you "shot to kill," you have just said that your purpose in firing the fatal shot(s) was to deprive a man of his life. It's a short step from there to determining presence of malice on the shooter's part.

But if you can demonstrate that you "shot to stop"—that your purpose in firing the fatal shot(s) was to stop someone from murdering you or another innocent person, you have demonstrated that your action in shooting that human being was justifiable.

That's why cops—and law-abiding private citizens who have put a little bit of thought and research into the matter of using lethal force in self-defense—have come to the conclusion that the rule is, "Shoot to stop," not "shoot to kill." It goes to the purpose for which the act in question was undertaken.

"Fingernails on the blackboard"

If there is anything that will make an old gunny grate his teeth as if he'd heard fingernails scraping on a chalkboard, it is saying "clip" instead of "magazine." Your great-grandpa's Savage 99 rifle had a rotary magazine integral to its mechanism to hold its cartridges. Your nephew's M4 rifle that he carries daily in Afghanistan has a removable box magazine. In either case, the magazine enclosed entirely the cartridges it held. However, the WWII vintage M-1 Garand battle rifle held its eight .30-06 cartridges in a clip, specifically an "en bloc" clip, so called because it stayed in the rifle to hold the rounds in line until the last one was fired, at which time the clip would automatically eject from the M-1 with a distinctive "ping." More common was the stripper clip, which held the cartridges in line at their bases or rims, and the cartridges would be stripped off it. They might be stripped into an integral magazine, as with a WWI-era Springfield 1903 rifle, or into the separate magazine, as your nephew might use them to load the magazines of his modern M4.

A widespread pet peeve is people who say "bullet" when they should say "cartridge." Each cartridge has a bullet: it's the projectile.

We gunnies ourselves argue whether what we grasp to fire a handgun are stocks, grips, or handles. Normally, calling it a "handle" marks you as a rank amateur, yet even experienced collectors will refer to "pearl-handle" or "bone-handle" guns. Connoisseurs themselves sometimes wonder why if they're grasping wood, the word is "stocks," but if they're holding rubber the preferred term is "grips." On a rifle or shotgun, however, that thing the action and barrel rest in will be called a "stock" regardless of whether it's wood or synthetic.

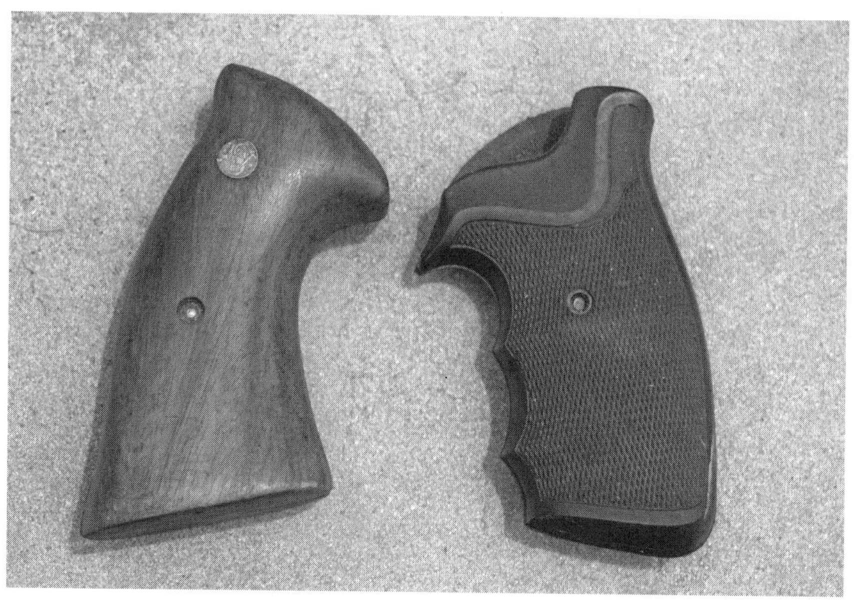

Wooden stocks (by Smith & Wesson, left) and rubber grips (by Pachmayr, right). Just don't call either "handles" in front of a purist. (A "common use exception" seems to be made for "pearl handles," however.)

The fact is, you could probably make a decent size book on the theme of "gun semantics." There's more than enough for a mere article, which is why I'm starting to run out of space. Suffice to say that some good, basic reading on firearms—at the public library, or on the Internet—will go far toward gaining fluency in arms-related lingo, and being able to "speak like a native" in the land of the gun.

For now, the rain here has stopped and I'm almost out of space, so it seems like an excellent time to go shooting. I guess I'll just have to stuff some bullets into some clips to stick up the handles of my automatics, and get to it. Δ

The Last Word

Getting the state out of marriage

There's a new TV "reality" show on TLC called *Sister Wives*. It's about a polygamous family: Kody Brown, his 3 wives, their 13 children, and a soon-to-be (maybe already) fourth wife as well as the 3 children she's bringing with her. Because I don't have a TV, I became aware of it as a news item on the Internet. In that news item, I also discovered that the Utah Attorney General's office is supposed to be looking into Brown and his family. Polygamy is illegal in all 50 states and it's a felony in Utah where the Brown family lives. Despite this, polygamy is still practiced in this country and, though the stereotype is that it's something only fundamentalist Mormons covertly engage in (estimates range from 8,000 to 60,000 polygamous Mormon marriages), it's also found among some American Muslims (estimates run from 50,000 to 100,000).

As a libertarian, I've asked against whom that kind of felony is being committed. As near as I can tell, it's committed against the sensibilities or religious beliefs of those who are against it.

However, it appears as though the the Attorney General's office is not likely to investigate it. They say they have just so many resources and they'd rather use them to investigate *serious* crimes. Good for them.

I've long thought I had the answer to the problems with polygamy (both polygyny — multiple wives, and polyandry — multiple husbands) as well as gay marriage, another one that seems to stir emotions. It's simple — get the state out of marriage. That's right, no more marriage licenses. Even when I applied for and got my own license some 30 years ago, I didn't understand why I needed the permission or blessings of the state, its politicians, and its bureaucrats to get married.

The reason the state is still involved in marriage at all, as far as I can tell, is that it's a religious holdover. But you don't need a marriage license to have babies, live "in sin," and live as gay couples. In fact, a guy can have a retinue of girlfriends all bearing his children, just like a polygamist, and nobody looks twice, even if he's not supporting them. But let him try to make them "legal" and, even if he's supporting them all, the authorities are at his door with their pitchforks and torches.

However, even if the state comes after Brown, he may dodge the bullet because he's only "legally" married to one of the women. The others, he says, are "spiritual unions." In other words, they're like the unions so many other people living, sleeping, and having babies together have who the police ignore.

But, in the event of arrests, the Brown family has engaged the services of a constitutional lawyer, Jonathan Turley. Why a lawyer who specializes in constitutional law? Turley has long been a critic of anti-polygamy laws. I would imagine, for starters, he might present a defense on the grounds that laws prohibiting plural marriages are based on religion and cite separation of church and state. But, more pointedly, he argues "unequal treatment." He points out, "... a person can live with multiple partners and even sire children from different partners so long as they do not marry. However, when that same person accepts a legal commitment for those partners "as a spouse," we jail them." Just what I've said.

One friend told me he thought we should have marriage licenses because the state has an interest in the family.

"What kind?" I asked. Do you want it to make marriage and divorce easier? More difficult? Make it illegal to have babies without its permission? What?

He didn't answer.

Another said his only gripe against gay marriage is that he feels as though members of a gay couple shouldn't get tax benefits if single people, like himself, can't.

"You're right!" I exclaimed to him. "When I say get the state out of marriage, I meant all the way. If an insurance company wants to confer benefits on married people, good for them, but getting the state out of marriage means getting rid of tax benefits or mandating that married and single people should be treated differently. Treat everyone equally.

There is only one reason the state should be involved in marriage. It's the only reason I can think of that the state should be involved in *any* contract: to act as arbitrator if the contract dissolves and is contested. As a libertarian, I see mediating disputes as one of the few legitimate functions of government.

By the way, I've got to mention, I finally saw an episode of *Sister Wives* at a friend's house. As we watched she said she didn't see how one man could keep four women happy; but one woman could keep four men happy. I see what's on her polyandrous mind. And in case you're wondering, I do not want multiple wives. However, if a bunch of consenting adults want to engage in such a marriage, I feel it's none of my business, your business, or the state's.

And, if you're religious, keep in mind, getting the state out of marriage does not necessarily get God out of *your* marriage. You can still get married in a church, have it blessed, sanctified, and French fried, for all I care. You *don't* have to pass up any of that. I just don't think your marriage, or anyone else's, has to be blessed by the state.

By the way, you do know what the actual punishment for bigamy is, don't you? Two mothers-in-law.

— John Silveira

Backwoods Home magazine

practical ideas for self-reliant living

Mar/Apr 2011
Issue #128
$5.95 US
$7.50 CAN

Propagating plants

Drive your own well
LED lighting
Morel mushrooms
Dehorning calves
Drinking goat milk

www.backwoodshome.com

DON CHILDERS

My view

Defunding government is a sensible voter solution to reining in local government

Like so many other communities across the country, my community of Curry County on the southern Oregon coast has rejected efforts by local government to raise taxes in order to fund itself. The latest rejection came in the form of a 3 to 1 thumping of the Law Enforcement Tax Levy, which was to fund the sheriff's office and criminal justice bureaucracy. The resounding thumbs down came in spite of an intense public relations campaign and editorial support from local newspapers, and despite dire predictions that failure to pass the new tax would mean a sharp curtailment in police protection for citizens and the potential bankruptcy of county government.

Immediately upon defeat of the measure, one of our three county commissioners, who comprise the top political posts locally, was quoted in the newspaper as saying, "The voters let us down!"

FACES OF ANGER — Paul Marko and Mindy Urken of Vermont just paid $142 tickets each for not wearing their seat belts while driving a distance of about 50 yards in Gold Beach, from one restaurant to another. They canceled their planned vacation in the area and said they would never come back.

I laughed out loud when I read it. It was not a matter of voters letting down county government, but just the opposite. County government, just like state and federal government, has lost the trust of the people. It is inept at best, repressive at worst, and local voters voiced their disapproval by defunding it.

My county is probably like a lot of other rural counties across the country. Most folks here are glad to make $15 an hour, but they have been funding a local government bureaucracy whose workers average, if you include their benefits and pensions, nearly $30 an hour. Not only that, but their pensions increase by 8% a year no matter what the economy or stock market does, thanks to a stipulation in their union contract. It's just one of the many perks overburdened taxpayers are tired of funding.

I took it upon myself to conduct informal interviews ("sleuth interviews" I call them, since nobody knew they were being interviewed) of several county officials, county workers, and many of my fellow tax-paying citizens to see how they felt about county government in light of the failure of the tax levy.

I got to interview only one other county commissioner, and he told me, "We did a poor job of selling the tax to voters." He thought a good idea would be to create a new taxing district that would fund the sheriff's office, and present it to the voters to see if they would pass it. I told him I thought that proposal would get defeated by about 5 to 1.

All three county commissioners, according to the local paper, are considering garnishing money set aside to repair local roads to help fund the sheriff's office. That may be illegal, however, as some of the money came from the federal government and was designated to fix roads. It would send local voters to new heights of fury if rain-damaged roads went unrepaired because the local bureaucracy "stole the money."

Several county workers told me they have begun looking for other jobs. It turns out that the county really is facing bankruptcy, although the gavel won't come down until the end of 2012. That's when the county will stop receiving federal funds intended to replace revenue from our long-ago-shut-down timber lands. A former county prosecutor told me that a likely scenario is that the county government will be forced to lay off all but a handful of its 225 employees, with those who remain being state-mandated officials, such as one judge, one sheriff, one public defender, and a few others. He said the county may even have to close the county jail and rent out space from a small California city just over the border.

There is no evident planning by county government officials for this predicted scenario. One local lawyer who has frequent business with the county told me, "They never plan for anything around here. It's full bore ahead like there's nothing around the corner."

But probably the most surprising result of my interviews was the bitterness I encountered towards local government by ordinary people. It ranged from the expected resentment of code officials, who residents complained hindered home improvement projects, to accusations that the local police were aggressive and abusive of their position when encountering the public. (I should point out that locals interviewed tended to group all the police together, namely, our several city police departments, the sheriff's deputies, and the state police. We are very top-heavy in policing agencies here, particularly in Gold Beach, which, as the county seat, has its own police department, is home to the sheriff's office and courthouse, and has a state police barracks just outside of town.)

You can almost not get through my town of Gold Beach without seeing the flashing lights of a police car next to a motorist, and you can barely drive from town to town (each town is about 27 miles apart) without running the gauntlet of state police cars issuing tickets where the 55 mph zone abruptly turns to a 40 mph zone. It has become an aggressive revenue-raising business, with cops vying with each other to control it. Some county bureaucrats want the city police departments disbanded and enforcement left to the county and state.

One out-of-town couple I ran into at the courthouse said they had planned to move to Gold Beach but now "would never set foot in the town again." They were paying a fine for "failure to wear a seat belt," after an offensive cop stopped them while driving from one restaurant to another. "It was all of 50 yards," the husband said. "It's absolutely outrageous." They let me take their photo for this article. (Our local towns, by the way, are essentially tourist economies. Some local businessmen complain that the cops are "collecting tourist scalps" and driving them away.)

The rate at which Gold Beach has ramped up handing out traffic tickets has attracted the attention of a prestigious national motorcycle club, which arranges high-priced touring trips for clients from all over the world. It began rerouting its tourist trips of the West Coast around Gold Beach, and in an online post it warned its members to avoid the area altogether "due to the heavy police presence."

The Gold Beach police chief, who was a new hire just about the time the economic recession hit, is not phased. He instituted a column in the local newspaper in which he regularly brags about setting local records for the number of citations issued to motorists. He even got the city to allow him to hire a couple more officers so he could issue more tickets. Over the past summer, he boasted, each month saw the issuance of more traffic tickets than the previous one, and the summer itself set a new all-time summer record for issuing traffic citations in Gold Beach.

The local county sheriff has now gotten in on the newspaper column business. His first column, which appeared shortly after the defeat of the tax levy, boasted about all the good policing his deputies were doing. Unfortunately, he made the mistake of boasting about using funds to eradicate marijuana plants in the local forests. That's not exactly what the public wanted to hear since surveys show 75% of voters believe marijuana eradication is a waste of public funds. When I asked another county official about the column, he said the sheriff needed some PR help, pointing out the more successful efforts of the Gold Beach police chief.

No wonder the sheriff's levy was defeated by a margin of 3 to 1 and the county is facing impending bankruptcy. The cops and the rest of the bureaucracy just don't get it! The voters are trying to defund them, but the bureaucracy is bragging in the newspaper how they are spending taxpayer money in ways the voters are fed up with. It's stunning when you think about the disconnect between the reality of what the voters want and the actions of those in the bureaucracy. It's the same at the state and national levels.

When it comes to the curtailment of police protection for citizens, several people I interviewed told me they were more afraid of the cops than they were of criminals. Of course, this is a community in which many people keep guns in their homes. One fellow said, "I can handle a criminal breaking into my home by shooting him, but an aggressive cop is a different matter. I can't do anything, or they'll take me off to jail."

Defunding government, especially defunding its police as the voters here essentially did, may be the only way to get through to government and its bureaucracies that it is no longer wanted. It's a big weapon voters still have. Unlike the federal government, local government can't just start printing money to fund itself.

My small community of Curry County, and my tiny town of Gold Beach, are the small, local reflections of what American society has become as a whole: a public overwhelmingly dissatisfied with not just a dysfunctional government, but an all too often aggressive, out-of-touch government that works against the interests of ordinary people. Defunding them locally is the beginning of the solution.

— Dave Duffy

Propagating plants

By Jackie Clay

We all love the idea of having a big, productive garden, full of all the nutritious, tasty foods our hearts desire. But the prices in the nursery catalogs can be enough to make you cry! Maybe you just can't afford that big garden full of berries, fruits, and other wonderful plants, after all. But wait! Here are some easy-to-learn plant propagating methods you can use to multiply your modest berry patch, orchard trees, and even some vegetables to have as many plants as you want.

When we first enlarged our new garden, I could only afford three black raspberry bushes — too much was going on building our new log house, and all the money went to that for a long time. *But* I did buy those three little bushes. Now, three years later, I have enough bushes from those initial three plants to plant a 50-foot row in our new berry patch up the hill, and also enough to give a bunch to my friend.

Here's how you can multiply your own garden plants without a degree in plant biology.

Strawberries are very easy to multiply from runners.

Multiplying plants by their runners

Season: early spring

This method works for strawberries, raspberries, blackberries, elderberries, and even lilacs and it is the easiest way of all to gain new plants. Only strawberries need a little help, because they produce above-ground runners which must root before they become a new plant. Left to their own devices, most strawberry runners will root eventually, but to help them out, just nestle each runner down into a nice bed of loose, fertile soil, then scoop up a bit of dirt to anchor the runner down to the earth. You'll know the runner has rooted when you tug on its leaf and it remains seated firmly.

To harvest strawberry runners, simply cut the runner free from the mother plant and gently dig up the new plant. Carefully transplant it to its new row, planting it as deep as it was previously, then water it and watch it grow.

Other plants send up shoots or "suckers" from underground roots. If there is adequate room, you can just let these suckers grow, forming a close-knit hedgerow, but sometimes too many suckers can weaken the mother plants. I often dig up and move my suckers. I did this with my blackberries, black raspberries, red raspberries, and lilacs. I got plenty of new plants like this.

Suckers are easy to dig and transplant. Just step a shovel deep between the mother plant and the sucker, severing the underground root that binds the two together. Then simply dig up the sucker and transplant it. When I do this, I always carefully pull out any grass or weeds so that I don't also transplant a crop of weeds, along with my new plants. Water the new plants well after transplanting to ensure that they get off to a good start.

Dividing plants with offsets

Season: spring or fall

Offsets are little "baby" plants that grow up around the mother plant. Some common garden plants that divide this way are rhubarb, wild plums, comfrey, multiplier onions, and chokecherries.

Offsets are only a little bit different than suckers, in that they don't have an underground root that tethers it to the mother plant. Offsets may be attached to the mother plant or have their own young root system. Rhubarb and comfrey offsets are closely attached to the mother root, but if you look closely, you can see they are their own individual plants. By using a sharp shovel, you can easily divide the offset from the mother plant, taking sufficient soil along with it to avoid stressing the plantlet. Wild plums, multiplier onions, and chokecherries often send offsets up a little way from the mother plant and are easily dug up and detached from it.

A wild asparagus plant yielded more than a dozen roots. After carefully separating the roots, I planted a nice row of asparagus.

Older, established asparagus plants often form a cluster of rope-like roots, tangled together, with old roots, young plants, and little baby plants all mixed together. Once when the county was clearing out roadside ditches, I dug up a "wild" asparagus plant from the side of the road, taking a bushel basket full of roots, dirt, and grass with it. At home, I soaked and washed the roots, then I pulled away all the grass and weeds, leaving only the tangled asparagus roots. By carefully separating the roots, I ended up with more than 20 asparagus plants.

I ended up with a nice bed of asparagus, all free. The next week, the county continued its ditch-digging and totally destroyed the asparagus plants that I had not taken.

Tip layering

Season: mid-late summer

Blackberries, red and black raspberries, and forsythia can be propagated by tip layering. The canes bend over naturally, and where they touch the soil, roots will form, eventually making new plants. We can hurry this process along by weighting down canes with soil or a rock, then burying the tip under an inch of soil. In a while, you'll notice new leaves and shoots beginning to poke up out of the ground. Let the new plant establish itself well, then tug at the leaves to see if roots are firmly grown. If they are, cut the new plant free from the mother plant with pruning shears, then dig it up and relocate it to its new spot.

Serpentine layering

Season: spring

Some plants, such as grapes, kiwis, hazelnuts, June berries, hops, and blueberries tend to grow roots from leaf nodes. You can speed this process along and harvest a number of new plants for your garden by serpentine layering a few plant stems.

First check to see which stems will easily bend down to lie along the soil. Then find the "knots," which are the leaf nodes you will be burying. With a sharp knife, carefully cut into the stem (near the knot) at an angle, about one third of the way through.

The cuttings are dampened, dipped into rooting compound, and poked down into moist potting soil, then placed in a sunny window until they take root.

Hold the wound open with a toothpick or other small object, then dab a little rooting compound on the wound with a small artist's paintbrush. Carefully bury the stem, holding it down with a rock or a U-shaped piece of wire clothes hanger. By doing this in several places on the same stem, you can gain several plants from one stem.

Be sure to keep the soil evenly moist and the soil firmly against the stem to avoid air pockets. Air pockets will often prevent roots from forming.

Cuttings

Season: late fall, early winter

One common method of increasing orchard and garden plants is by making cuttings and rooting them. This is used for grapes, kiwis, figs, quince, lilacs, cherries, peaches, and many other plants. The cuttings are taken in the late fall or early winter, when the plant or tree is dormant. Take your cuttings just below the leaf node where last year's growth ends and this year's growth begins. Cut straight across, then count up the branch, leaving about three to five nodes and make a diagonal cut just above the top node to remove the new, soft growth at the tip. It will only rot and cause your cutting to fail.

Plant immediately. If you can't, wrap the bottom in damp paper towels and place in the refrigerator. But plan on planting as soon as possible for the very best results.

Dip the bottom (straight) ends of your cuttings in rooting compound and bury the bottom two-thirds of the cutting in a good quality potting soil. Moisten the soil and wait for growth. If you live in a warmer climate, place the pots in an insulated cold frame over the winter. If you live in a cold-winter area, you can put your pots in a window in your house, but monitor the temperature and soil closely. Plants in a south-facing window can heat up too much and dry out very quickly, even during the winter.

In the spring, you may harden off your indoor plants gently, and plant them in a sheltered spot in your garden to begin life as a new plant. Sometimes it takes a while for the new cuttings to establish; be patient and give them good care. Once they are well-established you can transplant them to their final spot in the garden. Any plants that fail to thrive should be pulled up and discarded.

Besides these hardwood cuttings, you can also take root cuttings from your tomatoes. I've often taken cuttings from my best winter greenhouse tomatoes to get an early start on spring planting. You can take tomato cuttings from spring-planted tomatoes to get plants that will mature for a fall crop. Tomatoes are very easy to root, either in water, where they often root in as little as four days, or in moist potting soil.

With a sharp knife or single edge razor blade, take a four- to eight-inch cutting from either the growing tip or sucker, cutting straight across the stem. (Suckers are the little upright shoots between the main stem and a branch of the tomato plant.) Remove the lower leaves to avoid disease. Either place the cuttings in a jar of clean water to root or dip the end in rooting compound and gently plant in moist potting soil. From one strong plant you can harvest a dozen or more cuttings.

Tomatoes are simple to root in water.

Root cuttings

Season: spring or fall

Root cuttings are another very easy way to multiply your garden crops. Such perennial plants as comfrey, horseradish, and Jerusalem artichokes are extremely easy to multiply from root cuttings. Often, simply harvesting a mature plant and leaving the smaller roots in the soil will quickly spread the row or bed. In fact, many of these crops can actually become invasive through inadvertent root cuttings.

To make simple root cuttings, just dig up a mature plant and cut off one or more (depending on the root configuration) side roots. You will want to choose fairly thick roots. Replant the root, taking care to keep the "up" side up. Cut the root off the mother plant with a straight cut on the top side to make it easier to keep track of which end is up. Keep the soil moist, and in a week or so, you should see growth coming up through the soil from the cutting.

Starting fruit trees from seed

Apples:

When I was a very young child, my favorite book was the story of "Johnny Appleseed," a man who traveled through the wilderness wearing a pot on his head and carrying a bag of apple seeds over his shoulder to plant for the settlers who lived on the land or would shortly be coming. Born John Chapman, this missionary and horticulturist made it his life's work not only to preach to settlers of the wilderness (in what is now known as Michigan, Ohio, Indiana, and Illinois), but also to plant apple seeds as he traveled so that the settlers would have fruit to sustain them.

Today, with all the grafted apple varieties, we are led to believe that you can't plant an apple seed, as Johnny did, and have it grow into a bearing tree with good fruit. This is true to a certain extent, but it depends on the variety of apple you are harvesting seeds from and the parentage of those seeds. You may get a very good apple, resembling its "mother" tree, a good apple, but one that does not resemble its parent, or a not-so-

These nice tomato plants were started as rooted cuttings.

Here are some wild plum pits that Will brought from Washington. I'll put them in dampened moss in the refrigerator so they can get the chilling time they require before they can sprout.

great apple because the pollinator was a wild crab apple from across the fence. But even the not-so-hot apple isn't a total waste, as you can easily graft wonderful varieties onto those branches, turning it into a great tree. (See my article about grafting fruit trees in Issue #121, January/February 2010.) It is very important, when you live in Zones 2 through 4, to consider the hardiness of the apple variety you are considering planting seeds from. For instance, I love Fuji apples. But I wouldn't save seeds from one because it is not hardy in Zone 3 where I live.

You'll get more consistent results when saving seed from older varieties that have been around for centuries, such as Duchess of Oldenburg, Yellow Transparent, or Red Astrachan.

Harvest your apple seeds from mature, ripe apples (eat the apple first), then lay the seeds out on a pie plate in a warm, dry location to dry. When dry, you can plant them in a designated spot in loose soil that is rich in compost. A friend of mine plants his in an old tire so he can locate the young trees in the spring when they come up. Apple seeds must go through a period of cold in order to begin germinating.

You can also wrap the seeds in moist paper toweling and put them in a jar in the refrigerator. In a few weeks they will start sprouting. Plant them in a four-inch pot in a sunny window, and watch them grow. In the spring, you can set the baby trees out in their new home. It will be about four years before they begin fruiting, but with care they should reward you mightily.

You can use the same method with pears, although they often revert to "wild" pears, which are very astringent. Of course you can go ahead and grow some from seed and try the first fruits when they are ripe. If they are astringent, you can always prune the tree back and graft on branches from a great pear and still have your own creation.

Stone fruits like peaches, plums, and cherries:

Like apples, stone fruits can also be started from seed. Sure, you may get a no-good bum of a tree, but also like apples, you can cut back the poor fruiting tree and graft a wonderful variety onto it and presto, you've got a great tree. Back in New Mexico,

Not only am I harvesting wild plums for jam, but also for their pits, so I can plant a hedge of wild plums along our own woods.

one of the best nectarines I've ever eaten was "planted" in a ditch, probably by someone who ate a nectarine for lunch and tossed the pit. It grew, unnoticed, until it began to fruit. It was known far and wide for its wonderful, juicy taste.

One fall I canned up a bunch of peaches and dumped the pits out onto my garden, where they were tilled in. What a surprise it was when in the spring, among my tomato plants, there were nine little peach trees. I'm sure that if I had planted them in an area where they wouldn't get tilled under there would have been many more.

Like apples, stone fruits must undergo a period of stratification (being exposed to cold). The easiest way to do this is to simply plant the pits outside in the fall. During the winter, they will be exposed to the cold and in the spring, they'll emerge from the soil as Mother Nature intended.

You can also put your cleaned pits in a Ziplock bag of moist sphagnum moss in the refrigerator for six to eight weeks. Watch them carefully so that if they begin to sprout, you can plant them in pots immediately. You can pot up the little sprouts and hold them in a sunny window until spring, then plant outside in a protected, sunny spot.

The easiest (most sure) varieties to plant from seed are bush cherries, wild plums, Manchurian apricots, chokecherries, and older varieties of peach, cherry, and plum. Again, you may get a terrific new variety, a mirror-image "child" of the "mother" tree, or a tree that's just so-so that you graft onto, but the way I see it, it's a win-win situation.

Nuts, like these acorns, produce nice baby trees after a period of stratification.

Berries from seed

Although berries are more easily propagated by means of runners, layering, and suckers, it is possible to grow them from seed. Raspberries, black raspberries, blackberries, and blueberries are the easiest to start from seed.

To harvest seed from raspberries, black raspberries, and blackberries, mash them in a sieve and strain off the pulp under running water. Place the seeds in a bowl and slowly drain off the water; the seeds will sink, the pulp rise. Plant them in a cold frame in the fall. They will emerge in the spring. You can thin them out and continue growing on.

Blueberries are easiest to grow when the seed has been harvested from berries that have been frozen for 90 days. Thaw, then put in a blender with warm water on high speed for 10 seconds. Allow to stand for five minutes. Carefully drain off some of the water; seeds sink, pulp rises. Add more water and repeat until seeds are clearly separated. Remove seeds and place on a paper towel to dry. Plant in a three-inch deep flat filled with moistened, milled sphagnum moss. Lay the seeds on the surface and just sprinkle a light layer of more milled sphagnum moss over them and moisten. Cover with a newspaper and set in a warm, sunny location. Keep moist but not soggy. Seeds will germinate in about four weeks, but keep a close watch, as you must remove the newspaper as soon as they begin germinating. These plants are very small. After they are about three inches tall, you may transplant them into individual pots. Don't set them out in the garden until all danger of spring frost is past as they are tender at this stage.

Nut trees

Nut trees are very easily started from seed — so easy that even squirrels can do it! After all, this is how many nut trees get their start. As a child in Detroit, I spent hours watching squirrels grabbing black walnuts from the ground, where the nuts had fallen, and carrying them off to bury them in the black soil on the edges of our garden. Sure enough, in the spring, little walnut trees sprang up from the ground, as if by magic.

Now if a squirrel can do it, so can you. Just remember that nuts also need a period of stratification (exposure to cold), as they would naturally receive in nature. Nuts with husks need the husk removed before planting. Wear gloves when handling those green-black walnut husks though. I think I still have walnut-stained hands from handling walnut husks in childhood.

Nut trees usually have a long tap root, so it's best to plant them where you will let them mature. To be sure you *do* have a nut tree where you plant it, plant three or four nuts in the same general area. If all germinate, you can carefully transplant the smaller ones, leaving the best one in place. Remember that some nuts, such as black walnut and hickory, get to be very large trees, so allow room for them to grow. Unfortunately, they also take years to produce nuts, so you need to be patient; your children and their children will thank you.

Beware of squirrels; they will "harvest" your nuts before they have a chance to germinate. Before you plant them, try dampening the shells, then sprinkle them with hot pepper. Use gloves for handling and planting though, as it may burn your fingers. The squirrels can't usually smell the nut because of the pepper, and will not like the taste if they should investigate.

If you don't have any plants or trees to start with

Don't despair. That's where family, friends, neighbors, and sometimes complete strangers enter the picture. When you're visiting, don't be shy about asking about a "start" from your aunt's rhubarb, the neighbor's great raspberries, your friend's plum, or even strawberry runners from the guy down the street. Most gardeners are tickled to have you ask. Besides, there's only room for so many plants, then they become like weeds. That strawberry bed gets too overcrowded with lusty plants, the rhubarb becomes root-bound, and the horseradish threatens to take over the garden.

If you don't have a friend, relative, or neighbor that has the type of plants you want, don't give up. Tack up a notice in the grocery store, feed mill, or laundromat.

And remember your roots; when you have a bounty of plants in your garden, be generous about sharing them with others. It brings us together full circle.

Propagating your own plants will save you a ton of money, besides being a really enjoyable hobby. You'll learn a whole lot, along the way, as well. If you're interested in learning more, I recommend reading *The Plant Propagator's Bible* by Miranda Smith and *Secrets of Plant Propagation* by Lewis Hill. Δ

Morels for beginners

By Leon Shernoff

Morels are one of the most popular edible fungi to be gathered in the wild in the United States. While not many Americans hunt mushrooms in general, finding morels is a tradition in many parts of the country. If finding them is not a part of your family's tradition, this article offers background details and identification information to allow you to hunt morels with success and eat them with confidence.

Like all mushrooms, the morel is the fruiting body of a fungus. The main body of the fungus is a network of thin threads called a mycelium (think of the fuzzy mold on your bread); every so often, the fungus grows a fruiting body to drop spores—like single-celled seeds—onto the air currents, so that they can float away and start a new fungal individual. Most of us are only familiar with cap-and-stem mushrooms, like the button or portabello mushrooms we see in the grocery store, but the morel is a little different. A morel resembles a hollow, cylindrical sponge on a stalk.

The illustration on this page shows many of the important identification features of a true morel, a member of the genus *Morchella*: a clearly honeycombed head, divided by clear ridges; the fact that the whole fruiting body is completely hollow (like a chocolate santa); the fact that the head is continuous with the stem — the walls of the stem simply change into head as they grow upward. The morel's spores grow in the pits of the honeycomb, and are discharged in masses—if you blow a gentle puff of air on a morel that you find in the forest, you may be rewarded by having it puff a small cloud of spores back at you.

There are two broad groups of morels in the continent—the black and the yellow—and two generally-recognized species of each, plus one maverick. The black morels are more common on the coasts; the edges of their ridges are often black, and they get darker with age. They tend to be taller and more pointy than the yellows, and their honeycombs are set up on more of a grid pattern. They are sometimes associated with conifers, which the yellows never are. Finally, the ridges on black morels don't change much in thickness as they age.

The yellow morels are sometimes called grays; they start off a delicate greyish eggshell color, and turn yellowish as they age, if exposed to sunlight. Their heads tend to be more rounded than the blacks, and their honeycombs are more irregular in pattern. The ridges on yellows start out quite thick (when they are still eggshell-colored), then they get thinner and sharp-edged as they age and turn yellow. They are the dominant morel between the Rockies and the Appalachians, especially in bottomlands that see a lot of small elms and other scrubby trees.

The maverick that I mentioned is the half-free morel. It is the only morel that breaks the rule about the head being continuous with the base. The head of the half-free hangs off the stem at the bottom, making a sort of short skirt. Otherwise, it resembles a pointy black morel with an unusually small head (usually only about an inch tall). Since the flavor comes from the head and the spores that it generates some people pass up the half-free. But it is a fine fungus in its own right.

The east-coast black morel is currently called *Morchella angusticeps*; it is modest and cosmopolitan in its fruiting habits. The west-coast black morel is currently equated with the black morel of Europe, *Morchella elata*, and like the European morel it is famous for fruiting in tremendous quantities in areas that were burned the year before. As a college student in New York, I spent several years combing the woods near old lightning strikes and campfires, but east-coast morels just don't grow there. However, for the last decade people have been harvesting vast quantities of "burn morels" the year after forest fires in the Pacific Northwest.

The larger yellow morel of the central US is generally known as *Morchella esculenta* and the smaller, squatty-headed yellow of the south-central US is called *Morchella delici-*

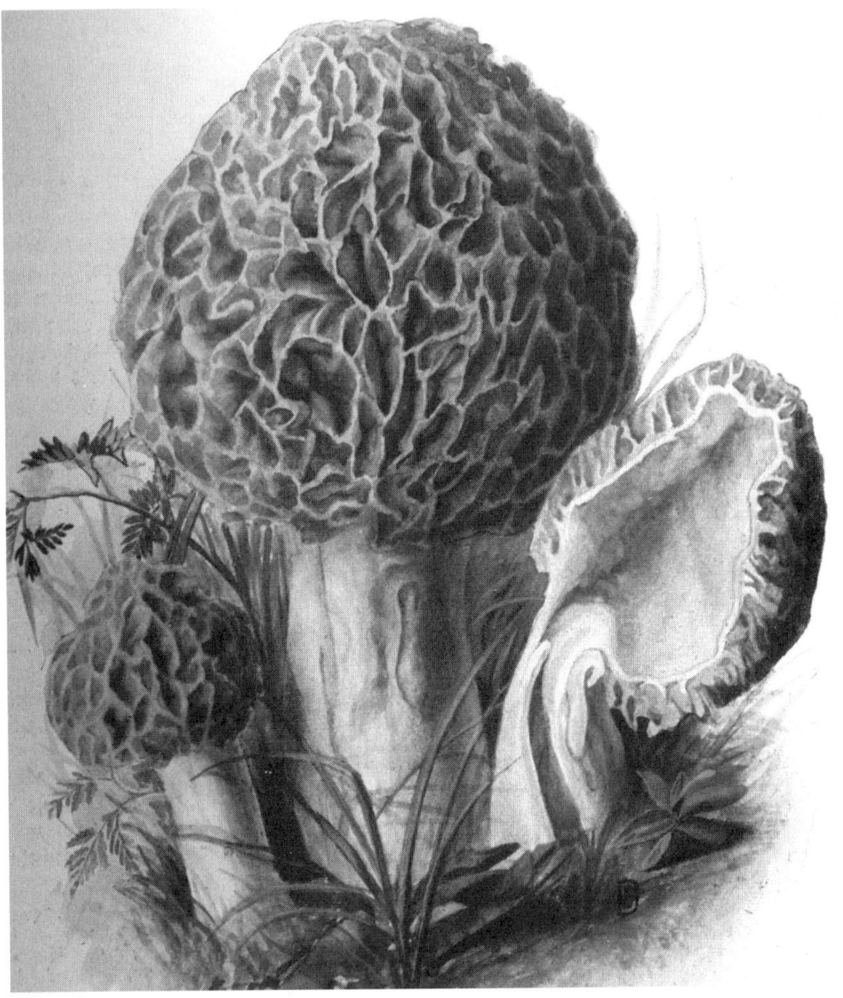

Above: This image of a yellow morel shows the honeycombed head and the hollow cross-section of a true morel. This image is from the 1896 German field guide Pilze der Heimat (Mushrooms of the Homeland), by Eugen Gramberg. At left: One of the yellow morels, ***Morchella esculenta.*** *Photo by John Denk.*

osa. Giant *esculentas* used to be called *Morchella crassipes*, but that distinction has gone out of favor. The half-free morel, in an unusually literal relationship between common and scientific names, is called *Morchella semilibera*. It is a maverick in habitat as well, growing almost anywhere, and in combination with any other morel species.

You may have noticed that I keep saying that these are names as "currently" used. Carol Carter, a mycologist in the Pacific Northwest, has been doing DNA testing on morels from around the country for the past few years now, and has currently isolated 14 separate species from the US. The four names listed here, though, are the ones in all the field guides, and they'll get you to where you want to go as far as collecting and eating are concerned. If you want the latest information check out Michael Kuo's website, *www.mushroomexpert.com*, which also has good morel advice, more pictures, and has even included a live weekly map of morel sightings across the country.

There is an annual succession of morels each spring: first come the half-frees, and then the other two. In the few areas where blacks and yellows occur together, the blacks come out earlier. There's about a week's difference between each group. Where to find them is a matter of some debate. Morels are unusual fungi in more than their shape; like many fungi, their mycelium is attached to the roots of trees, where it serves as a sort of extended root system. One of the most common (and essential) symbiotic relationships on the planet, the morels gather about a third of the tree's water, and most of its minerals from the soil. In return, the tree sends the fungus about an eighth of all the sugars that it produces. Most *mycorrhizal* fungi (as the relationship is called) send up their fruiting bodies continuously, whenever there is sufficient rainfall. Not so with morels, they store up the nutrients they receive from the tree for years, and usually only fruit when their partner is dying. What sort of tree death will stimulate them to fruit depends on the species and the area. On the west coast, the most stimulating form of tree death is forest fires. In the Midwest, their preferred location has traditionally been with elms; in the bottomlands along the Great Lakes and the Mississippi, there is a great abundance of small elms that grow for about 10 years, then get killed by bark beetles and fall over. The recently-killed trees are often surrounded by a crowd of yellow morels.

But in recent years, a new insect pest in the area, the emerald ash borer, has been killing ash trees. Suddenly, yellow morels are being found around these newly-killed ashes; before this, no one even knew that morel mycelium was growing with ashes. On the east coast, the classic places to look for morels are abandoned orchards, where the formerly domestic trees (apples are the most well-known) are slowly dying under the onslaught of the natural environment.

Having said that, there's also a substantial minority of morels that grow in places that no one can predict.

They will appear, seemingly out of nowhere, even in the middle of cities, on ground that has recently been turned over—construction sites, landscaping sites, backyard gardens. No one knows why; it's possible that the earth-turning snaps their connection to their plant partner, and makes them think that it is dead, prompting a panicked fruiting. The east-coast blacks often appear with apparently healthy trees, for no discernible reason—mostly with the ones named previously or tulip trees. Morels have been found from time to time growing with almost any tree except oak or maple. They tend to come up a few days after it gets warm suddenly, after a cold and damp period, but that's just in general. Once the trees start to bud, you might be able to find them at any time.

False morels

After all that about real morels, I'm not going to spend much time on the false ones, since I recommend avoiding them. But in many parts of the country, the false morels are simply called morels, and are eaten with enthusiasm, despite stories of poisoning. So this section is mostly so that you know what people are talking about if they call something a morel that you don't recognize.

A black morel, ***Morchella elata,*** *photographed by Pam Kaminski.*

False morels are in three genera: *Gyromitra, Helvella,* and *Verpa*. The *Gyromitras* are much larger and more widely popular. They are also more dangerous. Either kind of false morel has a wrinkled or convoluted head, unlike the honeycombed head of the true morel with its separate chambers. Their stalk goes up to the very top of the fruiting body, through the center of the head, and is connected to the top of the head, not at its bottom as in the true morels. Usually, *Gyromitras* either have a flaring edge to the head that makes it saddle-shaped, or the head curls back around the stalk, looking something like a deformed brain. A *Gyromitra* head has a reddish-brown color, which no true morel has. Because of this color, they are sometimes called beefsteak mushrooms, and because of the flaring irregular edge they are sometimes called elephant ears. A *Gyromitra* also has internal crosswalls and convolutions, both in the head and stem, unlike a true morel, while a true morel has the profile (in cross section) of a chocolate santa, a *Gyromitra* looks more like a chocolate santa that has recently eaten another chocolate santa.

A half-free morel, ***Morchella semilibera,*** *photographed by Pam Kaminski. Note the cross-sectioned specimen, showing that the edge of the cap protrudes out from the stem.*

Gyromitras are large fungi. It is not unusual to find them more than six inches tall and weighing more than a pound. A true morel, on the other hand, is typically only about four inches tall and weighs a few ounces. *Gyromitras* used to kill people regularly in Europe, until the mechanism of their poisoning was discovered. They contain a chemical similar to gasoline, called methyl hydrazine, often abbreviated MMH, for monomethyl hydrazine. It is the main ingredient in liquid rocket fuel. Like gasoline, it is very volatile, so it can be cooked off by cooking the mushrooms thoroughly. On the other hand, sometimes the cook has become very ill from inhaling the fumes. In western Europe, they are currently pro-

cessed by drying them for several months, giving the chemical time to evaporate; but in eastern Europe, where people stick more to the old ways, serious poisonings continue regularly.

The MMH, by the way, is not a contaminant from the "human-sphere," but a natural metabolite for these fungi. When they receive their sugars from the tree, the fungus immediately changes them into a form that the tree doesn't want back. Different fungi make different chemicals of this nature; as far as we can tell, their toxicity (or lack thereof) is a random feature, with evolutionary function.

Gyromitras are much less poisonous in this country than in Europe, where a 1967 survey found that 1/3 of people poisoned with this mushroom died. In the US, the mortality rate is closer to 15%, with most of them occurring before 1950. In the '90s, a mycologist went across the country, spot-checking and assaying *Gyromitras* along the way. In Kansas and Oklahoma, where they are most popular (along with Arkansas and southern Illinois), the few specimens that he collected turned out not to contain any MMH. This was a very sparse sampling of just a few fruiting bodies across a vast range of territory; it gives no information on how common this phenomenon is but it gives an idea of how many people can get away with eating them, for a while.

Why would anyone eat *Gyromitras*, with their known record of fatalities? First of all, their consumption is often a tradition in rural communities that mistrust the pronouncements of doc-

*Top: **Gyromitras** can have convoluted saddle-shaped caps, or more rounded brain-like caps. This collection has one of each. Note also the cross-walled interior — this false morel doesn't look like a chocolate santa, but like a chocolate santa that has eaten a few other chocolate santas. Bottom: This image of **Helvella crispa** shows the saddle-shaped cap of many false morels. These images are from the 1896 German field guide Pilze der Heimat (Mushrooms of the Homeland), by EugenGramberg.*

tors and medical studies. For a good-tasting mushroom that one can eat many times before suffering ill effects, it's often difficult to persuade people that this is a dangerous pursuit. Second, the toxin is extremely volatile, which makes the pattern of poisoning difficult to perceive. If you get the one undercooked piece at the table, you may get a dose of the toxin many times higher than that of anyone else eating the same dish. It can be difficult to persuade the other people at the table that your reaction is due to the mushroom and not something else. Finally, MMH is also a cumulative toxin; in some cases, it builds up in your body over years, and then you eat that one last bit and it puts you over the edge. It has also been shown to be carcinogenic and mutagenic in laboratory tests with cultured cells. Personally, I eat wild foods in order to avoid such chemicals.

The other genera of false morels are *Helvella* and *Verpa. Helvella* is a group of small mushrooms (usually just an inch or two high) with a saddle-shaped head, solidly colored in either eggshell white or dark charcoal, and a cross-walled stalk. They are not often collected for eating. *Verpas* are sometimes called thimble morels. They have a long stem and a small, skirt-like head (sometimes convoluted, sometimes smooth). The hollow stem comes up all the way inside the head, which hangs back down over the stem like a thimble over a finger (this is also their general size). The head is only attached to the stalk at the very top of the stem, the very tip of the finger. Both of these genera erratically cause strange symptoms in people, like lack of coordination, blurred vision, inability to write, and various levels of gastrointestinal distress. The toxins causing these effects are currently unknown.

In summary, to tell the false morels from the true ones, remember the real morels have a head with a distinctly honeycombed surface. This head is a simple continuation of the stalk, or is attached to the stalk near its lower edge. Furthermore, the true morels are hollow. False morels have a wrinkled or smooth head (not honeycombed), and it is free from the stalk—flaring out to form a saddle shape, curling back or draping over the stem—for most of its length. The chart on the next page summarizes the different kinds of "morels" in cross-section: the "chocolate santa" profile of the yellow and black morels in the lower right; the half-free morel in the upper right. *Verpas* are at top left, and the *Gyromitras* below. As the chart says, only the fungi on the right should be eaten.

Although the false morels are poisonous, they are not useless to the morel hunter, as *Verpas* and *Gyromitras* grow in similar habitats (and at similar times of the year) and thus are good morel indicators. *Verpas* in particular fruit in the right sort of area, just a week or so in advance of the half-free morels, making them useful indicators. *Gyromitras* tend to fruit after the half-frees, but before the yellows. These are just general tendencies, if there's a prolonged cold spell, past when the early fruiters want to come up, and then a sudden nice warm spell, they'll all come up at once.

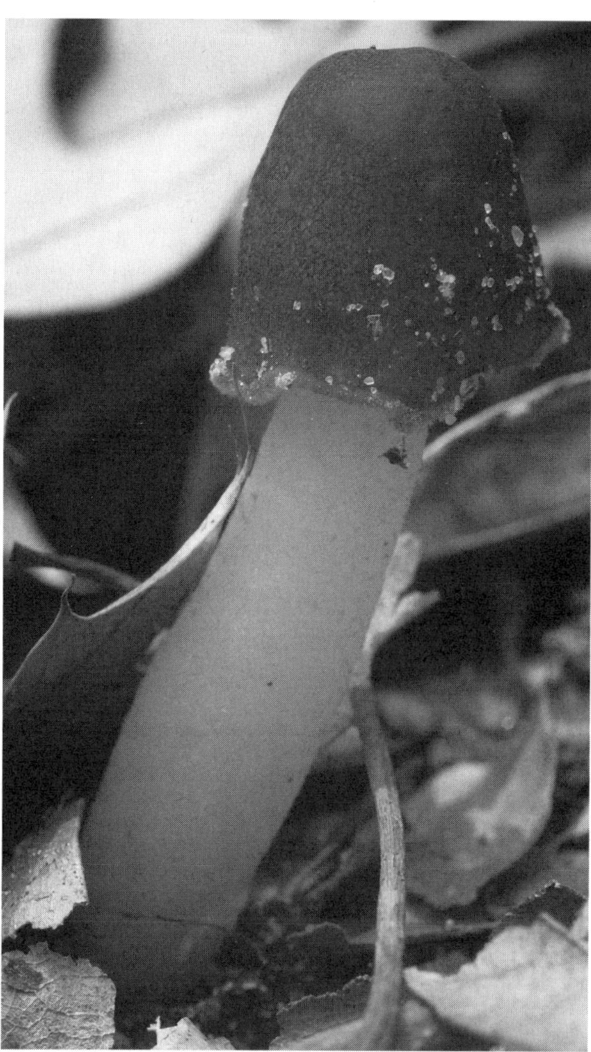

Verpa conica, *one of the false morels. It fruits before the true morels and in similar places, so it can serve as a morel indicator. Photo by John Denk.*

One other morel look-alike should be noted in passing — stinkhorns. Stinkhorns are a group of fungi that bear their spores in an odiferous slime on a honeycombed head. Flies and dung beetles are attracted to the stench and play around in the slime, getting it all over them. Then, when they fly to other places, the slime scrapes off of them and more stinkhorns grow from the spores. The easiest way to distinguish them is by season — morels fruit only in the springtime, while stinkhorns generally start fruiting in July and August. All reports of non-springtime morels in this country have turned out to be

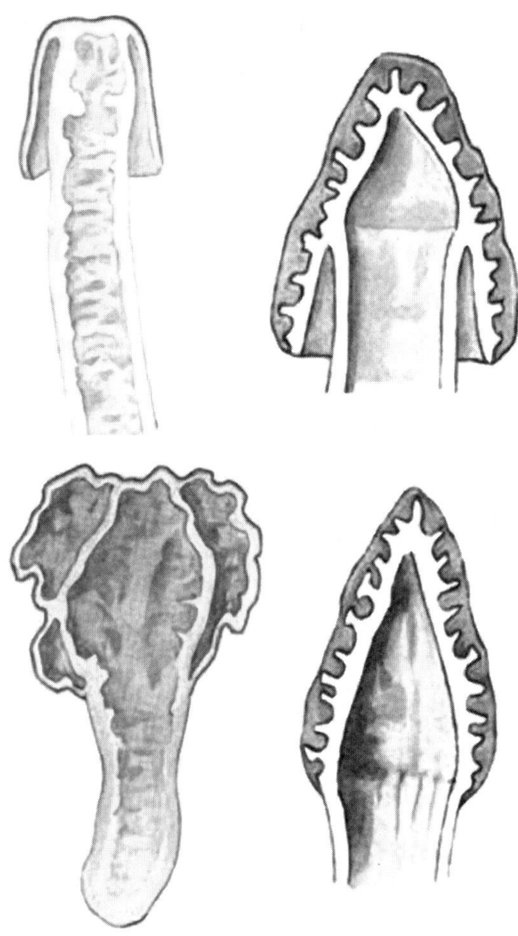

*This chart shows the cross-section view of true morels and false ones. The ones on the left are the false morels: **Verpa** at the top and **Gyromitra** below. At the right, you get the "chocolate santa" profile of a true morel: the half-free at the top, blacks and yellows at the bottom.*

honeycomb-headed stinkhorns that have had all of their slime removed by insects. Which brings us to the second way of distinguishing them — even with all their slime removed, they still smell pretty bad. Don't eat bad-smelling mushrooms; they're probably rotten. We'd never eat food from the store that smelled like a stinkhorn; we shouldn't eat wild foods like that either. I don't know about wild plants, but a substantial portion of wild mushroom "poisonings" each year are of people who collected edible mushrooms that were gone by, or let them sit in their refrigerator for too long but couldn't bear to throw them out. Actually, if it comes to it, stinkhorns are actually edible, but I doubt that it's a pleasant experience.

What to do with morels

First off, you must cook your morels. Raw morels have a strong track record of causing severe digestive upset. In fact, they were the presumed agent in the largest mushroom poisoning ever, which occurred in Vancouver, British Columbia in 1992:

"The guests included the chief of police, for whom this was a retirement dinner, and a number of members of the city health department. Many of the guests spent the latter part of the evening 'worshipping at the ceramic shrine' or at a nearby emergency room. Of the 483 persons present, 77 experienced some symptoms."(Denis R. Benjamin. *Mushrooms: Poisons and Panaceas.* W.H. Freeman, 1995)

The trick to cooking morels effectively is to use some sort of fat (usually butter) and to make sure that the spores (on the head of the mushroom) are exposed to it. This is where the flavor comes from. Just dumping them into a normal soup simply gives you a crisp, tasteless vegetable. There is a famous cream-of-morel soup, which is the default morel recipe if you ever search for one on the internet, and as you notice from the name, this involves a fat that the morels are cooked in. In the midwest, they are often batter-fried, or you can sauté them and put them on a steak. My favorite recipe is the following, a personal invention:

Leon's morels with toasted cashews and gefilte fish:

about a can of chicken broth
a large handful of rice
a large handful of cashew nuts
one large jar of gefilte fish, at room temperature
about an equal volume (to the jar of fish) of fresh morels
butter

Gefilte fish is a traditional Jewish food, fish balls that have been cooked by boiling them in fish broth. They are usually packed in the same fish broth, and since the fish bones have lots of gelatin, it usually gels around them. Using them in this recipe makes sense not just from the culinary standpoint, but (for most of the country) from an economic one: grocery stores that carry gefilte fish usually stock up for the holiday of Passover, which generally falls in April. After the holiday is over, the unsold gefilte fish is often available at a discount, which is the only time I buy it since it's rather expensive normally. And the time just after Passover is late April or early May, exactly when the morel season begins.

But now for the recipe:

In a saucepan, start cooking the rice in the chicken broth. Meanwhile, in a frying pan, toast the cashews over high heat, moving them around constantly so they don't burn. Add them to the cooking rice; they will make a nice sizzling sound as they slide in.

Lower the heat, add the morels, and sauté them in some butter, perhaps in two batches. By this time the rice should be done. Decant the gefilte fish, and cut the fish balls into bite-sized pieces. Add the cooked morels and the entire contents of the gefilte fish jar to the hot rice. The jellied broth will melt, and the gefilte fish will cool the dish to just the right temperature for eating.

Leon Shernoff is the editor of *Mushroom, the Journal of Wild Mushrooming* (www.mushroomthejournal.com). Δ

The stupid ladder incident

By Jim Van Camp

Almost everyone I talk to has a "stupid ladder" experience. Some are scary and some are worse, so anyone using ladders should take heed to avoid the following scenario I experienced.

A lot of water has gone under the bridge since I started working as a professional painter. I started out as an apprentice on my roommate's crew. They put me in the least visible place, rolling out closets in housing developments, masking off windows, and later working with other contractors. After 30 plus years I was pretty much on top of my game, or so I thought, before a hastily placed ladder came out from under me. After about a seven-foot fall I found myself laying in the dirt, not quite able to breathe, numb and hurting, with a fellow painter standing over me saying "Don't get up!"

I had broken my collarbone and two ribs. They had to operate on me to piece the collarbone back together with a metal plate, some screws, and another part that looks like a spring holding it all together. I was in the hospital for two days and I lost about two months of work, but I consider myself lucky after some other people started telling me about their stupid and scary ladder stories. The experience has taught me a few things which I would like to pass along to *BHM* readers.

Haste makes waste. In this case I almost wasted myself when I didn't check the stability of the ladder in some soft sand and gravel that was wet from a recent rain. I wouldn't say I was careless overall, but the quickly placed and untested ladder in a muddy working area is asking for trouble. Use footings, such as pieces of plywood, and lay them down on muddy or uneven patches of ground to shore up and level your ladder. Before going up the ladder, test it by moving the weight of your body up and down while standing on the first step of the ladder to make sure it's steady and gopher holes won't be a problem. Don't be in a hurry!

Sturdy, well-designed ladders and the right tools and equipment to brace your ladder will make you safer. Sometimes building scaffolds might be necessary. It takes time to build scaffolding, but in the long run it's safer and makes the job go faster.

Having the right tools and keeping them well-maintained also applies to ladders. I have a couple of old rickety aluminum alloy ladders with old worn-out foot pads that were undersized when they were new. These old ladders need new fasteners and new footings, otherwise they're not safe.

And something should be said about good ladder design. I can't help but think that if the ladder I was using had a little more "A-line" design built into it I might have had another second to react and get down a step or two. Single-pole ladders used for tree pruning and harvesting scare me. You just never know what's under that single pole part of the ladder as far as load-bearing capability. When in doubt, put a piece of plywood under it. Δ

Drive your own freshwater well

By Len McDougall

Whether it's home to animals or humans, every habitat must contain a source of drinking water. And because most homes in most places are not sited on the bank of a stream or lake, it has been a practice since biblical times to obtain the water needed by creating an access to aquifers concealed below the earth's surface. Before the industrial era made pumps and pipes common hardware items, wells were created by simply digging a narrow hole down to the water table, then drawing the water that seeped into its bottom upward in a bucket attached to a rope.

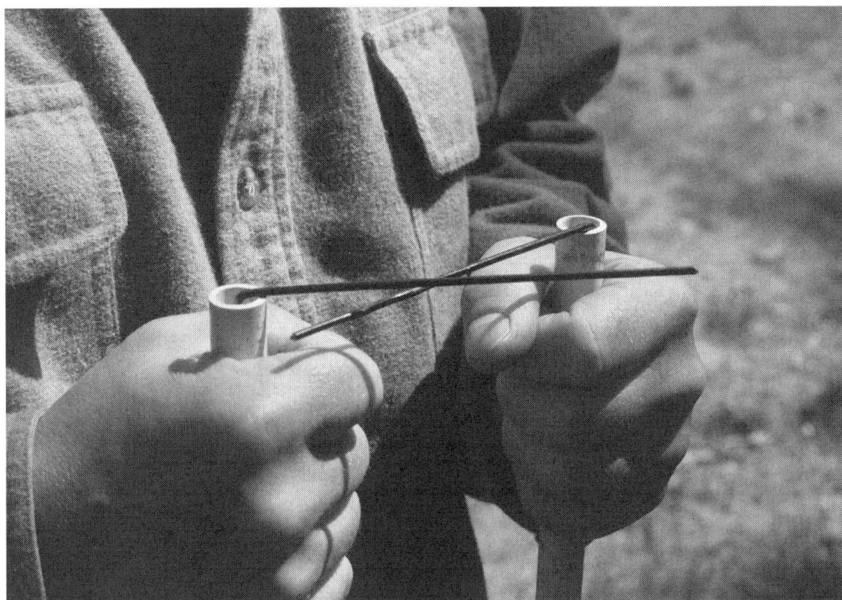

X marks the spot. How "witching" for water works is a mystery, but this time-honored method of locating good well sites is still in use today.

The well point's slotted holes permit water to enter, while stainless steel mesh inside keeps out abrasive sand.

An improved version of the open seepage well is the driven well. In its simplest form, this method of bringing safe groundwater to the surface uses a pointed, rocket-shaped "well point" to drive downward through soil until it reaches the water table. The well point is hollow, with slotted holes along its barrel to allow water to flow into it. Inside, these holes are covered with a heavy-mesh screen to keep out coarse sand and gravel.

Siting the well

The first step is to determine the best place to sink your well — where the largest deposit of water lies, and where it is nearest to the surface. The most time-honored method for accomplishing that is through "divination." This unexplained yet sometimes effective means of locating subterranean water was once practiced by well-diggers using a green willow "twitch." Water "witchers" would walk a selected area holding their twitches— which weren't necessarily

A good vacuum is critical to hand pump efficiency, so all threaded joints must be sealed with Teflon tape or pipe joint compound.

The physics of water-witching is unclear, and it is not always successful. A geologist uses more scientifically-based methods to help you locate where to dig.

Driving the well

There are several methods of getting a well point down to the water table, but the one most used by people in remote places today is the driving method, in which the point is driven downward like a nail. A pipe cap screwed snugly, but not tightly, onto the threaded end protects it from being damaged or deformed while being pounded from above. It is critical that neither the open end nor the threads below it are harmed while the point is being pounded into the earth.

A 100-pound "slam-hammer" drives the well point and pipe down to the water table.

made from willow — parallel to the earth; when the twitch began to vibrate or dip toward the earth of its own accord, there was water present underfoot.

Today's witchers tend to use a pair of L-shaped steel wires with equal-length sides about six inches long. To eliminate any chance of being influenced by the user, one side of each wire is placed inside a plastic PVC (water pipe) tube, and the tubes are held vertical so that the free end of each wire is parallel to the ground. With tubes held at an even height with about four inches between them, the witcher walks his chosen area until the wires swivel toward one another and form an X.

The first several gallons of water from your well will be muddy, until loose soil is pumped away to leave a cavity filled with clear water.

Begin by digging a pilot hole at least two feet deep using a hand auger or a shovel; the auger will make a pipe-size hole, but the wider shovel hole will require that soil be tamped around the well point to help hold it straight when pounding. A PVC casing placed over the well pipe — but kept above the point so that it doesn't inhibit water flow — keeps loose dirt from falling in around the well pipe as it is driven downward.

Well hammers can be as simple as a sledgehammer, or more preferably a large wooden mallet for softer soils. When punching through harder earth, some well-drillers prefer a pile-driver weight (a pipe filled with concrete) suspended from a tripod where it is hoisted upward then dropped onto the capped well point. More physically demanding versions include "slam hammers" comprised of a heavy, flat-bottom iron weight with a long steel rod that extends from it and into the well pipe as a guide.

When the well point has been driven down until only about ten inches remain above ground, remove the protective pipe cap and screw a

Well output is tested using a portable electric pump to see if it delivers the benchmark five gallons per minute.

four-inch nipple (a collar with internal threads) over the exposed threads. Use pipe joint compound or Teflon plumber's tape (wound in the direction of the threads, clockwise) to ensure a watertight seal. Screw a 6-foot-long pipe that is threaded on both ends into the nipple — actual length of the pipe can vary, but it has to be short enough to reach the upper end (you'll probably want a stepladder). Cap the upper end of the pipe, and pound it down until only about ten inches remain above ground. Remove the cap, apply joint compound to the threads, and screw-on another nipple, then screw another length of pipe into the top of the nipple. Pound this pipe down, and repeat the process, making sure to seal every threaded connection with joint compound or Teflon tape.

The pipe should move visibly downward with each blow from your hammer. If it stops and refuses to sink further after several blows, you may have hit a large rock. Do not continue hammering to force the pipe further, or you might damage the well point. It's easier and safer to pull up the well point by gently wobbling the pipe back and forth to widen the hole as you pull upward, then move the operation to another location.

When you reach the water table you will hear a hollow "bong" sound that issues from the pipe with every blow. To test it, remove the cap and drop a long string with a weight tied to its end (chalk line works well) down the well pipe until slack in the string tells you that the weight has reached the bottom of the well point. Draw the string back up, and measure how much of its length has been wetted to determine how deeply the well point has penetrated into the water table. To ensure good suction at the pump, it is important that the entire length of the perforated well point be immersed, and preferably at least two feet beyond that to account for seasonal variations in the water table.

When you reach water

When the drop-string is wetted to a length of at least five feet, it's time to screw on a pitcher pump (remember to seal the threads, or it may not draw efficiently). Prime the pump to create suction for its vacuum cylinder by pouring a cup of water into the pump's top, and jack the handle until water spurts from the pump with each downstroke. To be sure the well point is fully immersed in water, remove the pump, replace the cap, and hammer the pipe another two feet. Replace the pump, and jack the handle roughly 100 times to create a hollow filled with clear water around the well point. Alternately, you can use a portable electric water pump to create a water-filled cavity around the well point, and to test for a benchmark flow of five gallons per minute. When only clear water comes from the well spout, remove the pump and thread on a "check valve" between the well pipe below and the pump above; this will help to prevent water in the pipe from draining back down and will reduce the need to prime the pump.

The first drink of clear water from a well you've driven yourself is especially sweet.

How deep your well needs to be of course depends on how deep the water table is in a particular place. Depending on the type of pump, the depths to which manual pumps can operate is limited by the force of gravity and the length of its drawing stroke. In general, pitcher, jet, or centrifugal hand pumps are effective to a depth of 25 feet; larger stand pumps with draw cylinders will work to a depth of 50 feet.

Finally, check with authorities to be sure that there are no laws prohibiting wells where you live, and that the groundwater is not contaminated by toxic chemicals that have leached into it — this is not uncommon in more developed areas. Even where home wells are permitted, you will probably need to buy a building permit, and maybe have the finished well inspected and approved. Even with the red tape, a driven hand-pumped well is worth the hassle for the peace of mind it brings knowing that you can never run out of drinking water, come what may. Δ

More self-reliance in *Emergency Preparedness and Survival Guide*

Switch your family to goat's milk

By Tanya Kelley

If you milk goats, there's no doubt you've heard it—"Eww! Goat's milk! Gross!" To be perfectly honest, goat milk does taste different than cow milk. So? Different doesn't necessarily mean *bad*.

True, goat milk can taste downright "goaty." Goaty enough that even my dog wrinkles his nose at it. There are steps you can take to keep your milk sweet and delicious. There are also ways to break your family into the idea that goat milk might just be the best thing since sliced bread.

So, why not just get a cow and avoid all the family drama? First of all, a cow is a much bigger animal. Yes, they put out a lot more milk, but if your cow dies (and they do, believe me) you are out of milk. When your cow is late in pregnancy or has just freshened, you are out of milk.

It's easy to prevent that "goaty" taste in goat's milk. From left, Vision, Huckleberry, and Firecrackers.

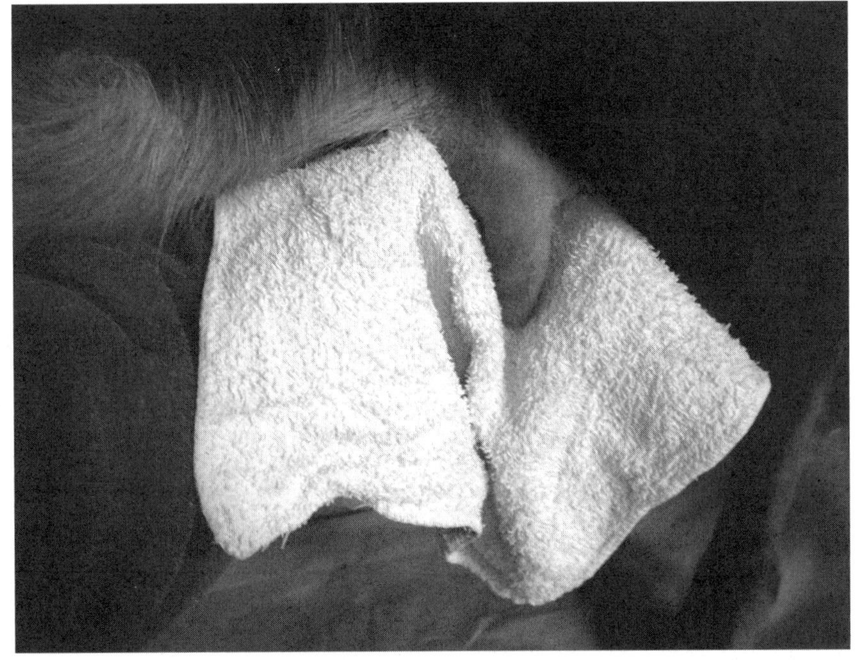

Wash and dry the udder before milking. Always use a fresh towel.

The expense and space required for one cow can keep a lot of goats. If a goat dies, you'll likely have more than one. You can stagger breedings to keep a year-round supply of milk.

The goat is often called the poor man's cow. Cow milk may be the norm in the United States, but across the world, goat's milk is more common.

So how do you get your family to *like* goat milk? For my family, it was a tough sell. I hated dumping a gallon and a half of rich goat milk to feed pigs and chickens, only to spend $3 a gallon at our local shopping center for cow's milk on an almost daily basis.

Keeping goat milk delicious

I attacked the problem from two directions. First, I had to make sure the milk never acquired that unpleasant goaty flavor.

Prevention starts with your goat. Remember, what goes in must come out. Good quality feed, water, and minerals are mandatory. I have heard some say that mineral deficiencies can cause off-tasting milk, but I have not personally experienced that. Goats that browse on wild onions, various mints, and garlic are also prone to unpleasantly-flavored milk.

If you've even been around a buck goat in rut, you'll have no trouble believing *his* musk could affect the flavor of milk from any does around him; however, that isn't always the case. I was shocked when I went into the barn at a large, commercial goat dairy near me. There were several bucks in rut hanging out in the same pens as the does. I asked the owner about buckiness in the milk and she said it had never been a problem. Since then, I have kept my buck with my does and found the same; however, my buck is still young. It might be a case-by-case situation.

I use a fine mesh coffee filter as a strainer over my milking bucket.

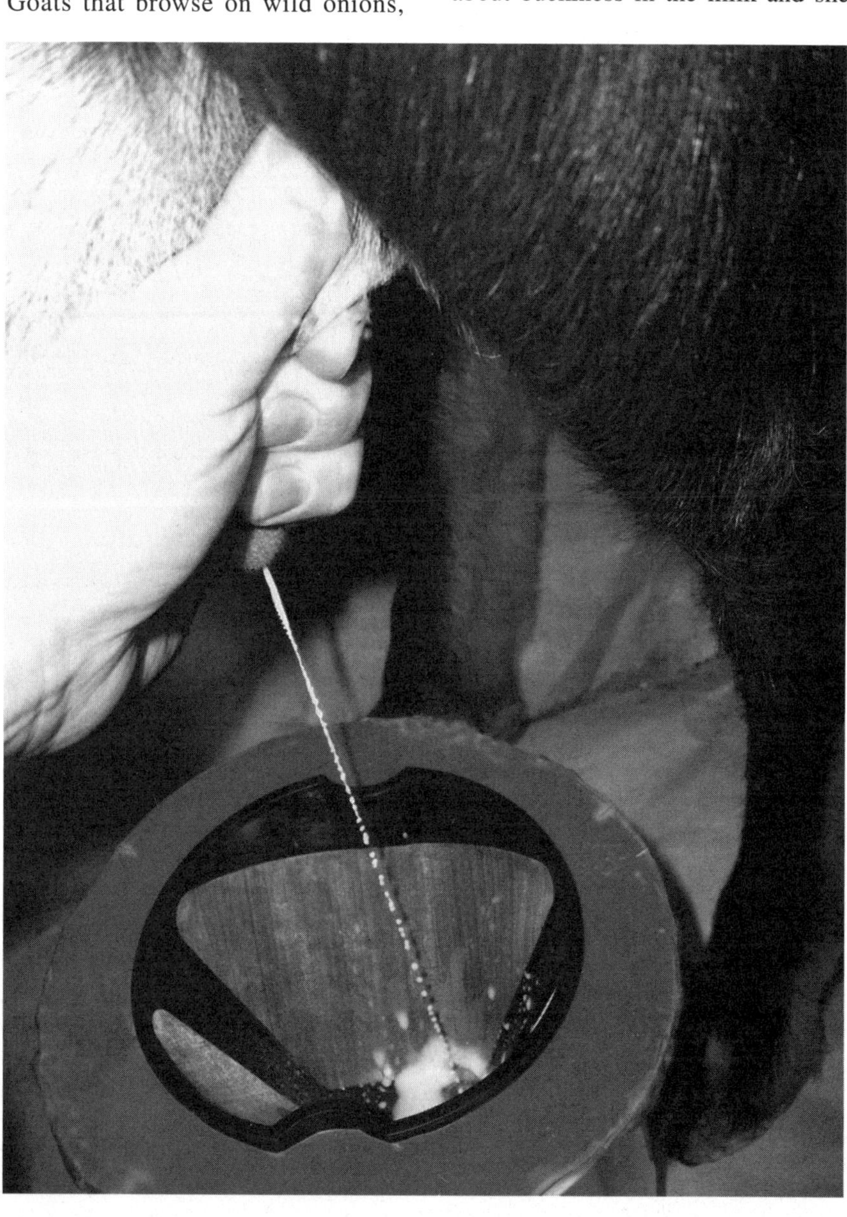

I milk directly into the strainer. This way, no wayward hairs or dirt make it into my fresh milk. After I bring the milk in the house, I strain it again to be sure.

Once your goat care is in place, prepare for milking. A clean milk pail is a must, as is a seamless stainless steel or glass container. Plastic absorbs flavors from the milk and will go from barely noticeable to downright goaty in a matter of days. Containers with seams have the same problem—you can't get them completely clean.

Many people milk into the pail and then strain the milk after, but if you think about it, milking can be dirty business. Your bucket of milk is sitting under an animal that has been lying around in straw, probably manure, and who knows what else. Add the natural sloughing off of skin and hair and it gets gross. I don't want that stuff floating in my milk, even for a little while. I strain while I milk. I know there are many options for milk pail strainers, but I made my own. I cut a circular hole out of a plastic lid from some long-lost mixing bowl. The lid fits onto my stainless steel milk pail and I can drop a fine-screened coffee filter into the cut out circle. The milk shoots through the screen and debris stays out. Later, I filter the milk again, just in case.

The faster you chill your milk, the better it will taste, especially during warm weather. I keep some lunch box-sized Blue Ice blocks in my freezer, and drop two into the milk

The quicker you chill the milk, the better. I put two blue ice blocks into my milking bucket to begin chilling the milk immediately.

pail before milking. The milk is chilled as soon as it hits the Blue Ice. After I milk, I wash the blocks off and pop them back into the freezer. They will be frozen again by the next milking.

The milk pail screen stops most debris from getting in the milk, but eliminating debris before it falls is even better. I use a cheap pair of people hair clippers to trim the hairs on the goat's udder. That eliminates any "dirt catchers." A trim every few weeks will be sufficient.

Once the udder is clipped, wash it with warm water before each milking. Dry it with a clean towel (use a fresh one every time you milk). Small, inexpensive washcloths work great for washing and drying and they are easy to launder. You can use unscented baby wipes too. Not only does washing the doe's udder prevent contamination of your milk, it also helps prevent bacteria from causing problems with your goat's udder. Wash your own hands, too.

Put a couple of squirts of milk into a test cup to check for any thickened milk, clots, or blood—warning signs that all might not be well. Not only will these affect the taste of your milk but also your doe's health. If everything looks good, milk the doe out.

After you milk, dip your goat's teats into a teat dip to further protect the udder from bacteria. There are many teat dip products you can buy, and you can even make your own.

Once you get your milk in the house, you may want to pasteurize it. There is a lot of debate about pasteurized milk vs. raw milk. You'll have to research and decide that for yourself. I don't find that pasteurizing prevents off tastes in my milk.

Put your fresh milk in the refrigerator as soon as you can. Store it in seamless glass or stainless steel containers. You can sterilize the containers if you like, but I've had good luck with jars that have been washed in warm soapy water and rinsed clean. Your container must have a tight fitting lid or your milk will absorb flavors from the refrigerator.

Your milk should taste fresh and delicious for several days or more. After a day or so you'll find cream on the top. You can skim it to use or shake the milk to mix it back in. Remember, this isn't store-bought, homogenized milk. It's the real thing.

Getting used to the taste

Is your family still stuck in the "different is bad" cycle? If your milk doesn't taste goaty, they may be unfamiliar with the fresh dairy taste. Even fresh cow's milk has that taste.

One way to get past that is to gradually introduce goat milk. Try mixing a cup of it into a gallon of store-bought milk. Then, with the next gallon, add more. Gradually increase the ratio of goat milk to store-bought milk.

I did this for quite a while, unbeknownst to anyone. Then, one day we were low on milk and I bought a gallon of milk and never got around to mixing it. Both my husband and my son were suspicious of the store-bought milk. They wanted to know if I had done something to it because it tasted goaty (even though it was straight cow's milk).

Another method is to mix a bit of vanilla flavor and a little sugar—just enough to change the taste to something a little more familiar. After a while, gradually reduce the sugar and vanilla.

Goat milk ice cream

I found an irresistible way to turn my family into goat milk lovers: Ice cream. My husband and my son are devoted ice cream fans. I came up with a simple recipe that won them over in no time.

Here's my "secret" recipe, guaranteed to change your family's mind.

5½ cups fresh goat milk
2 Tbsp. cornstarch
½-¾ cup sugar
1 tsp. vanilla

Mix ½ cup milk with cornstarch. Set aside. Heat five cups of milk in a heavy pan or double boiler. Stir frequently, as it scorches easily. When you see a crinkly skin form on top, stir the cornstarch/milk mixture into the hot milk.

Cook, stirring constantly, until mixture is thick, like honey. Stir in sugar and vanilla. You can remove from

Store milk in seamless glass or stainless steel containers with tight-fitting lids. It should remain fresh and delicious for several days or more.

heat now or, for a heavier ice cream, cook longer till it is a pudding-like consistency. Remove from heat and chill until cold. Freeze in an ice cream freezer until ready.

Variations:

Chocolate: Omit sugar and vanilla. Melt 6 oz. of chocolate (I use Hershey bars). Stir into hot milk.

Fruit: Make as directed. When ice cream is nearly frozen, add 1-2 cups diced fresh or frozen fruit.

This ice cream keeps great, but it will harden once put in the freezer. If you stir the ice cream an hour or so after putting it in the freezer, it will remain scoopable.

Follow these steps and your family will never say "eww!" again. You'll have lots of ice cream, fresh milk, and, if you get daring, fresh cheese. Best of all, you'll save money at the grocery store. Of course, those things don't even take into account all the health benefits of goat milk vs. cow milk—but that's a whole 'nother story. Δ

Make a better bucket butter churn

By Connie Rabun

When we first started in the dairy "business" on our homestead in Texas, we had dairy goats. They were very good milkers and taught us a bunch about dairy animals, and animals in general. I was happy with the goats, and really enjoyed them, but found myself wishing I could get more butter from my goat milk. When we moved to our happy 80-acre homestead in Missouri, we found that we already had "cow" fencing in place, but not "goat" fencing. So, we sold our goats and began the search for a Jersey cow. After looking for almost a year, I discovered a family in northern Arkansas who was raising a small herd of family milk cows, and just happened to be in need of a sorghum vat, which we could build (not we — my wonderful husband, who can do anything with metal!). So we bartered and brought home our first Jersey milk cow.

Our daughter, Dixie, churning butter

When we began making butter at home, we made it in glass jars, shaking and rolling them around. Then, I found a Dazey-style churn with broken paddles and shaft in an antique store for $10. I brought it home to Mr. Wonderful, who replaced the shaft with a stainless one and added stainless paddles on it. The original churn came with the short squatty jar, which succumbed to rough treatment, and rather than pay for another jar, Mr. Wonderful adjusted the paddles to make them fit into a regular gallon jar. Then, we could churn a half-gallon of cream at a time. Life was good on the homestead!

Some time later, we got the news that the daughter to our cow was up for sale, and we snatched her up. With two cows to milk, we were swimming in cream and it was time to consider a bigger churn. The second churn in our series was the old, round, wooden style, acquired through the barter system. This churn would allow a gallon of cream to be churned at a time, and this was a big help. The drawback to this churn was the cleanup. I never found anyone still using this kind of churn, and without regular use and thorough cleaning, mold can grow on the wood.

The next turn of events brought us into contact with an Amish fellow here in Missouri who pieces together old cream separators, and is very passionate about making them available for use, not for planters! We came home with an old McCormick Deering 2S cream separator. Now, we really had cream, and it was time to get serious about churning butter.

Parts of the homemade bucket butter churn

The bucket churn is born

While thinking one day of how to find time in Mr. Wonderful's schedule for him to make me a stainless steel churn, I got to looking at a plastic bucket with a rubber seal lid. The girls and I thought it might work as a churn, so we approached him with the idea. He was so glad I didn't ask for a stainless one, he immediately took a wooden dowel rod and marked the top of the bucket to cut a hole that just fit. Then, he grabbed two pieces of stainless scrap, welded together into an "X," put two holes in the middle of the "X," and screwed it to the end of the dowel. Voila! Instant butter churn.

We carried it back into the house to see how well it worked. We put two gallons of cream in and went to churning. The first batch churned beautifully, and was done in a jiffy. All was great until I went to wash it up. I kept feeling these little bumps in the butter. Upon closer examination, I discovered that our paddle clearance, which was close, on purpose, in order to churn as efficiently as possible, allowed our stainless paddles to rub the side of our plastic bucket, which was "shaving" our bucket. The little bumps were tiny pieces of plastic. I salvaged the butter by melting it and straining it through cheesecloth.

Butter completed in churn

The bucket went back to the shop. Mr. Wonderful said "No problem, we will make the paddles out of plastic." So, he cut out a little "X" out of the top of a plastic barrel, screwed it to the dowel, and we were fixed. We have now been using the butter churn going on six months and are very happy with it.

It is a wonder my husband gets any real jobs done out in his shop. To us, that is part of the beauty of homesteading. We are able to make do with less income because we make do with what we have and try to be inventive enough to get what we need. Δ

Delicious, dependable potatoes

By Linda Gabris

When I was a kid, my grandparents always grew a huge plot of potatoes in their backyard garden, enough for digging and eating fresh as "young" potatoes throughout the growing season. They also had plenty of rows of "keepers" for maturing and putting up in the root cellar for the long winter months ahead.

Grandpa vouched that "taters" root-cellared better than any other vegetable for winter keeping and thus earned their space more than any other plant in the garden.

Since my grandparents put up almost all of their own food for the winter months, when trips to town to buy store-bought groceries were few and far between, keeping a well-stocked root cellar was an important way of life.

I fondly remember when I was a kid how barely a day would go by that potatoes weren't on the menu in some form or another. Grandma made everything from potato soups, salads, biscuits, and dumplings to mashed, baked, fried, and scalloped delights that are as popular today in my kitchen as they were in Grandma's years ago. And Grandma's old recipe for luscious potato candies is still one of my family's all-time favorite sweets.

History

Potatoes are native to South America. History dates their cultivation back to early farmers, in what is now modern-day Bolivia and Peru, 7,000 years ago in the rugged Andes mountains, where fluctuating temperatures and poor soil conditions proved them to be a remarkably hardy plant.

By the 1600s, the potato had made its way to Europe, but since it was recognized as a member of the poisonous nightshade family, the potato was shunned and was considered not fit for human consumption. The crops were used mainly as animal fodder or food for the very poor.

By the 1780s, Ireland had become dependent upon their potato crops. The potato was a hardy plant that was easy to grow and dished up all the sustenance one's family needed in order to survive. Thus, two memorable events in Ireland's history are directly related to potatoes. One is the population explosion of the early 1800s, said to have come about by the self-sufficiency that potatoes provided; the other was the devastating potato crop failure of the mid-1800s that resulted in the great famine of Ireland, costing the country half its population through starvation and emigration.

In the rest of Europe, the potato was breaking ground as acceptable table fare. It quickly gained recognition as a reliable and tasty staple, earning its spot on the supper plate right alongside highly regarded meat.

Freshly dug baby potatoes or young potatoes only need to be washed in cold water before they are ready for the pot — no need to pare these gems.

Though it was originally a South American crop, the potato was introduced to North America by early settlers from Europe and the rest is history. How many of us today could imagine life without potatoes? I know

I couldn't, for potatoes are a big part of my family's diet. For those who occasionally indulge in the convenient world of fast foods, can you imagine the menu without "fries?"

Growing potatoes

The potato is an annual plant that is botanically related to the tomato, pepper, and eggplant. The edible tubers begin to form around 40 days after planting, about the same time the plant starts to flower.

It takes about 90 to 140 days from planting to maturity, depending on growing zone and variety. There are many different varieties of potatoes which are classified as early, mid-season, and late potatoes.

If you don't save your own seed potatoes for next year's crop, then you should try to buy potato stocks for planting that are inspected and certified. This will reduce the chance of disease and crop failure.

Stock potatoes can be cut into two, four, or even six pieces depending on the size of the planters. Each cut piece should have at least one or two "eyes." They will fare better if they are "cured" first. Put the pieces in a warm, damp place for about a week before planting. This encourages the cut surfaces to "heal over," makes them less prone to decay, and promotes faster sprouting.

Potatoes should be planted a couple weeks before the last killing frost is expected. Put them into holes about 6 inches deep and 10 to 12 inches apart. Start hoeing early, mounding little "hills" of soil around the base of the plants. This aerates the soil, deters weeds, and prevents developing potatoes from "greening" or getting sunburnt. The hills also protect the maturing potatoes from early frost.

Grandpa always said that a good potato crop calls for three actions. One is to weed, one is to water, and one is to rotate your patch every second or third season. According to Grandpa, if you plant your potatoes on the same ground year after year, diseases and pests are bound to strike. Moving the patch from one plot to another discourages problems in the potato patch. His old advice must be true, for Grandpa grew the best potatoes around.

Harvest and storage

Potatoes should be harvested before heavy frosts strike. When the tops of the plants become withered down, the potatoes will have reached full maturity and are ready to be dug. A well-matured potato will have firm, hardened skin which is less likely to bruise and thus will be better for long- term storage. An immature potato with thin skin will be more susceptible to injuries caused by digging and handling.

Potatoes should be dug on a warm dry day, as a damp day will cause soil to cling to potatoes, inviting rot. Dig a wide hole to avoid cutting into any of the potatoes with the spade. Turn the plants over and shake gently to retrieve all the tubers from the roots. After digging, allow the potatoes to dry in open air in a shady spot for about a week. Do not dry in direct sunlight as it can cause the potatoes to turn green, which produces a toxic, bitter taste.

Once cured, the potatoes can be moved into the root cellar. Grandpa stored his on cribs lined with straw. I store mine laid out on burlap bags. Never store them in plastic or on metal shelves. Ideal root cellar temperature is between 38 and 45 degrees F with good humidity. If you don't have a root cellar, store potatoes in a cool, dark place with good air circulation allowing them to breath. Use up potatoes that are bruised or blemished first, and always check the lot for a soft or rotten potato which can prompt the others to deteriorate. When conditions are just right, potatoes will survive the winter well and even last long into spring when the new crop starts to come in.

There are many popular varieties of potatoes which are often of more concern to the gardener than to the cook. From a gardener's standpoint, you may wish to plant those that are reputed as doing well in your growing zone. Or you may decide to plant a few hills each of Norland, Norgold Russets, or some other early season spuds for eating fresh from the garden.

Or maybe you prefer to plant some mid-season potatoes for summer fare, such as Jersey Royals, Red Pontiac, Viking, or Norchips. And, of course, if a hardy stash of potatoes for the winter root cellar is your number one concern, then you may choose a late season, well-respected winter saver such as Netted Gems, Russet Burbanks, or some other noted storage spud.

If you are unearthing your potatoes from the produce department of a grocery store, choose potatoes that are locally grown when possible, as these will be freshest. Look for firm, blemish-free potatoes. Avoid those that are wrinkled or bruised, are sprouting, or have tinges of green on their skins. They should smell pleasant and earthy fresh, never stale or distasteful.

When buying potatoes you may wish to choose a general multi-use potato. If you don't have ideal temperatures in your home for storing them (38 to 45 degrees F) do not buy more than can be used in a shorter period of time.

The recipes

Large round potatoes with pale yellow to brown and red skins and creamy "floury" flesh are ideal for mashing, baking, and frying. "Waxy" potatoes are better suited for salads. Fancy little round "baby" potatoes which can be bought in new fangled multi-colors, and those that look like "fingers" are excellent for gourmet dishes. They call for gentle cooking and look fascinating served whole.

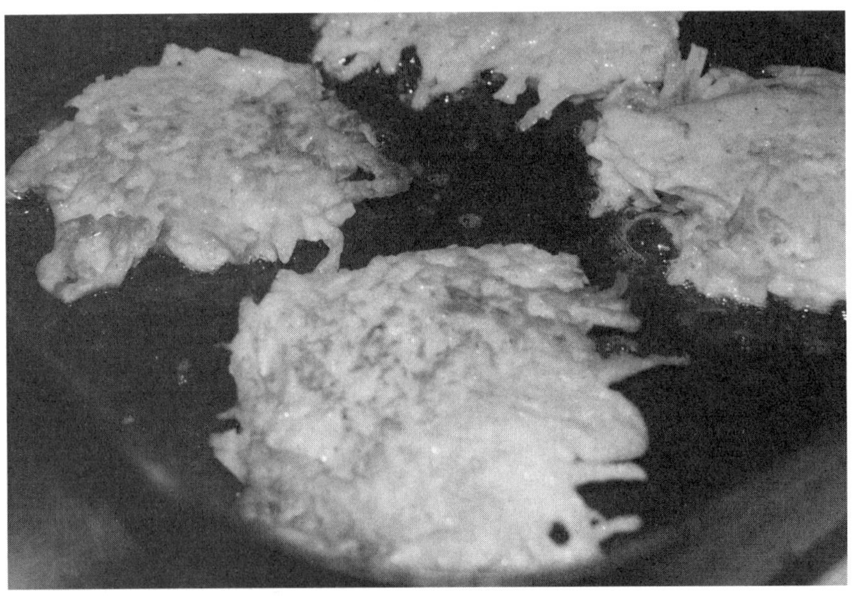

Fry potato latkes until crispy and golden on both sides.

But do not fret too much about variety, for one potato can easily stand in for another in the eyes of most cooks.

Fresh young potatoes and those with good looking, healthy skin can simply be washed in cold water before preparing — no need to peel. Older potatoes should be scrubbed well in cold water, and eyes should be dug out with the tip of a peeler or small paring knife and discarded, as should any blemishes and tinges of green which can cause a bitter taste.

Now it's time to dig up some great-tasting potato recipes. Here are a few of my favorite ways to cook and serve potatoes. Some are Old World recipes from Grandma's kitchen that I grew up with and still enjoy today. Others are newer recipes that I've rounded up from international cookbooks to showcase potatoes in a brand new light. Old or new, no matter how you cook them, potatoes are what good eating is really all about.

Fabulous French fries (chips):

There are four secrets to perfect French fries. One is soaking the traditional French-cut potatoes in cold water for at least two hours to turn the starch into sugar which produces a sweeter crispier chip. The second secret is to heat the oil to the ideal frying temperature (375° F) in the deep fryer or heavy-bottomed skillet before dropping in the potatoes. Vegetable oil produces a tasty chip. Thirdly, fry the chips in small batches, never crowding the pan. And lastly, drain each batch of chips on paper towels to absorb excess oil. Sprinkle with salt that has been ground fine in a mortar and pestle, and you are ready to serve the best chips ever. If you are making several batches of chips before serving, hold hot in a 300° F oven until all the chips are cooked.

Silver dollar potatoes:

I called these "silver dollar" potatoes when I was a kid, and the name has always stuck. Scrub four big potatoes and slice thinly. Put in bowl of cold water and soak while frying six slices of smoky side bacon in a heavy cast iron skillet. When bacon is crispy, remove from pan, pat with paper towels, crumble, and set aside. Dry potato slices on paper towels and slip into the skillet of hot grease. If you don't have at least two tablespoons bacon drippings, add enough butter or oil to make up the needed amount. Fry until undersides are golden, shaking the pan often. Flip and cook until evenly browned. Remove from pan and pat with paper towels. Sprinkle with salt, pepper, and crumbled bacon upon serving. Serves four.

Variation: Slice up leftover whole cooked potatoes in place of fresh.

Country-style mashed "taters:"

Grandpa loved mashed "taters" and I do, too. The biggest secret to making mouthwatering creamy-smooth mashed potatoes is to choose firm white or cream-fleshed good quality potatoes that are blemish-free. Pare

Herbed baby potatoes is one of the simplest, prettiest dishes ever. It's a great way to show off your freshly dug early potatoes.

about two pounds of potatoes. Put them in saucepan with enough cold water to cover and add a pinch of salt. Bring to a boil, reduce heat and simmer until fork tender. Do not overcook them. Drain, then blend ¼ cup heated buttermilk (or cream or milk) with three tablespoons of melted butter and add to the pan with the potatoes. Add salt and pepper to taste. Mash with a hand masher, or lightly beat with a rotary beater until creamy and smooth, adding a dab more buttermilk to reach desired consistency. Do not over-beat the potatoes as they can turn gooey. Serves four to six.

Variation: Add ¼ cup minced chives and sprinkle top with additional chives or decorate with a chive flower when in bloom.

Scalloped potatoes:

Nothing is more fragrant than a whiff of scalloped potatoes wafting from the oven on a cold winter day. Here's Grandma's simple recipe. Scrub four to six potatoes and slice thin. Mince a large onion. Heat two cups milk and melt ¼ cup margarine or butter in the milk. Set aside. Now, grease a deep 10-inch baking dish and layer the bottom with potatoes. Cover with onions, sprinkle with a tablespoon of flour, and season with salt and pepper. Repeat until the baking dish is layered to the top, ending with the flour, salt, and pepper. Pour the hot milk over the top, adding a little more if needed to cover. Bake in a 350° F oven for about an hour or until potatoes are tender and sauce is thick and creamy. Serves four to six.

Herbed baby potatoes:

Here's a very simple dish that is, as Grandma would say, "ever so pretty."

2 Tbsp. butter
2 Tbsp. bacon drippings or vegetable oil
1 minced onion
1½ pounds whole baby potatoes
fresh minced parsley, dill, basil, or other herbs of choice
salt and pepper to taste

Heat fat in sauce pan, add onion, and sauté until soft. Add potatoes and cook, shaking pan often, until tender. Add herbs, salt, and pepper. Transfer to serving platter. Serves four.

Potato latkes:

Grandma simply called these "potato cakes" but over the years I've come to know these tasty cakes that are deeply-rooted in Jewish cuisine by their proper name, latkes.

5 large scrubbed or pared potatoes
1 large onion
2 eggs
pinch salt
fresh grated black pepper
¼ cup flour
fat for frying

Grate potatoes and onions. Add eggs, seasoning, and flour. Mix well. Drop by tablespoons into skillet of very hot fat (oil or lard) and fry until browned on one side. Turn and brown other side. Work in batches rather than crowding the pan. Drain on paper towels. Serve with ketchup, or the traditional way with applesauce. Makes about eight cakes.

Poor man's potato soup:

This is a wonderfully thick, rich, and creamy potato soup that amazingly does not contain any milk or cream at all, thus its name.

6 large potatoes
4 Tbsp. butter, margarine, or oil
1 minced onion
1 stalk diced celery
1 carrot, chopped fine
¼ cup flour
salt and pepper to taste
3 cups boiling water
1 Tbsp. fresh minced parsley or 1 tsp. dried parsley

Scrub or pare potatoes and dice three potatoes into small soup-sized cubes. Cut the other three potatoes into larger pieces and put into a pot with enough water to cover. Bring to a boil and cook until mushy. Remove from heat and mash or puree these cooked potatoes until smooth. Set aside. In a soup pot, melt butter and add cubed potatoes and remaining vegetables. Sauté until onion is soft and carrot is cooked. Add flour and seasonings. Add boiling water and cook, stirring constantly until smooth and lump-free. Add the pureed potato mixture and cook until cubed potatoes are tender, but not falling apart. Taste and adjust seasoning. Garnish with parsley upon serving. Serves four to six.

Hungarian potato-kolbasz soup:

This is a thick, hearty soup that my husband, Sandor, fondly remembers from his childhood in Hungary during the years of war and revolution. It is a very economical soup to make, and when served with a thick slab of rye bread, is a full meal that really sticks to your ribs.

6 scrubbed potatoes cut into 1-inch cubes
3 Tbsp. shortening (or homemade pork lard for authentic taste)
½ pound thinly sliced kolbasz (Hungarian pork sausage or other spicy sausage of choice such as Italian chorizo)
3 minced onions
4 cloves minced garlic
1 chopped red, yellow, or green pepper
3 Tbsp. sweet paprika
1 tsp. salt
½ tsp. black pepper
3 large chopped tomatoes
½ cup red wine
1 tsp. caraway seeds
6 cups boiling water
sour cream to garnish

Heat the fat in a soup pot and sauté sausage, onions, garlic, and pepper until onions are golden. Add potatoes and paprika and cook until paprika is absorbed. Add remaining ingredients, except sour cream. Bring to a boil, reduce heat, cover and simmer until potatoes are tender, but not falling apart, adding a little more water if necessary to reach desired consisten-

Poor man's potato soup contains no milk or cream, yet it is thick and creamy.

Potato-salmon cakes make a quick, tasty supper dish.

cy. Ladle into bowls and swirl with sour cream, if desired. Serves six.

Potato-coconut candy:

1 cup mashed hot potatoes (if using cold potatoes, heat over boiling water until hot to work with)
3 Tbsp. melted butter
4 cups powdered sugar
¼ cup cocoa
2 tsp. vanilla
1½ cups shredded coconut

Mix all ingredients, beating until well blended. If mixture is too stiff, add more melted butter. If too moist to hold its shape, add more shredded coconut. Drop by spoonfuls onto waxed paper and set in fridge to harden.

Aunt Mernie's potato-dill bannock:

Grandma made this tasty bannock, too, but always called it "Aunt Mernie's" bannock. I never knew Grandma's Aunt Mernie, but I sure do love her bannock recipe.

3 cups flour
3 Tbsp. baking powder
pinch salt
⅓ cup room temperature margarine
1 cup buttermilk
2 cups hot mashed potatoes
2 Tbsp. fresh chopped dill (or dried dill weed to taste)
dab more buttermilk for brushing
additional dill for sprinkling

Combine all ingredients, except last two, in a large bowl. Mix well, adding a little more flour as needed to form a smooth dough, and knead lightly. Pat into a 10-inch greased cast iron skillet, or form into a circle and place on a greased baking sheet. Brush with buttermilk and sprinkle with remaining dill. Bake in 425° F oven until golden, about 20 minutes. This bannock makes a tasty breakfast or supper bread. Makes 12 wedges.

Potato-salmon cakes:

Here's a salmon supper that is quick and delicious. It's a really great supper for any weekday when you're running late.

2 cups cold mashed potatoes
1 cup bread crumbs
1 pint of salmon (if you can your own as I do) or 1 large can of store-bought salmon with juice
1 finely minced onion
1 egg
salt and pepper to taste
flour for dusting
oil for frying

Mix all ingredients except flour and oil. Form mixture into six patties, adding more bread crumbs if too wet, or more salmon juice if too dry. Dredge cakes in flour, and place on waxed paper in fridge until frying time. Heat oil in a skillet and fry cakes until crisp and golden on each side. These cakes can be served with salad and a cooked vegetable or serve them on buns like a fish burger. Δ

Ayoob on Firearms

The light at the end of the gun

By Massad Ayoob

My old friend (and publisher) Dave Duffy suggested my topic for this month in *Backwoods Home*. He had a bit of an epiphany in a critter eradication situation.

Dave writes, *"A few weeks ago I had to shoot a skunk in the chicken house, but the old long-barreled Sears semi-auto proved unwieldy as I tried to take aim at him.*

"Since then I attended a preparedness show in Utah where a gun seller was displaying a short-barreled Remington 870 with extended magazine and high quality LED light toward the front. It would have been perfect for the situation above. (I've had to shoot skunks and rats in the chicken house on at least a half dozen occasions.) It also looked way cool! You operated the LED light with your left thumb. He was charging about $1500 for it but it was all high quality. I'm thinking of buying one.

"It occurred to me that this shotgun would double nicely as a home protection gun. I've used my old Sears shotgun in "practical" situations more than any gun in my home, even though it's the least expensive of any firearm I own."

There's a lot to be said for a maneuverable firearm that has a light attached. (In police work, we've come to call it "white light," to distinguish it from laser sights and from handheld flashlights.)

When the SureFire company figured out how to attach them to pistols, LAPD SWAT quickly glommed onto them for their .45 caliber semiautomatic sidearms, starting a trend nationwide. The next cops to go with light-mounted guns were K-9 officers. During a dangerous manhunt in the woods, backyards, or alleys, the K-9 cops only had two hands with which to do three jobs: keep hold of the dog's lead, hold a gun, and hold a light. Attaching the light to the gun was a perfect fit for their mission.

The next step in development was smaller lights, sometimes combined with laser sights, which quickly slid on and off a rail that was integral to the gun. Heckler and Koch started the trend in the early 1990s with their USP (Universal Service Pistol), whose polymer frame was molded to take a proprietary quick on/quick off light unit. This soon gave way to the universal-fit Picatinny Rail, now available for military style rifles, standard on modern police service pistols, and even available on some shotguns. In Iraq and Afghanistan, the light mounted on a soldier's weapon can mean the difference between life and death.

And, as my friend Dave has noted, this concept has huge potential in routine rural living applications.

The backwoods gun & light

When you have to shoot a critter in the dark on your rural property, a light attached to the gun can be a huge help. Let's start by looking at the rationale of the concept.

The light allows you to confirm identification of the target before you press the trigger. You're awakened at 2 a.m. by furious barking, growling, and assorted commotion outside the house. You emerge to find your dogs fighting with a coyote. As you raise your firearm, you want to be damn sure that the gun is aimed at the coyote, not one of your own dogs. Powerful illumination that's running its beam in line with your gun barrel helps *greatly* to achieve this.

Massad Ayoob demonstrates the SureFire X200 light mounted left front on Picatinny rail on this S&W M&P .22 Long Rifle. Support hand thumb activates light from standard hold.

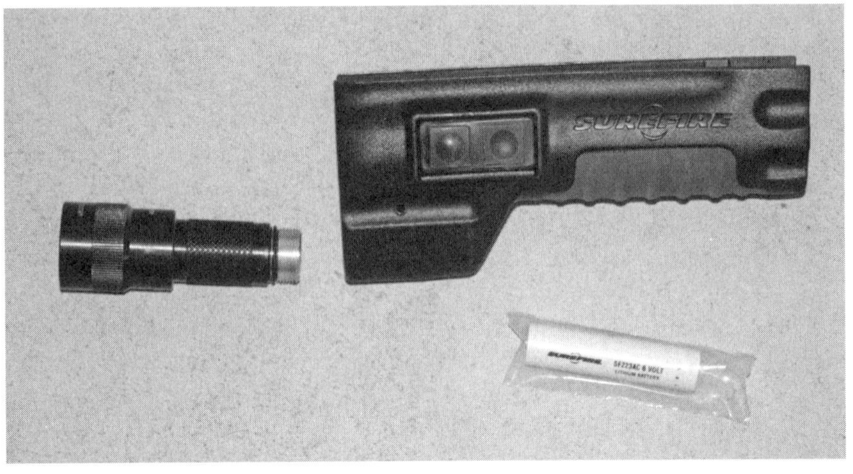

SureFire light system replaces "slide handle" on Remington 870 shotgun.

Even if you have glow-in-the-dark Tritium night sights, in serious darkness this just gives you a good aim at something you can't otherwise identify. Flicking on a powerful gun-mounted light allows you that critically important last-second verification that what you are about to kill, *is* what you intended to shoot. If it *isn't* what you came out to shoot, the light has saved the life of a loved one or a pet or some of your own livestock.

The light allows you to extend your field of view. One cornerstone rule of firearms safety is, "always be sure of your target *and what is behind it.*" As you emerge from your farmhouse after hearing the ruckus in the chicken coop, the light streaming out from your kitchen door may illuminate the predator from which you are trying to save your poultry...but the light fades at a distance, and what is behind the limited area of light is now in inky blackness. Are you *sure* that your son-in-law isn't running up behind the animal, in your line of fire, responding to the same commotion? Or that your beloved family dog isn't running toward the problem from the other direction? The powerful light mounted on the gun will pierce the darkness much farther, hopefully far enough to tell you whether or not you have a safe "shooting backdrop."

The light allows you to track your target. You've fired the shot. The recoil kicks the gun up into your line of sight, blocking your view, and when you bring it down the target is gone, though you can hear its running feet. With the powerful beam of light at the end of your gun, you are much more likely to find the threat, get it back in your sights, and make the finishing shot if that is necessary.

The light "changes the living target's channel." When an animal is caught in bright light, it tends to freeze. This is where the term "deer in the headlights" came from. It may just make the wolf that was entering the lamb's pen hold still long enough for you to make the perfect shot that ends the matter. With humans, I've found the reverse to be true: a man will tend to turn violently away from bright light that hits him in his eyes, particularly when his pupils are dilated after some time in the dark. If we're talking an armed two-legged intruder instead of a merely noxious four-legged one, you wouldn't be firing a deadly weapon at him unless he was about to kill or cripple you or your loved one. Wouldn't it be kind of nice if at this moment something could make him turn violently away from you or his other intended target, in a fashion that momentarily disorients him? What a coincidence: that seems to be *exactly* what bright light in the eyes in the dark causes people to do.

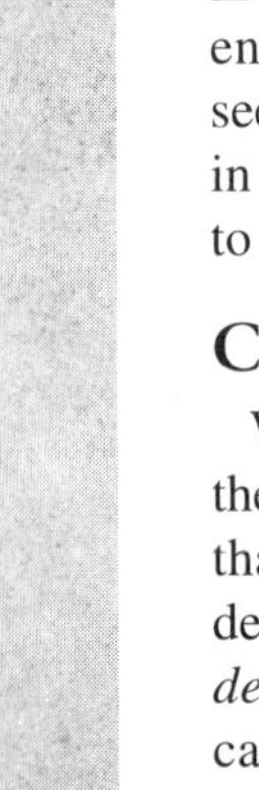

SureFire X200 light slips easily on and off this Springfield Armory XD45 pistol.

Caveat

When we mount a light to a firearm, the key thing we have to remember is that in the combination of light and deadly weapon, the operative term is *deadly weapon.* This means that we cannot use the combined unit as an ordinary flashlight to go out looking for things...because anything that's in the beam of the flashlight now has a lethal weapon pointed at it.

In a highly publicized case in Texas in 2010, an officer making a gunpoint arrest with a pistol fitted with a flashlight apparently fumbled when he tried to turn off the light, and accidentally discharged the weapon. The bullet struck and killed the compliant, surrendered suspect at whom the gun and the light were pointed. This sort of thing is the worst case scenario.

Let's say you've heard that proverbial "thing that goes bump in the night." You've grabbed your light-mounted gun to go looking for it, and the light coaxial to the gun barrel is the only illumination you have. You go searching room to room. Searching a room isn't looking at one thing, it's looking at dozens of things. Now, three or four rooms into the search, your bright beam illuminates the hundredth thing you've looked at … and it's an unexpected human being.

You are, naturally, startled. Startle reflex tightens our muscles. In the hands, the strongest muscles are the flexor muscles, and one is attached to your trigger finger. Before you know it, the gun has fired…and the person in the beam that's in line with your gun barrel, the person who startled you, is one of your kids.

Dunno about you, but there are folks who'd be thinking of using up one more bullet on themselves, at that point.

Right now, some readers into shooting discipline are silently yelling, "That stupid Ayoob! Doesn't he know that real professionals keep their finger off the trigger until they intend to shoot?" Yeah, he does. But he also is familiar with the European study of highly-trained SWAT cops who put their finger on their triggers during high-stress simulations when they didn't realize they had done it. He also is aware that only a perfect human being can be 100% certain of keeping their finger off the trigger, and a 100% perfect human being hasn't existed for at least 2011 years.

SureFire light is mounted on this Scattergun Technologies Remington 870, wielded by veteran police officer Tim Julian.

But let's say you're perfect right now, and you *don't* pull the trigger. Your kid still realizes that you pointed a loaded gun at him while searching with that light under the muzzle. You think the kid's gonna get over that by tomorrow? You think that won't be something the kid remembers at your funeral after you die of old age?

Thus the cardinal rule with this technology: *Don't use the gun-mounted light as a flashlight. It's emergency lighting for when the time to shoot is upon you.*

Right now, when I get up from this keyboard and go to bed, there will be a Springfield Armory XD pistol at bedside, loaded with 14 rounds of high-tech jacketed hollow point .45 ammunition and mounting an X-series SureFire light on its frame. But next to it will be a regular SureFire flashlight, and if I should feel a need to go looking for trouble, the gun with its turned-off light will

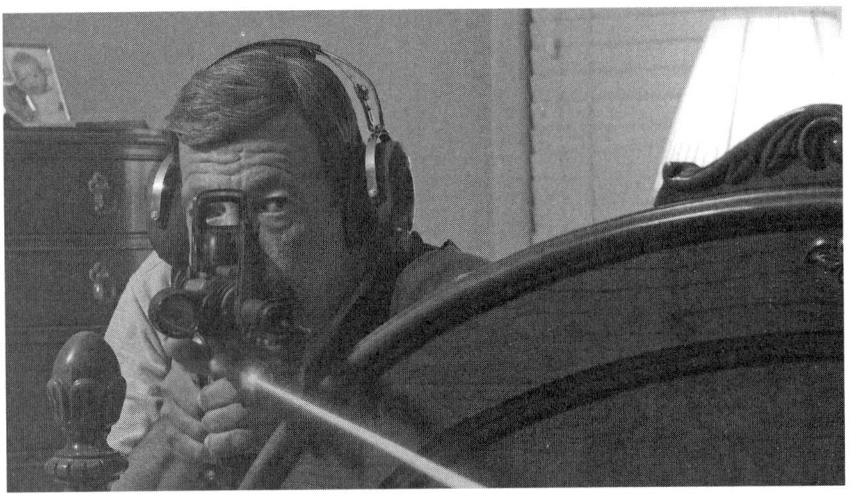

Light has not yet been activated, but green laser sight has, on this .223 S&W M&P15 rifle. Light is activated by button on fore-grip. Photo is "still capture" from home defense video in the "Make Ready" series from Panteao Productions.

be in my dominant hand in a retention position, and the separate light in the free hand will be the one that beams through the darkness, going quickly on and off as I move so it doesn't spotlight my own position.

Other gun/light options

There are lots of ways to coordinate a gun with a separate flashlight. I've developed a couple of techniques for that myself that are widely taught in law enforcement and the military today. But I'll be the first to tell you that being able to dedicate both hands to holding the gun steady, instead of one hand being partially or entirely dedicated to holding the illumination, results in faster, better hits.

One technique that everyone seems to miss (perhaps because it's not possible for a lone shooter) is the two-person technique. Partner A controls the gun, and Partner B runs the light. In a fast-breaking SWAT or self-defense situation, it's unlikely that this will be possible. But, if there are two of you responding when you have the proverbial "fox at the henhouse" in a farm situation, it can work remarkably well.

Let me share with you a situation I saw on my own rural property some years ago. It involved a fox, if not a henhouse. It was an outdoor barbecue party with dozens of folks in attendance. Night had fallen, we were still outdoors in balmy weather, and all evening we had been looking at a strangely-acting fox that had been circling closer and closer to where the people were at the periphery of the house. It was exhibiting signs of rabies, and we decided that "for the good of the order," if it showed up again it would be euthanized. (Foxes were a protected species, but the law made an exemption for obviously rabid animals.)

Sure enough, the furry little red dude showed up again. One of those present, an off-duty cop who worked that jurisdiction, drew a SureFire 6P and lit up the beast in the now-dark back acres, less than half a football field away from folks it could bite. Another of our party drew a Glock .45, took a strong two-handed Isosceles stance, and fired a single shot. The single Speer Gold Dot hollow point bullet hit it center chest and killed it, instantly and humanely. The shooter told me later that the other man's light on the animal silhouetted it perfectly in his sights, giving him a sight picture that looked like something out of a marksmanship manual.

Decades ago, on one of my safaris in South Africa, a friend on the grounds there asked us to come by and help us rid his farm of predators during a legal nocturnal hunt. We did so. The most efficient manner proved to be one person manning the light, and the other manning the gun. We didn't use shotguns, but it worked with rifle and it worked with revolver. Being able to dedicate both hands and all the fingers to holding the gun steady and making the shot was wondrously effective.

Will "one person on the light and another on the gun" work for combat? Probably not. The situation in front of the gun is too unpredictable, and coordination between two people in rapidly-evolving return fire situations will be too problematic. For two rural home dwellers working together in predator control on the property, though, it makes sense.

As a kid growing up in New Hampshire, I knew a lot of folks who stalked raccoons. The protocol for these "'coon hunters" was to tree the animal with dogs, then shoot it in the tree. Because it was perfectly legal to hunt them at night (and perfectly logical to do so, since they were nocturnal), all manner of light-and-gun combinations were cobbled together. But what most of the seasoned coon hunters came up with was the protocol of Hunter A runs the light, and Hunter B runs the .22. It was simply the most efficient way to handle that particular shooting scenario.

An analogy

In my younger days, I didn't like the idea of a gun-mounted light at all. Experience changed my view on that. One night in the early 1990s, Palm Beach County (Florida) Sheriff's Department hosted the annual conference of the American Society of Law Enforcement Trainers. I was that organization's chair of the firearms committee, a position I held for 19 years. During the seminar, I took a "busman's holiday" and went along with PBSO deputies for a raid on a drug house. As we were debarking from the SWAT van, one of the team members pointed to a window in the target house and yelled a warning.

All around me, guns were coming up, and my hand went immediately to the D.R. Middlebrooks Custom Colt .45 automatic in my own holster. But before I cleared leather, team leader Bill Testa had the SureFire light on his Benelli automatic shotgun on the window, and I saw the man behind the glass spin away from the blinding beam, his hands coming up empty. Moments like that teach you the value of gun-mounted lighting.

If you've been reading *Backwoods Home Magazine* for a while, you know one of the reasons I like a telescopic sight on a hunting rifle is the safety factor. Its magnification lets you see what you're shooting at. If you were negligent enough to use your riflescope as binoculars to scan the woods and look for things, you would eventually see an innocent human being in that scope. You'd be pointing a lethal weapon at someone you had no right to point a gun at. You could expect to lose your hunting license, and even be charged with the very serious felony of Aggravated Assault.

But, if you thought you had spotted a deer and aimed at it, the magnification of the scope would be a last-ditch verification of your target. Was it a legal buck with antlers, or an illegal doe standing where branches were behind her head? Was it really a white-tailed deer, or was it some guy in gray-brown Carhartts with a white handkerchief sticking out of his hip pocket? The multiple-times magnification of the scope can verify the target before it's too late, thus preventing a terrible mistake.

I submit that the light on the gun is exactly the same. You don't go looking for things with it, or you'll end up pointing a gun at someone you have no right to take at gunpoint. You use binoculars or a spotting scope to scan the hunting ground, and a separate flashlight for searching.

But, if you thought you spotted something you needed to shoot, the brilliant white beam of the attached gun light gives you that last-ditch target verification. It can help prevent tragic mistakes.

And for all these reasons, I think it can make huge sense for backwoods home firearms. Δ

Dehorning calves with dehorning paste

By Patrice Lewis

If you raise cattle either for milk or meat, you're faced with a dilemma: whether or not to let the calves keep their horns. Unless your animals are polled (genetically born without horns), this is an issue every cow owner must face.

We've had Dexter cattle since 1998. We started off with a couple of horned heifers who are now our herd matrons. After one of them got a little "testy" and learned to use her horns, we vowed never to have a horned animal on the property again, especially since we have children.

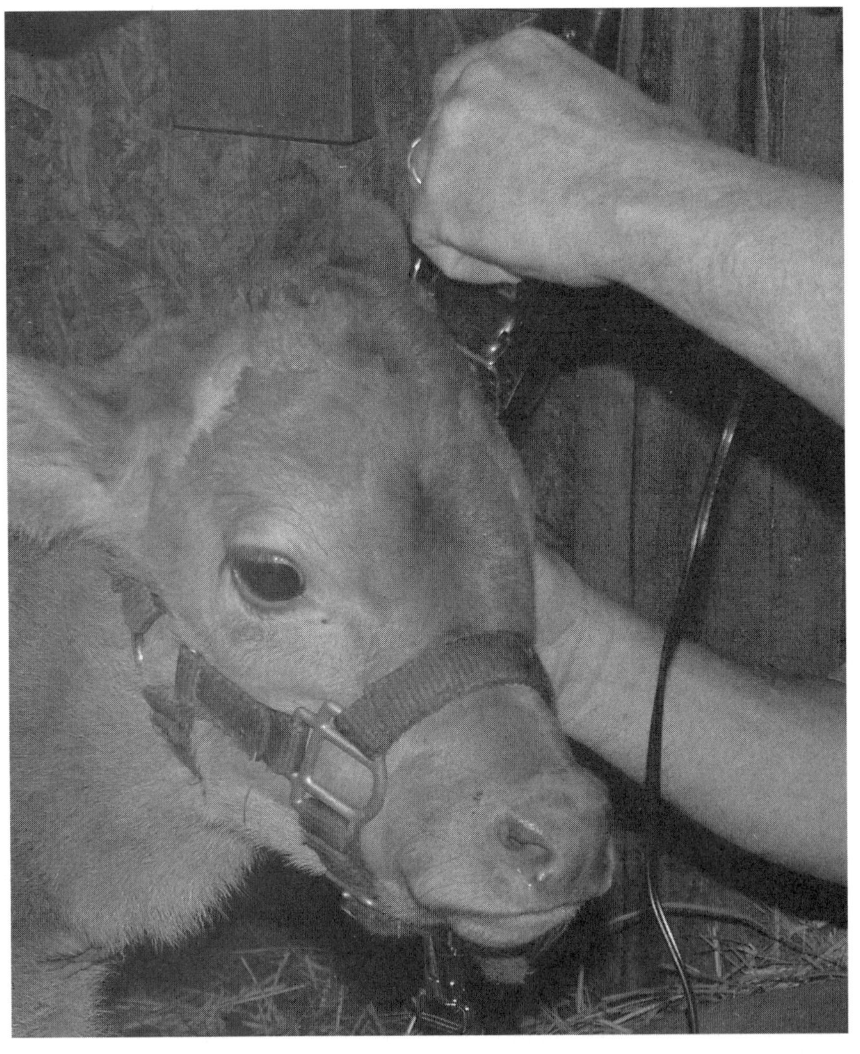

Shaving the hair over a calf's horn buds

So we've always dehorned our heifer calves. We don't bother dehorning the bull calves because we always turn them into steers which are put in the freezer at two years of age. Our steers have wonderfully sweet dispositions. And at two years, horns aren't big enough to be dangerous. Why waste a good dehorning on such critters?

But the heifers are a different matter. Heifers turn into cows, and cows are around for many years. So it isn't a question of "if" we would dehorn them, it is a question of "when."

Heifers need to be vaccinated between the ages of three months and one year against Bang's and other diseases. Since farm calls are expensive, we always waited to dehorn the heifers until we could combine it with vaccinations. That meant the calves were at least three months of age, sometimes older if we had multiple calves and were waiting for the youngest to turn three months. Then we would call in old Doc White.

Doc White was the beloved farm vet in these parts for decades. Though in his 60s, he could wrestle a calf into submission, dehorn, ear tag, tattoo, and vaccinate while hardly breaking a sweat. So we always relied upon his superior strength and know-how to get the job done.

Dehorning paste. Cost is about $6 in feed stores and only a small amount is needed for each dehorning. For the average homesteader with a few head of cattle, a jar of dehorning paste will last for years.

On our farm we don't have a squeeze chute, so we would herd the calf into a pen, put a halter on her, rope her up, and prepare for a rodeo. I always *hated* vet days, despite Doc White's competency.

The trauma of manual dehorning

The calves detested dehorning, of course. To dehorn a calf, you take these giant loppers with circular ends and crunch/whack/chunk the horn off. At three or four months old, calves have a pretty good "kick" to them, and let me tell you they kick for all they're worth. Naturally there was a lot of blood from the amputated horn, so Doc White would take his cauterizer (which was plugged in and heating during the dehorning) and cauterize the horn base. By this point the calf would be flipping and flopping and twisting in pain, attached by her halter to the railing, moaning pitifully. The mother cow would be outside the pen, bellowing in fury over the indignities to her baby.

The calves got over it, of course. But I *hate* to see an animal in pain. And needless to say, this procedure didn't exactly sweeten the calf's disposition or give her confidence in us.

The last straw was when we made the mistake of waiting *ten months* to dehorn a pretty little sweet-tempered heifer named Ebony. At ten months, her horns were six inches long — but we didn't realize this because she had all this curly fur on top of her head, burying the base of the horns and making them look shorter and smaller than they really were.

We waited this long because Doc White was ill and unable to make farm calls, and we were waiting for his health to improve. Unfortunately he passed away (may you rest in peace, Doc, you've earned it), so we called the only remaining large animal vet clinic near our farm and made an appointment for a vet to come dehorn Ebony.

The vet was a woman. Big mistake. I have the greatest admiration for women vets, so let me qualify that statement.

This vet just didn't have the casual arm strength old Doc White had after so many years of chomping off horns. Plus, the loppers hadn't been sharpened properly. Plus, I'm not sure she had a whole lot of experience dehorning older calves. What happened on that afternoon in the barn changed my views on manual dehorning forever.

It was a kicking, bloody mess, with a frantic, frightened, nearly year-old bovine bellowing in pain. The vet's assistant had roped the heifer and kept her hindquarters more or less on the ground, but her front half was heaving and flopping, dangling from her halter tied to a post. The poor vet took whack after whack after whack at those stubborn horns, with the animal struggling and bucking, blood pouring. Then she had to cauterize those huge gaping wounds…

Anyway, you get the picture. It was horrible.

To make things worse, once the animal was back on her feet and the

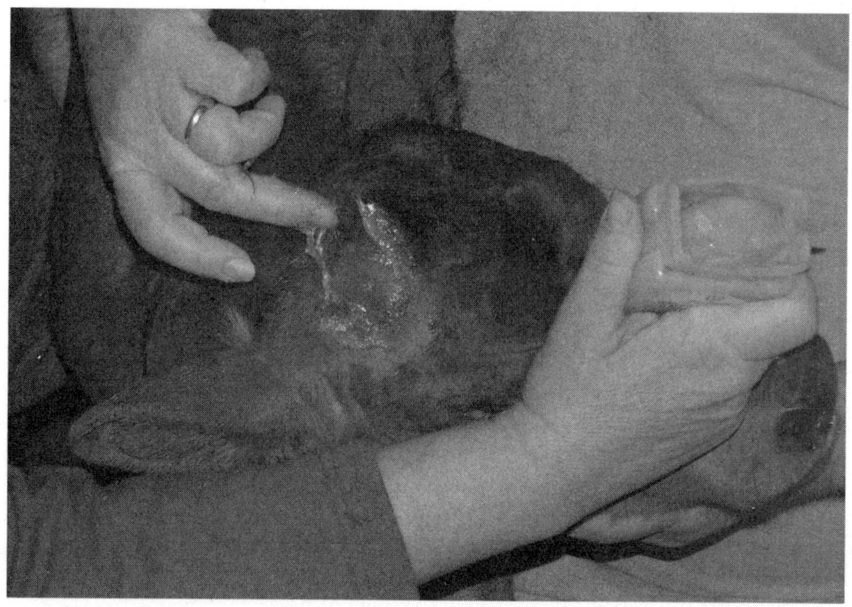

Making a ring of petroleum jelly around the horn bud to corral the dehorning paste. Dehorning paste is very caustic, and precautions need to be taken to make sure it stays where it's supposed to.

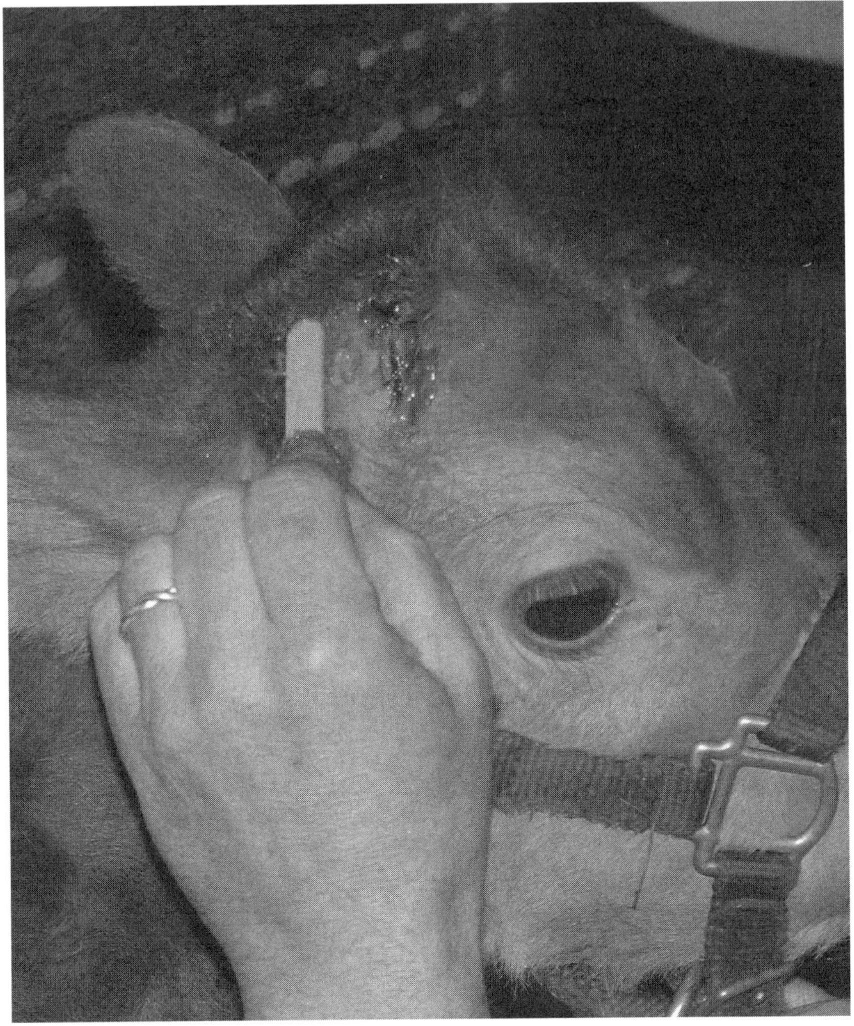

Applying dehorning paste with a popsicle stick. Use NO MORE than a THIN nickel-sized smear. Too much dehorning paste will eat away the calf's skull.

blood flaked off, we realized the dehorning was unsuccessful. One horn came off, but the other left a "scur," a partially amputated horn that grows back thick and misshapen and ugly. And for some reason, scurs usually grow backward and eventually grow into the animal's skull. Unless we try dehorning Ebony again at a future date, using anesthesia this time, (*cha-ching!*), she'll have a date with the freezer when she's about five years old.

In other words, because of a combination of our procrastination, inadequate farm facilities (like a head gate), and veterinary incompetence, this animal's life will be shortened. And, oh yeah, she's been suspicious of us ever since. Can't blame her, really.

There *had* to be a better way to dehorn cattle. We didn't realize it at the time, but there was.

An alternative: dehorning paste

Dehorning paste, which has active ingredients of sodium hydroxide and calcium hydroxide, is nothing short of a modern miracle. It's cheap (under $6 at most feed stores) and a small jar lasts a long time. And we could do it ourselves; no need to call the vet.

The material requires careful use. The paste is caustic and eats away the horn bud. The best time to apply it is when the calf is between three and ten days old, though I've heard that it can be applied to slightly older calves. (However, since I have no experience in pasting older calves, I cannot vouch for this.)

The critical thing to remember when using dehorning paste is to restrict the paste to exactly where it needs to go. Misapplication of paste is no small thing. I know a woman who dehorned a young calf, but the paste oozed down the side of the calf's head and left a horrible open lesion that required prompt veterinary attention to save the calf's life. The calf lived, but has an ugly scar.

So do *not* take any shortcuts or skip any steps when dehorning a calf. For God's sake, read the instructions before using the stuff. However, if all the proper procedures are followed, the method is safe, easy, non-traumatic, and — if the calf's behavior is anything to go by — minimally painful.

By the way, unless you have a stall and head gate capable of holding a baby calf, dehorning is a two-person job. Make sure one of those people is capable of restraining a calf. (In other words, your eight-year-old son may not be the right choice.)

How to do it

Start by isolating the calf at three or four days of age. Because our mature cows are not halter-broken, what we usually do is scoot the new mother and baby into the barn and lock them in for a few days. This has an added benefit of protecting them from any inclement weather or predators when the new calf is young and vulnerable. When the calf is three or four days old, it's a simple matter for one person to hold the cow at bay while the other person scoops up the calf and brings it into a pen. Have all your tools and equipment ready to go before separating the calf.

Here is what is required:

• clippers, to shave the top of the calf's head over the horn buds

• dehorning paste; have the container open and ready to go

• a popsicle stick, or something similarly flat and narrow

• vaseline

• vinegar and a rag, just in case some paste gets where it shouldn't be (vinegar will neutralize the caustic nature of the paste)

• duct tape

• embroidery scissors or other small, sharp scissors

Start by having one person hold the calf. Don't lay the calf on the ground; keep her on her feet. At this age the calf is usually pretty docile, though she'll struggle a bit. Keep your voices low and gentle and your posture relaxed; don't "Yee-ha!" or do anything that will make the calf freak. Believe me, the mother cow will be providing plenty of background noise already.

Feel the top of the calf's head, between her ears but a bit forward. The tiny horn buds can be felt as little bumps under the skin. These are the areas you want to shave with the clippers. Try to shave two good-sized circles over the horn buds as close to the skin as possible, but don't go crazy trying to achieve a perfect shave. The whole idea of shaving is to remove the excess hair that would otherwise be in the way and to allow you to see the horn buds more clearly.

A calf's head wrapped in duct tape to keep the caustic dehorning paste from touching the mother cow's tongue or udder. The duct tape should totally cover the horn bud region but leave the ears and eyes free. Make sure no petroleum jelly or dehorning paste is visible. The tape should stay on for about 12 hours.

A dehorning scab, approximately one month after dehorning.

Now take the Vaseline and make a circle around the horn bud, leaving about ¾ of an inch over the bud clear. The Vaseline is to corral the paste and keep it where it should be. The paste will warm with the calf's body temperature and get a little runny, so the Vaseline keeps it confined.

Now take the popsicle stick and scoop up some of the dehorning paste. Don't get any on your skin unless you want to be dehorned as well. (Remember, the vinegar will neutralize any accidental contact). Smear a thin, nickel-sized amount of paste over the horn buds. Do *not* use more than this; you don't want to eat through the poor calf's skull. This is *not* a case of "If a little is good, more is better."

Now here's an important part: take three or four strips of duct tape approximately 2½ to 3 feet long, and wrap it around the calf's head. The idea is to keep the dehorning paste from coming into contact with the mother cow's udder, or running into the calf's eyes. The calf will dislike this indignity as you wrap duct tape around her head, but do your best. Leave room for the ears to poke through, and of course don't cover the eyes. Wrap the duct tape over and around the calf's head until the horn buds are covered and the tape won't slip off, but don't make the tape so tight it strangles the calf or makes her uncomfortable.

Once you feel the tape is secure, the calf can be released to her mother. However, I would continue to keep the cow and calf confined in the barn or paddock for at least another 12 hours. Do NOT let the calf loose where you cannot re-catch her until you have a chance to remove the duct tape.

If we dehorn the calf in the morning, we leave the duct tape on until evening. If we dehorn in the evening, we leave the duct tape on until morning. Twelve hours is plenty of time for the paste to do its work, and then it will no longer be a danger to the mother cow either from licking the calf, or from the calf's head being in contact with the udder.

After those 12 hours are up, isolate the calf once more. With one person holding the calf, the other person should take small, sharp scissors and snip and pull away the duct tape. This will only take a minute or two. The horn buds will look ugly and raw and it will seem like the paste affected a larger area than you anticipated, but as long as the rawness doesn't extend beyond the general area of the horn buds (in other words, it hasn't dribbled down the side of her head or something) she should be fine. After this, the cow and calf can be released with the rest of the herd.

Over the next two weeks, you'll see the raw spots over the calf's horn buds scab over. The scabs will be there for two or three months, but will gradually fall off. By the time the calf is four or five months old, you'll never know she ever had horns or scabs or anything else. The result is clean and aesthetic.

And that's it! See how much easier this is than a manual dehorning? No blood, no struggle, no pain, no expensive farm call from the vet. And believe me, a three-day-old calf is a *whole* lot easier to handle than a three-month-old calf. The calves soon forgot they were ever manhandled by us and never acquired the suspicion the older calves had after being dehorned.

We've dehorned about eight calves with dehorning paste, with excellent results.

Now after a calf is born, I can say to my husband in a casual voice, "Tomorrow morning let's dehorn the calf" instead of "Oh God, tomorrow morning the vet is coming to dehorn the calf!" with stomach-clenching dread.

Just a little something to make your homestead life more peaceful. Δ

Grow gourmet salad greens

By Raymond Nones

Practically all gourmet restaurants today serve mesclun salads. Mesclun is a French term that describes a mixture of young lettuces and greens. This blend not only has a more appetizing appearance than plain lettuce but is also much more nutritious.

But you don't have to be French or eat out in fancy restaurants to enjoy these mixes; you can grow your own ingredients and have them at home every day. I grow everything needed in an area approximately four feet by four feet. You can do the same.

All of the lettuces and greens are harvested using the cut-and-come-again method. This system relies on the fact that leaf crops will regrow new leaves if cut at the largest seedling or semi-mature stage. The plants are usually cut when they are about three to four inches tall and are never allowed to grow beyond six inches tall.

Since the lettuces and greens involved are cool weather crops, two or more sowings can be made: one early in the season to be harvested in spring and summer, and another in late summer for fall harvest. Lettuces and greens are easily grown, usually without any disease or insect problems.

When harvesting salad greens, use scissors to cut them off above the neck of the plant, leaving some of the bottom leaves to continue growing. To thin plants, cut them off at the ground.

There are mixes and then there are mixes

Ready mesclun seed mixes can be ordered from gardening catalogs or purchased from retail store racks. Typically they will include loose leaf lettuces such as Black Seeded Simpson, Deer Tongue (both red and green), Green Ice, Lollo Rossa, Oakleaf, Red Sails, and Salad Bowl, plus greens such as arugula, endive, escarole, chicory, Corn Salad, mustard, radicchio, and kale. These assortments are then broadcast and harvested by the cut-and-come-again method.

Upon trying this system I was very disappointed. The mixing and scattering of seeds results in a hodgepodge, making it difficult to tell what is crop and what is weed. Slow-growing varieties immediately get lost in the crowd, and the strong, fast-growing plants quickly dominate the plot. Also, harvesting is confusing as everything is in disarray.

I now use my own system. I buy individual packets of each lettuce variety and green that is to be grown. Since the different lettuces and greens have different growth rates and needs, they produce better when each cultivar is grown and tended to in its own row.

In a four foot by four foot area I grow two varieties of lettuces and three different types of greens. I make two sowings per year. Over the years I have varied the mix. These are my latest selections.

Spring: I sow Green Ice and Lollo Rossa for the lettuces. I sow chicory, radicchio, and mustard for the greens. When cutting for a salad I supplement those ingredients with the wild dandelions that grow in my backyard. You can do the same provided you don't use any chemical pesticides or fertilizers on the grass.

Fall: Oakleaf and Red Sails fill the bill for lettuces. Arugula, endive, and kale complete the assortment.

These selections give a variety of colors, shapes, textures, and tastes to a salad. When deciding what to grow, strive for mixes that will not only be visually appealing but will also have a bit of a tang. You don't want bland.

I recommend buying your seed through a seed catalog rather than buying from a seed rack at the store. The seed mailed directly from seed companies has been properly stored under controlled conditions to retain viability. This is not always the case in a retail store where the temperature and humidity can vary greatly before packets are sold which will affect seed germination.

The French sometimes use as many as four varieties of red and green lettuces in a mix. They also use many different leaf crops for the greens. Some are quite exotic: Mizuna, Golden Purslane, Red Orach, Chervil, Broadleaf Cress, and some Japanese Mustards.

By using the cut-and-come-again method, your lettuces and greens will produce all season long. I grow all the salad fixings I need in a four by four-foot area.

Preparing the garden plot

Pick an area that gets at least five or six hours of direct sunlight a day. Soil preparation is especially important when sowing, as these are very small seeds. A fine seedbed is a must for good germination. The seeds need to be in good contact with the soil for a successful sowing, and this cannot be accomplished in a lumpy plot.

Once the plot has been dug up, go over the area, breaking up any lumps, then level it off using a rake. You may need to go over the plot several times in different directions to smooth the soil. At this point, if compost is available, sift some through a fine screen and spread a thin layer over everything.

A lath house will help protect your lettuces and greens from the sun and prolong the spring-summer harvest. It also helps shield young seedlings from the heat when making the hot weather sowing.

Sowing

The seeds can be sown in closely spaced parallel rows; since the plants will not grow to maturity, they don't need a lot of room. To make the furrows, use a piece of 1x2 lumber. Place the board across the seed plot, tilt the strip so that one corner faces down, then pull it back and forth until it makes a shallow V-shaped furrow. Repeat every two inches.

Sow the seeds one inch apart in the furrows, then firm the seeds into the earth with your finger and water. No need to cover the seed.

The spring crop should be sown as soon as the ground can be worked, about seven weeks before the last frost date. Generally, any frosts at that time will not significantly affect germination and growth.

These leaf crops have very shallow roots, therefore they require frequent watering for their entire life.

Harvesting

Normally, only minimum thinning is needed. When the seedlings have grown and are about three inches tall, they are big enough to eat. Harvest and thin at the same time. When harvesting, cut right above the stem, leaving a little of the bottom leaves with a stub in the ground. Thin where plants are too close together by cutting plants right at ground level. Eat all the thinnings.

As each cultivar has a different growth rate, cut the fastest-growing, tallest plants first. This means that the proportions of the varieties in your salad will change as time goes by.

Shading the crops lightly when the weather starts to heat up around the end of June will help to prolong the harvest. A lath house is the usual method to do this.

Hot weather sowing

The fall crop should be sown about ten to eight weeks, six weeks at the latest, before the earliest fall frost date. This sowing is a little trickier than the spring sowing because many cool weather crops have trouble germinating in high temperatures. Lettuce seed will not germinate at all if soil temperatures approach 80 degrees Fahrenheit or above.

There are a couple of things you can do to improve your germination success. First, put the seed in the freezer two days before planting. Make the furrows a little deeper, about ¼-inch, and wet them down with a hand sprayer prior to sowing. When the seed has been sown and firmed, spray again with the hand sprayer and cover with loose, dry compost.

Shade the entire area to prevent the blazing sun from drying out the seeds and heating up the soil. I use homemade lath panels propped up with a brick at each end.

Every morning remove the boards, water the seeds, and replace the boards; do not let the soil dry out. Once the seeds germinate, the sprouts need some sunlight. (*Some* is the key word here.) At this stage, to protect the young seedlings from the sun's hot rays, you can put up a lath house to cut the sunshine by about 50%. (I suggest that you make a few lath panels. Laths are sold in bundles of about 45 and are very inexpensive.)

By following this hot weather sowing procedure, I have never had any problem with the greens germinating and growing. But lettuces are another story. Sometimes lettuces absolutely, positively, refuse to germinate in the summer. The good news is, if the first attempt fails you still have a couple more weeks to try again before it is too late in the season. Wait a week or two and reseed. Remember, you can sow as late as six weeks before the earliest frost date. Unless you have incredibly bad luck, one of the later reseedings should be successful.

Jack Frost, the killer

Lettuce can take a few light frosts, and greens like endive, arugula, and kale are hardier and will withstand a little more. A hard frost will be the death knell for all.

So how long can you keep harvesting? One late sowing will see you through the earliest frost date, and usually a week or two beyond that with no sweat.

An extended harvest is possible by making an additional sowing around middle or late September. If you protect your crop in the event of a hard frost, you can enjoy a big bowl of delicious mesclun greens with your Thanksgiving dinner — *Bon appetit!*

Raymond Nones is a lifelong home gardener and author of the books; *Modular Vegetable Gardening, Green Thumbs for Everyone,* and *Grow Great Tomatoes.* Δ

Seniors, downsize your gardens!

By Alice Yeager

Once a gardener, always a gardener. We have an inborn something that makes us gravitate toward plants and fresh, tasty produce. We revel in our successes and learn from our failures.

However, as inevitable age creeps up, we begin to realize that we can no longer cope with the amount of gardening we used to do. Things have changed. It's no longer necessary to raise a big quantity of fruits and vegetables to feed our families. Chances are, children have grown up, married, and now have families of their own. Fortunately, some young parents have the desire to produce their own fresh food by remembering the good things that came from their parents' gardens. Others become very familiar with the produce and canned goods sold in supermarkets.

As for those of us who have spent more years tending gardens than we sometimes realize, it's time to downsize our gardening space to make our harvests compatible with our needs and our energy levels.

I can attest to the fact that age does eventually become a deciding factor. Even though nostalgia sometimes takes over and I remember the wonderful tasty vegetables that grew in our garden and wish I could grow them again, it's time to move on — just a bit more slowly and with a lesser amount of work.

Sadly, I lost my husband and best friend, James, in October 2008. We had been married 53 years. During that time we had harvested and enjoyed a lot of produce while availing ourselves of plenty of exercise and fresh air. That's not to say the weather was always perfect or the plants never needed watering or protection from bugs. Those things are just some of the challenges of gardening.

A prime example of easy-to-pick fruit may be found in something low-growing like blueberries.

We began to downsize our garden a few years ago and now I am becoming a container gardener, growing only my favorite vegetables in large pots and tending a few dwarf fruit trees planted near my house. I can easily reach the fruit when ripe. No more climbing on ladders or using fruit pickers on long poles at harvest time. Many fruit trees are available in dwarf size and I have, as usual, planted only the ones I favor and know will succeed in southwestern Arkansas (Zone 8). The selection of dwarf fruit trees is the same as for full-sized trees. Just avoid the varieties that don't perform well in your zone. For instance, apple trees don't do well in this area although they thrive in the northern part of our state where the climate is more favorable to them.

Luckily, and long before I began to think of down-sizing, I planted a blueberry patch only a short distance from my house. Now those bushes are worth their weight in gold. Most of them grow about four to five feet high making the fruit easy to reach.

Another good feature of blueberry bushes is that they are one of Nature's timeless plants that will continue to bear fruit from now on as long as the bushes are maintained and kept free of invasive vines and weeds. This is not a hard task and is well worth the effort. Nurseries are now offering some varieties of blueberries suitable for container growing in case one wishes to have the novelty of blueberries right at hand on a patio.

As to container gardening, there are rules to follow just as in regular gardening. Most of them are synonymous with the gardening we seniors have done in the past.

First: Plants grown in containers need attention and there's no better way than to have the pots positioned where you will normally pass by them at least once or twice daily.

That way you should notice anything going wrong — an onslaught of aphids, spider mites, or other hungry pests. Even tomato hornworms will attack container plants just as they will zero in on plants in the garden. So, don't think plants in pots are immune to pests.

My own container plants are placed alongside a front walk leading to my carport so that I pass them every time I go to my car. This arrangement not only makes it easy to keep an eye on the plants, but it's fun to be able to pick a ripe cherry tomato or two on the way to or from the car.

Second: At one time or another, plants are going to need water, so locate pots within easy reach of a water hose. Otherwise, you'll be making a pack-mule of yourself when Nature doesn't provide sufficient rain.

If plants need something to lean on as they grow taller, tomato cages make dandy props and they are available in several different heights. My experience has been to buy them early in the growing season as the stores don't usually restock them when they run out. One good thing about tomato cages is that they can be stored at the end of the gardening season and used over and over again. I consider this a good investment.

Third: Don't expect plants to perform well in small pots. Plants need some root room plus room for foliage to expand. I use plastic pots at least 17-18 inches in diameter. These pots will accommodate two or three plants depending on the varieties.

Fourth: Remember how good drainage is a must in a garden? It's also compulsory when dealing with container plants. Be sure that your pots have drainage holes and then place the pots where they are to remain. Begin filling them by first placing some small stones in the bottoms of the containers. You may also use broken bits of pottery, earthenware, etc. Don't use bits of bark, limbs, or anything that will decompose, as eventually they will clog, causing water to stand in the pots.

Fill the containers to within one or two inches of the tops with the best organic soil available and use plenty of compost — just as you used in your home garden. After you have selected your plants and put them in the pots, mulch them with grass clippings, shredded leaves, pine needles, etc. This procedure will let the soil remain loose and retain moisture just as it did years ago when we were harvesting heaps of good things from our large gardens.

Placement of containers is important, as big pots of dirt are not easy to move around. If you want added color, leave a bit of space between the pots and put in your favorite flowering annuals. I like the Inca marigolds as their height doesn't interfere with anything growing in the pots and they will produce their big beautiful blooms from early summer until cold weather arrives. If you like activity around the area, plant some red sage here and there. The plants grow tall, but they attract hummingbirds and butterflies. Use your imagination and you will find that there's an immense amount of pleasure to be derived from container gardening, to say nothing of creating a real conversation place as friends drop by.

At the end of the gardening season and depending on climatic conditions, the containers may be cleared of spent plants and replanted with cool weather crops such as various types of greens, radishes, onions, etc. There's nothing like adding something really fresh to a cold weather salad.

Garlic is another possibility in the cold season. Just plant some garlic bulbs in a pot in early autumn and soon you will see garlic's flat green leaves appear. This is a hardy plant and will produce green leaves all winter long unless hit by extreme cold. Just remove the badly damaged leaves and new ones will soon appear. These leaves add flavor to all manner of dishes in which you would ordinarily use garlic cloves. If you wish to harvest garlic bulbs, let the plants run their course in the spring, sending us their tall flower stalks and then dying back.

Container gardening, like regular gardening, may be as expensive or inexpensive as you care to make it. There are probably plenty of small tools such as trowels already on hand to be used in transplanting or cultivating. Larger ones — shovels, hoes, etc. — things one will probably never use again — can be passed on to heirs or sold in a garage sale.

If you want to jazz up your container space, there are plenty of bright colored ceramic pots for sale with prices beginning at about $20. However, plants grown in them won't produce any better than the ones given plenty of TLC in plain practical pots.

The Boy Scouts' motto, "Be Prepared," applies to many facets of life. At some point, gardeners become senior citizens. Before that stage of life is reached, why not do some planning to downsize? You'll be glad you did. Δ

Controlling cutworms

By Tom Kovach

Cutworms are pests that can do a lot of damage in a garden. Cutworms are especially fond of small seedlings and there are several different types of cutworms with different feeding habits. Tunnel-making cutworms feed just below the surface or where the seedlings emerge from the soil. Climbing cutworms move up plant stems and feed on flower buds, new leaves, and fruit. Army cutworms move in groups.

The cutworm larvae begin feeding in early spring, laying eggs on broad-leaved weeds or blades of grass. All cutworms feed at night.

Because of this night feeding, gardeners will often find the damage cutworms do before actually seeing the cutworm. The most obvious sign of cutworm damage is a row of seedlings with their stems severed. Other signs are chewed leaves and holes in the fruit.

The good news is these slow-moving, shiny, gray or brown caterpillars that feed on plants are easy to control.

Controlling cutworms

Preventive treatments are best if you have had problems with cutworms in the past. There are natural methods of control, such as digging up soil in the fall to expose the worms and keeping leaf debris to a minimum. This will help keep cutworms out of the garden.

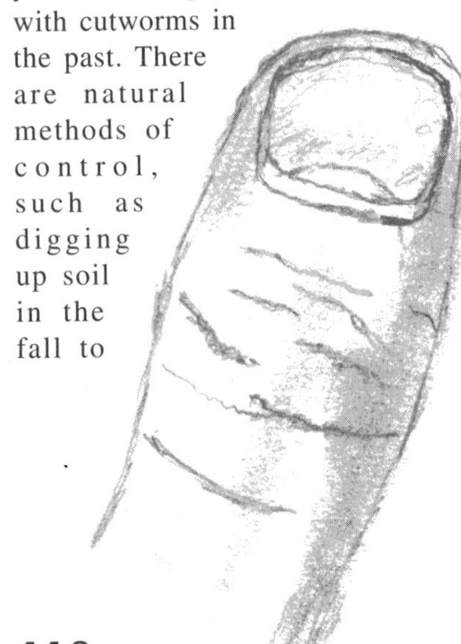

The insecticide Diazinon is quite effective in preventing cutworm infestation from becoming too widespread. You can mix it into the soil before planting, or apply it on existing plants to control chronic cutworm problems.

Bacillus thuringiensis (Bt), is a bacteria used in bacterial insecticides. The bacteria is deadly to cutworms, but doesn't have toxic effects on humans or other animals. Immediately after cutworms ingest the Bt, they stop feeding on the plants and begin to die.

In spraying Bt you will need: Bt, sprayer, sticker-spreader (surfactant), gloves, and a mask.

- Mix the Bt with water at the recommended rate. Always wear rubber gloves when mixing any insecticides.
- Add a sticker-spreader to the mix. This helps the insecticide spread easily and makes it stick to leaves better.
- Spray the plant. Cover the tops and bottoms of leaves and stems. Plant should be wet, but not dripping.

A tip on spraying Bt: Shake the spray container to keep the Bt mixed in the medium. When using a batch in the garden, apply the entire amount because the mix will only stay effective for about 72 hours. Bt is a living organism, so don't leave it in a hot car trunk or a hot storage room. Store Bt in a cool, dry place that is locked away from children.

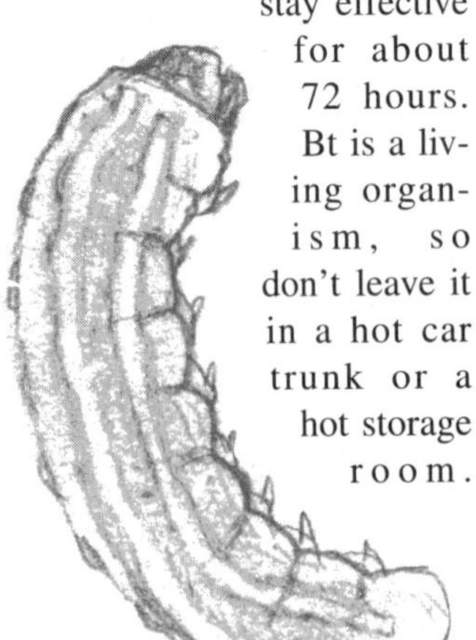

Always check safety precautions before using any sort of insecticide.

Natural control methods

- Handpicking: Cutworms are slow-moving and will usually curl up when touched, making them easy to remove. Pick them at night as they feed.
- Sticky bands: These sticky bands are available from garden centers. Place bands around the trunks of trees and plants. Cutworms will not be able to get by them to eat the leaves.
- Removing weeds: Eliminating broad-leaved weeds around susceptible plants will help decrease the possible locations for the cutworms to lay eggs.
- Baits: Bran is considered to be an effective cutworm bait. Mix some together with Bt and molasses in a bowl and spread around soil of susceptible plants.
- Barriers: You can protect young seedlings from cutworms by using simple, inexpensive barriers. Cut cardboard tubes (left over from toilet paper or paper towel rolls) in half and place them around the seedlings. Push the tubes into the ground so they are secure. As an alternative, use a tuna fish or cat food can with both the bottom and top removed. Use it as a "collar" to block out the cutworms.

If you haven't had experience with cutworms, keep in mind some of their favorite plants: ornamental flowers like gladiolis, petunias, pansies, and marigolds (to name a few) and edible plants like beans, tomatoes, peppers, peas, and cabbage.

Although they can cause a lot of damage, cutworms can be controlled simply and often naturally. Δ

Illustration by Sammy Duffy

A really cheap compost toilet

By Kai Moessle

"You do WHAT?"

"You use a bucket for a toilet? You're kidding, right?"

"Is your regular one broken and your landlord won't fix it?"

These are just the more print-friendly comments I get when I tell people about my "composting toilet for the masses."

The Sawdust Toilet was pioneered by Mr. Joseph Jenkins and is thoroughly discussed in his *Humanure Handbook*.

I stumbled across the first edition of his book when I was researching alternatives to the water-flushing toilet. Since I want to build an off-grid cabin and have a year-round spring on my property, I'm planning on just using a hand pump to get my water. Gravity feed flushing will not work since the spring is lower than the building site. Coupling that fact with the rather large price tag a conventional septic system carries convinced me to get started on the road to alternative sewage disposal methods.

Commercially-made composting toilets, while somewhat cheaper than a septic system, still require a hefty one-time investment and are quite cumbersome, especially the family-sized models. Since I'm tighter than a crab's rear end with my money (at least according to some of my friends) I kept on digging; in this case clicking on a library computer. I found quite a few references to the *Humanure Handbook*, the last one boasting that once you had read it you would "really know your &%#@!," so I decided to borrow it and see what I could learn.

After reading the entire book I still wasn't convinced that this system could really work; I was especially doubtful about the "no-odor-whatsoever" claim, but decided to try it out myself.

Today, five years later, I'm still using it and am happy to report that it does indeed work like the book says. It's also just as cheap as claimed: I didn't quite spend $30 in materials, including a brand new five-gallon bucket (I didn't have a used one on hand).

I used the materials to build the enclosure for the bucket. The book shows several different plans and styles (plain and fancy), but it's basically a box with a hole in the top large enough for the bucket opening to fit through and a regular toilet seat on top. I actually splurged and bought a wooden toilet seat ($12), not the $6.95 plastic one.

The last thing you need is what gives the toilet its name: sawdust. Mr. Jenkins recommends using sawdust from a sawmill, not from a woodshop. The sawmill works with green wood, so the sawdust contains a lot more moisture than the kiln-dried stuff a woodshop produces. This is important for the actual composting part, which I'll explain shortly. I get my sawdust from a big pile behind the local sawmill. It used to be free, but for the past year they've been charging me $2 for five 5-gallon buckets' worth. Those last me about three months.

To use your new toilet you "prime" the bucket with one to two inches of sawdust. Make your deposit as you do on a conventional toilet. Once the paper work is finished, instead of flushing, you cover everything with a generous amount of sawdust. This keeps flies out and odor in. Keep going like that until the bucket is full.

What happens next is the main difference between a regular composting toilet and the sawdust one. The former produces the compost right inside the toilet body. With the sawdust toilet you have to take the bucket (which is really a "holding tank") and dump it on an outdoor compost pile. There should be some kind of enclosure around it to keep your dog and other assorted critters from digging through it; I made mine out of seven pallets (free for the taking from many big warehouses). Since there will be some seepage into the ground, I would recommend some distance (about 100 feet) between the pile and any water source (well, stream, lake...). Before you dump the first bucket into the bin, Mr. Jenkins rec-

My sawdust toilet. The whole top with the bucket opening is hinged in the back to facilitate removing and emptying the bucket.

My two compost bins in the spring. The one on the right is being emptied out and used to fertilize my bucket garden and fruit trees. The one on the left is covered with a heavy layer of leaves to "rest" for another year.

ommends putting down a one-foot-thick layer of hay or straw as a filter. After dumping the bucket, its former contents have to be covered to keep insects out and the smell in. I use leaves that I rake into a big pile every fall, but hay, straw, sawdust, dirt, and any other organic material works just as well.

Clean the bucket out with soap and water; regular dish soap works fine. *Don't use antibacterial soap* since the water from the bucket is dumped on the compost pile. Antibacterial soap will kill the micro-organisms that convert your excrement to usable humus.

When adding more to the pile, always do so by making a hole in the center with a stick or shovel kept only for that purpose, dumping the bucket contents in the hole and covering it again with more leaves or hay. The inside of the pile will get quite hot because of all the microorganisms at work and will kill any harmful pathogens like E. coli, Salmonella, and Leptospires. The reason you use sawdust from green wood is that it helps the good bacteria to multiply rapidly by supplying additional moisture. After adding to the pile for about a year, start a new one and leave the old one to rest and fully decompose for one or two more years. Once that time is up, you have very rich, black humus for your garden. I've been using mine in my vegetable bucket garden for the past three years and it works great. Why pay for potting soil when you can have it for free? It also makes great fertilizer for fruit trees or flower beds.

The only problem with this "humanure recycling system" is the law (what else?). In my state I am operating in the gray zone, bordering black, according to the sanitary code, which I looked up after I was convinced this would work for me. It says that alternative systems are allowed after being tested and NSF-certified to meet the standards set forth in the regulations. None of this has been officially done with a sawdust toilet, so I'll keep it under the radar, more or less (my landlord knows about my doings and is okay with it).

The acid test for the "no odor" claim came about six months after I started using it — my mother came for a three-week visit! She was quite skeptical about the whole thing when I explained it to her on the way home from the airport. However, after the first week she had gotten used to "flushing" with a few cups of sawdust. The day Mom left I asked her what she thought of the whole bucket-toilet business. "You know" she said, "it doesn't sound very pleasant, like something they'd use in a Third World country, but once you get used to it, there's nothing yucky about it. I wouldn't want to empty it, though!"

The one thing that impressed her the most was that "even with the bucket almost full, I still couldn't smell a thing!"

In closing, I can honestly say that this is the most ecologically and economically sound composting toilet system I have seen to date. Also, after three years of eating all kinds of vegetables grown in my humanure bucket garden I am still alive and well, contrary to the dire predictions of some friends and co-workers. My thanks to Mr. Jenkins for putting it all in a book for the rest of us to read and use. Δ

LED LIGHTING

a breakthrough for independent living and emergency preparedness

PART 2: LED-based products

By Tim Thorstenson

In part 1 of Light Emitting Diodes (LEDs), (Issue #127, Jan/Feb, 2011), we examined the basics of the technology. But when we get to actual LED-based products, there are critical details that vary from one kind of light to the next. This time we will consider products which include: flashlights, headlamps, portable lanterns, work lights, and bulbs and fixtures for the home or cabin.

LED performance is still improving rapidly and this makes it a challenge to provide information that won't become obsolete down the road. Because of this, we'll avoid detailed reviews of specific products. I will mention some to illustrate important principles, but the principles themselves will be the focus because they will remain useful over time. I've listed some sources for product details and reviews at the end of the article.

"Flamethrowers" come in a range of sizes and shapes. Compared to the "compact" and "micro" LED options, they are a bit bulky. But next to the 2-D-cell incandescent flashlight at right, they are quite reasonably sized.

LED flashlights

The newest LEDs make it into flashlights pretty quickly. Considering that an incandescent 2-D-cell flashlight will produce about 20 lumens from fresh batteries, these LED options are nothing short of amazing: a compact light can produce 150 lumens (or more) for an hour or better from a pair of AA batteries. Many of these lights can be turned down to lower outputs and this can stretch the runtimes into tens or even hundreds of hours while providing enough light for routine tasks or emergencies. We do need to be aware of stuff that is of poor quality or which uses dated LEDs. But even if we eliminate the "junk," we are left with an overwhelming number of choices, so it can be a real challenge to find the best lights for your needs.

Available products

It is helpful to first put LED flashlights into some rough categories which include store brands, "gold standard" name brands, and better quality imports. Store brands include familiar names like Coleman, Duracell, Energizer, Ray-o-Vac, and Remington Arms. Some of these lights use more recent LEDs like the Cree XR-E, but they may come from the less efficient "bins." Store brands are also comparatively inexpensive and readily available. Some of these companies sell a range of products, so check the package for information on runtimes, lumen outputs, and the type of LED being used. At the other extreme, "gold standard" name brands offer rock solid products that are built like tanks and are made in the US. These options are generally more expensive but, as the old adage goes, this is a case where you *do* get what you pay for. The "gold standard" category includes well-known companies like Surefire and Streamlight, but there are also some small US manufacturers who deserve inclusion. Their names may not be as familiar, but their products are definitely "gold standard" and they are

A "compact" flashlight can be practical for routine on-person carry. And the 200 plus lumens now available from LEDs can really light up the yard for safety and security.

often quicker to incorporate the newest LEDs.

An excellent example of a small "gold standard" company is Malkoff Devices, which already has products with the new XP-G LED. Malkoff makes some complete flashlights, but the company also offers "drop-in" modules to upgrade Surefire and Maglight products. Back in the "incandescent days," everyone from police officers to armed citizens to a few backwoodsmen fell in love with Surefire's famous incandescent "6P" tactical flashlight because it put 65 lumens into a package roughly the size of a hot dog. But Malkoff's XP-G drop-in will provide 260 lumens and a much *longer* battery life from the same package.

The drop-in approach is clearly useful for the person who already owns compatible flashlights, but it can also be a good choice for those who are starting from scratch. To illustrate why, consider the compact tactical flashlight produced by a small US manufacturer called Elzetta Designs. The durability of this light is amazing and the price is comparable to many of the big-name gold standard products. But it still isn't cheap and it could really tick a guy off to buy a gem like that and then have it bested by future lights with newer LEDs. Elzetta's light uses Malkoff's drop-ins, so it could be upgraded down the road to keep up with LED advances for less than the cost of a better quality Chinese import. The same flexibility applies if you are considering one of Surefire's compact tactical lights or if you like the solid bulk of a good old-fashioned Maglight. But check on compatibility with specific flashlight models before trying to marry them to a drop-in. Note that there are other sources of LED upgrade products, but I use Malkoff's as the example because they are US-made, they are by far the best quality I have seen, and they pay proper attention to the important issue of heat management.

Between the extremes of "store brand" and "gold standard" there are a number of companies that fit in the "better quality import" category. The Chinese origin of these products is an understandable objection for some, but these lights do have their place. The prices can be affordable compared to the "gold standard" products, but the quality can be head and shoulders above the "store brands" (which are usually made in China, too).

With the newest LEDs, even "micro" flashlights like these examples from 4Sevens can combine impressive outputs with decent battery runtimes. A pen (top) along with AA and AAA batteries (bottom) provide size reference.

These companies are quick to incorporate the newest LEDs and they offer features like adjustable brightness levels and flexible battery options that can be very useful in some settings. Examples in this category include DereeLight, EagleTac, Fenix, NiteCore, O-Light, and WolfEyes, but this list is limited to the ones that I have had a chance to examine personally. A Georgia-based company called 4Sevens has been in business for several years selling some of these brands, but they have also started their own product lines and the company has shown a knack for sensible designs. Their products are still made in China, but design, quality control, and warranty service are handled in the US by 4Sevens.

In addition to the "better quality" imports, there are also some brands that suffer from poor or inconsistent quality. An additional caution is that some of the better Chinese manufacturers suffer from inferior Chinese counterfeiting! To separate the wheat from the chaff in this category, the "general information" resources listed at the end of the article will help. Some of these lights can be ordered direct from China through bargain websites and outlets like eBay, but I'd strongly suggest using a reputable, US-based vendor. Good vendors will allow you to avoid counterfeits, they can assist with product selection, many of them will provide warranty support, shipping is vastly quicker, the prices are often not that different, and, at least a slice of the pie will stay at home.

These EagleTac compacts use the new XP-G LED and they illustrate typical power options: The one at left uses two AA batteries. The other two take a pair of CR123A disposables as well as lithium ion rechargeables, but the fatter light at right will hold a bigger rechargeable and its larger reflector yields a tighter and brighter beam.

How big and how bright?

It is also useful to put the flashlights into rough categories of "compact," "micro," and what I like to call "flamethrowers."

The "compact" alternatives are the most abundant and the best all-around choice for most general purpose uses. These mostly use "single-die" LEDs and range from the size of a 20 gauge shotgun shell to roughly that of a bratwurst. Malkoff and a few of the imports are already offering products with the new XP-G LED and this can provide either a noticeable increase in brightness or a significant increase in battery life, depending on how the maker chooses to power the LED. Compacts often use either one or two standard AA batteries or one or two disposable lithium "CR123A" batteries. Typical maximum light outputs range from perhaps 50 or 60 lumens to 300 lumens. In addition, it is possible to squeeze upwards of 460 lumens out of the new XP-G LED, though most compacts use a lower maximum to maintain longer runtimes (and, especially with the smaller models, to avoid heat problems). A multi-die LED (or a Luminus "PhlatLED") can also be built into a larger compact and this can allow for a brighter output.

As the name implies, "micro" flashlights are smaller and they generally use one or two AAA batteries. With the latest LEDs, even these puny batteries can allow for impressive lumen outputs. For instance, the one-battery "Preon" from 4Sevens will produce about 70 lumens and the two-battery version will emit around 160 lumens. Both will run for 45 minutes on high and longer at lower settings. Micro lights are great for places like the shirt pocket where you *need* something that is as small and lightweight as possible, but they do also have some unavoidable drawbacks. Their small reflectors yield fairly broad beams that are great for close work but which have limited long-range utility. Also, they typically have rather thin bodies to minimize weight and this makes them less durable than a good compact. Since AA batteries have a much higher energy capacity than AAA, even though most stores sell both for the same price, I personally lean toward the larger "compact" lights for general purpose uses.

At the other extreme, we have the "flamethrowers." These use multi-die

Malkoff Devices' LED "drop-in" modules can provide top-end LED performance from existing SureFire (left) and Maglight (center) flashlights. They are also used in the rugged tactical flashlight made by Elzetta Designs (right).

LEDs, Luminus PhlatLEDs or an assembly of three or more single-die LEDs to produce much higher outputs than the compacts—500 to 900 lumens and more. The flamethrowers are still bigger than the compacts, but most are still smaller and lighter than a good 2-D-cell metal flashlight and, in spite of their outputs, many of them will run for an hour or more on a set of batteries. The flamethrowers are more than some folks will need, but they can be incredibly handy for certain applications. As with the smaller options, many provide adjustable brightness, so the same light that can be used for finding a cow or scaring off an intruder can also be used for rummaging in the toolbox without blinding you for the rest of the night. Malkoff Devices and the other import companies mentioned all offer one or more flamethrowers, but for technical reasons, many of them provide a relatively broad beam focus, so their effective *range* may not be as great as their lumen ratings can imply. For general use, a broader beam is usually better, but if you want maximum range for things like security, checking cattle, or spotting coyotes, use particular care with product selection.

For long-range needs, products like the Dereelight "DBS" and Streamlight's "Supertac" use goose-egg-sized reflectors to squeeze the more humble outputs of single-die LEDs into amazingly tight beams. The surprising result is that these lower-lumen options can greatly outreach many of the flamethrowers in terms of effective range. These choices are also much smaller and lighter than most flamethrowers, so they can be more convenient for weapon mounting or carrying in a belt holster. Such products are not the best choice for general purpose use because they can produce tunnel vision and blinding glare at close range, but they can be extremely handy for tasks like security and nighttime varmint hunting (where legal, of course). The Malkoff drop-ins for Maglight flashlights will also produce a tight beam. This is a bulkier option, but it also allows adjustable focus.

There are also "Super-Flamethrowers" that have raw LED outputs of 1400 to 2000+ lumens. This can be done by putting two or three multi-die LEDs (or six or seven single-die LEDs) into a single flashlight head. One of the better-regarded Chinese companies (OLight) has already put the "SST-90 PhlatLED" LED into a larger (and expensive) flashlight that provides an LED output of around 2200 lumens. But note that there is a competing technology called "high intensity discharge" (or HID) that can be a viable alternative in cases where huge amounts of light are needed at high efficiency.

Lumen ratings

There are two ways of rating lumen output—one is the raw emission of the LED and the other is the actual output of the flashlight itself. Most store brands and many of the imports cite LED lumens while the gold standard companies and a few imports will actually provide true flashlight (or "out the front") lumens. Because of unavoidable efficiency and optical losses, actual flashlight output will typically be at least 20% to 30% lower than the "LED lumens." In other words, a flashlight with an *actual* output of 200 lumens will likely be at least as bright as a product which quotes an LED output of 250 lumens.

Do not make *too* big of a deal out of brightness. The human eye does not respond to light in a "linear" fashion, so a flashlight that puts out twice the lumens will not appear "twice as bright." A brightness difference of 20% will not prove that significant in most practical settings.

Other features

You also need to consider things like beam pattern, adjustable brightness options, how brightness is adjusted, and the type of batteries used. With these variables, there is no "best" choice because that depends on individual needs. There is also the availability of useful accessories (colored filters, pocket clips, suitable holsters, etc.) that you may or may not need.

For example, a flashlight with multiple brightness settings is great for many uses, but it can be a negative when it comes to security or self-defense. One common design allows the user to toggle through the settings by tapping the tailcap switch and it is very easy to accidentally tap yourself into a candlelight output at the precise moment when maximum brightness is urgently needed. But others provide two or more brightness levels by rotating either the head of the flashlight or an adjustment ring. This may be a better choice if you want a defensive light that also offers brightness adjustment (just remember to leave the thing on the right setting).

It's important to mention battery options. Many "store brands" use AA batteries while the "gold standard" products more frequently use a small but potent lithium battery called the "CR123A." The imports frequently offer their compacts in your choice of the two formats. If you are familiar with the outrageous price of CR123A lithium batteries, you may have a very low opinion of buying a flashlight that uses them. But these batteries can be ordered at quite reasonable prices and they do offer some advantages, so it's prudent to touch on a few pros and cons concerning battery choice.

First, it should be understood that AA-format flashlights will work best with rechargeable "Nickel Metal Hydride" (NiMH) batteries. Alkaline AAs will work, but shorter runtimes (and probably a fading output) should be expected, especially at the higher brightness settings. NiMH is a far better chemistry than the old "ni-cads" (Nickel Cadmium) and the "pre-charged" variety will hold its charge for several months in storage. But if you prefer to avoid rechargeables, the CR123A format may be worth a look. A light that uses CR123A batteries will typically provide both a little longer runtime and a little more brightness than an equivalent AA-format product because of the extremely high energy capacity of lithium batteries. In addition, disposable lithium batteries boast a very long shelf life (10 years or so), a tolerance for high temperatures in storage (but with a shortened shelf life), and an ability to maintain good performance in the extreme cold (down to -40 F). Some (but *not* all) CR123A format lights can also use lithium-ion *rechargable* batteries and this chemistry is superior to NiMH in certain respects.

If you want the benefits of disposable lithium, you can find them in the AA batteries like Energizer's "Ultimate Lithium" and store prices for these are often more reasonable due to their popularity in electronic devices. In addition, NiMH rechargeables are also readily available from the local store whereas lithium-ion usually has to be ordered. As a result, the AA format can be a flexible and convenient choice: a few lithium AAs can be salted away in the emergency kit, NiMH rechargeables can be used for routine purposes, and alkaline AAs are available at any gas station or grocery store.

A couple of safety warnings: if you use disposable lithium batteries, I would suggest sticking with good name brands (Duracell, Energizer, Panasonic, Ray-O-Vac, Sanyo, etc.) and buying them from a reputable vendor to avoid counterfeits. Bargain lithium batteries have been known to explode on occasion but the name brands include internal protections. Use care, too, with lithium-ion rechargeables. In spite of their similar names, lithium disposables and lithium-*ion* rechargeables are *very* different critters and the disposables should *never* be recharged. Lithium-ion rechargeables have been known to burst when being recharged and can even start fires, so it is important to stick with good quality batteries and chargers and follow handling instructions carefully. In addition, there are several different battery sizes and formulations that fall under the "lithium-ion rechargeable" umbrella. These can vary in voltage and the

Common LED suppliers

Cree: www.cree.com
Luminus: www.luminus.com
Seoul SemiConductor Corporation: www.seoulsemicon.com

General information

www.light-reviews.com is a review site that contains reviews of a large number of LED-based flashlights.

www.candlepowerforums.com is a web forum that contains a lot of information on LED technology and products.

I am familiar with these product sources and confident in their reliability:
Elzetta Designs: 859-707-7471 / www.elzetta.com
4Sevens: 678-608-0308 / www.4sevens.com
FlashlightConnection: www.FlashlightConnection.com
FlashlightZ: 866-764-9900 / www.flashlightz.com
LED Supply: 802-728-6031 / www.ledsupply.com
Lighthound: 713-436-2609 / www.lighthound.com
MagnaLight: 800-369-6671 / www.magnalight.com
Malkoff Devices: 334-393-3717 / www.malkoffdevices.com
Pacific Tactical Solutions: 509-214-0302 / www.pts-flashlights.com
Streamlight: 800-523-7488 / www.streamlight.com

compatibility between different flashlights, chargers, and batteries is not uniform. The wrong combination can lead to poor performance, product damage, or even fires and injuries. Some import products are *only* intended for use with certain rechargeables and *not* with CR123A disposables. With the gold standard products, the reverse is often true—disposables are the only recommended choice and certain rechargeables can burn them out by supplying too high of a voltage. For safety—and to avoid the headache of needing multiple battery formats—please investigate lithium-ion rechargeables carefully before adopting them.

Gun-mounted lights

We should specifically mention this application because of its unique demands. For handguns, there are dedicated weapon lights that mount on the accessory rails now common to many pistols. Some of these can also be fitted to rail-less guns (like standard 1911s) by using an adapter kit. A given manufacturer will typically offer a range of such lights to fit different needs. For instance, Streamlight's "TLR-1" is suitable for full-sized pistols and emits an *actual* 120 lumens. Their TLR-2 uses an identical light source but adds a red aiming laser. For smaller handguns, they also have the very compact and lightweight "TLR-3" which produces 90 lumens from a single, smaller battery. Similar choices can be had from some other "gold standard" companies too, but the big caution in all cases is that the pistol makers definitely don't have their act together on a standardized accessory rail. Regardless of the brand of light you are considering, check your gun(s) with the light maker's compatibility information.

Elzetta Designs' mounts for long guns are particularly flexible because they come with spacers that will fit a wide range of flashlights. But care should be used in selecting the right light for this demanding environment.

When we get to long guns, such lights can also be used if the gun has an appropriate rail. But you can also use standard tubular-bodied flashlights. Companies like Streamlight and SureFire sell brackets and remote switches for certain models of their lights and there are also mounts available that will allow you to use your own choice of flashlights. For instance, Elzetta Designs makes some excellent mounts that can be used with their own super-tough flashlight. But Elzetta's mounts can also be bought separately and they will accommodate a wide range of other flashlights. This is handy, but it also gets us to the relevant warning. Lights sold by gold standard companies as suitable for weapon mounting are designed and tested to handle the recoil. But this may not be the case with generic, off-the-shelf alternatives. In addition to the LED, a flashlight also has electrical, electronic, and mechanical components and weaknesses in any of these could lead to failure. In this application, the gold standard products may be particularly worthy of the investment.

Headlamps

Much of what was said about flashlights also applies to headlamps, but there are a couple of special considerations. Heat sinking is a challenge, so you won't find many with multi-hundred lumen outputs, and there are fewer options in this category but there are still some good choices:

In the "gold standard" category, SureFire has recently released a very bright but very expensive model called the Saint. Streamlight has had an array of headlamps for a long time and now offers several LED models. There are also some companies (such as Black Diamond, Petzl, and Princeton Tec) that are specifically known for their high quality (and relatively expensive) headlamps. As with flashlights, the biggest and best-known companies are often a little slower at incorporating the latest and most efficient LEDs. The import companies have not really jumped into this market with both feet, but Fenix has models that use one, two, or four AA batteries. The four-battery model uses a little electronic trick to allow a maximum LED output of around 225 lumens: after a few minutes, it will drop down to 120 lumens to prevent overheating of the LED. "ZebraLight" is another quality import brand and they have several unique and flexible products. Note that these provide a broad and uniform flood of light which is great for close work but is very ineffective at longer range. 4Sevens offers a headband and a slip-on periscope contraption for their compact "Quark" lights and it can convert these into headlamps or pocket work lamps.

There are also some "store brand" products of decent quality and efficiency. For example, there is a "Remington Arms" branded product that uses four AA batteries and cites an output of 150 lumens (likely a raw LED output). The unit is bright and well built and it offers two brightness settings, a diffuser to spread the light for closer work, red LEDs for low light applications, and a "blood tracker" setting to aid in tracking wounded animals. Energizer, Coleman, and Ray-O-Vac branded products are also available with newer LEDs. As with flashlights, some store brands offer a range of quality options. Again, reading the packages will often reveal the ones that use more efficient LEDs like the Cree XR-E.

The durability and efficiency of LEDs make them the perfect choice for weapon lights like the Streamlight products shown here. Even a tiny, lightweight unit like the TLR-3 (top) can produce a very respectable output.

Area lanterns

There are dozens of LED-based lanterns, but many of these use older and less efficient LEDs. These options are not always a bad choice. If a person wants several inexpensive lanterns to have on hand for power failures or an occasional campout, some of these can be an affordable alternative that will provide adequate brightness and a much longer runtime than an incandescent equivalent. But when it comes to newer LEDs, the choices are more limited. The gold standard brands have never been in the area lantern market and the better-quality import brands have not offered anything that I am aware of. However, there are some store brand options worthy of note. Remington Arms has a 4 D-cell model that cites an output of 350 lumens. Ray-O-Vac offers a somewhat more compact alternative that uses 3 D-cells and also claims 350 lumens. Coleman has several lanterns that use efficient LEDs and they are available in a range of sizes and outputs.

In this product category, we also need to consider fluorescents. The efficiency of better-quality "compact fluorescent" bulbs can rival that of all but the newest LEDs, but they may not perform well in camp lanterns. In addition, LEDs eliminate the problem of fragile tubes and allow for more flexibility with brightness adjustment. If you have some fluorescent lanterns that you are happy with, it may be prudent to wait for the newest LEDs (like the Cree XP-G) to make their way into this product category.

Another option here is using handheld LED flashlights with diffusers to spread the light. Several companies offer attachments for their lights and it is also pretty easy to homebrew something with a sheet or tube of translucent plastic material. This approach can be especially handy in emergencies or where space is limited, but be careful of heat buildup. At maximum brightness, most flashlights

Some store brand products can be had with quite efficient LEDs. Shown here are a lantern and headlamp sold under the "Remington Arms" brand name.

run the LED at a pretty high power level and a flashlight body is not the greatest heat sink for extended operation, so damage to the LED is possible. An adjustable flashlight with lower brightness settings is a good idea for applications like this.

Area lighting is also a category where the build-it-yourself option could be rather appealing. For about $50-$70 you can get the parts needed to make a light source capable of 500 to 1,000 lumens (depending on your choice of components). The basic setup can be built into a housing that suits your fancy and operated from a 12-volt source while using roughly 8 to 12 watts of power at maximum brightness.

Portable work lights

Every reader can think of many uses for a decent work light or trouble light that can be operated from a 12-volt source (such as the car or a small battery). With the best of the LEDs, it would be pretty easy to design something that could belt out several hundred lumens while using only a few watts of power. Given the fact that many of the "consumer" products (such as the trouble lights which use large arrays of "pin type" LEDs) can be rather disappointing, building is also an attractive option here. The same light-making setup just mentioned could also be built into a package that includes suitable magnets, clamps, or hooks for mounting. Bare LEDs generally emit a broad flood of light, but a tighter beam may be desirable in a work light. If so, inexpensive focusing lenses are available to shape the beam to a pattern that meets your needs.

If we look to "commercial grade" products, we can find some very impressive options. A well-stocked example is "Larsen Electronics" (also known as "MagnaLight"). This US-based company has been in business for many years making and selling incandescent spotlights and other 12-volt lighting products and they now have an assortment of commercial quality LED work lights. Outputs of up to several thousand lumens are available (accomplished by ganging together multiple LEDs), but the drawback is that such products must be sold with a pretty high price tag because of the component costs. Extremely bright LED-based work lights have caught the interest of those in the trucking, mining, and heavy equipment fields and LED prices are expected to go down over time, so commercial quality options will hopefully become more available and less expensive.

One problem with new technology is that it can cause people to put on blinders and conclude that the *new* thing is always the *best* thing. This assumption can be especially dangerous when we get to lights for the cabin and home. For instance, a person working out of a vehicle could get quite a bit of light for a comparatively small investment by using some halogen incandescent "tractor" lights. Because of the poor efficiency, these use a lot of power and can kill a car or truck battery pretty quickly if you don't care to leave the vehicle running. But adding a good deep cycle battery to the setup could still prove cheaper than buying or building a multi-thousand lumen LED light.

If you need to light up a large area in a more efficient fashion, High Intensity Discharge (HID) is also an option to consider. This is basically the same technology used in everything from stadium and warehouse lights to portable light towers to the very irritating headlights found in some fancy cars. HID can provide an efficiency of around 100 lumens per watt and outputs are really limited only by the size of battery you are willing to drag around. 1,000 to 3,000+ lumens can be had from units sized like overgrown flashlights and bulky lanterns and even more is available from 12-volt corded products which are available in both spot and flood configurations. A potential drawback of HID is that most designs require a few seconds of warm-up time in order to hit full brightness and

Building it yourself can be especially attractive when it comes to work lights. It allows the use of the best available LEDs and you can design a light that actually fits your needs.

it is not the best choice for tasks that call for short bursts of usage and frequent on-off cycles. This can make HID a nuisance for *flashlight* use, but it is usually less of a problem with work lights. HID typically provides little or no brightness adjustment and it requires fairly expensive bulbs which will probably never wear out on most users, but could possibly break. Drawbacks aside, it can be a viable choice for some needs. Various HID products can be had from MagnaLight and other vendors.

Fixtures and bulbs for the cabin or home

We must not only compare different LED options to each other, we must also compare the LEDs to the other options when it comes to cabin and home use. Most notably, limitations like space, weight, and durability are usually not that critical and this allows for other alternatives like fluorescent and metal halide. In addition, we need to be extremely careful with the term "efficiency." As we saw in Part 1, the raw "lumens per watt" rating of a given LED is one thing, but the final useful efficiency of a bulb or fixture is another. Some loss here is simply unavoidable, but the difference between a good design and a sloppy one can be very dramatic.

In this respect, it is also important to be careful of "adjusted" efficiencies or creative ways of stating efficiency. Very importantly, this applies to other technologies as well as to LEDs. For instance, I've seen outdoor CFL (compact fluorescent) fixtures with efficiencies that have been "adjusted" based on a study which showed that cool white light sources will appear brighter than their raw lumen values would suggest. This is not exactly helpful because meaningful product comparisons become impossible. In a similar vein, one should be careful of bulb suppliers that simply parrot the ideal outputs and efficiencies of the LEDs themselves rather than providing realistic numbers for the actual final products. Another thing to watch out for is the "CRI" or "Color Rendering Index." This number has its uses, but it applies to color perception and *not* to efficiency. Finally, a statement that a certain LED bulb "is equivalent to" a certain incandescent bulb does *not*

Focusing lenses can squeeze the light from an LED into a tighter pattern and this can be particularly useful for work lights (note that the light itself is visible as the dot of light at far right). We'll examine this and other details related to building LED-based lights in the next article.

LED Technology Update

Brightness isn't everything, at least in some cases: the new "HP20" headlamp from Fenix (left) uses the XP-G LED, but its maximum output of 230 lumens is about the same as the "HP10" model (right) which is based on the older XR-E LED. By powering the new LED more gently, runtime from four rechargeable AA batteries is stretched from 2.5 hours to 3.5 and the heat-related limitations of the older model (see the "Headlamp" section) are avoided. These particluar examples also illustrate the importance of fitting other design details to your needs: the HP10's battery pack is attached to the back of the headband while the HP20's is separate and must be belt or pocket carried. An attached pack provides for more compact storage, quicker deployment, and the avoidance of cord-related snags and tangles. But a separate pack means less weight on your head, a potentially nice feature during extended use. It also allows the batteries to be kept inside a warm coat during cold weather operation.

mean that its lumen output will be comparable.

With these facts in mind, it is useful to ask: what is *reasonable* to expect in terms of LED bulb and fixture efficiency? We saw in our first visit that a very well designed bulb or fixture can provide an efficiency that is about 75% of the efficiency of the LED itself (this allows for optical losses, power used by the electronics, and efficiency losses which result from running the LEDs at higher than ideal temperatures). Applying this 75% factor to the efficiencies of the best available LEDs can give a reasonable, though perhaps optimistic, reference point. Recently, Cree released neutral and warm white versions of their new XP-G LEDs, so we can use these to establish a "best case scenario" for the top LEDs that are commercially available at this moment. In cool white, best low power LED efficiency is around 132 lumens per watt and 75% of this gives us a potential bulb/fixture efficiency of around 100 lumens per watt. Cree has demonstrated this level of performance in some prototype street lights and it suggests that 75% is not an unreasonable number to use. Neutral white XP-Gs come in at 124 lumens per watt, so we could expect bulb/fixture performance of around 90 lumens per watt. Finally, warm white XP-Gs can provide 102 lumens per watt, which leads to a possible bulb/fixture capability of 77 lumens per watt. It is important to understand that these estimates are based on best-bin LEDs being run at low power. Lower bin LEDs or higher power operation will lead to lower efficiencies. (For reference, recall from Part 1 that standard incandescent bulbs have an efficiency of around 13 lumens per watt and that halogen incandescent can provide 20 lumens per watt or a bit more).

It is also worth considering that Cree's best reported *laboratory* performance for a cool white LED is currently at 208 lumens per watt. If this could be translated into commercial LEDs, a bulb/fixture efficiency of over 150 lumens per watt would be feasible. Such performance (and even somewhat better) is almost certain to become available, but there is no guarantee as to *when*. It is good to have a handle on not only what is possible now, but also on what may be coming in the future.

Most of the LED bulbs found in the store at this writing can look pretty anemic. Clearly, it is not fair to compare them to the brand new XP-G, but LEDs like the Cree XR-E have been readily available for some time and, using our 75% factor, these could provide bulb efficiencies of 55 to 70 lumen per watt as we span from warm to cool white. In comparison, many retail products list efficiencies of between 20 and 40 lumens per watt and some bargain products don't even provide lumen ratings. There are some specialty products that cite higher performance capabilities—in the neighborhood of 50 to 70 lumens per watt or a little better. Such numbers (when accurate) suggest the use of good LEDs and pretty careful design. But they still pale in comparison to the 77 to 100 lumens per watt that are attainable from the new XP-G LEDs. Considering the cost of LED-based products, this is a *very* important thing to consider.

With these numbers in hand, we can also make a sensible comparison to other options. First, consider compact fluorescent (or CFL) bulbs. To draw a baseline, we can refer to the government's voluntary "Energy

Star" program which certifies products that meet minimum energy efficiency requirements. The minimum required CFL values are between 55 and 65 lumens per watt, depending on the wattage of the bulb. The potential efficiency of CFL will likely improve somewhat more with time, but note that these numbers are for *bare* CFL bulbs. The standards for fixtures and floodlights are lower to allow for the optical losses which result from things like lenses and reflectors.

When it comes to fluorescent fixtures based on traditional tubes, the Feds have mandated the use of newer, more efficient tubes and ballasts (electronic power supplies). The new "T8" tubes are skinnier than the old familiar ones and they offer efficiencies of 80 to 100 lumens per watt. Another alternative in some situations is "metal halide" (basically the same thing as "HID"). Efficiency here can be around 100 lumens per watt. Sodium vapor can provide 120 lumens per watt where its familiar yellow color would be acceptable. Another advantage of these choices is that they can provide a *lot* of light for a reasonable cost. It would require a number of high tech LEDs to provide the several thousand lumens that can be had from a two-tube T8 fluorescent fixture and that can get expensive.

In a nutshell, we find that a number of inexpensive, readily available alternatives can equal or beat the best currently available LED-based lights in terms of raw efficiency. Of course, this simple comparison ignores important considerations like the efficient dim-ability of LEDs or their potentially long service life. If you are starting with LED and CFL alternatives of comparable efficiency, but you would be happy with half-brightness except for intermittent needs like reading, card playing, eating, meal preparation, etc., then the LED option could prove vastly superior in the end. Operation at half-brightness could cut the power load by better than half and the cooler running temperature of the gently powered LEDs could mean a service life of well over 50,000 hours with little or no loss of output. On top of all this, the "directional" nature of an LED's emission could make it more efficient in the *delivery* of light and allow you to get better final lighting with fewer starting lumens. In order for LEDs to actually deliver these advantages, proper design is essential. For instance, many commercially available LED bulbs are *not* dimmable. In addition, a dimmable LED light will only be *efficiently* dimmable if the electronics are suitable.

This evolving technical situation means that a big project requires some careful thought. For instance, a person planning an off-grid home or big cabin could consider CFL bulbs (AC or DC) as a long-term-temporary solution until LED technology develops a little further. It should be noted that the standard screw-in bulb is not necessarily the best platform for LEDs because of their directional light emission and heat management issues. As a result, fixtures designed specifically for LEDs will probably provide the best performance in the long run. Thus, it might be best to mate the stop-gap CFLs with cheap plastic or ceramic lampholders instead of buying more expensive light fixtures with the idea of screwing in replacement LED bulbs in the future.

A problem with many of the high-efficiency options is that they are most readily available for use with 120-volt AC power. But considering them is still important, because it gives us an idea of what to look for when considering DC products suitable for direct battery use. RV and marine suppliers are often a useful source of such lights and there are also ones marketed specifically for off-grid uses. In addition, there is also the option of buying AC-based lights and using an inverter to power them. With a big project, this may be the final approach because of the need to power other appliances. When using this strategy (especially with smaller, portable inverters), take care to check compatibility. The AC current synthesized by inverters is not exactly the same as the stuff that comes out of a standard wall outlet. But if you need a lot of light, a proper inverter and off-the-shelf AC lights from the building supply store could prove to be both the cheapest and most efficient lighting strategy in some cases. Regardless of your choice with respect to a power source, it is important to assess the actual efficiency of the *specific* lights you are considering. The simple fact that a light is based on CFL or LED technology is not a guarantee of any particular lumen per watt efficiency.

LEDs will likely prove to be the hands-down choice for both off-grid and conventional lighting at some point in the future. But even then, there will still be more and less efficient choices, as there are now. For the time being, we also have to add in a careful comparison of other available technologies. As I said in Part 1, there are no easy answers here, but being armed with the right information is the essential starting point.

Next time

In Part 3, we will consider the alternative of building your own LED lights from components. This strategy can be particularly useful because it can allow you to put the best available LEDs into packages that will fit your specific needs. In addition, we will also consider the efficient *use* of light.

The author welcomes comments and feedback. You can reach him at timthorstenson@yahoo.com Δ

The Last Word

Justice Breyer is wrong about the 2nd Amendment

December 12, 2010, on *Fox News Sunday*, Justice Stephen Breyer said the Founding Fathers *never* intended for guns to go unregulated. His reasoning was that James Madison, often called the *Father of the Constitution*, actually didn't want the *2nd Amendment*, and he further claimed most historians would stand with him on this.

Let me start by saying Breyer is right, Madison *didn't* want the *2nd Amendment*. But what he fails to mention is that Madison also *didn't* want the *1st*, *3rd*, *4th*, or any of the other the first 10 amendments. He didn't want a *Bill of Rights*. Thus, using Breyer's logic, he must believe the Founding Fathers wanted to regulate speech and religion, require self-incrimination, etc. Perhaps in the future he's going to use this argument to rule in favor of censorship, self-incrimination, state-sponsored religion, etc.

But the reason Madison didn't want a *Bill of Rights* was that he didn't think it belonged in the *Constitution*. He and many of the other Founders held that since there are no powers in the *Constitution* that grant the federal government the power to take away our rights, it was unneeded. (See *Article I, Section 8* to see what powers were being granted to the United States.) Besides, the state constitutions almost all contained their own protections. So, including the amendments was not only a waste of time, it also provided the illusion that they weren't Natural or God-given rights; they were the gift of the federal government to bend, ignore, or abrogate as it wished.

However, what Breyer specifically said was that neither Madison nor the other Founders wanted the *2nd Amendment* and that Madison only included it to appease the other Founders who did want it.

Whoa! Others Founders wanted it? In one breath he said the Founders didn't want it, in the next he's willing to contradict himself.

But, if it must be known, Thomas Jefferson, George Mason, and many other Founders *insisted* on the *2nd*. More importantly, he fails to mention that Madison, one of the authors of what we now call the *Federalist Papers*, advocated the private ownership of guns by Americans in numbers *46* and *54*, both of which predate the *Bill of Rights*. So, it is odd that Breyer would claim Madison was against the *2nd*, and that most historians would stand with him on this, when it is so easily demonstrated his claim is false. Perhaps Breyer should read works of more competent historians or study some history himself.

Another claim of Breyer's is that Madison only agreed to the *2nd Amendment* so he could get the Constitution ratified, but the Constitution, written in 1787, was already ratified by June 21, 1788 — three and a half years before the *Bill of Rights*, where the *2nd* can be found, was adopted. So, the *2nd Amendment* could have been dispensed with had the Founders so wished, but there are no records showing that any one of them ever attempted to do so.

The last thing I want to point out (and I do this not only for Justice Breyer, but for others who claim that the *2nd Amendment* is about the right of the states to have militias and not an individual's right to bear arms), is that the Founders were very careful to distinguish between the *people*, the *states*, and the *United States*. The people are mentioned twice in the original *Constitution*, the states 26 times, and the United States 55 times. More telling, the people are mentioned five times in the *Bill of Rights*, the states three times, and the United States twice, and all three are mentioned together in the *10th Amendment*. That *Amendment* doesn't even make sense if the Founders weren't carefully distinguishing among the people, the states, and the federal government.

So, the wording of the 2nd Amendment is clear:

A well regulated Militia, being necessary to the security of a free State, the right of the people to keep and bear Arms, shall not be infringed.

We the people have the right to keep and bear arms and the federal government cannot infringe upon this right. And, since the passing of the *14th Amendment*, the states cannot infringe on any of our rights, either.

I should mention, thanks to Tammy Bruce at tammybruce.com, I was able to find wording from the Dred Scott decision that the Supreme Court's purpose in denying blacks full rights in that infamous case was because it "*... would give to persons of the negro race ... the full liberty ... to keep and carry arms wherever they went.*" In other words, free men have the right to keep and bear arms.

Frankly, I can't believe Justice Breyer investigated this issue himself. My guess is that one of his clerks handed him this baloney and he chose to believe it, not realizing that manifesting this degree of ignorance about the very document he is sworn to defend would come back to bite him on the butt.

If Justice Breyer is genuinely interested in basing his opinions on what the Founders *really* thought, he should read the *Federalist Papers*, stop trying to limit the rights of individuals, and follow *all* the guidelines of *Article I, Section 8*, which limits the powers of the federal government. It's hard to avoid the conclusion, however, that Justice Breyer is merely interested in following the liberal agenda, which includes taking away Americans' right to own guns. —***John Silveira***

Backwoods Home magazine

practical ideas for self-reliant living

May/June 2011
Issue #129
$5.95 US
$7.50 CAN

Saving seeds

A homesteader's journal
Medicating cattle
Build LED lights
Picking a pig
Fire starters

Jackie Clay's Pantry Cookbook
Pre-order now!

www.backwoodshome.com

My view

An American dollar worth two cents

Most Americans are unaware that today's dollar has the purchasing power that roughly four cents had back in 1913. That was the year the Federal Reserve (the Fed) was established. Just in the last few years, according to CNNMoney.com's Bailout Tracker, the Fed has created, out of thin air, at least $11 trillion in new money, some of which went to bailouts of Wall Street, the banks, and businesses like General Motors. Most of the money, however, is essentially unaccounted for, and when befuddled and often exasperated congressmen at congressional hearings have asked representatives of the Fed where all that money has gone, they get vague answers. What *is* known is that all that "new" money has devalued the dollar still further. In fact, in terms of the purchasing power of 1913, the dollar is on track to be worth around two cents in about two years.

What does this mean in a practical sense for the dollar to be devalued by so much in such a short period of time? For one, your standard of living, which you may have already felt slipping these last few years, is going to drop further. Food, energy, and the price of almost everything else you need or want is going to go up in price, but your paycheck, at least for most of us, probably won't.

Worldwide food prices are already higher than they were in 2008 when rising prices sparked riots around the globe. According to the United Nations' Food and Agriculture Organization (FAO), the *FAO Food Price Index* is at its highest level in the 21 years it has been used to track worldwide food prices — even after factoring in inflation.

According to msnbc.com, wheat is up 114%, corn 88%, soybeans 56%, coffee 65%, and sugar 79% over last year. Poor countries are being hit the hardest. You may not eat much in the way of corn and soybeans, but price increases are reflected in the meat you eat because meat animals must be fed some sort of grain or other agricultural products. It also drives up the price of wheat because it is diverted to feed animals, and that directly drives up the price of a loaf of bread.

The causes of these food increases are several:

Crop shortfalls

Summer droughts in Russia, flooding in Australia, and the third cold winter in a row in most of the northern hemisphere impacted big grain and rice producers such as Russia, China, Europe, and the United States. Also, failures of corn and vegetables in northern Mexico are resulting in higher food prices there and they will likely add to illegal immigration problems.

John Silveira

As a result of the shortfall in grain production, grain surpluses, meant to act as a cushion during bad times, are now at historically low levels. The United States and Canada are net exporters of grain, so we won't have the same problems that food-importing nations are already experiencing. But because worldwide demand has driven up prices of American and Canadian grains, that will eventually drive prices up at your local market.

Unintentionally manufactured shortages

An example of this in the United States is the Congressional mandate that food crops must be used to make biofuels. It's not solving the so-called energy crisis but it *is* making your food more expensive. The only people who are benefiting from it are the big grain producers and the politicians (both Republicans and Democrats) who created the biofuel mandate and get campaign donations from producers of biofuels.

The growing middle classes in poor countries

Factor in the burgeoning middle classes in both China and India, the world's two most populous countries, and it puts tremendous pressure on food prices. Millions of the formerly poor are acquiring middle class tastes for foods and other commodities. Unless the supply of these commodities increases, the prices for them will continue to rise.

Inflation

Even if we weren't experiencing worldwide crop shortages, and even if the weather was cooperating with farmers, prices would still rise because countries all over the world are diluting their money supplies. In the United States, our money is becoming worth less...maybe even worthless... and there is already the danger of hyperinflation. But it's also happening in Britain, China, Japan, and India because they've all created vast sums of money from thin air that dilutes their current money supply. The only reason the diluted U.S. dollar has not yet been replaced by another currency as the international medium of exchange is because other major currencies are being diluted also.

Rising commodity prices

Among the early symptoms of the coming rapid inflation are the rising prices on the commodities markets. Commodity markets involve "futures," the anticipated value of commodities such as wheat, gold, and oil. Rises in futures prices are because those who invest in them (and have money and are better able to spot trends than you and I) are betting the future prices of most commodities are going to rise.

The Commodity Price Index, a compilation of various energy, food, and metal indexes which reflect the costs of those products, has risen almost 28% in just the last 12 months. Part of this is also the result of bad weather, but the increased costs of metals — gold and silver in particular — reflect anticipated inflation, or the devaluation of our currency. That means that people with more money than you or I are taking their money out of paper and putting it into hard assets, among which are the precious metals. It's not just happening here, but in other countries, too. Those with money know what's coming.

In case you are wondering about specific indexes, the Commodity Food Price index is up over 32%, Energy over 20%, and metals over 57%.

The overall solution is elusive

The solution is elusive, at least on the national level. After the Federal Reserve has created trillions of dollars out of nothing, the Federal government, which is about to run out of money, seems to believe that the solution is to create even more money and add to an already unsustainable federal debt. In other words, the politicians' solution is going to exacerbate the problem. Part of the solution, then, is to keep getting rid of our politicians at the ballot box and voting in new ones such as the Tea Party candidates who seem to at least understand that government overspending must stop and that the Fed's printing of paper money must stop.

On the personal level, what can you do to protect yourself from the inevitability of rising prices? Do what the rich are doing, but on a smaller scale. Trade your money for hard assets. If you have money you can spare, buy some silver or gold. I buy junk silver coins, the pre-1965 dimes, quarters, and half-dollars. I also buy the .999 pure silver "dollars" the U.S. Mint has been producing since 1986. At this writing these "silver dollars" are worth about $33 apiece. Someday soon, it may be the only way to buy gas without a ration card.

Stock up on food, as you're always going to need it and it's going to become more expensive. If you don't have guns and ammo, buy some. Not only are they going to appreciate, someday soon you may need them.

—John Silveira

SAVING SEEDS

By Jackie Clay

I go through dozens of garden seed catalogs in preparation for each year's new (and better!) garden. I have a lot of "old reliable" varieties that I grow year after year. They taste great, are hardy growers in our cool, Zone 3 climate, either store well (such as squash and carrots), or they can-up and dehydrate well. Many are open-pollinated varieties from which I save my own seed. But I still try new things in the garden. Some are the latest "bells and whistles" hybrids, often costing upwards of $5 a pack or more, others are very old heirloom varieties I've never tried before.

A simple germination test will help you determine which seeds to save from year to year.

But one thing that strikes me hard is the steady and often shocking increase in the price of garden seeds. In a year of rocky economy, it seems like a whole lot of folks are going to be raising their own food. Several seed companies have already run out of catalogs, and the spring is yet young. I know we are getting very serious about our garden and are worried about the prospects of seed prices climbing even higher. So to fight that recurring expense, we've decided to again raise an increasing portion of our seed. After all, in the quest for a self-reliant lifestyle, the more a person produces what they use, the more sustainable life they will lead.

Seed saving is *not* complicated, although some seed companies make it seem so. After all, Native Peoples all over the world have been doing it for thousands of years. And out of all of this seed saving have come thousands and thousands of tasty, productive, beautiful, and hardy varieties. My, oh my, how these seeds have traveled from their beginnings! Take corn for example; it was developed in Central America from a wild maize, *teosinte*, which resembles a grass more than corn as we know it today. After years of selective planting, ear corn was developed. Soon, it was traded up through Mesoamerica (what is modern-day Mexico) and into what is now the United States, where it traveled quite rapidly and was quickly adopted by many Native American tribes. They, in turn, developed thousands of different varieties to suit their climates, growing seasons, and tastes.

The same thing happened, in different ways, with melons, squash, beans, and other vegetables. Squash started in the southwest, melons were brought by the Spanish explorers, and beans developed from wild beans of different cultures. Food has always been a chief trading stock and, because of this, new tasty foods traveled quickly.

The sad part is that during the 19th and 20th centuries, when commercial seed growing started, thousands of these superior, wonderfully tasty varieties were lost forever in the name of progress. In fact, this situation continues today. Most of the seed available through those beautiful seed catalogs are grown and marketed by a handful of huge companies. And most of it is hybrid (unable to produce an exact copy of itself), so seed saving is not a simple matter, as it should be.

Let's take a look at some oft-used terms and just what they mean to you.

Open-pollinated

Open-pollinated seeds are usually old, tried-and-true varieties that have been around for a long time. They are often called "heirloom" seeds because they were initially passed from one family member to the next, down through the generations. The first people in this country to have done this were, of course, the Native tribes, carrying their seeds from one camp to the next, from one garden area to another. Many times, these familiar seeds were so treasured that people faced starvation rather than eat their precious seeds. Cherokee women even sewed seed for their favorite pole beans in the seams of their skirts during the horrific forced march after the government "removed" them from their farms. This "walk" of hundreds of miles was later called the Trail of Tears, from which this variety of bean is now known.

I took this photo today, following my germination test on Hopi Chinmark corn I grew in New Mexico, 10 years ago.

Following the Indians, the European settlers often received some of this seed through trading, gift, or theft. Some immigrant families also brought seed from the old countries, trading with their neighbors as it grew and thrived. Seed was food and food was life. It held huge importance in times when, if you didn't grow it, you simply did not eat.

Open-pollinated seeds always produce the same plant and fruit as the plant the seeds came from. However, not all open-pollinated seeds are "heirloom" seeds. There is an increasing trend to create new and better open-pollinated varieties and to even breed back hybrids so that they will produce true types. One example is the "Indian" corn Painted Mountain. This was relatively recently developed by a Montana grower trying to develop a corn for cornmeal that would mature in a very short growing season. Diligently, he crossed dozens of native corns having good production, taste, and quick maturity, until he reached his goal. Then, by carefully choosing ears of corn closest resembling his goal each year, he stabilized this open-pollinated variety.

I have taken hybrid tomatoes, Early Cascade, and bred them back from the initial hybrid variety, in three generations, to reach a stabilized, open-pollinated variety. It only took choosing plants with the right type of tomato, pulling out the rest, and continuing to search for the ideal tomatoes.

Seed equals food; seed is like money in the bank.

Pumpkins and squash are the easiest of all seeds to harvest and save. Just look at this huge variety of last year's open-pollinated squash and pumpkins.

Hybrid

Hybrid varieties are crosses between two or more varieties. Seed producers hire experienced plant breeders to research and develop new and "better" varieties each year to market in the future, often at inflated prices. While hybrid stock often does exhibit more vigorous growth and disease resistance, it can sacrifice such things as taste, tenderness, and keeping ability. Today more seed is developed for commercial growers who sell to wholesalers, shipping countrywide. Such traits as a thick skin (for more successful shipping), holding ability (pick it green and keep it in a warehouse for a while), ease of mechanical harvesting (eliminate farm workers), and firmness (bruise less in the store and during shipping), mean more than do sweetness, tenderness, flavor, and total productiveness.

These hybrid varieties may be fine, but do not expect seed saved from them to produce "children" like the fruit you got the seed from. You may get a totally different plant, resembling one of the initial parent plants, something "kind of" like it or something in between. Although companies like Monsanto are developing varieties with a "terminator gene" that can not reproduce, hybrid vegetable seeds today are not sterile. But they don't reproduce exact copies, either.

Organic seed

Organic seed is simply seed that was produced without the use of chemicals in the growing of the "mother" plants. You can have organically grown hybrid seed, heirloom seed, or open-pollinated seed. It only means that the farm the seeds were grown on did not use chemicals, such as fertilizer, herbicide, or insecticide in the production of the plants.

Treated seed

Some seed is treated with a fungicide before being packaged. This is to prevent the seeds from rotting in the ground if planted just before a period of damp cool weather, which delays germination. Unfortunately, this seed treatment is also toxic (wash your hands after use, please!), and many people (me included) distrust putting it into their garden soil. Seeds often sold that have been treated are corn and muskmelon.

Which is best for me?

I'm asked that question a lot and my answer is always the same: "It depends."

I prefer to grow and save my own seed. We farm organically, although we will probably never be certified because we do not sell produce and do not need, or want to pay for, that certification; we know what we put into our soil — or what we do not. I try to stay away from treated seed by only planting when the soil temperature has warmed up enough to allow quick germination, and by paying careful attention to our trusty weather radio for a long-term forecast that we can usually depend on.

However, I also plant some hybrids each year, as many hybrids result in a much earlier crop than is available using open-pollinated varieties. (I *always* have "back-up" open-pollinated varieties in my seed boxes...just in case, for who-knows-what reason, hybrid seeds may be unavailable one year.)

I also always try a couple of new-to-me heirloom varieties to see how they perform for us, and how they taste. I like my food beautiful, too, so something new to me but an old and pretty heirloom always catches my eye, right off.

I firmly believe that every family should grow at least a portion of their own seed in order to be more self-sustaining as well as to cut garden costs.

Besides, saving seed is great fun. Most varieties of common garden crops produce seed that, if harvested and stored well, will keep viable for years. That way, if you have a good squash year and save a pint of squash seed, but then have two bad squash growing years, you'll still have plenty of seed for the next year. Remember, seed equals food; seed is like money in the bank.

Seed saving basics

For the most part, seed saving is very easy and you get a lot of seed for very little work. But remember that to save "pure" seed for any kind of crop you should know that different varieties of the same species can — and will — cross if not separated by an appropriate distance. Here are guidelines for producing pure seed, but you can sometimes reduce the distances I recommend by taking into account barriers between the gardens. For instance, I can grow one variety of a squash species in our lower garden and another in our berry patch. The recommended distance to keep them from cross-pollinating is half a mile, but the distance between these patches is only 600 feet. However, there is a large hill and a woodlot between the crops, so we feel confident that the insects that pollinate the squash blossoms will not readily travel between patches. And remember, a homesteader's need for "pure" seeds is not as high as is a seed grower's or serious hobbyist's.

Here I am, harvesting seeds from a very good squash. I "squish" out the seeds from the strings and pulp and place them on a pie plate to dry.

Here are some recommendations for spacing to prevent cross-pollination:

20-500 feet	beans, peas, tomatoes, peppers
half mile	squash, melons, sunflower
one mile or more	corn, fava beans, okra

In addition to planting different varieties of the same species at these distances, you can also build isolation cages from fine-screen mesh to cover the plants (this will keep pollinating insects out, so you will have to hand-pollinate the blossoms), plant different varieties at different times so they do not pollinate at the same time (works well with corn), or even hand-pollinate the blossoms.

To ensure that your seeds are plump and ready for collection, let your fruit ripen in the field. Unripe seeds will not germinate.

How long will my seeds stay good?

Most garden seeds, with the exceptions of onions and leeks, remain viable in storage for years, regardless of what some catalogs tell you. With older seed, there is a slow reduction in germination. Where year-old seed may have a 98% germination rate, four-year-old seed may have a 70% germination rate. When in doubt with some of your older seed, do a germination test. If most of the seeds germinate, great! If only a few do, you know you need to save seed soon. Simply plant more seeds to cover poor germination.

Test the germination of your seed by putting some seed on a damp paper towel, then wrapping it up and placing it in a closed jar. Put the jar in a warm place and check for germination (tiny roots and shoots). Some seeds germinate in as few as three days, where others require up to three weeks; check your seed packages or a

To save seed from this open-pollinated watermelon, pick out the dark, fat seeds and discard the white, immature ones. Put on a pie plate or cloth to dry.

catalog. Seed can remain viable a lot longer than commonly supposed. I have planted beans that were carbon dated 1,500 years and they grew!

Seed harvesting

We'll start with the easiest crops first and work up to the more difficult ones.

Squash and pumpkin: There are five major varieties of the species *Cucurbita*, grown in the United States: *C. pepo*, *C. maxima*, *C. mixta*, *C. moschata,* and *C. argyrosperma*. *C. pepos* are usually pumpkins and summer squash. *C. maxima* are usually larger, pumpkin-shaped squash and hubbard-type squash. *C. mixtas* can be cushaw, "sweet potato" or Japanese squash. *C. moschata* includes some Japanese and pumpkin-squash. *C. argyrosperma* includes many striped cushaw-type fruits.

It seems confusing, but you can still grow five different squashes in your garden each year, one of each variety, and still keep pure squash. For instance, I can plant my favorite *C. Maxima*, Hopi Pale Grey, along with a summer squash, a butternut squash, a cushaw, and a sweet potato squash. Or I can save seed from one of each, one year, then grow different ones the next. Infinite possibilities. *Or* when you have a great supply of seed, you can grow as many of the same species, but of different types, as you wish and just not save seed that year; they are just as good to eat, as the fruits will be purebred…just the seeds will be crossed.

To save squash or pumpkin seed, harvest the ripe squash late in the fall, before any hard frosts. Bring them into a protected spot that will not go below freezing and let them continue to "ripen" for a month or more. (I just stack them in a cool, but heated room, under a table, in a closet, or even in the hallway, then save seed as we eat them.)

Cut your squash in half with a sturdy knife or even a hand carpenter's saw if the rind is very hard. Be careful not to have an accident here. After the squash is halved, scoop out the strings and seed by using a large spoon. Then go through one piece at a time, squishing out the plump seeds by hand. Leave any that are flat and lightweight, as they are not viable and will not grow.

I place my seeds in a single layer on a pie plate. When finished, put the seeds in a warm, dry location. (Don't put in the oven; heating that much will kill the seed.) Every few days, stir the seeds by hand to keep them from sticking. After a week or so, there may be a thin, papery coating that flakes off. Work the seeds by hand until it all loosens, then blow the coating off outdoors. In another week, the seeds should be very dry and ready to store. Pour them into a jar and turn the lid down snug. If any condensation forms in the jar in the next day or so, immediately remove the seeds and dry them some more or the seeds will mold and be no good.

Squash and pumpkin seeds will be good to grow for many years if stored in a dry, cool place. You can also put your containers in the freezer for even longer storage. Be sure to label your seeds so you know what variety you have in the jar.

Muskmelon (and other melons) and watermelon: Most muskmelons are of the same variety and species, but they will not cross with watermelon or other garden crops. So each year you can grow your favorite melon variety, or alternate with others when you have plenty of seed saved that is pure.

Like squash, melon seed saving is very easy. Easier, in fact, as you don't have to continue ripening the fruit after harvest. We've all enjoyed a juicy melon in the summertime, spitting out the seeds as we go. All you have to do when you save melon seeds is to pick (or spit!) out the ripe seeds onto a piece of wax paper or non-stick cookie sheet. Pick out and discard any white, unripe seeds. Then put the seeds up until they are dry. I stir them around every couple of days with my hand or a spatula to keep them from sticking down.

In about two weeks (depending on the humidity), the seeds will be nicely dried and ready to put in an airtight jar for storage. Melon seeds remain viable for years.

Peppers: Most peppers, both sweet and hot, are of one variety, *Capsicum annuum,* so it's best to stick to growing only one variety (or a couple if you have a large area or plan on using isolation screens) each year. To harvest viable seed, you must let your peppers ripen thoroughly. This usually means letting them ripen deep red or the pepper's natural mature color. Some mature to orange, yellow, or even purple.

When the pepper is very ripe, harvest the pepper, cut it open, and remove the large, robust seeds. A few will be very thin and white; these are not viable so discard them. Of course, each variety of pepper has a different size and thickness of seed, so take that into consideration. Most bell peppers have a quite thick, larger, flat seed, where some smaller chilies have a much smaller, thinner seed. Take a look at a few seeds from your seed pack if unsure. I sprinkle my mature pepper seed out onto a kitchen towel, laid on a cookie sheet. The seeds don't stick as badly on a towel as they sometimes do on paper. Let them dry for a few days, then rub them gently to loosen them from the towel. Again, let them dry more. In about a week, they should be dry enough to remove from the towel and put in a pie pan for extended drying of another week or so. When thoroughly dry, pack away in a small, sealed jar with a variety label enclosed. Pepper seeds will remain viable for several years.

Beans: Nearly all beans, both bush and pole, snap, and dry, are of the same variety, *Phaseolus vulgaris.* Exceptions you may run into are runner beans (*Phaseolus coccineus*), soybeans (*Glycine max*) and cowpea, often called "yard-long bean" which is *Vigna unguiculata.*

Choose your best, ripe tomatoes to save seeds from.

While the recommended spacing distance for beans is listed at 30 feet, a few tall rows between beans is usually sufficient to save relatively pure seed. I plant my pole beans on one side of the garden, my bush beans on the other side, and separate them with rows of corn. They're only about 15 feet apart, but have never crossed yet.

All beans are saved for seed by letting them mature and dry in the pod, in the garden. This means letting a plant here and there, down the row, grow on and develop mature seeds, taking care not to harvest them when you pick your snap beans. I tie a piece of red yarn on all "save-for-seed" plants so I don't get in a hurry and pick them. The seed is ready to harvest when it rattles around in the yellowish brown pod.

Do be careful, though, as a few types of beans will split their dry pods and "self-seed" throwing beans far and wide. When the pods are ripening, keep a careful watch so this does not happen.

When in doubt, take your beans, dry plant and all, carefully into your garage, shed, or barn and lay the plants loosely on a tarp to finish drying. That way if the pods split, the beans will not have to be picked up, one at a time, from the garden rows.

By raising your own plants from your own seed, you have much greater control over what you eat. These are all open-pollinated tomatoes, grown in my little greenhouse from seed I have saved.

For a smaller amount of beans, you can just pick the pods, split the beans out, and lay the seeds on a tray to finish drying.

For a large amount of seed, it's easier to lay the plants or pods on a tarp, then walk around on them with clean shoes or rub the pods between your hands to loosen the bean seeds.

After harvest, the seeds should be cleaned and then laid out in a single row to finish drying for storage in airtight containers.

Peas: Peas, like beans, are of one variety, *Pisum sativum*, and will cross with each other. So if you plan on saving seed, stagger your plantings so that one will not flower at the same time as another. (Plant garden peas in the spring and then plant snap peas in the fall, for instance.) These peas include snap peas, edible pea pod peas, and garden shell peas. Soup peas are simply smooth seeded peas that are allowed to mature and dry.

To save pea seed, simply allow the peas to mature and the vines and pods to dry to a tan color. Be careful, as pea pods will split open, happily ejecting their seeds to reseed your garden. So when the pods are dry, either pick the pods or pull the whole vines to lay out in a dry area on a tarp to finish drying. Like beans, you can thresh out the seed by walking on the vines or whacking the vines with a plastic baseball bat or smooth stick.

Winnow the seed by tossing the seed from a basket, up in a strong wind. The wind will blow away the dry chaff and dust, leaving the clean seed behind. I further dry the seed on trays for a few days to ensure that it is sufficiently dry for long-term storage in airtight jars. Pea seed remains viable for years.

Cucumbers: All cucumbers commonly grown are of the same species and variety, so they will cross. If you are saving seed, it's best to grow only one kind each year. Yes, you *can* make pickles from cucumbers such as "burpless" or "Japanese" types and pickling cukes will grow long enough to use as slicers.

Cucumber seed may be harvested much like melon seeds. Allow the cucumbers from one healthy plant to ripen to the fat, yellow stage. Remember that when a plant has a couple of these "boats," it will stop blooming and producing pickle-sized cukes and slicers, thinking that its mission in life is done. So don't let many plants grow mature cukes or you'll lose out on a long harvest.

Cut the fat, mature cucumber open and squeeze the seeds out of the pulp by hand onto a clean piece of cloth, such as a kitchen towel. Remove any thin, unfilled seeds and discard them. Smooth the seeds out into a single layer and let dry in a protected, warm place. After a few days, stir the seeds around to dry them evenly and to prevent them from sticking. In a week they should be dry enough to put on a cookie pan to finish drying without sticking down.

After the seeds are very dry, pour them into a clean, airtight container and label them for storage. Cucumber seeds will remain viable for several years.

Corn: All corn grown in the U.S. is of the species *Zea mays*. So the different varieties of corn *will* cross. This includes field corn, sweet corn varieties, "Indian" corn, popcorn, and flour corn. As corn is chiefly wind pollinated, it is recommended that you isolate each variety from other corns by at least one mile. (Wind pollination is the means by which many "clean" corn fields are becoming contaminated by genetically modified corn pollen. It's getting harder and harder to find untainted corn seed.)

But when you are growing for your own family's use, varieties separated by about 100 feet, with a natural barrier such as a hill or woods between them, usually produce fine results. As most folks today grow sweet corn and don't have large pieces of land, you can always use sweet corn as a flour or cornmeal corn, as well. It makes terrific meal that is naturally sweet.

To harvest seed corn, choose several ears of your nicest corn and allow them to fully mature and dry on the stalk. If wet or very cold weather threatens, you can snap the ears from the stalk and bring them in to a protected area to finish drying on the cob. I usually husk the ears so I can watch for any signs of mold. When the seed is very dry on the cob, you can shell it off with your thumb into a tray. Remove any small kernels and discard them. Finish drying on a tray for a couple of weeks to ensure that the thick kernels are totally dry and ready for storage. Pour into an airtight container that is rodent proof (mice and rats *love* sweet corn seed, and so do weevils). Label the seed and put away in a safe storage area. Corn seed remains viable for years.

Tomatoes: Tomatoes are of the species *Lycopersicon lycopersicum*, and all varieties will cross if not separated by several feet or physical barriers, such as tall crops (corn for instance), trees, or hills. Tomatoes are easy to save seeds from. I grow my "seed saver" varieties in different corners of our huge garden, and also in our berry patch up the hill.

To save tomato seed, simply choose your best plants and nicest fruit. Let several ripen thoroughly on the vine, then harvest them. Cut the tomatoes open and remove the pulp and seed. Place in a bowl and mash the pulp with your fingers. Add water to fill the bowl. Let sit on the counter from six hours to two days. The pulp will float to the top and the seeds will sink to the bottom. Remove the pulp, pour off the water, and remove the seeds. Spread out on a cloth to dry. In a few days, work them loose with your fingers and move them around to ensure that they dry thoroughly. Remove any inferior seeds and debris, then place in a labeled, airtight container for storage. The seed will remain viable for years.

Okra: Okra is also easy to save seed from. All varieties will cross if not isolated in cages or by long distances (one mile is recommended), so it's best to grow only one variety of okra in years you plan on saving seed.

Simply allow some pods on your best plants to mature and dry. Harvest the pods when they are quite dry, but *before* they split open. Carefully remove the seed and lay on a pan in a dry, warm location to finish drying. When the seeds are very dry, place in a labeled, airtight container for storage. Okra seed will usually remain viable for more than four years.

Annual greens (lettuce, spinach, kale, Swiss chard, herbs, etc.): All lettuce is of the species *Lactuca sativa* and varieties will cross if not separated by many feet and physical barriers such as tall plants, woods, hills, or isolation cages. If you plan on saving seed, only allow one variety to bolt and bloom; keep the others cut.

Swiss chard is of the species *Beta vulgaris*, and may cross with beets, *Beta vulgaris*. However, beets require two years to produce seed — the first year, they produce leaves and the beet root, the second, the seed — so you have some flexibility here.

These greens usually bolt when the weather warms up and the season progresses. Leave a part of a row to go to seed when harvesting your salad greens, herbs for drying, or spinach and Swiss chard for canning. Soon after it is mature, it will bolt and send up blooming seed stalks, followed by seed heads. Keep watching these seed heads once they begin to dry. Some drop their seeds quite soon and easily; others hold them longer. Once the seed is mature (with thumb and forefinger, shell out a few seeds and examine them), clip the seed heads and place in a box or on a cloth to finish drying. When they are quite dry, rub the seeds from the husks onto a tray or pan. Winnow them gently to remove any debris, then continue drying them in a single layer on a pan.

When the seeds are dry, place them in an airtight, labeled container and put away for storage. Lettuce seed generally remains viable for a few years, while beets, spinach, and Swiss chard seem to remain good much longer

Broccoli: Nearly all broccoli is of the species *Brassica oleracea* so different kinds will cross if they are blooming at the same time. To save more than one, plant at staggered times or plant varieties with different maturity dates.

To save seed, simply allow your best broccoli to flower then form seed pods where the yellow flowers dropped off. In short-season climates, plant earlier broccoli or even start it in the house, as broccoli requires more than 100 days to form viable seed.

Protect your broccoli from frosts in the fall. Where broccoli itself is fairly frost tolerant, the seed pods seem to suffer damage from frost.

When the seed pods are fat and dry, watch them so they do not split and pop out their seeds. Clip off the seed onto a tray and bring into the house to finish drying thoroughly. When the pods are paper-dry, rub them between your hands to remove the seed. Winnow the seed gently to blow away chaff and debris. Continue drying the seed in a single layer on a pan in a warm, dry location. Pour dry seed into a labeled, airtight container for storage. Broccoli seed is usually viable for several years.

Biennial vegetables (carrots, beets, onions, celery, cabbage, Brussels sprouts, turnips, rutabaga, etc): Finally, we get to the "harder" vegetables from which to save seed from. These vegetables require two years to produce seed. The first year they produce leaves and roots, but no seed. They must be over-wintered in order to continue growing the second year, when they send up seed stalks and bloom. In mild climates, they can simply be left in place in the garden to winter over and continue growing in place the next year.

In colder zones, they can also be left in place in the garden and covered with a thick, protective mulch.

However, in the coldest zones, we must remove the plants from the garden, store them in a root cellar, then replant them in the spring. Root crops, such as carrots, onions, turnips, and rutabagas are simply dug and stored in the root cellar until early spring when the ground may be worked. All are quite frost tolerant so late frosts will not hurt them as they begin re-growing in preparation for seed production.

Cabbage and Brussels sprouts can not be harvested as we generally do, by simply cutting them. When you plan on replanting them next spring, carefully dig up a couple of your best specimens, replanting them in large buckets. Store over winter in a root cellar, sprinkling the soil with water as needed, to keep it from drying out. In the spring, after the hardest frosts are over, replant in the garden and encourage new growth.

This new growth gets "unusual." Many people think their plants have crossed with wild plants, as carrots get long stalks and look wild and unruly. Cabbages sprawl and send out blooming stalks that make the plants look alien. But it's all part of Nature's plan. Soon the stalks will have seed heads and, as the season progresses, they will begin to get fat and dry. Again, watch carefully so the seeds don't end up down in the dirt, spit out from splitting seed pods. Clip off the dry seed heads and place on a tray in a warm, dry location to finish ripening. Rub the seed heads between your hands to release the seed onto a tray or pan. Winnow to remove debris and continue drying for several days. Label your seed and place in an airtight container for storage. This seed will remain viable for several years before reduced germination becomes serious.

Of course there are many seed saving tips out there. One of my favorite books is *Seed to Seed* by Suzanne Ashworth. If you're interested in getting serious with your seed saving, this is the book for you.

And to find open-pollinated varieties in a seed catalog, check out Baker Creek Heirloom Seeds, Seed Savers Exchange, Native Seed/Search, and Fedco Seeds, among other great places.

Enjoy your trip down the road to more self-reliance, a cheaper garden, and tons of fun and good eating. Δ interplanetary travel

the gee-whiz! page

By O. E. MacDougal

Interplanetary travel has already happened, what with flybys and orbiters around several of the planets and their moons. There have also been landings on other bodies within our solar system including asteroids. Interstellar travel has been underway since the 1970s and Voyager 1 has officially passed through the heliosheath and is now in interstellar space, though given space's vastness, neither it nor any other interstellar probe we've sent out, so far, is likely to ever encounter another star. But other than orbital flights and the Apollo Program, all of these are unmanned. What most people are curious about is *manned* space travel. Here are the types of manned space travel we can look forward to and their likelihoods:

- Interplanetary — it'll happen
- Interstellar — perhaps, but not in our lifetimes
- Intergalactic — barring unexpected discoveries in physics, probably never.

Just sending men to the moon was an accomplishment and having people inhabit the International Space Station is no less a feat since it involved keeping humans alive in space for months instead of just days.

The ships will have to have their own "industrial base" because things wear out and have to be repaired or replaced. Outside medical aid will be impossible, other than medical advances broadcast to the ship (that will still take some years to arrive). Everything is going to have to be recycled, including the dead. So, your mother, who died yesterday, may be part of the sandwich you're eating today.

Space travel is all about time. Today, using conventional fuels, it takes months or years to get a vehicle to a planet outside of the earth-moon system. If Voyager 1, currently traveling at about 37,800 mph, were aimed at Proxima Centauri, the closest star to our solar system, it would take about 76,000 years. This is at least 15 times older than civilization itself. At 1 million mph, it's still going to take about 2900 years.

There may be faster ways to reach another star, including nuclear propulsion. Ion engines could create small, but continuous, acceleration. But acceleration can be, at most, halfway. The ship will then have to turn around and start decelerating.

How fast do we dare go? As we approach the speed of light, we encounter new dangers. Energy released in a collision with a ½-ounce pebble, traveling at 10% of the speed of light, would be equivalent to that of the nuclear bomb dropped on Hiroshima. At such speeds, even interstellar gases and dust will, over time, take their toll on the spaceship.

Space is so vast, there is the possibility that the only interstellar travel will be done by machines and the generation that launches one may never know the results of the mission.

Because of the incredible investment and power requirements, trips to other stars will probably be one-way.

Among the requirements for interstellar travel is that there will have to be simulated gravity for the entire trip. The effects of zero gravity on the body are gradually being documented and we will not do well on a voyage that will last at least decades, if not hundreds of generations, unless we can simulate gravity. New evidence even suggests that fetuses will not develop normally in zero gravity, so generational space travel will *need* to simulate gravity. A torus-shaped ship wheeling through space, so that centrifugal force simulates gravity, is a likely solution. People will literally walk on the walls of the ship and "up" will always be toward the middle of the torus while "down" beneath our feet will go on forever — just the opposite of what we have now, where down is to the middle of the earth and up goes on forever.

On the other hand, if we can create artificial gravity, we can use it as a propulsion system and make a ship "fall" through space with constant acceleration and, therefore, ever-increasing velocity. Is it possible? Not likely, but no one yet knows.

Will there ever be the space travel of science fiction with its faster-than-light warp drives? Worm holes that instantly transport us to other parts of the universe? Even time travel? I can only hope. In the meantime, none of it appears to be possible in our own lifetimes — and may prove to be impossible, forever.

FAMILY DINNER

AT BACKWOODS HOME MAGAZINE

By Richard Blunt

Richard Blunt prepares stuffed artichokes.

Last fall I was invited to Gold Beach, Oregon, to spend some quality time with my lifelong friend, Dave Duffy, and his family. On these visits it is customary for me to plan and prepare a meal for the Duffy family and any invited friends.

Over the years I've written, planned, and prepared dinner menus for a lot of folks while working in restaurants, hospitals, hotels, and other professional kitchens. However, cooking for friends and family has always given me the most satisfaction and pleasure. I use these meals to either introduce new recipes or present reworked versions of recipes from my existing files.

For this meal I reached back 16 years, to an article of mine published in the July/August 1995 issue of *Backwoods Home Magazine*. That article focused on the diversity, culinary appeal, and healthful benefits of foods served throughout the Mediterranean region.

Dave and his family have always enthusiastically embraced new foods, especially when they're healthful and appealing. A tour of their pantry and long-term food-storage area revealed a variety of dried beans, rice, dates, figs, raisins, dried cranberries, nuts, green and black brine-cured olives, extra virgin olive oils, and several varieties of pasta I could choose from. Ingredients like these are used to prepare many popular entrées throughout the Mediterranean region and, since they were right here in front of me, I decided to try and work them into my menu plan. I had previously developed versions of several North African dishes that were not included in the 1995 Mediterranean article, and one or two of these recipes would be perfect for this meal.

The extended Duffy family eagerly awaits the meal.

Both of the dishes I prepared are popular throughout North Africa and, over the years, have become popular entrées in many high-end restaurants. The main entrée is a chicken dish traditionally prepared in a specialty cooker called a *tagine*. My version of this dish is made with apricots and marinated Greek olives. I also decided to make a couscous pilaf, but added a bit of New England character by including dried cranberries in place of the raisins, dates, or other dried fruit.

I also asked John Silveira to help develop a stuffed artichoke recipe that incorporated sausage for the appetizer.

After returning home to Connecticut, I also developed a vegetarian stuffing for artichokes. I have included it here as a great alternative to the sausage stuffing.

Stuffed artichokes

The artichoke is a perennial thistle with a foggy origin. The general opinion is that it originated somewhere in the Mediterranean region, with North Africa considered a strong possibility. The edible portions are the lower portions of the leaves closest to the inner base, known as the heart, and the heart itself. There is a hairy-looking mass sitting on top of the heart called the choke. These are immature flowerets and should be discarded.

When shopping, look for artichokes that are tightly packed. The leaves should be plump, and should snap, not tear, when bent back. Don't be fooled into thinking that the small supermarket varieties, incorrectly labeled as babies, are something different. These are mature artichokes that grow in the shade of the plant's leaves and don't reach full size.

Artichokes require some trimming and steaming before stuffing. Steaming precooks the heart, allowing for the easy removal of the center leaves and the inedible choke. You can save time if you steam, wrap, trim, and refrigerate the artichokes the day before serving them. This will allow you to focus on the all-important stuffing the next day.

I use my water bath canning equipment to prepare five or more artichokes. For four or less, I use a collapsible steaming basket or a bamboo rack fit into a four-quart, heavy-bottom sauce pan with a tight-fitting lid.

The raw artichoke is prepped for steaming.

Ingredients:

- 6 large or 8 medium fresh artichokes
- 3 cups panko-style bread crumbs
- 4 oz. fresh-grated Romano cheese, divided
- 2 tsp. extra virgin olive oil, divided
- 2 medium yellow onions, diced small
- 2 celery stalks, diced small
- ½ tsp. table salt
- 1½ lbs. bulk-pack Italian sausage (pork, chicken, or turkey)
- 5 cloves fresh garlic, minced
- ½ tsp. dried sage
- ¼ tsp. dried oregano
- 1 tsp. fresh thyme leaves, minced
- ½ tsp. fresh rosemary, minced
- 1½ cups low-sodium chicken broth

Preparing the artichokes:

1. Preheat the oven to 300° F.

2. Using a sharp knife, cut off the stem of each artichoke as close to the bottom as possible. With the same knife, cut off the top third of the artichoke and snip the top third of the remaining leaves with a pair of kitchen shears.

3. Sprinkle the prepared artichokes with salt and place them, stem side up, in the steaming apparatus. Cover and steam over medium-high heat for 35 to 40 minutes or until the inner leaves pull away from the heart easily.

4. Gently remove the artichokes with a pair of tongs and place them on a wire rack to cool for at least 30 minutes.

5. While the artichokes are cooling, spread the bread crumbs on a large rimmed cookie sheet and toast them in the oven, stirring occasionally, until they are a light, golden brown, about 15 minutes.

6. Transfer the toasted crumbs to a small bowl and stir in three ounces of the Romano cheese. Set this mixture aside.

7. Grab the center clump of leaves and remove them from each artichoke. This will expose the hairy

Vegetarian curried lentil, mushroom, and rice-stuffed artichokes

clump at the bottom called the choke. Carefully scoop out the choke with a spoon to expose the heart at the bottom.

8. If the cavity created by removing the center leaves is not large enough to hold the amount of stuffing that you plan to use, you can remove additional leaves from the center to make it larger.

9. Cover the cooled artichokes with plastic wrap and set them aside while preparing the stuffing.

Preparing the sausage stuffing:

1. Increase the oven heat to 375° F.

2. Heat one teaspoon of olive oil in a 12-inch skillet, over medium heat, until it starts to ripple.

3. Add the onions, celery, and ½ teaspoon of table salt and cook, stirring frequently, until the vegetables are soft but not brown. Reduce the heat if they start to scorch.

4. Increase the heat to medium-high and add the sausage. Cook the sausage, stirring frequently to break up any large clumps. Continue cooking until the sausage loses its pink color and starts to brown.

5. Add the garlic, sage, oregano, thyme, and rosemary and cook, stirring constantly, until fragrant, about 30 seconds.

6. Remove from the heat and blend the bread crumbs and cheese with the sausage mixture.

7. Slowly stir in the chicken broth until the stuffing reaches a moist, but not soggy consistency. You can match the consistency of this with your preference for a poultry stuffing. My wife, Tricia, likes a moist stuffing similar to the type that is cooked inside a turkey. The rest of the family likes their stuffing a little drier like stuffing cooked in an uncovered casserole.

8. Spoon the desired amount of stuffing into each artichoke and sprinkle the remaining cheese on top.

9. Place the stuffed artichokes on a rimmed baking sheet, lightly cover them with a piece of aluminum foil, and bake for about 30 minutes.

10. Remove the aluminum foil and continue baking for an additional 15 minutes or until the internal temperature of each artichoke reaches 150° F when measured with a food thermometer. Serve immediately.

Curried lentil, mushroom, and rice stuffing for stuffed artichokes

My son Michael is a vegetarian. So whenever I plan a meat-based meal, at home or away, I plan on a meatless alternative that is both nutritionally adequate and satisfying. It wasn't necessary to prepare this recipe in Oregon. I did, however, prepare and serve it at a recent family meal to get some feedback from my review committee. All the comments were favorable, so I am including it here as an extra feature.

Ingredients:

4 medium artichokes
10 oz. frozen chopped kale or spinach, thawed
1 cup cooked jasmine or basmati rice
½ cup brown lentils
2 cups vegetable broth
2 Tbsp. extra virgin olive oil
1 medium yellow onion, diced
8 oz. white mushrooms, diced
1 small jalapeño pepper, seeds and stems removed, minced (optional)
2 medium cloves fresh garlic, minced
1 tsp. fresh ginger, minced
1 tsp. mild curry powder
¼ cup dry sherry
2 oz. crumbled Romano cheese
2 Tbsp. cilantro leaves, chopped
½ tsp. lemon zest
¼ cup chopped cashews or walnuts
salt and fresh ground pepper to taste

Method:

1. Trim and steam the artichokes as described in the previous recipe.

2. Preheat the oven to 375° F.

3. Place the thawed kale or spinach in a mesh strainer and squeeze out as much liquid as possible.

4. If you don't have any leftover rice in the refrigerator, cook ½ cup of jasmine or basmati rice, following the directions on the package. This will make one cup of cooked rice. Set the cooked rice aside to cool.

5. Combine the lentils and vegetable broth. Bring the mixture to a boil over medium-high heat, then reduce the heat and simmer the lentils for 30 minutes, or until they are tender but still retaining their shape. Drain the

lentils and save the remaining broth. You will need at least ¼ cup.

6. Add two tablespoons of oil to a 10-inch heavy-bottom sauté pan. Set the pan over medium heat. When the oil starts to ripple, add the onion and cook, stirring frequently until they begin to soften.

7. Add the mushrooms and continue cooking the mixture until they begin to soften, about five minutes.

8. Add the jalapeño pepper, garlic, ginger, and curry powder and cook until fragrant, about 30 seconds.

9. Add the sherry and continue cooking, stirring constantly, until the sherry is reduced and the pan is almost dry.

10. Stir in the ¼ cup of reserved broth and remove the pan from the heat. Gently fold in the cooked lentils, rice, Romano cheese, cilantro, and lemon zest. Season the mixture, to taste, with salt and fresh ground black pepper.

11. Stuff and bake the artichokes as described in the previous recipe and sprinkle the chopped nuts on top.

This will serve four people.

Marinated olives

Olives of all kinds can be found throughout the Mediterranean. Greeks seem to have more varieties than anyone else. Fortunately for us in this country, olive bars featuring high-quality olives, both imported and domestic, and cured both in brine and in oil, have become the latest rage in supermarkets.

I learned how to brine-cure olives many years ago from one of the most knowledgeable Italian cooks I've ever known. Mrs. Troiano was one of the many watchful mothers that checked the progress of my daily walk to and from school. In her backyard were two massive grape vines. The grapes from these vines were processed into bottles of homemade red wine which was served at most family meals. She also cured her own green and black olives every year.

Every Christmas she gave my mother two pint-jars of olives. One contained olives that were cured in basic salt brine, the second contained black and green olives marinated in spiced olive oil and Sambuca, an anise-flavored Italian liqueur.

These olives never lasted very long in our house. My mother served them on salads, as appetizers, or simply as snacks.

I now keep a jar of marinated olives in the refrigerator year-round, and use them in many of my recipes, including those for soups, salads, and many entrées. I prefer marinated olives I cure myself, but it takes about six weeks to properly cure a batch.

But whenever I discover I'm out of home-cured olives, I buy them at my local supermarket.

I included Mrs. Troiano's formula for home-curing olives in the Jan/Feb 1997 issue of *Backwoods Home Magazine*. If you decide to cure your own olives, raw olives can be found in some supermarkets, sold by the pound.

Marinated olives

Ingredients:

- 1 tsp. whole cumin seed
- 1 tsp. whole coriander seed
- ½ tsp. whole fennel seed
- 3 medium shallots, peeled and sliced thin
- 4 cloves fresh garlic, peeled and sliced thin
- 6 scallions (green onions), both the white and green parts, sliced thin
- 1 tsp. fresh rosemary leaves, coarsely chopped
- 2 tsp. grated zest from one lemon
- 1 tsp. fresh lemon juice
- 1 tsp. red pepper flakes
- ½ tsp. kosher salt
- 3 Tbsp. Sambuca
- ½ cup extra virgin olive oil
- 1 cup whole, brine-cured green olives
- 1 cup whole, brine-cured black olives

Method:

1. Toast the cumin, coriander, and fennel seed in a ten-inch heavy-bottom sauté or frying pan until golden brown. Transfer the toasted seeds to a heat-resistant bowl and set aside.

2. Prepare and combine the shallots, garlic, scallions, rosemary leaves, and lemon zest and set them aside in a medium size nonreactive (glass, plastic, or stainless steel) bowl.

3. Add the lemon juice, pepper flakes, salt, Sambuca, and olive oil along with the cooled whole spices and blend.

4. Add the olives and transfer the mixture to a Mason jar or plastic container with a tight-fitting lid.

5. Place the container in the refrigerator and marinate the olives for at least 24 to 48 hours.

I suggest using the olives within a week of preparation.

Braised Moroccan chicken with marinated olives

Ingredients:

6 cloves fresh garlic, about 4 tsp., minced
4 lemon zest strips, two inches long and about one inch wide (see sidebar for making lemon zest strips)
¼ tsp. cayenne pepper
2 tsp. Hungarian sweet paprika
½ tsp. fresh ground black pepper
1 tsp. ground cumin
½ tsp. ground coriander
1 tsp. ground ginger
¼ tsp. ground fennel seed
2 lbs. bone-in, skin-on chicken thighs
2 lbs. bone-in, skin-on chicken legs
salt and fresh ground black pepper
½ cup unbleached all-purpose flour
2 Tbsp. vegetable oil
2 medium yellow onions, skins removed, cut in half pole to pole, and sliced ¼ inch thick
½ cup dry white wine
3 medium carrots, peeled and cut into ½-inch-thick coins
1½ cups low sodium chicken broth
½ cup dried apricots, cut in half
½ cup pitted dates, cut in half
1 cup marinated Greek olives, cracked and pitted
¼ cup fresh cilantro leaves, minced

Braised Moroccan chicken with marinated olives

Method:

1. Prepare the garlic and lemon zest as directed. Set them aside in separate containers.

2. Combine the next seven ingredients in a small bowl along with half of the minced garlic and one lemon zest strip, minced. Set this mixture aside.

3. Dry the chicken pieces with paper towels and sprinkle lightly with salt and pepper.

4. Dredge the chicken pieces in the flour, shake off the excess, and place the pieces on a wire rack set inside a rimmed baking sheet.

5. Add two tablespoons of vegetable oil to a large Dutch oven set over medium-high heat. When it starts to ripple, place half of the chicken in the pot and brown on all sides. Reduce the heat if the chicken starts to burn. Set the browned pieces aside on the rimmed baking sheet. Return the pot to the heat, add additional oil if necessary and brown the remaining chicken and set it aside on the baking sheet, too.

6. Remove all but one tablespoon of oil from the pot. Return the pot to the burner set at medium-high.

7. Add the onions and the remaining three lemon zest strips. Cook until the onions soften.

8. Add the spice mixture to the onions and cook until fragrant, about 30 seconds.

9. Stir in the wine and cook until it is almost completely evaporated.

10. Add the carrots and broth. Scrape the bottom of the pot to remove any browned bits.

11. Add the chicken along with any accumulated juices back to the pot. Bring the mixture to a simmer, cover and cook over medium-low heat until the carrots are tender and the internal temperature of the chicken is at least 160° F. This will take about 45 to 60 minutes.

Making lemon zest strips

To make lemon zest strips, use a good vegetable peeler to shave off strips of a lemon's yellow skin, being careful not to take any of the bitter white pulp below.

12. Transfer the chicken to a platter and cover with a piece of aluminum foil.

13. Skim as much fat as possible from the surface of the sauce as you can. Add the dried apricots and dates. Return the sauce to a simmer until it thickens a little, about 10 minutes.

14. Return the chicken pieces to the pot along with garlic/lemon zest mixture, cilantro, and marinated olives. Simmer for an additional two or three minutes to heat all the ingredients. Adjust the seasoning with salt and fresh ground black pepper to taste.

Couscous pilaf

Mention North Africa to any food lover and chances are that couscous will be one of the foods that will come to his or her mind. This small grain pasta is without a doubt the most famous food of the North African region. Couscous is often referred to as a Moroccan dish, but folks in Algeria, Tunisia, Egypt, Libya, and Israel also claim that their countries are the official home of couscous.

This recipe has been a regular item at my dinner table since I wrote the Mediterranean article in 1995. Unfortunately, I didn't include it then, but since it has become so popular with my family and neighbors, I decided to share it with everyone.

Substituting dried cranberries for the traditional raisins, currants, or dates is my wife Tricia's idea. They add brightness to this dish that is reminiscent of many traditional New England dishes we grew up eating. There are hundreds of methods used throughout North Africa to prepare couscous. In Tunisia couscous dishes are usually hot and spicy containing fiery chili pepper seasonings along with coriander, cumin, and garlic.

This recipe produces a couscous that is exotic, mellow, and moist, as found in Morocco and Algeria. If you would like to spice up this recipe, simply add 1 teaspoon of cumin, ½ teaspoon of cayenne pepper, and ¼ teaspoon of ground cinnamon to the pan when you add the garlic. For best results, this recipe calls for a high-quality fine-grain couscous which is sold in many high-end supermarkets or specialty markets that feature Mediterranean and North African foods.

Couscous pilaf

Ingredients:

2 Tbsp. unsalted butter
2 cups fine-grained whole wheat or regular couscous
2 Tbsp. extra virgin olive oil
1 medium yellow onion, diced small
1 medium shallot, sliced thin
2 cloves fresh garlic, minced
½ cup dried, sweetened cranberries
2 cups low-sodium vegetable or chicken broth
1¾ cups water
1 tsp. fresh lemon juice
½ cup walnuts, roughly chopped and lightly toasted

Method:

1. Melt the butter in a 12-inch heavy-bottom skillet set over medium-high heat.

2. When it stops foaming, add the couscous and cook, stirring frequently, until the individual grains begin to turn a light brown. This will take about three minutes.

3. Transfer the browned couscous to a two or three-quart casserole with a tight-fitting lid, and return the pan to the heat.

4. Add the olive oil to the skillet. When the oil starts to ripple, add the onion and shallot. Cook, stirring frequently, until the onion begins to brown in about five minutes.

5. Add the garlic and cook, stirring constantly, until it becomes fragrant in about 30 seconds.

6. Add the cranberries, vegetable or chicken broth, and water. Increase the heat to high and bring the mixture to a boil.

7. Add the hot broth to the casserole with the toasted couscous, cover tightly with plastic wrap and the casserole's cover. Allow the couscous to sit for at least 15 minutes. Remove the casserole lid and the plastic wrap, gently stir in the lemon juice. Garnish the surface with the walnuts. Serve immediately.

Preparing this meal was a wonderful and uplifting experience for me. I am always at my best when cooking for friends and family. Especially when they are willing to pitch in and help like these folks did. I am looking forward to doing this again soon. Δ

Building Eric's house PART 5

By Dorothy Ainsworth

Last fall we wrapped Eric's house in white Tyvek like a cocoon to protect it through a harsh winter of rain, wind, and snow. From the outside it looked like a cold deserted box sitting on the hill, but on the inside a creature was stirring and it wasn't a mouse. It was me preparing for the final plumbing inspection.

There were two toilets, three sinks, and a hot water heater to install. But before any of that could happen, the flooring had to be laid in the kitchen and bathrooms, and cabinets had to be installed to hold the sinks and basins. That meant I'd have to start from the floor up.

Flooring

Home Depot is only 10 miles away, so I took the old covered wagon (my ancient Ford truck) in case I found some suitable flooring I wanted to haul home. Once there, I got a quick education from a salesman on some of my options: linoleum, ceramic tile, vinyl tile, and hardwood. Eric, who was busy working, said he trusted me to make a good choice as long as I kept his color scheme and budget in mind.

After looking at samples galore and asking lots of questions, I finally made the decision to buy vinyl tile strips (ambiguously called "planks") that would be *relatively* easy for a beginner to install.

"Traffic Master" brand was advertising a resilient floating-floor system called "Allure," and they lured me right in with their brilliant line: *"Anybody can do it!"* The sales-rep backed that up, and a printed poster on the wall behind the color samples erased all doubt.

It read: *"The ultimate do-it-yourself flooring! No messy adhesives or glue! Looks and feels like ceramic tile yet is waterproof even in moist areas! The planks adhere to each other, not your sub-floor, using the revolutionary GripStrip! To cut a plank simply score and snap! No underlayment necessary and the tile is quiet and warm underfoot! Follow the instructions and you'll be enjoying your new floor in just a few hours!"*

It sounded too good to be true and I should have known better, but I went full-bore ahead and purchased enough cases (15) to cover the kitchen and

We wrapped the house in Tyvek to protect it over the winter.

both bathroom floors — to the tune of $750 — and signed on the dotted line for Eric to pay it off interest-free in 12 months (regular promotional offers by Home Depot *and* Lowe's).

Allure tile was *not* cheap at $2/sq. ft., but was guaranteed for 25 years and was proclaimed to be the quickest and easiest flooring to install. Their claim would be true under *ideal* conditions, but when is that ever the case? Right away I ran into a problem. Our floor wasn't perfectly smooth because we had taken so long to build the house we had caulked the plywood floor-seams to withstand two winters before the roof went on. Consequently, a few of the seams were a little lumpy.

The instructions said an 1/8-inch variation in the sub-floor here and there was OK, so I set about to even things up. I chiseled and sanded the errant seams as flat as I possibly could without having to rent a belt sander, then decided to put down tar paper as an underlayment to completely smooth out the surface and hide any imperfections.

I had tried several times to call the company's customer service help-line to ask if using tar paper would void their warranty, but they never returned my calls. The plumbing inspection deadline wasn't going to wait for somebody back in Connecticut to finally answer the phone — and patience isn't one of my virtues when I get on a roll — so I proceeded with my plan.

I rolled out the 3-foot-wide 90# tar paper and stapled it down one course at a time, making sure the seams came perfectly together side by side so there would be no raised overlaps. The 12-foot wide by 24-foot long floor was now smooth and clean and ready to go.

Then the fun part began: laying the pretty tile. Each alarmingly heavy case of tile (whew!) contained 8 36x12-inch planks to cover 24 sq.ft. The first row had to be squared with the starting walls (beginning in a corner and working from left to right) to insure that all the subsequent rows would be square. It turned out — surprise! — that the wall corner was slightly out of square so after laying only two rows of tile-strips I was able to move and adjust the 2-foot by 12-foot "floating floor" to a happy medium by dividing the difference. That adjustment was necessary because the starting row was not exactly parallel with either wall which meant it would end up *way* off by the time I got to the other end of the room.

The vinyl tile strips were easy to "score and snap" to size with a utility knife.

They don't tell you in the owner's manual how to prevent this kind of disaster. They also don't tell you that the sticky "GripStrip" would rather stick to itself and your fingers than stick to the next tile strip. It also attracts dirt and debris like a powerful magnet, then *won't* stick to itself. I learned the hard way why they recommended buying an extra case "just in case."

One more thing they don't stress emphatically enough is that *before* you press the sticky surfaces together you must mate up the tile edges *exactly*. You can't be off more than hair's width from the edge of the previous-laid row as well as tightly against the tile just laid to the left, or you'll have an unacceptable gap. If this happens, they describe a way to fix it in the instructions, but who

> I enjoy working alone. I have more time and building experience than money, and Eric has more money than time and building experience, so it works out perfectly. He makes his living as a composer and pianist, and has to stay intensely focused on creative work when he's not out tuning pianos. I understand that, and I don't even want help with jobs that are best done solo, so I give Eric the heavy work and I do the light work. We have a communication code: When he's practicing his piano down in the basement and hears three staccato poundings on the floor up above, he comes running.

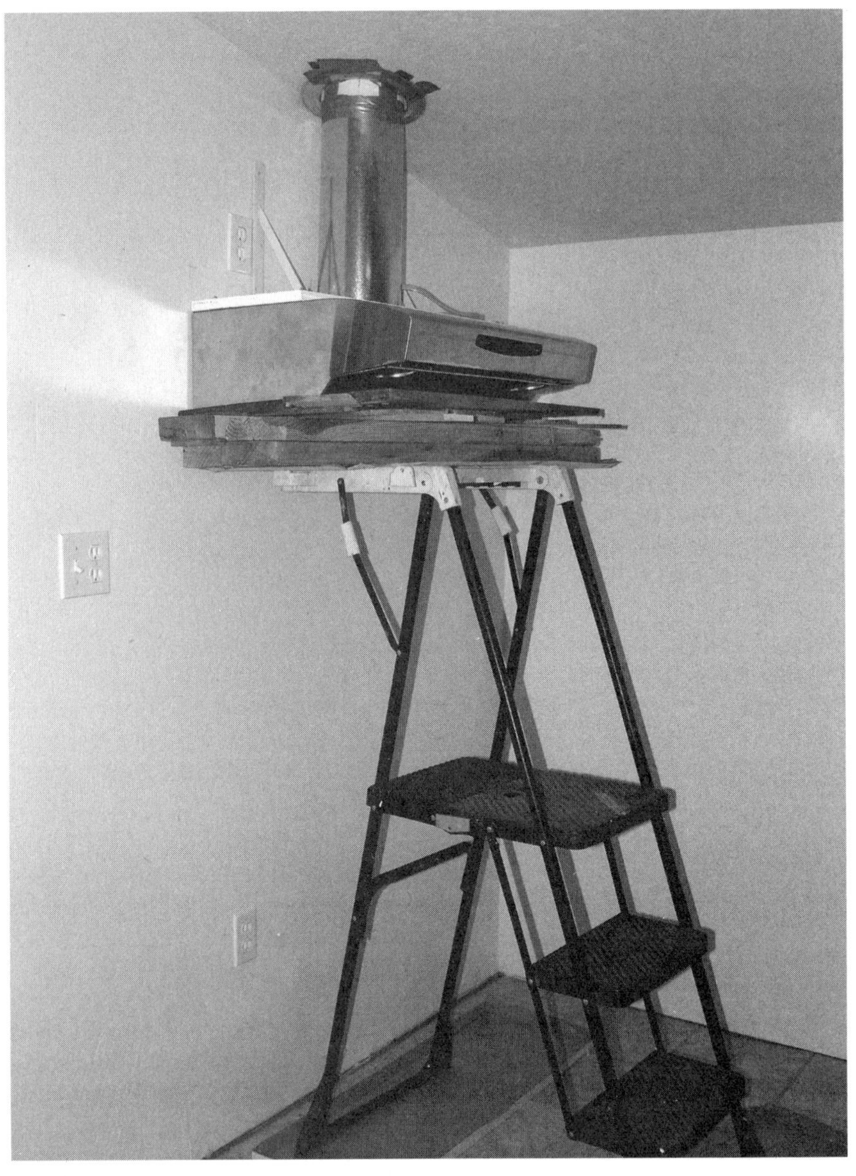

I used a stepladder and scrap wood to shim the exhaust hood to the right height to ease the hood pipe into the vent pipe in the ceiling.

wants to get out the hair dryer to heat up the glue and try to pry the GripStrip apart? Fortunately, I was so nervously careful in placing the tiles that I didn't have to resort to that trick of the trade.

The required procedure in laying this type of tile is to "stagger the joints." On alternate rows the wall-starter strip must have only two tiles in it instead of three, so one tile on the *left* side of the strip has to be cut off. Then the last tile in each row needs to be cut off wherever it ends up at the wall. There will be a lot of "scoring and snapping" going on, but make sure your utility knife is razor sharp or there will be a lot of "gnawing and haggling" going on.

I made the mistake of using a fine-tooth blade on my jigsaw to trim off one of the tiles, and every speck of vinyl that flew off landed right on the glue strip. I went right back to scoring and snapping!

It *is* true that the average person *can* do this — and I lived to tell about it — but I wouldn't say it's a piece of cake. To do a *perfect* job would require a perfect floor and factory-trained experts like you see in tutorials. That wasn't me, but I *was* able to do a darn *good* job.

I managed to get all three rooms done in record time, but only because I was a "maniac on the floor" like Jennifer Beals in "Flashdance." Well, not exactly. There's nothing exciting and glamorous about doing the duck-walk in Levi's, and there was no handsome guy in tights to pull me up and twirl me around.

Cabinets

After tiling all three rooms, I installed baseboard trim around their perimeters, and now I was hell-bent on getting the cabinets in. I heard that Lowe's carried unfinished oak cabinets and vanities for do-it-yourselfers for very reasonable prices. I climbed back in the old-mobile and it shook and shimmied me all the way to Lowe's, which was 20 miles away. Again, Eric was at work (*Somebody* has to pay for all this!) and again he gave me permission to run him into debt. If you can't trust your mother, who *can* you trust?

As soon as I saw the oak cabinets I knew he'd approve. They were fairly well made and best of all — affordable. I immediately spied one that was slightly damaged down low on the kick plate (easily replaced) so of course saw an opportunity to get a discount. It was the largest and costliest cabinet, the one we needed to hold the double sink, and the regular price was $200. The department manager said I could have it for $50. SOLD!

I had taken all the necessary measurements before going in so after deducting the length of the sink cabinet, I picked out a few others that would fit well together in the available space. When I asked for help loading them onto a giant flat cart, the manager took me on a detour to his desk where he entered my data into a computer software program and it immediately printed out a 3-D illustration of my kitchen to scale so I could easily visualize a workable cabinet arrangement and future appliances. It's a great customer service they provide and of course it boosts their sales. It worked so well on me that I was inspired to go ahead and buy a beautiful black and stainless steel gas range and matching hood I had my eye on that was on sale for 25% off ($500).

Before I was through I had run Eric's bill up to a grand total of $1000 — payable interest-free for an extended 18 month period. For only $60/month to Lowe's and $60/month to Home Depot, the kitchen and bathrooms would be basically complete and the final plumbing inspection *and* the final mechanical inspection (activated hood-fan) would be on time. Pay-as-you-go seemed to have up-and-went.

I am a big advocate of paying as you go but sometimes it's wiser to expedite progress by taking advantage of an exceptional opportunity. Interest-free loans on sale items were just too good to pass up, and the payments were within Eric's budget. If there's one thing I'm good at it's rationalizing.

I felt recklessly rich chugging home in my old pickup with the bed overflowing with cabinets and a stove. I marveled all the way home at what a great country we live in to be able to build such a nice house on sweat and promises alone.

Installing and leveling the cabinets (using shims) was not a difficult job, and finishing the oak surfaces was no work at all. I brushed on a couple of coats of a clear acrylic/polyurethane sealer called "Poly-Finish" by Ace. It's a water-based odorless mar-resistant satin finish and that's what Eric wanted in the kitchen and bathrooms — not the lingering fumes of a petroleum-based stain. He wanted to keep the wood grain light blond which would go nicely with the white walls, sandy-colored floor, and stainless steel appliances. When the sealer was dry I installed all the brushed-nickel cabinet pulls that match his decor and cost only $2 each.

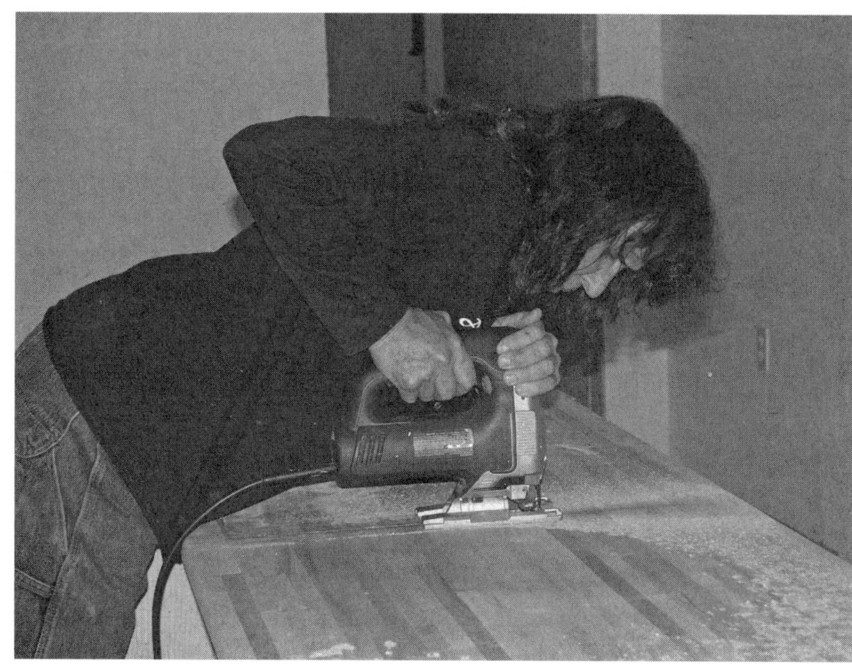

I cut out the sink hole in the butcher block drain board with a jigsaw.

Counter tops

Eric was working full time on a commercial soundtrack project so I continued to work on the kitchen by

The sink fit!

These heavy-duty brackets will support the butcher block counter

myself. The next step was to decide what kind of countertops and drain boards to use. I had heard that Lumber Liquidators stocked 8-foot-long hard-rock maple butcher-block countertops for $199 each. I decided to check them out on the internet.

When a photo of the butcher-blocks came up on Lumber Liquidator's home page, it was love at first sight, and without hesitation I ordered not just one, but *three* of them! So, again, while Eric was at his piano keyboard making money, I was at my computer keyboard spending money. But this time I paid the bill myself and informed Eric that 24 lineal feet of counter space would be his Christmas *and* birthday presents for the next three years. We both knew it was a lie, but that's the kind of thing a mother says when she wants to give a guilt-free gift.

They arrived by truck a week later and were exactly as I expected: Gorgeous! I couldn't wait to attack the project, but first I had to mount the range hood to the wall and connect it to its existing ceiling duct, then slide the range in place under it, perfectly centered. The range hood installation was *not* an easy job, but I had to grit my teeth and just do it. It was the last fan to hook up so I could get the *final* mechanical inspection signed off.

Now I was ready to get started on what I really wanted to do. I set the first countertop on saw horses and trimmed a few inches off to the exact length needed for the drain board, and then traced around the top-mount stainless steel sink and cut out the sink hole with a jigsaw.

Note: The sink-hole has to be marked extremely accurately or the sink could fall through, depending on whether it's a top-mount with a lip or an under-mount style.

I hefted the sink board over to the row of cabinets and set it on. I squared it up, made sure it was level along its length and width, then fastened it from underneath, screwing up through special holes in plastic reinforced corner tabs provided on each cabinet. I then trimmed up and used the sink hole scrap for a small butcher block to the right of the range.

Next I leveraged the second 8-foot countertop down flat on the floor on top of four 2x4 "stickers" (spacers). I had placed one at each end and one on either side of the cross-cut I was going to make in the middle, so there would be no binding of the blade. I cut the slab in half with a sharp new circular saw blade and with the help of a guide clamped to the block so I couldn't waver.

I used one 4-foot section of it for the top of a roll-around butcher-block island Eric had, and butted the other 4-foot section up against the third and final 8-footer, to create a 12-foot countertop along the east wall. I would join the seam later with a stainless steel T-strip.

The internet is a gold mine for DIY instructions, so simply google: "installing sink drains" (or whatever else you are doing yourself) and click on various websites that show exactly how to do the job with accompanying photos and tutorials. Hammerzone.com was my favorite.

I matched up the center of the counter length with the center of the 4-foot window, and drew a line on the wall at exactly the right height (36 inches) to be able to sit on a 2-foot stool and sip coffee and enjoy the view. I attached reinforced white brackets to support the 110-pound-each butcher blocks by lag-screwing them to the wall studs at 16-inch centers along that line. All the space under the countertop is free and clear so there will be no toe-stubbing in Eric's kitchen.

I rounded the corners on the countertop by first marking the curve with a large lid template, then cut the curve with a jigsaw and sanded it smooth. While the sander was still going I ran it along the sharp leading edge of the counter to bevel it a tad.

When the countertop job was completely done, I wiped on several coats of plain mineral oil, at 4-hour intervals, to bring out the colorful grain of the hard rock maple, and ooohed and aaahed with every application. Eric and I are both in love with the look, and we both think a house just can't have enough flat surfaces to pile stuff on.

Plumbing fixtures

I installed and plumbed the sink, toilets, and basins with standard plastic pipe drain kits and traps and hooked up the water supply lines with their required angle-valves (shutoffs). All the parts were available at the hardware store, and fairly inexpensive. Then I rigged up the shower fixture so it could be tested, even though I hadn't tiled the stall yet. Next I hooked up the hot water heater in the basement and installed the mandatory earthquake straps around it.

At long last I called for the final inspection and happily passed all the faucet and flushing tests, with water coming in and going out everywhere it should and not a drop where it shouldn't. The only thing I had forgotten was to put a bead of silicone seal around the base of each toilet, and I promised the inspector on Girl Scout's honor I would do it — and, bless his trusting soul, he signed me off.

The finished kitchen (sans refrigerator)

That night I celebrated by breaking out a miniature Coronita beer that had been in my refrigerator for a year, and had myself a little party.

Closing thoughts

There are 16 preliminary inspections and four finals listed on our big yellow "job card" issued by the county along with our building permit. We've passed all 16 preliminary inspections plus 3 of the finals (electrical, plumbing, and mechanical), but now have the *final final* to go. That's when they examine the entire building, and it's a biggie.

Before they will issue a "Certificate of Occupancy" we have a lot more major work to do. But then, after our final approval, we can take our time to finish up everything else, including floor coverings and awnings, and be able to pay for them as we go.

The inspector said that the interior doors can wait, except for the bathroom doors, which *have* to be in. The flooring, such as carpet or hardwood, can wait. The front and back entrances have to have stairs and safety railings, the wood stove has to be hooked up, and the siding has to be on the house. Roof venting must be done at the ridge and the eaves, and that's it.

We figure we can accomplish all that within a year — by 2012 — but it'll take yet another year to do all the cosmetic work and finishing touches that turn a house into a home. Eric's crowning glory will be moving his 9-foot grand piano from the basement into its final resting place in the living room.

Knowing Eric, at some point in his housewarming party, he'll don his Bach wig, play a Baroque fugue, take a deep bow, and the wig will fly off. After six years of building, a little slapstick will be refreshing, but hopefully this housewarming party won't be as HOT as the last one! (See "Out of the ashes" Issue #38, March/April 1996, available to read online for free at www.backwoodshome.com.) Δ

Medicating your cattle

By Melissa Nelson

As a cattle owner, eventually you will be faced with having to administer medicine to your animal. It can be scary when facing a thousand-pound beast and being expected to pop a pill down its throat or jab it with a needle. Even if you're against antibiotic use in your cattle, the wise owner will vaccinate their cattle against common diseases, so at some point or another you'll have to take the plunge and confront the task.

To save on veterinary expenses, or in places where livestock veterinarians are scarce, you can learn the basics in delivering medications and vaccines to your cattle. While some methods of administering medicine are fairly simple and easy to grasp, other methods are more difficult and best left to trained personnel to prevent injury to the animal.

Before you begin to treat your cow or steer, it is vitally important that safety takes precedence over treatment and that you know the temperament of your animal. If you are unable to handle your animal safely, let a more experienced person treat it. It is unwise for the average person without a strong, secure chute and plenty of experience to examine or treat bulls. They are too unpredictable and strong to handle safely. If your animal is docile and trained to a halter or you have a chute with a securely mounted head gate, proceed with caution as you secure it with a halter to a sturdy post or catch it in the head gate.

Cattle medication comes in many forms. There are oral medications such as pills, drenches, gels, and pastes. Injections can be given in the muscle or under the skin. Medicines such as antiparasitics (dewormers) can be poured directly onto the skin on the back to be absorbed. Some antibiotics and various types of fluids can be given directly into a vein, and medicine can be infused into the mammary glands via the teat canal.

Once the type of medication and route of administration is decided upon, you'll need to assemble the equipment needed to treat the cow. Oral treatments are administered via balling gun, mouth speculum, drench bottles, or gel or paste tubes. The gels or pastes come in tubes similar in shape to a caulking tube and are delivered into the mouth through the use of a caulking gun. Always have a bucket of warm water to lubricate the tools you are using.

You may have to loosen the halter or use a nose lead to relieve the constriction of the halter around the mouth so the animal can open its mouth for you. Standing to one side

Author's cattle herd on pasture

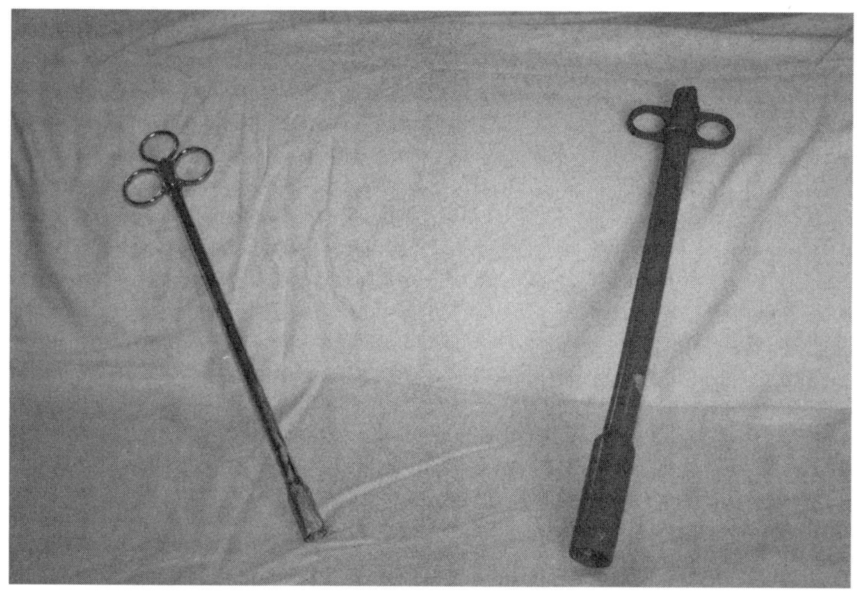

Two different style balling guns

of the animal, slowly reach over the head with your less dominant hand and grasp the edge of the lower jaw with your hand. Hold the head tightly to your body while you brace your feet at least a shoulder's width apart. Holding tightly to the animal's head will prevent her from swinging her head if she tries to butt you.

Advance the hand holding the jaw towards the mouth and place your hand between the lips right behind the lower incisors. There is a smooth gap between the teeth in front of the jaw and the molars in the back of the jaw. Pressing on the roof of the mouth will cause the animal to open its mouth. Gently introduce the balling gun or mouth speculum into the mouth and direct it towards the back of the throat. When you reach resistance, stop and administer the medicine. You can injure the animal's throat or roof of the mouth if you exert too much force in inserting the instrument.

Drench bottles or gel or paste tubes can be placed in the corner of the mouth in the gap between the teeth. The medicine then can slowly be squeezed from the bottle or tube. Allow the animal to swallow the medicine after a generous dose has been given. It may take two to three tries before the animal will swallow the entire dose. If you hold the head straight forward and parallel with the ground it will make administering oral treatments more successful.

Oral medications can also be given via a stomach tube which goes through the oral cavity, down the esophagus, and directly into the stomach. This is a much more complicated procedure and is best demonstrated before any attempt is made to treat an animal in this fashion.

Many medications are administered to cattle via injections. Antibiotics, vaccinations, anti-inflammatories, reproductive medications, vitamins, and calcium are all examples of medications given via needle into the muscle or under the skin. Read the medicine labels carefully to determine the route of administration or consult your animal care provider if you have questions. For muscle or skin injections you will need to assemble isopropyl rubbing alcohol, cotton balls, the medication, appropriate-sized needles, and syringes.

On full-grown cattle, a 16-gauge needle of 1 to 1½-inch length are needed for thick liquids, while an 18-gauge needle of the same length is appropriate for thinner liquids. Use shorter needles for subcutaneous (under the skin) injections and longer needles for intramuscular treatments.

Proper restraint and control of the animal is imperative with injections. With beef quality goals in mind, slaughterhouses prefer that cattle

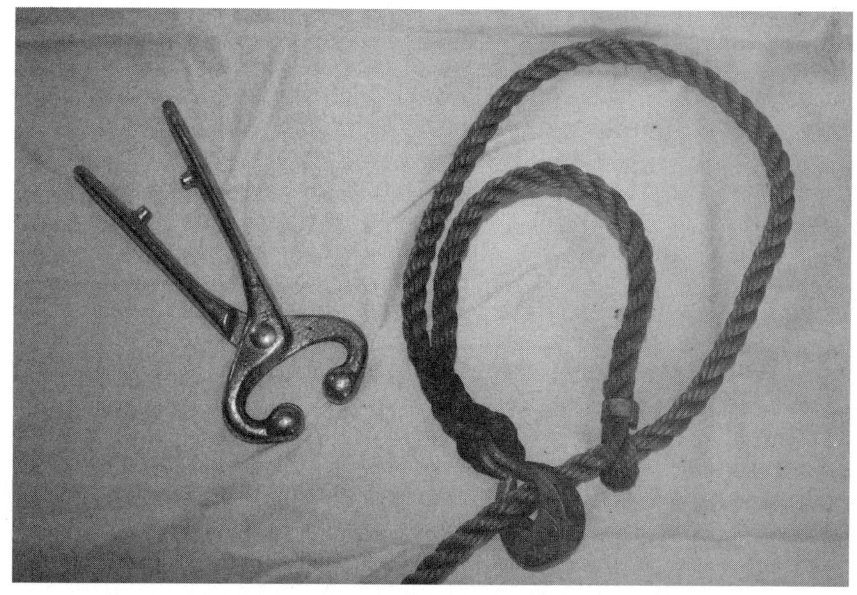

A nose lead and a halter with a quick-release honda (an important safety feature in a halter)

injections be given in the neck, about midway between the head and the front leg and in the middle third of the neck. Cattle can also be injected in the caudal thigh muscles, provided you can protect yourself from being kicked. Sometimes tail restraint, or tail jacking, can be used by a second person to add a little extra security. The tail is held near the base and is held straight up. Be careful not to put too much pressure on the tail as you can damage the nerves and muscles.

Once you have determined your injection site (an area free of manure and moisture) swab the area with isopropyl alcohol. Remove the needle from the syringe and remove the cap. Hold the needle by the hub with the thumb and forefinger and slap the area to be injected with the back of the hand and then quickly turn your hand and slap the needle into the selected site. Check that no blood appears in the hub. If blood appears, repeat the needle stick at a different site to avoid injecting the medication into the blood stream, which can be deadly. Attach the syringe to the needle and inject the medication. Up to 20 ccs of medication can be injected into one site in adult cattle. Subcutaneous injections of certain medications and some calcium solutions can be given in the loose skin in the neck in front of the front legs or in the loose skin in the chest area on the side of the cow behind the front legs. Safely secure the animal and prepare the site as above. Then insert the needle into the skin almost parallel to the body until it pops through the inner side of the hide. Up to 125 ccs of calcium solution can be given under the skin in this manner. For thicker medications, no more than 30-35 ccs should be given in one spot. Never inject irritating drugs or dextrose-containing solutions under the skin. Abscesses, cellulitis, or skin sloughing can occur in these cases.

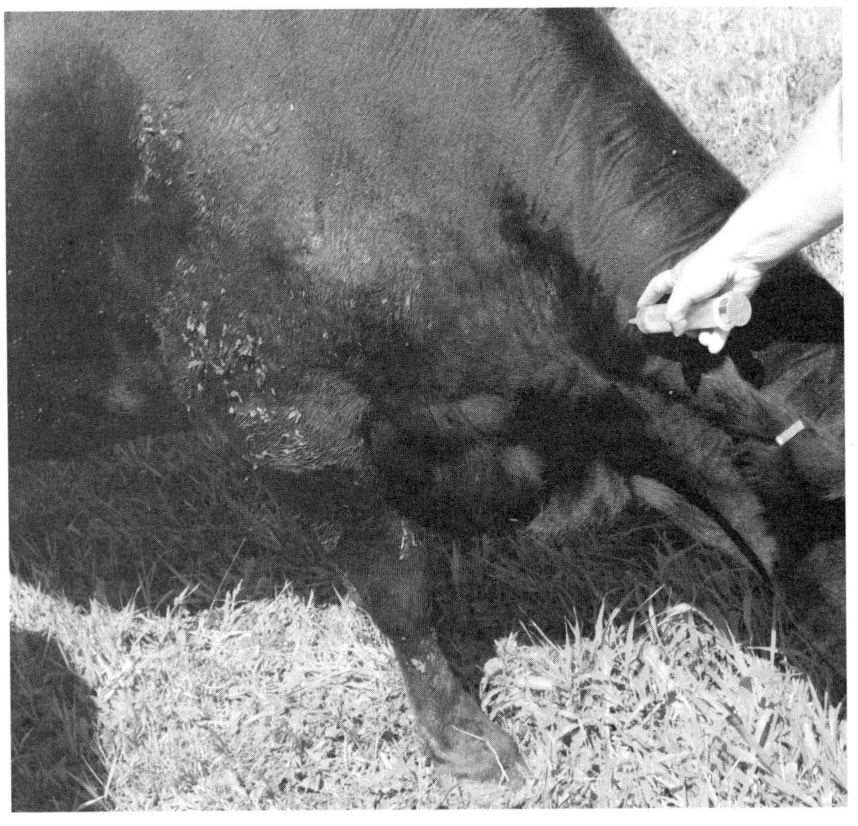

This photo shows the area on a cow's neck where an intramuscular injection can be given.

Many medications can also be given directly in the vein, but that is best learned by direct observation due to the danger of causing bleeding from an injured vein and the possibility of injecting medicine directly into the neck artery.

There are other routes of medicating cattle that the average cattle owner can tackle. Deworming medication and lice control have been conveniently formulated in a pour-on, which is, as the name suggests, poured along the top of the animal's back. Nothing could be easier, as long as you follow directions closely. Usually you will need to do this on a dry day and keep the animal dry for up to 24 hours after treatment to prevent the solution from washing off the skin.

Some cows develop mastitis, or an infection in their udders. Special mastitis tubes are widely available. These are tubes containing antibiotics with a special tapered end which inserts easily into the canal of the teat. It is imperative that the teat and the end of the teat be washed free of dirt, manure, and other foreign matter and the end of the teat repeatedly swabbed with alcohol before inserting the tube into the teat canal. Again, the cow will need to be restrained.

If the cow is not used to human handling of her teats, it is wise to have a second person perform tail restraint on the cow while you clean the teat and insert the tube end into the teat opening at the tip of the teat. After inserting the tube end, the plunger on the end of the tube is slowly pushed, in allowing the medicine to enter the teat canal.

Keeping a healthy herd begins with an educated owner. If you keep safety paramount, properly restrain your cow, and take your time, you can treat your own cattle, saving you both time and money. Δ

Is that a good pig?

By Kim Dieter

Lean ham, roasts, chops, savory sausage, and thick slices of bacon are the reason pigs are raised at home. A typical meat pig weighs 200 to 270 pounds and reaches that weight at five to six months of age. Because raising pigs requires time and feed resources, it is important to begin the enterprise with good quality, fast-growing pigs.

A desirable pig has a long body and deep sides. The side should be long and so should the length of the pig from head to tail. The pig should be meaty with bulging muscles in the shoulders and the ham (rear). Don't select a pig with heavy muscling in the shoulder and light muscling in the ham because the more valuable cuts of meat come from the rear of the pig. The loin (down the back) should be thick and wide. When viewed from the rear, the thickest part of the ham should be about two-thirds the distance from the top of the pig. Avoid pigs that are wide through the top of the ham but narrow through the lower part. Two additional indicators of muscling are the width of the chest, when viewed from the front, and the width between the hind legs, when viewed from the rear. A heavily muscled pig stands wide, both front and rear.

A desirable pig is a lean pig. Check the belly and jowl (under the chin) of the pig. They should be trim, not flabby. A desirable pig should be structurally sound. The pig should walk easily and freely with no signs of lameness or stiffness.

Young pigs are usually weaned from the sows at six to eight weeks of age and this is an age at which many meat pigs are purchased. Select a weaner pig that is long and thick. If a 40-pound weaner pig is purchased, the pig will need to gain two pounds per day to reach market weight at five to six months of age. If possible, check out the sow and boar that produced the litter. Do parents have desirable conformation? Talk to the breeder about the potential growth rate of the pigs. Did previous litters reach the desired market weight in five to six months? Did the pigs gain two or more pounds per day while on feed?

There are several popular swine breeds and individuals from any of the breeds have the potential to make a superior meat product. The white, erect-eared Yorkshire, the red-colored Duroc, the white, large-eared Landrace, and the white-striped, black Hampshire are four of these breeds. Often good meat pigs are crosses of these breeds.

If money is an issue, talk with a breeder and ask if any young "runt" pigs are available. There are often one or more small pigs in a litter. These pigs may require round-the-clock milk feeding until they eat solid food (four or more weeks of age). But some breeders will give these small pigs to someone who will take good care of them. If they have good genetics from the sow and boar, they will usually catch up in size with their larger littermates.

Healthy pigs are a necessity for a successful meat-raising enterprise. Consult a local veterinarian or county extension agent about common pig diseases found in your local area. Select a pig from a breeder with a sound health care program. Avoid a pig with a runny nose or other respiratory problems, diarrhea, or a pig that doesn't look thrifty.

If a pig is destined to be a breeding sow or boar, additional characteristics should be considered. Commonly, gilts (young females) and boars are used for breeding when eight months old. The gilts will have their first litter at a year of age. Check the underline of the pig. There should be two rows of six or more functional teats. It is especially important to watch the pigs walk. Avoid a pig with excessively straight legs, crooked legs, or an unusual gait, because that pig may not have a long, productive life. Since you will be working with the pig every day, select one with a good temperament.

With careful observation and a background check, desirable, fast-growing, and healthy pigs can be selected and the pigs will be "good pigs." Δ

A desirable 200-pound, 5-month-old Yorkshire and Hampshire crossbred hog

A homesteader's journal PART 1

By Dani Payne

This is a two-part series, the journal of Dani Payne as she, her boyfriend, his daughter, and a roommate made the move from Kansas to the Ozark foothills of northeastern Oklahoma where they would encounter scorpions, tarantulas, copperheads, unwelcomed visitors, wildfires, storms, floods, power outages; they would lose animals and suffer injury and unbelievably cold winters that would test their mettle. But they also began building, made repairs, fashioned labor-saving tools, built animal shelters, and planted a garden as they set out to make a new home for themselves.

We finally did it—made the move to a rural area. There were four of us: A roommate, my boyfriend, his 15-year-old daughter, and me. My boyfriend and I had been offered a job in northeast Oklahoma working in a machine shop. The two of us and our roommate drove to the area to scout out a place to live. The area is beautiful — Ozark foothills. While driving, we saw a huge hairy spider in the middle of the highway — a woodland tarantula, according to the locals. It was as big as a saucer and raised up on its legs as if to challenge the truck.

We used to listen to a radio show back in Kansas called *Coast to Coast* and heard a story about a trucker who reported a "Bigfoot" sighting on scenic Highway 412 near where we had driven. What on earth must be going on there in Oklahoma?

On that first search, we visited a beautiful 10 acres with a loft home. The place was so remote we had to drive across someone else's property just to get to it. We all knew what ticks were, but none of us had ever heard of seed ticks. These are tiny little critters that look like pepper, only reddish brown. They latch on just like an adult tick, and there were thousands of them. I started wondering what we were getting into. Tarantulas? Bigfoot? Seed ticks?

Our next scouting mission was conducted by a real estate agent who did the driving. We looked at several different places and finally settled on "the one." It's not primitive, just remote. It has all the amenities of the rat race — running water, electricity, modern appliances — with the bills to match, but at least it's out in the middle of nowhere. Thirty acres of Ozark foothills, part timber, part pasture. A book by Wilson Rawls, called *Where the Red Fern Grows,* was set a couple of towns over from here, and the gorgeous terrain is much the same.

The guys and the teen daughter moved in. I had to wait another few months in order to complete my 15th year at the old job in Kansas and also for preparations to be made to bring animals to the new place. Fencing for dogs and a shed and more fencing for horses was necessary.

A hiccup

When the day finally arrived, I loaded up our last few belongings and drove to Oklahoma. Upon arrival, I found that my government-issued Kansas ID was not honored in town. I could not open a bank account, write a check, or do any kind of business. Apparently, these folks only do business with locals; they wouldn't even accept a cashier's check.

Luckily, I had enough gasoline in the tank to drive on to a bigger town. All business was conducted there, an hour from the house, until I could establish "local" status.

A couple of quiet months passed. My boyfriend and I were working lots of overtime. Teen girl was doing well in school with straight As. Roommate was settling in nicely. He is partially disabled from a prior injury on the job.

Peace and quiet comes to an end

All of a sudden the quiet was shattered one evening. A vehicle came creeping up the driveway after dark with the lights off. We shined a spotlight on it, and the driver went crazy. He drove through the chain link fence and the horse fence trying to get turned around, then hightailed it out of here, spinning tires all the way.

The horses, curious critters that they are, spotted the downed fence immediately. Task number one was to patch the fence in the dark to keep the horses in, then task number two was to call the police like urban folks do.

This far out, police response takes awhile. By the time an officer arrived, they'd already found the truck a few miles away with the engine still running and the doors open. No sign of the driver, but the truck had been reported stolen from Tulsa, an hour and a half away. We found a few items that had spilled from the truck in our yard. A one dollar bill, a penny, and a playing card. Ten of hearts. Had we been "marked?" Perhaps we watched too much TV in those days because nothing more was ever heard about it.

Wildfires

Things settled down again, but not for long. A drought that year had taken a heavy toll, and wildfires began to break out all over. We could see the orange glow of them occasionally, but one of them approached a bit too close for comfort one night. It was about a half mile from the house. We got all the hoses and sprinklers out and got all of them going in the yard, even though it might be of no more effect than spitting on a volcano. My boyfriend got the lawnmower out and began expanding a "firebreak" while I checked the "git and split" bags and packed up dog supplies and other items in case we had to evacuate.

Fortunately, a fellow down the road who worked for the forestry department joined the firefighter crew with his heavy equipment. Those guys were right in the thick of the fire with their trucks and the forestry guy's 'dozer. Those men worked valiantly in the heat and the smoke and they did eventually get the fire under control. Hats off to those brave and gallant individuals.

No rest for them, though. There were more fires to put out. Come to find out later, many of these fires were intentionally set.

Deer and other neighbors

Peace and quiet soon returned. Sometimes we sat on the front porch and watched the deer come up in the yard. They seemed quite unafraid. The locals say that once deer season opens, they disappear and you won't see them again until spring. Sure enough, they were right. It seemed strange with the herd suddenly gone.

Straw bale dog houses

Meanwhile, we were hearing lots of activity from the next place down the road. Lots of traffic, shouting, and other commotion. Turns out, people were bringing all kinds of throwaway items to deposit there. This went on for some time, but the folks who lived there were finally evicted for nonpayment. Unfortunately, they left all their trash behind. Their 20 acres is adjacent to ours, so we decided to try to make a bid for the place. When we drove up, the owner had a 'dozer in there pushing all the trash over the ledge into a seasonal wash (excess water runoff). Kitchen stoves, refrigerators, air conditioners, car parts, couches, beds, chairs, toys, and all manner of home furnishings — mountains of the stuff going into the wash. The owner just wanted it gone so he could sell the place, but we live downstream. All that garbage washes down on us. We cashed in everything we had and put a down payment on the place if only to get the 'dozer to stop pushing trash off into the seasonal creek.

Afterwards we set fire to the rest of the trash but most of the damage was done. Even after several years, we still get garbage washing up after a good rain. Last time, it was a mattress, a commode, a cooler, some curtains, bedding, rotten 2x4 boards, cushions, sheet metal, and part of a tricycle. But, at least the "trash people," as the locals called them, were gone and not adding more to the dumping ground.

Building with straw bales

The weather was getting cooler and it was time to prepare for winter. The dogs all had store-bought doghouses, but they didn't much care for them. I decided to build them a straw bale structure based on an article in *BHM* (Issue #76, July/August 2002). Since this was a much smaller structure than the house in the article, I used lighter, more available materials. For example, we had ⅜-inch rebar electric fence posts to use instead of buying ⅝-inch rebar. Since this would be only three bales high, I figured it would hold. I placed 2x6 lumber under the bales to keep them above the moist ground, one at each side of each bale. When I attempted to pound the rebar through the bales and between the 2x6s, I forgot to account for the rocky ground. I needed a bigger sledge hammer. Oh boy, did I

Homemade hay bale spear

need a bigger hammer. Plans changed after the first layer. The second and third were pinned with smooth rod instead of rebar. Much, much easier. This whole thing was constructed under one of those cheap carport things, so no mudding or adobe was necessary. It was very quiet inside, very warm in winter, and cool in summer.

Copperheads & tarantulas

The copperheads made their appearance. There was a mating pair right on the doorstep, and when approached, the snakes became aggressive, leaving us no choice but to eliminate them.

Later on in the fall, the tarantulas began to migrate. Where they go, I don't know, but they are quite impressive to observe when on the move.

In the late fall, one of the horses started losing condition. The mare was pretty old — 45 or 46 years old, best guess. She'd lie down, then not be able to get up. I thought, perhaps, the muscles on her "down" side might be "asleep," so against all recommendations by the veterinarian, we'd roll her over to her other side. She could then get up on her own. The vet did not condone this, based on the risk of "twisted gut" but for this mare, it worked for about two years. Eventually, though, old age got the best of her. We lost her late that fall.

Due to the rocky ground, I hired a heavy equipment operator to dig the grave. Even with his big machine, he couldn't get very deep, so we collected stones to pile atop the grave. The hay crew mowed over them the following season, so we keep it mowed low all around now. Wouldn't be the last time I cussed at rocks.

Unexpected bounty

As fall drew to a close, we found ourselves again at the 20 acres next door where the "trash people" had grown a garden. There were late tomatoes of some sort and winter squash as big as watermelons. I don't know what kind they were, but they made excellent pie and the soup wasn't bad either. They tasted a bit like pumpkin, but better. They were the size and shape of a watermelon with dark green, very tough skin. Even a hacksaw wouldn't cut through without cooking them first. The flesh is orange, pungent, and pumpkin-like. The seed cavity is fairly small, but with lots of seeds. These seeds do not reproduce the parent plant so it must be a hybrid of some sort. Wish I knew what it was. I'd sure grow it again.

Surprise visitors

As the snow flew during winter, my boyfriend and I continued to work long overtime shifts, while also keeping up with woodcutting, fencing, horse maintenance, and other chores. One morning we saw that someone's cattle had escaped from home and wandered up our driveway. There's a fence on either side and a gate at the end. Our roommate walked out to the gate to "encourage" them to turn around and go back the way they came in. The bull had other ideas. He rushed the gate, rushed the fence on both sides, and got the rest of the herd stirred up. We're not exactly cow savvy, so I figured I'd just leave them alone for awhile. Sooner or later, they'd calm down and move on. Better that, than have the fences torn up or someone hurt.

Can you imagine calling in to work because someone's belligerent bull is blocking your drive? That's exactly what we did.

The herd did settle down after a little while, then moved back out to the road. Now the question was, "Where do these cattle belong?" Our roommate drove around the section and finally located the farmer. We found where the farmer's fence was down, and got it fixed while the farmer and our roommate got those cattle back home. We were a couple hours late for work, and I don't know whether they believed our "excuse" or not, but that's what really happened, no lie.

Homemade bale spear

A short time later, my boyfriend came up with an idea to make moving round hay bales easier. The old way was to pound an oil field rod through the center of the bale, attach a chain to the rod on both sides, then attach the chain to the truck and drag the bale. This often damaged the strings on the bottom and resulted in quantities of hay scattered along the path of travel.

He decided to build a bale spear for the pickup, so he could lift the bale off the ground for transport. Money was pretty scarce, so he bartered for materials and machine time at work and enlisted a little help after hours to construct it and mount it to the truck.

The contraption consisted of a rectangular steel frame that was bolted to the truck frame. A spear and counterpull apparatus was welded up to make one piece, and was mounted to the basic frame. A pulling ring was bolted to the truck bed so he could attach a come-along between the ring and counterpull. The contraption functions just like a store-bought unit. Lower the counterpull until the spear is parallel to the ground. Back the truck up to the bale and push the spear into the bale. Use the come-along to lift the bale off the ground, and drive away. Works great. You have to get out of the driver's seat and up into the bed of the truck to raise the bale, then again to lower it, but it's a huge improvement over the old way.

Fishing fever and loss of a small friend

As winter rolled into spring, fishing fever struck. I've not been bitten by this bug myself, but many others have been, including my boyfriend. Around here in spring, it's spoonbills. I'd never heard of them before, but fishing for them sure is a craze here. Seems like every waking moment not occupied by work is spent at the river. I don't quite get it. For such a large fish, there's only a small amount of meat and sometimes some roe. I guess these guys (and gals) love the sport of it.

Meanwhile back at the ranch, with all the fishing, the overtime, and extracurricular activities at school, the smallest member of our canine companions had fallen into a state of grooming need. The dog belonged to the teen girl, who was battling migraine headaches at the time, so she took the dog to the vet who had a groomer on staff.

A call came for the girl a couple of hours later. The little dog was dead. They said she had just died on the table for some reason unknown to them. Talk about an uproar in the house. She'd had this little dog all her life. She and her dad picked up the dog from the vet's office and brought her home for burial. They had gone ahead and finished the grooming. She was buried out back. She wouldn't be the last.

Taxes and trimming

We received our tax due notice on the 20 acres next door and, boy, were we floored. Taxes last year were $14 and some change. This year they want $460. I made an appointment at the courthouse to protest, to no avail. They knocked off $10 out of "the kindness of their hearts" and I walked out of the place wanting to spit on their sidewalk.

I just couldn't understand such a huge increase. Double or triple maybe, but this was unfathomable. We had made no improvements whatsoever. No electric, no well, no nothing. We put in excessive overtime at work to satisfy our tax-happy government.

With all this overtime required, other things fell behind. The "down front" of our property became overgrown with weeds, tall grass, and small trees of the oak variety. The folks that used to own this place would bush hog it down, but no such luck for us. We didn't have a tractor and bush hog and had no money left to hire it done, thanks to the tax man. I went out there with one of those little string trimmers on wheels and a pair of pruning shears. Took me 2½ days and I wound up with a nasty case of poison oak. I'd never been allergic to poison plants before, so I was quite surprised. I also stepped on a copperhead snake in the process. Thank goodness the mower ran over it first.

A new member and more government B.S.

Our roommate's brother asked to stay with us for a while after being hurt on the job. He'd suffered an injury while transporting horses and needed somewhere to recuperate while going through the worker's compensation rigamarole. He had a 5th wheel that he lived in and brought it to our place. He shared the electricity and water and all. Always paid a share to cover. Wasn't long before he was one of us.

Our roommate had been battling with Social Security disability for a couple of years by this time and finally, with a lawyer's help, he succeeded. With his settlement, he would buy a 4WD tractor with a front loader, bush hog, and back blade. Work that used to take days could now be done quickly and efficiently. Also, that year, my tax return was larger than expected and we bought a DR® brush chipper. Another efficient machine. There is a huge benefit in ganging up together on bills, home, and large equipment, rather than each one trying to go it alone. I know that not everyone can live this way, but it works for us, and so much more can be accomplished.

Snakes and sand plums

One of the dogs lit up one evening, creating a ruckus in which all six dogs joined. Upon investigation, we found that there was a copperhead right up by the house. Trying to get those dogs called off was like trying to stop a mob after a riot has begun. Finally, though, all the dogs were collected and put in the house. My boyfriend dispatched the snake with a throwing knife. The throw impressed

"Step over" for the garden fence

all the rest of us. First throw — clean kill.

Summer heat continued. While driving along the "upper 20" I saw something that looked suspiciously like the sand plums I used to see back in Kansas. I don't know what the locals call them, but I get the feeling they don't think they are fit to eat. Granted, they are quite bitter off the tree, but they make the best jelly.

We picked and picked and by the end of the season we had about 40 pints of the jelly. I've been giving the jelly away for Christmas and birthdays since then and folks really seem to like it. Must have been a good year for them, because they haven't produced a thing for the last three years.

Scorpions and cancer

Dog days were in full swing. We started to see scorpions. They were everywhere. Not the big black ones like in the desert southwest, but small brown ones. They are about an inch and a half long and blend right in with the color of the dirt. Their sting is not fatal, but, believe me, you know it when one "gotcha." They were on the porch, in the house, in the garage. One was hiding in the weedeater vent — boy, was that a surprise.

As the weather cooled, the scorpions retreated, we waited for wildfires, idiot pickup drivers, etc., but it stayed fairly quiet. Well, until the snow fell. One of the dogs had been fighting cancer under the radar. Once his symptoms appeared, it was too late. We had to have him euthanized. The only thing worse than digging a grave in rocks is digging in *frozen* rocks with a foot of snow on top. Just like with the horse last year, we had to collect stones to go on top of the grave, because we just could not dig deep enough. There are big boulders and shelf rock about two feet down in that location. We still keep it mowed in summer so the hay crew won't damage their equipment.

Ice storm and generators

December folded into January. The weather turned. Sleet began, then icy rain cut in. It kept going and going. Next day, my boyfriend and I went slowly and carefully to work. The roads were already treacherous and by the end of the shift, even 20 mph was too fast. This is hill country with lots of curves and hairpin turns. There are no guard rails or shoulders. It was still icy in the morning. We tried to get out for work, but could not. The hill at the end of the drive was too much. Even our 4WD couldn't do it. We had to call in to work. The power went out shortly after that. All the motels filled to capacity and folks were going to friend's homes where power was still on. Not us, we had wood for heat, hurricane lamps for light, and a hand crank radio. Water was the hard part since we are on a well. In the mid-morning, it warmed up just enough that the ice on the roof started to melt. Every pot, pan, kettle, trash can, and bucket was set out under the drip line. Towards noon the sun went over the house and the melting ice refroze. We brought the containers into the house. Two empty buckets were reserved to chop ice out of the horse's water tanks. They were then brought indoors to thaw, and returned to the tank next day, only to chop out more ice for the next day's water. Also, I chopped ice out of the pond to thaw for flushing toilets. It wasn't solid ice though and I broke through twice. Even with all the ice coming indoors to thaw, it wasn't enough. As soon as we could get out, we brought in several 5-gallon containers of bottled water for cooking and drinking.

The teen daughter went to stay with friends who had a generator after day two. Too primitive, I suppose. The dogs, however, were ecstatic. They all got to come indoors and were delighted. These are *not* small dogs, by the way. They range in weight from 70 lbs. to 190 lbs. Fun times with the dogs even though there was no electricity or running water.

We finally got back to work after day three. We were late that day because the frozen food from our freezer was close to thawing, so we decided to donate all the frozen items to a shelter. Temps outside were fluctuating, getting into the 20s and low 30s during the daytime, so outside storage was not an option.

Our roommate's brother bought a generator for his 5th wheel. The thing was pretty noisy, but at least he had lights, TV, cooking, heater, and news. It wasn't big enough to run a 220 volt deep well pump so water was still scarce. Generators sold out by the end of that day.

Next day, on our way to work, we saw folks selling generators, chainsaws, etc. out of trucks and trailers by the roadside (making quite a profit for themselves). They were bringing them in from out of state and charging exorbitant prices for them.

We had an old Lehman's catalog lying around and decided to dip into savings and buy an Aladdin lamp. After ordering by "snail mail" we still received the lamp days before the power was restored.

This all came to an end though as the electric crews got the power restored. Our house is the last one on our circuit, so we knew it would be a while before they got to us. They had crews here from all over. The guys who cleared our lines were from Louisiana and at the end of the eleventh day we were back on the grid. Kudos to them and to all the other crews.

Having the power back on was a little strange at first. All the little noises that modern appliances make seemed to be a cacophony. Doesn't take long to get used to it again though, and boy howdy, *did somebody say hot shower?* What a treat that was.

The ice finally melted and the damaged trees were cleared. Spring finally showed. I started a garden using Wallo' Waters after reading a *BHM* article by Jackie Clay. Good thing, too, because we had a very late freeze. Temps dropped to low 20s. There would be no strawberries, blackberries, sand plums, peaches, etc. this year. The blooms and leaves blackened and died. The Wallo' Waters did their magic and the tomatoes and peppers grew right through it all.

Two labor-saving devices

Our garden was situated outside the dog fence (no digging, no poop, etc.) so you have to either climb the dog fence and then the horse fence or go the long way around. My boyfriend had by this time blown a couple of discs in his back, so fence climbing was out of the question. He decided to make a "step over" for the fence. He had a small supply of oil field pipe that he'd been using to make corners for fencing and decided to build the step out of the same material. He welded up a simple "A" frame about seven feet tall, then welded crosspieces to make a sort of ladder. One side is inside the fence, the other on the outside. A few steps up and then a few steps back down and, presto, you are on the other side.

Another thing became difficult for the big guy, and that was picking up logs from ground level and lifting them to the log splitter, not to mention bending over them while splitting. He thought, "Why not raise

Log splitter on a riser

Hoist and tong installed in pickup to assist in moving logs

Our flooded driveway

the splitter up to tailgate height and split right off the truck?" So he bartered for materials at work and built a riser. He made it from channel iron, various lengths of pipe, and strap iron for bracing. The log splitter rests on top of this contraption at almost the same height as the truck tailgate. No more bending down and no more lifting from ground level.

Floods

May spilled into June and the rains began. And continued. The ground became so saturated, there was nowhere for the water to go except to run off. And run off it did. The creeks rose higher and higher. Rivers broke crest and still it kept raining. The water over the "low water bridge" down the road from here rose to record highs. Debris on the trees afterward indicated it had been more than 20 feet high, and this was only a seasonal run-off creek.

New chimney cap

We tried to go around the long way but the water was over the road that way, too. Same creek, different road. We had to call in to work. No way to get there. Soon after we returned to the house the water rose again and our driveway was overtopped by another run-off creek. Now we were housebound as it was running deep and fast. No way to get a vehicle across and I wouldn't try to swim it if you twisted my arm behind my back.

No one wanted to look out the back porch. The garden was under a foot and a half of rushing water. The Wallo' Waters might be a miracle for cold temps, but they are no match for floodwater.

The rain finally took a breather. Nobody knew at the time that the respite was temporary, so we got to work and fixed the driveway, replanted the garden, and cleaned up the debris that had washed from the upper 20 acres, only to have it all washed away during the next wave of rain. More work missed at the job, more fixing, more replanting, etc. Garden was way late for Zone 6. We were starting plants in mid-July! The heat arrived with a vengeance and keeping young plants going in 100 plus degrees produced less than desirable results. Some made it, but not many. Fortunately, the previous year had been a bumper year and we still had canned veggies in jars.

Another welding project

Coming back from the garden one afternoon, we looked up and noticed that the chimney cap could use some work. Ours is a sheet metal square tube about three feet tall with a horizontal sheet across the top and a rising opening at each side. We lifted the thing off the chimney and lowered it to the ground for inspection. It was too rusted out to repair so we took it to the shop where we worked and bartered for materials and equipment to build a new one. Measurements were taken from the old one and applied to the new materials. Sheet metal was bent at four 90° angles to form a square tube then the seam was welded. The top parts were cut, then welded to the top of the unit, then "stays" were welded to the tube so that the apparatus would fit inside the chimney, but could only sink to the "stays" (or stops). When we got it home, we painted it with high-temp wood stove paint. After it cured, we hauled the thing up on the roof and placed it. Now for the moment of reckoning. Would it fit right? The fit was so tight, we had to pound it into the chimney, being careful not to break the fire tiles. When cooler weather arrived, we tried it out and it worked great.

Pack rat & other pests

We went out one day intending to drop a few trees so they'd cure in preparation for firewood season. The truck wouldn't start. She's a '73 Dodge and cold blooded, but this time, she wouldn't go at all. My boyfriend raised the hood and no wonder. She had been sitting for a couple of months and a pack rat had moved in. He (or she) had sticks, leaves, acorns, paper trash, and what all packed around the breather and carb (well, everywhere else too). My boyfriend scooped out a bunch of the stuff by hand, then got a shop vac out after the rest of it. Now she started. When the chore for the day had been completed, we parked the truck away from trees and structures, and also we'd raise the hood every couple of days. We'd see the little bugger every now and then, but sooner or later the dogs got the rat.

With the summer heat, the undesirables made their appearances. The copperheads came. We got into the habit of making a groundsweep before letting the dogs out. I'd hate to think what would happen if the dogs got to them first.

Anybody need a pack rat?

The scorpions came out in droves. They were everywhere indoors and out. One of them got me in the bottom of my foot. I couldn't walk for three days. The *only* good thing about winter is no snakes, no scorpions, and no ticks.

A new addition & more ice

Our roommate drove out to check the mail one fall day and this tiny pup bounded out from under the rural mailbox with teeth bared and a big bark. Poor little thing's eyes were barely open. He was a little blue-tick hound and heaven only knows how long he'd been there. Apparently, people think it's OK to dump their unwanted pets out in the country. "Oh, some farmer will take care of it." Well, they're right. Most farmers do take care of them. With shotgun, rifle, pistol, poison, etc. Whatever it takes to kill them. This little guy was lucky though, and as he grew up, he turned into a great watch dog.

The tarantulas were on the move again, so we knew winter was closing in soon. It turned colder and we had another crippling ice storm. This time the power was only out for four days. Much of the vegetation had been removed the year before.

My boyfriend had blown out a third disc in his back and could no longer perform his duties at work. He was off on short-term disability. Since the third disc was concurrent with the other two, his doctors said surgery wouldn't help. We were told it was degenerative disc disease and can't be fixed, so with his doctor's help and a lawyer, he applied for Social Security disability. What a fiasco that turned out to be.

It's a three-ring circus, complete with hoops to jump through, trapeze acts to perform, and a two to three year waiting period. Even with his doctor, a lawyer, and Social Security doctor, it's still in limbo. Meanwhile, he's blown a fourth disc. That's the nasty nature of a degenerative condition.

In the next installment, we will see how Dani and her family faced more fires, freaky bad weather, the loss of beloved animals, unemployment, trespassers, and thieves — among other "inconveniences." But Dani has also had more successes as she and her brood forge out their self-reliant lifestyle. Δ

LED LIGHTING
a breakthrough for independent living and emergency preparedness
PART 3: LED lighting alternatives — Build it yourself

By Tim Thorstenson

(This is the third and final installment of this series. The first part, LED technology essentials, appeared in issue #127, Jan/Feb 2011. The second part, LED-based products, appeared in issue #128, Mar/Apr 2011.)

In this LED series, we've touched on the idea of building your own lights. The merits of building vs. buying are always very dependent on individual circumstances. With LEDs, building allows one to use the most efficient LEDs in the design of lights that are suited to specific needs. But to help you decide if building is right for *you*, Part 3 on LEDs will consider the details. We will also examine a related and critical topic: *delivering* light efficiently.

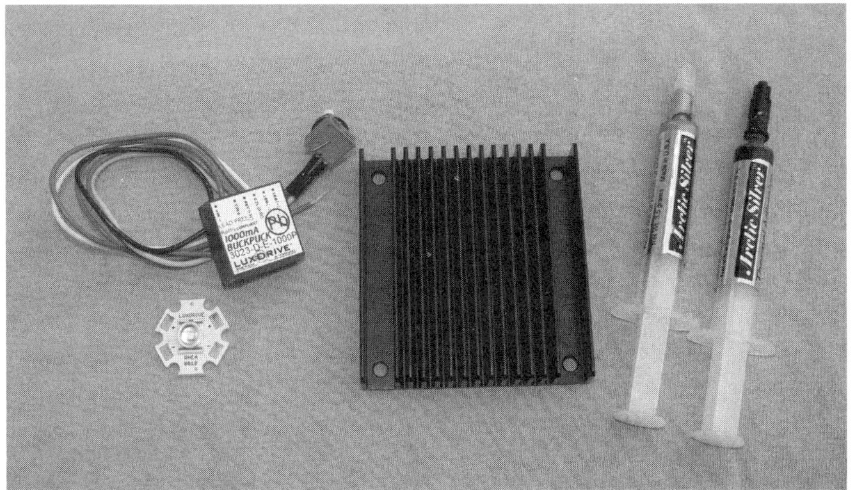

Here are the basic components needed to assemble an LED-based light source. From left to right: an LED and driver, a heat sink (shown fins-up), and heat-conductive epoxy or paste for mounting the LED.

Basic requirements

We'll discuss projects that require only some fine soldering and a little basic electrical and mechanical technique. The final light or fixture is limited mainly by your needs and imagination, but the basic light-making assembly will be similar regardless of what you want to build: you need an LED or LEDs that will meet your requirements and a driver (electronic controller) that is matched to both your power source and LEDs. Finally, a heat sink is required to keep the LEDs from getting cooked. Once you have these basics, they can be built into an almost unlimited array of lights. This could include portable lanterns for camping and emergencies, trouble lights for use on car power, portable spotlights or floodlights with handy mounting attachments that could be run from a small rechargeable battery, and various fixtures for use in a camper, cabin, or home.

A battle plan

In Part 1 and 2, we've tried to focus on general principles. With the changing nature of the technology, pages filled with details about specific LEDs and products could quickly become useless. But it is also necessary to use real-life examples in order

CAUTION: Voltages, electrical currents, and other values cited here are subject to change as well as to errors on the part of the author, so please confirm them for specific products. These projects involve low voltages, but it is still important to use proper wiring methods and appropriate fuses or circuit breakers in order to prevent fires and damage to batteries, chargers, and components. To avoid headaches, make sure to consult local electrical codes before starting a project in a home or cabin.

to talk sensibly. We'll use the best currently-available LEDs to illustrate the principles, but the principles themselves will remain useful even if (or when) these specific LEDs become outdated.

Sources of components

The most straightforward source of components is a retail supplier, such as LEDSupply (www.ledsupply.com, 802-728-6031). This company supplied components for the example projects pictured here and they receive very positive reviews for service. Of course, there are other good vendors, too. There are also bargain components available from discount outlets and websites like eBay. You can get some good deals, but there is a huge range of quality and customer service may be difficult or impossible. Remember that, especially in a cabin or home, even low voltage electronic components could pose a fire hazard if they fail. I'd suggest considerable caution and some appropriate research on forums like www.candlepowerforums.com prior to using "bargain" components.

LED selection

There are several different categories of LEDs (see Part One) and any of these could be considered, depending on the amount of light you need and the availability of suitable drivers. Here, we will stick with single-die LEDs because they are relatively easy to configure and because drivers are readily available. Brighter "multi-die" LEDs can also be useful in some applications, but suitable drivers are more limited at the moment. In addition, single-die LEDs have at least a couple of general advantages. First, for area lighting, several single-die LEDs can often be the better choice because they allow both the light and the heat to be spread out over a larger area. Second, continued improvements in efficiency are likely to turn up first in the single-die category.

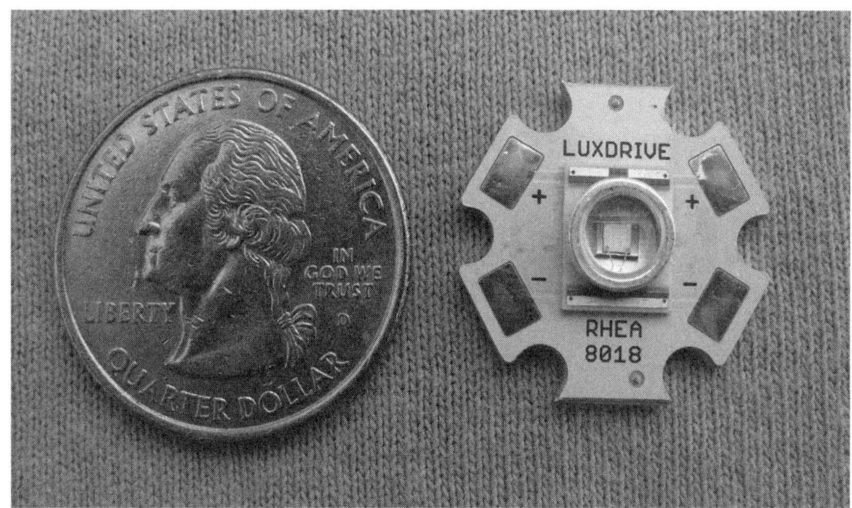

The LED itself is actually just the small dome and rectangular piece at center. But this one came pre-mounted to a "star board" and this makes for MUCH easier mounting and soldering.

Previously, we used the Cree "XR-E" LED to illustrate many concepts, but we also learned about a newer and more efficient Cree LED called the "XP-G." When I started working on this series of articles, the XP-G was only available in cool white and its availability was limited. But neutral and warm white color tints have now been released. Cool white is readily available and, by the time this article gets to print, it is likely that the same will be true of the more pleasant color tints. Because this LED represents the best efficiency available at this moment, we will use it for our examples. But, as I mentioned earlier, the principles of building will almost surely be similar when the "next new thing" rolls out.

Regardless of what type of LED you select, there are a couple essential numbers that are needed. One is the maximum current that it will handle, which is usually provided in milliamps (mA). The second is the voltage (usually called the "forward voltage") required to run the LED at maximum or at lower current levels. Such information, along with lumen outputs and lumen per watt efficiencies at various current inputs, can be had from a vendor or from the manufacturer's data sheet. As we go, we'll see examples of these numbers and how to use them. For home brewing, purchasing LEDs pre-mounted on what is called a "star board" (see the accompanying pictures) is often a sensible idea. Good mounting and connections can be a real challenge when trying to use tiny, bare LEDs. In contrast, a star board is easy to solder and it allows for simple mechanical mounting. In most cases, you can simply secure it to the heat sink with a heat-conducting epoxy or with a non-hardening heat transfer paste and some small self-tapping screws. Vendors that sell LEDs can also supply these materials.

It should be noted that there are also pre-made assemblies that can be useful for some projects. For instance, there are pre-made strips available that have LEDs mounted every so many inches on a long, narrow piece of "printed circuit board" (PCB) material. Some of these strips even include on-board drivers, so firing them up can be as simple as mounting the strip to an appropriate heat sink, providing a power feed, and adding a suitable cover or diffuser. Note that some of these options require the unit be electrically isolated from the metal

Here is an LED work light: the heat sink (top) with mounted LED has been attached to an electronic project box which holds the driver and electrical connections. The metal bracket can swivel for adjustment (note the wing nuts) and allows mounting options like the magnet shown here. As a finishing touch, the exposed LED should be covered with a lens or diffuser to protect it from damage.

mounting surface. Make sure to consult the technical information.

Heat management

As we saw in Part One, heat management is essential. For many applications, there are pre-made heat sinks which are readily available and fairly inexpensive. The back of the heat sink (the cooling fins) should be left exposed to the open air and should not be enclosed in any sort of housing. In addition, the heat sink will work best if it is mounted with the fins pointed up or on its side with the fins running vertically. Within these limits, the heat sink and mounted LED can be incorporated into virtually any sort of lantern, lamp, fixture, or housing that you can brew up for your needs. A single small heat sink (about 2.5 inches square and one inch tall) will be adequate for a single small LED like the XP-G and it would be sufficient for a couple of them if the intended use will generally involve operation at lower power or for fairly short periods. If you are experimenting with your own materials, note that surface area is generally more important than mass and that a flat black surface will actually emit heat much more efficiently than a shiny one.

Powering the LEDs

Most LEDs can be operated over a wide range of electrical currents and there are some huge tradeoffs. As the current is increased, more light will be produced. But more heat will be produced, too. In addition, there is a diminishing return: total lumens will increase, but the lumen per watt efficiency will decline as the current input is ramped up. On top of this, published outputs and efficiencies (the ones I will cite) assume a relatively low operating temperature for the LEDs. As the LEDs are pushed to higher current levels, it becomes progressively harder to maintain a low operating temperature, even with good heat sinking. As a result, the gap between "ideal performance" and "practical field performance" will likely widen as we go to higher current inputs.

In any case where maximum efficiency is a must, lower operating currents are a necessity. To prevent thermal deterioration of the LED, they are also a good idea when a very long service life is desired. The LED itself has some inherent "thermal resistance" and more is added at the interface between the LED and the star board and at the junction between the star board and the heat sink. This all means that the LED will unavoidably run at a temperature that is at least somewhat higher than the surroundings, even if your heat sink is a fifty pound chunk of copper with huge fins. As the current input is increased, this temperature elevation will also increase. If we throw in the additional fact that home-brew heat management is likely to be less than ideal, the conclusion is that modest current inputs are the best way to insure a long service life. Of course, the drawback is that more LEDs will be needed to produce a given amount of light.

But when we get to things like trouble lights, camp lanterns, and cabin lights, the situation can be somewhat different. Even at fairly high operating temperatures (within reason), LED service life can still be many thousand hours before any significant reduction in brightness will occur. In these uses, it can be perfectly acceptable to run the LEDs at full power (assuming that adequate heat sinking is in place) because such lights may not get a thousand hours of use even in several years of service. Efficiency *will* drop off, of course. But, as a practical matter, it may be both easier and cheaper to use a little bigger battery for such projects than it would be to build lights that use larger numbers of more gently-powered LEDs.

It is important to understand that this does not need to be an either/or choice because an *adjustable* driver with a top current output equal to the maximum rating of the LEDs can be selected. For cabin or home, the lights could be designed so that a moderate brightness setting would prove adequate for most needs. But when you need extra light for intermittent tasks like cooking or reading, it would be available by turning a knob. Portable lanterns and work lights may get run at maximum brightness for routine use, but they could be turned down if an emergency requires you to conserve battery power. Of course, generous heat sinking should be used to allow good heat removal during highest-power operation. Electrical current measurements with a good meter can give you a handle on how much juice is being used by adjustable lights at various brightness settings.

Diffusers & lenses

A broad, uniform field of light is usually desirable for general area lighting and the natural pattern of the bare LED may be fine in some settings. But if the LED is subject to possible damage, it would be prudent to cover it with a clear plastic or glass cover. If glare is a problem or an even more diffuse light is desired, a textured or frosted diffuser may be preferable. However, extreme care should be used in selecting diffusers because heavy frosting or texturing can greatly reduce the emitted light.

In some settings, a tighter focus than the LED's natural output may be desired and a particularly useful accessory here is the "focusing lens." These small, inexpensive plastic lenses mount over the LED and they function by bending the light into a tighter pattern. Several different patterns are available and the right one can greatly improve the *useful* efficiency of your project because it will squeeze the light into the area where it is needed. For example, an unfocused LED might make an excellent area light. But when it comes to a trouble light, you may find that a lot of the lumens will wind up landing outside of where you really need them (be it a fuse box or an engine compartment). In contrast, a "wide" focused lens will provide a pattern that is still broad enough for such tasks but which is quite a bit tighter (and therefore brighter) than a bare LED. Lenses with a "medium" or "tight" focus could prove very useful for vehicle-mounted work lights or when you want to light up something like a walkway or outbuilding via a fixture located at some distance. One caution with these lenses: a given model of lens will be designed to work best with a certain type of LED. When ordering, make sure that you are getting the correct ones.

It's helpful to mention the difference between a focusing lens and a reflector. A focusing lens sits in front of the LED and it can be designed to gather the vast majority of the light output into a specified pattern with a very sharp cutoff between bright light and virtually no light. In contrast, a reflector sits behind the source (and to the sides), so it will only catch *part* of the LED's light and put it into a beam. The rest (which can be a major portion of the total output) will escape directly out of the front of the LED without being captured and focused. The result is a bright central beam and a broader, dimmer surrounding area of "spill" light. In many flashlight applications, this spill light is by no means wasted. The central beam allows you to spot things at a distance, but the spill light simultaneously allows you see closer hazards over a much wider area. In a defensive situation, this could be a menacing intruder. In more pristine environments, it could also be the tree branch hanging at forehead level or the gopher hole at your feet. But when it comes to an area lighting job (i.e. lighting up the path to the outhouse), the spill light from a reflector may indeed be wasted. Here, the right focusing lens can provide much more efficient use of the light.

This is the back of the LED work light. The wires from the driver to the LED were routed through small holes drilled in the face of the heat sink. They run between the cooling fins and into the project box (make sure to protect the wires from sharp edges). A cheap woodworking clamp is shown here as another mounting option for use in the field.

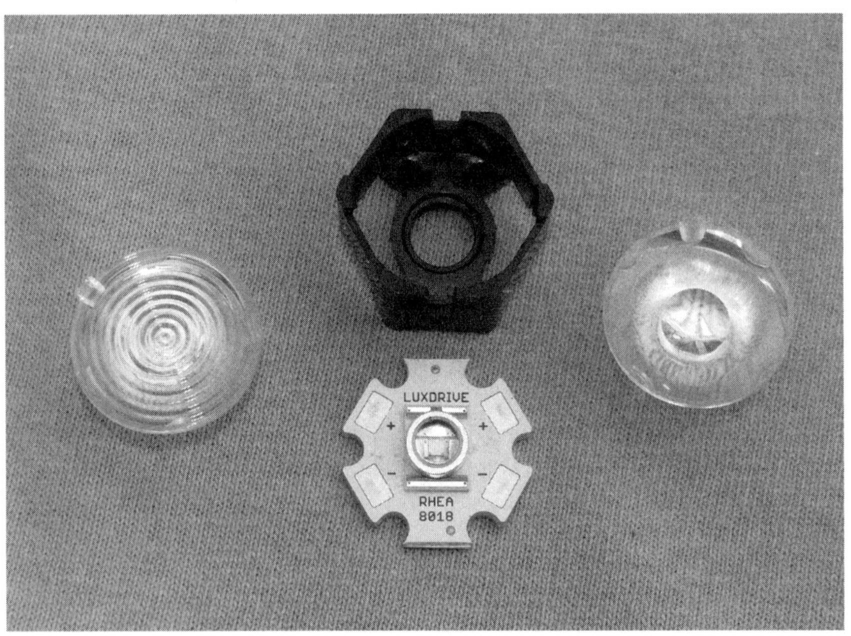

The black plastic lens holder at top center will fit over the LED at bottom. Focusing lenses (left and right) can be snapped into the holder to provide different beam patterns from the LED.

Drivers

Good commercial drivers are available for single-die LEDs. Because the current inputs are fairly standard, drivers designed for older LEDs like the Cree XR-E will work just fine with the new XP-G. Because most readers are probably interested in using power sources such as 12-volt batteries, we will focus on the "buck" drivers. These take voltages which would otherwise be too high and reduce them so as to push a constant current flow to the LEDs. "Boost" drivers are also available for battery sources that would otherwise provide too *low* of a voltage.

A good example of a buck driver is the BuckPuck which is made in the USA by a company called LEDdynamics. It is no larger than a piece of bubble gum and can have standard outputs of 350, 500, 700, or 1,000 milliamps (mA). Drivers like these are available with pre-attached wiring harnesses and, if desired, a "trimpot" (adjustable resistor) that allows the brightness of the LED to be varied (turning the knob on the trimpot will progressively reduce the driver's current output from its specified maximum). The driver can be mounted in a small box and the trimpot is designed to be mounted through a hole in the enclosure with the adjustment stem sticking out. Attaching a knob to the stem will then provide easy adjustment. The standard DC version of the BuckPuck will handle up to 32 volts, so it is very suited to 12- or 24-volt DC batteries. Some drivers may draw a very small amount of power even with the trimpot turned all the way down, so an on/off switch or other positive means of disconnect is a good idea to prevent a small drain when the lights are not in use. One very important thing to note is that drivers like the BuckPuck can often power more than one LED. The maximum number will depend on things like the voltage supplied by the source and that required by the LEDs.

Design considerations for drivers

There are some extra precautions that should be taken when the drivers will be connected to a battery that is simultaneously attached to a charging system. Most importantly, a charger can provide up to several volts more than the "nominal" rating of the battery system, so it is important to insure that the voltage will *never* exceed the driver's rating. Some charging systems can introduce an "AC ripple" and this can be a problem with electronic devices like drivers. Better quality off-grid systems may provide filtering to eliminate this "ripple" along with regulation to prevent harmful voltage spikes and other problems, but this is always a good thing to check out specifically. Care may be required if the driver will be mounted remotely from the LEDs or if there is a long wire run from the driver to the power source. Long connecting wires can act like an antenna and pick up electrical "noise" that could interfere with the driver's electronics. Manufacturer's data sheets can provide information on how to deal with problems like this. It should be noted that the efficiency of a given driver can vary depending on factors like the input voltage. For applications like a camp lantern or work light, this is probably a fine detail to lose sleep over. But if you are planning a more extensive project, driver efficiency can become significant. The manufacturer's data sheet will once again provide helpful details and a good vendor can often assist with finding the best driver for a given project.

A caution about homemade drivers: designs for simple current-regulating circuits can be found in many basic electronics manuals (they are sometimes called "constant current power supplies"). These can provide a stable current output over a wide range of voltage inputs, but the pitfall with many simple circuits is their efficiency. They often do their job by essentially dissipating some of the input power and turning it into wasted heat. Depending on factors like the input voltage of the source and the voltage required by the LED, it is possible for a simple current regulating circuit to use as much power as the LED itself, or even more!

Configuring the LEDs and drivers

NOTE: Our use of the Cree XP-G LED as an example can lead to some confusion. Cree originally specified a maximum current of 1,000 mA, but they raised it to 1,500 mA after further testing. However, I am going to treat 1,000 mA as "maximum" for a few practical reasons: first, the higher limit only applies to *cool white* XP-Gs. Second, simple drivers are not as readily available at higher outputs, at least as of right now. Third, for reasons mentioned earlier, higher inputs could result in a high operating temperature under typical homebrew conditions. Finally, even at ideal temperatures, operation at 1,500 mA will result in an efficiency drop of around 40% relative to performance at 350 mA and this is somewhat self-defeating.

When it comes to powering LEDs, the first thing to address is the number of LEDs that can be connected to a single driver. To determine what is possible, we need the voltage required by the LEDs, the voltage required by the driver, and the minimum voltage that will be supplied by the power source when it is at a state of maximum discharge. Here's an example: At 1,000 mA, an XP-G LED requires a "forward voltage" of around 3.3 volts and a BuckPuck driver specifies an "overhead" of about 2.0 volts. This means that two such LEDs connected in "series" with a single driver would only require a total of 8.6 volts (2 LEDs at 3.3 volts + 2.0 volts for the driver). This could be supplied very comfortably from a 12-volt lead acid battery (which should never be discharged to a voltage anywhere near that low). If your battery won't be discharged too heavily between charges, it is possible to power *three* XP-G LEDs at 1,000 mA (required voltage would be 11.9 volts). It is important to note that a battery run down below this voltage (such as during an emergency) will still continue to power the LEDs, but their brightness will decline progressively as the voltage drops further.

When connecting multiple LEDs in this kind of setup, they are wired in series: the (+) output lead from the driver is connected to the (+) terminal of the first LED, the (-) output lead from the driver is connected to the (-) terminal of the last LED and all intervening LED-to-LED connections are made in an alternating (-) to (+) to (-) fashion. Of course, a proportionately larger heat sink (or multiple small ones) is essential when setting up multiple LEDs. A higher voltage system can allow even more LEDs to be powered from a single driver, but there are a few cautions here. First, it is important to make sure that the maximum voltage of the power system never exceeds the voltage limit of the driver. Second, even though the driver is still delivering the same amount of current through the LED string, the total *power* it is handling will increase as the LED string is made longer. Thus, it is important to check with a good vendor or with the manufacturer's data sheet for the acceptable maximum number of LEDs.

Output vs. efficiency

As we know, higher current will give us more lumens, but with a reduced efficiency. To see the impact of this tradeoff, let's consider the performance of a string of three XP-G LEDs. As discussed earlier, it becomes progressively harder to

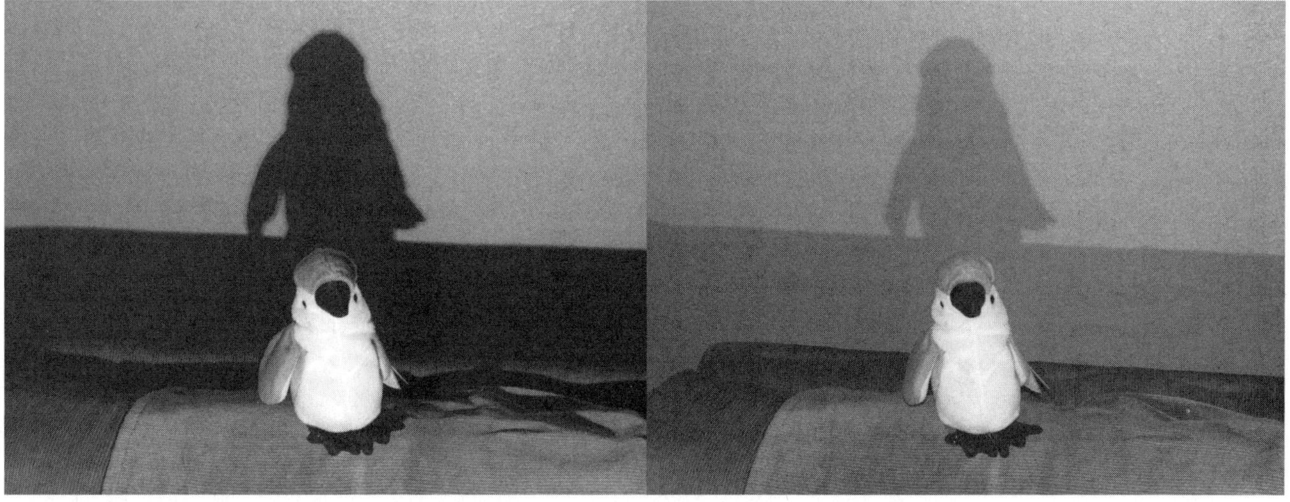

The output of an LED is naturally "directional." This can allow for highly efficient DELIVERY of the light, but it can also lead to sharp, dark shadows (left). Combining an "omni-directional" source for general lighting with directional ones for tasks like reading and fine detail work can soften the shadows and result in more pleasant lighting (right).

A bare LED like a Cree XR-E or XP-G will emit a broad pattern of light. Depending on your needs, this may or may not be desirable.

maintain low operating temperatures for the LEDs as current input is increased. Thus, the spread between these ideal values and typical field performance will likely become bigger as the current input is increased. The numbers cited here are ideal LED outputs for the "R5" bin (best available at this writing) in *cool* white. We'll consider the performance of neutral and warm white tints in a bit. If you are visualizing what you might need for a project, it is handy to recall that a standard 60 watt incandescent light bulb will produce about 840 lumens.

At a 1,000 mA input, three XP-G LEDs could provide an ideal LED output of 1,040 lumens and efficiency of around 103 lumens per watt. In contrast, operation at 350 mA would produce only 420 lumens, but efficiency will climb to about 132 lumens per watt (a 25% increase). In many practical settings, operation at a compromise current somewhere between these levels can provide a good balance between output and efficiency while keeping the heat output reasonably modest. For instance, operation of the three LED string at 500 mA would generate about 585 lumens while retaining an efficiency of around 120 lumens per watt. Increasing the current to 700 mA would result in about 730 lumens with efficiency in the neighborhood of 108 lumens per watt. Remember that operation at higher current inputs will result in more heat, so it is important to plan your heat-sinking accordingly. BuckPucks are available in a choice of the current outputs just mentioned.

Advanced wiring strategies

If you are certain that you *only* want to run the LEDs at lower levels (350 or 500 mA), there is a slightly more complicated wiring arrangement that may be worth considering. In a series-wired string of LEDs, each LED will receive the full current supplied by the driver. But if two identical, series-wired strings are connected in electrical "parallel" to a single driver, the driver's output will split between the strings and each LED will receive about one-half of the driver's current. Using the example of a 12-volt system again, this means that you could power six XP-Gs at 350 mA by purchasing only one 700 mA driver instead of having to buy two 350 mA drivers. Alternately, a single 1,000 mA driver could be used to power six LEDs at 500 mA. Drivers with adjustable outputs can still be used and data sheets will provide schematics for wiring strategies like this.

It is easy to miss important points in the midst of all the numbers and there is one that definitely needs to be emphasized here. This technique allows for the use of few drivers when the goal is to run the LEDs at lower current anyways. But we lose the option of cranking the LEDs up to "maximum" for occasions where the extra light would be handy, so it is good to be clear about what we are giving up. Powering six LEDs from one 1,000 mA driver (as just described), will allow for a maximum output of about 1,170 lumens (six LEDs at 500 mA). But using *two* adjustable drivers to power the same LEDs as two separate strings of three would allow for up to 2,080 lumens (six LEDs at 1,000 mA). The question here is whether having access to the extra light is worth the cost of the second driver. The answer, of course, depends on your intended uses.

Color tints and relative efficiency

In Part 1, we saw that neutral and warm white LEDs can provide light that many will find more pleasant, but that they also suffer from lower lumen outputs and efficiencies relative to cool white. This remains true with the new XP-G LEDs: best bin efficiencies for the XP-G LEDs at 350 mA are 132 lumens per watt in cool white, 116 lumens per watt in neutral white, and 102 lumens per watt in warm white. Cree is also offering an "outdoor white" which sits between cool and neutral white and provides an efficiency of 124 lumens per watt at 350 mA. There's still a tradeoff between aesthetics and efficiency, but it's definitely worth noting that even the warm white XP-G (102 lumens per watt) is more efficient than the cool white tint of the older XR-E LED (92 lumens per watt). As with cool white, the neutral and warm tints are available in a number of bins that vary in efficiency.

One more power strategy—but use with caution!

It can be tempting—and it *is* possible—to connect an appropriate string of LEDs in series and feed it directly from a given power source without the use of a driver. *This approach has some serious limitations and it is very easy to burn out some expensive LEDs if it is done improperly.* But there are a couple of reasons for mentioning it. First, those who pursue this topic further are likely to run across it, so a discussion of the pros and cons is in order. Second, as we will see, the operating specs for the XP-G work out nicely for this technique, so it could actually prove useful in a few cases.

Most of the problems with "direct feed" are a result of the touchy relationship between current and voltage in an LED and the XP-G can be used to illustrate the problem: about 3.0 volts is needed to drive the LED at 350 mA, but 3.3 volts will increase the current to 1,000 mA. In other words, increasing voltage by 10% will almost triple the current flow. The numbers vary with different LEDs, but the same general touchiness holds true and this makes it very easy to accidentally overpower the LEDs. Of course, this can lead to a shortened service life and, in extreme cases, it could even burn out the LEDs in pretty short order. Making matters worse is the fact that the published forward voltages for a given LED are "nominal" values. As with brightness and efficiency, the exact required voltages will vary somewhat from one LED to the next. So even if you are supplying the correct voltage in theory, it is still possible that the LEDs could be getting an excess dose of current. It is for these very reasons that the LED makers strongly suggest powering their products by controlling current rather than voltage.

That said, the XP-G is about as good as it gets for this approach. First, the voltages are convenient: a string of four such LEDs wired in series would require about 13.2 volts in order to produce a 1,000 mA operating current (4 LEDs at 3.3 volts each). This, as many readers will know, is in the neighborhood of the maximum voltage supplied by most 12-volt lead acid batteries when in a state of full charge (various types of "12-volt" lead acid batteries will specify somewhat different full-charge voltages, but most of them are at or below 13.2 volts). In addition, the XP-G has a maximum current rating of 1,500 mA (in cool white). To get the current this high, a nominal voltage of around 3.5 volts per LED is required and this works out to about 14.0 volts for a four-LED string. This is above what we are likely to get from most "12-volt" lead acid batteries and it provides a cushion with respect to accidentally overpowering the LEDs. *If considering this approach, please make sure to confirm the actual maximum voltage output of the power source you will be using!*

Here are some precautions for those thinking about this strategy. First, it would be very prudent to conduct actual current measurements with a good meter to insure that the LEDs are not being overpowered. Second, I personally would avoid a setup that involved the simultaneous connection of a charger. In a setting like a cabin

Focusing lenses will tighten the output of an LED by varying degrees and they can be selected to suit a given use. Shown from left to right are the beams that result from "wide," "medium," and "tight" lenses.

where the batteries will be charged by sun or wind while you are away, the charger and lights could be connected to the battery with a "double throw" switch so that one or the other (but *not* both) would be engaged to the battery at any given time. Third, a battery in a full state of charge will run the LED strings at fairly high current inputs, so generous heat-sinking should be used for such setups.

It is also important to understand that this strategy has some other problems that are less dramatic but are still very significant from a practical perspective. First, there is no way to *efficiently* dim the LEDs. An adjustable resistor could be placed in series with the LED string, but this illustrates the problem with using resistors to directly control the current to LEDs: as the resistor is turned up and the LEDs become dimmer, the power that would otherwise go into the LEDs is simply being dissipated by the resistor in the form of heat. So much for efficiency! The other big snag is that brightness will fade dramatically as the battery voltage drops during discharge. The output of four XP-Gs at 13.2 volts will be over 1,300 lumens. But at 12.8 volts, it will be a little under 1,000 lumens. At 12.4 volts, it is only around 800 lumens and at 12.0 volts it is a humble 550 lumens (these numbers are calculated from "nominal" LED voltages, so actual results could vary by a fair bit). In contrast, a three-LED string with driver control will be able to maintain full brightness (or a reduced output of *your* choice) down to at least 11.9 volts. With a two-LED string and a driver, constant full brightness would be available down to 8.6 volts.

The problem of fading brightness can be minimized by using a battery that has a capacity well in excess of the minimum needed for a typical usage cycle; this will minimize the voltage drop that will occur between charges. Whether your intentions are routine or emergency uses, good drivers can allow for much more flexible power conservation along with convenient (and *efficient*) brightness adjustment. In addition, the cost of some decent drivers can pale pretty quickly in comparison to the expense of a few cooked LEDs!

That having been said, this strategy could be useful in some settings. If you can tolerate the brightness swings (and/or minimize them with system design), then this approach could save some money in places where the lights will either be "on" or "off" and where adjustable brightness (at least of the intentional kind) is not needed.

Please watch the numbers!

It is fortunate that the specifications in terms of electrical current and forward voltage are *generally* consistent within a given LED product line and it is only the lumen output and efficiency that vary as we go from tint to tint and from bin to bin. However, check the numbers carefully for any specific type of LED that you will be using. For instance, the "older" Cree XR-Es have a maximum current limit of 1,000 mA in cool white but only 700 mA in neutral and warm white. At the moment, only *cool* white XP-G LEDs have received approval from Cree for operation at 1,500 mA. The suggested limit is still 1,000 mA for neutral and warm white.

Cost

At retail from LEDSupply (as of this writing), an adjustable BuckPuck driver will run about $20 and one with a fixed output will be a little less. Cree XP-G LEDs are around $9 apiece (best bin versions pre-mounted on a star board). Small heat sinks are $4 apiece or less. In other words, figure about $60 to brew up a basic skeleton that uses three XP-G LEDs and a BuckPuck driver (I'm figuring three heat sinks). Of course, this does not include components like lenses, housings, power cords, and so forth. As with other home-built projects, value often lies in the eye of the beholder. The other powering alternatives described above can reduce the number of required drivers in cases where the ability to run the LEDs to maximum output is not needed or eliminate them entirely when the consequences of "direct drive" are acceptable.

Delivering light efficiently

Efficiency has clearly been an important topic in this series of articles, but the truth is that we've actually covered only half of that story. Lumen per watt ratings can tell us how efficient a source is at *making* light. But we also need to consider the critical issue of *delivering* that light efficiently. We can get a grip on this topic by imagining a bare incandescent light bulb hanging in a rustic cabin with open rafters. Simply replacing this bulb with a good quality compact fluorescent (CFL) bulb could easily increase the lumen per watt efficiency by a factor of three or four or more. But the point we are considering now is that the improvement, as described so far, is not nearly as good as it *could* be. The CFL, like the incandescent bulb, will emit light in essentially all directions. Much of that light will shine up into the rafters and be wasted.

An easy and effective solution is to mount a suitable reflector over the bulb. This will capture the light that would otherwise be lost and redirect it down to where it will be useful. A reflector *is* a very good thing in a situation like this, but note: even the shiniest reflector will not be perfect. Even good quality, mirror-smooth, silver reflectors will often reflect only 85 to 90% of the light that hits them. Polished aluminum, stainless steel, or white-painted reflectors can be even less efficient. A related concern is diffusers mounted in front of the light source. These may sometimes be a necessity in order to prevent objectionable glare, but they can also absorb and scatter a significant amount of light and reduce overall efficiency. In fact, even a plain sheet of glass or plastic can absorb around 10% of the light that strikes it and an opaque white diffuser can soak up 20% or more.

It is important to appreciate the significance of these "optical losses," so let's consider an example. I'll note up front that this is oversimplified, but it is also very instructive. Let's say that we have a fixture with a 90% efficient reflector and a 90% efficient diffuser. We are going to put a 1,000 lumen CFL bulb in the fixture and, for simplicity, we will assume that half of the light (500 lumens) will shine directly down to the diffuser while half will shine up to the reflector before getting redirected down to the diffuser. Of the 500 lumens that hits the diffuser directly, 90% will make it out of the fixture (450 lumens). But the 500 lumens which hit the reflector first will fare somewhat worse. The 90% efficient reflector will reflect only 450 of those 500 lumens. On top of this, only 90% of the 450 lumens which survived the reflector will make it through the diffuser, so our net here will be 405 lumens. Of the 1,000 lumens we started with, only 855 will make it out of the fixture (450 "direct" lumens plus 405 "reflected" lumens). In other words, even this optimistic example will eat up almost 15% of the available lumens! A poorer reflector with 85% efficiency and an opaque white diffuser with 75% efficiency would increase the total optical loss to around 30%. If we were starting with a bulb that had an efficiency of 100 lumens per watt, our final *fixture* efficiencies would be 85 and 70 lumens per watt, respectively.

An immediate lesson to be drawn from this is to be careful about making apples to oranges comparisons when selecting products. The efficiency rating for a bare bulb will not include the optical losses that result when said bulb is put into a separately purchased fixture. But an honest and accurate rating for a pre-made fixture (that includes its own light source) should factor in these additional losses. In the same vein, things like extremely opaque diffusers, tinted lenses, and colored shades should be avoided if your goal is maximum efficiency, and this applies whether you are buying or home-brewing.

This discussion also leads us to seeing a definite advantage of LEDs, at least in *some* settings. Conventional bulbs and tubes—whether they are incandescent, fluorescent, or metal halide—will emit light in all directions. Using a reflector is far better than nothing in situations where some portion of the light would otherwise be wasted. But, as we have just seen, even the best reflector will not redirect *all* of that light and some of the lumens will still be lost. In contrast, an LED emits almost all of its light in one direction—out of the face of the chip. In a setting like our rustic cabin example, an LED mounted in the rafters and pointed downward would naturally send the majority of its light into the area where it was needed. In addition, it may be possible in some cases to avoid the use of heavily frosted lenses or diffusers because the LED can be situated to produce minimal glare when viewed from the side.

Now the "aimed" or "directed" lighting provided by an LED (or by a CFL with a very good reflector and no diffuser) will provide the most efficient delivery, but it is also important to consider the other side of this coin before designing a lighting system: a potential problem with such directed lighting is that it can produce very sharp and very dark shadows. In some cases, such as with yard lights or trouble lights, we live with this because the benefit of efficient light delivery is worth the drawback. In other cases, the shadow problem can be reduced or eliminated by using several dimmer sources placed at different locations instead of relying on a single brighter one. LEDs are perfect for this approach, but there are cases where this may not be practical.

To see the benefits of "un-directed" lighting, let's move from our rustic cabin to an off-grid home with finished walls and ceiling. Let's say that we want to light up a pretty decent-sized room from a single location, so we can't use the trick of sprinkling several LEDs around in the ceiling (perhaps we don't have decent access to the attic or maybe we just don't want to fool around with multiple fixtures). If we hang a bare CFL bulb in the middle of the ceiling, it will emit light in all directions. The light that gets thrown up to the ceiling and out to the walls will not get used with the greatest efficiency, but at least some of it will get reflected and bounced back into the living area. This means that any given spot in the room will actually receive light from multiple directions—both directly from the bulb itself and indirectly as a result of light that has been reflected from the walls and ceiling. The net result will be much fainter and softer shadows.

If you've never thought about the significance of this effect before, find a room that is decently lit by only a central ceiling fixture. Sit down with your back to the fixture, put your magazine in your lap, and see if you can still read it! The reason that you are not looking into a pitch dark shadow is because indirect light from the ceiling fixture is reaching the magazine after being reflected from the walls and ceiling. In an area where good *quality* light is important, the benefits of this type of lighting may be worth the sacrifice. To salvage as much efficiency as possible, there is one fairly obvious thing to keep in mind: white walls and ceilings may not be 100% efficient reflectors, but they are a far cry better than darker alternatives.

LED Update

The Part One update introduced the new Cree XM-L LED. Since it is now available in flashlights and as a separate component, some details are in order:

First, maximum current input is three amps (3000 mA). This yields about 900 lumens and puts the XM-L on par with "multi-die" LEDs (see Part One). At about $9, it could simply be used in place of the XP-G. But the XM-L could also be run at higher power to reduce the number of LEDs, drivers, and other components needed for any given project. One snag here *was* the lack of higher output drivers, but LEDdynamics (makers of the "BuckPuck") plans to have 1,400 and 2,100 mA units available by press time. With proper heat sinking, such power levels are not imprudent for the XM-L and they equate to 500 and 700 lumens per LED, respectively. An XM-L at 1,400 or 2,100 mA will be roughly as efficient as an XP-G at 700 or 1,000 mA.

In flashlights, the XM-L can put "flamethrower" performance (see Part Two) into a compact light. For instance, the Lumintop TD15-X (available from www.sbflashlights.com) delivers an LED output of up to 720 lumens and a nice general-purpose beam while being small enough for convenient carry. In a flamethrower-sized reflector, the XM-L can provide a notably tighter beam than a multi-die LED and several import products are available in this category. Those who want gold-standard, US-made options can look to Malkoff Devices: an XM-L version of their long-range "Hound Dog" flashlight is in production and lamp modules for Surefire and Maglite products are in the works.

The compact, XM-L based Lumintop TD15-X (left) can rival the output and beam focus of the multi-die based "flamethrowers" at right. Extension tubes (left center) can be added to stretch runtimes and accommodate various battery options.

Such shadow-free lighting could also be accomplished with a single LED fixture by either buying or brewing something that uses reflectors and/or diffusers to spread the directional light produced by the LEDs. Alternately, one could bounce the LED light off the ceiling instead of aiming it directly down into the room. But in doing so, we are *forcing* the naturally directional LED to behave like an omni-directional bulb. This can create the same kind of optical losses that result when we force a CFL into behaving as a directional source. The conclusion here is that an LED has a natural advantage with respect to delivery efficiency when directed lighting is desirable, but an "omni-directional" bulb or tube (CFL or otherwise) can enjoy a similar advantage where diffuse, shadow-free lighting is needed. If you are choosing between options that have a roughly similar starting efficiency in terms of raw lumen per watt output, this is something to consider.

Of course, this ignores other potentially significant pros and cons (such as the efficient dim-ability of LEDs or the cheaper current purchase price of CFLs). When you start looking at the actual products, it is important to consider a large number of factors to find the best options for your needs. To recap what we've covered, these include total lumen output, lumen per watt efficiency, service life, purchase price, the "natural directionality" of the source, and the availability of *efficiently* adjustable brightness. All of these need to be evaluated and dovetailed to fit with your needs. There are no perfect or easy answers here, but I hope that this background information will be of some help. Δ

Cabbage for good health and great eating

By Linda Gabris

When I was a kid, the number one reason Grandpa and Grandma grew row after row of cabbages in our backyard garden was simply because we loved cabbage on the table. Of course, Grandpa claimed that cabbage earned its space more than any other vegetable in the garden and that it was the best keeper for wintering in the root cellar (an important storage method in our rural neck of the woods before hydro came through).

According to Grandmother, a well-respected herbalist who was relied upon by folks from miles around, cabbage not only dished up a whole lot of healthy eating but was also a number one pick for treating a host of everyday ailments and common complaints such as constipation, listlessness, heartburn, bad stomach, lack of appetite, and poor circulation.

Cabbage belongs to the family of cruciferous vegetables known as *Brassica oleracea* of which broccoli, kale, Brussels sprouts, kohlrabi, and cauliflower are also members. There are four main types of cabbage with countless hybrids which, in my book, are of more concern to gardeners than they are to cabbage eaters.

The most popular type grown and eaten in North America is green cabbage which has tightly compressed, sturdy crisp leaves. The outer leaves of a healthy green cabbage are bright green with the color of inner leaves being paler to white as they are peeled away from the core or "heart" as Grandma called it.

Green cabbage was the familiar head in my grandparent's garden and it is the prized head in mine, too, for not only is it a good choice for root cellaring, but is also a super hardy plant that can stand up to early frost and even snow, which is always a hovering threat to gardeners in colder growing zones.

Types of green cabbage include *Grenadier* which is super sweet and crunchy and a preferred choice for slaw lovers, *Charmant* noted as being an early head for harvesting, and *January King* which is well-suited for

Green, red, and Savoy cabbage

late harvesting and is a very good keeper. In more temperate zones, it can even be left in the ground over winter and dug out as needed.

Green cabbages are perfect for the soup pot, braising, for shredding into coleslaws, and are the traditional cabbage for pickling whole and making into sauerkraut which is an Old World creation that originated in Germany from where it got its name. The leaves of green cabbage can be steamed to make them pliable enough for stuffing and rolling into cabbage rolls, a popular Hungarian and Ukraine dish, or used in place of grape leaves in the Mediterranean creation known as *dolmas.*

Red cabbage has tight leaves like green cabbage but has a coarser texture and a slightly sharper flavor. Red cabbage adds appetizing deep purple color and super crunch to tossed salads and makes a very pretty bed for vegetable platters. It is well-suited for braising and for making into sweet and sour dishes. Red cabbage is also a popular pick, especially in Asian cuisine, for fermenting or pickling which is one of my favorite summer salads.

Popular types of red cabbage include *Meteor* which has wonderful rich purple color and is most eye-pleasing in the salad bowl, *Red Rodan* reputed as being the hardiest of the redheads and easiest to grow, *Ruby Ball* which is a nice sweet early cabbage, and *Scarlet O'Hara* with a hefty, pretty, burgundy head.

Keep in mind that red cabbage, like beets, can stain other foods and often turns a tinge of blue upon cooking so choose green cabbage instead of red in recipes where you do not wish to change the color of the dish but still want to add exciting cabbage goodness and flair. Adding a drop of vinegar to the cooking water can help to keep red cabbage from fading. When you do want to play with color, red cabbage is the one to opt for in recipes such as jellied salads and traditional Old World borscht (beet and cabbage types of soup) where vibrant color is desired.

Savoy cabbage has yellowish-crimped leaves which are more delicate in flavor than green and red cabbages. Common types of Savoy cabbage are *Salarite*, *Wivoy*, and *Promasa.* They are a good choice for stuffing and rolling since the leaves are more pliable than green cabbage and hold their color well upon cooking.

Since Savoy cabbage is more delicate, it does not lend itself well to the salad bowl as it can go wimpy especially under heavier dressings such as those with a mayonnaise base which is often used in slaws. It is, however, delicious on sandwiches — adding an exciting crunch as it stands up better than leaf lettuce for lunchbox sandwiches that have to sit a spell before being eaten.

Chinese cabbage varieties known as "snow" or "napa" cabbage, and bok choy are readily available in larger supermarkets across the country making them another delicious choice for cabbage connoisseurs. These varieties of milder flavored cabbages have softer, tenderer leaves than other types of cabbage, making them ideal for Oriental dishes calling for quick cooking such as stir-frying.

Cabbage is one of the world's oldest known cultivated vegetables with its roots tracing back to 4,000 BC. Cabbage was introduced to Old World from Asia by the Celts and it quickly became a major crop throughout Europe. According to history, it was brought to the Americas in the mid-1500s by French explorer Jacques Cartier.

Since cabbage, especially common green cabbage, is well adapted to colder climates and only takes three months to fully mature, it is a favorite of gardeners, especially those in colder zones with shorter growing seasons.

If you don't grow your own cabbage, buying organically-grown cabbage at a vegetable stand or supermarket is the next best thing, especially if you load up on it from local growers during the fall when it is at its prime for table use and super bulk buys can be had.

When selecting green and red cabbage, look for firm, heavy heads that have healthy color. Leaves should be tight with no discoloration or dullness. Check the root end of the cabbage to be sure the leaves are not starting to separate from the stem as this is an indication of age.

Do not choose cabbage that is already shredded as some of the nutritional value will be lost and its shelf life will be shortened and steer clear of those with outer leaves stripped away as this is an indication that the head has already started to deteriorate. Savoy and Chinese cabbage should be firm with good color—no fading or tinges of brown.

Green cabbage is the best choice for long-term storage and will save up to five or six months in the coldest corner of your root cellar or up to two months in the fridge. Savoy cabbage keeps about one month in the fridge before it starts to lose its character. Chinese cabbages are more perishable and will start to go limp after a week or two.

To help maintain freshness, especially after the head has been cut, wrap it in a plastic bag, punch the bag with holes in order for it to breathe, and store in the vegetable crisper of the fridge. Jacketing the cabbage in a paper bag also helps to prevent moisture loss and fading.

Freezing excess cabbage

When there's a bounty of cabbage to your avail, it can be frozen for future use. Trim the coarse outer leaves from the head and save for stock making. Core the cabbage by quartering it and then slicing out the hard heart from each portion. Do not discard the core as it can be eaten out of hand as a special treat or added to the stock pot along with the outer leaves. It is a little stronger flavored than the rest of the head but full of nutrients too good to waste

Cut the cabbage into wedges or shred as desired. Blanch three to four minutes in boiling water. Drain, pat dry, and cool before putting needed amounts into zip-lock freezer bags or cartons. Frozen cabbage has a shelf life of up to one year in the freezer. It can be used for soup, added to stews or casseroles, or dressed with cream or cheese sauce. It loses crunch upon thawing so it is not well-suited for slaws or other recipes calling for fresh, crisp cabbage.

Tip for cabbage roll lovers: Simply wrap a whole head of green cabbage in plastic wrap, jacket in a paper bag, and freeze for future cabbage rolls. Once thawed, the leaves will be pliable enough for stuffing without steaming the head first. I always freeze four or five whole cabbages in the fall from my garden especially for this purpose. The inner portion of the cabbage that's too small for rolls can be used in soup or stew.

Since Grandmother didn't have a deep freezer when I was a kid, some of the cabbage heads that weren't destined for wintering in the root cellar would get pickled whole by covering in brine while others were shredded and made into sauerkraut.

To make sauerkraut

You will need a crock, large glass jar, or wooden barrel as Grandpa and Grandma used. Don't use metal or plastic as the cabbage can draw an off-taste from these materials.

A general rule of thumb is to use 14 pounds of cabbage per one cup of pickling or kosher salt. Of course, you can increase or decrease the recipe to suit your needs. Shred the cabbage. Place a layer in the crock, salt lightly, and pack down with your hands. Repeat until all the cabbage and salt has been used. Weigh it down with a rock or other heavy object to ensure that cabbage stays under the brine as it is formed and be sure to leave a little headspace for brine to rise.

To make sauerkraut, shredded green cabbage is layered with salt in a crock and weighted down with a clean stone.

Once pickled, the sauerkraut can be stored in a cool place, frozen, or canned for safekeeping. I make a crock of sauerkraut every fall from excess garden bounty of cabbages and it is delicious cooked with smoked venison meats and pork ribs. It is also a traditional filling for perogies and when fried it makes a tasty side dish for homemade pork or store-bought sausages.

How to dry cabbage

Dried cabbage is a versatile staple to have on your pantry shelf and another great way to put up some of your extra heads. Grandma dried hers on homemade wooden drying racks that sat behind her kitchen woodstove. I dry mine in a food dehydrator

Drying cabbage in a food dehydrator

Grandma's green cabbage soup

and use it in the same recipes and medicinal concoctions handed down to me from Grandma.

When I was a kid, I'd often grab a handful of chewy cabbage to nibble on. Dried cabbage has a delightful jerky-like texture, minus the salt, making it a healthy trail snack for outdoor enthusiasts. Instead of traditional GORP (good old raisins and peanuts), I add dried cabbage to my homemade trail mix for a super healthy chew.

Dried cabbage is an excellent staple for campers and backpackers as it is nonperishable, light, and adds exciting flavor, texture, and extra nutritional boost to other dried camp foods such as rice, pasta, and bean mixes. I create my own food mixes and dried cabbage makes all the difference in the world between the mixes being good and being really great.

Healthful benefits and Old World cabbage cures

Recent studies have indicated that cabbage is a powerful antioxidant helping the body to ward off various types of diseases and cancers, especially those of the colon. It is reputed as helping to boost the immune system which is the reason Grandma upped our cabbage servings in the wintertime during cold and flu seasons.

It is a rich source of vitamins C and E, fiber, iron, calcium, and potassium. The pungent odor that comes from cabbage as it begins to cook is due to the sulphur content which is an element that helps the body fight bacteria and, according to the writings in Grandma's old doctoring journals, keeps the hair strong and shiny and also helps flush impurities out of the body.

To make a dose of Grandma's medicinal cabbage tea (said to be good treatment for those who can't keep food down, for helping to break up a chest cold and congestion, and, according to Grandma, "good for almost anything that ails you...") put a couple of tablespoons of dried cabbage into a preheated teapot. Add a few sprigs of dried basil or thyme. Cover with one cup of boiling water and let steep until cabbage is soft. Serve in a teacup with a spoon for getting up the cabbage after the tea has been drunk. This tea is excellent for calming the nerves and treating chilblains. I like mine with a dash of soy sauce and a pinch of black pepper.

A leaf or two of raw green or red cabbage dipped in apple cider vinegar and nibbled on before mealtimes helps curb the appetite of those who tend to overindulge and also helps ward off heartburn, as Grandma has it written.

It is also noted in her old doctoring journals that folks suffering from numb fingers or toes, or poor circulation in their arms, legs, or feet should include more cabbage in their diets. She also recommended cabbage plasters for those suffering from rheumatism and arthritic aches and pains.

To make a cabbage plaster, pound several outer green leaves until they are well bruised. Grandma used a big round stone for pounding the leaves; I use my meat mallet. Wrap the prepared leaves around the afflicted area and hold in place by a piece of flannelette. I can vouch that this Old World cure brings fast relief for swollen, aching joints as it has warming properties that not only ease pain, but also help reduce swelling. I have depended on it for years for relief from twisted ankles and wrists, sore knees, and sprains.

Modern day research backs Grandma's old cabbage claims as studies have indicated that external applications of raw cabbage leaves are useful in helping to improve circulation and for reducing inflammation, thus useful for treating rheumatism and arthritis, chest infections, tonsillitis, sciatica, and other related afflictions.

I learned from Grandma that a cabbage poultice can be used for drawing infection from wounds. You simply shred a handful of green cabbage and pound it until mushy using a pestle and mortar. Spread the cabbage on the infected area and wrap it in a clean lint-free cloth. Leave for 30 minutes to an hour, depending on the severity of the infection and then rinse the wound in boiled water that has been allowed to cool until tepid. This can be repeated using clean cabbage each time until pus is drawn out. If the sore is caused from a foreign object, such as a splinter, the poultice will draw the offender to the surface where it can be removed. I remember my grandma using this treatment many times to draw out berry thorns, thistles, and slivers from my hands and knees when I was a kid!

Cabbage on the table

When it comes to cabbage on the table, the good news is that it's an inexpensive vegetable that's readily available year round and since there are so many delicious ways to enjoy it you'll never tire of sampling the healthful joys of dining on the cabbage patch family.

Below are some Old World recipes from Grandmother's collection and some new-age recipes that showcase cabbage in gourmet fashion.

Grandma's green cabbage soup:

This is a versatile soup that is a supper in itself when served with wholesome homemade whole wheat bread. Sprinkle with grated cheddar or Parmesan upon serving, if you wish. Serves 6.

3 Tbsp. vegetable oil
1 minced onion
4 cloves minced garlic
4 peeled diced potatoes
½ head green cabbage, cored and shredded
½ cup barley
6 cups homemade vegetable stock (I make mine from saved up scraps such as outer cabbage leaves and hearts, carrot ends, cauliflower stalks, celery leaves...)
1 pint canned tomatoes with juice
salt and pepper to taste

Heat oil in soup pot, sauté onion, garlic, and potatoes until onion is soft. Add cabbage, sauté until it starts to go limp. Add barley, stock, tomatoes, and seasoning. Bring to a boil, reduce heat, cover and simmer until barley is tender.

Quick Oriental cabbage soup

Quick Oriental cabbage soup:

4 cups water
¼ cup soy sauce
1 tsp. sesame oil
drop or two chili oil
3 dried shiitake mushrooms broken into bits
2 cloves minced garlic
small knob grated ginger
2 cups shredded Savoy cabbage
salt and pepper to taste
minced green onions

Put all ingredients, except green onion, into saucepan. Bring to boil, reduce heat, simmer 5 minutes or until cabbage is barely tender. I like it when the cabbage still has a bit of "bite." Sprinkle with green onion before serving.

Cabbage cakes:

Grandma made these often. They are crispy on the outside, tender and moist inside. Serve them with sour cream on the side.

Fry cabbage cakes until golden on each side.

3 cups finely shredded green cabbage
1 minced onion
1 beaten egg
3 Tbsp. sour cream
4 Tbsp. flour
salt and pepper to taste
vegetable oil

Steam the cabbage until tender. Drain and pat excess moisture out of the cabbage. (Grandma steamed hers on top of the woodstove but this can be done in the microwave). Add onion to cabbage. Mix the egg, sour cream, and flour, blend into the cabbage. Add a little more flour if mixture is too moist or a little more sour cream if too dry to form cakes. Heat oil in skillet, drop batter into the pan, and cook the cakes until bubbles form on the top side. Flip and cook the other side until golden. Makes about 6 cakes.

Braised green cabbage:

Here's an old recipe from Grandma's files — a vegetable side dish to go with roast venison or other roasted meat or poultry.

3 Tbsp. vegetable oil
1 minced onion
1 head green cabbage, quartered and shredded
2 Tbsp. brown sugar
¼ cup apple juice
salt and pepper to taste
1 Tbsp. apple cider vinegar

Heat the oil in saucepan, sauté onion until soft. Add cabbage and sugar, cook until cabbage begins to wilt. Add apple juice, pepper, and salt. Bring to a boil, reduce heat and simmer until cabbage is tender and liquid is evaporated. Sprinkle with apple cider vinegar, add seasonings and heat through. Serves 4.

Red cabbage and feta cheese salad:

My favorite salad — no measurements to fuss with! Simply put a serving of shredded red cabbage on a salad plate. Add crumbled feta cheese. Top with nuts or seeds of choice and sprinkle with balsamic vinegar and a drop or two of olive oil — and a good dose of fresh minced raw garlic if romance isn't on the menu!

Cabbage, prawn, and pineapple stir-fry:

Another recipe that is so versatile, you will never make it the same way twice! I always use whatever vegetables I have in the crisper and prawns or whatever other seafood I have available. Chinese and Savoy cabbage are perfect for this recipe but green cabbage is good, too! Serves 4.

3 Tbsp. vegetable oil
3 cloves minced garlic
1 onion, quartered and separated
2 cups pan-ready prawns (or other seafood suitable for stir-frying)
2 stalks diagonally-cut celery
1 sweet red pepper, cut into chunks
1 thinly sliced chili pepper (optional)
3 cups chopped Chinese or Savoy cabbage
1 thinly sliced carrot
small knob grated ginger
handful snow peas
1 cup canned drained pineapple chunks, juice saved
green onions to garnish

Heat oil in wok, add garlic and onion and stir-fry 1 minute. Add prawns and stir-fry about 3 minutes. Add remaining vegetables, continue stir-frying until vegetables are barely tender and prawns are cooked. Stir in the sauce and cook until thickened. Garnish with thinly sliced green onions and serve over steamed rice.

Sauce:

¾ cup pineapple juice
4 Tbsp. soy sauce
3 Tbsp. sweet chili sauce
1 Tbsp. cornstarch blended into 2 Tbsp. cold water
honey to taste

Mix ingredients, taste, and adjust sweetness.

Oriental pickled red cabbage:

A refreshing salad for summer dining. It saves well for several days in the fridge and improves with age.

1 head red cabbage
knob fresh grated ginger
¾ cup rice vinegar
3 Tbsp. soy sauce
2 Tbsp. mirin (Japanese cooking wine)
honey to taste

Grate cabbage finely and put into a glass bowl with ginger. Mix remaining ingredients and pour over salad. Weigh down with a plate so cabbage is submerged. Marinate in fridge at least 4 hours before serving.

Fried cabbage with homemade noodles:

This simple, hearty main course dish comes from Hungary. It is always a big hit at my supper table.

Noodles:

2 cups flour
pinch of salt
2 eggs
cold water

Put flour into a bowl with a pinch of salt. Break in eggs and blend with a fork. Add just enough cold water to form a ball, knead until smooth. Put dough on floured board and roll out thinly. Cover with clean towel, let dry several hours. Cut noodles into 2-inch strips, dust with flour, pile atop of each other, and slice into about ¼-inch noodles. Drop noodles into boiling lightly salted water, cook 3 minutes. Drain, toss with olive oil or a little butter. Set aside.

Fried cabbage: Heat 3 tablespoons of oil or fat in skillet. Old World cooks use homemade pork lard or bacon grease, but olive or vegetable oil is the healthier choice. Sauté 4 cups shredded cabbage until soft. Turn heat up and continue cooking until cabbage turns tan. Add the cooked noodles and heat through. Season with salt and pepper and serve

Fixings for cabbage, prawn, and vegetable stir-fry — Savoy cabbage is excellent in stir-fries as are traditional Chinese types of cabbage.

sour cream on the side. Soy sauce is excellent sprinkled over top, in which case omit the salt.

Spicy Indian cabbage:

This spicy cabbage dish comes from India and is sure to become a family favorite.

4 Tbsp. butter (or margarine)
½ tsp. cumin seeds
½ tsp. coriander seeds (you can use ground spice, but I like the burst of flavor that biting into a whole seed produces)
crushed dried red chilies to suit taste
1 minced onion
3 cups shredded green cabbage
3 grated carrots
salt and pepper
lemon juice

Heat butter in saucepan, sauté seeds and chilies for about half a minute. Add onion, fry until soft. Add cabbage and carrots and stir-fry until cabbage is soft, about 3 minutes. Season, sprinkle with lemon juice. Serves 4.

Old World cabbage-cheddar biscuits:

A savory biscuit that is sure to please. Serve these with cabbage soup for a double good dose of cabbage.

2 Tbsp. butter
½ Tbsp. sugar
2 cups finely shredded cabbage
2 cups flour
1 Tbsp. baking powder
pinch of salt
¼ cup shortening
½ cup grated cheddar cheese
milk (about ½ cup)

Melt butter in frying pan, sprinkle in sugar. Brown it but don't burn it. Add cabbage and cook over low heat until it is tan, about 15 minutes. Set aside to cool. Put flour, baking powder, and salt into bowl. Cut in shortening until crumbly. Stir in cheese and cabbage. Add just enough milk to bind. Knead lightly, pat on floured board into ½-inch circle. Cut out biscuits and place on baking sheet. Bake in 450° F oven for 15 minutes or until puffed and golden. Makes 12 to 15 biscuits. Δ

Make your own firestarters

By Claire Wolfe

I bought an old house last summer and inherited lots of the former owners' stuff — some of it good and welcome, some strictly landfill-fodder.

Among other things that the sellers left were bags of stove pellets. Now, that's a good thing. Unfortunately, the stove for those pellets has a broken igniter and some of the pellets were stored in damp conditions and are dissolving back into the sawdust they were made from.

I asked readers of my *Backwoods Home* blog (www.backwoodshome.com/blogs/ClaireWolfe/) what they thought I should do with bags of ruined wood pellets. Suggestions were varied and creative. At first I didn't pay much attention to one suggestion: make your own firestarters.

Why bother, I thought? Firestarters are cheap. Why spend hours on something I can get at the hardware store for a few bucks? (Yes, I know that's not the best backwoods thinking, but there it is.) Not until somebody else laughingly suggested that I make my own and market them as "Firebrand Firestarters" in recognition of my political heckraising did the thought of homemade firestarters spark my imagination. Besides, since I wasn't about to pay $200 to repair my stove's igniter, I was going to need a lot of firestarters to get the thing going. At least one a day during heating season for years to come.

Well, I can tell you I'll probably never market "Firebrands," but I've discovered that making firestarters is a lot of fun. Not only that, the homemade type have several advantages over storeboughts:

• They tend to work better.

• They're less expensive — virtually free when made from materials already on hand.

• It's easy to make several months' supply in one session.

• You can custom-design your firestarters to have characteristics you want. Make different types for backpacking and home use, for instance, or one type for lighting charcoal and another for wood.

• They're a great project to make with your older children.

The plate in the foreground contains all the different types of firestarters from the egg carton plus some small wax-coated pinecones. I suspended most of them from pieces of cotton yarn and dipped them in purple wax. The remaining bits of yarn (also wax-saturated) serve as wicks. The bowl in the rear contains chunks of firestarter from the pie tin.

• You can make them plain for everyday use or fancy (and fragrant!) for gifts or to sell.

Here's what you need

• Some form of wax. This can be paraffin bought from your local canning supply. But I'll bet you've got a bag of old candle ends around somewhere. Those will do just as well. So will those broken crayons your children no longer use. Or wax seals you've removed from old canned foods. Or beeswax.

• Some type of combustible material in small bits: sawdust, dryer lint, evergreen needles, wood chips, crumbly stove pellets, cotton balls, thick shredded paper or cardboard, cut up bits of old cotton rags — even the soft undercoat you've brushed out of your dog's fur. Don't use anything that might be toxic (like sawdust from treated lumber, for instance); otherwise, if it's small and it will burn, it's probably good.

• A large pot (a water-bath canner with a rack in the bottom does nicely, but a stewpot will do)

• A quart-sized jar

• Something you can use for a mold: egg cartons, muffin pans, aluminum pie dishes, miniature paper cupcake cups, shot glasses, or votive-candle cups (if you have a bunch of them), or anything else that can hold the materials. Cut-down sections of toilet-paper rolls could work. Ice cube trays are a possibility; just make sure yours won't melt!

• A cookie sheet or some other material to protect your kitchen counter from spilled or leaking wax.

How to make them

One important thing to remember: Although this project is easy and safe if you use reasonable precautions, you are working with flammable (and hot) materials. So melt your wax at medium to low temperatures (never use high heat). Keep an eye on it as it melts; don't walk away and forget it.

Fill a mold with your combustible material. Here I'm using an egg carton, but many other types of containers will do, from pie pans to toilet-paper tubes. From left to right the materials in the carton are: dog fur, evergreen needles, dryer lint, sawdust from crumbling stove pellets, cotton balls, and torn bits of the egg carton itself.

Handle hot materials with oven mitts. Work carefully to avoid spills. And keep small children and animals away from the stove and the rest of your work area.

1. Assemble your materials.

2. Place just two to three inches of water in your pan — no more.

3. Fill a jar about halfway with wax and place the open jar into the water. Note: If the jar tries to float when you put it in the pan, either add more wax to the jar or lower the water level in the pan. Otherwise, you could end up with wax in your water and water in your wax.

4. Heat the water on medium *just to simmering*. As soon as you see rising bubbles in the water, turn the heat to low and watch as your wax finishes turning liquid.

5. While the water is heating, place your combustible materials loosely into the mold or molds. Place the molds on the cookie sheet or other protective surface.

6. Once the wax has completely melted, lift the jar carefully from the pan (wearing oven mitts on both hands) and pour just enough wax into the molds for your combustibles to absorb. Don't worry about completely covering the materials; it can actually help to have some bits sticking out from the wax; protruding material can serve as a wick.

7. Once the wax has cooled, you can remove your firestarters from their molds. How you do this will depend on the materials you've used. If your mold was made of paper (like an egg carton or muffin cup), the mold may end up becoming part of the firestarter. Just cut or tear the excess away and use the remaining paper to help light your creation. If your mold was rigid metal or glass, put it in the refrigerator for half an hour and your new firestarters will pop right out. If your mold was flexible metal like an aluminum plate, just

Melt your wax over medium to low heat. Keep the water level in the pan low enough to prevent the jar from trying to float. If you prefer, you can use a double boiler instead of a jar and kettle to melt the wax. But that could take quite a bit of cleanup. The jar has the advantage of giving you a place to store leftover wax until your next firestarter-making session.

bend it until the waxy creation within pops loose.

Some tips and some fun additions

Once you have the basics, you can customize your future creations. Each material has its own characteristics, and by changing materials and sizes, you can make firestarters that are best for certain purposes.

For example: Cotton ball firestarters can be among the hardest to light. But because they're lightweight, compact, and don't crumble, they may be your best bet for backpacking trips. Also, if you're using an egg carton or other paper mold, the saturated cotton balls may pop out without the need to destroy the mold.

I like to make the starters for my pellet stove using an aluminum pie pan. Just layer ½-inch or less of combustible material in the pan and pour in enough wax for the material to absorb. When it sets, you have one big pie-sized lump. It ain't pretty. But it's fast and you can break the "pie" into any size chunks you need. The irregular edges and protruding combustibles also make these pie-plate "Firebrands" very easy to light. The pan is good for several uses before it develops cracks.

If your only aim is to get a campfire, barbecue, or stove going, you probably don't care how your firestarters smell. But be aware that some materials (like pine needles) produce a lovely aroma. Others (like dog hair) may stink when they burn.

If you want to get fancy with aromas, consider adding one of the following to your melted wax: oil of clove, cinnamon oil, peppermint oil, or some other aromatic oil.

When color matters, use colored candles. Or use white or clear wax, then add a crayon or two. A single crayon can create surprisingly vivid color. If you add more than one, be aware of the effects of mixing colors. A yellow crayon and a red one will yield orange. A blue one and a green one gives you turquoise or aqua. Red and blue make purple, and so on. But some colors only make a mess! Mix red with green or purple with yellow and you'll end up with an ugly mud color.

If you discover that your newly made firestarters are hard to light (unlikely, but it can happen), wrap them in a twist of paper like a candy. Apply a match to one or both ends of the paper and you're on your way.

You can also make firestarters by tying a length of cotton string or yarn to a small combustible object and dipping it several times in the melted wax. Pinecones are the most common for this, but you could get creative with any small, easily burnable thing — cut cardboard shapes, little scrolls of rice paper, small wooden game pieces, or wooden beads, for instance. Once the wax dries, cut the string (leaving enough to serve as a wick), then pack your finished firestarter in a gift basket for a friend. (If you're giving firestarters away, it's a good idea to test that your particular kind works first.)

Decorative firestarters could also become items to sell at a local craft fair or farmer's market. You're not likely to earn a lot of money on them, but you'll have had fun creating them. Δ

the under-appreciated sweet potato

By Vernon Lewis

An elderly acquaintance was reminiscing one day about the Great Depression and how poor her family had been. Her family grew a garden, like so many others at that time, and one of the vegetables they raised was the sweet potato. My wife, Isabel, a native of Taiwan, shared that the sweet potato had been a valuable staple in her parents' day as well — from before WWII to the days of Taiwan's subsequent prosperity. The tubers and the leaves were a large part of the average diet, especially among the poor. Our friend commented that she had always thought the leaves and vines were poisonous to humans. Isabel and I felt it was a shame that this lady's family had not taken full advantage of the sweet potato's bounty and wondered how many others needlessly went hungry and malnourished.

The sweet potato is often mistakenly called a yam. The yam has brown or black skin which resembles the bark of a tree and has off-white, purple, or red flesh. In contrast, sweet potatoes are elongated yellow or orange tubers with ends that taper to a point. The sweet potato is what Americans commonly eat for Thanksgiving and Christmas. The Irish potato (what we Americans bake or mash) is different. It is a member of the nightshade family and you must not eat anything but its tuber, as the leaves and stems of Irish potatoes are poisonous and could kill you.

You can grow your own sweet potato slips by placing a sliced sweet potato in a shallow dish of water. When the sprouts grow to about six inches long, break them off and place in a glass of water for a couple of weeks until roots develop.

Sweet potato leaves and tender vine tips can be used as a cooked green just as spinach would be used.

Good for you

Sweet potatoes — both the tubers and the leaves — are one of the most nourishing vegetables we can eat. The Center for Science in the Public Interest (CSPI) ranks the sweet potato tuber "number one in nutrition of all vegetables." USDA data show low sodium and very low saturated fat and cholesterol, high dietary fiber, vitamin B6 and potassium, as well as very high vitamin A, vitamin C, and manganese. It has a low glycemic load and is strongly anti-inflammatory. Eating your home grown sweet potatoes with the skin allows full benefit of the nutrients.

As good as sweet potato tubers are, my favorite parts of the plant to eat are the young, heart-shaped leaves and vine tips. The soft, pleasant consistency is somewhere between spinach and chard. The taste is vaguely reminiscent of spinach, but not as pungent and with its own unique character and taste. These greens are widely consumed in many parts of the world, including Africa and Asia. Sweet potato leaves and vine tips are high in vitamins A and C, and are a good source of vitamin B2 (Riboflavin). They are also an excellent source of the antioxidant lutein.

Easy to grow

The sweet potato also happens to be one of the easiest vegetables to grow successfully. Starting sweet potatoes is simple. Those in the southeast, and perhaps other areas as well, can buy bunches of sweet potato slips — short rooted vines with small leaves — at a local garden supply store when it is time to plant. Alternatively, you can start your own slips. About four to six weeks before planting time, slice a tuber into two-inch slabs and place each slab in a shallow saucer of water. Place these slabs where they will receive some light, (such as on a window sill) yet remain warm enough for this warm-weather plant to sprout. In a few days you will observe sprouts forming. Add water as needed.

As the sprouts reach six to eight inches tall, break them off and place them in a jar of water so they will form roots. Place the jars where they will receive full light for at least part of the day to prevent sun scald once they are planted in the garden. Adequate roots should form in a week or two. The sprouts should be planted soon after they form a small set of roots or they tend to rot. If the weather looks like it will remain cool longer than anticipated, you may extend the time the sprouts are on the tuber or plant the slips temporarily in a pot of dirt.

If you grew sweet potatoes last year, you may find that the roots, small tubers, buried vines, and other leftovers emerge as small vines with the warm weather. These can be dug up and placed in this year's sweet potato bed.

Sweet potatoes will grow in less than ideal soil, but to maximize your harvest, fertilize well. To enhance tuber growth, limit nitrogen and enhance phosphorus and potassium. To enhance leaf growth, use more nitrogen. You may want to grow part of your crop for the tubers and part for the greens. Do make sure your sweet potato bed is deep and loose, amending with organic matter. The tubers will grow down and some of them will reach a foot or longer and weigh several pounds. Growing in compacted soil causes them to push out of the ground where they are more easily damaged by rodents. It also forces them into distorted shapes that are more easily broken and harder to prepare for eating. In addition to that, wrestling them out of the ground during harvest wastes effort and damages tubers.

The biggest problem I have had with growing sweet potatoes is predation from mice and voles. The first two years I raised them, the varmints ate more than my family did. This was easily remedied, however. During the winter and growing season I kept rodent poison in bait stations. Pets, birds, kids, and the occasional wayward chicken could not reach the poison, but the mice, voles, and rats did. Worked like a charm.

Harvesting

Harvest leaves any time you want, daily if desired. Just leave enough leaves for the plant to feed itself. If your sweet potato plants are healthy, harvesting the leaves will not harm them. In fact, harvesting the leaves is the perfect opportunity to keep the vines in check, as they like to take over a garden area. Cut vines that are escaping their boundary, then strip the dark green leaves and the tender tips. The vine remaining on the plant will branch and sprout new growth. Rabbits and goats love the leftovers and so do the chickens if they are chopped into small pieces. You can also compost them, but the vines will establish roots and start growing again.

The tubers can be harvested and eaten any time after they form. To maximize the harvest, allow them to grow as long as possible, but dig before cold autumn weather, as freezing will damage the tubers. When digging the tubers out of the ground, loosen the soil with a shovel or garden fork, being careful not to damage them. Set damaged tubers aside for short-term consumption, or feed them to the livestock; we almost always cut off the damage and eat them. As you remove the tubers from the ground, brush off the loose soil. After harvest, lay the tubers out and allow them to cure for several days, keeping them dry. After curing, place the tubers in covered storage containers (I use cardboard boxes) and place the containers in a cool, dark location. The tubers will become sweeter and more flavorful over the first few weeks after harvest. They are supposed to keep for six months or more, but we always eat them long before that. Do not neglect the smaller tubers that look like fat roots. They are very edible and Isabel says they are sweeter than the larger ones. She just washes them, boils them, and eats them, skin and all.

Cooking sweet potatoes

Most of us eat sweet potatoes at holiday meals, peeled, baked, and smothered in brown sugar and marshmallows. But the versatility of the sweet potato is unparalleled. The young tender leaves can be used just like cooked spinach and other greens are used.

Sweet potato tubers can grow up to a foot long, in loose, deep soil. Compacted or rocky soil will cause the tubers to push out of the ground or grow in odd shapes.

The tuber can be used in place of winter squash since it has a similar consistency, just a little drier. It can be used in breads, cakes, pies, pastries, casseroles, soups, stews, and made into fries and chips. The tubers and leaves can also be preserved by canning or cooking and freezing. Here are a few of my family's favorite ways to eat sweet potato tubers and greens. These are also simple and require minimal preparation.

Sautéed sweet potato leaves:

Wash the leaves and tender vine tips in cold water several times until clean. Put a flat pan or wok on medium heat and pour in a dab of olive oil or other cooking oil. Add several cloves of garlic — whole, crushed, or chopped as preferred. Fill the pan with a slightly heaping pile of the greens. Stir the greens now and then to keep them from scorching until they are wilted. Unlike spinach, sweet potato leaves do not lose a lot of water when cooked, so you may need to add a bit of water to the pan to aid the wilting process. When the leaves have wilted, stir in a pinch of sugar and salt to taste. Serve hot.

Baked sweet potato:

Wash the tubers thoroughly before preparing. There are a couple of ways my family bakes sweet potatoes. The first way is to place any size tuber in an oven heated to 350° F until soft all the way through. The second is to select medium to large tubers and wrap in heavy aluminum foil. Cover them in a bed of coals for about 20 minutes. You may need to turn them once to cook evenly. The tubers are done when they become soft all the way through. Unwrap, then eat them skin and all.

Sweet potato broth:

Peel a tuber and cube it into one-inch or smaller chunks. Boil water equal to about two to three times the volume of the tuber cubes. Place the chunks in the boiling water for 20 to 30 minutes. When the chunks are soft, add the sweetener of your choice (honey, brown sugar, or granulated sugar) to taste and serve. Very nice on a cold day. Δ

Lenie in the kitchen

Dutch oven stew for Sunday night supper

By Ilene Duffy

When my sister, Sally, moved away in order to begin her teaching career in 1976, she gave me our Aunt Belle's Dutch oven. Since then it has been one of my most treasured pieces of cookware. Whether on the stove or in the oven, with soups, stews, rice, or beans, the Dutch oven gets frequent use in the Duffy household. Aunt Belle would be delighted to know how much I have used it.

A few weekends ago, I came across a stew recipe that I wanted to try using my Dutch oven. The directions say to brown the meat on top of the stove, then finish cooking the stew in the oven. I used the basic ingredients called for, but modified the recipe with the addition of root vegetables. The original recipe called for beef broth, but I changed it to chicken broth with wonderful results. After the addition of all those great vegetables, there was no room for potatoes, so I just steamed some red potatoes as a side dish. Our Sunday night dinner got a resounding thumbs up from my Duffy men.

Oven beef stew

2 lbs. beef stew meat, cut into 1-inch cubes
½ tsp. salt
¼ tsp. pepper
⅓ cup flour, divided
2-3 Tbsp. olive oil
½ tsp. dried sage
2 sprigs of fresh rosemary leaves, chopped
1 large onion, chopped
6 cloves garlic, chopped
2 cans (15-oz.) chicken broth
2 bay leaves
3 carrots, chopped in large chunks
3 parsnips, chopped in large chunks
3 rutabagas, quartered

Hearty beef stew with carrots, parsnips, and rutabagas makes a great supper.

Preparations:

Preheat oven to 350° F. In a cast iron Dutch oven, heat olive oil. In a large bowl add the stew meat, sprinkle with salt and pepper, then add about half of the flour. Mix until well coated. Add to the hot oil and stir to brown meat on all sides. Add the dried sage and fresh rosemary leaves. Stir in the onion and garlic and cook about 4 minutes, stirring occasionally. Add the remaining flour, mixing it in well. Add the broth and bay leaves. Stir gently while scraping the bottom of the pot. Bring mixture to a gentle boil.

Cover the Dutch oven securely, then transfer it to the warm oven. Bake for at least 1 hour. Remove from the oven and add carrots, parsnips, and rutabagas. Cover and return to oven for about 45 minutes. Check vegetables to see if they're done, but not too soft.

This stew is great served with warm cornbread. The nutmeg and cinnamon adds a nice touch.

Jack Fazio's cornbread

1½ cups flour
1½ cups cornmeal
1 Tbsp. baking powder
½ tsp. nutmeg
½ tsp. cinnamon
¼ tsp. salt
¾ cup sugar
2 eggs
½ cup canola oil
1 cup milk

Preparations:

Preheat oven to 375° F. In a large bowl, mix all dry ingredients. In another large bowl, mix eggs, oil, and milk. Add dry ingredients to egg mixture until just blended. Pour into greased 9x12-inch baking pan. Bake for about 25 minutes or until it tests done with a toothpick. Δ

Backwoods Home magazine

practical ideas for self-reliant living

July/Aug 2011
Issue #130
$5.95 US
$7.50 CAN

Wash day
with Jackie Clay

Storing and using wheat
Blueberry cash crop
The low cost of beef
Survival storeroom
Buying a backhoe

www.backwoodshome.com

DON CHILDERS

My view

A government with not enough to do, but lots of hungry mouths to feed

Most people look in the wrong places for threats to society, and their perceptions are easily manipulated by the mass media, which is often spoon-fed its stories by politicians and government bureaucrats who have a vested interest in having people look in the wrong places.

Just this morning I read a *New York Times* story about an Appalachian community in Ohio that was "home to some of the highest rates of prescription drug overdoses in the state" and that had "growing numbers of younger victims." The story was an all-too-familiar government rant about drugs destroying families. Its cleverly selected anecdotes about children whose lives have been ruined by prescription drugs — "including a seventh grader" — may contain some truth, but in a society of 300 million there are always some poor souls destroying themselves with bad behavior.

The sources quoted in this story were some of the usual government misinformers: a health bureaucrat who warns, "Around here, everyone has a kid who is addicted," a police chief who cautions, "We're raising third and fourth generations of prescription drug abusers now," and a state assemblyman who cries, "It's the darkest, most malevolent thing you've ever seen." And the usual government solutions have been proposed: new state and federal laws controlling prescription drugs, arrest and incarceration of offenders, and, of course, increased funding to do it all.

The story states that authorities are already making progress against the prescription drug problem by arresting doctors who prescribe them. One has already had his license revoked and another is on trial in federal court for "illegally dispensing prescription painkillers." Unfortunately, the article complains, "the drugs are legal, and it is hard to prosecute the people selling them." So the police chief has called for a "coordinated effort by local, state and federal law enforcement agencies," Ohio Governor Kasich "declared the county a pilot project for combating addiction," and the "Obama administration announced plans to fight prescription drug addiction nationally."

Lord help us, the government and the bureaucrats are coming to the rescue again, this time to keep us safe from prescription drugs. The article even cites three elderly drug pushers — a 64-year-old veteran, a 74-year-old Social Security recipient, and a lady called Granny who is in her 70s and is selling prescription drugs out of her house. These old folks and their doctors, the government says, are all part of this new threat to society.

But some of us know what's really going on. Big Government, in particular its obese drug enforcement underbelly, has too many bureaucrats with not enough to do. They need to justify their existence and appetite for our tax dollars, so they are following the business example of their more productive civilian counterparts by going out and creating more business for themselves.

This is the problem with government bureaucracies. Once they are in existence, they not only never go away but they expand into areas where they have no business. The current bureaucracy that enforces the government's *War on Drugs* is left over from *Prohibition*. It didn't go away once *Prohibition* ended, but merely changed its mission to combat marijuana, the devil weed that was threatening to destroy our youth. Now that the public is sick of the *War on Marijuana*, the bureaucracy needs a new enemy so they are trying to sell the public on the prescription drug menace. If it means carting Granny and her doctor off to jail, so what. It's business!

Unfortunately for us freedom-lovers in society, there are enough easily misinformed voters around that the government will probably succeed in convincing them that "something must be done to save our children from this new threat." Ordinary people who yesterday were law-abiding citizens will suddenly be deemed criminals for the sake of keeping the bureaucracy employed.

This is how government bureaucracies evolve, and how a tyrannical state ultimately emerges. Already, doctors are hesitant to prescribe many types of painkillers for their patients due to the undercurrent of suspicion the *War on Prescription Drugs* has created. Next time you need a painkiller for more than a month, ask your doctor to make your prescription renewable at the end of the normal one-month period. He most likely won't; it is simply too risky to be labeled by the feds as a doctor who may "overprescribe" prescription drugs.

It's a sad state of affairs in the formerly most-free country in the world, and I think it's going to get worse. When these government bureaucrats are done terrorizing old folks and doctors, they'll manufacture a new threat to keep themselves employed, and the cycle will continue until enough people understand that their turn to be a target of our unnecessary and underemployed government bureaucracy could be next.

All too few of us understand that the real threat to a free society comes from the society's own government and its ever-growing bureaucracy which must always be on the hunt for money to feed itself. It needs domestic enemies, so it preys on the rest of us like a pack of wolves among a flock of sheep.

Our military just killed bin Laden, who was a real threat to our society, but all the while we have been hunting him, our domestic army — the bureaucracy — has been waging a guerilla war against us. Today it's Granny and her doctor, tomorrow it will be you. — ***Dave Duffy***

brew your own ROOT BEER

By Tim Murphy

Ah, root beer! That sweet, dark elixir of kidhood, majestically topped with a beige pillow of foam. It's the perfect companion to Bazooka bubble gum, baseball cards, wiffle ball, and hot summer days. I grew up quaffing Canfield's, Hires, A&W, Faygo, Frostie, Dog & Suds, and Dad's. Today you'll find Barq's, Mug, IBC, and Henry Weinhard's in my fridge. Just like in the nineties for beer, today there is a growing home "root brew" movement.

Variations on root beers and sassafras teas have been made for centuries. Its origins go back well before our country was founded, but it wasn't until 1876 that Charles Hires produced the first national brand. "Hires Root Beer" was unveiled at the United States Centennial Exposition. His was the first drink to use the name "root beer" and it was sold in bottles, at drugstore soda fountains, and as an extract to mix at home.

There are hundreds of recipes out there today, from the very simple to the complex. Root beer ingredients are as varied as alcoholic beer components. Flavorings include vanilla, sarsaparilla, licorice, anise, ginger, birch bark, dog grass, wintergreen, sassafras, burdock, juniper, spikenard, and dozens of others. In the early 1960s it was discovered that safrole, a component of sassafras (a major root beer ingredient), was carcinogenic. Root beer manufacturers dropped it from their recipes and scrambled to find substitutes. This altered the drink's "old-fashioned" taste. However, if you've ever wondered why Barq's Root Beer (the one with "bite") is so distinctive from most national brands, here's the secret: They use sassafras with the safrole removed, retaining a closer tie to those original root beers.

Brewing your own is quite easy for the beginner and the price can be equal to or cheaper than the popular brands. A 2-ounce bottle of extract costs me $6.99. Depending on the recipe and strength of flavor, this will yield 3½ to 4 gallons. I use a brand called Old Fashioned Homebrew Root Beer Soda Pop Base made by Rainbow Flavors, Inc. in Osage Beach, Missouri. Here are three of the simplest recipes to get a beginner started.

Super-kwik super-cooled root beer:

6 cups sugar
3¼ gallons cold water
2 ounces root beer extract
4 pounds dry ice

In a large cooler or tub, mix sugar and water together until sugar dissolves. Stir in the extract. Gently put dry ice into the liquid and cover with a lid, loosely. Don't tighten it down or pressure may build up. Let the mixture "brew" for about an hour, then serve. Store the remainder in gallon jugs or bottles.

Home-brewed root beer:

3 Tbsp. root beer extract
2 cups sugar
1 tsp. dry yeast
1 gallon warm water, divided

Pour root beer extract over sugar and add enough water to dissolve. Add yeast to ½ cup warm water to dissolve. Add both mixtures together and pour into gallon jug. Top off jug with warm water and let set for 6 hours uncapped. Tighten lid and refrigerate. After 24 hours, it's ready to drink.

1-2-3-4 Root Beer:

2 cups sugar
1 tsp. yeast
2 Tbsp. root beer extract
1 gallon warm water, divided

Put dry ingredients in a one-gallon jug and pour in one quart of warm water. Stir, or cap the jug and shake until well mixed. Finish filling the jug with warm water, cap, and store in a cool, dry place. Let sit for two days to two weeks, then refrigerate.

The first recipe is by far the easiest and is the most fun for kids to make. So good luck, hoist a frosty mug, say cheers, and enjoy! Δ

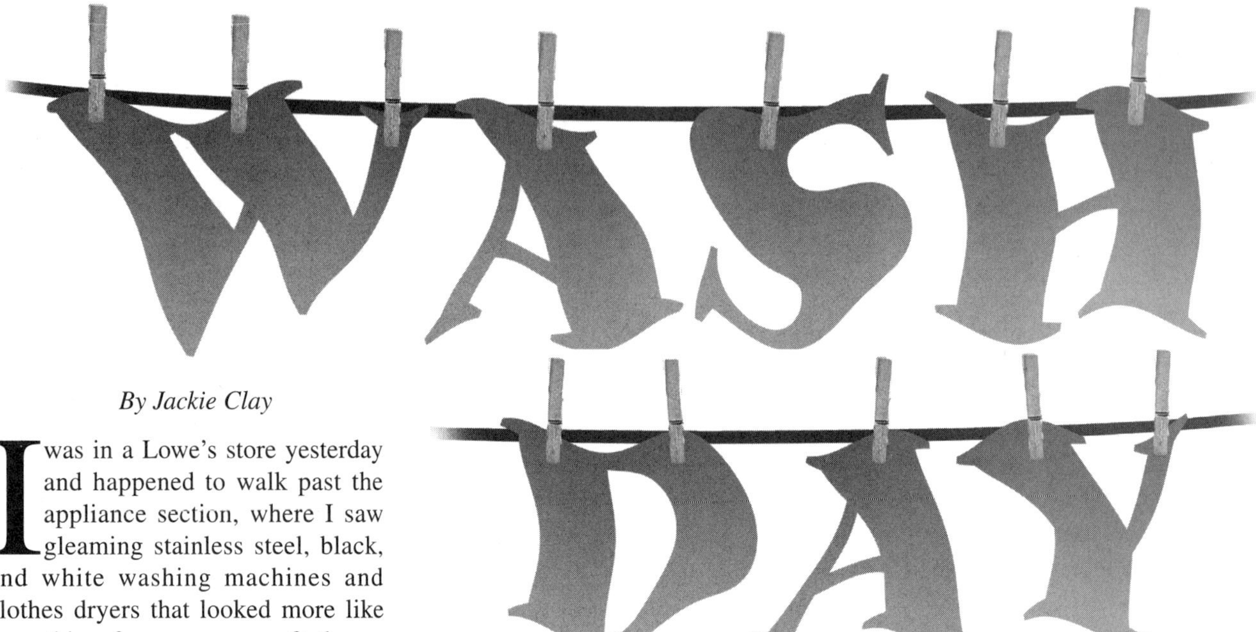

By Jackie Clay

I was in a Lowe's store yesterday and happened to walk past the appliance section, where I saw gleaming stainless steel, black, and white washing machines and clothes dryers that looked more like something from a spacecraft than a laundry room. They all had hefty price tags yet boasted of their energy and water savings. If I used that much energy and water to do laundry, I'd be horrified. My money can be spent on much better things than that.

So how do I wash and dry clothes, you may ask? A scrub board in the creek? Pounding clothes on rocks? Naw. Been there, done that; but didn't like it much.

I wash and dry my clothes like both of my grandmothers and my mom did when I was young. I have a wringer washer and a clothesline just a few feet outside the front door. I don't use the clothesline in mid-winter anymore, although I have in the past. Now I have a propane clothes dryer to use during rainy spells, winter, and when I'm in a hurry.

Advantages of a wringer washer

While using a wringer washer is a little more labor-intensive than using an automatic washer, on the homestead the wringer washer wins, hands-down. First of all, it uses much less water. I fill the wash basin with 15 gallons of water. The rinse tub holds 30 gallons, but I only fill it with 15 or less. That may seem like a lot of water, but with that water, I typically wash six or seven loads of laundry. I start with whites, I progress to light-colored t-shirts and towels, then to darker, but not-so-dirty shirts, darker towels, and good jeans, then move on to dirtier shirts and work jeans, and finally to really dirty work jeans and rugs.

So those 30 gallons of water wash six or seven loads of laundry. And the water doesn't have to be hot, either. Beat that, automatic washers!

Did I mention that my clothes really come cleaner in a wringer washer than they do in an automatic? Well, it's true. While we were in "camping" mode on our new homestead, I took

Washing in a wringer washer and hanging out clothes to dry saves tons of cash, plus your clothes come cleaner and smell oh-so-good.

our clothes to the laundromat in town. Not only was it horribly expensive, but also my clothes never came as clean as I was used to. I tried stain removers, scrubbing before washing, and hotter water to no avail, but as soon as I got my wringer washer set up, my clothes once again came clean.

And for those "dainty" or fragile washables — which I have very few of — you can easily swish them around in the tub for a few minutes, wring them out, and be happy that they didn't fall apart or shrink.

Likewise, for those really, really dirty work jeans, you can leave them in to agitate for an hour if you need to and they come clean enough that your neighbors think you beat them on rocks in the creek all day.

Best of all, you can find a good used wringer washer on sale for less than $100. Mine came from the dump. It had the cord cut off, but we put a new one on and it has worked perfectly for years. I've seen them at yard sales and in newspaper shoppers for $25 to $50.

Once you bring home a wringer washer, you can expect it to wash clothes for you for years, trouble free.

Here is the washer, in progress. Note the on/off knob on the lower front of the washer and the rinse tub next to the washer to receive washed clothes.

Tips on buying a wringer washer

Although you can still buy new wringer washing machines, including a gasoline motor-driven washer that Lehman's Hardware, among others, carries, most of us choose an "experienced" (used) washer, for financial reasons. And, while most used wringer washers are in good shape, it pays to know a little bit about them to make sure you're getting what you want.

The wringer washer has a large tub with a removable agitator in the center. Under the tub is an electric (or gas, in a few cases) motor with a plug on it. The motor drives the agitator and wringer. The gearbox is under the tub, next to the motor. There is gear oil in the box to lubricate the gears. This box sometimes leaks dark oil; check for signs of leakage. You can always add more oil, but if the box is dry, your gears won't last too long.

Some wringer washers are equipped with a pump to pump the water out of the tub after use. The pump will pump the water up and into a drain pipe, similar to that of an automatic washing machine. Or it will make quick work emptying the tub if you choose to empty the dirty water into your rinse tub or even out onto the ground. My aunt washed clothes in her kitchen and pumped the dirty water out into her kitchen sink to drain. After she was done washing, she rolled her wringer washer back under the stairway and hung her tub up on a nail, pulling a curtain across to hide them. There are many various ways to handle a wringer washer, other than having a designated laundry room.

If your washer doesn't have a pump, the tub will drain by gravity. Mine never had a pump and we have plumbed it permanently into a PVC pipe, to drain out into my flower bed next to the house. My old wringer in Montana had no pump either, but I washed outdoors and just drained the water out onto the ground. Think about this when you go to look at your prospective washing machine; you don't want a gravity drain if you *must* have your washing machine inside, in a conventional laundry room, and don't want to re-plumb to suit your new machine.

The tub should be relatively clean. When plugged in, the knob on the outside of the tub should turn on the agitator when pulled out, stopping it when pushed in. The motor should run quietly, with no odd clanking or squealing.

The cord should not be cracked or have bare spots. Of course, you can

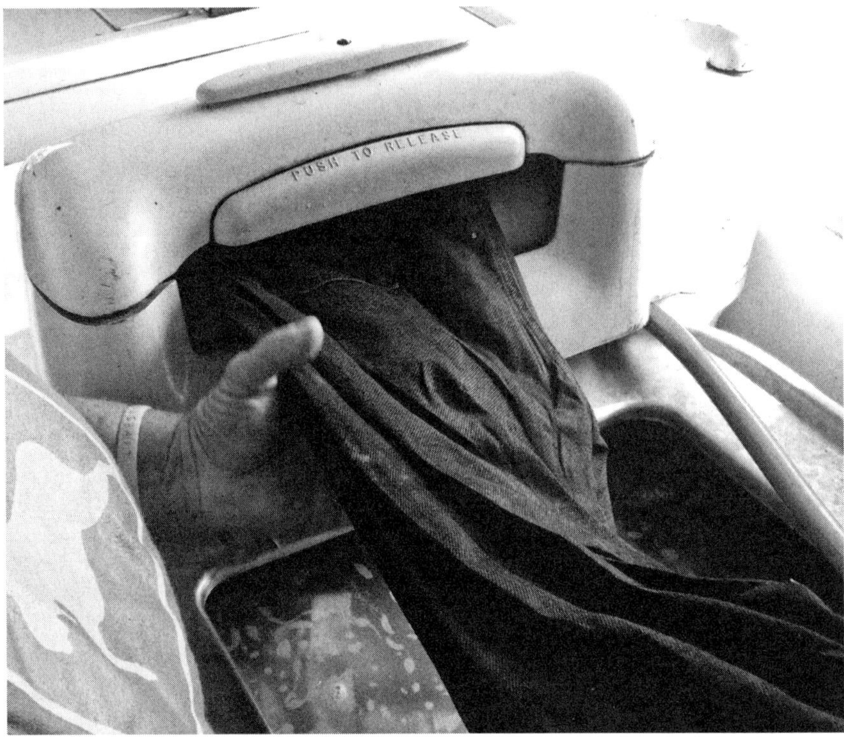

To protect zippers and buttons during wringing, fold the clothing in half, with the fasteners inside. The added bulk of the clothing protects them.

always replace a frayed, broken, or missing cord, as I have done. It is quite an easy and quick job. Because water and a bad cord can cause a fatal electric shock, never use a wringer washer with a faulty cord.

The wringer is removed by pulling it straight up off the driving shaft. Set firmly in place, the top roller and bottom roller of the wringer should meet firmly when the top is pushed evenly down and the tightener on top turned down. The rollers of the wringer should roll smoothly when the handle on the side is turned. One way makes the wringer pull the clothes away from the washer into a rinse tub, the middle is *stop,* and the opposite way will make the clothes back up into the washing machine again.

There is a safety release above the rollers, usually a blue or chrome flat bar. In the event that clothes (or your fingers!) get trapped in the wringer, you can smack this bar with your hand and the pressure will instantly release from the wringer. The rollers will pop apart with a loud noise; to put the rollers back in place, just press down so that they are even, then turn the lever on top to lock them back in place.

You should check all of these features, if possible, before buying your new washer.

Advantages of drying clothes on a clothesline

Like washing clothes with a wringer washer, drying clothes on a clothesline is a little bit more work, but it isn't work-work. It is quite peaceful and rewarding. All you need are clotheslines, a sturdy clothes basket, and a bunch of good clothespins. How cheap is that?

Your clothes smell so good after drying outside in the sun and wind that people actually sniff you when you stand nearby, wondering why you smell so good. No dryer sheet can ever imitate that wonderful fragrance. When I take my clothes down off the line, I can't resist burying my face in the clothes, just to inhale that windblown perfume.

Yes, your clothes sometimes come off the line stiff and with some wrinkles, but modern fabrics are quite resilient and the wrinkles will come out soon after you get dressed, even without ironing.

Towels may not look as "fluffy" as those out of the drier, but boy, do they ever absorb the water when you use them. You'll dry off in half as much time by using these nature-dried towels, and enjoy the process as they retain their great outdoor fragrance.

You can even hang clothes all winter, as I have done in the past. Despite snow and ice, they will eventually "freeze-dry" on the line, without having to bring them in first. Of course, you can also use a clothes-drying rack in front of the wood stove or in your bathtub to substitute for your clothesline in the winter. I've also had clotheslines in my basement, to use during the winter. The clothes dry very well, although they don't have that outdoor, windblown fragrance.

Installing a clothesline

The simplest method of hooking up a clothesline is just to run it between two sturdy tree trunks or a tree and a building. You'll want a clothesline made of plastic-coated wire so it won't stretch. The plastic will keep the wire from rusting and staining your clothes and will also soften the "bite" on your clothes. A rope will work in a pinch, but it will eventually stretch and sag to the point of being useless.

A long line of wet clothes is extremely heavy. Couple that with the flapping these heavy clothes will do on the line and you'll quickly see why you need to anchor the clotheslines with sturdy fasteners, such as screw eyes or strong hooks. With long lines, you will also need a propping pole, as even the strongest clotheslines will sag down under this weight to the point that some clothes may drag in the grass and dirt. A simple sapling with a Y in it is sufficient.

Although you can use the tree-to-tree or building-to-tree anchoring method, often you'll want your clothes-hanging area in a spot devoid of trees. The alternative is to set in your own clothesline poles. These can be treated 4x4s, or steel 2-inch pipes. (You want your lines about 1 to 1½ feet above your head, for ease of reach; for me, lines 6½ feet high are just right. The posts should be sunk 3 feet in the ground. To gain extra line room, a 4-foot cross bar is fastened to the top.

When you have your post cut to length and cross bar fastened securely to the top, drill holes through the cross bar, spaced evenly. Through these, put eye bolts, to which your clotheslines will be fastened.

Dig a 3-foot-deep hole at least 6 inches wider than your post. Either pour a 4-inch concrete pad on the bottom of each hole or sit a 4-inch rock on the bottom of each hole, on which to rest your post. Cut some braces and stakes, then plumb and level your posts, one at a time. Mix up a wheelbarrow load of cement, a little on the sloppy side, and shovel it into the holes, being careful to work out air pockets and keep the posts plumb and level. Bring the cement up just a little above ground level and trowel it off so it slopes away from the posts. Let the cement cure for two days, then remove your braces.

Measure and cut your clotheslines, making sure to leave sufficient line to anchor each end. You can simply tie one end with two good knots, then stretch it tightly to the other end and tie that too, but I've found that it's better to include a tightening turnbuckle on one end, as even the best of clotheslines will stretch and sag with use. With the turnbuckle, you can easily and quickly re-tighten your lines.

Yes, you could just dig a hole, put in a post, and tamp the dirt around it, but that post will eventually fall over under the weight of the clothes, even with a bracing wire run to a stake in the ground. Take the time to use the cement and you'll be happy for many years to come.

Wash tub, clothes basket, and clothespins

To rinse your clothes, you'll need a wash tub. You can either buy a new one from a large store, such as Home Depot, Menards, or Lowe's, or use an old galvanized tub you've bought at a farm store or yard sale. Now that I have my new laundry room, I opted for a new plumbed-in plastic-on-legs tub. Before you plumb in a new tub, check out which side of the washer you'll need your tub to be located on. The wringer on a washer can swing around to several locations; just be sure the knob to turn the agitator on and off is handy and that the wringer swings easily to both the wash-to-rinse tub location and the rinse tub-to-laundry basket position.

While you can use just about anything to carry your clothes, I prefer to use a good willow clothes basket, lined with a piece of old sheet. The sheet keeps the clothes from snagging on the basket and can be taken out and washed, if need be. Any water will drain through it. The basket is lightweight and airy, and dries quickly after use.

Some people like the wooden clothespins that simply shove down over the clothes. While I have used them, I really prefer the spring loaded ones that you squeeze open with thumb and finger. The one-piece pins seem to split and break easier, where the others last longer.

If you keep the pins handy in a clothespin bag on the line, hanging clothes is so much easier. You can just push the bag down the line as you hang clothes, with the pins always ready at hand.

Washing clothes

In the olden days, ladies washed their clothes, especially their whites, in boiling water. Back then, it not only ensured very clean clothes, but it also killed any lice in them. Today, that's not usually much of a concern with us, but hot or boiling water will make washing with homemade lye laundry soap easier.

Fill up your washing machine with water, either hot or cold, to within about an inch of the top of the

Here are our new (used from the dump) clothes poles, ready to hang lines on in a day or two after the cement has cured.

Even in winter, clothes freeze dry nicely outdoors.

agitator. Add bleach, if desired, and laundry soap or detergent. Pull out the knob on the side of the tub so the agitator engages. Add your white clothes. Pre-treat stains before adding to the washing machine, if you wish.

Unlike the automatic washing machine, you have total control, down to the second, of how long you leave your clothes in to agitate. I usually leave my whites in for about 15 minutes. If you are using very hot water, you'll do well to have a clean stick handy to fish the clothes out of the water in order to wring them. Turn on your wringer so that the rollers will pull the clothes from the tub toward the rinse tub.

Always be extremely careful when wringing clothes, as your fingers, hands, clothes, or even hair can be pulled into the wringer. For this reason, watch any children nearby, as well as your own fingers. My late husband, Bob, was "helping" his grandmother wash clothes when his hand got pulled into the wringer. By the time his panicked grandmother reacted and hit the emergency bar, his whole arm had gone into the wringer! Luckily, other than pain and bruising, Bob got off easily. Just be careful. I've used a wringer washer for more than 40 years and neither I nor any of my children has ever gotten into the wringer, but I *always* think about it.

Wring your whites into the rinse tub, then swish them around with your hand well. Swing the wringer around to the into-the-laundry basket position and wring the clothes dry. Put your next load of light-colored, lightly soiled clothes on to agitate and go hang the first load.

Washing tips

To keep bra and other hook-and-eye clothing from having the hooks squashed flat, run a sock, towel, or other larger, soft piece through the wringer with the hooks. To keep buttons from popping off as you wring the clothes, fold the buttons inward and also run a soft, large piece of clothing through the wringer at the same time to cushion them. Buttons are usually "pinched" off when the cloth goes through the wringer and the buttons are trapped on the outside, popping them off back into the washer.

Zippers can be a bugger in a wringer washer. But if you fold the zipper to the inside as you fold the waistband in half, burying the zipper, it will help prevent damage.

How to hang your laundry

Let me tell you right here, I don't think any two women agree on how to hang clothes on the line. I'll tell you how I do it, and you'll have to take it from there. I don't argue religion, politics, or how to hang clothes.

I hang my socks in pairs, by the edges of the cuffs, underwear by the waistbands, and T-shirts by the hem (being careful not to stretch them too much). Twin and double sheets are draped lengthwise over one line and pinned on each end and in the center on windy days. Queen or king-sized sheets are draped over two lines, using pins on each line. This keeps them from dragging in the grass or dirt. I hang pillowcases by the end seam. Back when I had diapers, I hung them by one end.

By holding the edge of your wet clothing in both hands and giving it a vigorous snap, your clothes will have fewer wrinkles.

I hang my shirts by the collar, folded over the line, so the shoulders don't dry with a clothespin "pinch" mark in them. Jeans and pants are hung by the waistband. If you want a nice crease in your pants, fold the legs, making the crease, then hang the pants by the cuff. It does leave a pinch mark on the cuff, but that usually wears away quite quickly and the pants need no ironing to keep the crease.

Laundry soap and detergent

While you can use any store-bought laundry soap or detergent, you might like to use your own homemade laundry soap, made with your own bars of lye soap. It's what Grandma used, and I've used it for years. It doesn't suds up like store detergent does, but it does clean clothes. This recipe does work best with hot or boiling water, though. Hard water will result in even less suds, but it will still clean.

To make your own laundry soap, grate up a bar of lye soap. I use the medium holes in my food grater, not the finer ones; you'd be grating all day! Then add just enough water to the soap to dissolve it. Heat the soap-water to hot, but don't boil it. Stir it well and when it is totally dissolved, add this to three gallons of water. Add one cup of washing soda (available at your grocers in the laundry area; not baking soda!) and mix well. Pour into gallon jugs. You'll be using about a cup of this per washing in your wringer washer. So you see, this recipe goes a long, long way...and is cheap, too!

By using your own homemade laundry soap, along with a wringer washer and a set of good old clotheslines, you'll quickly see a huge savings in your household expenses. Your clothes will look and smell fresh and clean. And you will actually get some enjoyment out of laundry days. It's one of those little pleasures that too many people have forgotten about or never learned in this hurry up world. Remember to smell the wind in your clothes! Δ

Making lye bar soap

Lye bar soap is very easy to make, but like most things you do have to be careful and watch what you're doing. The great thing about making soap is that a big batch will last a long time, even when you grate it and use it for your laundry. Keep in mind that lye burns and the fumes are strong enough to make your eyes water and your lungs burn. So be careful not to splash the lye about, have all young children and pets out of the area, and make your soap in a well-ventilated area. You can make soap from any amount of fat, but like any recipe, there are certain amounts of lye, fat, and water that must be used to get a good, usable product.

There are many different "recipes" for soap making, and here is one that is very basic. The soap won't be "gourmet" quality, but it's easy and quick to do. First render your fat. Grind it, then heat it gently until it becomes liquid, straining off any bits of meat or debris. Have your soap forms ready. I use shallow boxes, like the kind that canned pop comes in. Line them with heavy plastic sheeting. You can also use any non-metal bowl, disposable plastic carton, etc. Grease your molds with petroleum jelly to get the soap to release easier when it hardens.

Slowly stir 16 oz. of lye into 5 cups of cold water in a large enameled pan with no chips. Never use lye with a metal pan of any kind; it about eats it up. There are real strong fumes at this point, so don't hang over the pan. I use a wooden spoon to gently stir them together. It will heat up as the crystals dissolve. When they are all dissolved, cool the lye water to 70-75° F — lukewarm, but use a thermometer to make sure. If you are using tallow (venison, beef, or sheep fat), instead of lard (pig fat), only cool the temperature to 90-95° because tallow melts at a higher temperature than lard.

Heat 10 cups melted fat to 120° (lard) or 130° (tallow). You want the lye water and the melted fat at close to the ideal temperatures when you mix them. Pour the melted fat slowly into the lye water and stir round and round (don't go back and forth or you'll splash) till the mixture gets about like honey. Expect it to take about 15 minutes. The soap is ready to pour into your molds when your mixing spoon will stand upright without tipping over.

When it's ready, quickly pour the mixture into your molds and work it until it's pretty flat. Don't worry if it's a little dark; it bleaches itself out in a few days. The longer soap cures, the harder it becomes. In about 2 weeks it should be just about right to take out of the molds. At this point, you can easily cut it into bars with an old knife.

I grate a bar of older homemade soap with an old cheese grater for laundry soap. If you want to use it for dish soap, I've had better luck by making soft soap out of the grated pieces by adding boiling water enough to melt the soap into a thick gel. The dishes come sparkling clean, but don't expect it to bubble like dish detergent. When you wash your dishes with hot water and rinse them well with hot clear water, you'll be amazed at how nice it washes.

Survival storeroom

By David Eddings

This story begins in the mid-nineties when the Y2K threat was in the news. Several members of my family thought it would be prudent if we started stocking food just in case Y2K turned out to be the major problem that a lot of people predicted it would be.

We contacted a company that specialized in providing long-term foods to the public. Our order was not large enough, so we contacted a Mormon group that lived in a nearby town. They were delighted to have us go in with them on an order because they were just short of enough to place the order.

A few weeks later, we met in the small town and watched as an 18-wheeler rolled in with 73,000 pounds of food. This is how our food storage program began. We left there that day with more food than I had imagined. We had made some provisions for storing the food by buying some shelving, but it was barely enough to hold the two-year supply of food we had brought home.

As you all know, Y2K turned out to be a non-event. As time went on, a lot of our friends began doing away with their stored foods, either by giving it away or consuming all of it with no thought that it might come in handy later on. We knew that what we had was long-term foods and they would still be good for years. The problem was that we didn't know very much about planning a storeroom for people that lived in a city. We wanted to keep what we had and make it the core of a storeroom that would provide for us and our extended family.

Each 2x4x6-foot unit has 20 running feet of shelf space and is rated to hold 5,000 pounds.

Backwoods Home was a great help along the way. The information we gained from the magazine and other sources kept us from making a lot of mistakes and gave us ideas that we could put to our use. I recognized the need for a plan for a storeroom for city folks. The key for that storeroom was shelving.

Shelving

Most of the information that I had read dealt with building shelving from scratch using wood. Living in a subdivision and not having the tools or skills to make our own shelving, I ruled out that option. Since we had already bought some shelving to store our long-term foods, we decided to continue with that method. This works out well because the shelves can be taken down and moved, if necessary. In our case, that was a plus because we did buy a place in the country and had to move all of our food at that time.

I like to call a set of shelving a module because my plan is expandable by adding modules as they are needed. That is also why I wanted to write about this project, in hopes that it might help others get started with a storage program of their own, by starting with one module and doing it one step at a time.

The shelving kits we used are the Muscle Rack 5500 series. They cost around $70 at Lowe's. The shelving is rated at 5,000-pound capacity. They are 48 inches long, 24 inches wide and 72 inches tall and have five shelves. The shelves are adjustable in 1.5-inch increments.

The box states that the unit can be assembled in 30 minutes. Once you get the hang of it, you can do it in less time. The only tool needed is a hammer. I have gotten good results with a rubber mallet. One person can do the job, but it is much easier and safer if two people do it. I strongly recommend that the shelf boards that come with the kit not be used. The shelf boards are heavy-duty particle board but they will not support the weight of canned goods for very long without sagging. Lowe's carries plywood sub-flooring that works fine for shelf boards. I wouldn't use anything less than 5/8-inch thick. One 4x8 sheet will make four shelves and they charge a nominal fee to cut it for you. Buy the cheap grade of plywood. It doesn't have to be pretty, just strong. Once completed, you will have 20 running feet of shelf space and the start of a storage program. Since this shelving is free standing, it is important to always load the heaviest items on the lowest shelves to reduce the chance that the shelves will tip over.

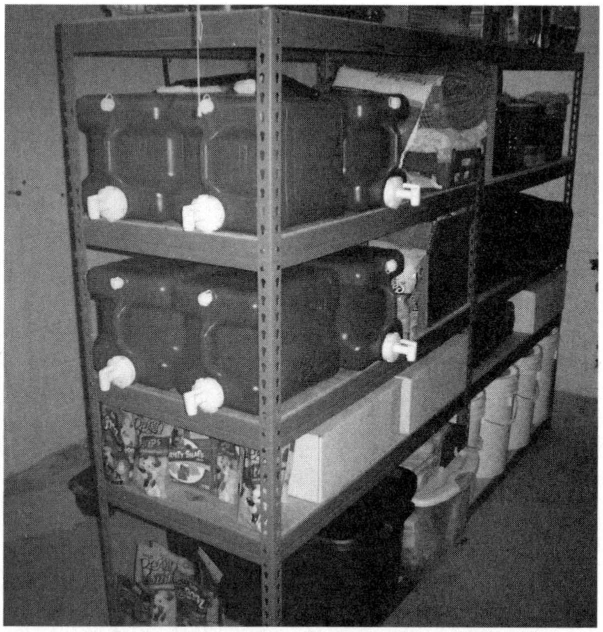

Each "Aqua-Tainer" holds seven gallons of water and has a convenient spigot.

Never use the lower shelf as a step up to reach something from a high shelf.

Warning: The shelving used in the construction of this storeroom is industrial-strength steel. Using any shelving not rated such should not be used for obvious reasons.

One big advantage of a shelf module is that it can be loaded from either side. We date every perishable item that is placed on the shelf. You can load from one side and remove from the other if you want to. The rule is "first in, first out." This will help you with a rotation plan and keep your stored foods fresh. We prepare our grocery list by walking through the storeroom and listing each empty space and buying a replacement item with a trip to the grocery.

Water storage

We all know that food storage is important, but you should make arrangements to store as much water as you can, also. A person can live for a long time without food. Water is critical for survival. We have two methods for storing our water that will provide several days' worth of water for our needs. We purchased Aqua-Tainer brand water containers. These can be purchased from several places, but we bought ours from the sporting goods section at Walmart. We got two prices even at the Walmart stores. One Walmart had them for $10.80 and the other was a dollar more for some reason. I have seen them online for $16.95 plus shipping, so it pays to shop around.

I have found the Aqua-Tainer to be a quality product. The box shape makes them very easy to store on your shelves. Each one holds seven gallons of water. It comes complete with a spigot and an air vent. You must open the vent before opening the spigot or the water won't flow. When the container is full, the water will come out almost as fast as from a kitchen faucet.

The second method we use to store water is saving plastic soda bottles and large juice jugs. Even 32-ounce Gatorade bottles make excellent water containers. We keep around 70 gallons in those alone. We keep our water for about six months before replacing it with fresh water. It is important when filling the plastic containers to fill them to the brim and to splash some of the chlorinated water into the lid. We try to avoid having any air space between the water and the lid.

Water filtration kit

We have a water filtration system that is made from a kit we purchased from Cheaper Than Dirt! (800-421-8047, www.cheaperthandirt.com). The kit is a Camp-352 by Monolithic and will filter to .5 microns and meets NSF standards. We plan to treat the filtered water, just to be on the safe side. The kit consists of a ceramic filter, a filter sock, and a spigot. The kit sells for $29.97 and does not include the buckets needed to assemble the filter. We purchased the two five-gallon buckets from Emergency Essentials for $7.95 each.

For less than $50, you can have a filter system that rivals one that costs around $200 and filters 14 gallons of water per day. The filter can be cleaned with a soft brush and by back flushing. By adding a Gamma Seal lid, you have the convenience of a screw-on lid. This system should last a pretty good while.

Food savers

I feel that one of the best investments a person can make for a storage

Two shelf units bolted together have 80 square feet of shelf space to house bulky non-food items.

program is a vacuum sealer for foods. It will pay for itself in being able to buy foods in bulk and re-packaging in smaller quantities. It can be used to seal dry foods also. We buy rice in large bags and freeze it for several days, then divide it into smaller bags and vacuum seal it. It is as hard as a rock and stacks very well on the shelves. Foods that are vacuum-sealed stay fresh for months without freezer burn. A good unit can be purchased at Walmart for around $70 dollars. I can't say enough about this product.

Combining modules

By placing two modules side by side and bolting them together you can create space to store bulkier items. Each shelf is 4x4 feet and gives you 16 square feet of space. We use this space to store paper towels, toilet tissue, cleaning products, paper plates, and any other non-food item that doesn't have a use-by date. We also stock items for ladies' special needs. We store paper plates and cups to help conserve our water. Because water is critical, you don't want to be wasting it to wash dishes.

Alternative cooking

We had all the food stored, but we didn't have a viable method for cooking it. A two-burner Coleman camp stove didn't provide the cooking time needed to cook a lot of the foods we had on hand, plus it is labor intensive because it requires constant attention by pumping the fuel tank and also the small tank. Gasoline is dangerous and breaks down over time, so we ruled that out and decided to go with kerosene. Kerosene will also be useful in space heaters and emergency lighting. It will store for long periods without breaking down. It will turn yellow, but that doesn't seem to affect its quality. We live in an area where ice storms can happen anytime during the winter and we have been left without power for days at a time, so fuel reliability over the long term is critical.

I contacted a fuel oil company in our area and they gave us a 55-gallon drum and came out and filled it for us. I went to Northern Tool and bought a hand crank pump that screws into the top of the drum. This setup has kept us warm, snug, and fed when the power goes out.

I went online and located a two-burner kerosene stove that looked promising. It's called the Butterfly Stove, and I got mine from St. Paul Mercantile (888-395-1164, www.stpaulmercantile.com). The stove sold for $120 with a small shipping charge. My brother wanted one also and the company gives a 10% discount for two. If you purchase four you get a 15% discount, so if several people want to go together you get a pretty good discount. The stove is 30 inches wide and 30 inches tall — a nice height for cooking. The instructions for assembly left much to be desired, but with a little patience, one person can do it. The company also has a three-burner model.

The stove has a center reservoir which supplies both burners by gravity feed. The glass tank holds 1.8 quarts of fuel and can be refilled while the stove is in operation. While testing the stove I found fuel wasn't going all the way around the wick. The burners are adjustable, so that wasn't a problem. I had to loosen the adjustment screws and tilt the burners back and that solved the fuel flow problem. It is important that the stove be set up on a level surface. The height of the flame depends on the rate of fuel flow, so there is a lag between the time you turn the valve until you get the desired result. When first lit, the burners do smoke a little. Once the combustion chambers get hot, the smoke stops. In my opinion, this a dandy little lightweight stove that can cook a lot of food.

The Butterfly oven is a companion for the Butterfly stove. The oven was designed to fit on top of one of the burners. St. Paul Mercantile sells it for $55. The instructions are pitiful; you almost have to look at the picture to assemble it. It is a two-person job to put together. It warns that the sharp metal parts can cut and I will attest to that. After it was assembled I added some sheet metal screws to the corners at the top and a few other places. Even with all the problems I had putting it together, I have to say it's a darn good little oven. The oven has inner baffles that make it very efficient for its size. It has a temperature gauge on the door. The temperatures are shown in centigrade, but you can find a conversion chart online to convert it to Fahrenheit. I decided to test the little oven by cooking two frozen biscuits. That is a pretty tough test and it passed with flying colors. The Butterfly oven works well on the side burner of an outdoor gas grill.

The Alpaca kerosene heater/cooker is a heavy-duty single burner stove with a tank capacity of .9 gallons. The top of the stove is configured like a gas range burner. We got it from Nitro-Pak Preparedness Center (800-866-4876, www.nitro-pak.com). We have used ours several times and it does a great job as a cooker as well as a room heater. As a heater, it works best with a pan of water over the burner because you can turn the burner up high without it smoking. The Butterfly oven will work on this stove. When we bought ours, the price was $65. Now the price is approaching $100. You can sometimes find them on eBay for much less. These two stoves and the oven should take care of all your cooking needs.

Should you decide to go with kerosene as your energy source, you should contact your local codes department to see if there are any restrictions on bulk storage.

Grain mill

Our long-term food supplies include around 300 pounds of wheat. Our problem was we had no means of milling the wheat. We ordered the best mill that Lehman's Hardware had for less than $200 dollars (877-438-5346, www.lehmans.com). This mill came with both stone and iron burrs, and does a fine job of milling wheat almost as fine as store-bought flour. Lehman's still carries the mill, but it only comes with iron burrs now. If you want good flour from your wheat you really need the stone burrs. Another mill that will fill the requirement having both types of burrs is the Wondermill Junior Deluxe from Homegrown Harvest (866-900-3321, www.homegrownharvest.com). I'm not going to list the features of this mill, but the company claims it is "the world's best," so it must be pretty good.

An electric grain mill is nice to have, if your budget will allow it. There are several good ones out there, but remember you won't always have electricity available, so the hand-powered mill should be your first priority. I suggest that you mill some wheat and practice making bread. It is a good feeling to know that you can make bread from your storeroom if you ever have to.

Butterfly oven, Alpaca kerosene stove, and Butterfly two-burner kerosene stove.

SuperPails

Emergency Essentials carries most any dry food you would want in your storeroom in 6-gallon "SuperPails" which are equal to eight #10 cans. They have wheat (both hard and soft), corn, and all types of dried beans. We added popcorn and soybeans to our long-term storage. We use popcorn for corn meal and soybeans have many food uses.

When ordering SuperPails from Emergency Essentials (800-999-1863, www.emergencyessentials.com), your order must weigh at least 200 pounds. A few SuperPails will add up pretty quick. They charge $12 dollars shipping for any order over $120 and you can't beat that.

Vitamins

One of my reference books advises that your storeroom should contain a large quantity of vitamin C. This is one vitamin your body doesn't store and it is possible a survival diet won't provide enough of this vital vitamin. Store it where light can't get to it. It has a shelf-life of about five years.

For quite some time I have wanted to write about our storeroom and how it came about. Is this the best possible storeroom? Probably not. Is it flexible? Yes. Can anyone do it without any special skills? Yes. Is it expensive? No. Anyone can do it without busting the budget if it is done in baby steps like we did, one module at a time. I would caution that if this type of storage room is built in an above-ground room on a wood floor that some consideration be given to reinforcing the floor from underneath. Stored foods are extremely heavy.

Other books we found helpful when stocking our storeroom were *Gateway to Survival is Storage* by Walter D. Batchelor and *Passport to Survival* by Esther Dickey. Δ

There are few foods and crops that homesteaders consider as essential as wheat. In these days of pasty loaves of over-processed "store-bought" bread, the mere phrase "whole wheat" evokes thoughts of wholesomeness, healthfulness, and quality.

It shouldn't be too surprising to learn that wheat is the most important and widely-grown grain crop in the world. It is also the best type of grain to use for bread making — and this comes from an old country boy who has eaten his share of bread! Indeed, this life-giving grain can be made into hundreds of nutritious breads and other foods. It is deserving of that number one spot on the food scale. It is equally deserving of a prominent spot in the homesteader's larder.

Although it varies according to variety and type, a kernel of wheat contains approximately 11% protein. It also contains carbohydrates, fiber, vitamins, and minerals. Of course, those nutrients are present in the wheat in its natural state. The more it is processed, the more of those nutrients are removed. So it stands to reason that the less it is processed, the better.

Taking into consideration the quality of much of the country's bread offerings, storing a supply of wheat and grinding one's own flour not only is good for our health, but also for our pocketbook as well.

As for freshness, the ordinary bag of flour that is stored at room temperature in the pantry will lose practical-

wheat

By Charles Sanders

ly all of its food value over the period of about a month. If you have your own buckets, cans, or jars of wheat stored, you can quickly grind a week's worth of high quality, fresh, whole wheat flour in minutes.

For many of us, a stored supply of wheat offers yet a greater degree of self-sufficiency and independence from the increasingly fragile food supply chain. In any event, one can benefit from having the nutritional food source right at hand.

Let's discuss some different types of wheat, their characteristics and uses for the homesteader.

Types of wheat

Here in the United States, there are seven or so main types of wheat that are grown. They have different growing characteristics and adaptations. They also offer different qualities for cooking.

One of the best is **hard red winter wheat**. This type of wheat is widely grown in the traditional grain belt of the United States — the Plains states. It is one of the best for bakers and makes up about 40 percent of the wheat grown in the country.

Hard red spring wheat is next. It is a northern crop, grown through the northern states and Canada. It is high in protein and is another great type for baking flour. It makes up about a quarter of the wheat grown in the country.

Soft red winter wheat is mainly grown in the eastern part of the country. It is lower in protein, but offers excellent milling and baking qualities. It also makes up about a quarter of the wheat grown in the United States.

Hard white winter wheat is the newest type of wheat in the United States. It has a sweeter flavor and lighter color than the varieties of red wheat, but offers a high protein content. Growing in popularity, it currently makes up only about 1 percent of the U.S. wheat crop.

The next type of wheat is **soft white spring wheat**. This type of wheat is grown in some of the east and in the Pacific Northwest and California. It produces a very white flour with a sweet flavor. It makes up only about 7 percent of the nation's wheat crop.

Durum wheat is the hardest variety of wheat. It is also the highest in protein. It is highly desirable for "high grade" food products. It makes up about 3 percent of the U.S. wheat crop.

How much to store?

Now that's a good question. A lot depends upon how big your family is and how much wheat you can or will use. I am going to give you a variety of ways to use the grain, but just exactly how much wheat to store is for you to decide. Below, I have listed the guidelines given by FEMA (Federal Emergency Management Agency).

One year's supply of wheat according to FEMA recommendations: Adult males, pregnant or nursing mothers, and active teenagers aged 14-18: 275 pounds each. Women, youths aged 7-13, and seniors: 175 pounds each. Small children age 6 and under: 60 pounds each.

As you can see, the amount of wheat needed for storage can add up pretty quickly. If you are an average couple with three children, you can expect to store anywhere from 600 to 1100 pounds of wheat. That translates to between 12 and 25 buckets of wheat. An important factor to remember when laying in your supply is simply this: Use it! A year's supply of wheat will not do any good just growing old on the shelf. If your family is not used to the processing and using of fresh raw wheat, then phase it in over a period of time. Make a special event out of grinding, sifting, and baking with it. (This is a good time to tell your youngsters the story of the Little Red Hen).

For those who wish to obtain their wheat in bulk, in the unprocessed form, I offer the following suggestions: First, locate a good source of the grain. If you can grow your own, so much the better. You will then have total control over your wheat from seed to finished loaf. Growing, harvesting, processing, and using wheat on the home scale may be impractical for many, due to acreage, time, or desire. However, if you live in an area where wheat farming is common, you can usually work out a deal with one of the farmers to purchase a few bushels from him. If you are a stickler for using organically-grown grain, you will probably have a more difficult time locating a source, but keep looking. They're out there, and becoming more common. Another source to consider is the local feed mill or agricultural co-op. There you can probably get the grain already dried, although you may wish to clean it a bit before storage. There are also commercial suppliers of bulk grains and foods for home use. Check a few of these out and compare their products, prices, and shipping costs. Some are listed at the end of this article.

After deciding on the type of wheat you need and obtaining the amount you need, you must turn to storing it in a manner that will keep its nutrients and quality stable until used. Remember that for most of us, dark red winter or spring wheat is probably the best choice. Those varieties also tend to store better than other varieties.

To get your wheat ready for storage, you must first determine that it is clean enough to use for baking purposes. Granted, chaff and straw can provide a lot of fiber in one's diet, but it isn't very palatable. If you have purchased your wheat from a commercial bulk food supplier, it has likely already been cleaned; you can ask when you purchase it.

If you have purchased raw, bulk wheat from a neighboring farmer you will need to clean — or winnow — the grain. The simplest way to do that is to spread it out on a large sheet of plastic and toss shovelfuls of the wheat into the air and let the wind carry the chaff and straw away. If you don't have enough wind to do the job, a good electric fan will suffice. I have winnowed several bushels of wheat in just this manner. It works very well.

Next in importance is to store grain that is sufficiently dry to resist rotting and molding while in storage. For home storage purposes, wheat should not contain more than about 10% moisture. The low moisture will also inhibit insects from taking up residence in the grain.

As I mentioned above, you may be able to get wheat that has already been dried from your local feed mill or co-op. But unless you are drying an extremely large quantity or live in an especially humid area, you should be able to easily dry more than enough to suit your needs.

To dry grain yourself, try this simple method. Simply spread out a large piece of black plastic sheeting in a sunny spot — I used the deck on the south-facing side of my house. Spread a quantity of wheat to make it not more than an inch or so deep. After spending a hot afternoon on the plastic, both the direct heat and that reflected from the side of the house had sufficiently dried down the wheat to about 11%. To measure the moisture percentage, I used an agricultural moisture-testing meter borrowed from an uncle.

If you purchased wheat from a local farmer, he might test your dried wheat for you. The local grain elevator will have the moisture meter and will probably test it for you, as well. If you are really serious about regularly laying in a home wheat supply, you might purchase your own tester, but expect to pay at least $150 for it.

If the solar-drying process takes more than a day, simply cover the grain in the evening, and then uncover it again late the next morning. Be sure to conduct this drying operation during the driest, hottest part of the season, since wheat will readily draw moisture during humid times.

Once you have your wheat crop dried down to about 10-11%, it's time to store it. I like to use plain 5-gallon buckets as storage containers. They are durable, will seal tightly, and will hold a good, usable quantity of wheat. When stacked and stored, they allow good air circulation around them. A further advantage is that you can often get them cheaply or even free. Ask around at your local restaurants, bakeries, delis, or pizza joints. Those businesses get a lot of their ingredients in plastic buckets.

Do not put the wheat directly into the bucket. First line the bucket with a 13-gallon kitchen garbage bag. Fold the excess bag over the sides. Next, fill the bag in the bucket with enough wheat to come to within an inch or so of the top ***(The USDA does not recommend using trash bags, as chemicals can leach into the food. Food-grade Mylar bags are available. — Editor).***

Today, dry ice is often used to preserve the wheat. It works by releasing carbon dioxide as the material evaporates. It will kill any bugs in the storage container.

To treat your bucket of wheat with dry ice, place 2-4 ounces of the material on a piece of heavy brown paper or waxed paper on top of the wheat. The fumes created during the evaporation are heavier than air and will settle throughout the bucket. Place the lid loosely onto the bucket. Allow about 30 minutes, then secure the lid to create an airtight seal. Check the bucket to see if it is bulging. If so, crack the seal and wait another five minutes or so, then reseal.

Another practical method of wheat storage is in tin cans. I have participated in group canning sessions where dried wheat was used to fill a #10 can to within a quarter inch or so of the top. Next an oxygen absorber packet was placed on top of the wheat. A lid was put in place and the can was placed on the electrically-powered canner. The machine rolled a perfect crimp as it sealed the can lid onto the can. The cans store nicely on shelves in the basement and are conveniently-sized.

One problem with having cans, jars, or buckets of wheat stored on the shelf is: "Now that I have it, what am I going to do with it?"

Once you are staring at a bucket of wheat, wishing for a loaf of bread, you come up with an obvious quandary: How do I turn the grain into flour? The home miller has several different small mills available that will do the job. You can get simple hand-cranked steel-on-steel mills all the way up to

In my Amish neighbor's field, these shocks of wheat await threshing.

electric-powered stone mills. You can also spend a little to a lot in purchasing your mill. I have had a Corona hand-powered mill with steel burrs for many years. It still turns out wheat flour that is very usable in any dish or bread I've tried. I did consider adding a pulley and some bicycle power to it at one time.

Evaluate the different mills and how much you plan to use it. Do you want stone burrs that will produce a finer grind, or will steel burrs suffice? (You can often run the flour through twice if it isn't fine enough to suit you.)

As a food, wheat is very versatile. Its most popular use, of course, is in bread making. Countless bread recipes from all over the world exist as a testament to the usefulness of the grain and the dependence that people over the ages have placed upon it.

However, one of my personal favorite uses of wheat is actually a by-product of the flour-making process.

After grinding a batch of wheat flour, it is sifted and put aside or stored for use in baking. The coarse "leavings" are poured into a pan and either soaked overnight or started directly in the morning. Simply set the covered pan on the stove to simmer for about 35-40 minutes. Uncover and allow it to thicken. Then ladle a bowlful, add a big dollop of butter and some honey. This hot cereal will keep you going all morning.

Another good use for wheat is to use the whole kernel or berry to make bulgur. Bulgur originated in the Mediterranean region and Middle East. It is made by steaming or soaking the entire wheat berry. The resulting cooked kernel is softened and swollen and can be used in soups or crunchy snacks, in side dishes or main courses.

Try making your own batch of bulgur by placing a rack into the bottom of your cold packer. Add water up to about the level of the rack. Place a pan or pot atop the rack and add a cup of wheat, a cup of water, and a pinch of salt. Cover the cold packer and

Cans of wheat line the storage shelf.

cook on high heat for about 15 minutes. Then reduce the heat and allow the steam to cook the wheat. Once the wheat kernels absorb the water in the smaller pot they will fluff up. Then simply remove them and use or store them for up to two weeks in the fridge. Note that in place of the cold packer, you may also use a saucepan and steamer combination, if you have that.

Your prepared bulgur is tasty as a breakfast cereal by adding milk, fruit, and honey. It can also be used in soups or any dish calling for barley or rice.

Another way to enjoy bulgur is to season a couple of cups of bulgur and spread it evenly over a cookie sheet. Toast it in a moderate oven until it is nicely browned and crunchy. Sprinkle the seasoned kernels over a salad. If you season the bulgur with a sweetener before drying, it becomes a healthful, crunchy snack.

The most popular use for wheat is in the baking of bread. Bread is certainly a simple, basic staple that can be baked in any homestead home. Once you have tried your hand at bread baking, it becomes a sort of quest, to fine-tune the recipe, the oven, and the loaf to try to come up with that perfect loaf. In any case, the loaves you produce will bear little resemblance to those white, pasty loaves found in the local market.

Here are a few recipes for whole-wheat bread that you should enjoy.

Whole wheat bread #1:

This is a good, basic whole wheat loaf to get you started. This recipe will turn out one golden, crusty loaf.

2 tsp. honey
1 Tbsp. vegetable oil
1 cup warm water
1 tsp. salt
2 Tbsp. dry milk
2 Tbsp. wheat bran (kept over from sifting the flour)
1½ tsp. dry yeast
2 cups whole wheat flour

Stir together the honey, oil, and water in a large mixing bowl. Stir in the salt, dry milk, bran, and yeast. Add the flour and mix all together. Turn the dough out onto a lightly-floured surface and knead. Add a bit of flour if needed. Knead for about 5 minutes. The dough should be slightly sticky. Put the dough in a greased medium bowl, and turn it over so that the top is lightly greased. Cover with a light cloth and set it to rise for about 45 minutes or until it is doubled in size. Turn the dough onto a breadboard and knead for about 3-4 minutes. Shape into a loaf, and place into a greased loaf pan. Cover and let rise for about 30 minutes or until it is doubled in size. Bake for about 40 minutes in a 350° F oven. Turn the finished loaf onto a rack and allow to cool.

Whole wheat bread #2:

2¼ tsp. yeast
3 Tbsp. dark brown sugar
2¾ cups whole-wheat flour
¾ cup warm water
3 Tbsp. nonfat dry milk powder
3 Tbsp. vegetable oil
1 tsp. salt
1 large egg or
2 large egg whites

Stir the yeast and sugar into the water and let it stand until foamy, about 5 minutes. Into a large mixing bowl put the rest of the ingredients and mix well. Make a depression in the center, pour in the yeast mixture, and work it into the rest. Put it out onto a floured board and knead until smooth and elastic (about 10 minutes). Transfer the dough to a large plastic bag, squeeze the air out, and seal the top of the bag. Place the dough into a bowl to rise in a warm location. Allow it to rise until doubled in size, about 1 hour. Punch the dough down and shape it into a smooth ball. Place the smooth side up on an oiled baking sheet and cover it loosely with oiled plastic. Let it rise in a warm spot until doubled in size, about 45-50 minutes. Preheat your oven to 375° F. About fifteen minutes before baking, put the rack in the center of the oven. Lightly dust the top of the loaf with flour. Place the loaf in the oven and bake until the bread is well-browned and sounds hollow when rapped on the bottom. This should take about 30-35 minutes. Remove the loaf from the oven and pan. Place it on a cooling rack. Makes 1 loaf.

Grinding wheat into nutritious flour

Whole wheat bread #3:

8 cups scalded milk
6¾ tsp. yeast
⅔ cup water
1 Tbsp. sugar
12 cups whole wheat
¾ cup shortening, melted
½ cup molasses
1 cup sugar
2 Tbsp. salt

Scald the milk. Dissolve the yeast in 2/3 cup water while the milk is cooling. Dissolve 1 cup sugar in the hot milk. Stir all the ingredients in a large bowl, turn out onto a floured board and knead for about 5 minutes, adding flour a little at a time, if necessary. Knead the dough for about 5 minutes. Let the dough rise until doubled in bulk (about 1½ to 2 hours). Knead the dough down and shape it into 6 loaves. Put in greased loaf pans. Let it rise again until doubled in the pans. Bake in a preheated 375° F oven for about 40 minutes. Turn the loaves onto a wire rack and let them cool.

There are many more recipes and uses for wheat. Your own experimentation will yield great results in cooking with this great cereal grain.

If you are interested in trying your hand at growing your own wheat patch, then I recommend locating a copy of *Small-Scale Grain Raising,* by Gene Logsdon. This standby text has all the information you'll need to raise your own grain crop. The book has been published in a Second Edition and is available from *Backwoods Home Magazine.*

If you want to purchase wheat, either in bulk or ready to store, but cannot find a source for buying wheat locally, check out these mail-order suppliers:

- Walton Feed, 800-847-0465, www.waltonfeed.com
- Emergency Essentials, 1-800-999-1863, www.emergencyessentials.com
- Wheat Montana, 800-535-2798, www.wheatmontana.com Δ

The low cost of beef

By Jared Bedke

As a fourth generation cattleman, I get a lot of questions about raising cattle and the beef business. The majority of questions I get asked are similar enough that I can see most people want to be informed, but need a little help. That's why I'm here, to answer your questions, so let's start at the beginning.

The basics

The major classifications that cattle fall into are: bulls, cows, heifers, and steers.

Bulls are male animals that still have their testicles and can reproduce.

Cows are female animals that are usually at least three years old and have had at least one calf.

Heifers are female animals that are usually under three years of age and have *not* had a calf.

Steers are male animals that have been neutered. The interesting thing about steers is that they never stop growing and can reach weights upwards of 2500 pounds. Large steers like that are called oxen. I don't know when they turn from steers into oxen, but I'm guessing at around four years of age.

When steers (and for the most part heifers raised for slaughter) are killed commercially, they are graded based upon the amount of fat, or marbling, in the muscles. The major grades are: Prime, Choice, and Select.

Prime beef has the most marbling and is the most tender and flavorful grade. It is also the scarcest. Only a small percentage of all the steers killed will grade Prime, and therefore they command a premium. When you go to the steakhouse and get a Prime rib dinner, you are getting a slice of a rib roast from a Prime carcass. If you go to a high dollar steakhouse and get a $30 T-bone steak, you're probably getting a steak off of a Prime carcass.

I was in a "steakhouse" one time and on their menu they put that their Prime rib was cut from selected prime or choice carcasses. I smiled. Clearly, they didn't know what a Prime rib really was, so when it was my turn, I ordered the Choice rib. The waitress was naturally confused but the others at the table got a chuckle out of it.

The next grade of meat is Choice. Choice beef doesn't have the heavy marbling that the Prime carcass does. It's still on the upper end of the grade scale, but isn't as tender or flavorful as Prime. It, too, commands a premium at the restaurant or butcher, but not as great a premium as a Prime beef would.

Select grade meat is right in the middle of the scale of grades. It has very little marbling and is extremely lean meat. Most of the time in the grocery store you will see them advertise Select meat at "special" prices. Most likely these are the types of steaks or roasts that the average consumer buys. The vast majority of commercially-slaughtered beef falls into this category because it costs the least amount to feed a steer to reach this grade of beef, and it's all about the "Benjamins" for commercial feeders.

I can't even remember what the other two lowest grades of beef are; we'll just call them tougherthanheck and shoeleather, and leave it at that. You want to avoid these if at all possible.

Also we must throw into this discussion old cows that have been killed and converted into beef. Cows are not graded like steers or feeder heifers are. They are simply inspected and stamped as edible beef. I don't know for a fact, but I'm willing to wager that most of the packaged hamburger patties that you can buy for a nickel a piece come from cows. Probably a lot of your fast food joints serve it, too. It's the cheapest burger you can buy, and you don't know whether that particular hamburger came from an old Holstein milk cow or something else.

Types of livestock operations

For the most part, the commercial beef industry falls into three main types of operations: The cow/calf producer, the feeder, and the finisher.

The cow/calf producer is the beginning of the process. These types of operations have a herd of mother cows that have a baby calf. A cow's gestation period is nine months, just like a human's. That means that a cow will have a calf once a year usually, and most of these types of operators program for that.

About six months after the calf is born, the calf is weaned from its mother. The producer then has to decide whether to sell his "calf crop" to somebody else and concentrate on his new crop, or keep the calves (retained ownership) and feed them to a larger weight and size. If the producer sells them, he usually sells them to the feeder.

The feeder is the next step of the process. Usually the feeder has what is known as a feedlot. A feedlot is basically an acreage with many different pens of cattle grouped according to size and weight. They don't require as much space as a cow/calf producer does because the cattle are concentrated and the feed is delivered to the calves in the various pens.

Usually feeders take the cattle from weaning weight up to about 800-900 pounds. Then they either continue to feed them a different ration in order to get them up to around 1200-1400 pounds or they sell them to the finisher.

The finisher is another type of feedlot that buys cattle from the feeder and then continues to feed them up to the point where they are sold to the various packing houses for slaughter and eventual distribution to restaurants and supermarkets around the country.

Grass-fed vs. grain-fed

Because of the current commercial structure of the beef industry, most cattle are grain fed. The reason for this is that both a feeder and a finisher make their money on a quick turnaround. The quicker they can get an animal from the base weight to the end weight, the quicker they get paid and the less it costs them to keep the animal. Also, they can then purchase another smaller animal to replace the one they just sold because there's more room in the inn. The more they cycle through, the more they make.

Grain fed means that the animal is fed a ration consisting of some hay, grain (barley, corn, etc.), or other by-product such as potato waste or distiller's mash. The ration is specifically designed to make the animal gain the most weight it can in the shortest time possible.

Grass fed means that an animal eats only grass or hay (dried grass) for the entire duration of its life.

There are definite advantages and disadvantages to both. In order to fully address these differences, we've got to look for just a bit at the digestive tract of the cow.

The inner workings of a cow

A cow is a ruminant. What this means is that a cow will ingest her feed as quickly as she can and it is stored internally in what's known as the "rumen." Later on, the cow will then regurgitate the partially-digested feed and chew on it for a while. This is known as a "cud." After she's done chewing the cud, she swallows it and it goes into her "third stomach," where it passes into the intestines and is digested. Here's where it gets technical.

Technically, the cow doesn't digest the feed. What happens is that her rumen contains certain microbes that thrive on the partially digested feed. These microbes have a lifespan of about 24 hours and in that lifespan, they are born, eat, reproduce, and die. The microbes digest the cow's feed and convert it into nutrients the cow can digest. But the microbes themselves are also a source of nutrition for the cow, providing around half of the dietary protein the cow consumes each day.

Now within a cow's rumen there are all sorts of microbes that thrive on all different kinds of feed. If a cow is used to eating grass or hay, the microbes that thrive on grass and hay become dominant.

When her feed is suddenly switched to grain, the "grass" microbes die because it's not the type of feed on which they thrive and the "grain" microbes take over. The only problem is that it takes the "grain" microbes a

> I know a lot of people that just live for New York Strip steaks, but turn their nose up at a T-bone. That always makes me smile, and here's why: A T-bone has two different pieces of meat on it, the large side, and the little side. The big side of a T-bone is actually the New York Strip, and the small side is a piece of the tenderloin (or filet mignon). Also, there's a little crescent out of the top of the bone in the T-bone. That little crescent is actually the spinal channel of the animal. When you see that, you know that the animal the steak was cut from was less than two years of age. Any animal more than two years of age cannot have the spinal channel on the meat because of the risk of passing mad cow disease. Therefore, anything more than two years of age will never be cut into T-bones, but rather will be cut into New York Strips instead. This is true for a two-year-old animal and also for a ten-year-old animal. When you see a NYS advertised for $4.99, you're most likely getting the NYS off of an old cow. That's why they're always tough.

bit of time to populate and get to the same point that the "grass" microbes were a few days earlier. During this period of time, the animal has to consume its own fat reserves to take up the slack. This is why there will always be a bit of a drop-off whenever you switch feeds.

Advantages and disadvantages

The main advantage to feeding an animal grain is that it is a quick way to put on pounds after the initial feed-switching process. Most feeders will start their newly-purchased animals on a "starter ration" where they slowly increase the grain content while lowering the hay content so there's not as much transitional loss.

The disadvantage to grain feeding an animal is the cost of the grain. It also has a tendency to change the color of the fat of the animal and the flavor of the beef. If you're used to eating grain-fed beef, the flavor is something you're accustomed to and you probably won't notice the difference. This, too, depends on what other types of feedstuffs or by-products are in the mix. Most feeders use everything at their disposal that is cheap and can be fed to an animal. It increases their profit margin. Another drawback is that there is evidence out there that shows a diet high in corn can lead to the development of a resistant strain of *E. Coli* bacteria in the digestive tract of the animal. If your animal develops this and then you spread the manure on your garden, you run the risk of spreading and ingesting the *E. Coli* on your raw vegetables. Watch the documentary, *Food, Inc.*, sometime if you'd like to know more.

The main advantage of grass-fed beef is that the animal is on a consistent diet and isn't exposed to feeds they wouldn't normally eat. After all, a cow is designed to eat grass. The beef is very tasty and a bit leaner than grain-fed animals; however, earlier this year I sold a grass-fed beef that was wonderfully marbled. The butcher had a hard time believing that the animal was actually grass-fed, because it looked better than others that were grain-fed hanging alongside of it. As an aside, the family that bought half of it told us they've never had such good beef.

The main disadvantage to grass-fed beef is that it takes the animal a longer time to reach the point where they are ready to butcher. Grain-fed animals can be pushed so they are slaughtered at 15 months of age but grass-fed animals require around 18 months.

Raising your own beef vs. buying one

I would never tell anyone that wanted to raise their own beef not to. But before you get started, there are several factors to consider. Ask yourself the following two questions: Are you better off raising your own? Or are you better off buying a beef from someone else?

If you want to raise your own, you first need to decide whether you're going to buy a cow so that you can have a calf every year, or whether you just want to buy a weaned calf and finish it out yourself.

If you want to buy a cow, you've got several concerns that go along with it. The first is initial cost.

If you buy a young cow or heifer that has been bred and has a calf inside of her, it will cost you somewhere in the neighborhood of $900-$1200. Then you are responsible for making sure that the cow delivers the calf without any problems. Sometimes this means pulling the calf and, in the worst case, having a cesarean section. Both aren't much fun, especially if you're not set up for pulling a calf or don't really want to spend the money to have a veterinarian do it for you. With these possibilities out there, it's easy to see that before long, you'll have $1500 into the cow and the calf might be born dead to boot.

Of course, there is the possibility that nothing will go wrong and you'll get a calf with no problems at all. My motto is "plan for the worst, hope for the best," especially in the livestock business.

If you're not willing to risk the birthing process, you can buy a "pair," or a cow that has already given birth and is nursing a calf. Pairs currently run around $1400 on average for a young cow in the four-year-old range.

Of course, once you buy the pair, you've got to provide care and feed for them. On average, a cow needs about 25 pounds of feed a day. That means that during the year the cow alone will consume around 4.6 tons of feed. Eventually, the calf will grow to a point where he'll need just as much. Remember, you'll be weaning the calf at around six months of age so that the cow can get ready to have another calf for you. You've got to also think nine months ahead and make sure your cow gets bred, either by artificial insemination or by a bull (another cost). The calf will need to be separated from his mother until he's weaned, so you'll need to provide the feed for each of them separately at this point. This takes between four days to a couple weeks, depending on the animals. After the cow has quit lactating, you can put them back together if you want.

How much hay you'll need really depends on where you're located. For example, in Florida you might get by with a small pasture because of your annual rainfall and mild winters. If you live in the cold desert of southern Idaho, like I do, that means you'll need a lot more than a small pasture. Last I heard, in my part of the world the average is 60 acres per cow per year. No, that's not a typo. It takes on average 60 acres of sagebrush side-hills to provide the feed required by one cow for one year, if those side-hills weren't covered with snow for six months or so. If you have an irrigated pasture, you'll get by with less, but you'll still need to think ahead about hay production. If you're considering this, talk to your county extension agent and he'll be able to tell you what your average is.

So, up to this point you've got $1400 in the pair, 4.6 tons of feed (total between hay and pasture) for the cow each year, and 4.6 tons of feed for the calf because you're raising him to around 18 months of age if you want it grass fed. If you want it grain fed, you've got a shorter time span, but the additional cost of purchasing grain. Hay usually sells for around $100-$130 per ton, but I have seen it as high as $200 in 2008. For the purpose of figuring, we'll assume that you've only got to feed your animals hay for 100 days on average every year and they're on pasture the rest of the time. I understand that there's an opportunity cost associated with the use of the pasture but those figures will be variable based on location, so it's hard to put a figure on it here, but for the sake of example we'll say that it's half the cost of hay. That means the initial cost of raising one beef by yourself would be on average $1400 for the pair + $250 for hay + breeding fees + $150 pasture costs + time, effort, and energy + butchering fee (if you have someone else kill it) + cutting and wrapping fee (if you have someone else age, cut, wrap, and freeze it) = around $2350 -$2650 for one complete grass-fed beef in your freezer via the "pair" route. However, the longer you keep the cow and if she keeps having live calves, the initial cost of purchase can be averaged down over a 10-year span.

Now, if you decide not to buy a "pair" and avoid the initial and residual costs, you can usually buy a weaned calf for around $600. You'll still have to provide for the animal for the additional year it will take, and as Patrice Lewis pointed out in the March/April 2010 (Issue #122) of *BHM*, cattle like company. You'll have a hard time keeping one lone animal calm and content without some sort of company. An animal that runs away or you can't keep in the pasture will quickly reach the point of diminishing returns. Given the same types of costs, we have $600 for the weaner + $125 for the hay + $125 for the pasture costs + time, effort, and energy + butchering fee + cut and wrap = $1250-$1450.

So, these are the rough costs involved with raising your own beef. The biggest downside is, of course, the risk of death. If you do everything right, there's still the chance that your animal will just lay down and die. Then you're just out both the money and the beef. Also there are the intangible costs that you can't account for.

I once had a neighbor who called me up one fall. He'd bought a few calves earlier that spring to graze down his pasture and then after having them for the summer, he sold them. He was a farmer, and he wasn't sure he was doing the math right, so he asked me how to tell if he'd made any money on the calves. I told him you take the amount you sold them for and subtract the amount you bought them for and he'd have his answer. He laughed and said, "I know that, but the numbers are upside down and I don't know if I've missed something or not." I told him nope, that's the way it worked and then he told me that it cost him $100 to mow his pasture all summer. The moral? Don't always plan on them gaining as much as you hope.

Buying a beef

If you just don't want the hassle or don't have the space needed to raise your own, you should look into buying a beef.

You can either go to the store and buy medium-grade beef for what I would call exorbitant prices, or you can go to a feed lot and purchase a live beef there and then pay to have it killed, cut, and wrapped for your freezer. All of the animals that you buy from a feed lot will be grain fed.

The other option is to locate a family ranch near your location and arrange to have them raise a beef for you. If you want a natural or grass-fed beef, this is your best option.

How do you find a family ranch? That's a good question because they're rarely listed in the yellow pages under "family ranch." Go to a farmer's market in your area and ask around. Somebody always knows somebody who knows somebody. Just remember, if you are making a "cold contact" with the rancher, you need to be willing to do some things for him.

Raising a grass-fed beef is about an 18-month process, so be willing to give the rancher a down payment to let him know you're serious. From my own personal experience, I won't take on any new customers without a non-refundable down payment and I'll tell you why.

Last year, I had 13 beeves that I could have sold in the spring but I had nine families commit to taking them for fall delivery as grass-fed beef. I took them at their word and put the time, effort, and energy into them to feed them through the summer. Last fall, six of the nine backed out at the last minute when the steers were ready to be killed. This left me sitting on more than I could eat in a year, not to mention I was out quite a bit of money when they left me hangin' and there wasn't much I could do about it. I was able to call around and get them sold to other people, but I learned a valuable lesson.

Remember, you are entering into a contract with the rancher and he is entering into a contract with you. He is contracting with you to provide you with beef and you are contracting with him to provide a market for the beef he spent the time raising for *you*. When you leave him high and dry, you've screwed it up for everyone. The rancher that at first might have been amenable to establishing a relationship with people interested in grass-fed beef now won't be. He can't take the risk, and he's not going to go broke based on your promise to pay him next year when they're fat. This is serious business for serious people. The uncommitted need not apply.

There is a flip side to that coin as well. You need to ask around and find out if your family farmer is trustworthy and won't take your money and run, but I doubt he'd get far off of your deposit anyway.

How big of a deposit, you ask? I'd suggest you plan on paying around $700, with the balance due on delivery of the beef. That's roughly just over $1 per pound because the average grass-fed steer will give you between 600-700 pounds of meat and it fills a freezer up quite nicely.

What would I do with 650 pounds of meat?

This is the next question I get asked all the time. The short answer is — eat it.

Most people I run into don't eat a lot of beef because it's cost prohibitive when buying it from the supermarket. But let's think for a minute about the costs and benefits.

I was driving by the local store one day and they had a "special" on hamburger. It was $2.50 a pound, and their T-bones were $7.99 a pound. I was aghast. Let's just say, for the sake of example, that you had $1800 to spend on beef. That means you could buy about 700 pounds of hamburger from sources and locations unknown, or about 200 pounds of select or choice T-bone steaks. For that same $1800 however, you could probably buy a whole grass-fed beef cut and wrapped. That means you get the roasts, steaks, ribs, burger — the whole kit and caboodle. You just have to buy it all at once. It's a no-brainer to me.

Now, I can tell you this as a fact: If you can buy steaks for the same price as hamburger, you're going to eat more steak. If you can buy a roast for the same price as hamburger, you're going to eat more roast beef. If you've got 650 pounds of meat in the freezer, you'll be surprised how easily you'll consume it.

But what if you're just a young couple and can't eat a whole beef in a year's time? Split it with somebody. Talk to your parents or in-laws. You take a half; they can each take a quarter. My experience has taught me this, once you eat good beef, you never have any trouble finding willing mouths.

So what do you suggest?

If you have plenty of ground to take care of the animal and have a ready source to obtain the animal (such as a friend in the livestock business), then you should seriously consider it. You will be able to cut your cost of beef down a little. However, you do assume all of the risk.

If you don't have much land, then you'll be far better off finding somebody to purchase a beef from. Just remember, if you're buying one from a commercial feedlot, it will most likely be grain fed and might have been given hormonal implants to increase the rate of gain. Make sure you ask. If you want a grass-fed animal, it will cost a bit more and be harder to find.

If you've got land enough to take care of one animal and you're trying to decide between a milk cow and a beef animal, I'd say go for the milk cow. You will realize a return on your investment quicker with a milk cow because she'll start giving milk right after she calves, whereas a beef animal is at least a one-year investment from the time it's weaned before you get any meat.

If you're just not sure, then buy it instead of raising it. As I've said, you'll spend at least $600 to buy a weaner, then you've got to care for and feed it for the next year or so and hope things go well. It will take a lot more of your time and money than you think, too. All in all, you're definitely putting all of your eggs in one basket whereas someone in the beef business can capitalize on economies of scale and raise them for about the same price and assume all of the risk. Don't limit yourself in the area you look, either. Even though I live in southern Idaho, I've had beef go all the way to Tacoma, Washington. The logistics take some work, but it can be done.

There's plenty more to think about, but that's enough for now. I wish you all the best of fortune and hope that now you are at least a little more knowledgeable and can make a more informed decision.

Jared Bedke is a cattleman in southern Idaho and can be reached for inquiries or comments at bedkebeef@starband.net. Δ

Buying a backhoe

By Ian McCollum

As the builder of an underground house, I've had a lot of experience moving dirt — more experience than I'd really like to have. When I started building, I had a lot of time and very little money, so all but the biggest jobs were shovel work.

A backhoe might just become your favorite homestead tool.

Do you really need an earthmoving machine?

I'm really in a pretty good position to eschew technological help. I'm a young guy in good physical shape, and I can heft a shovel when I need to. But even so, there are many times when a good digging machine makes the difference. In some cases, it's the difference between a job taking several days of hard work versus just a few hours, and sometimes it's the difference between a job getting done versus being put off indefinitely.

The obvious use for a backhoe is, of course, digging holes. Building a homestead of any decent size requires digging quite a few different holes. You'll need to dig your house foundation, plus the foundations for your shop, barn, greenhouse, guest house, and any other permanent structure you have in mind. You'll need to dig trenches for water lines, power lines (and being off the grid only means more power line trenches between your buildings and power shed), and network cables. You'll need to dig drainage channels around the house, and cut a driveway and associated culverts to keep it intact in the rain. You'll need to dig out stumps to clear land. Those are just the obvious things that will need to be dug. It's also worth remembering that in many places, you don't need a special permit to put in a septic system. If you can dig, you can install your own septic system and save quite a lot of money — especially if you need a long distance between the tank, house, and leach field.

A good digging machine is also a good lifting machine. Need to lift your trusses up onto your house frame? Move large rocks? Lift heavy laminated beams or logs? Pull your truck out of a mud hole or sand wash? Pull your neighbor's car out of the open water line trench they accidentally backed into? Repair a washed-out road after a storm? Rip out the thin concrete slab to replace it with a thicker one? Dig holes to plant small trees? Move large manure piles? You'll find all kinds of uses for a backhoe.

Why a backhoe over the alternatives?

If that last section hasn't convinced you of the usefulness of a backhoe, then you surely haven't spent enough quality time with your shovel. The question by now should not be *if* you get one, but *which* one you should get. There are really quite a few choices for the homesteader looking for earth-moving equipment. At the large end are the full-size commercial backhoes. But there are also a myriad of options for mini-backhoes, mini-excavators, skid steer loaders, and even modified antique garden tractors.

When heavy machinery first became viable for individuals in the United States, the primary market was for farming tractors. By the

1930s and 40s, developments like the 3-point hitch made it possible to use a motorized tractor for many labor-intensive farming tasks, and tractors like the iconic Ford 8N became commonplace. These tractors were designed to pull implements, but some were modified to add front loader buckets. These tractors are readily available and can often be found in decent running shape at low prices. This makes them look like a viable option, especially for the homesteader on a serious budget. However, these machines were not intended to carry heavy loads in front or use now-standardized hydraulic backhoe attachments. They generally lack front-wheel drive and power steering, which makes them difficult to maneuver while carrying a load. The lack of a backhoe arm seriously limits their practical utility. Unless you intend to use it primarily for maintaining a farm field, the antique tractor is a false economy for today's homesteader.

Not all aged machines are obsolete, however. There is a thriving market in used full-size backhoes, especially in today's rough economic times. A machine that may have cost tens of thousands from the factory can be bought 10 years later for a fraction of its sticker price. Construction businesses regularly upgrade their machinery to newer models to take advantage of more comfortable or powerful models, and to have the tax write-off. If the previous owners took good care of their machines, these older backhoes can have thousands of hours of good service left in them, and are built to serious industrial standards. They will still have all the (substantial) capabilities of a full-size backhoe, but at a much more affordable price. I believe this is the best way to get a machine for the person who is at all mechanically inclined and doesn't have big piles of money to spend.

One of the more common routes people choose when looking for a backhoe is the large market in mini-backhoes. These are small gas or diesel tractors (30-40 horsepower) with front loader buckets and various rear attachments including backhoe arms. These machines are more affordable new than their full-size commercial relatives, and offer all the modern bells and whistles, plus the confidence of a new machine and a factory warranty. They also have the ability to use a variety of modular tools like forklift loaders, augers, etc. The downside is that these machines cost significantly more than larger used backhoes, and are less useful. The small size makes them less intimidating to the new operator, but that advantage quickly wears off when you discover that they take two or three times as long to do any job. They can carry less in the loader bucket, have narrower backhoe buckets, and less reach. Less power to dislodge rocks and stumps as well. Used ones occasionally come up for sale around me for reasonable prices, though, and that might make sense for some people.

Mini-excavators are an option as well. These are generally tracked instead of wheeled, and have a small backhoe arm and a small dozer blade. Very small compared to tractors with backhoe arms, these machines are excellent for suburban landscaping and digging trenches. They're not too useful for other things, and are as expensive as anything you can get. Leave these to the specialists — a homestead needs a more general-purpose earthmover.

Finally, you could get a skid steer loader (aka Bobcat). You can get these either wheeled or tracked, and they can be fitted with all sorts of modular tools. A loader bucket is the standard, but you can also get augers, forklifts, backhoe arms, and numerous specialty pieces. They can certainly be very useful, especially for working homesteads. What they lack is serious excavation ability. A skid steer loader can move around material well, but it can't dig a big hole well. The backhoe attachments, while

Before you buy, try digging a test hole with the arm fully extended, and lifting a full front bucket to its maximum height.

available, are not large and are best suited for trenches or small jobs. I would consider a skid steer loader if I knew I was done building — but as long as there are foundations to dig, I want something with some serious excavating muscle.

Why not rent?

Two additional options are renting and hiring backhoes. Most towns of moderate size have businesses that will rent out heavy equipment, like backhoes and skid steer loaders. This is certainly the cheapest way to get a machine for a single project, since you only need to pay for the day or two that you will be using it. Renting also generally gets you a fairly new machine, with many of the nice modern features like an automatic transmission. Finally, of course, it means that you don't have to worry about any maintenance costs. The cost of rental, however, does add up pretty quickly if you need the machine for multiple projects. You also have to consider delivery costs, particularly when your property is off the beaten path. In my case, the nearest rental company is about 50 miles away, so I would be paying about $250 each time just for delivery. Going back over my receipts, I found that the money I had spent on rental backhoes before I bought my own would have paid three quarters of my purchase price.

The hose on the left leaks, as evidenced by the accumulated oily dirt. The one on the right is old but in fine working order.

An oil leak on the engine could be minor or serious. This one is an easy fix with some RTV sealant.

If you are considering a rental, think about whether it would be wiser to hire an owner/operator instead. If you don't have much (or any) experience working with heavy equipment, a skilled driver will get your job done much faster than you could, especially if it is a trickier piece of work such as leveling ground or digging around obstacles. Hired operators are also generally paid by the hour or job, whereas a rental machine comes on a per-day basis, whether you can use it the whole time or not.

Regardless of whether hiring or renting makes more sense, if you anticipate more than a couple jobs for the backhoe, the smart move is to buy one early on, before you've dumped thousands of dollars on someone else's. I guarantee you'll find far more uses for it than you expect.

Where to look and what to look for

So, have I convinced you to get a big beefy backhoe? If so, there are some things to look for and some things to definitely avoid.

First off, where to look? The place I would (and did) start is the internet. Sites like eBay (www.ebay.com) and especially Craigslist (www.craigslist.

com) can be a treasure trove of potential deals. Even if your local town doesn't have a Craigslist site, looking in the nearby cities can give you a feel for prices in your area, and you might always find a seller willing to deliver or to make a deal good enough to make a long trip for. Print classified ads like *Equipment Trader* (a spinoff of *Auto Trader*) are worth looking at, but I wouldn't depend on them, as the good buys will be snapped up quickly. In more rural areas, always keep an eye on Post Office and grocery store notice boards. Ask around among people with connections to the local good ol' boy network — shop owners, swap meet regulars, and mechanics. You never know who has a something they would be willing to sell but haven't bothered to advertise.

Engines: Diesel is much preferred over gasoline. A diesel engine will provide more power at low RPM (which means less fuel consumption), have easier maintenance (no carburetor to tinker with), and have a longer life.

Mobility: Four wheel drive is a nice improvement over 2WD. Consider the terrain you will be using the backhoe on; 4WD might be essential for you, or it might just be a perk.

Cab: I'm out in the desert, so a roof on the machine for shade was a must-have for me. It may not be for you, but I would strongly recommend one. In addition to shade, it will also provide protection in case you roll the backhoe or something falls on it. A fully-enclosed cab can also make it more comfortable to use in cold or windy weather.

Problems to watch out for

Get a mechanical inspection up front. I won't cover the engine itself — that's a subject worthy of many articles by itself. If you don't have the skills to evaluate an engine, I would strongly suggest finding a friend or hiring a professional mechanic to help you inspect the machine. There are some issues specific to backhoes that are easy to check as long as you know what to look for.

The core of a backhoe is its hydraulic system. If that has problems, the machine will not work the way you need it to. Fortunately, the main elements of the hydraulic system are easy to test and inspect. Begin your inspection by starting up the engine and putting it in neutral. First, look at the hoses — most of them will be exposed and easy to see. Look for how many are new, and how many are dulled and older. Look for frayed or worn hoses; you can safely assume that any hose with its outer sheathing worn off is going to need replacing fairly soon. There may be nicks and chunks taken out of the hoses from being inadvertently scraped against trees or rocks. Leaky fittings are evident from the build-up of oily dirt they attract. Next, extend all the attachments so you can see the full length of the cylinders, and look for deep pits or gouges in them. Any sharp edges will destroy the cylinder seals and cause leaks, and replacement cylinders aren't cheap.

If you don't find any deal-breakers with a visual inspection, get back in the cab. If you don't know how to operate the controls, this is the time to find out, and any decent seller will show you how. Use the front bucket to lift the machine off its front wheels, and then turn your seat around and use the two outriggers to lift the rear wheels off the ground. Now turn the machine off and let it sit for several minutes. If the hydraulics are in good shape, they won't move at all, and the backhoe won't sink towards the ground. If it does, you have problems and will need to replace parts.

If the seller has an area where you can dig a test hole or two, definitely do so. This will let you get a feel for how the controls work, and if there are any problems with them when used under a load. Try digging at full extension of the backhoe arm, and lift a full front bucket to its maximum height.

In addition to the hydraulic systems, it is important to test the basic mobility of the machine. If it's a 4WD model, lift it up off the wheels and make sure all four have power when you are in 4WD. Check the brakes, both on flat surfaces and a slope. Fixing brakes is pretty easy on automobiles, but with a backhoe, it is much more labor intensive (those rear wheels weigh 300+ pounds each). Also check the parking brake — digging on a slope can be a real pain if you don't have a parking brake in good working order. Make sure the machine will start smoothly from a standstill when going uphill, and make sure the clutch works smoothly if you are looking at a manual transmission machine. Transmission issues should be a deal-breaker, and brake issues are at least worth haggling the price down. I'm not equipped for serious mechanical work, so brakes were a deal-breaker for me.

Repair prices will vary quite a bit with the different vintages and makers of heavy equipment, but make sure to check parts availability online before purchasing. For example, I discovered that some Ford backhoes like mine were made in England, and those parts are harder to get than the similar (but not interchangeable) American-made models.

So you bought a backhoe — now what?

Because it isn't used on a daily basis around the homestead, heavy equipment is vulnerable to deterioration but also has the potential to provide years or decades of good service. The key is good preventative maintenance. When you first get your machine, do a thorough basic servicing on it. Change out the fuel filter, oil and oil filter, air filter, and hydraulic filter. Top off or replace the

This hose holds pressure for now, but it will need to be replaced sooner or later.

hydraulic fluid if necessary. Make sure the fuel in it is good, and drain the fuel tank if it is stale or contaminated. Get a grease gun if you don't already have one, and give all the lubrication zerks a good dose. Start a maintenance log, and continue to change those basic items at the recommended intervals.

Other basic preventative steps include covering the tires to prevent damage from sunlight, and moving the machine periodically to keep seals lubricated and tires from cracking. In addition, make sure the exhaust is protected from rain or snow that could get into the engine.

When using your machine, treat it with some respect. Don't under-throttle it, but also don't run it at higher speed than really necessary. Use the controls gently and smoothly, and don't jerk the arm around. If a rock or stump won't be budged, look for a different way to get it out instead of beating the machine up with the brute force approach. You're not paying an hourly fee, so you have plenty of time to go slow and steady, and overcome obstacles safely.

Treat your backhoe well, and in return it will save you an enormous amount of labor and become one of your favorite tools around the homestead.

Ian McCollum holds a degree in Mechanical Engineering Technology from Purdue University, but wishes he had spent the tuition money on a big Caterpillar excavator instead. He currently spends his weeks in civilization working in the solar power industry and his weekends building his off-grid homestead in the boonies. Δ

This hose has been nicked on a tree or rock. It's not a problem now, but could be indicative of abuse.

Grandma's soup from your garden

By Joyce Lindsey O'Keefe

Remember those old-fashioned soups that Grandma used to make with deep flavors that echoed the essence of the earth?

Grandma took time to make her soup stock from scratch and she used produce from her "kitchen garden" to give her creations a satisfying richness. Too often soups encountered on grocery store shelves, in restaurants, and even those made at home by hurried cooks all carry that same, flat "processed" taste.

Could Grandma's soups be made today without spending hours slaving over the stove? Yes! With an organized approach, it's possible to produce flavorful seasonal soups using vegetables and herbs from your refrigerator, freezer, or your backyard garden.

The keys are freshness and flexibility. As a gardener, you already know your crops are unlikely to come in exactly as planned: you'll get less of one veggie, more of another; something will ripen ahead of schedule, something else will fail to sprout. So, there is no single recipe for Grandma's soup: she used whichever vegetables and herbs were growing abundantly in her kitchen garden at the time, in whatever combination she thought would taste good. Most of us can — and probably will — add foods from our pantry or the grocery store to our soups. Fresher ingredients equal better taste, so using seasonal produce makes sense.

Shortly after we married, when my husband smelled the enticing aroma from the kitchen, he often asked me, "What kind of soup are we having tonight?" Invariably, the answer was "surprise soup," for rarely will two soups turn out exactly the same.

Despite the lack of a specific recipe, there are steps for efficiently concocting a modern version of Grandma's soup:

1. Prepare the stock: homemade if possible; commercial, if necessary.
2. Prepare the vegetables, herbs, and meat, (if desired).
3. Cook the soup.
4. Keep it safe: boil, reboil, and store.

Prepare the stock

The soup stock is probably the single most important ingredient that gave your own grandmother's soup its rich, authentic taste. The use of canned or powdered "pre-fabricated" soup stock and "starters" is most likely the reason so many soups today seem to taste alike. Use your freezer to help you prepare homemade stock:

Save trimmings and peelings from vegetables in plastic bags in the freezer. When you cook vegetables

Ingredients used in Grandma's soup: stock made from saved vegetable juices and vegetable scraps, organic commercial chicken broth, ½ cup raw long grain white rice, about 1 cup diced cooked turkey meat, and home-grown organic garden vegetables and herbs.

and meats, save their juices in containers in the freezer. It's okay to mix meat juices such as chicken and beef together, but keep fish and seafood juices in a separate container and use only for fish soups. It's fine to store meat and veggie juices together, if desired. Save meat scraps and leftover slices in plastic bags in the freezer. Save meat bones separately, but not tiny ones that might slip through a strainer.

When you are ready to make soup stock, first put the juices in a large pot or pressure cooker. Add about ¼ inch of water to the bottom, so nothing burns, then cook on medium/high until the liquid is boiling. Slide in your saved vegetable scraps and meat bones, if any. When you include meat bones, pour in about one tablespoon of vinegar (any kind) to leach the gelatin out of the bones. Boil everything vigorously at least five minutes to kill any harmful bacteria. Then let the scraps simmer for another half hour or until the vegetable peelings are mushy.

Using a strainer, colander, or sieve, drain the liquid from the large pot into your medium-sized soup pot. Mash the veggie scraps against the strainer with the back of a wooden spoon (or other large spoon) to squeeze the last of their juice into your soup pot. If possible, compost the remaining veggie scraps.

If you don't have quite enough homemade soup stock, or none at all, use commercial vegetable, chicken, or beef broth. With the addition of fresh vegetables and herbs from your garden, you should be able to form an acceptable stock without adding any processed "soup stock flavorings."

To remove fat from the stock, refrigerate the soup pot for several hours or overnight. Fat will rise to the top and solidify, then it can be skimmed off. You may concoct a soup at that point, or freeze the stock for later.

Before making soup, check the flavor of the stock. Is it robust or feeble? Now look at the vegetables and herbs you have collected from your garden. If the stock tastes a little weak, strongly-flavored veggies such as cauliflower or cabbage can give it a boost. So can additional herbs or some commercial meat broth. If the stock seems too intense, you might divide it into two or three batches, freezing some for later use, then diluting the amount you plan to use now. Or, you can add more neutral-tasting ingredients to the stock, such as potatoes or rice.

Garden ingredients for Grandma's soup:
Top row, left to right: collard greens, red winter kale, Swiss chard, lettuce leaf.
Bottom row, left to right: lavender, French tarragon, golden thyme, sage, Vietnamese coriander, Shiso, chives, Walla Walla onion

Prepare the vegetables, herbs, and meat

If the soup stock is not already hot, boil it for five minutes while you rinse and dice your garden vegetables and herbs and prepare the meat. Remember that ingredients going into a soup should always be spoon-sized or smaller; larger pieces tend to slip off a diner's spoon and splash into the soup bowl.

To make it easy to add them to the soup in the correct order, set prepared veggies on a plate near the cooktop, each type in its own pile. Cut herbs into tiny pieces to help distribute their flavor throughout the soup. Remove excess fat from meat before you dice it. Trimmings and peelings from veggies can go into a freezer bag for your next soup stock.

Cook the soup

I like to add onions and garlic, if available, to the stock first. Some cooks swear that these must be sautéed in oil beforehand, but that's a matter of choice. I also add my herbs now, to allow the flavors to blend into the soup longer. However, never add salt to a soup until just before serving, if at all. It is best not to add salt if the soup may be frozen later because the salty flavor will intensify while the soup is in the freezer. I cook all my soups without salt, then make salt available at the table.

Next, put in your choice of grains or legumes: beans, peas, pearled barley, lentils, rice, couscous, pasta, potatoes, corn, etc., then cook for the required time.

Once these are done, add meat, if desired. If you are using either raw meat or uncooked fish instead of leftovers, you might brown these separately in a little oil before adding to the other ingredients. Or you can do this in the soup pot, as a first step, before adding the stock. In any case, be sure meat or fish becomes thoroughly cooked. Grandma's soup is not the place for steak tartar or sashimi.

Finally, slide in your prepared vegetables. If you put in the longer-cooking ones, such as potato chunks, first and save the quicker-cooking pieces, such as chopped spinach, for last, it's more likely everything will heat through at the same time.

Avoid the dreaded "one-vegetable soup." Even if you have a bumper crop of kale, your soup will be more interesting if you can round up at least three veggies, in addition to the flavoring ones such as onions. Tomato juice or pieces help keep veggies crisp. Okra thickens a soup stock.

Colorful is tasteful. A monochromatic soup is boring. If your garden is giving you white onions, turnips, Daikon radishes, and some anemic-looking Swiss chard, it's OK to raid your pantry for yellow corn kernels and canned tomatoes to enliven your soup.

Once all your ingredients are in the soup, set it on a rolling boil for five full minutes. Then you may sample your creation, adjusting the seasoning, adding favorite spices, as desired. Occasionally, I've rescued a lackluster soup by pouring in the contents of a small can of spicy vegetable juice or by adding dried shiitake mushrooms.

Vary ingredients in rhythm with the season, but also to suit the occasion. For example, when I knew a gourmand friend of ours was going to stop by, I added wild rice and a variety of dried mushrooms to my soup; he was delighted.

Lucky Time

Since April I'm 77; this year
is '07 and this July Fourth all
six of our children and some of theirs
filled this old house with life. They ran go-karts
in the meadow, built a float for the parade,
churned ice cream in a worn-out freezer, drank
pop and beer by the case, went on float trips
down Meramec, filled night skies with fireworks,
laughed, gobbled up their mother's cooking, washed
dished, argued politics, relived the past.

And now they've gone back to their homes
and far off countries and we've got settled
in our comfort rut again and we're glad
they're gone and can hardly wait until next time.

— *Jim Thomas*

Keep it safe: boil, reboil, and store

Soup will keep safely in a 40° F or colder refrigerator for two nights. On the third day, if it is not all gone, you must eat it now, freeze it, or reboil it. If possible, eat the soup sooner rather than later, because it loses some nutrients each time you freeze or reboil it. If you have a microwave and freezer-to-microwave bowls, this can be an easy solution for those leftovers. Pour the leftover soup into containers and place those into the coldest part of the freezer to harden. Unless you are fond of odd surprises, label all containers with type and date. If you don't, you may find yourself serving potato-onion soup with baked potatoes for dinner, or navy bean soup alongside a three-bean salad.

If you plan to finish the soup soon, but not that day, or don't have room in the freezer, reboil the soup. Bring it to a rolling boil for a full five minutes. Don't cheat on either the intensity of the boil or the time — this high heat is necessary to kill any unwelcome organisms that may have taken up residence in your creation. Once the soup has weathered a hard five minute boil, it's good for another two nights in the refrigerator. Hopefully, by that time it will have been consumed. If not, you can choose again: freeze or reboil.

This modern way to make Grandma's soup isn't difficult or expensive.

Pair vegetables and herbs from your garden with a little time and organization, and you can enjoy the deep, rich flavors of a seasonal soup that would make your grandma proud. Δ

These dogs can hunt

By Michael D. Faw

Hunting dogs often serve double-duty as a family pet and provider.

Dogs are popular with rural residents but, unfortunately, many of those dogs have become full-time pets that are always contained in fenced backyards. At one time, however, dogs were foremost work animals that were relied upon to help put food on the table and keep beasts out of gardens. If you want a dog that serves as a pet, and can also aid with the hunt, then you have options. There are many dog breeds that can give chase *and* unwavering friendship.

One breed of dog that can hunt and be a cherished family pet is the Labrador retriever, or Lab. It's America's most popular dog breed. Your choices with this breed soon become one of color with black, brown (or chocolate), and yellow as the top options. There are also other dogs that can deliver the goods while being family-friendly, such as beagles, pointers, and some hounds. Picking and training a dog can be rewarding work if you do your research before you pick up a pup or snap on a leash.

The Labrador retriever is the most popular dog breed in the United States. Not only is it an even-tempered family pet, it also makes an excellent hunting dog.

Top breeds

There's no disputing that a Labrador retriever is the top dog by ownership of registered breeds in the United States. It's held this position with the American Kennel Club registrations for 20 years. Most dog owners — and those with an interest in dogs — recognize the Lab as a breed with an even temperament, and a dog that can be used to hunt upland birds like pheasants and quail, as well as a long list of waterfowl species when sent forth from blinds and across fields. As a species, Labs generally love to play fetch and this translates into game retrieves in the field with some training. Joining Labs in popularity are Golden retrievers that can also be used to hunt birds.

The beagle, another popular pet and hunting breed, ranks No. 4 with the AKC. Most Americans are aware of this fun-loving energetic breed, thanks to Snoopy, of *Peanuts* fame. Beagles, as small hounds, are predominately used to chase rabbits, and can be trained to tree squirrels and track wounded deer. Unlike large breeds, however, beagles are small — the average weight for a male is 20 to 35 pounds — so they will be cheaper on a yearly basis to feed and house.

Also on the AKC's 2010 popular dog list are the Dachshund and Poodle. Believe it not, these species were once hunting breeds, and the Dachshund still performs field duties in its native Germany. (Note: *hund* means hound in German.) Dachshunds can chase and sometimes retrieve squirrels if you initiate the pursuit and practice. Poodles were used for hunting once, and one innovative dog musher has used them as sled dogs in recent times. Cocker spaniels are another breed that was once popular with hunters, and this breed seems to be returning to good graces with some upland bird hunters. Most spaniels are also known for being close-at-hand family pets that are easy-going inside the home.

Other dog breeds that are popular as pets and pursuers are German Shorthairs, Vizslas, Weimaraners, and some setter breeds. These dogs are still used in parts of Europe as hunting hounds to pursue boar, but in North America the breeds are generally used to locate, point, and retrieve birds. The Shorthairs, Vizlas, and Weimaraners are all known for their intelligence and for being devoted family members.

Before you select a dog to serve double-duty as a hunter and family friend, research the breed in your local library or on the Internet. There are many breed-specific clubs that have valuable information about a breed's traits, quirks, and temperament. A breed like the Weimaraner, for example, was made popular as a top photo model in New York while wearing human clothes, but the breed is very high energy and needs a lot of exercise and human interaction. It has too much energy for some home environments. In the field, however, this dog's energy surplus becomes a source of non-stop hunting, impressive agility, and determined drive.

Remember that most dog breeds in the U.S. are imports, and some breed lines have been far removed from their hunting heritage. Unfortunately, select breeding in some lines has produced dogs that are stars at standing around and looking pretty, but those dogs will have no concept of being afield or hunting. On the other side of the coin, some breeds were never developed to be pets, such as the American Foxhound, a breed that George Washington is credited with developing.

Picking a pup

After you've completed the breed research, it's time for on-the-ground research. Call and interview breeders, check references, and go take a look. It might be best to leave the kids at home in this process or emotions could overpower reason. You should also make a pup or dog selection from hunting stock with a proven record of hunting. That rules out most mall and chain pet stores as sources. Some dog lines have become show dogs and might be afraid of squirrels or gunshots.

When you visit a dog breeder, look at the dog's living conditions and watch the parents, if present. Shyness, leg problems, or excessive aggression could be unwanted traits that your new dog could inherit. Note also how everyone interacts with the pups you are inspecting, because the kind of human interaction received in those early days of life often sets the stage for how the dog reacts to humans in the future. Make your first trip an on-site inspection and research mission. Return for a second look after you narrow the sources. While all pups are cute, remember that they will grow up — sooner than you think — and you'll spend up to 15 years with your new family member.

Yellow lab pup

If the dog will also be a family pet and possibly live in your home, take the kids along on the second visit and closely observe the interaction. If the breeder has kids, note how they interact with the dogs. Pups learn to avoid humans and kids if they have been sources of pain, and this can be a very difficult obstacle to overcome, and could possibly be a problem before any hunting training begins.

If you will use your dog for hunting, inject hunting-related items into the interaction, like a bird's wing or squirrel tail, and observe the pup's reaction. You can buy squirrel tails and bird wings at outlets that sell fly tying materials or in some sporting goods stores that offer dog training supplies. If the pup pursues and latches on to any wing or tail that you pass before it, you are well on your way to having a dog that has an interest in game.

You should also prepare your home, vehicle, and family before buying or acquiring a dog. Small pups like to chew up anything they discover, especially shoes, and they need a place that they can go and find peace and solitude, like a dog crate or kennel.

Weimaraner training to retrieve

Along with potential problems with house training, you'll need to fully understand what will be expected of the new dog, and who is responsible for what in your household. There are many methods and informative sources on training dogs to behave in or around the home, and when making contact with humans.

Training to hunt

All hunting dogs should know command basics, such as heel, sit, and stay. This is very important before heading afield.

The development of a hunting dog depends on many factors. You must decide what you want the dog to do, your amount of time to train, how receptive the dog is to commands, and other factors. For some hunters, the reward is in training and hunting with their dog. The obvious benefit is to develop a dog that adheres to your commands, your pace, and your likes and dislikes. And you can save a lot of money by training your own dogs. There are many great books and DVDs on training hunting dogs, so research before you take on the task.

If you use a dog trainer, however, you will also have to be trained. You — and all family members — will need to understand the trainer's commands, how to reinforce them with the dog, and what is and is not acceptable. Your dog may be absent for months if it goes to a trainer's camp, but the incoming training bills will remind you that you have a dog. It will be up to you to reinforce the training once your dog returns home.

One important factor with hunting dogs is their reaction to gunshots and loud noises. Some dogs couldn't care less, and for other dogs the sudden loud bang creates true terror. Some trainers have tempered a dog to gunshots and loud noises by banging or dropping a metal food dish while the dog eats. You can also take the dog to a gun range and feed treats while others are shooting, or have the dog present while you practice plinking. Offer treats along with pats and rubs to present the message that you are comfortable, and the dog should be comfortable in a noisy environment. If your dog panics at gunshots, stop and ease the fear, and consider training from a long distance and moving closer to the shooter over a period of time.

A dog that's expected to be afield or in the forest and hunting should be introduced to those environments as a pup. Tall grasses create confining areas that upset some dogs, and a dark forest with tall trees and strange sounds and sights can unnerve some timid dogs. Take them afield to play and explore, and make the introduction fun. Repeat walks in the forest and field as often as possible to build confidence and familiarity.

One other issue is how far — or close — you'd like a dog to hunt ahead of you. Obviously squirrel and rabbit dogs need to range out to make discoveries and tree or chase the game. Bird dogs that range too far, however, could go on point upon finding a quail or pheasant but are so far away that you never realize it. A long check cord tied to a pup's collar and a small bell on the collar helps you keep track of its location, and hold it in place when you approach. Some hunters also place their pup in the field with mature hunting dogs when possible.

A final controversy is whether dogs that reside indoors can go outdoors and hunt. Yes, they can. In fact the more "partnership" you create with a dog often means it will work harder to please you, or possibly better understand your voice tones.

The hunt

Walks afield in the forest should be times to introduce your pup or dog to smells representing animals you are interested in. For a beagle, stopping to sniff rabbit droppings or den entrances lets a pup know you have an interest in this smell and all things related. Stopping to explore a pheasant feather found in the grass or to observe ducks on the water will let your dog know you have an interest — and so should they. Most dogs learn quickly.

Many states have regulations covering dog training, so discover the guidelines before heading afield. Some areas are closed during certain months, or firearms can possibly only be carried at certain times. You'll also want your dog to be ready to perform when legal hunting seasons are open, so preseason training is important.

There are also shooting preserves that can release birds so you know where they are and can introduce your dog to the sounds and smells of a hunting experience. You can find hunting preserves near you at *www.wingshootingusa.org*. Some areas also have enclosed areas to train beagles with resident rabbits and brush piles included. These training areas often offer game when it could be scarce on your ground, and often permit shooting before and after the standard hunting season dates. Some places require membership, and others permit access after you pay a day fee.

Of course, hunting on your property and in the neighborhood or region can be rewarding if you have habitat for wildlife. You can improve habitat for nearly every species, including squirrels.

Chasing the buck

In addition to using your dog to place food on the table, you can also use some dogs to put cash in your wallet and pay for dog food. You'll need to check your state's laws before selling edible meat and some animal parts, but there's a market for some of these items.

Fly tying enthusiasts — and the sources that supply them — buy squirrel and pheasant tails, and entire rabbit skins with the ears attached. Entire pheasant skins can be crafted into decorative wreaths, and these fetch a handsome price. There are also contests that award prizes and cash for dogs that tree squirrels and chase rabbits. And there are places that host hunters and also hire guides with dogs that pursue game, such as shooting preserves that release upland birds. If you use your dog to hunt coyotes and tree raccoons, the hides from these species can be sold as fur.

And finally, if you become skilled at training dogs to hunt specific species, other hunters could search you out to hire your expertise and services. Good dog trainers demand a hefty premium.

Hunting dogs that serve double-duty as family pets can lead to many options. Many dogs are up to the challenges. Δ

These two dogs have done their part to put food on the table.

Kebabs
fancy-free summer fare

By Linda Gabris

I love entertaining, especially in summertime when we all eat outdoors where we can kick our shoes off, leave our hats and shades on, and prepare food in one of the simplest and oldest fashions known to man — threaded onto skewers, cooked over coals, and eaten directly off the stick. This is what I call "footloose and fancy-free" summer dining.

The word, kebab (also spelled *kabob*, *kabap*, *kibob*, and *kebhav*) is derived from the ancient Akkadian word, *kababu,* meaning to burn or char. The cooking method is believed to have originated in the Caucasus where mountain men speared meat onto the end of their swords for quick cooking over an open fire, eliminating the need for packing cooking gear and utensils into the treacherous high country.

When the cooking method made its way into Turkey, the term *shish kebab* was adapted, *sis* or *shish* meaning "spit" and kebab meaning "roast." The cooking method is deeply-rooted in the cuisines of the Middle East and Greece, Pakistan, India, and Southeast Asia where it has held ground for centuries as a convenient way to prepare delicious meals in bite-sized portions, cutting down drastically on cooking time which helps to conserve fuel, which is often scarce.

Although sheep and goat were the traditional ancient mountain meats for spearing, chicken, as well as other white and red meats, seafood, fish, vegetables, and fruits have all become popular picks for "kebabing."

As for the heat source, the backyard barbeque is ideal for cooking kebabs on but if rain sends your party packing indoors or if you like to indulge in kebabs all year round, the loaded skewers can be placed on a grilling rack and broiled in the oven or cooked on an indoor grill (which I often use when a kebab craving strikes in the midst of winter and my barbecue pit is buried beneath a foot of snow).

You can use metal or bamboo skewers available in various lengths. Food seems to adhere better to wood than it does to metal, thus holding it more firmly in place during rotation. Also since inexpensive wood skewers are disposable, cleanup is that much easier!

On the other hand, metal skewers (even though they need scouring after use) are sturdier and less apt to catch fire. If using wooden skewers, soak them first in cold water for about an hour before loading them to deter the sticks from catching fire during cooking.

My general rule of thumb is this: If the food is lightweight and requires

Big-stick beef kebabs

quick cooking, such as prawns or fruit, I'll go with bamboo. If it is heavier fare like chunks of beef that need a sturdier stick and longer cooking, I'll choose metal skewers.

When I entertain larger gatherings kebab-style, I like to set up a kebab bar near the grill which allows my guests to load up their own skewers with a selection of whatever their hearts desire — meats, seafood, vegetables, fruits, or whatever other foods are on the cookout party menu along with a selection of breads or buns, salads, relishes, as well as barbecue, basting, and dipping sauces along with spoons and accompanying brushes.

A little tip to remember: If cooking both seafood and other types of meats at the same feast, one side of the grill should be reserved for fish only and the other side for meats so flavors don't mingle. If you have a second grill, such as a portable camp grill, it comes in handy for the purpose of cooking the seafood separately.

I also have an extra grill rack reserved especially for dessert kebabs which ensures sweet bites don't pick up trace tastes of meat, onion, or garlic. I hunted down the extra rack at a local salvage store for a few dollars. If you only have one rack available, scour it well to remove savory flavors before grilling sweet foods intended for desserts.

After each guest assembles their kebab it can be placed on the grill and cooked to personal satisfaction — rare, medium, or well-done. Let's face it, some folks like their beef barely warmed while others, including my kids, would freak out at a bite of meat with a touch of pink showing. Since it's impossible for a chef to distinguish the varying degrees of desired doneness to suit the taste of each individual diner, I find the best solution to achieving satisfaction for all is to let everyone "time their own stick."

Hungarian meatball kebabs

When it comes to choosing appropriate foods for kebab making, my motto is, "If it'll thread onto a stick, it's kebab-able." Below is a selection of some of my favorite kebab combinations.

If you have a garden, plan your kebabs around whatever the garden is producing — zucchini, cherry tomatoes, peppers, corn, baby potatoes, or what-have-you.

Some of the kebabs below are super kid-friendly while others are a little more on the gourmet side of town. All are delicious and, if you work with what the season has to offer, (both in your garden and at the produce stand), you can serve top quality food without breaking the family budget.

Another little tip to keep in mind is that foods should be paired up or cut into suitable-sized pieces that will cook evenly. For instance, prawns are quick-cooking. They only require a few minutes per side. So do not pair them up with potato chunks that take about 15 minutes longer than the prawns to cook as one food will be overdone by the time the other is tender.

Instead, I like to pair prawns up with melon balls, cherry tomatoes, pineapple chunks, zucchini, and other quick-cooking bites. The potato chunks go better with cubed meat such as beef, pork, or lamb which require about the same amount of cooking time.

Hot dog kebabs:

Here's a simple, very versatile recipe for kebabs that is always a big hit, especially with the younger set. You can judge how many hot dogs and how many vegetables it'll take to feed your crew. I find that one pound of hot dogs makes enough for about 14 kebabs. Of course, the vegetables mentioned below are only a guideline — you can add or omit anything you wish.

hot dogs, frankfurters, or European wieners, cut into 1-inch slices
husked corn on the cob, cut into 1-inch sections
quartered onions
zucchini slices
pepper chunks
whole button mushrooms
small baby potatoes, parboiled until almost tender
pineapple chunks

To assemble — thread hot dogs and vegetables alternately onto the skewer. Grill kebabs for several minutes per side or until hot dog is golden (or until sausages are cooked) and vegetables are tender, brushing with the basting sauce below upon turning.

Basting sauce:

½ cup butter
1 Tbsp. prepared mustard
2 Tbsp. ketchup
¼ tsp. garlic powder

Melt butter in small bowl in microwave. Add prepared mustard, ketchup, and garlic powder. Blend well.

Big-stick beef kebabs:

These kebabs, so named because I always use the biggest skewers I can find for threading the luscious meat onto, are always popular with beef lovers. You can use any type of cheaper cut of lean beef in this recipe, because the secret to tenderness lies more in the lengthy marinade than it does in the cut. Along with rendering the meat super tender, the fragrant soak instills wonderful flavor and aroma into the meat.

2 pounds beef trimmed of excess fat and cut into 1-inch cubes
cubed acorn or other squash of choice
red, green, and/or yellow peppers cut into bite-sized pieces (using multicolored peppers adds visual appeal to the stick)
whole button mushrooms
halved baby potatoes
quartered onions

Marinade:

¼ cup olive oil
2 Tbsp. balsamic vinegar
¼ cup red wine
4 cloves minced garlic
2 Tbsp. soy sauce
1 small minced onion
¼ tsp. black pepper
1 tsp. seasoned salt

Put marinade ingredients into a bowl. Add cubed beef and mix well. Cover and marinate in fridge for at least 5 hours, or overnight. Thread meat alternately with prepared vegetables of choice. Place on grill rack and cook, turning often, for 10 minutes or until desired doneness is reached. Near the end of cooking time, brush both sides with barbecue sauce, if desired. This is enough meat for about 8 servings. How many kebabs it makes depends on how many vegetables or mushrooms join the meat on the stick.

Honey-orange salmon kebabs

Variation: Any venison meat — moose, deer, elk, or bear — can be used in the above recipe and the name changed to suit the game. If using bear, however, be sure to cook it thoroughly as you would pork to safeguard against trichinosis.

Be sure that separate utensils are used for handling raw foods and cooked foods to prevent cross-contamination. For instance, a fork that has speared up raw meat to lace onto a skewer should not be used for eating from or for forking a pickle from the pickle crock.

Foil-wrapped lemon chicken kebabs:

These tangy, succulent chunks of threaded chicken on a stick are delicious. The secret — the loaded skewers are wrapped in aluminum foil before grilling to lock in juices and flavor. I serve these kebabs with lots of crispy bread, tossed dandelion or other type of wild and wacky green summer salad leaves, and little bowls of yogurt dipping sauce called *tzatziki* (recipe below).

4 skinless, boneless chicken breasts, cut into 1-inch cubes
¼ cup lemon juice and 1 tsp. grated zest
2 Tbsp. olive oil
4 cloves minced garlic
1 tsp. each ground coriander and ground cumin
½ tsp. salt
¼ tsp. black pepper

Put chicken in a bowl. Mix remaining ingredients well and pour over chicken. Cover and marinate in fridge for a couple of hours. The longer you marinate, the more infused with flavor and aroma the chicken will be. It can stand overnight, if you wish. Thread the chicken onto 4 skewers. Wrap each skewer securely into a square of lightly-greased aluminum foil. Grill 8 to 10 minutes, turning frequently. Peel off the foil and dip each luscious bite into the *tzatziki*.

Variation: Any vegetables you desire can be threaded alternately with the chicken, in which case you can make up to eight of these delicious kebabs instead of just four "all chicken" kebabs as above.

***Tazatziki* dipping sauce:**

1 cup plain unflavored yogurt 5 cloves minced garlic (That's right — this Greek dipping sauce is meant to be garlicky and delicious.) ¼ cup finely diced cucumber (if using young garden or English cucumber, the skin can be left on. Otherwise, peel if the cucumber is mature as the skin may be tough and bitter.) 1 Tbsp. olive oil 1 Tbsp. lemon juice

Combine all ingredients into a bowl. Cover and let stand in fridge at least an hour before serving to allow flavors to "marry."

Hungarian meatball kebabs:

A few years ago, I developed this recipe quite by accident and now it's a family favorite. One day my husband and I were making Hungarian sausages and we had about a pound of ground pork sausage mixture left when we ran out of casings. So I formed the sausage mixture into meatballs and threaded them onto skewers alternately with green pepper chunks and onions and grilled them for supper. They were delicious. Now when we make Hungarian sausages, we always set aside a good portion of the sausage mixture to form into meatballs, which we pop it into the freezer and save especially for kebab making. If you like this recipe, you can make up larger batches of the sausage mixture and freeze for future use as I do. A tip: If you wrap these kebabs in aluminum foil before grilling, the meatballs will be extra moist and juicy, especially useful if using lean ground pork as mentioned below.

1 pound ground regular pork (When we make sausages we are grinding a whole leg of pork so there is plenty of fat. Regular ground pork works better than lean ground pork; however, if you are watching your fat intake, the latter will produce a leaner bite.) 3 cloves peeled garlic 3 Tbsp. sweet red paprika ¼ tsp. cayenne pepper ½ tsp. salt ¼ tsp. black pepper 1 tsp. onion powder red pepper chunks onion chunks

Put garlic onto a small microwavable saucer with 2 tablespoons of water and cook on high about 1 minute or until garlic is soft. Using a

Prawn and melon ball kebabs

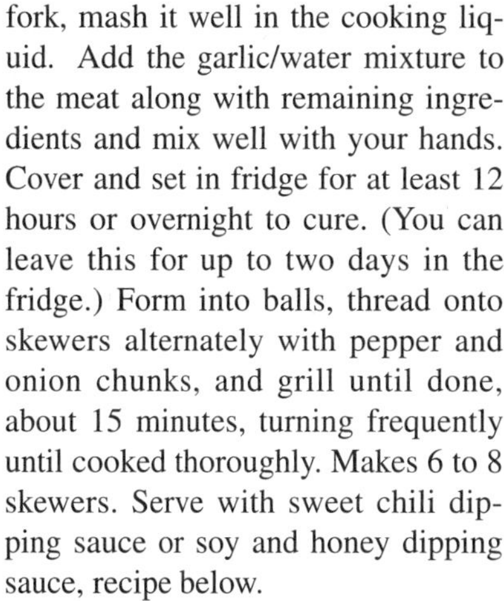

fork, mash it well in the cooking liquid. Add the garlic/water mixture to the meat along with remaining ingredients and mix well with your hands. Cover and set in fridge for at least 12 hours or overnight to cure. (You can leave this for up to two days in the fridge.) Form into balls, thread onto skewers alternately with pepper and onion chunks, and grill until done, about 15 minutes, turning frequently until cooked thoroughly. Makes 6 to 8 skewers. Serve with sweet chili dipping sauce or soy and honey dipping sauce, recipe below.

Soy and honey dipping sauce:

¼ cup soy sauce 2 Tbsp. honey 2 Tbsp. ketchup 1 clove minced garlic

Put soy sauce into a bowl. Add honey, ketchup, and minced garlic, blend well. Let stand at least 2 or 3 hours before serving. Serve as dip with the above kebabs or with other types of meat or chicken kebabs.

Honey-orange salmon kebabs:

These sweet, fragrant kebabs are always a winner with fish lovers. They are so light, bright, and refreshingly good that you'll reel in tons of raves every time you serve them.

1 pound skinned, boneless salmon cut into 1-inch cubes orange slices cherry or grape tomatoes **Marinade:** ½ cup orange juice 2 tsp. grated orange zest 2 Tbsp. lemon juice 1 tsp. freshly grated ginger 2 Tbsp. honey 2 Tbsp. soy sauce 1 clove minced garlic freshly grated black pepper

Basting sauce:

2 Tbsp. each of honey, soy sauce, and melted butter, blended together

Strawberry kebabs

Put salmon in bowl and add marinade ingredients in order given. Mix well. Cover and marinate in fridge for 2 or 3 hours. Thread salmon onto skewers, alternately with orange slices and tomatoes. Place loaded skewers onto grill rack that has been lightly oiled or sprayed to prevent sticking. Grill kebabs, rotating and brushing frequently with basting sauce, until fish is tender and well-glazed, about 4 minutes to each side. Makes 4 to 6 kebabs.

Ham and pineapple kebabs:

These are tasty and inexpensive, and are always a big hit. They look as pretty as they taste.

1 pound ham, cut into 1-inch cubes (I like to use cured, home-smoked ham but any store-bought ham that is ready to eat is suitable, thus the kebabs only need to be "glazed" on the grill.)
3 cups pineapple chunks

Marinade:

¼ cup pineapple juice
3 Tbsp. honey
1 Tbsp. soy sauce
pinch of ground cloves

Put ham into bowl. Mix marinade ingredients, pour over ham. Cover and marinate in fridge for several hours. Thread ham and pineapple chunks alternately onto skewers. Place on oiled or sprayed racks and let drip 10 minutes. Put marinade juice into a bowl and add 2 tablespoons melted butter. Use as a basting sauce. Grill until ham is glazed. Makes 6 to 8 skewers.

Vegetable kebabs:

For those who lean towards vegetable kebabs instead of meat or fish kebabs, here's a recipe that is sure to please. This is especially nice when the summer garden is producing more fresh vegetables than you can keep up with! The bottom line on this one is to choose whatever vegetables you have to your avail and in amounts to suit your needs.

zucchini, sliced into 1-inch pieces
sweet peppers, cut into bite-sized pieces
cherry tomatoes
whole button mushrooms
quartered onions
eggplant, cut into chunks
ears of corn, sliced into 1 or 2 inch sections
chunks of pumpkin or squash
potato chunks
olive oil
salt and pepper
crushed basil

Thread vegetables alternately onto skewers. Brush generously with olive oil, sprinkle with salt, pepper, and basil. Grill the kebabs, brushing with additional olive oil or melted butter until tender. Serve with *tzatziki* dip-

Apple kebabs

ping sauce (recipe mentioned earlier) or with a dipping sauce of your choice.

Prawn and melon ball kebabs:

These are very elegant and delicious. I find that tiger prawns work nice, as well as any larger type of shrimp. If you love scallops, they can be used with, or in place of, the prawns.

12 to 14 pan-ready prawns
2 cloves minced garlic
2 Tbsp. soy sauce
¼ tsp. black pepper
½ tsp. grated fresh ginger
2 Tbsp. lemon juice
pinch grated lemon zest
1 tsp. crushed chili flakes
1 cantaloupe or honeydew melon

Put prawns into a bowl, add remaining ingredients, except melon, of course, and mix well. Cover and marinate in fridge for several hours. Cut melon in half, remove seeds. Using a medium-sized melon ball scoop, scoop out the flesh into as many balls as you can make. (Remaining melon in the shell can be eaten with a spoon.) Thread prawns alternately on skewers with melon balls. Brush with lemon butter (melt ¼ cup butter in small bowl and squeeze in juice of half a lemon) and grill about 3 minutes per side, basting often, or until prawns are cooked. Makes 4 to 6 skewers. Serve with sweet chili sauce (I make my own) or other dipping sauce of choice.

Strawberry kebabs:

Here is one of the most elegant of all summertime desserts. Not only is it "to die for" good, but it's also so easy that it's almost sinful!

fresh strawberries (of course, for this recipe the berries must be large tame berries, not the little wild ones that are better suited for eating with a sprinkle of sugar and a dot of cream)
lemon juice
sugar

Wash strawberries and pat with paper towels. Leave stems on, if you wish. Thread strawberries onto skewers. Brush all sides with lemon juice and sprinkle generously with sugar. Let air dry for about 10 minutes in order for sugar to adhere. Place on grill rack and grill on all sides until sugar begins to caramelize and imprints of the grill are embedded into the berries. Serve with a dollop of yogurt or whipped cream for dipping.

Apple kebabs:

When the backyard apple trees are laden with fruit or when the fruit stand is selling apples cheaply by the bushel, make some apple kebabs! Wash apples but do not peel. Using a melon scoop, make as many apple balls as you can out of the flesh of each apple. Thread apple balls onto skewers. Squeeze lemon juice over top to prevent discoloration. Sprinkle generously with sugar and a pinch of ground cinnamon. Grill until imprints are left on the apple balls, brushing frequently with the honey-cinnamon butter glaze (recipe below). Serve with whipped cream sprinkled with additional ground cinnamon for dipping. Make lots — they go fast.

Honey-cinnamon butter glaze:

Melt ¼ cup butter in microwave. Blend in 3 tablespoons honey and 1 teaspoon of ground cinnamon. Use as brush for fruit kebabs or apple kebabs.

Fruit kebabs:

banana chunks
apple cubes or balls
cubed orange with rind left on
strawberries
pear chunks
melon balls (watermelon, honeydew)
grapes
pineapple chunks
lemon juice

Thread assorted fruits onto skewers, brush with lemon juice to prevent discoloration. Place on rack, brush with honey-cinnamon butter glaze (recipe above) and grill, basting with the glaze until imprints are made. Serve with chocolate dipping sauce.

Chocolate dipping sauce:

12 ounces sweet chocolate
¾ cup heavy (whipping) cream
1 tsp. orange extract

Melt chocolate in double boiler and cool to lukewarm. Blend in the whipping cream and extract. Makes about 1¼ cups. Δ

Ayoob on Firearms

Use the right ammunition!

By Massad Ayoob

The purpose of the gun is to fire ammunition. It follows that the ammunition should be the correct ammunition. This is simple. It is not hard to understand. But it's amazing how often people make mistakes in that regard — often people who should have known better. And, yes, that includes this writer: total disclosure and *mea culpa* right up front here.

Sometimes, the choice of a particular cartridge just isn't right for the purpose, even though the caliber of the ammunition may be correct for the caliber of the firearm. I studied a shooting case in Illinois many years ago when a crazed killer armed with a shotgun engaged police officers in a gun duel. One deputy was in a perfect position to drop him, got him in his sights, and pressed the trigger of his 12-gauge riot gun. Unfortunately, it wasn't loaded with the heavy buckshot pellets it was supposed to have in it on duty; someone had left it loaded with light birdshot from the last range training session. The gunfight took place outdoors in a snowstorm, and once they'd gotten through the gunman's winter clothing, the tiny pellets couldn't go deep enough to do anything more than irritate him. The gunman kept coming, firing all the way, until a cool-headed state trooper killed him in his tracks with a perfectly-placed 9mm pistol bullet.

The problem with full metal jacket

Keep practice ammo and target ammo for practice and for target shooting, and use the right stuff for more serious purposes. Consider that many Fish and Wildlife laws in the United States actually ban the use of full metal jacket rifle bullets for hunting big game. This is because bitter collective experience has taught us all that such ammunition sometimes just punches through the animals like an icepick, allowing them to run far enough that they'll never be found, and will die later in agony from their wound and rot on the forest floor. That's not sport. That's not true hunting. A hunting rifle bullet will generally have a soft-nose configuration, designed to expand as it passes through flesh. It anchors the animal sooner, and more humanely, and better guarantees venison in the freezer instead of carrion for Nature's scavengers.

The same is true of defensive handgun ammunition. The 9mm Luger cartridge, when it was only available in a pointy-nose full metal jacket configuration, earned a reputation as an impotent man-stopper in WWI, and that has continued through the long years since. Illinois State Police Ordnance unit members told me that during the years they issued the 9mm with full metal jacket (late '60s, into the early '70s) they never had an instant one-shot stop on a violent felon unless that bullet hit him in the brain or spine. This led ISP on an odyssey through soft-nose bullets, to hollow points at standard velocity, to the extra-fast 115-grain +P+ hollow point (1300 feet per second), and finally the .40 caliber jacketed hollow points that the department issues today. Since full metal jacket (FMJ) ammunition is seen by the Pentagon as mandated by the international rules of warfare, American soldiers and Marines have complained about its

Massad Ayoob

poor stopping power in 9mm since the adoption of the Beretta M9 service pistol more than a quarter of a century ago. Those complaints are still coming in from the field in Iraq and Afghanistan. Our military has responded by experimenting with a variation of Federal Cartridge's "expanding full metal jacket" (EFMJ) 9mm round, by issuing hollow points to at least some base security and Military Police personnel stateside, and allowing Marine Expeditionary Unit-Special Operations Command (MEU-SOC) and Army Delta Force to use .45 caliber pistols that throw bigger bullets than the 9mm Beretta can.

This is also why the American police establishment has gotten away from full metal jacket and other types of non-expanding handgun ammunition. In 1999, the nation was outraged by a shooting in the Bronx where NYPD officers fired 41 shots at a man, hitting him 19 times. The fact of the matter was, the man didn't fall until he was hit the 19th time, at which point the four involved officers all stopped shooting. All were vindicated at trial. The ammo they had been using was full metal jacket 9mm, issued by the department for reasons of political correctness. Today, NYPD issues Speer Gold Dot 124 grain +P jacketed hollow point, and the only (few) times anyone has taken anything close to that number of hits have been cases where the target was ensconced in a vehicle, and the auto bodies slowed down the bullets and reduced their power by the time they hit flesh.

Use enough gun

Famed novelist and big game hunter Robert Ruark wrote a classic book about his hunting experiences in Africa, and its title, *Use Enough Gun,* became a byword of advice for others who stalked dangerous animals. Ruark noted that a round designed to kill small animals as if they were hit by lightning bolts, such as the .220 Swift firing a tiny bullet weighing only 45 grains at a velocity of over 4100 feet per second, would virtually explode a woodchuck, but on a larger animal might blow itself up on the shoulder, creating an ugly flesh wound but not breaking through heavy shoulder bones and getting into vital organs for a clean, humane kill.

The wonderfully versatile .30-06 rifle cartridge depends on its user to know which particular load in the caliber is appropriate for the quarry. If you want to use your ought-six to hunt woodchucks in the off-season to make you more ready for deer season, you want to load it with something like a 110-grain bullet at 3300-plus feet per second. It will decisively kill the chuck. A generation of hunters learned in the mid-20th century, when cheap military surplus .30-06 full metal jacket ammo was available for as little as a penny a cartridge, that it would often shoot through a woodchuck leaving an "icepick wound," and the animal would crawl back into its burrow to die a long, painful, guilt-producing death. The 110-grain varmint bullet would possibly blow up on the shoulder of a moose or an elk. For those big-antlered, big-bodied critters, you'd use something more like a 220-grain bullet at 2400 feet per second. For your ordinary whitetail deer, a 150-grain at 2970 foot-seconds would do fine, and for a bigger mule deer, maybe a 180-grain at 2700 foot-seconds, with the 165-grain bullet at 2800 feet per second being a good all-around compromise.

Cartridges are aligned like this in a tube-magazine rifle. The recoil from firing a chambered round could jar the pointy nose of the right cartridge into the primer of the left cartridge shown here, creating a catastrophic chain detonation in the magazine. Don't use this type of ammo in that type of magazine.

Avoiding catastrophe

So far, we've been talking about getting the best effect downrange. Now, let's discuss avoiding the kind of mistake that leaves shooters blinded or otherwise maimed because they put the wrong ammunition in the gun and then, to their everlasting regret, pulled the trigger.

Ever notice that .30-30, .32 Special, and .35 Remington ammunition always comes with flat noses in factory loadings? That's because it's made for guns with tubular magazines, and a spire-point bullet could act like a firing pin when its sharp nose jarred the primer of the cartridge in front of it during recoil. The result could be a chain detonation in the magazine that could amputate the shooter's forward hand. Hornady came out with a line of cartridges called LEVERevolution with soft rubber nose caps, that gave the ballistic advantage of spire point bullets without the danger pointy rounds normally pose in tube-magazine rifles.

Back in the day, when I was on the board of directors for a local gun club, I got an urgent phone call requesting me to report to the range, where a shooter had been seriously injured when his rifle blew up. I showed up with camera and notebook. It turned out to be an easy thing to reconstruct, though it would prove to be a hard thing for the shooter to recover from.

He was a hunter more than a shooter, and had come to the range to sight in his two favorite hunting rifles for deer season. Both were top-quality bolt-actions. One was chambered for the .270 Winchester cartridge, the other, for the .308 Winchester round. Not thinking he could possibly mix up the rounds, he had both rifles and boxes of both calibers of ammunition on the same shooting bench.

The moment came when he slipped a .308 cartridge into the .270. The stage was now set for tragedy.

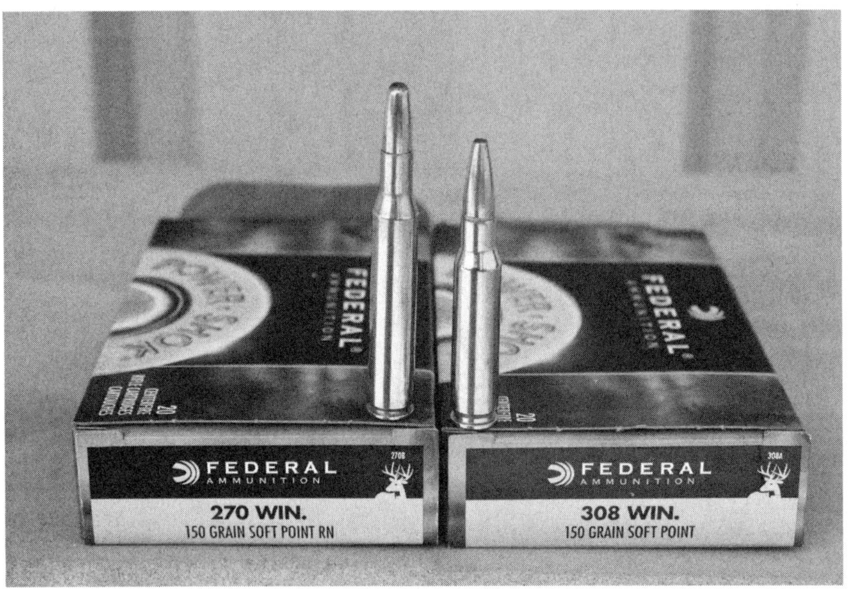

A rifle chambered for .270 Winchester, left, was able to chamber a round of the shorter .308 Winchester, right, with a thicker bullet. When fired, the rifle exploded with devastating and permanent consequences.

At first thought, you'd figure that a .30-caliber cartridge could not go into the exactly-sized firing chamber of a rifle with smaller bore diameter. However, while the .270 and the .308 both evolved from the .30-06 cartridge that came along earlier in the 20th century, each evolved in different ways. The .270 is the .30-06 "necked down" to take a smaller diameter bullet, but with similar overall length. This is why a .270 and a .30-06 will both require a "long action" rifle. The .308 (also known as 7.62 mm. NATO) came along in mid-20th century, using the same bullet diameter as the .30-06, but with a shorter overall length. This is why the .308 will usually (but not always!) be encountered in what is called a "short action" rifle.

In this instance, when the stubbier .308 cartridge was placed into the .270 rifle, it was sufficiently shorter that the action locked it into the firing chamber. However, the far end of that chamber and the bore (internal diameter) of the rifle were too small for the bullet. Standard pressure for cartridges in this category is in the range of 50,000 pounds per square inch. When the oversize bullet hit the too-narrow part of the chamber-into-bore continuum, the steel of the rifle was stronger than the copper-jacketed lead of the bullet and refused passage — and pressure spiked to an uncontainable level. Basically, the rifle violently exploded.

There was blood on the table and on the ground when we got there, and pieces of the rifle had been blasted over a wide radius. I doubt that we recovered them all. The shooter was severely lacerated, and because he was not wearing adequate eye protection, he suffered serious injuries to both eyes. He was not totally blinded, but he sustained injuries which, the doctors said at the time, would result in permanent visual impairment.

There is a lesson here.

That case involved a rifle. "Blow-ups" happen with shotguns, too. From the 19th century into the early 20th, it was in vogue to use Damascus steel in shotgun barrels. This was a legacy of lower pressure black powder. Modern smokeless powder that became state of the art in the late 19th century created greater pressures, and soon Damascus steel was rendered obsolete in the manufacture of shotguns. Unfortunately, guns are the ultimate "durable goods," and old shotguns were fired with new shotgun shells. People started noticing that they blew up when this happened. As the old guns got older and the steel deteriorated, and the new shells became more and more powerful, they blew up more often.

By the time this old man started learning about guns in the 1950s, it was already understood that *you didn't fire modern shotgun shells in old Damascus barrel shotguns!* Unfortunately, this wasn't understood by *everybody*, and the tragic gun blow-ups kept happening. Half a century later, this writer owns exactly one Damascus barrel shotgun. It's a fine old Lefever double-barrel I inherited from my dad. When I was young, Dad would fire light trap loads through it. The gun is a half a century older now, and so am I. I follow a simple rule with it: I don't fire it at all. It remains silent, a legacy of the past, like the stand-up 1940s radio I also inherited. It's a decoration, not a tool anymore. I would advise anyone reading this to treat their Damascus barrel shotguns the same way.

With shotguns, even modern ones, there can also be problems with loading the wrong size of shell. If a 20-gauge shotgun shell is inserted into the larger-diameter barrel of a 12-gauge shotgun, it can slip down that barrel and stop about halfway, where the rim of its cartridge head begins to hit the constriction that is built into a shotgun barrel. The shooter pulls the trigger and nothing happens because, after all, there is no longer a shell with a primer held in front of the firing pin...or maybe the shooter checks the chamber, sees nothing there, and thinks he forgot to "chamber a round." So, a live 12-gauge shell is now inserted.

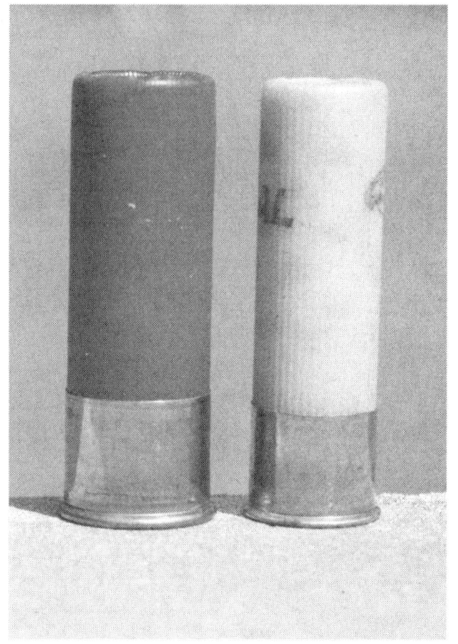

Left, a 12-gauge shell, color coded red. Right, a narrower 20-gauge shell, color coded yellow. If a 20-gauge shell gets into 12-gauge chamber, it may slide forward and get stuck halfway down the barrel, causing a catastrophic explosion when the shotgun is fired.

A quarter-inch difference isn't obvious, unless you can visually compare the shells, but the boxes clearly state that the 12-gauge shell at left is a 3-inch Magnum, while the one at right is 2¾ inches. A mixup like this nearly got an Idaho cop killed.

Later, it comes time to fire the shotgun. The trigger is pulled. A powerful 12-gauge shell discharges its payload in the chamber, sending it toward the muzzle and it hits the primer at the base of the trapped 20-gauge shell that is lying unseen partway down the barrel.

Two horrible things happen at once. First, the lead payload is now stopped inside that "pressure vessel," and pressure spikes explosively. Second, the 20-gauge shell is simultaneously detonated, not inside the heavy circumference of steel that is the firing chamber, but in the tapered portion of the gun barrel that may not be strong enough to contain the resulting pressure.

The result is a devastating explosion halfway down the barrel, right about where the shooter's forward hand is located in a normal firing hold. I've heard stories of all the fingers being blown off, and entire hands being amputated by the blast in a "field avulsion."

This is why it is *imperative* to keep 20-gauge shells separate from 12-gauge shells. It is why the ammunition industry color-codes 20-gauge shotgun shells yellow, and 12-gauge shells other colors (red, green, black, blue, whatever).

With shotguns, remember that shotshells come in different lengths. Standard length for 12- and 20-gauge shotguns is 2¾ inches. However, 3-inch Magnum 12- and 20-gauge shotguns have existed for a very long time, and we now even have 3½-inch Magnum 12-gauge shells, duplicating the payload of larger-diameter 10-gauge shotshells. With a break-open single- or double-barrel shotgun, you'll see and feel the incompatibility immediately if you try to load a shell that's too long. However, with a shotgun that feeds from a tubular magazine, such as the typical semiautomatic shotgun or pump gun, you can run into a treacherous problem: the ammunition will go into the magazine, but it won't cycle into the firing chamber. A longer shell simply isn't going to want to go from the magazine of your pump or auto into a chamber that isn't long enough.

In the early 1980s, I ran across a scary example of this in Idaho. The volunteer Auxiliary Police attached to the regular local police force offered to clean all the department's shotguns, an onerous chore which the full-time cops gratefully allowed them to do. The enthusiastic volunteers realized that the department's ammo was getting pretty old, so they chipped in to buy some new shotgun shells. Figuring the cops would want the most powerful ammo available, they bought new ammo of the most potent kind available at the gun shop: 3-inch Magnum 12-gauge buckshot.

Which would have been fine, except that the department shotguns had 2¾-inch chambers. Because shotguns in police vehicles are traditionally carried with empty chambers and full magazines, they reloaded the magazines with the long shells until no more would go in, and put them back in the patrol cars.

Between then and regular shooting qualification, the guns remained in that condition. Then the time came when one of the career cops was arresting a man who didn't want to be arrested. There was a fight and the bad guy got the cop's service handgun out of his holster and started firing it at the policeman. The officer ran around the car, dove into the front seat, and grabbed the shotgun out of the dashboard rack so he could shoot back. He tried to pump the first shell into the chamber and it stuck in place before the action could close.

The young officer involved was apparently a very impressive physical specimen, and the strength of adrenaline was upon him. That's the only way I can explain what happened: he managed to physically *force* the oversize 3-inch plastic shell into the 2.75-inch steel chamber, and fire one shot. That shot fire-formed the wrong-size shell into the chamber and hopelessly jammed the shotgun but it also struck and instantly killed the would-be cop-killer, saving the officer's life.

Handguns, too...

Handguns are not immune to "wrong ammo" problems, either. In the latter 19th century, Colt manufactured many revolvers in caliber .38 Long Colt and, not realizing that Smith & Wesson would soon develop the longer and more powerful .38 Special cartridge, bored the cylinder chambers straight through. They could not have known that a far more powerful cartridge of the same diameter, would come along in 1935, Smith & Wesson's .357 Magnum. The cylinder dimensions would allow these much more powerful cartridges to be fired, with the potential of turning a gun designed for low-pressure black powder cartridges into a small hand grenade that might be more dangerous to the shooter than to his opponent.

Today, the most popular police pistol cartridge is the .40 Smith & Wesson, and among state troopers, the .357 SIG cartridge is close on its heels in popularity. You can put a .40 barrel in a .357 SIG, or a .357 SIG barrel in a .40, and they'll work fine: useful versatility, there. Unfortunately, the .40 with a .357 SIG barrel may still be marked ".40" on the slide, and vice versa, and if someone puts .40 ammo in a .40 with a .357 SIG barrel, the cartridge won't chamber and the gun won't fire. If someone puts .357 SIG ammo in a gun marked ".357 (SIG)" but fitted with a .40 barrel, the shot will fire, but the undersize bullet will rattle down the barrel and go wide of its target, and the pistol will most likely jam.

General advice

If you're a parent, you've probably heard yourself pontificate to your children, "Use things the way they're meant to be used!" When you're dealing with guns, get in touch with your inner child and remind yourself of the same advice. We must use the ammo the gun was designed for, and the load appropriate to the purpose.

The bottom line? Use the right stuff. Plan ahead. When you *need* to fire that gun for something serious, you don't want it to blow up or jam, you want it to function as intended. Δ

BROWN RICE

The staff of life for half of mankind

By Habeeb Salloum

Rice is one of the most extensively cultivated plants and is the chief source of food for much of the human race. Records indicate that at the dawn of civilization it was domesticated in the Indus Valley of India. From there, its cultivation spread eastward to China and the neighbouring lands of southeast Asia.

In China and its surrounding countries, it quickly became the main staple. Even today, this region is still the heart of the rice-consuming world. In the Far East, it is the most important cereal and is practically synonymous with food. Over 90% of the globe's rice supply is produced and consumed by a third of mankind in that part of the world.

To the west, in the Greek and Roman eras, the cultivation of rice became common in the Middle East. However, in most of the Mediterranean countries it never became popular as a food until the 8th century, when the Arabs introduced it into the Iberian Peninsula. The Spanish and Portuguese name for rice, *arroz*, from the Arabic *ruzz,* attests to its origin.

In later centuries, the Spaniards carried it to Italy where it became a staple in the Italian kitchen. From Spain, the Conquistadors also took this grain with them to the New World where it became an important part of the Central and South American cuisine. In North America, rice was introduced by the British in the 17th century. However, in the subsequent decades, it never became a daily food of the people. Nevertheless, it was cultivated on a large scale for export to other parts of the world. Today, the United States produces some 10 billion pounds of rice, and is the world's leading exporter of this cereal.

Rice is the only grain that needs flooded fields to grow and thrive. It is an annual cereal; under ideal conditions it can yield three crops a year if the land is saturated with water.

Rice and chickpea soup

Seeds are planted in nurseries, then the seedlings are transplanted into fields covered with a few inches of water. The plant, growing to about three feet high, has a hollow stem, long leaves, and seeds at the top. It takes almost four months' growth to be ready for harvesting. During the growing season, water is kept constantly in the fields until a few weeks before reaping when the land is drained.

The seeds are enclosed in a husk. Inside, the kernel consists of an outer and inner bran, a germ, which incorporates most of the minerals, vitamins, and starch — by far the largest component.

In the mostly underdeveloped lands where rice is the main food, only the husk is removed. The brown rice that remains still incorporates the bran and germ, retaining all the nutrients. On the other hand, in more affluent countries, the rice is polished and, at times, coated with a mixture of glucose and talc. This results in the loss of almost all the minerals and vitamins, leaving the cereal with nearly 90% starch content.

Brown rice contains calcium, iron, phosphorus, protein, potassium, sodium, and the vitamins thiamine, riboflavin, and niacin. It is easily digested

Brown rice and vermicelli

and aids in the assimilation of other foods. Also, it is nutritious and very palatable. When milled by hand, as the farmers of Asia do, it is a better source of protein than wheat.

Almost free of cellulose, brown rice leaves very little residue in the intestines. For diabetics, it is a good source of carbohydrates because very little insulin is needed to assimilate its starches. For hundreds of years, its high thiamine content (a B vitamin) protected the peasants of Asia from the dreaded disease *beriberi*.

The only drawback of brown rice is that it takes longer to cook and it is easily infected with weevils. Hence, great care is needed in its storage.

Like the white polished types, brown rice comes in three kinds: long, medium, and short. During cooking, the water content of a recipe should be increased by between one quarter and one third, and the cooking time doubled. In the same fashion as the white varieties, when cooked it expands up to three times its normal size, giving it a large water content. Much tastier than the polished types, it can be used for all recipes which call for white rice.

Brown rice can be cooked by itself or with all types of other grains, meats, and vegetables, and can also be utilized for stuffing. In addition, it is excellent as a breakfast cereal and as an ingredient in salads and desserts.

No matter how it is cooked, brown rice is a very nourishing and delectable grain. A staple of half the earth's population and, at times, the only food of the poorer peasants, it contains almost all the elements needed for survival. Its healthy nourishment of a large segment of humankind in the past centuries has proven that it is truly an important staff of life.

Plain brown rice:

4 Tbsp. butter
1 cup brown rice, rinsed
½ tsp. salt
2½ cups water

Melt the butter in a frying pan then stir-fry the rice for 2 minutes. Stir in salt and water, then bring to boil. Cover, then cook over medium/low heat for 20 minutes, stirring a number of times to make sure the rice does not stick to the bottom of saucepan, then re-cover. Turn off heat, stir and re-cover, then allow the rice to further cook in its own steam for 30 minutes. Serve as a main dish or side dish.

Note: Substitute olive or vegetable oil for butter in any of these recipes as a healthier choice.

Serves 4.

Rice and chickpea soup:

4 Tbsp. olive oil
2 medium onions, chopped
4 cloves garlic, crushed
1 small hot pepper, finely chopped
1 can (5.5 oz) tomato paste, diluted in ½ cup water
1 can (19 oz) chickpeas, undrained
1 tsp. salt
1 tsp. thyme
1 tsp. pepper
1 tsp. cumin
8 cups water
¾ cup brown rice
4 Tbsp. finely chopped coriander

Heat oil in a saucepan, then sauté onions, garlic, and hot pepper over medium/low heat for 10 minutes. Add remaining ingredients, except coriander leaves, then bring to boil. Cover, then cook over medium heat for 50 minutes or until the rice is cooked. Stir in coriander leaves, then serve.

Serves about 10.

Rice salad:

2 medium tomatoes, diced into ¼-inch cubes
4 Tbsp. chopped chives or green onions
2 Tbsp. finely chopped fresh mint
2 Tbsp. lemon juice
1 Tbsp. olive oil
½ tsp. paprika
½ tsp. pepper
pinch of cayenne
one recipe plain brown rice
½ cup pimento-stuffed green olives

Thoroughly combine all ingredients, except the rice and green olives, in a salad bowl, then add rice while it is still warm and mix. Decorate with green olives and serve immediately.

Serves 4 to 6.

Rice, lentil, and spaghetti stew:

- 4 Tbsp. olive oil
- 1 large onion, finely chopped
- 4 cloves garlic, crushed
- 1 small hot pepper, finely chopped
- 1 cup lentils, rinsed
- ½ cup brown rice, rinsed
- 4 Tbsp. tomato paste
- 1 tsp. salt
- 1 tsp. basil
- ½ tsp. pepper
- ¼ tsp. allspice
- 8 cups water
- ½ cup spaghetti, broken into small pieces
- 2 Tbsp. finely chopped fresh coriander leaves

Heat oil in a saucepan then sauté onion over medium/low heat for 10 minutes. Add garlic and hot pepper, then stir-fry for 3 minutes. Stir in remaining ingredients, except the spaghetti and coriander leaves, then bring to a boil. Cover, then cook over medium heat for 20 minutes. Stir in spaghetti and cook for another 20 minutes or until the lentils, rice, and spaghetti are done, adding more water if necessary. Stir in coriander leaves (optional) and serve.

Serves from 8 to 10.

Rice and vermicelli:

- 5 Tbsp. butter
- 1 large onion, finely chopped
- ½ cup vermicelli, broken into small pieces
- 2 cloves garlic, crushed
- 1 cup brown rice, rinsed
- 3½ cups water
- ½ tsp. salt
- ¼ tsp. pepper
- ⅛ tsp. cayenne
- 2 Tbsp. toasted sesame seeds

Melt butter in a frying pan then sauté onion over medium heat for 10 minutes. Stir in vermicelli and garlic, then stir-fry for another minute. Add rice, then stir-fry for one minute. Stir in remaining ingredients, except the sesame seeds, then bring to boil. Cover, and cook over medium/low heat for 20 minutes, stirring a number of times to make sure the rice does not stick to the bottom of saucepan. Turn off heat, stir, and re-cover to allow rice to cook in its own steam for further 30 minutes.

Place on a serving platter, then sprinkle with the sesame seeds. Serve hot as the main course or as a side dish.

Serves 4 to 6.

Rice-stuffed peppers:

- 8 large green or red sweet peppers
- 6 Tbsp. olive oil
- 2 medium-sized onions, chopped
- 4 cloves garlic, crushed
- 1 cup brown rice, rinsed
- ½ cup slivered almonds, lightly toasted
- 2 medium tomatoes, chopped
- 1 tsp. salt
- 1 tsp. ginger
- 1 tsp. dried basil
- ½ tsp. pepper
- 2½ cups water
- 2 Tbsp. finely chopped fresh mint
- 4 eggs, beaten
- 4 cups tomato juice mixed with ⅛ tsp. cayenne
- 4 Tbsp. finely chopped fresh coriander leaves

Cut out about 1 inch in diameter piece from the stem end of peppers and reserve, then remove the seeds and set peppers aside.

Heat oil in a frying pan, then sauté onions over medium heat for 10 minutes. Add garlic, rice, and almonds, then stir-fry for 2 minutes. Stir in tomatoes, salt, ginger, basil, pepper, and water and bring to boil. Cover, then simmer over medium/low heat for 20 minutes, stirring a few times and adding more water if necessary. Remove from heat and allow to cool, then stir in mint and eggs to make a stuffing.

Fill peppers with stuffing, and cover each one with its reserved stem end. Place peppers side by side in a casserole, then combine the mixed tomato juice with coriander leaves and pour over top of tomatoes. Cover and bake in a 350° F preheated oven for one hour. Serve with a portion of the sauce accompanying each pepper.

Serves 8.

Rice and honey dessert:

- 1½ cups brown rice
- 5 cups water
- 4 Tbsp. butter
- 6 Tbsp. honey
- 2 Tbsp. powdered sugar
- ½ tsp. cinnamon

Place rice and water in a pot, then bring to boil. Cover, and cook over medium heat for 25 minutes. Drain, then set aside.

Melt butter in a frying pan; stir in rice and honey. Cook over medium heat for 10 minutes, stirring often to make sure rice does not stick to pan.

Place on a serving platter, sprinkle with powdered sugar and cinnamon, and serve warm.

Serves 6 to 8. Δ

Blueberry cash crop

By Ed Mashburn

There are low-bush, high-bush, and rabbit-eye blueberries which grow naturally in different parts of the country.

My almost two-year-old grandson loves blueberries. Put a bowl of those round blue jewels in front of him, and he's a happy little man. He's not alone. Many folks love blueberries, whether they are used in whole wheat muffins, fresh in cereal, or over ice cream. Not only are blueberries delicious, but they also give us a number of health and nutrition benefits. They can be successfully grown in nearly every part of the country.

Blueberries freeze better than just about any other fruit or berry, so a summer crop of blueberries will continue to feed a family for months after being harvested.

One of the best things about growing blueberries is that they have proven, no matter where we have lived, to be our most reliable cash crop. In the Ozarks of Arkansas and Missouri ,where we lived and raised our kids, and way down south on the Gulf Coast, where we now reside, those little round blueberries have brought us some welcome cash income.

When I first planted my most recent berry patch, I just wanted some berries for our home use. We sure got that, and a lot more. From just a few dozen blueberry plants, I have picked several hundred dollars' worth of cash-crop blueberries in the past five years. I have found that each year, I can sell every berry I don't want to eat.

I don't hesitate to say that blueberries should be on every small-farm grower's list of cash crops to be considered.

Blueberries are easy

In the United States, there are basically three types of blueberries for the small-farm grower to consider: low-bush, high-bush, and rabbit-eye blueberries. Growers have used these native berries as the origins of the multitude of hybridized commercial blueberries.

Most blueberries used for home and commercial production are of the high-bush type because of the larger size of the fruit and the easier growth habits of the high-bush.

Small farm growers should do a bit of study before they run to the catalog to order a few acres of blueberry plants. It really does make a huge difference where in the country a farm is located as to the selection of blueberries to be grown. Small-farm owners should work closely with local university extension agents when selecting specific type of blueberries for a location. For instance, when I lived in the Ozarks, "Blueray" and a few other varieties did well. However, down here in the deep South where I now live, other varieties such as "Climax" do much better. It really is very important to do some study before planting. Time spent in determining the best variety of blueberry for a specific location can save a whole lot of time later.

It's not too hard in most places in the United States to make blueberries happy. They like an acid soil, and they don't like their roots to be wet. If these minimal requirements are met, blueberries will grow and produce. Most blueberries are quite cold resistant, and they don't mind hot, humid weather such as we get on the Gulf Coast. There are varieties of blueberry which are very well suited to higher, mountainous climates.

In very dry places, some sort of irrigation will need to be anticipated. Drip systems seem to work very well with blueberries, and a low-rate drip system makes the best use of available water with minimal run-off or evaporation.

As mentioned earlier, blueberry plants are acid lovers, and they appreciate fairly heavy fertilizing with low pH fertilizers. Growers need to be careful not to over-apply nitrogen to blueberries; this can be quite harmful to the plants. Again, very good advice can be obtained from local extension agents. The state of Missouri, for instance, does a good job of getting good, useful information to blueberry growers.

Here's the bottom line: make the plants happy and they will produce heavy crops for a long time with really minimal care and work on the part of the grower.

The first job for any potential berry grower is to determine how much time and space that can be devoted to a berry patch. If space and personal time is abundant, a grower may choose to plant several acres of blueberry bushes which will develop into a full-time job — at least during growing and picking seasons. If time and space are limited (as in my present situation) a couple of dozen bushes planted in odd corners of the yard may be the extent of the blueberry growing. Either way, blueberries will reward the grower in most cases.

No matter where we have lived, blueberries have provided our most reliable cash crop.

Blueberries as a cash crop

I will start my discussion of sales and money by stating from the outset that blueberries can, in certain cases, generate a good bit of money. The United States Department of Agriculture says that a mature planting of blueberries can return as much as $3,000 per acre with correct marketing, management, and growing.

Of course, the best choice for the small-farm grower with a good crop of blueberries is direct sales. Selling straight to the consumer by the grower generates the most cash. This is best accomplished by having a passer-by see the gorgeous, ripe, and shining berries in baskets and then sample a few. Cash changes hands, and everyone goes home very happy. Quite often, once local residents discover a berry grower's prime, fresh product, word of mouth and repeat sales to individuals will consume the entire year's production.

I have seen very large blueberry operations in the Midwest and deep South which relied almost entirely on "You-pick" procedures. This selling technique really requires minimal grower time in the field actually picking. It works like this: When the berries ripen, the field is opened up to visitors who come in and pick as many berries as they want. Gallon pails are provided by the growers, and folks come and pick until they get tired. When the picker is finished, he or she returns to the starting point and pays for the berries. This type of operation can be run on the "honor system" where the picker not only picks but measures and leaves payment in a secure drop-box or jar for the berries while the grower is elsewhere.

Many small farm growers use local farmer's markets and flea markets to sell their berries, with very satisfactory results. I love to sell this way, and I'd sell all of my berries this way if possible. Unfortunately, I must work away from home, so my direct sales opportunities are limited to weekends.

Sometimes, dealing with a local fruit stand or produce market can be a very happy experience. I have sold most of my berries to local markets over the past five years, and by establishing myself as a reliable and conscientious grower who delivers product when promised, I know I have markets where I can sell every berry I grow.

For instance, Dennis Young, owner of Burris Fruit Market in Loxley, Alabama, who buys most of my excess blueberry production, gives potential home-farm growers some very good advice. "We need good, fresh, carefully picked and packaged berries," he says." We don't want berries in gallon buckets — we buy by pints only." He recommends that growers check with the eventual seller to see what packaging size and form will be best. To help the grower out, most fruit markets will provide the

By establishing myself as a reliable and conscientious grower who delivers product when promised, I know I have markets where I can sell every berry I grow.

grower with the desired containers for the product for no charge.

Young also advises home-growers to try to select varieties of berry which ripen and mature sooner than others. Berries which come ripe even a few days sooner than the main flood of produce will bring a higher price from fruit markets, so growers should try to grow early-ripening varieties. Again, check with local extension agents to determine which varieties will ripen sooner in a specific location.

When asked what the biggest benefit a fruit market offers small-farm berry grower's, Young says it's because markets buy in quantities. "I have a customer base which is very large. I provide a grower with a place to sell in bulk."

There's no reason not to go blue

I believe blueberries are just about the perfect fruit for small-farm growers who want to not only improve their personal and family nutrition, but also generate a little extra cash at the same time. Although the average small-farm owner probably won't get rich selling blueberries, that little extra cash in summertime always seems to come at a good time at our house.

If properly planned, planted, and maintained, a blueberry patch will provide great benefits to the small-farm owner for many years to come. Spend a little time speaking with local university extension agents, walking over the property looking for good planting areas, and then plant good, suitable bushes. In just a few years, the berries — and the cash — will start rolling in. Δ

Backwoods Home magazine
practical ideas for self-reliant living
Sept/Oct 2011
Issue #131
$5.95 US
$7.50 CAN

Stash silver
FOR HARD TIMES

Extend your growing season
Prevent the winter blahs
Raising kids simply
A sawmill business
Buckboard bacon

www.backwoodshome.com

My view

Reinterpreting the Constitution

Since the 1930s, it's become fashionable, particularly among liberals, to advocate "reinterpreting the *Constitution* when that document gets in the way of their "progress." There has arisen a whole school of thought that advocates reinterpretation, when *they* think it's necessary, and it recently became a cover story in the July 4, 2011 issue of *Time* magazine in an article by Richard Stengel.

Stengel's essay pretty much encapsulates many of the current arguments that the *Constitution* should be "reinterpreted" by new generations, not *amended*, as in accordance with *Article V*.

In an attempt to win the reader over to his side, Stengel begins by asking what Washington and the other Founders would think of all of our newfangled technology and the new problems that face our nation that he seems to think overwhelm or are outside of the purview of that document. It's a rhetorical question. He doesn't provide an answer. He infers that, in light of the changes that have taken place in our society since 1787, when the Constitution was adopted, each generation should reinterpret its words to deal with its unique set of circumstances.

Article V

The Congress, whenever two thirds of both Houses shall deem it necessary, shall propose Amendments to this Constitution, or, on the Application of the Legislatures of two thirds of the several States, shall call a Convention for proposing Amendments, which, in either Case, shall be valid to all Intents and Purposes, as Part of this Constitution, when ratified by the Legislatures of three fourths of the several States, or by Conventions in three fourths thereof, as the one or the other Mode of Ratification may be proposed by the Congress; Provided that no Amendment which may be made prior to the Year One thousand eight hundred and eight shall in any Manner affect the first and fourth Clauses in the Ninth Section of the first Article; and that no State, without its Consent, shall be deprived of its equal Suffrage in the Senate.

Well, Stengel may not know what Washington, Jefferson, Franklin, Mason, and the others would say if new ideas and new problems conflict with that document, but *I* can tell you what they'd say: "If you want to change the 'law of the land,' we've included the steps in *Article V*, where it says you have to submit your changes to the states. Through this process, the people can debate them and decide if that's how they want to live."

Of course, the real reason those who want to go the easy route of reinterpretation is so that a few experts — *their experts* — can amend the rules by which this country is run, without having to go through the lengthy and arduous process of letting the people and the states determine if we really want their changes. Keep in mind, the *Constitution* is the blueprint by which this country is supposed to be governed. Change should not be so easy that it can be done rashly or frivolously.

I will say I don't think most liberals have nefarious intentions when wanting to sidestep the amendment process. I think they truly believe their hearts and intentions are so pure that they should be allowed an easier route than the amendment process, a route they would, I assume, deny to those whose motives are not as pure as their own.

Ironically, Stengel disparagingly refers to those who oppose reinterpretation as having an "almost fanatical focus on the founding document...", but he seems to omit the fanatical focus liberals have on it when troglodytes from the far-right try to reinterpret parts to suit their own tastes, such as reinterpretations of our freedom of the press, freedom of speech, or how citizenship should be interpreted in the *14th Amendment*.

Did the Founders ever consider including reinterpretation as a valid way to change the *Constitution*? Would they have included it had they thought of it? I don't know. But try to imagine, for a few moments, how they would have worded it had they wanted to include change by reinterpretation, and you'll see the problem. Who is to do the reinterpreting? Do the people and the states get to vote on it or is it to be imposed on us by the courts or other "experts?"

Even when the *Constitution* was originally written, in secret and outside of the inputs of others, the final document was still submitted to the states for approval — a vote by the states— before it was adopted. But I have *never* heard those who argue for reinterpretation suggest that the people or the states will have any say in how it's reinterpreted.

I think you can see it's no accident that the Framers didn't include something so absurd in the document.

I'll be the first to admit I don't think the *Constitution* is perfect and there are parts of it I'd like to see changed. But I've never said we should ignore those parts nor have I ever suggested we reinterpret or change the meaning of the words we find there to accommodate me.

If *anyone* wants to change that document, he or she should read it first, then follow the dictates of *Article V*. And changes they propose should be publicly debated and have to be approved by the people who are going to have to live under the changes, through their state legislatures, not have them forced down our throats by a minority of politicians, judges, zealots, or special interests. ***— John Silveira***

A small-scale sawmill business for the homestead

By AJ Reissig

Running a small-scale sawmill can be a great homestead business. Besides the income generated, the mill also has the benefit of providing low cost, rough cut lumber — an asset to any homestead. In an area such as ours where there are few small-scale mills, custom sawyers are often in great demand. Because of this, it is very easy to recoup start-up costs quickly (if the business is set up correctly). And for the rural homesteader or farmer, much of the necessary equipment that complements the sawmill — chainsaw, cant hook, tractor — may be already owned. This is the story of how my homestead sawmill business evolved.

In 1996, my brother and I purchased 37 acres of land that was for sale next to my parents' farm in southwest Ohio. The acreage was part of an old farm, and the piece that we purchased had everything that we would want in rural property. Big Indian Creek flowed past the south side of the land, within view of the house. The land had about 12 acres of good bottomland fields; the rest was wooded land that was a mix of oak, maple, sycamore, and cedars. We even had an old tobacco barn that was big enough to hold a basketball court. It seemed the perfect place to establish a small farm. However, like many dreams, it was too good to last.

In late June of 1997, a tornado hit southwest Ohio, cutting right through the middle of our land. While our home went unscathed, we lost the old tobacco barn, and there were an untold number of trees down on our acreage. While many of the trees would be cut up into firewood, my brother and I realized that a lot of the trees could be milled into lumber. (We are talking about some really big trees.) Unfortunately, the few local mills in the area seemed only to want to screw us over. So, after a little research, we decided to take a gamble and buy our own band saw mill.

The saw is mounted in a large metal chassis. The saw is mobile and the log is stationary.

The saw chassis is pushed down the rail to make a cut. Turning the log, like everything else on this mill, is done by hand.

Like a majority of small scale mill operators, we use a band saw mill. In principle, these mills work the same way as the band saw that could be found in a woodshop. However, the saw is mounted in a large metal chassis. This chassis rides down a pair of horizontal rails that straddle the log. So, unlike a woodshop bandsaw, the log is stationary and the saw is mobile. There are a wide variety of mills on the market, ranging in price from a few hundred dollars to more than thirty thousand dollars. Most of the mills I looked at use a Briggs and Stratton (or a similar) engine to power the saw. We decided to go with a manually controlled mill at the low end of the price range, which has worked out well for us.

Since we lost our barn in the tornado, we decided to take over part of the garage for the sawmill operation. Our mill is set up to cut logs up to 14 feet in length, and can handle a log diameter of 28 inches. The garage location has prevented us from setting up the mill to handle longer logs, but that doesn't seem to be a problem. In fact, I can't think of one time when we have had a need to cut a log longer than the 14 feet.

Luckily, I already owned much of the equipment that I would need to set up the milling operation. Since our family has always heated with wood, we were already equipped with chainsaws (as well as the necessary gear to keep them sharp and running), cant hook (a hand tool used for rolling logs), and logging chains. Between myself and my parents, we have two tractors for moving logs (Dad has a Ford 8N, while I own a Ford 2000). I did purchase a set of skidding tongs, which have been useful on the tractor for lifting logs. Later on, I bought a metal detector to check logs for imbedded metal.

Running the sawmill is extremely simple, but does require a fair amount of manual labor. Having a helper (or two) to work with you will ease things considerably. I start by dragging a log into the empty garage bay with the tractor. Then, using a pair of ramps that my father built for the mill, the log is rolled onto the mill's railings. After positioning the log and clamping it down, the blade height of the saw is set, and the milling can begin.

Since my mill is completely manual (no hydraulically powered anything), I have to push the saw chassis down the rail to make a cut. After each cut, the saw blade is raised, and then the chassis can be backed up to the starting point. Now, if this was the first cut on a log, the log will need to be turned over to square the opposite side. (Turning the log, like everything else on this mill, is done by hand.) Once the log is turned, the blade height can be reset, and milling can continue. Now there are mills on the market that are completely automatic, but for my business, I can't justify the expense for that type of mill.

At first, neither my brother nor I had any intention of starting a business. Our goal was simply to put to use the trees lost to the tornado. (After all, you can only use so much firewood.) However, word soon spread, as it often does in small, close-knit communities such as ours. Soon, we not only had people wanting to buy rough cut boards from us, but we also had individuals who were bringing logs to us for milling. And so, our little project evolved into a business.

We mainly mill logs that a customer brings to us. Sometimes, this includes milling old barn beams. The old beams are generally cut into planks for flooring or other projects. The thing to watch out for with the old barn beams is nails. The destruction of several bandsaw blades by old nails is what prompted me to invest in a metal detector. I now thoroughly check out everything we mill (especially old beams) with the metal detector (and I haven't lost a blade since).

We also do some logging on our own land. Most of the logs that come from our land get milled into lumber that we use for ourselves, but we do sell some of the excess. Over the years, we have also picked up a few regular customers that buy the boards that come from our land. I have one remodeler who regularly comes to me for cedar (which he uses to line or trim out closets). Another remodeler has become a regular customer because I will supply large oak timbers (6x6 and 8x8) for timbered porches and entries for far less than any home center. There is also a woodworker who regularly buys sycamore, buckeye, and Eastern Red Cedar.

Due to a lack of space, we do not dry boards for customers. We do have a small amount of space that we can use over at my parents' place (a little corner of their barn), but for the most part that is reserved for our personal use lumber. While we could make more money by selling boards that are dried, we just do not have the space for that right now. We are talking about building a greenhouse that would double as a solar kiln during the summer months, but right now the project is still just talk.

Our mill is set up to cut logs up to 14 feet in length and can handle a log diameter of 28 inches.

How to charge customers was an issue that we had trouble with for a while. I did a lot of internet surfing to find out how other small mills charged. Some charged a rate per board foot, some per linear foot. Others even charged a board foot rate plus an hourly rate. I finally settled on a price based on an hourly rate. To me, it seemed like the easiest thing to keep track of. Also, it did not matter if we were milling customer logs or logs we harvest ourselves (for the logs that we harvest, we add in the extra time taken to cut the logs and haul them to the mill). This also allowed customers to save themselves money if they wished to help me turn logs or stack boards. (It also compensated me if a customer decided to just hang out and get in my way.)

The mill has not only provided me with extra income, but has also allowed me to remodel the house to an extent that I could never have afforded otherwise. All of the bedroom closets of my house are lined with Eastern Red Cedar, and I have replaced all of the baseboards and door/window trim with oak that I have milled. I have also built a bed for myself, several bookcases, and a butcher block countertop in the kitchen. We have also built one mid-sized shed, which has seen multiple roles over the years (tool shed, goat barn, and firewood storage, to name a few).

Since I am an avid recycler, the waste from the mill is put to good use. I generally cut up the initial slabs (the ones made when we "square" the logs) to be used as firewood, although I save a few of the nicer looking ones for woodworking projects. Some of our sawdust is mixed into the compost pile to increase its carbon content. I also use some of the sawdust for bedding in my goat barn. The rest of the sawdust is sent over to my parents' home, where my mother uses it as mulch for her flower beds.

Running a sawmill business can be a wonderful way to earn money on the homestead. While running the mill does entail a large amount of labor, the experience of watching a log transform into a useful product creates a great sense of fulfillment. So, if you are looking for an avenue to add some income to your homestead, definitely consider running a mill. Δ

Stashing junk silver for bad times

This is a pile containing $100 face value of pre-1965 "junk silver" coins, but it could represent 400 gallons of gasoline or 400 loaves of bread.

By John Silveira

When I was a teenager, a gallon of gasoline was about 25 cents and so was a loaf of bread. Now, each costs around $4. However, there are gas stations today (one is in Medford, Oregon) that will sell you a gallon or more of gas for a mere 25 cents — but *only* if that quarter is a pre-1965 "junk silver" quarter. They call those pre-1965 silver dimes, quarters, and halves "junk silver" because, having been circulated, they are worn and have no real numismatic (coin collecting) value. But they are far from "junk" as each coin is 90% silver, and silver is becoming more and more valuable.

If money becomes worthless, and it's becoming worth less and less every day, possessing junk silver currency in a collapsed economy may bump you to the head of the line for medical services, food, or for a host of other goods and services for your family. There may come a day when $100 face value in junk silver coins are worth 400 or more gallons of gas. In a car that gets 25 m.p.g., that can be at least 10,000 miles of travel. On the other hand, it can be more than 400 loaves of bread for your family to eat or maybe 500 to 600 cans of soups and veggies.

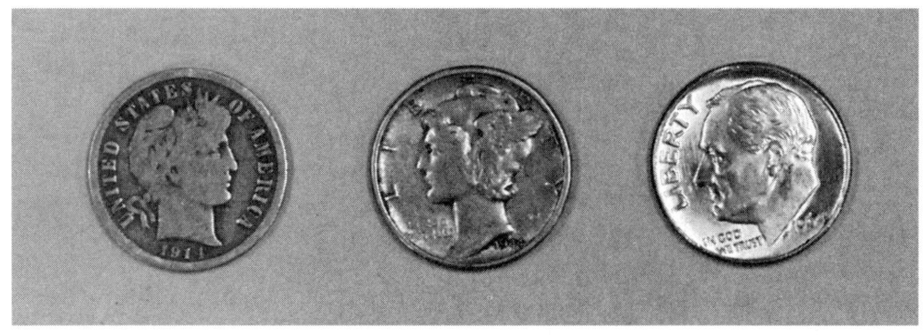

From left to right: the Barber dime, the so-called Mercury dime, and the Roosevelt dime. The figure on the Mercury dime is not the Roman god of that name. It is actually "Lady Liberty" and the wings are part of what's called a Phrygian cap and they represent freedom of thought.

Though large corporations, like the electric company, may not be able to take your silver (bureaucracies will have rules and their employees have little latitude to make decisions), the guy who owns the local gas station, the bakery, the grocery store, or even your doctor *can* and, if he or she is any kind of businessman, will value silver over the "legal tender" the Federal Reserve is passing off nowadays.

As I write this, pure silver is worth about $36 a troy ounce (see sidebar on "Weights.") and $1 face value of junk silver has about .715 ounces of silver, the same purchasing power as approximately $25 in Federal Reserve Notes. (That's the funny green stuff that's in your wallet now.)

A hedge against inflation

Junk silver is a good hedge against inflation, which we are now experiencing in almost every area, especially at the supermarket.

One of the few areas in economy where deflation, rather than inflation, is occurring is in the housing market, which is why the U.S. Government is able to claim that the U.S. inflation rate is low. Of course, they neglect to say that for the first time in history, they have included depressed housing costs in the formulae they use to calculate inflation.

Inflation is now hitting us harder than it has in three decades and the price of silver, gold, and practically everything else has taken off. When the latest rise in the price of silver started a few months ago, I discovered I only had about $115 in face value in junk silver stashed away. Today I've got more than double that and I'll buy more as the price drops back.

How much junk silver?

How much junk silver should someone own for bad times? The answer, of course, depends on your circumstances. I'd like at least $300 to $400 worth. However, if you're just beginning, you should only consider buying junk silver *after* you've laid in food, medical supplies, and whatever tools — including guns and ammunition — you feel you may need for the circumstances you and your family are in.

If you haven't bought junk silver before, you're going to encounter several issues.

The first is that you're going to pay a premium of some sort to get it. But given its potential value in bad times, it'll be worth it. Besides, other factors I'll mention later will likely make your silver appreciate more and compensate you for the cost of the premium.

The second problem is the same problem all precious metals have: They are not "productive investments," that is, they don't earn interest, nor do they pay dividends. They are inflation hedges and "real" cash as the dollar declines. If it weren't for those two factors, I wouldn't buy it.

Which junk silver coins?

The junk silver dimes, quarters, and half dollars are an alloy made of 90% silver and 10% copper, as are the new "proof" coins.

When originally made, $1 face value — that is, ten dimes, four quarters, two halves, five dimes and two quarters, or any other combination that adds up to $1 — contained .7234 troy ounces of silver. Today, because of wear and tear, the convention is that $1 face value contains about .715 ounces. In other words, it's assumed that the average silver coin has lost about 1.16% of its mass and, therefore, 1.16% of its silver.

Still, coins of the same denomination do not all weigh the same. Older dimes weigh less than newer dimes, and so on.

To ascertain the weight differences, I decided to buy a scale and weigh my own junk silver coins. I bought an RCBS 505 reloading scale which has

Weights

There is a variety of weight measures used in the United States. One involves avoirdupois ounces and pounds which we use to measure everything from our body weight to potato chips. There are 437.5 "grains" of weight in an avoirdupois ounce and as there are 16 ounces in an avoirdupois pound, so that pound is 7,000 grains.

Another weight system, troy ounces and pounds, is used for precious metals such as gold and silver. A troy ounce is 480 grains and there are 12 troy ounces, or 5,560 grains, in a troy pound.

In comparison, a troy ounce is about 9.7% heavier than an avoirdupois ounce.

From left to right are the Barber, the "Standing Liberty," and two Washington quarters. The second Washington quarter is a silver proof of the 2005 Kansas quarter which the U.S. Mint makes for collectors.

a capacity of 511 grains. (One troy ounce is 480 grains.) "But," I asked myself, "how will I know for sure that my scale is accurate even after zeroing it?" So, after spending $112 for the scale and shipping, I spent more than $100 for a set of Class 6 calibration weights and discovered my scale is accurate to about one part in 4800, all the way out to one troy ounce, accurate enough for what I'm doing.

I expected to find quite a bit of variation in coin weights, with the older coins — those which have been circulated longer and have seen the most wear — to weigh less than the newer coins. What I wasn't expecting was the amount of variation in weight within the same year of issue, even when the coins showed no wear. Quite a few people didn't believe this could be true. They felt, as I had before I used my scale, that coins fresh from the Mint should all weigh "the same." They don't. Fresh from the Mint, silver quarters should weigh about 96.45 grains. But the 40 uncirculated 2005 Kansas State quarters I have weigh from as little as 95.2 to as much as 99.1 grains. That's as much as 1.3% less to as much as 3% more. That's quite a range of error. I can only attribute it to the fact that the blanks from which the coins are pressed are not uniformly thick. Later, I would discover that the new Silver Eagle bullion coins, uncirculated, average about .5% more than spec and virtually all 40 that I own are overweight.

And this is not a new phenomenon. I've got some old dimes, quarters, and halves which are actually heavier than spec, even though they show more than 20 years of wear.

I'd avoid the older coins like the Barber dimes, quarters, and halves (so named because they were designed by Charles Barber, head engraver for the Mint, and circulated from 1892 to 1916). The Barber coins I have show anywhere from more than 8% wear to almost 14% wear. That's 8 to 14% less silver, but you won't be paying less for them. You may even be paying an added premium because they're "old."

The same goes for the "Standing Liberty" quarters. They show excessive amounts of wear.

Part of the wear on the old coins is because of their age, but part is due to their intricate designs. The so-called "Standing Liberty" quarters are among the prettiest coins the Mint ever produced, but the raised edges and intricate detail wore off fast. The figures blurred and detail wore away. Frequently, the dates were obliterated. With all that wear, silver disappeared.

> If you're wondering how the Silver Eagle dollars equate to the junk silver on the basis of silver content, figure one Silver Eagle is worth about $1.40 face value in junk silver coins, more if the junk silver is really worn.

Personally, I think the old "Walking Liberty" half dollars, designed by Adolph Weinman, are the most beautiful design for any of the silver coins the Mint has ever made. But, with all that detail, wear was inevitable. So I wouldn't get too many of them unless the premium is low or you like them just because they look cool.

I should add that the Walking Liberty design has been returned on the Silver Eagle bullion coins the Mint has made since 1986. However, the beautiful eagle which appeared on the reverse side of the Walking Liberty half was not carried over to the Silver Eagle. The Silver Eagle has a much duller eagle on the reverse side.

Later silver coins, those from the '50s and '60s — these include Roosevelt dimes, Washington quarters, and the Franklin and '64 Kennedy halves — don't show that much wear because soon after the Mint replaced silver coins with the modern (and almost worthless) "clad" coins in 1965, shoppers rapidly gleaned the silver coins from circulation. Thus, many of those coins, though over a half-century old, often look almost like new and even the worn ones have lost less than 1% of their weight. Another reason these coins show less wear is because, unlike earlier coins, they have less intricate detail, so there's that much less to be abraded off.

> If you're buying coins for their silver content, stay away from numismatic coins — those coins with collector value. You'll be paying too much of a premium if you do buy them.

As a result of my "studies," I try to stick to Roosevelt dimes, Washington quarters (especially those from the mid-50s to 1964), almost any of the

In the top row, from left to right, are the Barber, "Standing Liberty," and Ben Franklin half dollars. From the left, in the bottom row are a 90% Kennedy half dollar and a 40% Kennedy half.

Franklin halves, and all the 1964 Kennedy halves.

Where to buy

I won't tell you where to buy your silver because prices, shipping costs, and other costs are constantly in flux.

I've found local stores, both coin stores and some antique stores, with fair prices, but some online stores and some local stores are grossly overpriced. One antique store in Coos Bay, Oregon, is selling junk silver for just over spot (the price of a commodity such as an ounce of gold or silver at that very moment), but another, just a few miles away in North Bend, was asking $4.50 for Mercury dimes — ridiculously overpriced — and buying them from the public for $1.70. Not a bad racket if you can pull it off.

I suggest googling "junk silver" online and visiting some of the sites to see who's offering the best deals. Lately, I've been buying mine from www.providentmetals.com, but I keep checking prices at other sites.

To figure out what kind of premium you're paying on junk silver, divide the price of $1 face value of the 90% silver coins by .715 and you'll see what you're paying for the silver content. Today, not including any shipping, I can buy $1 face value in Franklin halves from one online site for $26.32. Dividing that by .715, I see I'm getting the silver content for $36.81/oz. At the moment, that's 80 cents over the spot price of silver. Not a bad deal, especially when I buy enough so that the shipping is free.

I don't have much to do with the so-called war nickels, coins made with 40% silver which include the Kennedy halves made from 1965 to 1971 and the Eisenhower "S" dollars made from 1971 to 1976. If I find a really good deal on them, I may buy some. For the moment, I'm keeping the ones I've collected from my change the last 40 years, but I'm not buying any.

Silver bullion coins

Although everyone's survival larder should contain junk silver coins, you may decide to consider silver bullion, too. If so, consider the Silver Eagle "dollar" coins made by the U.S. Mint. They contain one ounce of .999 fine silver. Though they are designated as dollar coins (because, by law, all coins issued by the government must have denominations on them), they are worth whatever an ounce of silver is currently going for which, today, is about $36. And, yes, I have some.

But there are two problems with Silver Eagles. First is that, like the new silver proof coins, they are not as recognizable to the general public as junk silver is and this *may* make them more difficult to spend in hard times.

The second problem is a more difficult one to deal with: Silver Eagles are now being counterfeited, in China among other places, and as they become more valuable, expect the quality of the counterfeits to improve.

Though they say "one dollar" on them, the two Silver Eagles are actually silver bullion coins made by the Mint for collectors.

Many people are also investing in silver bullion rounds (they look like coins) and bars made by private mints. I'm not. The trouble with them is that they are going to be more difficult to spend because they are unlikely to be recognized by the general public, and to sell them they generally need some kind of authentication. In the meantime, like the Silver Eagles, they are and will continue to be counterfeited.

If you're going to put money in bullion, make it separate from the junk silver coins that you can be sure are going to be spendable, if and when the world goes to pot.

Americans are always going to recognize dimes, quarters, and halves, and junk silver coins, especially those that have seen years of circulation, and they are going to be difficult to fake.

When to buy

The price of silver is high, just now, and though I wish I had laid in my stash when it was a lot cheaper, I'm going to buy about $10 face value each month for the next year. However, I believe there's a "correction" coming and the price will come down. And if the spot price goes below $33 an ounce, I'm going to buy a little more than $10 face value each month. How much more depends on how low the price goes.

So, how low do I think it might go? I think the spot price of silver will dip back into the $20 to $30-per-ounce range and there's a remote chance it'll visit the teens, one more time. But don't wait for that. It may not happen.

What about gold?

Gold is good. But the biggest problem with holding gold is that it's difficult to spend. Unless you're buying a large-ticket item or making a massive purchase of food, guns, ammo, etc., how do you get change? If a guy wants junk silver quarters for a few gallons of gas, I can easily fill my tank with some silver change. I can't as readily do that with gold.

Also, if you're like me and you've only got a little money to spend, start with junk silver. Right now, for $1500 I can get about $55 face value in silver or a 1-ounce piece of gold bullion. Tell me which one you think is more useful.

Silver will outpace inflation

With the recent bailouts, during which the Federal Reserve Bank poured about $11 trillion into our economy to bail out its Wall Street cronies, the value of the American dollar is going to decline faster than it ever has. There is no way that that amount of money, created out of thin air, can be introduced into our economy without creating inflation, and inflation is going to guarantee that, over the long run, your stash of junk silver will become worth more in Federal Reserve Notes. Inflation is not going to go away.

Theoretically, the rise in the price of gold or silver will, over the long run, stay in step with inflation. (In the short run, it doesn't.) But there are other forces which, over the long run, *may* make your stash of junk silver go up even faster than inflation and even faster than gold. This is what will make the premium you have to pay for your silver today less painful tomorrow.

One of the forces that will make silver's price rise is that silver is in demand because it has a multitude of industrial and consumer uses. Silver conducts heat and electricity better than any other metal. Because of this, it's used in the production of computers, cell phones, monitors, chips, automobiles, etc., and more uses are being found every day. Sometimes a lot is used, but usually it's very little. But even in minute amounts, millions of computers, monitors, cell phones, etc., add up to a lot of silver.

Silver is also valuable for use in the purification of water and air, and it's got antibacterial properties. It has uses for which no decent substitutes have yet been found. Modern civilization just wouldn't be the same without this precious metal. And because of the way it's used in such small amounts in so many industrial products, it's often not economical to recycle, so it's lost.

Foreign demand

With roughly a third of the world's population between them, both China and India are industrializing and both are trying to provide more consumer products to their citizens. One commentator has pointed out that about 10 years ago, the per capita consumption of silver in China was a mere $1/70^{th}$ of that in the West. But now, they're catching up.

In the meantime, the world's supply of new silver has not kept pace with silver consumption. Since 1990, more silver has been consumed every year than has been produced. To make up for the shortfall, silver reserves have been depleted and the price of silver has increased — well ahead of inflation.

In the future, the world's two most populous countries are going to be eating up gobs of the metals as both their industrial bases and consumer demands increase.

And if that's not enough, China is *finally* allowing its people to own silver bullion. Until recently, private ownership of the metal was illegal. There are roughly 1.33 billion people in China and even if you take only a small percentage of that figure taking possession of silver for savings, numbers like that can do nothing but drive up the cost of this precious metal.

All of these reasons and more are going to drive up the demand on silver and, along with it, its cost, promising to make your silver stash more valuable to you in bad times. Δ

Journey to the backwoods
part 1

— By David Lee —

It was 1975. The young man was 29 years old. It was time for another change in his life, a big one. He had spent the last eleven years trying to choose a career he really liked and he had tried several.

All during high school he was mentored by his parish priest who tried to persuade him to enter a seminary after graduation and go into the priesthood. Four years of hard work by the good priest was ruined when the young man found out the meaning of celibacy. That was his first try. He was not priest material.

His next career venture was in the military, right after high school. It seemed like it would be exciting and the opportunity for advancement was good if he stayed for 20 years. But army life was 95% boring, 5% terror, and 100% being bossed around. It was not for him. That was his second try. He was not going to be a soldier.

He decided he needed to further his education. His family was too poor to help him go to college and they weren't inclined to encourage him in that direction. His father's reaction to this plan was, "We didn't go. You don't need to either." Scholarships were minimal and few were available; he didn't want to go into deep debt to get a degree.

The young man's first homebuilding effort, built using salvaged materials from the flood

He always liked fixing and building things and, by exploring options, he learned there were apprenticeships available that taught high-level skills in a number of practical trades. He would be able to earn a paycheck while learning, a trademark of most apprenticeships as far back as there have been skilled trades. He got busy researching these opportunities that were a godsend to him and many other poor but ambitious alternative knowledge seekers.

His research paid off. He found a trade school. After getting hired and spending six months proving himself a good and smart employee, he was accepted into a machinist apprenticeship program at an aircraft manufacturing company in Connecticut, the best one he found after considerable investigation.

It took three years of work and study to graduate and receive his Journeyman Machinist Certificate. He now had a trade as good as any degree and better than some. He went on to teach other employees of the company how to operate machines that shape metal into jet engines. It was a good paying job but working in a factory was gloomy. The union rules and company management system controlled his every move and left him little opportunity to express his creativity, something he felt he needed to do in life, especially with his new skills.

Fast car necessary for detective work

The Detective

As a country boy from Vermont, living in the city of Hartford, Connecticut was new and strange to him but a necessity if he wanted to keep this job. It was hectic, expensive, and sometimes dangerous living there. He was young though, and the entertainment and excitement of city life led him, by curiosity, into a part-time job working for a private detective agency.

After a few months learning the basics, he was assigned cases involving industrial espionage. During the late 1960s, NASA and other technology companies were extremely busy. So many contracts for machined parts were put out for bid that the crime of stealing patented industrial secrets mushroomed. Winning contracts from the information those secrets revealed could make a lot of money for a rogue machine shop at the expense or ruin of the legitimate patent owner. Companies were hiring detectives to find spies within their own organizations.

This was exceptionally interesting work so he left his position at the machinist school to work full-time for the agency. He was not going to be a factory worker.

The young man's machinist experience allowed him to fit into machine shop settings easily because he could operate all of the equipment and his affable country boy demeanor encouraged friendly conversations. By paying attention to shop gossip and following up on clues, he could learn whether or not a company had thefts, leaks, or employees selling information to outlaw shops.

He did this and other detective work (actual title: Professional Witness) for three years before deciding it was a markedly inappropriate career choice if he wanted to live a long peaceful life and maybe have a family someday. During that time he learned from the inside how entrenched corruption is in the business, government, and criminal areas of society. He was becoming jaded and world-weary. Even though he was at his highest income to date he resigned from the agency. He was not going to be a detective.

WWII BSA British Army motorcycles, later turned into "Choppers"

One of the derelict military BSAs transformed into an exotic mortorcycle by high school students.

The teacher

He decided to try something else with his new education. Something wholesome.

At the age of 26 the young man moved back to his hometown in Vermont when he learned the Industrial Arts teacher position was available at his old high school, a situation for which he was well qualified. The pay was much lower but so was the cost of living. He was back in his own peaceful hometown with the respectable career of teaching kids a trade — what could be better? It was exciting.

He inherited an unruly group of eight senior boys too rowdy to associate with other students. This was a shock to the new teacher. When he was a student some years before, the Industrial Arts teacher was good at his profession and "The Shop Course" was respectable, preparing students for work in local factories. That good man had died and shop class had turned into the default detention center for wayward boys. In addition, all the valuable tooling that made the machines useable was now missing.

The new teacher knew what to do. The useless machinery was sold to local machine shops that could it put back into service after making necessary repairs. He used the proceeds from sales to buy mechanics' tools and began teaching the boys how to work on cars, something they were more interested in doing than causing trouble.

This was grossly unacceptable to the school administration. They wanted these boys to accept the classes meant to send them on to higher education. Cars were forbidden at school. Fear of paving the parking lot with rubber from the boys doing 'burnouts' was expressed. Rules had to be followed.

Undeterred, the young teacher started an Alternative Motorcycle Building course. He brought in eight derelict British army motorcycles that had seen service during WWII in Europe (leftovers from his part-time import/export business) and donated them to the students. For the rest of the year he and the 'greasers' (a nickname the shop boys accepted with pride) built choppers from the antique machines. The young teacher's efforts attracted so much interest that by year's end 75 students had signed up for the class to help his eight greasers build the distinctive machines.

The school administration and the town government department that managed the schools now viewed him as a radical nonconformist. Bureaucratic roadblocks were put in his way. Most of his budget money was 'redirected' to the Woodworking Shop. There were not too subtle hints that he was 'upsetting the system.' However, eight young thugs became accomplished students, learned to teach other students mechanical skills, and were popular celebrities at the end of the school year, gaining diplomas instead of Attendance Certificates.

His first home

Another opportunity presented itself during the school year that brought big changes to the young man's life.

He felt apartment living was a waste of money and decided to buy a home. Not a new or expensive place. He wanted one that needed a little fixing. He liked the idea of turning an old place into a comfortable home. A little four-room bungalow was available on a quiet side road on the outskirts of town and he bought it. Working on his house during evenings and weekends was a real pleasure to him. It was the most satisfying work he had ever done. When the school year ended he decided to spend the summer working full time on the little house.

Summer went by fast. As the new school year approached, the young man had to make a decision. Teaching high school students was rewarding and the students loved him, but the discord between him and the inflexible, meddling administration made the job distasteful. Bickering over funds and petty power feuds among teachers spoiled his belief that teaching was the noble calling he had believed it to be. The administration reclassified the Industrial Arts Department in such a way that he was no longer qualified for the position.

Local politics played a part in school decisions too. A retired machinist who was influential in town business wanted to be the Industrial Arts teacher and, rather than fight over it, the young man decided to move on. He was not going to be a high school teacher.

It was time for another career attempt.

He had a plan. He would finish fixing up his house, sell it, and build another one. A brand new one, and maybe sell that one too. This could turn into a career he would gladly take on. The country was coming out of a recession and people were buying things again, including new homes. This might just work.

Now that he was self-employed he worked very hard for long hours every day. There was so much to do. He bought an old truck and fixed it up, tuning the engine, installing new parts, and putting on good tires. Now he had a reliable truck, an important tool he needed in his new line of work, and he learned how to take care of it himself so he would not have to take it to expensive repair shops.

He decided to put an addition on his little house to more than double its size. He drew plans for the addition and revised them over and over, even as it was being built. Having the power to bring his creative ideas to life was gratifying. Organizing the operation was complicated but rewarding. Buying the right materials at the right time, keeping lumber dry during the rainier-than-usual summer, and making the most of sunny days kept him occupied. The satisfaction all this gave him was wonderful.

The flood

Then came a local disaster.

It rained like never before. Rivers and streams rose up and flooded the land surrounding them. Vermont is a hilly place. High ground was plentiful so not many homes were damaged, but everything along local rivers was flooded.

About two weeks after the rain stopped and the waters receded, the young man happened to be taking a walk through the low land where a river entered a lake just outside of town. Havoc had visited here as debris, washed away by the floods, settled in the swamp. Huge piles of every type of lumber were snagged around the trees that had held their ground and not been uprooted, and every item was scrubbed clean by the rushing water.

This was a Eureka moment for the young man! Though he did not realize it at the time, finding those piles of building materials was his first big step toward backwoods living.

He made a mental note of the materials. Great long hand-hewn beams, too many to count, were everywhere. A number of old barns had been lost — but not totally lost. Here they were, right in front of him, disassembled, cleaned, and ready to be used again. The young man had visions of the old beams becoming a new barn or, even better, a new house, or used in the addition to his home.

Along with the beams were weathered barn boards, thousands of board feet of them. As he investigated each pile, new treasures turned up. A lumber mill next to the river had been flooded out. Thousands of feet of brand new lumber, some rough-cut, some finish-milled, lay all over the swamp.

And more surprises appeared. Many bridges on back roads in Vermont were decked with sawn timbers six inches thick, 8 to 12 inches wide, and at least 14 feet long. Each bridge had 50 to 100 or more of these timbers and each one was treated with a preservative. Here were several hundred, maybe a thousand of them, right in front of him.

There was enough three-inch thick curved tongue and groove lumber to rebuild the silo it had once been. Even the cone-shaped roof was there, though in pieces. Along with all that he found two-inch thick planking that he would later take home to become a floor and some of the walls of the new addition to his little home and still there would be enough left over to use in another building.

After a couple hours spent roaming through God's building supply yard, the young man realized there was far too much treasure for just himself. He knew three other men who were building their own homes and could use these materials, so he called them. For almost six weeks the four of them spent most of the daylight hours driving down the little dirt road to the edge of the swamp, carrying out lumber, loading their pickup trucks, and taking it home. Each salvaged three or four truckloads a day. It was seriously hard work but well worth it.

The young man's pile of materials grew large and varied. Folks noticed. One visitor stopped by to inquire about buying a nice hand-hewn beam to use as a mantle. Another wanted two old weathered wood barrels and several antique wagon wheels. He sold barn boards to people for remodeling their homes. Weathered wood was popular then. His builder buddies and fellow salvagers were having similar experiences. Salvage work could be a business all its own.

Then they caught the attention of the local government.

As the enterprising young men were salvaging goodies in the swamp, other people heard about the treasure trove and showed up to see what they could find. It wasn't long before more people around town heard the story and salvaging from the swamp was in full swing. It became almost a party atmosphere. Neighbor helping neighbor, they carried their treasures home to be put to better use than letting them decay into swamp mulch.

Several businesses in town — the building supply stores, an antique dealer, and a construction company owner in particular — learned what was going on and complained to the selectmen and town manager about the new, unregulated salvage business. It had to be stopped. It was dangerous for people to be taking stuff out of the hazardous swamp. The citizens had to be protected from themselves by the local government. Moreover, it was taking business away from them. Yes, they insisted. Town management must put an end to this free-for-all! There was no law against what the people were doing. Anyone could go there. But there had to be a way to stop it.

At a selectmen's meeting attended by 'concerned' citizens, it was determined the swamp should be 'cleaned up' to prevent future floods from being dammed up by the debris.

The construction company owner was awarded the contract to do the job. In an uncharacteristically short time for such municipal business, bulldozers and trucks were at work in the swamp, pushing the 'debris' into three huge piles which were then set on fire. The burn took four days because there was so much to fuel the flames.

At the next selectmen's meeting there was some discussion that perhaps the materials removed from the swamp by the young men who started it all should be confiscated by the town. This plot was abandoned when it was made known the contractor who was doing the swamp rehabilitation had taken many huge truckloads of valuable materials out and added them to his personal stash at his company storage yard to be sold later.

A good thing had come to an end. Or had it?

The four enterprising young men were sitting on the bank above the swamp, having a couple of beers and watching the last of the big fires burn when one of them said, "Hold my beer and look at this."

He pulled out a map of the area surrounding the town. In red ink he had circled seven more places where a river or stream entered a lake or pond. "What do you say we go check these places out?"

Within three days the four of them were again salvaging materials. Only this time, they told no one and kept a low profile while doing their work. The treasures were not as numerous as in the big swamp but each of them managed to double what they had previously accumulated.

Thanks to this adventure, Our Guy figured he now had enough to build the major parts of at least four homes. As he was designing structures in his head for ways to use the superb building materials he had collected, he realized his life path was there before him. He took this windfall of treasure as an omen that home building would be his new career.

So far he had learned that a career in an environment as controlled as the church or the military was not for him, although his experience in those organizations gave him a sense of right and wrong, discipline, and a knowledge of guns, all of which he appreciated.

He gained a valuable education at the aircraft manufacturing company, but the repressive structure of a big corporation was not for him either.

Detective work was simply too dangerous for him to consider it becoming a long-time profession.

Nor was he willing to make a career of teaching, where power struggles ruled the work environment. But he did learn that teaching was enjoyable.

His oppressive experience with local government was irksome too. It occurred to him from his encounters with it that government was not there to help anyone but itself and its friends.

Building homes

All of these lessons had steered him toward a life of self-employment where he could be his own boss. Building homes might just be the ticket.

Putting the addition onto his little house kept him busy from early morning until after dark, and after that he spent time planning the next day's work. He kept a list on a clipboard of everything there was to do and everything he needed to buy. That clipboard would become his competent secretary for life. It kept him from wasting any time wondering what to do next or worrying about forgotten jobs, items, or appointments.

As summer passed into fall, the framework of his addition rose up from the foundation that he had dug and poured by hand. The old axe-hewn beams looked even better now that they were neatly stacked and ready to be put in place and he designed the structure to showcase them.

Rough-cut old lumber from the swamp could have been used for his framing but it would have made bumpy, hard-to-insulate walls and created too much extra work to look good, plus its beauty would be buried inside the walls. He had seen homes built with rough lumber. Some looked good in an artistic but inept sort of style and the amount of detail work to get them even that good was unacceptable to him.

He built the walls and roof framing the standard way and used his special lumber for added strength and in ways that showed off its beauty. He made his front door of magnificent weathered hardwood. Interior doors, closet and cabinet doors, window casings and frames were made with weathered barn boards.

Instead of using standard windows he bought bare panes of glass and made his own window sashes. This opened up new ideas for ways to use glass. He could put a window of any size any place he wanted. It was during brainstorming sessions about windows that he thought of making screened vents with doors of weathered wood. They could also be any size and installed anywhere.

One idea led to another and his little house and the addition were taking on a very distinctive style similar to a very old, charming cottage in a storybook.

The best part of his new career was the liberty of being his own boss. He worked from dawn to dusk and beyond, falling asleep exhausted but satisfied at night and waking up excited, raring to go each morning. Weekends and weekdays were no different from each other. Defining moments in the building process marked time for him. The foundation completed, the framing done, the sheathing attached, the roof finished so that the interior of the house stayed dry, and the windows and doors closing the last openings of the building were memorable moments, more so than calendar dates.

Fall was warm and stayed late that year, lucky for Our Guy. When December came, the shell of his addition was done on the outside but the interior was empty. It needed insulation and interior walls, wiring, and plumbing and... a whole lot of things. Most of all, it needed a heat source. He built a wood stove from a 55-gallon steel drum. What a treat that was. Working in warmth when it was cold outside and making it happen all by himself was inspiring.

It was about then that the young man approached his first financial crisis. He had made do with an old skill saw, a hammer, and a few tools he had collected along the way. He was saved a major expense by using the treasures from the swamp instead of having to buy a lot of building materials. But now he needed insulation, drywall, electric and plumbing supplies … all kinds of things, including more sophisticated tools. And he needed to figure out how to acquire the money to buy them.

He decided to mortgage his property. This would be the next lesson in the problems entrepreneurs face.

The banker listened to his story, told him he admired what the young man was doing but no, he could not get a loan because he didn't have a job. It seems building a house to sell wasn't considered employment because it didn't bring in a weekly paycheck. And even though the young man had no other debts, that's just the way it was.

"Rules are rules," said the banker.

But luck was with him. Back in high school he was a member of his church credit union and he still had a small account there. The manager, hearing the young man's need, told him the credit union would lend him money. This was a lifesaver. It also taught the young man another lesson. His chosen career would require unconventional sources for funds, at least for his first home building project. He assumed that after the first house was sold he would have enough money to build his second house without needing to take out a loan.

Unfortunately that would not be the case but he didn't know it then. Still, he was always on the lookout for ways to find money when needed.

The house project was back on track. He bought materials and some tools. The new table saw made possible whole new ways to make things. A chainsaw made it easier to provide wood to heat his home. Smaller tools like drills and planers gave him the ability to do exacting work almost to the precision he could perform back at the factory. He combined his metal working knowledge, his new woodworking skills, and some imagination to create wooden hinges that performed better than metal ones of any size, from kitchen cabinets to garage doors. This specialty would be one of his trademark building techniques throughout his career.

It was a heady experience when new ideas came to him, further proof he was on the right career path. He was already anticipating his second home building project.

During the winter months another shift in circumstances arrived.

In a small town news travels fast. People heard what the young man was doing and stopped by to see his progress and chat with him. Most respected his need to keep working and didn't stay too long. However, there were so many visitors that it did slow his progress. By Thanksgiving he had to put up a sign that said, "Visiting Hours 6 to 8" which only barely diminished the parade of sightseers. But, with 6 to 8 being mealtime, some of them thoughtfully brought pizza and beer. Spontaneous parties broke out at times.

Among the visitors were a few who were interested enough to want to try doing the same thing as our young entrepreneur. There were eleven of

Stone was collected from stream beds. Boards from the flood zone sheath the upper wall. Window casings and doors were made from salvaged lumber.

Big wooden spools that once held heavy duty electric wire were used to build the tower. Seven were rescued from the flood zone, as was the cable holding the tower together.

them — four young married couples and three who were single. They visited so often, learned so much, and were so enthusiastic that Our Guy put them to work. They were glad to help him each time they stopped by. One thing he especially appreciated was their giving other visitors 'The Tour' of his unusual home, which allowed the young builder to keep working.

By Christmas the eleven steady visitors and the young man had become good friends, and they held a big party in the shell of the new addition. Under the influence of the festivities a plan was hatched. The eleven wanted to join forces and form a group with a common goal. In order to make it work, Our Young Man would be their teacher and mentor.

In that long ago time of the early 1970s, going "Back To The Land" was a movement popularized by Helen and Scott Nearing and other 'Age of Aquarius' prophets and gurus. Armed with practical information gleaned from the pages of *The Mother Earth News* and many books on the subject, it seemed a good and logical life choice.

The Group's plan was to take a year's time to build three houses, sell them, then buy a piece of land together somewhere out in the country, set up a "Back To The Land" community and live happily ever after.

Our hero's role was to be the leader and coordinator of this plan since he had the most experience and his house was not far from being finished. After that he could focus his full attention on the success of the venture. Members of the Group would start building homes at the start of the new year. Their goal was to be off to the backcountry within a year's time. They would all help each other, sharing skills, funds, materials, and work.

The end of December rolled into 1973. Enthusiasm was high. Group members began construction on two building projects. Weekly meetings kept interest high and progress steady. By springtime the two new homes were well underway.

The young man finished his own project in late spring and already had a buyer when the next blow to his trust that business and government were mostly honest arrived.

Having been in the Navy, the homebuyer qualified for a loan backed by the Veterans Administration. Obtaining the loan required an appraisal by a VA inspector. A week after the appearance of this potential buyer, a letter informed our young homebuilder that the VA would not approve the loan because the inspector estimated the house to be worth only about 60% of the sale price.

This was a major shock to the young man. How could he have missed the inspector's visit when he had been home the entire week?

Two days after receiving the appraisal letter the real estate dealer who originally sold him the little house came by for a friendly visit and offered to buy his new house for a thousand dollars above the VA appraisal. He refused the offer.

The young man became suspicious. He called the VA office and started asking questions. He learned his friendly real estate dealer was also the VA appraiser in his area. He was being scammed.

A complaint was filed and a new appraisal for the full price made it possible for him to proceed with the sale of his home.

Further investigation of this real estate dealer revealed he had carried out this fraud numerous times in the past. He was especially adept at acquiring apartment buildings this way. Our Guy pursued the matter for months, trying to have charges filed against this man. Nothing happened. The real estate dealer was also a selectman and well connected with everyone in the local government including the police chief, who informed the young man that he should stop bothering people about this 'nonsense' or there would be problems for him.

The most he managed to accomplish was to get the VA to take away the real estate agent's job as appraiser — but for only six months!

It was a hard lesson. The young man was learning not to trust people in power, whether they were in government or business. He vowed to involve a lawyer in all future business deals. Good plan, though not the surest strategy in life. But he did not know that then.

In fact, he forgot his own advice almost immediately. The Group's projects were going very well and it didn't occur to him at the time that lawyers would be needed in transactions among friends.

He was about to learn more life lessons as his journey to backwoods living proceeded.

To be continued... ∆

Homemade electric power

By Jim Van Sant

Ever wonder how you could live off the grid when the sun isn't shining on your solar panels?

Our homestead alternative energy system is based on 12 volts direct current. That is what your car battery supplies. Many smaller store-bought generators supply only 115 VAC alternating electricity. They are great for powering up your power tools or standard home appliances but are pretty inefficient for charging 12-volt batteries.

If you are into 12 VDC (volts direct current) for charging your car battery or powering up your off-the-grid alternative energy system you need a 12-volt DC generator.

As a homesteader having no special training, licenses, or badges, I wanted an inexpensive solution for electricity that does not require any special skills or tools.

We all know our cars and trucks contain a 12-volt alternator or generator that is powered by the engine. It keeps the lights, radio, and heater fan supplied with electricity.

I wanted to generate some electricity and not spend a lot of money. My goal was to charge a dead car battery, play my radio, light up some indoor and outdoor lights, run my computer, charge up some flashlight batteries, and run some other low power gadgets.

A fun destination for us these days is a trip to the local hardware store. We walk the aisles and get ideas for new projects we hope to do someday. On a recent trip I spotted something unusual. In a row of $200-300 pressure washers, I saw a unit sporting a large handwritten $25 price tag. The manager said the new washer had been returned and did not work, and the estimated cost of the repairs would be more than the unit had sold for originally, so they were just trying to get rid of it. It had a new Honda gas engine and that alone had to be worth more than $25. The water pump had failed, but I didn't need a power washer. I had another project in mind.

My homemade 12-VDC generator

On the way home, I stopped by the local auto dismantler yard. I was looking for the largest, cheapest, cleanest truck alternator I could find on the part shelves. The owner quickly understood what I was trying to do, handed me a large truck alternator, and rang me up for $20. Back at my workbench, I dug around and found some scrap heavy-gauge sheet metal pieces to make some mounting brackets. By cutting and pasting I was able to match where I would mount the alternator so its drive pulley would be lined up with the drive pulley on the vertical shaft gas engine. I used my electric drill to drill some holes in the metal brackets to match up the mounting holes on the alternator. The sturdy brackets were attached to the metal engine frame and the used alternator with ¼-inch machine screws, lock washers, and nuts.

A challenge for me was fitting the pulleys to the correct size rubber belt. The belts come in many shapes and sizes and it took me three tries to get the right one. The size and depth of the pulley grooves is important to prevent early belt wear from slippage.

I was going to rig a strong spring for a belt tensioner. For now I just used some shims behind the mounting bracket to tighten up the belt.

Now for the big test run. The nearly new gas engine fired up with the first pull on the starter cord. Despite the load resistance from the pulley belt and the alternator, the engine turned the alternator at a good steady RPM.

Voltage meter in hand, I checked the voltage output and it was zero. No power. Shock and panic! Naturally my first thought was that my bargain alternator wasn't working, but then I remembered that an alternator must be connected to a 12-volt battery to establish a "field current." When I connected the alternator terminals to my storage battery with jumper cables, all was well. The battery

The alternator was positioned so the drive pulley lined up with the one from the engine.

charged to full capacity after a few minutes.

Now it was clear that I had a new electric power-producing capability. On a dark, cold, rainy day when my solar panels or wind generator are not producing charging current, I now have another option for self-reliance. Any lawn mower engine from a garage sale could be used with any used car alternator for this project. Δ

Extend your growing season

By Jackie Clay

Having lived most of my adult life in relatively inhospitable gardening areas, it seems like we never had enough time in our growing season to grow anything. I've seen a foot of snow on June 27th, a blizzard on the Fourth of July, and a killing freeze the second week in August.

I've had to use some helpful techniques to get crops growing fast and keep them growing, while at the same time, protecting them from surprise nasty weather. We've never had a lot of money, so as much as I would have liked to, I couldn't buy a greenhouse kit to put up in the garden. I had to improvise, doing the best I could with what I had.

Starting your own plants

Very early in the game I learned that I absolutely had to start my own plants from seed so I could grow the best varieties for our climate to get a harvest at all. Mid-winter sees me comparing seed catalogs for the best deals on the varieties I want to grow the following spring. As we grow increasingly more open-pollinated heritage varieties, I have a huge assortment of seeds that I have saved over the years: squash, tomatoes, peppers, carrots, beans, cucumbers, melons, and corn, plus lots of herbs and flowers. My first humble seed starting was growing some tomato plants on our enclosed sun porch, way back in Sturgeon Lake, when my oldest son, Bill, was still in diapers. From there, I expanded my little seed starting to include peppers, melons, squash, cucumbers, herbs, and flowers each year. By starting my own seeds, not

By starting your own plant varieties, you get an eight week jump on your growing season.

Wallo' Waters protect tender plants in the garden from unexpected cold weather.

only was I assured of getting the varieties I needed and the flavor and performance I wanted, but perhaps most importantly, I got an eight week jump-start on my garden by planting indoors.

To start seeds, fill containers at least two inches deep (preferably four inches) with a good quality seed-starting soil. Punch small holes for drainage in the bottoms of your containers to let excess water drain out. This prevents the seeds or tender young plants from rotting. Water the soil well (it's usually quite dry), let it soak in, then carefully place your seeds an inch apart each way in the container. You don't have to plant the whole pack of seeds. Plant what you wish to grow, then seal the envelope again and store it in a jar for next year. Seeds stay good for many years, and you save money this way.

Sprinkle about 1/8-inch of seed-starting soil over the seeds and gently sprinkle warm water over the container, dampening the soil well. You don't want it heavy and soggy, just nicely moist. Put the container in a used bread bag or white/clear plastic shopping bag and close it with a twist. Tuck the end under the pot and set it in a warm location. Watch the container carefully; tomatoes can germinate in as few as four days or take as long as two weeks, depending on the temperature. The optimum temperature is around 75 degrees; cooler makes things slow down, but too hot can actually cook the seeds, so keep them out of direct sunlight.

Once the plants are up, remove the plastic and place them where they get sunshine for most of the day. Watch out so they don't dry out, as a sunny window will tend to suck the moisture out of the pot. Once the plants have two sets of true leaves, it's time to transplant them to a larger container of their own. I find that Styrofoam coffee cups work well for this. Just poke a hole in the bottom and fill with good potting soil. (Avoid cheap soil — it is solid peat and very dense and acidic. Plants don't like either.) Plant the seedlings just as deep as they were in the starter containers (or deeper if it is a leggy tomato plant — it'll form roots up the stem, too, making it stronger). Put the Styrofoam cups in a pan or other container to hold excess drainage water. These can be old cake pans, plastic wash basins, or nursery flats with no holes.

When your climate has warmed up enough to set the plants out, gradually harden them off. This means to gradually get them used to outdoor growing conditions, including sunshine, wind, and rain. At first, set your plants out in a protected location for an hour or two. Then gradually increase the time outdoors and move them to a less protected location. Soon they'll be ready to set out in the garden and begin growing.

But what if you live in an area with unexpected, frigid springtime

The temporary greenhouse we built on the new log cabin

weather or pop-up frosts, and even snow storms, like us?

Hotbeds

Way up in the mountains in Montana, I kept my plants growing strongly in a hotbed until the weather had moderated. After all, I still had three feet of snow on my garden in mid-May! True, the weather was sunny and usually warm. The snow was going fast, but I still had plants that wanted to grow out of my kitchen window and get going. So I shoveled a spot out in the sunshine that was protected from the wind by pine trees, and made a hotbed.

A hotbed is basically a box over a rectangular hole in the ground. The box is partially filled (about 18 inches) with fresh horse manure, which is then covered by about a foot of good garden soil. The box is raised above ground and has a sloped roof made of an old wood and glass storm window, hinged on the back. The manure heats up as it rots and keeps the hotbed warm when the nights (and days) are cold, while the soil protects the roots from getting burned by the hot manure. The sides hold in the heat, and the window lets in the light and warmth from the sun.

By hinging the window frame to the back, you can prop the window open, as needed, when the inside temperature gets too warm.

I made my first hotbed from old railroad ties; later I made another out of logs. The hotbed works great, not only for keeping tomatoes and other plants growing strongly, but also to start early lettuce, spinach, and other salad greens.

Another year I built a cheap temporary greenhouse attached to the outside of our kitchen. It was built of only poles from the woods and plastic left over from another project. It wasn't pretty, but it worked great. I was able to open the kitchen window to allow heat from the house to keep the plants warm at night.

My greenhouse was only 8x8 feet and six feet tall, but it helped get my plants going well when there was still a deep covering of snow on the garden.

But even after the weather warmed up, a high-country garden is subject to snow and frost. Of course, some crops, such as peas, spinach, turnips, broccoli, and cabbage don't mind a bit. But those cold events would have killed my tomatoes and peppers.

We are able to grow vegetables year around in the green room.

I don't take chances, so my tomatoes went into Wallo' Water plant protectors. When I ran out of them, I planted the rest of the tomatoes in plastic "tents" made by driving a stout wood post in the ground at each end of the row to a height of about four feet, then nailing a rail across the top. I carefully trimmed off every single sharp stub, then I draped plastic over the tomato row, letting it hang down in the back and front. I held down the edges of the plastic with some soil, and held the front shut with a rock. On nice days, I'd open the front and back or pull the sides up.

As we lived so high, and the weather is so unpredictable above 6,000 feet, I only grew determinate tomatoes (bush type, not vining), so I could easily protect the mature plants. To our friends' amazement, we had a great garden!

Even my small patch of Earlivee sweet corn was housed in plastic tents all spring, until it began to tassel out. We didn't have much sweet corn, but we appreciated each and every ear.

Cold Minnesota

When we moved here to our woodland homestead in northern Minnesota it was February. We were camping out in a 30-foot travel trailer with an old fish house for an addition, where we had a wall-hung propane heater. A couple months later, while we were still in "camping" mode, my my elderly parents came to live with us. My oldest son's friend found us a free mobile home. I hate trailers, but sometimes you have to do what you have to do. We had it moved to our property. As it was located east and west, that left the back door facing south. The wheels were soon turning ... greenhouse?

Our carpenter friend, Tom Richardson, built a deck on the south side of the mobile home, then we built a temporary greenhouse on top of that deck. I splurged on clear corrugated fiberglass roofing, as I knew we would be using the greenhouse for a while until we got the house built. We used screws for the entire construction, as I knew that it was going to be temporary and we would be reusing all the material at some point.

The permanent green room attached to our new log home has plenty of windows to let in light. On cool nights, the house heats the green room; on warm days, the green room heats the house!

The side walls were framed to fit the odd windows Tom and I had saved from various places (mostly Tom's other jobs and the dump). It wasn't pretty, but it sure worked well.

I built benches to fit against the walls and we were in business. Mom loved plants and enjoyed sitting out there in her wheelchair on sunny days, admiring her growing things.

This greenhouse cost about $800, but the deck was later recycled to be used on our existing deck, the roof was reused, first on our temporary greenhouse on the new log home, and later on the roof on our chicken coop. The old windows went first into the temporary greenhouse on the log home, then to various locations on the homestead, such as the chicken coops and goat barn. It could have been built cheaper, using non-treated lumber and sheet plastic on the roof, but I considered it a good investment, considering how much use and enjoyment we got from it, and we were able to reuse everything.

Heat for the greenhouse came by opening the back door of the trailer to let the heat flow into the greenhouse. Likewise, on a warm, sunny day, the door let heat from the greenhouse flow into the mobile home, saving propane.

Our green room

In the years to come, many changes came into my life, but we did get our new log home built. The following spring, I decided I had to have another greenhouse, as there was no heat in the old mobile home now, and the greenhouse couldn't be used up there. Carefully, Tom dismantled the temporary greenhouse and we moved it down to the south facing side of our new home. Using similar construction techniques, we soon had a recycled temporary greenhouse, using most of the same materials over again. It served happily for another

Here's one of my small hoop houses that fits over a 4x4-foot raised bed in our house garden (without covers of either floating row cover or plastic, as needed).

year, raising not only our vegetable starts for the garden, but many herbs and Mom's flowers. It was heated by leaving the back door of the house open, just like we did in the mobile home.

The following spring I had saved enough money and we were ready to build our permanent green room. Once again, Tom carefully took down the second temporary greenhouse (I'm sure he thought I was nuts at this point), saving the material to re-use.

The permanent green room was framed with used power poles. Tom had some used double pane patio door windows and I had found some at the dump. These make excellent windows for a greenhouse as they are heavy, strong, and double-paned. (If you shop for some, check for moisture and dirt between the panes, as these windows have a compromised seal and will fog up considerably on warm days.) We selected the best of the used patio door windows and used one horizontally in the green room and three vertically in the enclosed porch, along with a few sliding windows for ventilation. I splurged for a skylight in the green room and another in the enclosed porch. They are nice and do let a lot of sunlight in.

Both the floor and ceiling are insulated. We still have to finish off the outside wall of the green room and porch with half log siding, but we have to buy a little at a time as we can afford it.

Our greenhouse not only lets us start plants in the spring but also grow tomatoes and peppers year around. I hope to grow dwarf citrus as well and am encouraging my tiny trees every day.

Due to the location of the windows, we get plenty of sun/heat in the winter, but not much heat in the summer months, so the green room doesn't overheat the house in the summer. The air flow through opposing windows always creates a nice breeze when we need it most.

You'd think that we'd be happy with that, wouldn't you? Well, yes and no. Our seedlings were getting off to a great start, but we were having trouble getting our peppers and melons to ripen. The plants would get to bearing nicely just as freezing weather hit, and we'd only get a few fruits.

Will's hoop house

Several years ago, I bought a neighbor's old hoop house. Not much was

A close-up of the conduit brackets holding the hoops

Here you can see the framework and supports of the hoop house.

left but the ¾-inch PVC plastic hoops. They laid around for several years, but I never got around to building the hoop house. Then this spring Will got it built so we would get more peppers than just barely enough to season our salsas and tomato sauces.

Will used two 16-foot 2x4s and two 12-foot 2x4s for the base. The two long boards were tilted in so that the hoops would fit nicely against them. He screwed an upright 2x4 in the center of the back and framed in a stoop-through door on the front. Over the top of these, he screwed a 16-foot 2x4 to act as a ridgepole to support and keep the plastic hoops in place. Using aluminum conduit fasteners (the ones with a screw hole in each end and hump in the middle), he screwed each hoop into place, first on the base and then to the ridge beam.

When that was complete, we draped a leftover piece of 4 mil plastic sheeting over the whole works. We had just enough to cover the roof/sides and back, draping the ends up to both sides of the door opening. We then drew it snug and stapled it in place everywhere there was a piece of lumber to staple onto. Wow! We instantly had a great hoop house, with a total of only four hours' work in all.

The ¾-inch PVC is a little flimsy. If we bought new material, it would either be 1-inch metal electrical conduit or 1-inch PVC. But even though it is flimsy, it works. It even held together when a freak storm popped up, blew it over a 6-foot fence into the goat pasture, then sent it crashing into two 3-inch diameter popple trees, uprooting one and breaking the other. The hoop house was a little damaged, but the hoops and plastic survived. The lesson learned: be sure to drive pipes or metal posts into the ground to firmly anchor the hoop house against strong winds.

We planted six rows of peppers in the hoop house when there was still a danger of frost. One night, a freeze was predicted and we put a propane heater in it, just in case.

As I write this, it's the second week in July and we're already eating peppers from our hoop house. That's unbelievable. And hundreds are set and even more are blooming. The peppers really love the hot days and warmer nights. They do tend to dry out quickly, so we are taking special care to keep them well watered every week. We just are using a little square spray lawn sprinkler, set in the center of the hoop house aisle. It mists won-

The peppers LOVE our hoop house!

derfully and the peppers think it's a hot summer rain.

We're already planning another hoop house for our melons next spring. This one works so beautifully it's unbelievable.

Other season extenders

I've also got some mini hoop houses that I find invaluable. They're only 4x4-feet, built out of 2x4s as a base, with ¾-inch PVC hoops running through another 2x2 ridge beam with holes drilled in it. I've not only used this to good advantage for starting hills of squash or melons, with plastic stapled over it, but with plastic replaced by floating row cover material. It is perfect to put over one of my raised beds of broccoli to keep cabbage moths from laying eggs on the leaves. No sprays, no powders, no work. When I weed or harvest, I just lift off the cover and go to it. I have three of them (so far) and when put in a row, they'll also protect a row of broccoli or cauliflower.

Again, in the fall, I can add a layer of plastic and protect the pepper plants in my house garden's raised beds or a bed of special flowers I don't want to get hit by early fall frosts.

Bill and Carolyn Presley, friends of ours, developed a few great season extender ideas that they said I could share with you. One is simply a pair of heavy-gauge wires, bent to form hoops about 9 inches wide. By crossing a pair of them over a tender pepper or tomato (or other) plant, you can then slide a used plastic shopping bag, such as the type you get at Wal-Mart, over the hoops, anchoring the bottom with garden soil. They protect and warm the plant and soil and it's so easy to remove them when the weather's warm or you want to work around the plants.

Another of Bill and Carolyn's great ideas is to cut the bottom out of larger plastic coffee containers. Then remove the top. Their celery grows stock and strong, blanching nicely, with little damage from the slugs as it's hard to get to the plants. Carolyn's celery is three times as large and nice as mine. Although celery does survive a frost or freeze, it sure likes the warm, cozy protection of the plastic container.

Another thing I have often used is a plastic milk jug with the bottom cut out. This can be placed over a tender plant to protect from frost and heat the soil. Shove it into the soil a bit so it doesn't blow away. When the days are hot, remove the lid. When nights will be cool, put the lid back on in the late afternoon. Plants love it and grow quickly, hastening your harvest.

My garden is getting harvested earlier and earlier every year, due to our using several of these helpers every year. We still live in cold Zone 3, with about 90 days of growing season, but I'm growing abundant 90-day tomatoes, 110-day squash, and getting red peppers. It's great to be able to grow some of these longer-season crops. All of these methods will help extend your growing season by months, and help ensure that you get a crop to harvest at all. Δ

Ayoob on Firearms

Tailoring guns to females

Bill Van Tuyl built this custom 20-gauge auto shotgun for his wife Jennie. It features a short stock with a cushiony recoil pad at the butt.

By Massad Ayoob

So, I'm sitting here in a hotel writing this, less than three hours after getting off the witness stand in a manslaughter case. The defendant was a 5'3", 130-pound female who was being stalked by her sometimes-abusive estranged husband. It was a "backwoods home" kind of incident: the ex accosted her, with a male relative along (for moral support presumably), when she was trapped on a narrow dirt path on her dad's rural shooting range. There was no escape: her car was blocked in by his, and he had deflated one of her tires. Things escalated; he punched her, threw her to the ground, and kicked her. She took the beating in a fetal position, curled up to keep him from getting the gun that was tucked center-front inside her waistband. He left her on the ground and strode triumphantly back to his car, snarling "stupid bitch!" over his shoulder as he went. As he reached the car where she feared he had a weapon, he spun to face her, shouted a challenge, and appeared to be about to lunge at her again. At a range both prosecution and defense stipulated to be fifteen and a half feet, she fired from the ground. A .38 Special bullet cut his spinal cord, and he fell. The assault was over.

One reason I believe she was able to get the hit that probably saved her from being killed or crippled was that she was given that revolver by a father who was wise in the ways of firearms, and understood that the gun has to fit the shooter. It was a Colt SF-VI, an uncommon late variation of the D-frame revolver Colt introduced in 1907 as the Police Positive, and brought out with a short barrel like the SF-VI's in 1926 as the Detective Special. It's one of those very rare handguns that seems to fit small female hands and large male hands equally well. As I sit here waiting for the verdict, I'm reminded of a basic fact:

For equipment to work, it has to fit the user.

If you put a five-foot-tall woman behind the wheel of a truck or automobile whose seat has been adjusted for a six-foot-six male driver, she's not going to be able to drive that vehicle as safely or as well as she could if the seat was properly adjusted. The reach to the steering wheel won't be right for her shorter arms, nor the reach to the pedals for her shorter legs. It might even get to where she's not safe for herself or others running that poorly-fitting machine.

It's exactly the same with guns. When I learned that editor Annie Tuttle — a willowy, petite female herself — wanted an article on this topic, the same week I was in court for the above-mentioned case, supporting information was more readily at hand than usual.

Basic physical differences

In Volume 66, Number Three of the *European Journal of Applied*

Five-foot-tall shooting champion Gail Pepin adjusts telescoping AR15 stock "short" and exhibits masterful control. Rifle is Ruger SR556.

Telescoping stock of AR15 is a boon to petite females and other smaller-statured shooters. This one is Ruger's iteration, the SR556.

Physiology and Occupational Therapy, we find an article titled "Gender Differences in Strength and Muscle Fiber Characteristics" by A.E.J. Miller, J.D. MacDougall, M.A. Tarnopolsky, and D.G. Sale. They write of their research on the title topic, "The women were approximately 52% and 66% as strong as the men in the upper and lower body respectively. The men were also stronger relative to lean body mass."

As a rule of thumb, it seems that few experts predict a woman to have more than two-thirds of a man's strength, even if the woman in question is the same height and weight as the man. Where does upper body strength come into it? If you're firing a rifle or shotgun from what we call "offhand," the standing position, one arm (usually the weaker, non-dominant arm) is out in front, supporting the weight of the gun and trying to hold it steady on the target.

Accordingly, a rifle or shotgun that's lighter in the front makes sense for someone whose long suit isn't upper body strength.

There's also the element of stock length. Col. Charles Askins, Jr., the legendary 20th century gun expert, was sent to Vietnam to train our allies there in riflery back in the 1950s. He found a population of soldiers whose height, on average, was about that of the average American female. The US Army had equipped them with surplus WWII Garand rifles, long guns that weighed nearly 10 pounds loaded. Col. Askins experimented with shortening the stocks at the butt and found that it helped, but the guns were still muzzle-heavy and hard for them to hold steady on target from an offhand position. When I discussed it with him back in the mid-'70s, he told me that the little M1 carbine — a much shorter gun, weighing only six or so pounds — was much easier for them to manage. The .30 carbine round was anemic compared to the powerful .30-06 cartridge fired by the Garand, but the Colonel wisely reckoned that a hit from the carbine would do a lot more damage to the enemy than a miss from the more powerful, larger rifle.

Shortening the butt

In days of old, the traditional way of fitting a kid to a rifle or shotgun was to carefully saw off the back end of the stock, perhaps in slices like sliced bread. As the youngster "grew into the gun," lengths of the stock would be glued back in place, like adding bread slices, until it was eventually back to full length. Spend enough time cruising gun shops and gun shows — or just checking the gun cabinets in some rural families' homes — and you'll see shotguns and rifles which exhibit lines on the stocks where those segments were glued back on. You can almost count them as growth rings, like the rings inside the cross-section of a tree trunk. Often, for esthetics, a slip-on recoil pad like the Pachmayr would be applied, covering the glue lines and softening kick a little bit. (Those slip-on recoil pads can be handy things, sort of like rubber galoshes for guns. Like galoshes, they look ugly and sometimes fit sloppily, but also like galoshes they more or less get the job done.)

By the mid-20th century it came into vogue for gun manufacturers to offer rifles and shotguns with "youth stocks," pre-shortened to fit smaller folks. The theory was, as the kid grows up, the parent simply removes the metal-ware, the "barreled action," and fits it to an adult-size stock.

It turned out that "youth stocks" tended to fit petite to average-size females remarkably well. That is still the case. And of course, since the adult female won't be getting any taller and her arms won't be getting any longer, the need to buy a longer stock in the future is eliminated.

Adjustable stocks

1994-2004 was the decade of the late and unlamented Clinton Assault Weapons Ban, which among other things forbade adjustable length stocks for rifles like the ubiquitous AR15. The multiple-position collapsing stock allows it to instantly adjust for arm length. It is a simple and remarkably effective solution to the stock length problem. The most common caliber for the AR15 rifle is .223 Remington/5.56mm NATO, which most of us consider a bit light for a deer rifle, but the AR platform is available in 6.8mm, a cartridge more suitable for deer-size game. Ergonomic in most other respects as well, an adjustable stock is the key for fitting such rifles to the physically smaller shooter. The telescoping stock is available for some other semiautomatic rifles as well, including one of our most popular .22s, the Ruger 10/22.

Telescoping stocks are also available for slide-action and semiautomatic shotguns. They're a functional alternative to the youth stock, if non-traditional looks don't get in the way of the given shooter's enjoyment of hunting and shooting experiences.

The dimension we're looking at is called "pull." On the gun, it is measured from the butt to the trigger. The quick "rule of thumb" test in the gun shop is to confirm that the rifle or shotgun is empty, bend your shooting arm 90 degrees, and place the butt in the inside crook of the elbow. If the trigger finger comfortably reaches the trigger, its fit for that shooter is generally considered "good to go."

The Winchester Model 70 Featherweight bolt action hunting rifle has just been reintroduced in a short stock format. The manufacturers' PR folks write, "With smaller-framed shooters and those who like a lightweight compact rifle in mind, Winchester Repeating Arms has introduced the Model 70 Featherweight Compact. The new rifle features a 20-inch barrel, a 13-inch length of pull, an overall length of 39½ inches and weighs just 6½ pounds. The Model 70 Compact is the perfect rifle for ladies, young shooters, and those looking for a light-weight mountain rifle."

For a rifle or shotgun, that thirteen-inch pull measurement seems just

Short-fingered female Florida state trooper gets the feel of her new Gen4 Glock 37 .45 at FHP Academy in Tallahassee. Photo courtesy Harris Publications.

Petite teenage competitor Nikki Pinto deftly wields her S&W M&P 9mm, its backstrap adjusted for "size small" hand, at 2009 International Defensive Pistol Association's US National Championships.

about right for the smaller-statured shooter. The Model 70 can be had in such popular hunting calibers as .243 and .308. Most of the other makers of bolt action rifles produce similar-size guns in a similar array of calibers. If you prefer a lever action, Marlin offers a shorter-stocked version of their classic .30-30. Remington and other makers have "youth-stocked" autoloading and slide-action shotguns.

Handguns

While I was writing this article, the jury brought in a quick, clean verdict: Not Guilty on all counts. As noted earlier, that life-saving little Colt .38 fit the petite shooter's hand well.

Over the years, we've found some other handguns that work very well in smaller hands. One is a classic 1935 design, the 9mm Browning Hi-Power, now also available in caliber .40 S&W. Another, counterintuitively, is a classic "big man's gun," the 1911 pistol, a/k/a the Colt .45 automatic.

After WWI, the US Army Ordnance board conducted an assessment of small arms used in the conflict. Many doughboys complained that the trigger on the 1911 .45 pistol was too long. In the 1911A1 update of that handgun in the 1920s, the trigger was shortened considerably and the frame was niched out at the back of the trigger guard area, so the shooter "could get more finger on the trigger." This turned out to be an ideal trigger reach for short fingers. 1911s are also available in calibers that kick more softly than .45, such as .38 Super and 9mm.

As "pull" in terms of stock length is the key to the shooter finding a rifle or shotgun that fits her, "trigger reach" is the most important dimension for fitting the pistol or revolver to the hand. Holding the unloaded handgun with its barrel straight in line with the long bones of the forearm, the index finger wants to be able to comfortably reach the trigger with enough leverage to pull it straight back without deviating the muzzle off target.

That finger placement is in part dependent on the weight and length of the trigger pull. With a semiautomatic target pistol that might have a "light trigger" of less than four pounds pull weight, the tip or the pad of the finger may be sufficient. (The "pad" of the finger is generally described as where you would find the whorl of the fingerprint.) This is also a suitable finger placement on most rifle and shotgun triggers. However, if the shooter has something like a double action revolver whose trigger pull is long and relatively heavy, she'll want to be contacting the trigger at the crease of the

Jennie Van Tuyl shows rapid fire recoil control with her short-stocked custom Remington 1100 20-gauge autoloading shotgun. On her hip is another gun that fits small hands well, a J-frame Smith & Wesson revolver.

index finger's distal joint. This will give the finger more leverage with which to bring that trigger straight to the rear while still holding the muzzle on target.

Adjustable grip pistols

In addition to the older handgun designs mentioned above, it is definitely wise to check out the modern generation of polymer-framed semiautomatic pistols with interchangeable "straps" on the back of the gripframe. The concept dates back to Walther of Germany in the early 1990s, and in addition to that company's products can be found on several more: the Smith & Wesson Military & Police auto pistol line, some of the Heckler and Koch pistols, the XD(m) imported to the US from Croatia by Springfield Armory, and the recently introduced Gen4 Glock series. The interchangeable hard backstraps allow the guns to be fitted to a wide variety of hands. The adjustment potential greatly improves the shooter's ability to achieve a trigger reach that fits her hand.

My friend Melissa Oman is in charge of firearms training for the Florida Highway Patrol. Not too long ago, her agency became the first department in the country to adopt the Gen4 Glock 37, a service pistol that holds eleven rounds of .45 GAP. The GAP (Glock Auto Pistol) round is a shortened version of the great old .45 ACP (Automatic Colt Pistol) cartridge which duplicates the ballistics of a full power, standard pressure ACP round. Melissa formed a selection committee that included veteran troopers and district post firearms instructors from all round the state, to evaluate a number of different firearms when it came time to select a new pistol.

The Gen4 Glock was the majority choice because, in part, of its interchangeable backstrap feature. It was imperative that the gun fit the hands of the many petite female troopers on the force. The committee felt that the Gen4 Glock achieved this better than anything else they tested.

Melissa tells me that since the adoption, virtually all the smaller-handed female troopers issued the new gun have gone with the shortest trigger reach its optional fit offers. Interestingly, a significant majority of larger-handed troopers of both genders have made the same choice.

The pool firearm

A "pool" gun is one that will be used by multiple people. The rifle and shotgun my department has in every patrol vehicle may on a given day have to be used by a day shift officer, an evening shift patrolman, and a midnight shift cop: therefore, each is a "pool weapon."

If a farmhouse has only one rifle or shotgun available, that's also a "pool gun" situation. When the fox is in the henhouse or when a home invader is kicking in the door, that gun may have to be used by six-foot Dad, five-foot Mom, or a responsible adolescent well-trained by parents in emergency management. The gun will have to fit them all adequately.

My advice for a pool firearm is this: SET IT UP TO FIT THE SMALLEST PERSON AUTHORIZED TO USE IT! Yes, the all caps and the exclamation point DO mean I'm shouting, because this point is deserving of special emphasis.

A stock that's too long for the shooter is absolutely destructive to their ability to effectively use the rifle or shotgun. Many of us have seen (or been) the little kid who fires Daddy's 12-gauge and gets knocked flat on his or her butt. The reason is that to hold the long-stocked gun up, the shooter has to rock her shoulders back. This takes her off-balance. I've seen physically strong but short-statured women trying to rapidly fire "man-size" 12-gauges with their front foot literally off the ground after the second or third shot. I've seen them staggered backward by the recoil. The reason is that the too-long stock forces them off balance.

A SHORTER than optimal length stock, by contrast, presents a much smaller problem to the larger shooter. One simply tucks into the gun. (Taking the shotgun down to 20 gauge, by the way, affords softer recoil, and still is amply powerful for many shotgun tasks.)

With handguns, a too-long trigger reach is destructive to accuracy because the shooter has to make one of two unsatisfactory accommodations. Either the finger isn't on the trigger enough, which will tend to cause the finger to "push the shot" to the left for a right-handed shooter (vice versa for a southpaw), or the hand has to twist around to where recoil is channeled painfully into the thumb instead of the web of the hand, which can severely impair recovery from recoil between shots.

However, when the gun with shorter trigger reach is in a larger hand, it's no big trick for the shooter to simply flex the median joint of the trigger finger outward a little bit, to make the trigger pull manageable. Thus, with handgun as well as long gun, the larger shooter adapts to the shorter person's firearm more easily and effectively than the smaller person can adapt to a firearm fitted for a larger shooter.

Bottom line

Fit. It's a critical factor in the interface between us humans and the machines and tools we use. The firearm is a tool. Fit it right to the user, and it will serve you well. Δ

More good reading:

The Coming American Dictatorship

By John Silveira

Preparing to battle the winter blahs

By Claire Wolfe

I know the perfect, guaranteed way to beat the winter blahs. If you're in the northern hemisphere, leave on November 1st and spend the next six months on a South Pacific island. If you're in the southern hemisphere, stay there for now, then head to the California coast next May. Big Sur is nice.

Oh. Wait. You say you haven't won the lottery yet? Your Uncle Scrooge hasn't died and left you all his gold coins? Well, darn. Guess we need a Plan B.

Although the sun may still beam benevolently as you read this, it's wise to start getting ready for winter long before winter is ready for you. That's true whether your plan involves buying a ticket to Tahiti or staying put. So this article is going to focus on advance preparation for personal health and happiness in the year's dark months.

Most of us need extra help during the cold months to stay in the best mood and the best physical shape. The two go together.

We all know about Seasonal Affective Disorder (SAD), that mysterious malady that leaves some unfortunate souls so depressed they can scarcely function in the dark months. But did you know that researchers have recently verified what most of us have suspected all along? In winter, the average person — not afflicted with SAD — tends to be more grouchy, unhappy, and anxious than in the lighter months.

We also know — perhaps more than we wish — about winter comfort-food cravings, lack of exercise, and weight gain. Unfortunately, winter blahs and winter blimp-outs often go together in a nasty negative feedback loop: Feel bad? Eat. Feel bad? Lie around like a lump. Eat and lie around like a lump? Feel bad.

Cold, dark weather brings cravings for comfort foods. Instead of indulging in cakes, cookies, pies, candy, or starchy vegetables, plan to keep healthy alternatives around. Raw, unsalted nuts can be as richly filling as any treat. Spicy cheese lights up the tastebuds. And vegetables, even when served with high-calorie, high-fat sauces or dips, are still better than carb overload.

Good weather, especially in the backwoods, forces us into activity. The veggies must be planted, weeded, harvested, canned. Lawns mowed. Vehicles washed. Houses painted. And on and on. When the days turn dark and cold, even folks who profess to enjoy all four seasons may have to force themselves into action. Even in the active country life, inertia tends to take over.

We can't banish seasonal demons entirely, any more than we can banish rain, wind, and ice. Yet the worst that winter has to offer when it comes to bad mood and bad habits can be managed with some advance planning.

What do I know about it? you might ask. Well, I've spent most of the last 30 years in the dreary, drippy Pacific Northwest, where "winter" drags on for nine months (in a good year). I also lived many years in Minnesota, where the sun tends to shine even in January, but somehow manages to pull all the warmth out of the earth the more it glitters. People in Minnesota claim to love their winters. They prove it by cross-country skiing on city streets, ice fishing (i.e. getting drunk in cramped shacks on top of frozen lakes), spinning their cars for sport on the surfaces of said lakes, thumping their chests with Nordic hardihood — and still going completely bonkers by February. And then there was Wyoming. Let's not even talk about Wyoming.

I am no doctor, nutritionist, or therapist and you shouldn't take my words as authoritative. But believe me when I say I speak from experience about making the best of winter.

Let there be light

Until 15 years ago, there was no treatment for severe cases of winter's emotional blahs. You just had to tough it out. In the 90s, scientists discovered that short, intense exposure to certain types of light (especially in the morning) eliminated or reduced the depression of SAD. People with severe winter moods began sitting in front of light boxes with their eyes open for half an hour or more. It helped.

In 2010, further research indicated that the bluish light often used should be replaced by green or white for greater effectiveness. But the fact is that not many people have the time or inclination to sit in front of a light box every morning.

Fortunately, for both SAD sufferers and the rest of us, there's a more simple, inexpensive way to get light: bundle up, grab the dog's leash, and take a walk. Do it at mid-day for maximum sun exposure. This benefits you even if you don't have much sunshine in your part of the world. The diffused light of a cloudy day is still vastly more powerful than household light. Not to mention that both being outdoors and getting exercise are known mood lifters.

Another thing you can do: build reflectors that direct winter sunlight into the windows of your home. This not only improves mood, it may also help save on energy costs. The time to build those reflectors is now, before you need them.

If the darkening months affect you so badly that you have to drag yourself through daily activities and you spend your spare time stuffing cookies and cake down your gullet, you may have SAD and light is just one of several treatments. Others include negative-ion generators used during sleep, cognitive behavior therapy, and as a last-ditch, SSRI antidepressants. If past winters have depressed you to that degree, now is the time to start exploring options. Specialized light fixtures for SAD are expensive to buy, but you can purchase the bulbs cheaply online and make your own. Start now and before the days get dark you'll know whether you have the time or patience to sit in front of a light box every day. If not, you'll still have time to check out other options before enduring seasonal depression.

For SAD sufferers and the rest of us, a winter boost may also be found in nutritional supplements.

Vitamins and minerals for winter

Even if you don't normally take supplements, there are a few you should consider for the dark, cold months. It's time to lay in your supply and begin dosing yourself as soon as the days start feeling short. Among the most important supplements for winter are:

Vitamin D (specifically D3). "The sunshine vitamin," your mother may have called it. Your body generates it when sunlight comes in contact with the oils in your skin. In winter, even in sunny, Minnesota-type climates, our bodies make less vitamin D, partly because we go outdoors less, partly because we're wrapped in jackets, mufflers, hats, and mittens when we do, so our skin and sunlight have less chance to interact.

There is no direct evidence that vitamin D lifts our seasonal moods. But the importance of vitamin D becomes more apparent with every study. Among other things, it appears to be a powerful cancer preventative. Yet nearly all Americans are deficient

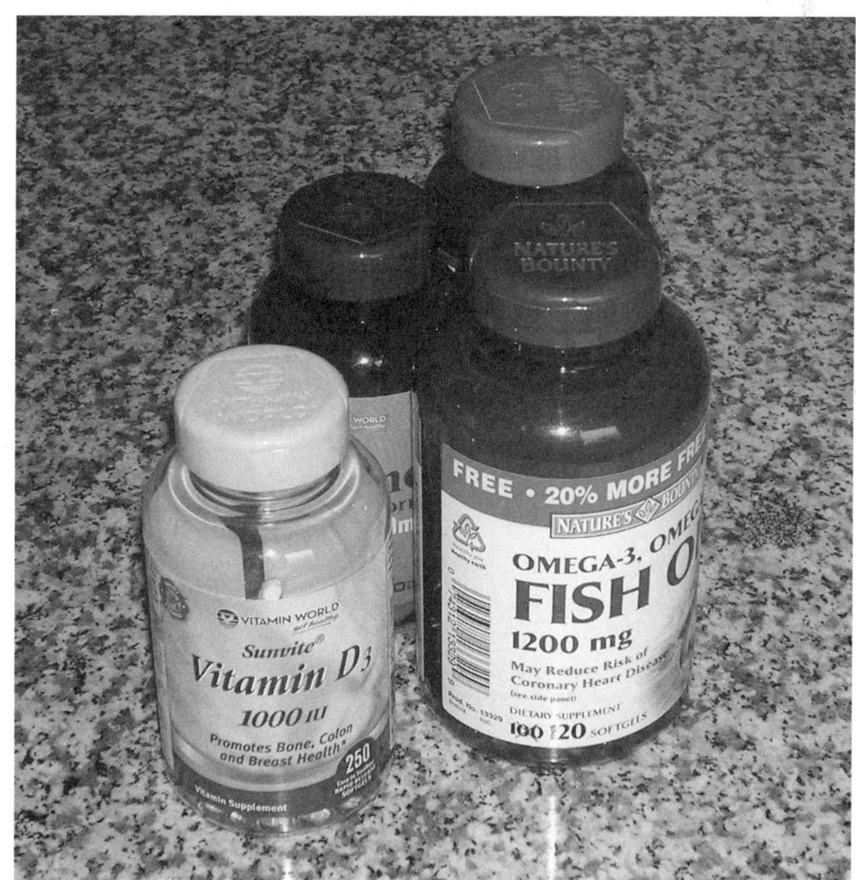

Supplements can help offset both the long-term and short-term effects of winter. Vitamin D capsules make up for the lack of sunlight on our skin and fish oil helps keep our brain tuned up. Both have other vital benefits, as well.

in it, and the problem is worse in winter than in summer.

Short of a blood test, there is no way to know whether we're actually getting enough vitamin D. Recommended levels vary by age and are different for pregnant and nursing women. A dosage of 5,000 IU may be a good seat-of-pants level to start with. This is higher than the government-recommended level, but a lot of people believe the government has badly missed the mark on its guesstimated dosage. In any case, do your own research before deciding on the right amount for you. New information on both the impressive value and proper dosage of vitamin D seems to come out weekly.

Fish oil. A fish-oil capsule with every meal is good for battling winter's brain-fog and may help prevent both heart disease and Alzheimers.

Melatonin. Melatonin is a hormone generated by our pineal glands, which helps to regulate our daily body clock. Normally, melatonin levels start to rise in the evening. They stay elevated for most of the night, then drop in the early morning, helping us to wake up. Shorter days may cause us to produce melatonin off-schedule, affecting both sleep and mood. Taking a melatonin supplement in the late afternoon or early evening may produce a better night's rest and happier days.

Other winter helpers: Biotin to keep skin healthy; vitamin B-12 to fight depression and stress; magnesium (especially for cold dry climates) to combat dehydration; vitamin C, which won't cure colds but can shorten their severity and duration; zinc, also good for colds and the immune system; vitamin A for helping your eyes adjust and for general health.

Something as simple as wearing bright colors can help battle the blahs. Here, cheerful hand-spun, hand-dyed wool waits to be knitted into a hat and mittens. Beside it, a playful scarf with foot-long fringe is already made out of glittery storebought novelty yarn.

Good food, good weight

You crave carbs in the winter, admit it. So do I. Nice, filling baked potatoes. Rich, home-baked breads. And desserts. Oh my, those desserts!

Carb cravings are natural. Our bodies are probably telling us to store fat, as our ancestors so badly needed to do through the lean late winter months. Only problem is, we're privileged not to have those lean months any more. And our daily diets, year-round, are already so carb-heavy that we're killing ourselves.

(A disclaimer: I practice primal nutrition — aka neanderthal or caveman diet. "Going primal" means eating vegetables, nuts, seeds, meat, fish, eggs, fruits, and some dairy. It also means keeping carb intake low and avoiding grains — which is not necessarily for everybody. My body does great on this regime, and even forgives me when I occasionally give into my #1 carb craving, great bread or crackers. So keep in mind that I have an anti-carb bias. Make your own choices as your mind and body dictate. But it's undeniable that our plunge into horrific rates of obesity, diabetes, and fatty-liver disease came along just as the federal government began pushing us to eat "healthy" carbs and avoid supposedly unhealthy fats. Just something to think about.)

In any case, the combination of decreased activity, extra calories, and winter carb-gobbling leads to a lot of problems, from depression to heart disease to hating ourselves when we look in the mirror.

The solution? Don't try to deny your seasonal cravings for richer, more filling food. Just direct yourself in a slightly different way. If cakes and cookies are your thing, try a little multi-grain bread and butter instead. If you pig out on bread slathered with high-calorie toppings, switch to rice cakes or switch to a healthier topping like almond or cashew butter. If you just can't live without something rich and warm, go back to old issues of *Backwoods Home* and make some of the lovely casseroles, stews, and soups created by Ilene Duffy, Richard Blunt, and many other *BHM* food writers.

This is yet another area when advance planning can help. Lay in healthy foods. Don't even get the ingredients for your biggest dietary "sins." Take a look at your pantry and see what needs to be used up (it's more likely to be carrots than sugar). Clip those filling-but-healthy recipes and lay out a plan for using them from November through March. Look forward to making and eating dishes that are comforting, but not sugar-loaded.

And keep moving!

Let there be bright

It's a small thing, but it can make quite a difference. In choosing your winter wardrobe — whether you're making your own, buying at thrift stores, or splurging at the mall — look for brighter-than-usual colors.

Forget black or gray or brown. Even forest green or deep purple may be too dull. Go for burnt orange, bright red, hot pink, sky blue, grass green, magenta, yellow, or any other color that says, "Winter, you won't win."

If you like the dark, subdued, traditional fall and winter colors (as I do), or if your cold-season wardrobe is already full of them and isn't ready for a re-do, get or make some brighter accent pieces — a gold vest for a guy's suit, a red tie, a mint green scarf, a silver belt. Thrift stores — and plenty of lead time for shopping — are your friends.

And more!

Starting now, plan several winter excursions. They don't have to be anything fancy. You don't have to go to a ski resort or take a Caribbean cruise. Just tell yourself that — once a month, say — you'll take a weekend and do something fun. Then make specific plans to do it. Get snowed out one weekend? Move the plan to the next available date; don't cancel it.

Buy or make your holiday presents early. Begin planning or finding supplies now. Avoid the frantic feeling, the pressures, the incredibly annoying repetitions of "The Little Drummer Boy" piped into every store. You might even save money by not putting yourself in the position of having to buy something at a bad time.

Plant fall bulbs. Lots of them. Even if you're not normally a gardener. You'll feel better in January knowing you'll soon be seeing crocuses and daffodils poking their heads through the snow and mud.

Hold a late-season garage sale to clear the clutter. You're going to spend a lot of time indoors; make your environment pleasant.

Chop wood. (But you already know all about that, don't you?) Sew up some insulating window shades — in cheerful colors. Plan a quilting bee or an old-fashioned community corn-husking.

There's plenty you can do to ward off winter blahs. But whatever you do, planning ahead really helps. Once winter inertia sets in, it's harder to come up with new ideas and get moving on them. Have some plans ready — for eating, playing, making things, or whatever — and you'll find it a lot easier to keep yourself and your family active, happy, and healthy while you wait for the sun to return. Δ

Let there be light

Extra help for bringing light into your winter world can be found on the Internet. Some are especially helpful for anybody who suffers from Seasonal Affective Disorder (SAD), but other options can bring in light and cut down on winter heating bills for anybody.

Build your own inexpensive lightbox with compact fluorescents
http://borislegradic.blogspot.com/2008/12/lightbox-construction.html

Build your own inexpensive non-fluorescent lightbox
http://www.sean-crist.com/personal/pages/sad/

A light shelf may help reflect sunlight into your rooms if your windows are on the sunny side.
http://www.wisegeek.com/what-is-a-light-shelf.htm

A heliostat can also reflect light into your home even if your windows aren't on the sunny side.
http://www.iwilltry.org/b/projects/build-a-heliostat-for-solar-heating-and-lighting/

Solar tubes: More energy efficient than skylights
https://tedstips.wordpress.com/2011/03/04/suntubes/

More self-reliance in *Emergency Preparedness and Survival Guide*

Lenie in the kitchen

Bean, rice, and chicken soup

By Ilene Duffy

My mother was a teenager during the Great Depression and although her family never went without food on the table, she often talked about having to wear shoes that were too small for her growing feet and needing to wait until she was in her 20s before getting necessary dental work done. She learned to be frugal while growing up which served her well many years later when she became a widow when I was 15 and my younger sister only 11. Overnight, our middle class household needed to tighten its financial belt.

But she persevered and in her quiet way taught my three sisters and me timeless lessons — thoughtfulness, patience, determination, generosity. I'm sure relatives and family friends would agree that one of her most endearing qualities was how she made her kitchen so warm and welcoming. It wasn't just the delicious food she prepared, but the kindness that she exuded that made her kitchen table a memorable place to visit and linger.

I think of her often when feeding my own family. With today's recession and food prices going up almost daily, I wanted to conjure up a soup recipe that might have been served at her family's table back in the early 1930s. My requirements for this soup were that it would be easy on the budget, predominantly use fresh produce from my vegetable and herb garden as well as storage foods from my pantry, be healthy, and make enough to feed our family including three hungry teenage boys.

This bean, rice, and chicken soup is a keeper — easy to prepare, delicious, uses a lot of ingredients from my pantry, and feeds a houseful.

We have a small herb garden behind the parking lot at the *BHM* office. Before making the soup at home, I snipped off six sage leaves and a few sprigs of thyme. I've got the dried herbs at home in my spice cabinet, but the fresh herbs really make a huge difference. The oohs and ahhs I heard from my soup tasters have inspired me to put some neglected pots on my deck to better use. I'm going to plant some sage and thyme in them so I'll have fresh herbs readily accessible for my next pot of soup.

Bean, rice, and chicken soup

8 cups chicken broth
½ large onion, chopped
1 carrot, thinly sliced
3 stalks celery, chopped (leaves included)
1 zucchini, chopped
1 yellow summer squash, chopped
½ tsp. dried basil
6 leaves fresh sage, chopped
1 tsp. fresh thyme leaves
⅓ cup parsley leaves, chopped
½ tsp. freshly ground pepper
1 can (15 oz.) black beans, rinsed and drained
1 can (15 oz.) white cannellini beans, rinsed and drained
2 cups cooked chicken, diced
6 cloves garlic, finely chopped
2 cups water
1 pat of butter
¾ cup uncooked brown basmati rice, rinsed
salt to taste

Preparations:

Measure broth into a large Dutch oven or stock pot and heat to a low simmer. Add remaining ingredients in order listed except the water, butter, rice, and salt. Stir occasionally. In a separate pot, add 2 cups of water and a pat of butter. Cover with a tight fit-

These biscuits are especially good when they are hot out of the oven.

ting lid and bring to a boil. Add rinsed rice, stir, replace lid, turn heat down to a low simmer, and cook until all water is absorbed, about 30-35 minutes. Turn heat off, keeping lid on and let sit for about 10 minutes. Spoon rice into soup and cook on very low heat about 10 more minutes. Add salt to taste if necessary.

Herbed bread or biscuits go very nicely with this soup. I found a new biscuit recipe I wanted to try and changed it in order to incorporate a bit of whole wheat flour. I also added dried herbs.

Herbed biscuits

1 Tbsp. dry yeast
¼ cup warm water
½ tsp. honey
1½ cups flour
½ cup whole wheat flour
2 tsp. baking powder
1 Tbsp. sugar
½ tsp. salt
½ tsp. dried oregano
¼ tsp. dried thyme
2 Tbsp. butter
2 Tbsp. shortening
½ cup plus 2 Tbsp. room temperature milk

Preparations:

In a ceramic bowl, dissolve yeast in warm water, stir, then stir in the honey. Let sit until bubbly.

In a large bowl, sift together flour, whole wheat flour, baking powder, sugar, salt, and herbs. Cut in the butter and shortening with a pastry cutter or two knives. Add the room temperature milk to the yeast mixture and then add it to the flour mixture. Toss gently with a fork until incorporated. Place the dough on a floured board and knead gently a few times.

Flour a rolling pin and roll out the dough 1/3-inch thick. Cut with a biscuit-cutter dipped in flour and place the rounds on a greased baking sheet. Gather up the scraps of dough left on the board and roll out again to make more biscuits. Let the biscuits rise, lightly covered, about an hour. Preheat oven to 375°F. Bake about 10 minutes until light brown on top. Serve warm. Δ

Millet: An economical and healthy food

By Habeeb Salloum

Of little importance in the diets of North Americans, millet, the least popular of grains in the Western Hemisphere, has been relegated to the lowly feed for birds. Yet, for the inhabitants of Asia, Russia, and sub-Saharan Africa it has been a top food for hundreds of years. A staple in the Orient long before rice, it has remained for centuries an ideal grain for those with little financial means.

In Ethiopia the national dish, *injera*, is made from millet and in the Indian sub-continent where it was cultivated in antiquity it has continued on the daily menu until our times. It has been long valued by the masses in that part of the world for its wholesome and healthy qualities. In the foothills of the Himalayas the long-lived Hunzakuts attribute their longevity to its nutritional elements.

Known as Guinea or Kaffir corn, it comes in various types, the most important being: pearl or bulrush, foxtail, and finger or red; and in shades from white to green and yellow. In the preparation of food, all species can be utilized as a replacement for other grains..

Called "the poor man's cereal," millet is easy to grow in almost any type of soil and is extremely productive. Each plant produces a number of stalks with a single head that, at times, yields about two ounces of seed.

In terms of mineral and vitamin content this ancient food is one of the richest grains available. Besides calcium, carbohydrates, fat, fiber, iron, phosphorous, potassium, niacin, riboflavin, and thiamine, it contains a nearly complete protein which goes well with dairy products and legumes. Even though it lacks vitamins A and C, it is still a valuable cholesterol-free and healthy food.

It is low in starch, easily digestible, and aids in the relief of constipation, is beneficial for weight gain, and is good for general emaciation. Its amino acids closely resemble those of eggs and some types contain more than ten times the calcium of wheat. In Africa the seeds are brewed into a beer that is drunk to relieve stomachaches and rheumatic pains.

An appetizing grain with a pleasant flavor, especially when pan-roasted, millet is sold whole, hulled, cracked, or as a flour. It is usually found in natural food stores or health food sections in large supermarkets. Very resistant to rotting and insects, it stores well in a dry place for long periods of time without losing any of its flavor or nutrients.

Millet cooks quickly and adds a sapid nutty taste to foods. It can be prepared with rice or in place of rice and is excellent in salads, soups, or with any type of meat. Above all, as a porridge it has few rivals.

On the other hand, its flour lacks gluten and cannot be baked into leavened bread but it blends well with wheat flour — a mixture that is very good for breads, cakes, and puddings. It is said that cooks who give this grain of the ancients a try are entrapped with its fluffy texture and toothsome qualities and, thereafter, add it to their storehouse of foods.

Left, uncooked millet; right, plain cooked millet

Plain millet:

4 Tbsp. butter
1 cup millet, rinsed
¾ tsp. salt
¼ tsp. pepper
2½ cups water

Melt butter in a frying pan, then add millet and stir-fry for 3 minutes. Stir in remaining ingredients then bring to a boil. Cover and cook over medium/low heat for 20 minutes, stirring a number of times to ensure that the millet does not stick to the bottom of the frying pan, then re-cover. Turn off heat then allow millet to further cook in its own steam for another 30 minutes. Stir with a fork to loosen the kernels. Serve as a main dish, side dish, or in salads. Serves 4.

Millet with vermicelli:

4 Tbsp. cooking oil
⅓ cup vermicelli, broken into small pieces
1 cup millet, rinsed
¾ tsp. salt
¼ tsp. pepper
3 cups water

Heat oil in a frying pan, then stir-fry vermicelli over medium heat for 2 minutes.

Add millet and stir-fry for a further 2 minutes. Stir in the remaining ingredients and bring to a boil. Cover and cook over medium/low heat for 20 minutes, stirring a number of times to ensure that the millet does not stick to the bottom of the frying pan, then re-cover. Turn off heat then allow millet to further cook in its own steam for another 30 minutes. Stir with a fork to loosen the kernels then serve as a main dish or side dish with stews. Serves 4.

Millet and chickpea salad:

2 cups cooked plain millet
1 can (19 oz.) chickpeas, drained
2 medium tomatoes, diced into ¼-inch pieces
4 Tbsp. finely chopped green onions
2 Tbsp. finely chopped fresh coriander leaves
4 Tbsp. olive oil
4 Tbsp. lemon juice
½ tsp. salt
¼ tsp. pepper

Millet and chickpea salad

Place all ingredients in a salad bowl and thoroughly mix, then serve immediately. Serves about 6.

Millet and lentil soup:

3 Tbsp. cooking oil
2 medium onions, chopped
4 cloves garlic, crushed
1 small hot pepper, finely chopped
4 Tbsp. finely chopped fresh coriander leaves
½ cup lentils
2 tsp. salt
1 tsp. pepper
1 tsp. cumin
8 cups water
½ cup millet, rinsed
1 zucchini, 6 to 8 inches long, diced into ½ inch cubes

Heat oil in a saucepan, then sauté onions, garlic, hot pepper, and coriander leaves over medium heat for 10 minutes. Add remaining ingredients, except millet and zucchini, then bring to boil. Cover and cook over medium heat for 20 minutes, then stir in the millet and zucchini and re-cover. Cook for further 40 minutes or until both lentils and millet are done. Serves 8 to 10.

Fried egg and millet:

1 cup millet, rinsed
4 cups water
4 eggs
4 Tbsp. finely chopped green onions
¾ tsp. salt
½ tsp. pepper
⅛ tsp. cayenne
4 Tbsp. butter

Place millet and water in a saucepan then bring to boil. Cover and cook over medium heat for 20 minutes, then drain millet completely and set aside.

In the meantime, thoroughly mix remaining ingredients, except the butter, then set aside.

Millet pudding

Melt butter in a frying pan, then stir-fry millet over medium heat for 3 minutes. Stir in egg mixture, then stir-fry for a further 3 minutes. Serve hot. Serves 4 to 6.

Millet with shrimp:

4 Tbsp. butter
2 cups shelled fresh or thawed frozen shrimp
4 cloves garlic, crushed
1 Tbsp. finely chopped fresh coriander leaves
2 Tbsp. flour
¼ tsp. salt
¼ tsp. pepper
⅛ tsp. cayenne
1½ cups water
2 cups cooked hot plain millet

Melt butter in a saucepan, then stir-fry shrimp, garlic, and coriander leaves over medium heat for about 6 minutes or until shrimp begins to turn pinkish. Add flour then stir-fry for a 2 minutes more. Add remaining ingredients, except the millet, then, stirring constantly, bring to boil and cook over medium heat for 3 minutes.

Place millet on a serving platter, then cover with the shrimp and their sauce and serve immediately. Serves 4 to 6.

Chicken and millet paella:

4 Tbsp. olive oil
1 pound boneless chicken, fat removed and cut into ½ inch cubes
1 tsp. salt
½ tsp. pepper
1 large onion, chopped
2 cloves garlic, crushed
½ small hot pepper, finely chopped
1 cup millet, rinsed
1 cup chicken broth
2 cups water
½ tsp. ground ginger
¼ tsp. ground coriander seeds
½ tsp. turmeric
1½ cups fresh or frozen lima beans

Heat oil in a frying pan, then sprinkle chicken with ½ teaspoon of salt and ¼ teaspoon of pepper. Sauté over medium heat until chicken cubes begin to brown, then remove cubes with a slotted spoon and set aside.

In the same oil, sauté onion, garlic, and hot pepper over medium heat for 10 minutes then add millet and stir-fry for a further 3 minutes, adding more oil if necessary. Add the chicken broth, water, ginger, coriander, turmeric, and the remaining salt and pepper then bring to boil. Transfer frying pan contents to a low-edged casserole then spread chicken pieces and lima beans evenly over top. Bake uncovered in a 350° F preheated oven for 40 minutes or until millet is done, then serve hot from casserole. Serves about 6.

Millet pudding:

4 cups milk
½ cup millet
4 Tbsp. butter
1 cup raisins, rinsed
½ cup shredded coconut
½ cup brown sugar
1 tsp. vanilla

Place milk and millet in a saucepan then bring to a boil, stirring a number of times. Cover, then cook over medium/low heat for 30 minutes, stirring a number of times. Stir in remaining ingredients, cook for further 5 minutes, adding a little more milk if necessary, stirring often. Serve hot or chilled. Serves about 8.

Note: All the above recipes call for the whole millet seeds. Δ

Buckboard bacon

By Tanya Kelley

Last year, our family processed a hog for the first time. We made roasts, pork chops, bacon, Italian sausage, breakfast link sausages, and hams. All of the results were quite tasty, but there was one thing that, for our family, just wasn't worth the effort: Ham.

Now, I know that isn't going to be the case for a lot of people, but we aren't big on ham around here. We'll eat sliced deli ham on sandwiches, but I sure don't want to cook a whole ham for making into sandwich meat. Not to mention the fact that, out of all the products we processed from the pig, the ham was the most time consuming.

When butchering time rolled around this fall, I intended on making all the hams into fresh roasts, instead of curing and smoking them. After all, what else could you do with them? Then a friend told me about buckboard bacon. Traditional bacon is made from pork bellies. Buckboard bacon uses other cuts of the hog, but is cured and smoked just like bacon.

Our family might not be ham lovers, but we will happily devour bacon. Buckboard bacon was the perfect solution, it seemed. Because we had never sampled buckboard bacon, I didn't want to make all of the hams into bacon, just in case we didn't like it. I decided that I would divide the hams into three portions — one third for sausage, one third for roasts, and the last third for buckboard bacon.

Buckboard bacon is every bit as easy to make as regular bacon. As we processed the pig, I set aside the ham meat according to its intended use. Once I had enough meat for the buckboard bacon, I cut it into 2-inch-thick slabs, so that it looked somewhat like the pork belly slabs.

Once the meat was weighed, I made the curing mix — ¼ cup canning and pickling (non-iodized) salt, 1 cup of sugar, ½ cup table mustard (not powdered), and 1 teaspoon ground black pepper for every 5 pounds of bacon. I mixed it well, then rubbed it into the meat, making sure it got worked into any crevices.

It might seem odd that the curing mix contained mustard. I know it made me nervous. I like mustard on sandwiches, but did I want mustard-flavored bacon? Definitely not. However, the finished product doesn't even hint of mustard, so you can use it with confidence.

I made my own curing mix but you don't have to. I checked out the hunting supplies section of our local farm store and found a variety of packaged cures to choose from. If you can't find something you like locally, there are countless choices online. I also found many curing mix recipes online.

I layered the slabs in my plastic dish pans and covered them with plastic wrap. I had three pans full, so I stacked them. That forced the meat down, so the curing solution pressed into it.

I'm fortunate enough to have a root cellar that stays between freezing and 40 degrees, so I could park the pans in there to cure for 10 days. If you don't have a root cellar, a refrigerator works just as well, as long as you keep the containers sealed so they don't absorb any flavor from other foods in the fridge.

I turned the meat once a day, re-layering so the top pieces rotated to the bottom. I also rotated the order of the stacked dish pans. The cure draws the liquid out of the meat, so it is soon sitting in its own juices. Rotating the stacks makes sure all the meat gets completely soaked in the cure.

On the tenth day, I brought the pans inside. I rinsed the meat, making sure to wash out any crevices. Then I put it back in the dish pans and filled them with cold water to soak.

I soaked it for an hour, then fried a sample piece to test for saltiness. Wow! It tasted like bacon, without the fat and with just a hint of pork chop taste. It was so good, my husband voted to *not* smoke it. Call me lazy, but I agreed. Why tamper with perfection, I thought. Perhaps we'll smoke it next time.

I put the slabs in the freezer until they were chilled (but not frozen) and then brought them out for slicing. Chilling the meat, almost to the point of freezing, makes it stiffer and easier to slice. I wanted to slice it thin, like bacon, so that was important.

Since buckboard bacon isn't from pork bellies, some of the slices weren't exactly bacon strip shaped. Actually, very few of the pieces came out looking like bacon strips, despite my attempt to cut the meat into slabs. That doesn't affect the taste, though. I sliced all of it, in various shapes, and then realized I had another challenge. Where was I going to put it all? Our freezer was already bursting at the seams.

I wrapped and stuffed what I could into the nooks and crannies in the freezer. About half of the bacon didn't fit. Time for Plan B.

Buckboard bacon doesn't have much fat on it, compared to traditional bacon, so I figured it would dehydrate well. I spread the meat on the dehydrator trays. Ten hours later, I had some delicious "bacon jerky." Or something like that. It's great to eat dried, that was for sure. It reconstitutes and fries up for breakfast well too.

The dehydrated bacon keeps without refrigeration. That meant I could send some samples to my sons in California and Florida. Imagine their surprise when I told them I had just shipped them some bacon from our pig — in the mail!

Because the buckboard bacon has very little fat, you have to add a bit of fat to the pan when frying it, whether dehydrated/reconstituted or frozen. Even so, there's less fat than regular bacon — good news if you're trying to cut back. It also cooks much faster than bacon so keep a close watch on it while you're cooking it. Once the bacon is cooked, you can still scramble your eggs in the drippings, for a tasty breakfast.

So far, we've eaten the buckboard bacon as jerky, fried like regular bacon, and boiled in a pot of beans. The flavor is great and we've never been disappointed. The reconstituted or freshly fried bacon is great for sandwiches — much better than ham, if you ask me!

Just like anyone can get pork bellies and make bacon at home, anyone can make buckboard bacon at home too. However, if you aren't able to raise your own pig, buckboard bacon may be even easier to make. You can use any cut of pork, so you don't have to special order pork bellies. Another advantage? I see a lot of grocery store ads for pork roasts — but I never have seen the grocery store have a sale on pork bellies.

The only disadvantage I have found to buckboard bacon? It is disappearing at an alarming rate. If this keeps up, I may have to make all of the ham into buckboard bacon next fall! Δ

Raising kids *simply*

By Patrice Lewis

Have you ever wondered what it would be like to live simply? When asked what constitutes a simple life, nine out of ten people will answer something along the lines of "living in the country" or "no commute" or "having no mortgage."

By this definition, however, those who live in the city, commute to a job, or have a mortgage are excluded from the simple life… right?

Wrong. Simple living is none of those things. A truly simple life can be accomplished virtually anywhere, by virtually anyone, under virtually any circumstances. No need to live in the country, though I'll admit from experience it's (mostly) a lot of fun.

So what precisely does it take to live simply? The answer is, well, simple. In fact it can be distilled down to three words. Got a pen? Here they are:

MAKE. GOOD. CHOICES.

That's it. A simple life is nothing more than the accumulation of sound, sensible, rational, thoughtful choices.

And make no mistake, good choices are *the* single most important factor for a simple life. If you *choose* to rob a bank, don't be surprised if your life gets very complex. If you *choose* to live within your means, your life will be simpler than those who don't.

The concept of making good choices goes across the board for all aspects of our lives, including who we marry and how we raise our kids. And frankly, raising our kids simply is one of the greatest gifts we can give them.

Some may ask — how can we raise kids simply in today's complex culture? And what precisely does it mean to raise simple kids?

What simplicity is not

First let's examine what simplicity for kids is *not.*

Simple living is not "green living" or otherwise saving the planet. I've read books on raising "simple" kids which focus solely and exclusively on being green. Bunk. Personally I don't care if you impart these values to your children or not — but please note this constitutes a *belief,* not a *behavior.* Beliefs may or may not simplify one's life; but behaviors (which after all are based on *choices*) will make or break a person.

Simplicity is not giving your kids unlimited freedom to (cough) "express themselves." Naturally I'm not suggesting you stifle their childish impulsive emotions or creativity — far from it. But too many parents think "expressing themselves" means children should be allowed to behave like horrible brats, unrestrained by their parents or other adults. I've often found that parents who want their children to "express themselves" are just too lazy to discipline them.

As an example, I know a homeschooling family whose two boys were always encouraged to express themselves and were seldom disciplined. The mother took pride in her sons' spirited behavior and actually *would not allow* her husband (the boys' father) to discipline "her" boys. (You can see the problems already, just with this information.) As a result, the boys often "expressed" themselves by screaming four-letter curse words at estranged playmates in public, or taunting a handicapped child in an art class to the point where the teacher had to expel them. The boys are now teens and have become young thugs, verbally abusing their mother and despising their emasculated father. It's a sad and rather extreme example of a lack of discipline. These young men are not likely to ever have a "simple" life unless they can correct their own course … which seems unlikely.

What simplicity is

So just what leads to a simple life for children? The following are some ideas:

Decrease household drama

In this day of easy divorce, it's becoming a rare child who grows up in the same home as both his biological parents. Children who grow up in homes full of strife and/or with multiple marriage partners ("This is your new daddy!") develop a shaky, unstable foundation that will affect them forever.

This is often the elephant in the room no one wants to see because too many adults are caught up in their own wishes and desires. No one wants to admit that multiple divorces, marital strife, and tense emotions damage children. In today's "feel good" culture (That means "feel good" for the parents, *not* the children), adults are encouraged to do whatever they like without considering the needs of their kids.

Our daughters planting seeds in the garden

Needless to say this doesn't apply when a spouse has harmful addictions, is violent, or other manifestations of *choosing badly to begin with.* But by limiting the drama in a home, children can funnel their emotional energy into growing up, developing their talents, and becoming productive members of society — rather than funneling their emotional energies into hiding from drunken abusive parents or wondering who mama will bring home next to be their new daddy.

Sorry if this offends, but the statistics are indisputable: an intact home is possibly *the* single biggest factor to raising secure children who will have the ability to make those critically good choices that will contribute toward a simple life.

Moral foundation

Raise your children with a strong moral foundation. Often a religious upbringing contributes to this, but all the churching in the world won't help if the parents don't model strong ethics themselves.

These ethical choices should include keeping one's word, working hard, being honest, being kind, and other important and intangible behaviors. Children who have a strong moral foundation upon which to stand grow up more likely to make good choices as teens and adults. It is astounding how much kids internalize the values of their parents, and how strongly this will influence their adult lives.

I recall two seemingly minor examples from my childhood. In one instance, my mother was on the phone with a store who had undercharged her for a particular item. That's right, *undercharged.* The store was generously trying to waive the difference, but my mother wasn't having it. "You folks have to make a living too," she told the representative, and insisted on repaying the price difference even though it was only a few dollars. It was an example of ethical behavior I've never forgotten.

The second instance came when my mother was rebuking one of my teenage brothers after a boyish scrape. She told him, "Your behavior is a reflection upon your father, and I will *not* have your father disrespected in this manner."

This simple sentence carried astounding weight. It showed us an example of marital respect and unity, how our actions reflect upon our family, and how the choices we make have an impact. Again, it was an example I've never forgotten … and which I've carried into my own marriage.

Training

I expect decent parents to raise their children wisely, and this means *training* children on how they are expected to behave. Obviously, this is best done starting at a young age and should include all aspects of the kind of behavior you expect. Manners, politeness, respect for elders, not interrupting, not whining … all this takes training.

And training takes *consistency.* Too many parents do a half-assed job teaching their children proper behavior. But just as you can't "train" a puppy to heel or stay with one or two sessions, neither can you expect your children to learn a life-long habit of respectful behavior or self-control by enforcing it once or twice when they're toddlers. Believe me, training children takes *years.*

As an example, I know a woman who hails from the south where children are expected to address their elders as "sir" and "ma'am." She and her husband have three daughters: two teens and a toddler. I find it refreshing how the mother will gently correct the toddler whenever she forgets these respectful terms. The two older teens have this down pat and therefore model the behavior for their youngest sister. The toddler's parents are consistent in their firm expectations for how they want their children to behave, and the teenage girls are living proof that it works.

Training should include respect for parents. Our children were *never* permitted to speak or act disrespectfully towards us when they were young. Now that they're teenagers, they still act respectfully and we have *no* teenage rebellion. Not even a hint.

A side benefit of consistent training is that children learn self-control. If young kids are not permitted to butt into an adult conversation and demand instant gratification for a wish, they learn the world does not revolve around their whims. Needless to say, this self-control serves them well when adolescent hormones are bulging at the seams.

Set boundaries

The whole idea about raising children is to set firm boundaries and parameters and not to let the children step outside those boundaries. Contrary to a more progressive view on such issues, boundaries do *not* represent a prison for children. They represent freedom.

Naturally these boundaries will shift and change with a child's age, maturity, and trustworthiness — but there are always boundaries. Boundaries are critical for teaching self-control, and self-control is critical to making the proper choices in life. Boundaries are merely the reflection of expected behavior that allows people to get along in a crowded, complex world.

And kids, being kids, will test those boundaries. When they step outside that invisible line, you correct them and bring them back in. Then children will grow up happy and secure in the knowledge of how they're expected to behave.

Here's an example: My mother used to teach Sunday school for Kindergarteners. One morning she gave the children a tour of the church. One child was consistently loud, obnoxious, and rowdy. Finally my mother — an experienced woman who raised three boys of her own — took the child by the shoulders and said sternly, "Stop that. You are supposed to be quiet and respectful in church. *Do you understand me?"* She spoke in a strong and forceful tone that implied such dire consequences that I winced (because she used that same tone on me when I misbehaved).

And you know what? It worked. Not only did the boy stop his misbehavior, but he cuddled up to my mother for the rest of the class. Once the boundaries for his behavior and actions were laid out in no uncertain terms, he knew what was right and what was wrong. That knowledge brought him security.

Education

One of the most critical decisions in any parent's life — and remember, this decision is a *choice* — is how to educate our children. Most people simply send their kids to public school and assume all will be well. Nothing could be farther from the truth.

The relentless peer pressure kids experience is almost guaranteed to change your children into fashion-conscious, disrespectful, over-sexualized beings. They can't help it. Since they're away from your care and influence for the majority of their waking hours, what else can you expect? Peer pressure can be one of the most destructive forces at work in a child's life. For the sake of your son or daughter, do whatever you can to minimize that influence — or at least substitute peers whose pressure will be good, not bad.

To this end, I would strongly urge you to consider homeschooling.

Homeschooling has long ago been demonstrated as academically superior, and homeschooled students do *not* (contrary to ignorant criticism) lack socialization skills unless you count the "skills" of bad language or lack of respect.

Raise them

But of course if you're going to homeschool your kids, it means one parent needs to be home. Believe me, I understand how that's not always possible in today's economy. But for Pete's sake, *try*.

Perhaps you can alternate your work hours (this is the tact my husband and I took when our girls were small). Perhaps one or both of you can tele-commute. Perhaps you could *really* buckle down and live frugally so one of you can stay home. Whatever it takes, do your utmost to raise your own kids.

Limit media

Children today are frighteningly media-savvy. But is this a good thing? Does it contribute toward a simple life? I don't believe so.

Children become wired at such an early age — first to television, then to games, then to cell phones and texting, then to social media — that they never learn to look within themselves to harvest the richness of their imagination. If a child does nothing but stare at screens all day, how will he ever figure out how to build a city out of blocks, or construct a car out of Legos, or build a go-cart? How will she ever have a chance to climb a tree and let her imagination turn it into a castle from the Middle Ages?

While I believe it's necessary for children to have *some* media exposure — they're going to have to get along in this world, after all — it's important to consider what will benefit them versus what will not. For example, a knowledge of computers will benefit children when they become adults. A knowledge of television sitcoms will not.

Children who grow up with their eyes constantly glued to a screen — any screen, from an iPad to a cell phone — do not develop the communication skills necessary to become gainfully employed as adults. If your kids speak and write

Our daughters doing math work

like texting monkeys, it's time to yank away the electronics.

Bury them with books

One of the single biggest gifts you can give your children is the love of reading. There is nothing more wonderful in the world than to fire their imaginations through the stories they read in books. But a love of reading will almost *never* happen unless the parents model this behavior.

This is where limiting their media exposure will be a big bonus. Only when the kids don't have the passive, easy lure of mass electronics will they turn to books to feed their hungry souls. Only when kids see their parents turning to books instead of television or the internet will they learn to view books as the ultimate companion on rainy days and to escape from stress and problems. The richness that grows from within cannot be duplicated with movies or video games.

To this end, buy books by the cart-load. They can be purchased for pennies at library sales, thrift stores, and yard sales.

I believe a home without books is a sterile, bleak environment because it's a home usually dominated by electronics. But books are warm and friendly. We have more than 5,000 books in our home and seldom deny ourselves the pleasure of buying more.

Don't deprive your children of this resource. Encourage reading at all opportunities.

Demonstrate your own good choices

All the advice I've given — limiting media, devouring books, etc. — are pretty much worthless unless parents are willing to step up to the plate and model the values you're trying to impart. What's the use of telling your children to go read a book if you do so to get them out of your hair while you're watching TV? What's the use of refusing them a cell phone when you're glued to yours?

Remember: The essence of a simple life is to *make good choices.*

Raising children is hard enough as it is. Raising children to be confident, strong, honest, moral, and ethical is virtually impossible unless the parents are the ones making good choices themselves, and thus guiding their children through today's complex culture.

Naturally we can't achieve perfection when raising our kids. Life tends to get in the way. We all make mistakes. But showing your kids the impact of good *and bad* choices will help them simplify their future in unimaginable ways.

In the end, what kind of children do you want facing a complex world? You *choose* to create another human being. Your children are your legacy. What kind of legacy are you leaving? The world is going to heck in a handbasket, and your kids are going to have to deal with it. Arm them the best you can by giving them a simple, solid upbringing. Δ

A small space yields a BIG crop of garlic

By Howard Tuckey

In less than an hour last fall, I tilled up a 4x8 foot garden bed and planted 250 seed cloves of Chesnok and Russian Red garlic. I've been doing it this way for several years, and am very satisfied with the yield, which gives us plenty of garlic for the table, as well as seed for the next year.

A few years ago I found a 4x8 foot piece of treated wood lattice. The holes are approximately four inches on center, which is excellent spacing for planting garlic and other crops, too. I till up a different spot in the garden each year, smooth it off, and lay the lattice flat.

I put one garlic clove in each hole and poke it into the ground (the pointy end goes up). Just poke them all in — don't spend a lot of time trying to cover them. After all the holes are filled, remove the lattice and put it away for next time. I keep it hanging on a couple of screws on the side of the garden shed.

Now cover the bed with about an inch or so of good compost and tamp it down, then mulch the whole bed with two or three inches of pine needles. The needles will settle over the winter, and the garlic comes up right through them in the spring. Pine needles will keep the weeds at bay for most of the summer. The only other maintenance comes during the summer, when I cut the scapes to ensure larger bulbs. (Scapes are the flower stalks that grow on hardneck garlic varieties.) Those scapes are good in stir fry, so don't toss them.

We get around 250 heads of garlic from that 4x8 foot bed — a pretty good use of space, I think.

I usually harvest 250 heads of garlic from one 4x8 foot bed.

What to do with all that garlic?

We like garlic in all of its forms: roasted, dried, cooked in sauces, or one of my favorite ways, pickled. Here's one of my favorite garlic pickles:

4-6 whole heads garlic, divided into peeled cloves (I use mostly softneck garlic for this, as the hardneck cloves tend to be too large.)
1½ cups white wine vinegar
5 Tbsp. sugar
½ tsp. salt
1 tsp. pickling spice
fresh thyme or tarragon (optional)
½ to 1 habañero pepper (optional)
2 half-pint sterilized jars with lids

Peel the garlic cloves, cutting any very large cloves in half lengthwise. In a small saucepan, bring vinegar, sugar, salt, and pickling spice to a boil, stirring until sugar is dissolved. Add garlic cloves, return to a boil and cook, stirring, for about one minute. Put tarragon or thyme and habañero in jars, then evenly divide garlic, liquid, and spices between the jars, filling to within ¼-inch of top, making sure garlic is covered. Cover tightly. Let sit at room temperature for 24 hours then refrigerate for up to two months. Makes two half-pint jars. Δ

Anatomy of an edge

By Len McDougall

My grandpa used to say that he knew only six people who could properly sharpen a knife, and that he'd taught the skill to three of them. He probably wasn't exaggerating by much; the science of making knives sharp hasn't been part of the average person's life since a fixed-blade sheath knife was part of almost every American's daily work attire. A rugged knife is the original multi-tool, enabling its owner to cut, chop, whittle, skin, butcher, and drill, and it was a prudent sidearm in the days when there was more wilderness than civilization. As the need to use a knife tapered off, so did the need — and the ability — to sharpen a cutting edge back to working condition.

The original knife and tool sharpener is a dense, abrasive sandstone. It served people who relied on their blades well into the 20th century.

Honing a knife (or lawnmower blade, axe, or scythe) to shaving sharpness demands first knowing why a sharp edge is sharp. The key to sharpness lies in bringing both sides of a blade to meet at a very pointed and highly polished apex. A dull blade is one that has had that pointed joining of its two beveled sides rounded off by wear, which basically translates to driving a broader surface area into a material being cut, and requiring more downward force to penetrate a given material. Restoring, then polishing an edge to its original (or sharper) bevel is accomplished by slowly removing sub-microns of blade material until the sharpest and most-pointed meeting of the two sides has been achieved.

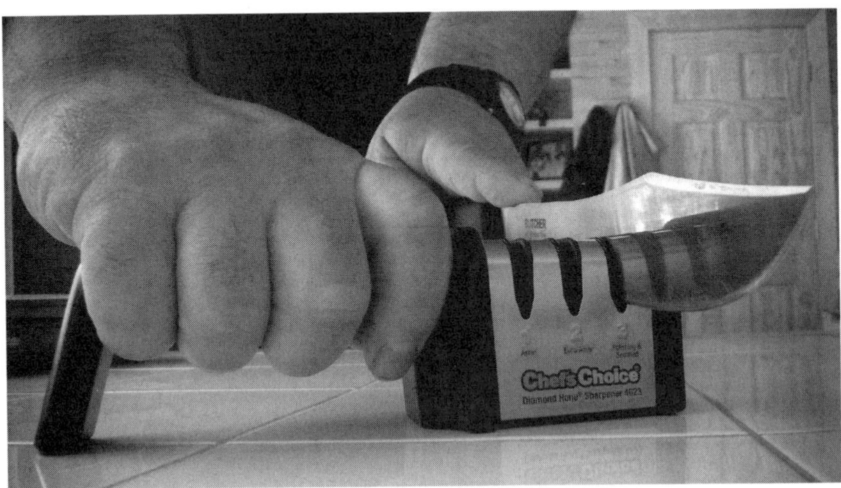

This inexpensive Chef's Choice manual sharpener has three blade guides with pre-angled diamond hones at their bottoms to sharpen and smooth the edge of virtually any knife to skinning sharpness.

The traditional re-sharpener is a stone, coarse enough to abrade a few molecules at a time from a blade when the two are rubbed against one another. If you can keep the angle between knife and stone constant while smoothly grinding the sides of a blade to terminate in a smooth, even point from handle to blade tip, you can achieve an edge keen enough to demand respect from its handler. By polishing the bevels against a harder honing surface — like the traditional Arkansas oilstone — even an axe can be honed to hair-shaving sharpness.

I believe you can forget all of those confusing instructions about keeping a blade at a specific angle to the honing surface. Most American and European blades have cutting edges ground to twenty degrees, while Asian knives are historically angled to fifteen degrees, but that really doesn't matter, because gauging precise angles by eye alone is virtually impossible. The secret of an expert honesman is a learned ability to "feel" the edge as it slides against a honing surface. If it slips, catches, or slides jerkily as you grind the blade against it, then there is not a broad enough or flat enough surface against the stone to create an even bevel that drags smoothly. A skilled knife sharpener can restore his or her knife's cutting edge in the dark, just by feeling how smoothly the blade drags. Veteran skinners sometimes intentionally increase the angle of their knives' edges to create a steeper point where the sides meet, which increases the amount of wear needed to make it dull (but makes it more prone to chipping when used for chopping).

Smith's Pocket Pal has carbide bevel-cutting and ceramic polishing blades, and a fold-out diamond-impregnated tapered rod hone for serrated edges, and gut and strap hooks.

There is no wrong way to create the sharp bevel of a keen edge. The classic honing motion is to begin at the choil, where the sharpened edge ends, just ahead of the handle. Move the blade in a circular motion that grinds it against the honing surface at a narrow angle, as though you were trying to slice a very thin layer from the hone. As you rotate the blade in even-size circles, draw the knife back from handle to tip to grind an even cutting edge with a needle-sharp point. As the circling blade rounds the "belly" that leads to its point, raise the handle to increase the honing angle as cutting angle changes.

It's usually easier to sharpen a knife by grinding its edge against a hone, but some blade metals like D2 tool steel and beta-titanium tend to roll off to one side when they meet at a thin point. These metals get sharpest by honing with the edge, with most friction applied away from the cutting edge. All edges can be sharpened by honing with their cutting edges, but they must first have an evenly-beveled cutting edge.

To save time when sharpening a very dull knife, I use a coarse aluminum-oxide "stone" (it's actually man-made), available at most hardware and department stores for around $10. A larger stone, three inches by at least six inches, provides a safer and more efficient grinding surface. I wet the stone with water (never put any type of oil on an aluminum-oxide hone or its porous surface will soon be clogged by non-abrasive varnish), and then grind a blade hard against it in a back-and-forth motion, toward the edge then away from it. This motion permits a forceful push against the hone that maximizes the amount of metal ground off, and quickly "sets" its edge. I repeat the back-and-forth motion up and down both sides of the blade until the beveled cutting edges are even on either side, and the blade feels sharp, but rough. It doesn't matter if the bevels are a little rough, so long as they are even, because a finer hone can polish a rough edge better than it can create a new one.

A keen edge drags against a thumb dragged crosswise over it — never run your thumb lengthwise with the edge, because a sharp blade literally splits skin with only slight pressure. Finally, you can "strop" a good edge to hair-shaving sharpness by polishing it with the edge against a wide

The simple to use Quick-Fix pocket sharpener from Lansky can keep knives of every size cutting effectively in the kitchen or in the field.

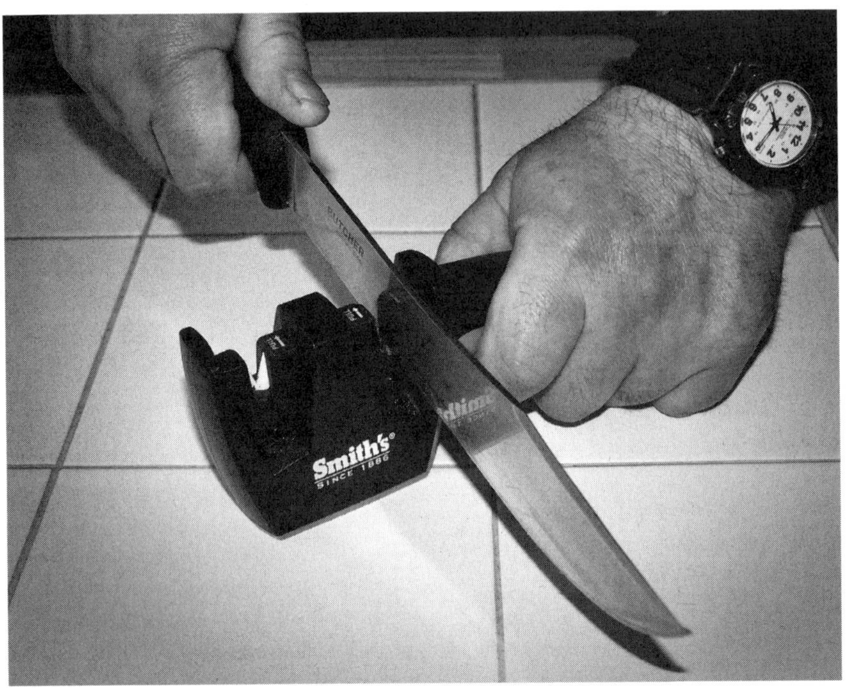

In actual trials, Smith's Edge Pro manual knife sharpener enabled men and women who had no skill with conventional honing stones to apply hair-shaving edges to a broad range of blade styles.

leather belt or strap to stand it up and create a surgically-sharp blade.

Sharpening tools

Many attempts have been made to create a sharpening tool that enables anyone to put a shaving edge on a knife, but only recently have a few succeeded at making almost everyone nearly as good at sharpening knives as the best honemasters. The latest generation of manual sharpeners are typically pull-through designs, with two V-shaped notches comprised of two intersecting blades that form each notch; the carbide side mills nice, even bevels onto the dullest straight-edge knives, while the ceramic side does a bang-up job of polishing straight- or serrated-blade knives to a keenness that might raise your eyebrows.

Using the latest sharpeners is simple: place the blade being sharpened in the appropriate notch, starting at the choil, and draw the knife backward smoothly toward its tip. Light downward pressure is best, especially in the aggressive carbide notch; if the blade chatters and catches as you pull it through, ease up on the pressure being applied. Try to keep the blade at right angles to the sharpener to ensure even cutting on either side, and raise the handle upward as you round the blade's belly, toward the point. Notch blades are ambidextrous to accommodate left- or right-handed users, and blades are reversible to extend their lives. Blades can also be replaced when (if) they wear out. Replacement carbide or ceramic blades are available, but the originals are likely to last several years with regular use.

If you prefer the control and versatility of traditional honing stones, it's hard to go wrong with a simple round (knife) or rectangular (axe) aluminum-oxide honing stone, double-sided with coarse and medium grits, and priced at about $10 to start. About twice as expensive are crystalline diamond-impregnated Diamond hones. Some hones are rods, which can sharpen strap-cutter and gut hooks, some are flat like conventional honing stones; all are touted to last forever.

Smith's Diamond Tri-Hone Sharpening System is an example of how sharpening tools have improved

An improvement on a time-honored method, Smith's Diamond Tri-Hone Sharpening system can put surgical edges on knives and scissors for many years.

in recent decades. The Tri-Hone's 2.5x8-inch Coarse (325-grit) and Medium (750-grit) diamond stones, and a Fine (800-1,000-grit) Arkansas oilstone mounted onto a rotating triangular spindle make it simple to take a knife from completely dull to razor-sharp with one convenient tool. An advantage of the Tri-Hone design over conventional honing stones or ceramic-rod sharpeners is that it offers superior stability and angle control — critical for tough, hard-to-sharpen steels like ATS-34 or D2. The Tri-Hone's stand holds whichever stone is used five inches above the surface it rests on, the ideal height for a kitchen table or countertop. Rubber feet help to keep the unit from sliding as blade is worked against stone. Price of the Diamond Tri-Hone is $99.99.

For field sharpening there are now pocket-size sharpening tools that are ideal for anglers and hunters who might dull their knives in places where the bulk and weight of conventional sharpeners is inconvenient or prohibitive. Two of the easiest to use and most effective go-everywhere sharpeners are Lansky's Quick-Fix and Smith's Pocket Pal. The Quick-Fix uses two notched guides with a coarse carbide bevel-cutter on one side of a large easy-to-grip tab, and ceramic polishing blades in the other notch. The Quick-Fix retails for $6.

Smith's Pocket Pal uses coarse carbide and 600-grit ceramic blades set into V-shaped notches to quickly repair dulled or damaged cutting edges, then polish them to deer-skinning sharpness. The blades are reversible and replaceable, but it's not likely most of us will ever need to replace them. Adding to the sharpener's usefulness is a 2-inch long, 400-grit tapered rod, set jackknife-fashion into the opposite side, for sharpening straight or serrated edges. The Pocket Pal retails for $10. Δ

Beefsteak tomato sauce

By Robin Nessel

If you are like me, you often have a lot of extra slicing tomatoes that you cannot possibly eat as fast as they ripen. What do you do with all those tomatoes besides making salsa and catsup? How about sauce?

Tomato sauce is traditionally made with paste tomatoes and for good reason — paste tomatoes have less water and do not need to be cooked down to a thick consistency. Many times I tried turning my extra beefsteak tomatoes into sauce by cooking them down and ended up with a bitter sauce that left a bad aftertaste. Most of this got thrown to my chickens who are less than discerning about such things.

I looked through cookbooks, and they all basically said the same thing: cook down the sauce until it thickens. If it is slightly bitter, add some sugar or baking soda. The baking soda is supposed to counteract the acidity in the tomatoes. I tried adding sugar. Too little and it did nothing to get rid of the bitterness. Too much and I ended up with a sugary sauce that was only masking the bitterness. I added baking soda a pinch at a time until the foaming stopped, but ended up with a dull sauce that left a bad aftertaste.

Eventually I found an article that said that sauces should not be cooked down because that only concentrates the acids and the bitterness of the tomatoes. That is why it is best to use paste tomatoes. They make a naturally thick sauce that does not need to be cooked down to thicken.

With this bit of information I concluded that my problem was that the tomatoes I was using had too much water and when cooked to thicken this only contributed to the bitterness and acidity.

I reasoned that removing the water would make the resulting sauce thick without cooking it down and possibly without the acidity and bitterness I was getting in my previous sauces.

I filled a juice steamer with slicing tomatoes, turned on the stove, and waited for it to do its thing. About an hour later the water had collected and I put the separated tomato flesh through a food mill, removing seeds, cores, and peels.

What came out of the food mill into my pan was a beautiful thick tomato sauce. I put the sauce pan on my stove and warmed it a bit and tasted it. To my delight it was naturally sweet with a bright tomato taste sans the acidity and bitterness. I cooked the sauce a bit more adding my favorite seasonings, then cooked up some pasta and sat down to eat. This was one sauce my chickens would not be getting. I can honestly say it is the best sauce I have ever made. Δ

Love, sweat, and determination

By Mary Marvin

When two of our sons had outgrown the nest and the third was finishing college, my husband and I started looking for a place in the country.

We found an ad for a bank foreclosure and the bank was anxious to sell. The ad read: "A beautiful place in the country with waterfalls. All offers considered." So we went to look.

It had waterfalls alright, but only when it rained hard. At the edge of the back yard was a creek and behind the creek was a steep hill. Each time it rained, water gushed down that hill. So the waterfalls were not a plus, but they got us there to look.

The house as it looked in winter, after we had been there about three years

The house had been empty for quite a while. Where once the lawn had been, there was a hayfield. A large barn had burned, and the foundation and half-burned beams were still there. Woodchucks had been having a heyday digging under the old barn foundation.

Behind the barn area were old cars and car parts, and among them were several piles of rotting lumber. We discovered that a sawmill once had existed there beside the creek, leaving a deep hole where the mill pond had been.

However, when we got past the cars and car parts there was a road that meandered along beside the creek. There were beautiful woods on each side of it. A careful look through weeds revealed a rock fence along the side of the driveway.

Because the house had been empty, some of the windows were broken. The former owner had moved out without shutting off the water; pipes had frozen and broke.

We debated. "Should we or shouldn't we?" We were getting close to our retirement years and this place looked like a lot of work; but we could see a lot that we liked also, including 20 acres of land with timber. We offered $20,000, expecting that it wouldn't be accepted, but it was.

We worked together indoors and outdoors. As each project was completed we felt happy. The kids were grown, but we had some good years left, and we felt like newlyweds as we worked to make the old derelict house become a home again.

We loved the place even though the mice chewed in the walls and the first year that we had a garden the woodchucks ate it all.

We loved listening to peepers, watching lightning bugs, and hearing the owls hoot as darkness descended.

As time went on I began noticing that my husband tired easily. He had congestive heart failure.

When he died a friend said to me, "Certainly you're not going to stay in this God-forsaken place now that your husband is gone."

I raised my eyebrows and said, "Why do you say God-forsaken? God is everywhere here. Of course I'm going to stay." Δ

The Last Word

The Un-*PATRIOT Act* renewal

By Claire Wolfe

On May 26, President Obama signed the latest extension of the *USA PATRIOT Act.*

He didn't exactly sign it. He was in Europe and ordered the bill "robo-signed" into law by machine. There was a brief, indignant flurry in the media. Was robo-signing actually legal? Did it violate the *Constitution*?

It's funny. Pundits worried about the wrong thing. Certainly Obama's hands-off act reeked of irresponsibility, but the real dereliction of duty was signing the extension at all. The *PATRIOT Act* itself is the real abuse of the *Constitution.*

The Act became law on October 26, 2001 in the aftermath of 9/11. It was a behemoth, passed in rage. Nobody read it. Ten years later, we ought to be calm enough to examine it and ask whether such a law has any place in a free country.

Many parts of the *USA PATRIOT Act* are permanent. But three provisions were so controversial that Congress agreed to sunset them. They have to be re-authorized every few years, and that's what Congress and the president did last May.

Those sections include roving wiretaps (your innocent conversations may be recorded if you have even peripheral contact with someone under investigation), the "lone-wolf" provision (federal agents may conduct surveillance of any non-citizen, even if that person has no known terrorist connections), and the so-called "library provision," Section 215.

Section 215 is one of the most hated parts of the *Act.* It allows federal investigators to demand information on you that is held by third parties — credit card companies, car rental firms, bookstores, hotels, Internet service providers, banks, and more. Investigators may demand "any tangible thing" including "books, records, papers, documents, and other items." Furthermore, Section 215 places a "gag" that forbids recipients of these demands from revealing that you're a target.

You may agree or disagree with these parts of the *PATRIOT Act.* But the need to vote on them every few years is supposed to give time for consideration — and that isn't happening. Each time they've come up for re-authorization, the vote has been rushed, with little thought about how the law has been used or might be used.

I mentioned earlier that all other portions of the *PATRIOT Act* are permanent. That's not precisely true. Any parts of the Act can go away if Congress repeals them. Congress rarely repeals anything, but they should. Take the infamous Section 505, for example.

During the run-up to this spring's vote, Sen. Ron Wyden (D-OR) warned that, "When the American people find out how their government has secretly interpreted the *PATRIOT Act*, they will be stunned and they will be angry."

A few days later, the news brought us a glimpse of what Wyden meant. This glimpse shows how rapidly federal mission creep destroys our traditions of due process and individual rights.

Section 505 of the *PATRIOT Act* concerns so-called national security letters (NSLs). To understand how dangerous these are, we need to back up in time.

The *Fourth Amendment* to the *Constitution* states, "The right of the people to be secure in their persons, houses, papers, and effects, against unreasonable searches and seizures, shall not be violated, and no Warrants shall issue, but upon probable cause, supported by Oath or affirmation, and particularly describing the place to be searched, and the persons or things to be seized."

In 1978, federal officials decided to sneak around the *Fourth Amendment.* The FBI, CIA, and Pentagon began using self-generated "demand letters" in financial crimes — national security letters — to get companies or organizations to turn over data. They evaded the *Constitution* by saying that compliance with the demands was voluntary and applied only to "transactional data" (e.g. who you called and when, but not what you said).

In 1986, Congress made compliance mandatory, but didn't create penalties. In 1993, they added punishments for non-compliance. You see the mission-creep? You see the gradual, "Well, if X is tolerable, then Y and Z can be imposed, too"? But it gets worse.

In 2001, the *PATRIOT Act* greatly expanded the power of NSLs. They now can be used to dig up dirt on "US residents, visitors, or US citizens who are not suspects in any criminal investigation" (Wikipedia).

Remember that this requires no oversight by a judge. Every NSL comes with a gag order, too. But it gets worse.

In 2007, an investigation by the Inspector General of the Justice Department showed that the FBI had misused NSLs literally thousands of times. They expanded the already-broad provisions of the *PATRIOT Act.* Then in 2008, the FBI created for itself a new category of investigation called an "assessment." This is what they use if they have no solid reason to suspect us of wrongdoing, but they want to be able to go through our trash, search databases for information on us, or send out a surveillance team to monitor our activities.

In 2011, according to Charlie Savage of the *New York Times*, the FBI is writing itself a new set of investigative guidelines. Under the 2008 rules, an agent would have to open an official inquiry — create a data trail — when starting an "assessment." Under the new rules — nothing. No warrant, no subpoena, no NSL needed. The FBI won't even have to put a notation in a file before it starts plowing through our trash cans and the records of our email transactions. It can all be done in secret without oversight. If you're a celebrity and an agent wants to dig into your life, no problem. If you're an agent's ex-spouse or the boyfriend of his daughter or a good-looking neighbor, he can begin snooping into your life without even creating a record — let alone swearing an oath before a judge based on probable cause.

The FBI's proposed new powers aren't written directly into the *PATRIOT Act*. But the Act is the great enabler. Sections 215 and 505 are subject to impossibly broad interpretation. By their very nature, they kick the *Fourth Amendment* when it's already down. They give federal agents *carte blanche* to trample on every part of the rule of law.

This is how the STASI worked in East Germany. It is not how a government should function in a free country. Δ

Backwoods Home magazine

practical ideas for self-reliant living

Nov/Dec 2011
Issue #132
$5.95 US
$7.50 CAN

Solar-powered chicken coop

Savory supper pies
Living with wolves
Best apple pie
Unplanned homebirth
Build a "holz hausen"
Reloading

www.backwoodshome.com

CHILDERS

My view

How we battle the effects of a recession

Like other communities across America, mine has been suffering from the current recession. The county government is near bankruptcy, many of the cops have been laid off, schools have let teachers go and cut classes and sports programs, and small businesses have furloughed long-time employees or cut their hours. It can be a bit depressing in a small community that wasn't that prosperous to begin with.

But in my town we decided to do something about it, at least in our small way. A few of us local businessmen and semi-retired publishers like me set out to create something positive. Since I'm a golfer, I bought into the idea of fellow retiree and golfer, Grant Hornbeak, that we start a youth golf club to not only replace one of the sports the local schools cut but also to get the community involved in something that had the potential to boost the local economy.

We called the club *Wild Rivers Junior Golf (WRJG),* and Hornbeak quickly linked it to the *PGA's First Tee* program by starting up a *First Tee* class at our local elementary school. One of the teachers there, Glen Litterell, agreed to take *First Tee* training from the *PGA*. *BHM* provided the $3,000 seed money needed for the specialized *First Tee* equipment and child-sized golf clubs.

Hornbeak then launched a *WRJG Summer Golf Camp* at the local Cedar Bend Golf Course that attracted more than 20 kids and volunteers like Jake and Audrey Jacobson, course manager Toby Stanley, and the entire girls' and boys' high school golf teams. I was the publicity guy, making sure the camp got adequate press coverage in the local newspaper. Parents brought their kids out to attend.

Then I put on my publisher's hat, first enlisting the sympathetic voice of our popular local newspaper's sports columnist, Randy Robbins. Then I challenged Dewey Powers, the owner of our biggest restaurant, *Spinner's Seafood, Steak, and Chop House,* to a thousand dollar match, proceeds to be donated to *WRJG*.

Dewey was aware my company had sponsored the high school boys' golf team the last four years, and he had read about the success of the *WRJG Summer Golf Camp* in the local newspaper. And I was aware that Dewey, like other business owners in the community, was always being approached for donations to help good causes, so I didn't want to just go begging for support. Instead, realizing he was an avid golfer with two golfing sons, one of whom is the local club champ, I challenged him to a match involving some of the best golfers in the county. The winner would claim a beautiful trophy that *WRJG* would provide, and the loser would donate $1000 to *WRJG*. I pointed out to Dewey that his team would have the advantage since he himself was a good golfer and I (a well-known terrible golfer) intended to play for my own team.

The initial First Tee Cup teams, from left: Toby Stanley, Matt Anderson, Toby Stanley Jr., Robby Duffy, Brett Martin, Dave Duffy, Alfonso Powers, Dewey Powers, Dennis Allen, Dane Ross, Jim Toth, Dewey Powers III

But for spice, I broadened the wager: "The loser also buys both teams dinner in your own restaurant!"

He agreed and we played the match two weeks later, his six golfers against mine. Randy Robbins gave us the necessary publicity to get the local golfing community involved, and many people came out to watch it. His team won, but that didn't bother me, nor did I mind ponying up the thousand bucks for *WRJG*, because I had already lined up Spinner's next opponent, *Gold Beach Lumber*, which had agreed to the same format. In fact, I had lined up the next contender after that, *Jerry's Jet Boats*, and the next, *The Corner Drug,* and the next, my dentist Dr. Tom Westfall.

Randy Robbins wrote a dramatic story about the first match in the paper, highlighting the beauty of the crystal glass *Curry County First Tee Cup* that *Spinner's* had won. The trophy is now proudly displayed in *Spinners'* entryway where hundreds of diners see it daily.

The result of all this activity is that we're filling the coffers of *WRJG* at the rate of a thousand dollars a match so we can fund the school's *First Tee* program, another summer golf camp, and both the boys' and girls' high school golf teams. Grant Hornbeak and I took his original idea to create a *First Tee* program and involved a lot of other community members in a fun way that gave something to the donors as well as to the kids we wanted to help.

In our small way, we're helping replace what a bad economy had taken away. We're now making plans to start two more *First Tee* programs at schools in the nearby towns of Brookings and Port Orford. Hornbeak is going after *PGA* grants available to programs like ours that have already shown success, and that could create money for golf jobs. To heck with the bad economy! — ***Dave Duffy***

Midwinter madness

Coping with that two-faced time of year

By Claire Wolfe

Last issue we talked about how to prepare to keep our best health and mood through the dark winter months. Now comes the hard part: December and January.

December — that month when you *will* be jolly (and busy!) whether you like it or not.

January — that month of … well, a whole lot of January-ness; one of the longest, emptiest times of the year.

Other than being cold and dark, these two months have nothing in common. They're opposites. Yet we must leap from one to the other with the agility of a tightrope walker. That leap can be a feat even in the best of times.

These, it goes without saying, are far from the best of times. Most of us are entering our fourth winter of depleted resources, diminished credit, and shaky hopes. Politicians have been nattering about "recovery" for two years, but the rest of us wonder what the politicians have been smoking. Pundits now fret that we might be entering "another" recession. What have the pundits been smoking? Sixty-eight percent of Americans in a recent poll said we've never gotten out of the 2008 recession — and no matter how the government cooks the books, that 68% know in their bones the reality of the situation. We are in a depression. And things will almost certainly get worse before they get better.

So… now comes December. *Be jolly! Spend money!*

Riiight …

But hard times can make for good times. Ask your Great-Granny; most likely she has warm memories of growing up in the Great Depression. It just takes a little creativity and the right attitude.

So here's a small Hard-Times Survival Guide to December and January.

December — frenzy

The holiday season may be joyful. It may be depressing. But it tends to be frantic no matter how you take it. Even if you truly love Christmas, Hanukkah, or the politically-correct winter celebration of your choice, there's an inevitable element of *force* to it all. Forced joy. Forced visits with relatives you don't get along with. Forced scheduling. Forced shopping or gift-making. And inescapable repetitions of the same 10 holiday tunes that the dull-minded people of the Muzak company think you want to hear.

If force is too strong a word, call it pressure. But even for people who have elf DNA or can sing "Fah who foraze! Dah who doraze!" along with the Whos down in Whoville, this is a "pressury" season — as the thousands of articles on coping with holiday stress attest. Expectations that you *must* be happy, *must* spend money, or *must* feel worshipful are all harder when wallets are so empty that even moths can't live in them anymore.

So how to cope?

1. Make this a year to adopt new traditions. If your holidays end up as escalating gift-buying contests, with each child demanding more or each adult trying to outdo the other in lavishness, opt out. If your holidays tend to feature visits with relatives you can't abide, free yourself. Don't go. If any part of your holiday tradition has just become habit, break the habit.

Sure, it takes work and guts and may create some temporary stresses (and even not-so-temporary stresses among your more judgmental relatives). But this is *your* life. These are *your* holidays. They're for you and the people you love to enjoy. If you've fallen into traditions that aren't enjoyable or practical, hard times give you a perfect justification for change: "I'm sorry, we can't afford to travel this year." "No, this time we can't host the big dinner alone; we need more people to pitch in." "Do we really need expensive presents? How about giving each other gift certificates for personal services, instead? You know ... I'll bake you cookies and you give me a half-hour massage."

No matter what new tradition you establish, do your best to make this a big part of it: Do nothing out of a sense of obligation.

2. Be kind — to yourself and others. Every mid-winter holiday in every tradition is based around one concept: the return of light after a time of darkness. Bringing some personal light into the world counts for more than 1,000 forgettable presents.

And again, hard times become a great justification for finding deeper "reason for the season." There's nothing wrong with presents, of course. We all remember the Christmas when we got the bicycle. Or the BB gun. Or the golden-haired doll. But when times are hard and money tight, what greater gift can you give than the gift of time and caring? And what greater lesson can you teach your children?

3. Enjoy low-cost, low-stress activities. Go look at other people's Christmas decorations instead of wrestling with your own. Attend a free or low-cost concert; there are lots of them this time of year.

4. Put the credit cards on ice for the holidays. Literally. Put them in a plastic tub of water and freeze them until the shopping season is over. And practice other forms of fiscal sanity. Stick to a budget. For gifts. For meals. For parties. Make lists of what you're going to buy and don't deviate from them without extremely good reason.

5. Make simple gifts, emphasizing creativity, do-it-yourself values, and the fun of shared work.

If you don't have the time for that, make the Internet your friend. Buying online keeps you out of malls. And staying out of malls saves hours, stress, and possibly money. And at Amazon.com or eBay you won't have to listen to piped-in versions of "The Little Drummer Boy."

6. Do your best to keep your healthy diet on track through all the changes. Everything we covered in issue #131 (Sept/Oct 2011) about diet and exercise remains important. The holidays don't have to change that. Go ahead and have that second helping of turkey or ham. Slurp up that egg-nog. Even accept that extra dollop of whipped cream that Aunt Sarah wants to put on your pumpkin pie. There's no harm in a little indulgence. There may be a lot of good in allowing yourself some extra treats in these depressing times.

Just don't make the entire month an orgy of carb consumption. Or alcohol consumption. Or anything else. Aim for moderation in the amount you consume. Aim for quality in the foods you eat. Be moderate with sugars, refined starches, and alcohol. Emphasize protein, healthy fats, nuts, and vegetables.

7. Say no. Say no to parties you'd rather not go to. Say no to insistent, whiny kids. Say no to relatives whose demands tax your resources and your patience.

Know your limits. Know the things that might trigger a stress overload, a temper tantrum, or a teary collapse. Back off your level of activity before you stress out. Do your best to avoid "trigger" activities or people who bring out the worst in you. Ask for help when you need it.

Remember: you can't control how your relatives and friends or bosses and coworkers behave, but you can decide how *you'll* behave. Give yourself all the breaks you can.

January — aftermath

Then comes January. They don't call this the "dead of winter" for nothing. Here come the dull days when you might wish you had a little of that frantic activity back in your life.

Yet January brings its own kinds of stresses. With new possessions abounding, tree trimmings coming down, and bits of wrap and ribbon still lurking in the crannies, your house might look like a flash mob hit it. Being jolly for a whole darned month has left you grouchy and exhausted.

Worse, if you splurged at the holidays, these dead days are when the bills come due. Worse yet, if you overindulged at the holiday table, the "bill" for that comes due, also. January is when you look at yourself in the mirror and pledge to live on dry crusts and water for the next three months and never allow yourself to have any fun again — ever. No, instead you'll just capital-W Work on yourself. You'll diet. You'll give up alcohol. Or cigarettes. You'll hit the Stairmaster every morning at 5:00. You'll take a class, learn a new skill, become a better human being, a better parent, or a better cook. You'll finally rebuild that old car your wife's been nagging you about. You'll finally get down to a size 6. You'll change your ways overnight. It's January! Out with the old, in with the new!

You line yourself up with a punishing list of New Year's resolutions and regulations and restrictions that you couldn't fulfill even if you were a candidate for sainthood. For about two days, you brim with the pride of strong will and determination. Then inertia takes over and all that resolving and pledging just weighs on your conscience. All the self-betterment projects you don't do become as draggy as the chains Ebenezer Scrooge was scheduled to bear in the afterlife.

Oh weep! I don't have any will power. I'm such a Bad Person!

Then you comfort yourself by eating a quart of ice cream while slouching in front of the TV. Well, maybe *you* don't. But certain persons I won't mention have been known to do something like that.

But this is the backwoods in hard days. These are no times for sinking into the blues. These are the proverbial tough times when "the tough get going."

So ...

1. Clean and simplify. This is a terrific time to clean house. Or organize the workshop. Simplify, too. The influx of Christmas *stuff* is a perfect excuse to get rid of the old. Donate it to charity. Hold an off-season (and indoor!) garage sale. Move junk out to the barn to recycle it into firewood or project material.

Creating an uncluttered environment unclutters the mind. It brings out creativity. The physical aspect of sorting and moving *stuff* can be healthy all by itself. When you lighten your physical load and lighten your rooms you also lighten your heart. And more light is precisely what we all need right now.

2. Don't pressure yourself to do anything big. You might think this is a good time to start some new activity you've been promising yourself — learn a language, take up oil painting, begin building up your body, or whatever. But it's a good time to start such things *only if you're really going to enjoy and pursue them.* If you're just making one more resolution that'll be shattered the next time you get in a time crunch, don't do it.

3. Get outside as much as possible, particularly for healthy activities. Emphasize ones that are simple to do so you'll have fewer excuses. Or ones you love, like skiing. Your body needs the movement. Your mind needs the stimulation. And *all* of you needs the extra vitamin D from outdoor light. Is there a winter sports league in your area? Even an informal one? This might be a good time to join it.

4. Brighten your indoor experiences, too. Not the outdoorsy type? Weather too awful to go out? Okay. Then set up a bird feeder, get yourself an Audubon guide, and watch cardinals and juncos brave the storms. This might also be a good time to apply a fresh, brighter coat of paint to a room or two. And don't forget bright accents in your clothes or your home.

5. Don't beat yourself up over broken resolutions. Again, be kind. If you make resolutions but don't keep them, don't condemn yourself. Consider this: in the long run, even repeatedly broken resolutions can be useful. For one thing, they can help you know what to cross off your list. (I am never going to speak Italian, no matter how many times I resolve to learn. *Que sera sera.*) But sometimes even the resolutions you don't keep can serve as guideposts. Important resolutions, those you keep coming back to ("I will quit smoking;" "I'll find a more fulfilling career;" "I'll move to the backwoods.") point the way to the future. You may find (I have) that a resolution that really matters might not get fulfilled *right now*, but in the long run, it puts you on the right path.

6. Relish the down time. This is the moment to enjoy those non-material gifts you gave each other for Christmas — to give or receive those massages, to fulfill or collect on promises. It's also a great time for old-fashioned board games — games that can be played *together*, and not with the solitude of a glaring computer screen. Oh, and every true romantic knows that January is the finest time for candlelight and long, cozy evenings by the fireside.

7. Prepare for next season. Start saving your change in a jar. Don't touch it until next Christmas comes around. All winter (and all year) you'll have the sense of accomplishment of watching the jar fill. Come December, you'll have less financial stress when it's time to buy gifts and host gatherings.

8. And don't forget the porn! No, silly, I don't mean sexy pictures (and even if I did, the good folks of *Backwoods Home* wouldn't let me say that). I'm talking about that classic country form of lust, that prime source of juicy fantasy to take you away from the realities of Darkest Winter — January's seed catalogs. Read 'em and plan ... Δ

Solar-powered chicken coop

By Jeffrey R. Yago, P.E., CEM

I am sure many of you have raised large flocks of chickens for years as a normal part of rural life. However, many suppliers of baby chicks today have reported their spring sales have doubled every year for the past five years, and the majority of these increased sales are going to urban homeowners who have never raised chickens before.

Distributors of chicken supplies and feeds are also reporting a significant increase in requests for training and educational materials related to raising chickens. Part of this recent interest appears to be associated with the increased demand for natural foods with no pesticides or hormone additives, while others just want to leave the city and live a simpler life.

Pre-manufactured chicken coop with roof-mounted solar module

Sales of pre-manufactured and ready-to-use chicken coops have also dramatically increased. Unlike the large room-size chicken houses many of us may remember from visits to our grandparents' farm holding 50 or more chickens, the majority of these pre-manufactured coops are sized to house only four to twelve chickens. The primary difference between raising farm chickens and a few backyard chickens is many first timers still have regular nine-to-five jobs in the city and are constantly on the go in the evenings and on weekends.

To meet this limited time challenge, many pre-manufactured chicken coop suppliers are adding time and labor-saving options which significantly reduce the need to have somebody home at all times to care for the chickens. Not only are automatic feeders and waterers available that hold days of nourishment, but also automated doors and lights operated by timers and photocells almost totally eliminate the day-to-day tasks associated with caring for these live animals.

Chickens are, by nature, chicken and are afraid of everything, which is not a bad instinct to have when almost every other animal with four legs or large wings seem to find chickens both tasty and easy prey.

This means you need a secure chicken coop that locks them in each night — and locks everything else out. Having an inside light that comes on before dark not only helps draw chickens inside each evening, but can also improve egg production by staying on at least four hours after dark.

While these new automatic and labor-saving devices can make raising chickens much easier for the urban homeowner, this also means you will need a reliable source of power to operate these electrical devices, something not found on our grandparents' chicken coops. If you live in an area with long periods of deep snow and freezing temperatures, you will most likely need to extend utility power from your house to your new chicken coop to provide heat, or at least prevent freezing of drinking water containers. However, if you only need to power a light and automatic door you can easily power these devices with a solar module. This means running a long electric line to your new chicken coop will not be required. Using a remote area of your property has the advantage of reducing potential complaints from neighbors who may not share your enthusiasm for your new back-to-basics lifestyle, and solar power makes this possible.

Solar-powered electric door has just opened for the morning.

Sources of materials

Electric door:
www.poultrybutler.com
724-397-8908

Solar components:
www.dtisolar.com
804-457-9566

Free advice for raising chickens:
www.backyardchickens.com

Pre-manufactured coops:
www.myamishgoods.com
800-635-4619
www.ezcleancoops.com
888-442-9326

Backyard chicken suppliers:
www.mypetchicken.com
888-460-1529
www.raisingchickensright.com

Books on raising chickens:
www.backwoodshome.com
800-835-2418

Manufacturers of automated coop doors also offer models designed to operate on 12 volts DC, and there are numerous 12-volt light fixtures available from RV and boating suppliers. Since you will want to minimize cost, I suggest buying a 12-volt DC light fixture designed to use an LED-style lamp. Although more expensive than a standard light bulb, they will significantly reduce the cost of a larger solar module and battery which would be required to power a conventional light fixture.

I selected a surface-mounted LED fixture designed for interior boat lighting, and a sealed 12-volt battery typically sold as backup power for commercial fire alarms and computer UPS (uninterupted power supplies). Pick a solar charge controller designed to charge a sealed battery, since a standard solar charger has a higher voltage output that will over-

An LED light fixture requires very little battery power to illuminate the chicken coop interior.

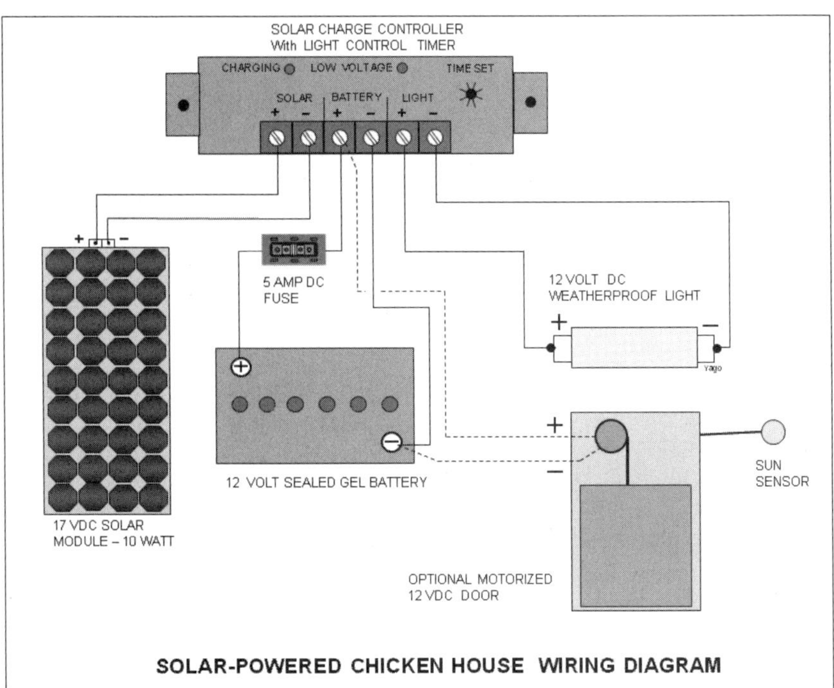

SOLAR-POWERED CHICKEN HOUSE WIRING DIAGRAM

Interior electric sliding door powered from solar-charged 12-volt battery

charge and dry out a sealed battery. If you want to also automatically turn the light on and off, some solar charge controllers include a timer function that is triggered when the solar module senses sunset. This type of control can provide both dusk-to-dawn lighting control as well as timed-off hours of operation after sunset.

Although it takes some fine-tuning and a learning process for the chickens, ideally the light will turn on before dark and bring in the chickens before the door sensor decides to close the door for the night. I must admit that some of my chickens still have not gotten with the program and end up standing outside at the closed door half the night. I am not sure any automatic system will totally eliminate the need for some personal attention from time-to-time, just to make sure all the ladies are safely in for the night.

System electrical design

This design assumes all of the electrical devices you want to power will operate from a 12-volt DC battery. For this application you will need a solar module to mount on the roof, a sealed battery to locate in an unused interior corner, and a solar charge controller. Due to the low voltages and limited power required, most of this wiring will be in the #16 to #18 size range and can be easily stapled to the interior walls and ceilings of the coop. Just remember that chickens are curious and will peck at anything that looks interesting, so keep the wiring and electrical components out of reach when possible.

A solar module in the 10 to 20-watt range should meet most of your power needs, and will have a very low shock or fire hazard. However, even a small sealed battery can cause wires to glow red and start a fire if shorted out, so I strongly recommend including an automotive-style DC fuse between the battery "positive" and the rest of the electrical circuit. Finally, even the best automatic controls that operate motorized doors and lights can get out of sequence with the day/night cycle, so I suggest including a manual switch that you mount just inside the main door or you may find yourself crawling inside the coop when the automatic door gets stuck.

Conclusion

Raising chickens is no longer limited to 100-acre farms and commercial chicken growers, but as you bring chickens into more populated areas and on smaller tracts of land be sure to consider your neighbors' concerns and local ordinances. Giving away fresh eggs can help, but you still may need to obtain a special use permit, meet property-line setback limits from neighbors' homes and wells, and finally, limit noise and smell. This usually means no roosters waking everyone up in your cul-de-sac at 5 am and frequent house cleaning with fresh wood shavings.

You will not believe how resourceful area dogs and foxes are at digging under a fence, or how quickly a hawk can fly in and carry a young chicken away. There have been cases of predators breaking glass windows to get into a chicken house and killing every chicken they can reach. Provide a safe environment for your chickens and you will be rewarded with more fresh eggs than you can possibly eat while letting the sun power everything.

Jeff Yago is a licensed professional engineer and certified energy manager with more than 30 years of experience in the energy conservation field. He has extensive solar photovoltaic and emergency preparedness experience, and has authored numerous articles and texts. His website is www.pvforyou.com. Δ

Sealed 12-volt battery, solar charge controller, and in-line fuse

Build a *holz hausen* to dry firewood

By Doug Fluckiger

I have a confession to make: I'm in love.

My secret passion is tall, dark, and handsome. I may find her lying luxuriantly among a dark grove of firs. She may be standing proudly on a sunny mountainside with flowers at her feet, waiting for me to arrive for a secret rendezvous in the woods — just me, a dead tree, and my chain saw.

Yup, I love firewood.

I love every aspect of the firewood scene. I love dropping a dead tree among its lush green neighbors, leaving more light and air for healthy trees to grow. I love blocking the wood up and splitting it, an art that takes a little bit of muscle and a lot of skill. I love to see wood dry over the season, watching it darken from the creamy yellow of fresh-cut wood to the browned and cracked ends of a well-dried log. I love the exercise that comes from working with wood (not to mention my farmer's tan — stand back, ladies); and the few ashes I gather monthly form a dandy ice-melt for the driveway or fertilizer for the garden. I love starting the 200th fire of the season almost as much as I love starting the first; and as for the bone-soaking heat of a wood fire, the faint perfume of woodsmoke in the winter air, the magic of embers in the night — well, you won't get those with your forced-air gas furnace, no matter what its website says.

There's another aspect of wood-burning that almost drives my cheapskate heart giddy with delight. Firewood is cheap heat. If you live near the woods and can get it yourself, it's ridiculous how little you can spend to keep your tootsies toasty all winter long. Even if you have to buy your firewood, a well-insulated home stretches that wood a long way. Last year in our neck of the woods, we enjoyed one of the longest, snowiest winters on record. I went through more than five cords of wood. The cost: $20 for a permit to cut wood, $75 for chain saw maintenance, and $50 or so for transportation, chain saw fuel, oil, and various supplies. That's $145 for eight months' worth of heat. You won't get that with hydronic heat in your floor, no matter what the neighbors say.

The "foundation" of your holz hausen is a layer of bark or gravel and a perimeter of boards to keep the first course of blocks tipped towards the center.

I have another confession to make: When it comes to stacking firewood and keeping it stacked, I have a checkered past. I'm not too good at stacking up my winter's heat and keeping it there. Up where we live, the summers are short. The brief time available for drying wood leaves little room for restacking toppled woodpiles. Wood shrinks as it dries. It shifts and cracks, and knots and broken branches become fulcra that slowly tilt the stack. Bark dries out and slips loose under the pressure of stacked logs. Wind pushes on the stack. And every so often, I would come out to find that my carefully stacked line of logs has toppled down onto the ground. Not good!

I came across a traditional Old World method of drying firewood and decided to try it. After all, some of those folks live well up north and probably know a thing or two about stacking wood. It's a circular woodpile called a *holz hausen* (German for "round house"). The *holz hausen* is started with carefully stacked wood on the exterior, loosely filled with wood blocks, tied together with interior cross poles, and topped with "thatched roof" circles of split wood. I love the results.

Efficiency

One boast of the *holz hausen* is that it dries wood more quickly than a traditional woodpile. The theory goes that its cylindrical form causes a chimney effect, in which air entering the *holz hausen* is drawn upward by the heated mass of wood in the center, speeding the drying effect. My experience backs up this theory. We live in an area that has short summers and is typically wet and cold in the spring, and our wood does not have much opportunity to dry out. Nevertheless, with only a few weeks' worth of drying time I have seen very green wood in a *holz hausen* dry out until it cracks. With a few months of hot weather, even wet wood dries to a cracking dry state, perfect for winter burning. When it reaches that stage, I move it into the woodshed where it's stored for the season.

Stability

Circles are naturally stable. Ever wonder why bubbles, tanker trucks, or water drops are round? It's because the circle exerts equal pressure on all sides. No part is weaker than any other. That's not the case with a line, which is vulnerable along its length; the longer it gets, the more vulnerable to pressure. That's as true with woodpiles as it is with geometry.

The circular form of a *holz hausen* means that every block of wood exerts roughly equal pressure on every other block at its level. The blocks help hold each other in place. If the wood is stacked carefully, the *holz hausen* not only retains its shape as the wood shrinks, it actually becomes stronger as the individual pieces settle in together, grabbing on to each other and to the cross pieces inside.

Space conservation

A wood stack for one cord of wood — 128 cubic feet — is not much problem if you have limited space. But if you heat with wood, finding room for five to eight cords of wood to dry out over the summer — or over a year, if necessary — becomes more of a problem. We built our home on a fairly steep mountainside, and level spots are hard to come by. Every summer I had long stacks of firewood down by the garden, up by the house, and wherever I could fit it. When I strung out a Great Wall of Firewood along the driveway, my wife drew the line. Three or four handsome cylinders of wood out back are a much better use of space.

Beauty

That brings us to another benefit of the *holz hausen*: They're nice to look at. Everyone who sees our wood stacks comments on their unexpected shape, often followed by something like, "You know, that's kind of pretty." Something about the snug, compacted shape suggests the very snugness that the firewood will create when the snow begins to fall.

Building a *holz hausen*

Start your *holz hausen* on level ground, with maximum exposure to sun and wind. Cover the ground with gravel or a thick layer of bark, or some other material to keep your firewood away from the moisture in the soil. Pound a stake into the ground, and tie a string around it. Cut the string off four feet from the stake, and knot it to prevent unraveling. This is your measuring string — the radius of the *holz hausen.*

At the end of the string, place a small piece of flat wood at right angles to the string. I use scrap lumber sawn about 18 inches in length. Next to that flat piece place another one, whose center is also perpendicular to the string. These pieces of wood form the outside radius of your *holz hausen,* and also keep its outside edge tipped inward. Move around the circle, placing wood pieces; the string keeps your radius constant, forming a circle about eight feet in diameter. Depending on the height of the stack and how tightly you stack it (you don't want it too dense, you want the air to move through it), your *holz hausen* will hold about a cord and a half of wood.

Begin stacking your firewood with the outside of each block aligned with the far end of your measuring string. This way, your beginning row of blocks will be tilted in toward the center, helping ensure the stability of your stack.

You'll soon notice that the natural tendency of the wood is to tilt outward, not inward. That's because the blocks of wood, being roughly rectangular, will radiate from the center point of the circle like the petals of a flower. This causes V-shaped gaps opening outward between each block of wood. The wood above the gaps wants to settle into them, tipping the wood blocks outward and weakening

Cross braces placed at a height of three and six feet help hold the holz hausen together.

This holz hausen holds about 1½ cords of wood.

the stack. This is the single biggest challenge of building a *holz hausen* (really, it's the only one I can think of). You'll need to battle this tendency with your ingenuity and a bit of care, but since you are smarter than a block of wood, it's not hard to do.

One way to keep your wood always tilted inward is to make sure that the fat part of every block is on the outside of the circle. This extra width may be caused by knots or broken branches sticking out of the block; also, split pieces will often flare around a large knot, causing one end to be wider than the other. You can use a smaller-diameter piece of wood to wedge into a pesky gap to maintain your angle. I have also found that shifting a piece so it's slightly diagonal to its neighbors will often cause its inside end to drop down, which is what I want.

You can also prop up a sagging block with a smaller stick placed perpendicular to it, to boost its drooping ends. Just make sure that your prop log goes in split side down, so that it isn't forced out under pressure.

When the stack is about three feet high, place two 8-foot cross poles right across the stack. I make these from natural wood poles I cut from my property. Place them at right angles to each other, and make sure the ends are aligned with the outsides of the blocks. This will help hold the *holz hausen* together as it rises. Place a second set of cross poles between the 5- and 6-foot levels, and continue stacking at least two more feet of blocks above this to hold it steady.

Once there's enough weight on the first set of cross poles to hold it in place, you can begin tossing wood blocks of firewood loosely into the center (some people suggest that you can stack it vertically there). The substrate of gravel or bark will keep these blocks from ground moisture, and their loose configuration will help allow air penetration through the entire stack.

This inner woodpile serves two purposes. One, its bulk helps hold the mass in place and increases its stability even further. Two, it allows you to dry more wood in the same area than if the *holz hausen* were hollow. I like to throw drier pieces into the center. This reduces the total amount of moisture that needs to be removed from the stack, and ensures that if the drying process is slower than anticipated, I still have well-dried wood in the center.

Finish your *holz hausen* by first heaping up the loose center pieces to form a mound. Then, on top of your top circle of wood, complete a circle of blocks split in half with the bark still on. Create a second tier of similar blocks inset 8-12 inches in from the first circle, and a third circle in from the second. These circles will begin climbing the mound you made as you move inward, raising inner tiers above outer tiers. Continue to shrink your circle right into the center. This will give you a "thatched roof" top to your *holz hausen.* Bark is waterproof, so this covering will shed much of the precipitation that may fall on your stack during the summer. The rising concentric circles finish off your *holz hausen* nicely.

As for drying wood efficiently, I'm hooked. The *holz hausen* does a great job of reducing fresh, wet wood to crackin' dry fuel in reduced time, and its handsome and sturdy shape ensures that everybody who sees it knows all about my love affair with wood heat. Δ

Living with wolves

By Len McDougall

Luminous numbers on my bedside clock told me that it was just four a.m. when I awoke to the frantic barking of sled dogs from their chain-link kennels next to the house. Like any parent, I could differentiate between the voices of my huskies, and it was clear that Cuda, our largest and strongest "wheel" dog, was sounding most urgent. His was the only one of our ten 10x10-foot kennels that opened to the outside, and because obedient Cuda never wandered beyond the boundaries we'd taught him, or got into mischief, his gate was sometimes left open at night.

This apparent savagery is a normal part of the gray wolf's vocabulary; pack mates snarl and tussle frequently, but no blood is drawn.

Rubbing my scratchy eyes and feeling around in the darkness for slippers with my feet, I grabbed one of the several bright LED flashlights we keep at strategic points between cabin and barn. Cuda's bark was shrill, almost panicked, as I threw on a jacket and headed out into the snowy night.

When I reached his kennel, Cuda was inside, backed against the rear fence panel, a look of authentic terror in his rolled-back eyes. I swept the flashlight's beam through the woods in the direction the dog was trying to back away from, and stopped it on an adult gray wolf, standing atop the hardpack about 25 yards distant. The wolf was a young adult, judging from the contrasts of its mask and saddle markings, probably three or four years old, wandering alone while the Alphas — its father and mother — were off establishing a den site for their newest litter of offspring. From December through March, it wasn't uncommon to see lone wolves wandering the pack ice of Whitefish Bay, hunting squirrels, especially, that could be maneuvered onto the open ice, where a wolf has the advantage.

The young, apparently male, wolf was fixated on poor Cuda, its head lowered, hackles raised, and lips curled back from impressive canines. It seemed not to notice me or my light in the heat of this testosterone-filled challenge for territory. Fortunately, 85-pound Cuda was nearly the size of his challenger, which probably explained why there hadn't been bloodshed yet. Still, the dog seemed to recognize that this wouldn't be a contest merely for social status, and he appeared to realize that a physical conflict here would be equivalent to pitting a street brawler against a professional killer. Cuda had never brought down anything larger than a red squirrel, while the fact that this wolf stood before me was confirmation enough that it was proficient at taking lives to feed itself.

I stepped between wolf and dog, and shined my light directly into the lobo's eyes. That got its attention, finally. But the wolf didn't regard a confrontation with me in the same way it had my dog; it held its position for a brief moment, but when I began walking heavily in its direction, it fled into the woods before I took three steps. I spent a few minutes comforting my scared dog, then latched his gate, and it has been latched every night since; at least until this wolf's pack regroups in early May and moves on.

There was nothing bold in my actions. Running off this probing wolf didn't demand courage, but it did employ an understanding of wolf behavior — an ability to "speak wolf," if you will. Having lived with a captive pack (kept under state permit) for more than a decade has provided some insight into the unique behaviorisms and habits of timber wolves. I don't believe a wolf can actually be owned by anyone, but having had the privilege of interacting with and observing one of nature's largest predators on a daily basis for many years has been an experience filled with epiphanies.

A common misconception about predators in general is that they like to fight. Predators that rarely eat without killing always target the weakest prey, because survival demands avoiding the possibility of injury as much as hunger permits. A broken jaw — not uncommon in animals that hunt hoofed prey — leads to slow, painful death. Gray wolves are legendary for taking care of their own injured, but solitary hunters can be in dire straits from a variety of wounds that might impair their ability to feed themselves — a fact that has made the cat family efficient at dispatching prey with a minimum of fight.

Starvation causes desperation in every species (ours not least of all) but wolves always choose the path of least resistance when it comes to violence, preferring small, weak, or injured prey. All members of the Canid family universally scavenge already dead animals (here in the Upper Penninsula, many road-killed deer are removed from roadsides within a day by large carnivores), and may even shadow weakened ungulates until they are too near death to struggle. Lone wolves have been known to run down yearling deer in a snowbound forest, or onto lake ice where having hooves is a disadvantage, but most make a living under human radar, feeding on voles, mice, and other plentiful (but smaller) prey.

The apparent savagery displayed by members of even the same pack toward one another — so beloved of movie makers — is one example of how different *Canis lupus* and our own best friend, *Canis familiaris,* are from one another. A dog that lowers its head, fixes its stare on your eyes, and bares its teeth is prepared to bite you at least once; a wolf that does the same is merely expressing dislike, and is unlikely to stand its ground if pressed. Snarling, growling, even what have been described as furious fights among pack mates are only squabbles, communicated in wolf-speak; neither animal is ever injured, and blood is drawn only by accident. The pack mentality is a product of pure survival, and each member instinctively refrains from detracting from the strength of the unit; dogs, however, have often displayed a willingness to kill their own kind — a phenomenon of which every dogsled driver is aware.

Its belly full, this wolf is rolling on meat that it can't eat, laying claim to it with a signature scent.

Another behaviorism that is unique to wolves is their historically-proven reluctance to harm humans. Tales of old are replete with stories of wolves doing all sorts of unbelievable things, but in real life, mountain men of old who were injured or starving have fed themselves by driving wolf packs from a kill. No other large predator would permit that, and wolves won't relinquish kills to any other carnivore, not even brown bears, without bloodshed.

A recent news article told how a state employee was "attacked" by a wolf in the Upper Peninsula when he happened upon a small pack feeding on a deer. The alpha wolf approached the man, he said, and he backed away until he was against a pile of brush; the wolves then left the scene without further incident. Like most similar encounters, the man was not harmed; he was merely a perceived competitor who had been driven away from the wolves' food cache. Had the wolf's intent been more serious, the man would have found himself beset on all sides by the entire pack.

Having appropriated meat from wolves myself, I would have selected a long, stout stave from that brush pile, and wielded it like a staff while I made my retreat, never allowing the wolf to see my back. Wolves are fearful of anything that is new or beyond their understanding, and our ability to transform inanimate objects from the surrounding terrain into weapons is incomprehensible to most species. Holding a long, stout stave (shovel handle) in front of myself has always caused a wolf to regard it, not me, as the enemy, and just swinging it through the air to make a whooshing sound has set both wolves and bears to running. A second long stick waved behind as you withdraw makes pack mates think you have eyes in the back of your head, and a wolf that does get behind you is likely to bite at the stick first.

If you find yourself confronted by a wolf — or any predator — try to remember that nature is logical, and for a usually shy animal to confront a species that has always been its most lethal enemy infers that the animal has something that it believes is valuable. Wildlife experts universally agree that the best advice for any such confrontation is to back away slowly; don't turn your back, and never run — your chances of actually outrunning a larger quadruped are nil, anyway.

If the animal confronting you approaches, and you don't have a long stave, make yourself look larger by spreading your jacket out from the sides, or by holding a backpack or other large object over your head, and roar at it with as much volume as you can muster. The goal, as taught to me by old Amos Wasageshik, my Ojibwa grandfather, when I was a boy, is to make yourself look dangerous, and capable of inflicting serious injury, but not threatening enough to trigger a fight.

This wolf stood its ground for just a moment, but fled when the author approached.

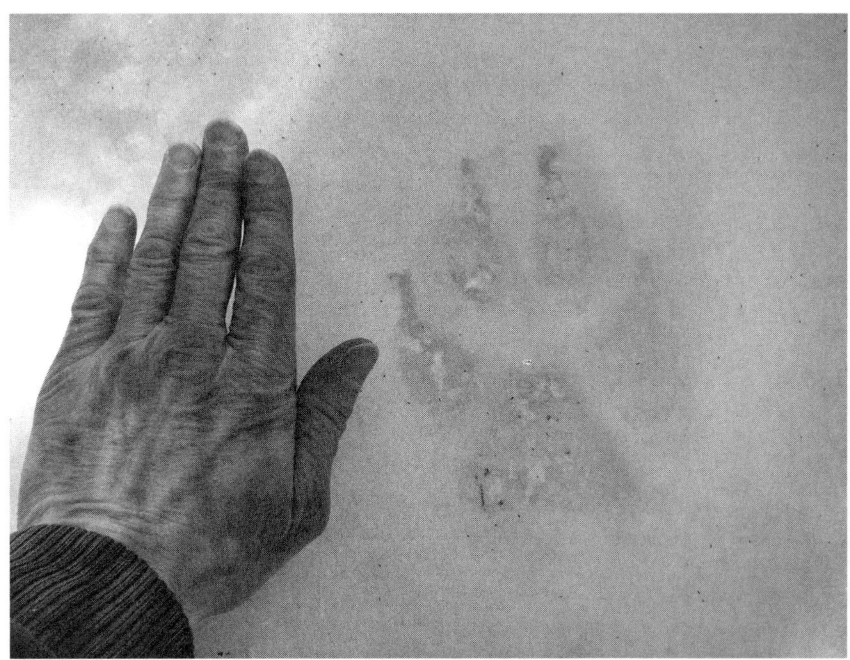

A right front wolf track in snow; a typical adult has forepaws that are at least four inches long, discounting claw marks — much larger than coyotes or dogs.

Based on experiences gathered from interacting with captive wolves in a large enclosure, where they cannot run away as wolves in the wild would, one action that you should never take when confronted by a wolf is to kick at it. Wolves consider that to be an active attack, and another lesson I've learned from captive wolves is that if you take on one, you'll deal with the entire pack. A long staff is regarded with fear, but striking out with hands or feet is an invitation to fight.

After more than a decade of working with wolves in captivity and in the wild — where I've been blessed with three face-to-face encounters — and sleeping hundreds of nights on snow and dirt in woods where wolf packs howl, I do not believe that wolves are a threat to humans. The death of Kenton Joel Carnegie in Saskatchewan in November of 2005 prompted Mounties to shoot two of three wolves that locals had been feeding, but when Dr. Lynn Rogers arrived on the already trampled scene, he quickly proved that the killer had been an old bear.

The mauling death of jogger Candice Berner, near Chignik Lake, Alaska on March 8, 2010 was "probably" caused by wolves, but Alaska State Police Colonel Audie Holloway stated, "If we're able to actually prove which animal, it will be through some kind of DNA analysis or through some expert that can maybe testify or explain how they know that it's a wolf." The Alaska State Police have refused further comment, but the fact that few wildlife authorities believe that wolves — who are inquisitive, and known to investigate corpses — are to blame is reflected in the lack of press this story received.

Me, I believe what wolves have taught me. Based on that, I'll continue to share the woods with them without fear. Δ

The *best* apple pie you'll ever bake

By Richard Blunt

Dave Duffy, the publisher of *Backwoods Home Magazine*, asked me to review some of my early recipes and see if any needed updating. After rereading a few, I selected several that have undergone changes since *BHM* first published them. Most of these changes have been the result of comments and suggestions made by friends, family, and *Backwoods Home* readers. Over the years I've made a habit of recording these comments and criticisms. So, recently, I decided to review these notes and select the recipes that have generated the most comments.

To my surprise dessert recipes, especially pies, seemed to garner the most attention. The apple pie recipe I included in my article on great American foods in Issue #30 (Nov/Dec 1994) received at least 60 suggestions and other comments. Several came from my wife's mother, Gertrude. On one occasion, after eat-

Limiting gluten formation makes a better pie crust.

ing a piece of my pie at a family Christmas dinner, she offered a few suggestions she said would make my pie almost as good as hers, if I followed her instructions. After reading that comment, I decided that my immediate goal would be to get beyond "almost as good." What follows is my latest attempt to reach this goal.

Since Thanksgiving and Christmas, two great occasions for making pies, are almost upon us, and apple season is currently at its peak, this is a great time to update this favorite and frequently-prepared dessert.

Over the years I have often relied on my mother's old recipe file for guidance, especially when preparing dessert recipes. Once she found a recipe she liked, she would copy it on an index card and place it in an old mahogany cigar humidor. From that day on, the selected recipe became a standard in her kitchen. She very seldom made changes to these recipes unless she had to make a substitution for an unavailable ingredient. My mother was one of those rare individuals with a never-fail long-term memory. She never recorded any of these changes on the card. Unlike my mom, I have a terrible memory, but I am constantly revising recipes as I discover ways to improve them and when I make any changes to a recipe, I record that change on the recipe card. The changes to this apple pie recipe were so extensive I decided to share them with everyone in a new article.

This revised recipe produces a pie with mounds of tender, juicy apples surrounded by a rich and flaky pastry crust. However, handing folks a new recipe that includes only changed ingredients and an updated assembly procedure is not going to be enough. I want to make you a better cook, too, and understanding why these changes are necessary is also important. This updated pie does not replace my mom's original. I grew up loving all of her pies, and will continue to use her original recipe from time to time.

My wife, Tricia, and daughter, Sarah, helped pick enough apples for 10 pies.

My mother would make her first apple pie around the first of October, when the new crop of New England apples appeared in the local markets. She was very selective when choosing the apples for her pies. Her favorite was a tart, grayish-green apple called the Roxbury Russet, believed to be the oldest apple bred in this country. We also lived in the Boston neighborhood where this apple was first planted, Roxbury, Massachusetts, and across the street from a church that had two of these trees in back. Unfortunately, this apple is not widely available on the market today, probably because it isn't a very attractive apple, and it only produces fruit in alternate years. Her second choice was one of the sweet varieties, usually Golden Delicious or Braeburn. These three apples are excellent choices for a pie because they hold their shape during baking.

Her pie crust is basic. It is made with vegetable shortening, flour, salt, and ice water and is easy to prepare and produces reliable results. The apple filling contains about two pounds of apples, sugar, cinnamon, salt, butter, and flour, and is easy to assemble and tastes great. My updated version doesn't stray far from the original, but it produces a better pie that solves most of the perceived shortcomings in the original.

I live in New England and apple picking in the fall is an established tradition in my family. There is one orchard in my area that grows Roxbury Russet apples and my first apple picking adventure includes a trip to this orchard to see if these apples are available. I hold to mother's standard of using only fresh, crisp apples in my pie, so the Blunt family looks forward to our first fall apple picking adventure.

Last weekend, my wife Tricia, my daughter Sarah, and I went apple picking. My sons, Jason and Michael, are away pounding the books at their respective universities and missed this annual event. As usual, after we finished picking and handing our bag of apples to the owner for weighing, we discover that we had picked enough apples for 10 pies. Of course everyone was looking at me with that, "What are going to make with all of these apples" look on their faces. Before Sarah could voice her post-apple picking plea, I offered my suggestion for an apple pie as a starter.

"Daddy," she said, "you're supposed to wait for me to ask that question."

This first apple picking adventure has been a family ritual for 22 years. Almost every aspect of it has become a tradition etched in stone, including suggestions about what to do with the apples. Speak out of turn and you will be put in your place. I apologized for speaking out of turn and we paid for our apples and headed for home.

Immediately after unloading our apple cargo, I took both my mother's original apple pie recipe and my revised version out of the working file, and began separating and peeling enough apples to make both pies. From October through early spring all types of pies are favorite desserts in my house, with apple pie at the top of the list. So, determining which version of this pie would be the standard had to be decided.

Once again, the final decision would be made by the recipe review committee: my wife and my three children. Over the years they have tastefully yet methodically deconstructed the old standard for this favorite dessert. The most recent observations came from Michael and Sarah last fall. We had finished dinner and I announced that I made apple pie for dessert. I cut everyone a piece, and, as usual, we all cleaned our plates.

After dinner, Michael wanted to know why there was a huge air space between the top crust and the apple filling.

I told him that the apples lose moisture as the pie bakes, causing them to shrink.

"Oh," he said, "so that is why there is so much juice on the bottom of the pie." He also pointed out that this juice made the bottom crust a little soggy.

Since I had always believed that a somewhat soggy bottom crust is an unavoidable consequence of making an apple pie with fresh apples, I didn't consider this a real problem.

A few weeks later I made another apple pie and Sarah came to me with another observation.

"Dad," she said, "the crust on this pie is not the same as the last one. It isn't as crispy; it also seems to be a little tough and pale."

This pie usually receives blanket approval, so these constructive criticisms caught me a little off guard. In spite of my surprise, I promised Sarah and Michael I would consider their observations and see if there was a solution.

A couple of days after my conversation with Sarah I posed these questions to a professional baker who has a solid knowledge of baking science. He gave me several suggestions he thought would help me improve the crust and filling. The combination of his advice and some interesting facts I learned while researching whole grain breads led me to a complete revision of my mother's apple pie recipe. The basic food science applied here is really simple, but the effect on the finished pie is dramatic. The most radical changes are in the crust recipe, so let's start there.

New never-fail pie crust

The original version of this crust formula is simple and results in an easy-to-assemble pie crust and yields predictable results. This new formula uses almost the same amount of flour, salt, and shortening as the original recipe. I replaced half of the vegetable shortening with unsalted butter, which adds flavor. Also, I have added one common pastry ingredient, sugar, and one not so common ingredient, 80 proof vodka. Yes, VODKA! Okay, let's talk about the vodka first.

All workable formulas for pie crust contain some brand of all-purpose flour. Depending on the brand you use, this type of flour has a protein content of about 11 percent. Protein is essential to the formation of gluten. When making bread, the formation of a strong gluten network is a definite plus. However, when making a pastry, like pie crust, limiting gluten formation can yield better results. As I explained in my last two bread articles, gluten is formed when two partial proteins (gliadin and glutenin), present in all wheat flours, link together when water is added to the flour. When making pie crust gluten can, if not kept in check, make for a tough pie crust. I first tried to solve this problem by incorporating a portion of cake flour, which contains about half of the protein of all-purpose flour, into my crust formula. The result was a crust that was somewhat dry and had a sandy texture.

My baker friend told me that professional bakers have long understood the need to limit gluten formation when making a pastry crust. The most efficient way to accomplish this is to carefully control the amount of water in the formula. Too much water will yield a tough crust. However, without proper hydration the crust will be dry and difficult to roll. With the amount of flour in my formula he calculated that I would need 9 tablespoons of cold liquid, and suggested that four tablespoons of that liquid be some type of alcohol. His preference was 80 proof vodka. He explained that since 80 proof vodka contains only 60 percent water, the remaining 40 percent is ethanol. Gluten will not form in the presence of alcohol as it does with water. So four tablespoons of vodka added only about 2½ tablespoons of water to the dough, while the total liquid volume remained the same. This small, but significant, reduction in water volume will result in pie dough that is both easy to roll and tender when baked. If you are worried about the alcohol, it vaporizes in the oven during baking.

He told me, "Adding sugar and salt to most baked items is essential to the development of flavor. Also, adding a little lemon zest will add brightness to the finished crust. Sugar also insures proper browning of the crust during baking." He went on to say, "Mixing the fat with the flour should be done in two stages. The first mix should include all of the fat, and nearly half of the flour blended with the sugar and salt. The remaining flour can be added after the first batch is fully incorporated, and mixed just enough for it to become evenly distributed. Combining the ingredients in this manner creates small pockets of fat that are only coated with flour. These pockets of unincorporated fat melt when the crust is baked, resulting in crisp, flaky layers."

While working my way through the recipes in my previous bread articles, I discovered that scooping with a measuring cup was an unreliable method for measuring flour. Professional bakers use a balance scale to accurately weigh the principal ingredients of a recipe, including liquids. By applying this wisdom of weighing the flour that I use in my bread recipes, I solved all of my consistency problems with my pie crust.

I usually use my 11-cup food processor to mix pie dough. But, after talking to several neighbors and family members, I realize that some folks prefer a standing mixer fitted with a paddle to perform this task. Still others, like my mom, use a dough cutter to blend the fat with the flour mixture. I made this crust using all three methods with good results. The food processor and standing mixer both produced excellent dough with about the same effort. If you have plenty of time and don't mind a little hard labor, the dough cutter produces dough very close to one mixed by machine.

When using a food processor or manual dough cutter, the fat must be refrigerator-cold. With the standing mixer the fat should be allowed to come to a cool room temperature. This will prevent the paddle from throwing flour all over your counter. Like any other carefully-crafted recipe, this one requires a little more work and attention to detail than other pie crust formulas. But once you have mastered the technique, I am sure that you will find the extra effort rewarding when your pie comes out of the oven.

New never-fail pie crust

Ingredients:

11½ oz. unbleached all-purpose flour (Note: I use King Arthur all-purpose flour in all of my baking formulas, because I believe it produces the most consistent results.)
1 tsp. table salt
2 Tbsp. light brown sugar
6 oz. chilled vegetable shortening, cut into ½-inch pieces
3 oz. chilled unsalted butter, cut into ¼-inch pieces
½ tsp. grated lemon zest
4 Tbsp. chilled vodka
5 Tbsp. ice water

Method:

1. Combine the flour with the salt and sugar in a large bowl and blend.
2. Transfer 6 ounces of this mixture to a food processor or standing mixer with the paddle attached.
3. Add the chilled shortening and unsalted butter. Process until the dough starts to develop uneven clumps — about 15 seconds. The dough will look like large curd cottage cheese and all of the fat will be coated with flour.
4. Scrape the bowl and evenly distribute the dough around the blade or paddle.
5. Add the remaining flour and pulse in short bursts until the ingredients are evenly distributed. This should take only five or six pulses or 15 to 20 seconds at medium speed with the standing mixer.
6. Empty the mixture into a medium bowl. Add the grated lemon zest to chilled vodka and ice water. Sprinkle this mixture over the dough.
7. Using a rubber spatula begin folding the dough and pressing down on the mixture after each fold. Continue folding until the dough sticks together and forms a tacky ball. You will have about 25 ounces of dough.
8. Divide the dough into two balls of equal weight, and flatten each ball into a 4-inch disk. Wrap these disks in plastic wrap and refrigerate them for at least one hour.

The Blunt family's new favorite apple pie filling

As I said earlier, there are no wonder ingredients in this updated pie filling. I have doubled the amount of apples, added a little lemon zest and one tablespoon of instant tapioca. The only other flavor in this filling is ground cinnamon and white and brown sugar. Sugar performs several tasks in this filling. It works in cooperation with the salt to extract moisture from the apples, boosts the sweetness of the apples, and acts as a binding agent to hold the filling together.

Let's begin with the problems I discovered in the original formula. The most noticeable problem, with the original pie, was the huge empty space between the crust and the filling after the pie was baked. This was caused by heat extracting water from the apples during baking. The volume of this extracted water is one reason why most two-crusted apple pies only contain about two pounds of apples. In a vain attempt to prevent this liquid from soaking the bottom crust, some form of starch thickener is traditionally added to the filling. I have tried several concoctions like plain gelatin, cornstarch mixed with lemon juice, and a butter/flour roux with limited success. On a couple of occasions I overdid it with these starches and

New-age deep-dish apple pie

ruined the pie. This approach to thicken the extracted liquid gave the filling a texture that made it taste like it came from a can. It really didn't do much to solve the soggy bottom crust problem.

I wasn't sure if there were any satisfactory answers to these problems, so I went back to the baker for advice. His answer to what I thought was a complex problem was simple and to the point. "Double the amount of apples in the pie," he said. "Then cook the apples over low heat to extract most of the water. The water will be flavored with the brown sugar, lemon zest, and cinnamon. This flavored apple juice can then be drained from the tenderized apples, thickened to the desired consistency and folded back into the cooled apples. You will only need about one cup of this flavored juice to properly stabilize the filling."

"Why low heat?" I asked.

"Apples naturally contain a generous amount of pectin, a complex carbohydrate that gives them structure. When the apples are cooked at the right temperature, the pectin is converted to a heat-stable form, which will continue to add structure to the apples. If you cook the apples at high temperature this natural pectin loses much of its binding ability, resulting in mushy and overly soft apples. Drain the cooked apples in a large colander and save the juice. If you want a pie with a concentrated apple flavor, discard this juice, cool the apples to room temperature and make your pie.

"Personally," he added, "I like the subtle flavor boost the added liquid provides, so I put it into the pie.

"Finally, when you preheat the oven, place a large rimmed-cookie sheet on the rack to heat up. When you are ready to bake, set the pie on the hot baking sheet. This simple step quickly liquefies the solid fat in the bottom crust and distributes it evenly between the particles of flour, creating a tight seal that prevents the juice from the apples from seeping and making the bottom crust soggy."

Since that conversation, I have made at least six versions of this pie, starting with the seasoned, precooked apples and no fortified sauce, followed by three pies using various amounts of tapioca-thickened liquid. Deciding on which one of these pies would become the standard was not easy. You see, I only had two members of the recipe review committee as tasters: my wife Tricia and my daughter Sarah. They are two of the toughest pie critics I know. We were unable to make a final decision until I made two of these versions a second time.

The notes that I make on recipe cards are usually just a few sentences long. Because there are so many comments about this recipe, the notes filled eight index cards. I am confident the procedures I outline here will produce the same results for you as they did for me. Besides the extra time needed to cut the additional two pounds of apples, this pie requires no more effort than the original recipe. Please give it a try. I am sure that you will be satisfied with the results of your efforts. I still love the original version of this pie, but I will admit that this updated version is better.

New-age deep-dish apple pie

Ingredients:

- 2½ lbs. Golden Delicious apples
- 2 lbs. Cortland or Granny Smith apples
- 5½ oz. granulated sugar
- 2 oz. light brown sugar
- 1 tsp. ground cinnamon
- ½ tsp. lemon zest
- ½ tsp. table salt
- 1 tsp. lemon juice
- 1 cup extracted apple juice (This is the juice you'll be creating when you're cooking the apples.)
- 1 Tbsp. instant tapioca, ground to a powder in a spice grinder or coffee mill
- 1 large egg, lightly beaten with 2 tsp. of cold water (which will be used when assembling the pie)

Method:

1. Peel and core the apples, then cut them into ¼-inch slices.

2. In a large bowl combine the apples, granulated sugar, brown sugar, cinnamon, lemon zest, and table salt. Gently toss this mixture with the apples.

3. Place the apples in a large Dutch oven, cover and cook the apples over

medium heat, stirring frequently, until the apples are just tender and still hold their shape. This will take about 15 to 20 minutes. The juice being extracted from the apples should be maintained at a gentle simmer. Adjust the heat up or down as necessary.

4. Transfer the apples and juice to a large rimmed cookie sheet and cool to room temperature. This will take about 30 minutes.

5. While the apples are cooling, heat the oven to 425° F and place an aluminum foil-covered rimmed cookie sheet on the middle rack.

6. Drain the juice from the apples through a large colander set over a large bowl. Gently shake the colander to extract as much juice as possible. (This will be your "extracted apple juice" listed in the ingredients.)

7. If you haven't done it already, grind the instant tapioca to a fine powder in a spice grinder or coffee grinder used for this purpose.

8. Combine one cup of the extracted apple juice and the lemon juice with the instant tapioca in a small sauce pan and mix well. Bring this mixture to a simmer while stirring constantly until the mixture thickens, about two to three minutes after it starts to simmer.

9. Cool this mixture for about five minutes and gently mix with the cooled apples.

Assembling and baking the pie

Let's put this pie together and bake it to find out if all this new-age science works.

1. Reduce the oven heat to 400° F.

2. Remove one of the chilled dough disks from the refrigerator, place it on a generously-floured work surface, and roll it into a 12-inch circle.

3. Gently drape the rolled dough on the rolling pin and transfer it to a nine-inch pie plate. Position the dough so that there is a one-inch overhang around the edge.

4. Working around the circumference of the dough, gently press the dough into the bottom contour of the plate. Then put the dough-lined pie plate in the refrigerator for at least 20 minutes.

5. After 20 minutes, remove the pie plate from the refrigerator and transfer the cooled apple mixture to the pie plate. Return the filled pie to the refrigerator to keep cool.

6. Remove the second disk of dough from the refrigerator and roll into a 10-inch circle on a floured work surface. Remove the filled pie from the refrigerator and transfer the rolled dough disk to the pie, leaving an even one-inch overhang around the plate. Pinch the edges of the top and bottom crusts firmly together to seal the pie. Trim away excess dough with a sharp knife. Cut four or five two-inch slits in the top of the pie with the same knife for vents.

7. Brush the entire surface of the pie with the beaten egg/water mixture.

8. Set the pie on the preheated cookie sheet and bake until the crust starts to brown — about 30 minutes.

9. Reduce the oven temperature to 375° F and continue baking until the pie is golden brown and the filling is bubbling — about 25 to 30 minutes.

10. Remove the baked pie from the oven, place it on a wire rack, and cool it for at least two hours.

Please give this apple pie a try, but don't abandon your old standard recipe, if you have one. As my son, Jason, says, "Apple pie is the best and it is almost impossible to make a bad one." Δ

Mushing

By Len McDougall

The air is cold enough to freeze your nostrils together when you inhale, and exhaled moisture hangs in a dense white cloud for a few seconds before dissipating. The dogs bark and dance around as the gangline is clipped to their harnesses, then to a neckline extending from the gangline to their collar rings. The team is eager to go; if the sled wasn't snubbed to a large red pine, and anchored on the opposite side by a steel snow hook stamped into the hardpack, the dogs would drag it driverless down the trail.

Satisfied that none of the dogs are tangled, the driver keeps them in place with a shouted "Hold!" and moves to the rear of the ash-frame racing sled. She steps on the runners with the lightweight Steger mukluks favored by competitive mushers who spend time running behind, or "pedaling" behind the sled. A tug against the quick-release hook of the snubline releases the rope from its anchor tree. Finally, she pulls up the snow hook and sets it into the handlebar holster. The lunging, anxious team is kept in check by only a steel-clawed foot brake driven into the snow under her weight.

The driver steps off the brake and onto the runners. The command to go is "Hike!" but the dogs are scrambling forward as soon as they feel the brake release. All is quiet now, except for the scraping of paws and runners against snow, and the panting of dogs who live to pull a sled.

Steel is in the lead; he's a wiry, cocky young fellow who struts around the kennel like a rooster, but becomes all business when he's on the job. Behind him are the "swing" dogs, Littlefoot and his sister Ducky, gentle animals who would prefer to follow rather than lead, but who could lead if it were asked of them. In the "wheel" positions, directly ahead of the sled, are the powerful brothers, Cuda and Saber, who provide the sheer muscle needed to keep the sled moving over rough terrain.

With a light sled and driver, these five Alaskan huskies deliver sufficient power to set a flying pace through

These Alaskan huskies love to pull. When team and driver are working in unison, it is a sight to behold.

You can't start a young musher's education too early.

Lake Superior State Forest. Although all of them are from long-distance racing teams, the dogs know their job today will be to simply pull first-time mushers around a three-quarter mile circuit. Being happy dogs, perhaps a little spoiled and a little fat by racing standards, the team members perceive their job as play, and are eager to please the driver.

The first leg of the circuit leads through 300 yards of pine and oak forest, then onto an abandoned logging road straightaway to a wide turnaround, a half-mile from there. The driver slows the team on a corner by pressing one foot down onto a "drag brake" — a section of snowmobile track mounted between the runners — while leaning inward to counterbalance the sled against centrifugal force that could otherwise overturn the rig. In the event that the sled does overturn, a driver is obligated to never release the sled's handlebar, and must instead drag along behind it until the dogs tire and slow enough for it to be righted again.

That isn't going to be a problem today. The trail is hard frozen and well packed under numerous snowshoe tracks, and a fresh dusting of snow softens it against the dogs' weather-toughened paws. The team is fully into the business of dogsledding now, mouths wide open and pink tongues lolling as they haul against the gangline with all the muscle each of them possesses. Snow flurries upward from behind 20 scrambling paws, settling onto the sled basket as the driver leans in hard on the final curve, skewing the sled's flexible frame as it skids to the outside edge of the trail.

One last ridge, and they break out of the forest onto the wide straightaway. To the huskies, it's a superhighway, and they kick in the afterburners, whisking the driver along at a pace that makes the wind whistle in her ears. The dogs race along almost in ecstasy until the driver again slows them by stepping onto the drag brake. They've reached the turnaround, where a man with a walkie-talkie waits to help teams negotiate the loop.

This driver needs no assistance. "Gee!" she shouts as the team approaches the trail split, a command to Steel, the leader, to guide them onto the right fork. He obeys, needing no further instruction as they engage the looping turn that leads back to the straightaway. The driver leans far into this long curve, managing to keep the sled on its runners as it skids along behind. The sled would be easier to handle if she applied the brake, but taking corners fast on a dogsled is part of the thrill. The man with the walkie-talkie sputters a bit at the wave of kicked-up snow that washes over him when the team races past.

The dogs are a bit less frantic on the return trip; not tired, but less insane in their desire to pull the sled. Steel sets a quick pace that none of the other dogs finds challenging, and the return trip flies by smoothly. The driver has to jump off the runners and "pedal" behind while pushing the sled over the first ridge when they reenter the woods, but after that, it's an easy run through snowy forest back to the staging area.

Back at the kennels, a shouted "whoa!" confirms to the dogs that they've reached the end of this run. The driver sets the snow hook, then snubs the sled to the anchor pine, before petting and congratulating the dogs individually as they are unhooked from the sled. Once loose, each dog runs to its own gated 10x10-

The power and speed of well-trained huskies as they pull driver and sled almost effortlessly along a snowy trail is an experience that drivers never forget.

foot chain-link kennel, where a warm, triple-wall insulated doghouse and a bucket of fresh, slightly warm water awaits them. To the dogs, this is home, and they're happy to be there.

Inside their kennels, the driver removes the pulling harness over the head of each dog, and each of them habitually raises a paw to allow the chest strap on that side to slip past its foreleg. She hangs each harness neatly from the chain-link outside. Finally, each dog receives a few ounces of frozen red meat, which they all relish, as reward for a good run. The dogs who haven't run yet are clamoring for their turns in harness.

The driver strips off her fleece hat to reveal a shock of straw-blonde hair. Cheanne Chellis has been running and training Alaskan huskies for nearly a decade, and she's good at what she does — good enough to teach a dogsledding workshop that trains beginners to harness and drive a sled solo.

After doing a good day's work, all the dogs get a warm supper of athlete-formula kibble, moistened and warmed with a half-dozen ladlesful of soup made from venison or beef scraps, sometimes boiled chicken broth. More than just working dogs, these huskies are part of the family, and their appearance denotes good care.

Cheanne loves teaching the nuts and bolts of mushing to people who might otherwise never get to drive a dog-sled, but she cautions that actually owning a team isn't for everyone. Mushers must be fit enough to jump off the runners and pedal to help the team crest a hill, and flexible enough to shift their weight quickly from one foot to another on uneven terrain and corners — it doesn't hurt to be on the athletic side. They also need to be comfortable working long hours outside in cold weather, and prepared to spend much or all of each day working with dogs.

Between the costs of food, medical care, and time, having one's own mushing kennel is a serious commitment, and the best-loved dogs are the best working dogs. Cheanne says she gets several calls a year from people who ask her to adopt whole teams because the responsibility of caring for them has overwhelmed the owners. Sadly, most of these dogs end up in a pound.

But you don't have to own a dog team and sled to experience the thrill of mushing. Fans can feel that thrill vicariously at dog sled races, like the Mackinaw Mush in Mackinaw City, Michigan, or the U.P. 200 (a qualifier for Alaska's Iditarod race). Local Chambers of Commerce can provide information about race locations and dates, and about mushers who might be operating dogsled tours or workshops.

Snowmobiling is exciting, and snowshoeing is serene, but no other winter activity provides the same romance, excitement, and satisfaction as mushing a team of huskies through a snowbound wilderness. It's an experience everyone should have, or even just observe, at least once. Δ

Dogsledding Organizations:

International Sled Dog Veterinary Medical Association
PO Box 828, Putney, VT 05346
http://www.isdvma.org
Information about dogsledding activities and organizations around the world.

Iditarod Trail Committee
PO Box 870800, Wasilla, AK 99687
http://www.iditarod.com

Great Lakes Sled Dog Association
http://www.glsda.com
Information on scheduled races, race results in the Great Lakes region.

Michigan Dog Drivers Association
http://www.michigandogdrivers.org
Dedicated to providing aspiring mid-distance dog drivers with organized events.

M.U.S.H. (Mid-Union Sled Haulers)
http://midunionsledhaulers.com
Recreational, family-oriented sled dog racing association.

Upper Peninsula Sled Dog Association
http://www.up200.org
PO Box 15, Marquette, MI 49855

Making Yogurt

By Patrice Lewis

When you get to the point where you're milking your own cow, you'll need to figure out what to do with the excess milk. One of the easiest and tastiest options is to make homemade yogurt.

Yogurt is nothing more than the bacterial fermentation of milk using specific cultures. As far as I know, any milk can be used (cow, goat, yak, water buffalo, whatever). Yogurt in one form or another has been around for literally thousands of years. Curdled milk, after all, is nothing new. Because the fermentation process changes lactose into lactic acid, people who are moderately lactose-intolerant are often able to eat yogurt without a problem.

Making yogurt requires two main ingredients: culture and heat. Both must be controlled in order to produce a successful batch of yogurt.

Theoretically, any commercial yogurt (bought at a grocery store) that contains live cultures can be used to culture your milk. However, I've had little success following this option and prefer to purchase a yogurt culture in powder form from a supply company.

While there are a number of yogurt cultures available from suppliers, I wanted something I could re-culture myself so I wouldn't have to keep purchasing new culture. After a bit of research, I found a Bulgarian Yogurt culture through the New England Cheesemaking Supply Company (www.cheesemaking.com). It can be

Heat milk on the lowest setting to no more than 180° F.

Stirring in half a cup of nonfat dry milk gives the finished yogurt a creamier texture.

re-cultured indefinitely without the need for fresh culture powder.

So...ready to make some yogurt? Let's start from the beginning. I'll pause for a while so you can go milk your cow...

...Now that you're back, strain and chill the milk and let's get started.

Let the milk cool to 105°- 110° F — don't stir. Scrape off and discard the skin that forms on top.

Start with about two quarts of milk. You can use skim or whole, fresh or store-bought. I prefer fresh skim. Put it in a pot on the lowest heat setting on the stove. You don't want to heat it too quickly or it will have a burned taste. Keep a thermometer in the milk to watch the temperature. Do not use a microwave.

I like to add half a cup of nonfat dry milk when I get started. This gives the yogurt a creamier texture. Stir the dry milk into the fresh milk until dissolved.

Heat the milk to no more than 180° F. Don't go any higher than this or the milk will taste burned. This temperature is high enough to kill off any undesirable bacteria and to denature the milk protein so it won't form curds (as with cheesemaking).

When the milk reaches 180° F, turn off the heat and let the milk cool to between 105° and 110° F. Don't stir the milk while it is cooling. It will form a thick nasty layer of skin on top. After the milk has cooled, scoop off and discard the skin (don't try to mix the skin back into the milk; it will only result in strings of skin in the yogurt). Don't let the milk cool to less than 105°F or it will be too cool to culture the milk. Re-warm if necessary.

Add the yogurt culture. Do *not* add the culture before the milk has cooled to at least 110° F. Trust me on this; you will kill your culture if you add it to the milk when it's too warm. Stir the culture in thoroughly.

Now the milk has to be incubated for a minimum of 5 to 6 hours. The longer it incubates, the tarter the yogurt. (I usually incubate mine about 12 hours because I like a tarter yogurt.) Anything can be used as long as the milk stays warm. Several years ago I bit the bullet and bought a Yogotherm Yogurt Maker because it's non-electric and simple to clean (it's literally just a plastic bucket that nests inside a Styrofoam sleeve and cover). You could probably put the milk behind the woodstove in order to stay warm, or inside a gas oven with a pilot light, or wrapped in towels and tucked inside a small ice chest. Use your creativity to come up with some way to keep the milk warm. But low-grade heat is necessary for the milk to culture and thicken properly.

When you are sure the milk has cooled to at least 110° F, add the yogurt culture.

After the yogurt has incubated for several hours, chill the yogurt for about 12 hours.

Before flavoring the yogurt, scoop out a few ounces and put it in a small container. Cover and keep this in the fridge. This is your starter for the next batch. The starter is best used within a couple of weeks — the older it is, the less effective it is. If you don't make yogurt very often, you may have to purchase some more starter culture for your next batch. However, the starter can be frozen and then thawed at room-temperature (*not* in the microwave!) to store it for longer periods of time.

The hot cultured milk must incubate for a minimum of 5-6 hours.

The yogurt can be sweetened and flavored to your preference. You can use honey, sugar, Splenda, or eat it unsweetened. You can add vanilla flavoring or puréed fruit. My favorite combination is one cup Splenda plus two cups peach purée.

Fresh yogurt will store in the refrigerator far longer than fresh milk. I've eaten yogurt that is two or three weeks old and the only problem is it needs a little stirring and has a tarter flavor than fresh-made yogurt.

Making yogurt is such an easy task that it will become a routine way to use up some of the excess milk from your dairy animals. Δ

Building Eric's house PART 6

By Dorothy Ainsworth

"*It doesn't matter how slowly you go as long as you don't stop.*" This saying by Confucius is definitely my *modus operandi*. It has taken six years to build Eric's house, but this ol' tortoise with lipstick is getting very close to the finish line.

Several wild hares I know told me I was nuts to start another long, drawn-out building project. They chose to buy instant houses, and now, sadly, a few of them are in foreclosure. Eric and I *do* have some credit card debt, but it's manageable.

"Building Eric's House, Part 5" (Issue #129, May/June 2011) left off with the kitchen and bathroom tile laid, cabinets and countertops installed, and the sink and toilet plumbing hooked up. After that expense, we needed some time to save up for the siding ($3,000), so I continued to work on the interior of the house. I decided to install the door jambs and doors because we *did* have enough money for that relatively small job. The idea was to keep moving.

Installing doors

My old haunt, Builders Bargain Center, had a nice supply of beautiful solid pine doors — with small imperfections here and there — at half-price. I bought six of them for $60 each, six locksets for $20 each, and 12 hinges for $3 each. I also bought some 1x8 pine and ran it through the table saw to rip an inch off the width of each board to fit the 6½-inch wide jambs (2x6 framing is 5½ inches wide plus two thicknesses of ½-inch

Dorothy using a hole-cutting jig so lockset can be installed

At left, counter-boring bit and plugs to hide screw heads in door jambs. At right, handmade jambs, doorstops, and trim.

sheetrock). I fastened the jambs to the door framing with screws, but first countersunk the holes ¼-inch deep with a special bit so they could be plugged with attractive hardwood bungs.

To save money, I also made my own ¾x1¾-inch doorstop molding out of pine and rounded the edges with a router. After the doors were hung, I used small-gauge finish nails to attach the stops to the jambs while pressing them against the *closed* doors. I used a nail-set to sink the heads below the surface, and filled each tiny hole with wood putty.

A new building code required that we install a door or window

At left, Eric uses a Sawzall to remove sheathing from fire escape opening. At right, the fire escape is made from half of a pine door.

Dorothy saved about $200 by reconditioning a second-hand front door.

fire escape (called "egress") out of the bedroom. It had to be big enough for a 300-pounder to jump out of, and placed no more than 40 inches off the floor. The 2x4-foot existing bedroom window is 60 inches off the floor (for privacy) so it would be hard to climb out of.

This emergency exit was in the original plans and already framed-in, but had been sheathed over during the winter. Eric cut the sheathing out with a Sawzall, and I installed one half of a pine door in the opening after fastening cedar jambs. I made a slanted sill out of a hunk of redwood I had lying around unemployed, and weather-stripped the stops. Because the recessed door opens *in*, we'll put a screen on the outside. When the "dutch door" is open, a nice breeze wafts through the room, so what seemed like a ridiculous code requirement turned out to be a good idea after all, not to mention attractive and useful.

Eric's dad gave him a heavy-duty metal front door with a built-in jamb and threshold. It was second-hand and needed some repair and restoration but was a good-looking residential style. I completed the work in just a few hours, then painted the door and hung it. We saved about $200 and it looks as good as new.

As soon as I finished installing all the doors and their hardware, I trimmed them out with pine-grained molding secured with small-gauge finish nails called brads. I cut each section to length by hand and mitered the 45-degree corners using a fine-toothed saw and miter box. Then with medium-gauge finish nails I installed all the pine-grained baseboard 3/8 inch off the floor around the perimeter of each room so the carpet could be pushed into that crevice when the time came.

Finishing the interior

The time came faster than I had planned. I myself turned into a wild hare one day and called a carpet guy I knew for an estimate. He came out, measured, and brought samples. For $1900 (including labor) he said he would pad and carpet the whole house with 110 yards of affordable 28 oz. commercial-grade carpet — which is what Eric wanted — and have it done in four hours. (His estimate was $500 less than Lowe's and Home Depot's for the same quality.) We couldn't resist the temptation of going ahead and getting that job done via a low-interest credit card. It would mean the interior of the house would then be completed — so we went for it.

While I was still in the hopping mode, I also called a propane installer (Suburban Propane) and had a 125-gallon tank brought out, and had the orifices in the kitchen range converted from natural gas to propane. The good news was that a 125-gallon tank can be installed right near the house so we didn't have to dig a trench and bury a pipeline — as is required with larger tanks. Yay! The serviceman hooked us up to the gas pipe stub sticking out of the wall. The pipe had been installed during the plumbing job and had already been inspected and pressure-tested. At this point only the kitchen range is propane so a tank full of gas (100 gallons) should last a year — to the tune of $300. Installation of the whole system, including the annual tank rental, was an affordable $200.

Eric's basic color scheme is blue/gray flooring and blonde wood against white walls, and his hardware and fixtures are brushed nickel and stainless steel. It's a conservative industrial look and that's what he likes. I built a raised hearth for the woodstove, tiled it with a variegated blue/gray ceramic tile, and trimmed it in blondish molding to match all the other trim in the house. The total cost of materials for the hearth was $200 and the job was totally doable for any semi-skilled do-it-yourselfer.

I installed a 4x8-foot section of tongue and groove hardwood bamboo flooring in the entryway because it will wear well under traffic. It was on sale at Home Depot for only 88 cents a square foot, and took about two hours to install with construction adhesive. (I chose not to use nails.) The whole job cost $50.

When all the interior finish work was done, I couldn't wait to get out my sewing machine and make curtains. I've probably fooled a lot of people over the years because of my massive (seemingly masculine) building projects, but if the truth be known, I am *not* the tough gal type who loves to strut around in a carpenter's belt. I would rather wear an apron and bake cookies than saw a board in half. I'd rather hold a baby any day of the week than pound a nail. It doesn't mean I didn't enjoy building my own house, but my biggest pleasures in life are soft and maternal and have to do with nurturing. I'm the Little Red Hen story but with a different ending: I'd happily

Dorothy shows the hearth framing and plywood.

For the hearth, ½-inch cement board was glued down over the plywood with special adhesive. Seams were also taped and filled.

Dorothy grouts the hearth tile with sanded grout.

This small propane tank will be placed right next to the house — no need to dig a trench and lay a gas line.

share the bread even if I had to build the kitchen to bake it in. And I did.

The crisp white chino-cotton curtains are simple, light, and airy. The house is on a hill so they are mainly there to dress the windows and to keep the blinding sun from peeping in — rather than Tom from peeping in. (But anyone creeping around this property will do so at their own peril!)

Next

We've decided to use board 'n batt siding to match some of the other buildings on the land (ie., pole barn, storage shed, and shop). We like the rustic look and it holds up very well over the years.

A big lumber yard and building supply place called Fields Home Center in Murphy, Oregon sells exactly what we want. They carry a huge supply of rough-cut, kiln-dried, sugar-pine siding. It's a true 1-inch-thick by a true 12-inch-wide, and comes in 16-foot lengths. It's 99 cents a foot and they deliver for only $95 a load (within a reasonable distance). We'll order 2500 board feet of siding by September 1st, 2011, and install it with a nail gun to beat the fall rains.

After the siding is on, we'll build an entrance deck on the north side where we enter the house, and a stairway and railing off the south side of the house (required emergency exit). Then at last we'll call for the final inspection.

We're inching along as fast as we can, but, like any girlie girl, I take time to put on lipstick and curl my eyelashes once in a while — and Eric, being a serious classical musician, keeps playing the piano even when it seems like the Titanic is sinking! If this unlikely duo can build a house from scratch, anybody can! Δ

The Zen of building

Philosophical encouragement by Dorothy

Building a house needn't be an intimidating undertaking. It is simply an organic process of assembling some of earth's most basic elements into geometric forms to create the microcosm we call home. Trees supply the wood, iron supplies the nails, silicon sand provides the glass, copper carries the current, wood and natural gas supply the heat, concrete is rock, and water flows freely in and out by gravity. It's all very elementary and almost primitive. It only gets complicated when we aspire to arrange these elements into a structure that satisfies our aesthetic taste; otherwise we'd be happy to live in a hut.

The real fun of building one's own house is designing it. The rest is good old hard work, which has its own priceless rewards. My message is this: Life is tenuous so enjoy the journey! Nature is capricious and has the ability to disassemble the whole thing in a few short minutes or hours by turning it into a pile of splintered sticks, washing it away in a flood, or burning it into lumps of carbon and melted metal — as happened to me when my house burned down in 1995 — but I still believe what I said a couple of years later: "It's better to have built and rebuilt than never to have built at all.

Enjoy the work! No matter how it turns out, you will be forever changed in a positive way by the experience.

The Last Word

The threat of electromagnetic pulse!

I like "doomsday" scenarios — even ridiculous ones, such as the supposed Mayan calendar prophecy for 2012 or what had been Y2K doom-and-gloom leading up to the year 2000. Of course, there are some genuine doomsday threats to worry about, such as the possibility of another flu pandemic like the one of 1918-1919 or other pandemics health officials worry could be caused by drug resistant "superbugs" that could kill tens of millions, if not hundreds of millions, worldwide.

There are also unlikely but *plausible* catastrophes I like to mull over, such as the eruption of one of the world's super volcanoes, the impacting of a large asteroid, or the onset of another glacial age, all of which are going to happen — *eventually* — and, if one of those happened now it could wipe out as much as 90 percent of humanity, and we're powerless to stop them.

But what if there was a well-documented, but preventable threat, that could bring this country to its knees and kill as many as a quarter of a billion Americans, yet we were doing nothing to prevent it. In fact there are fixes we could put in place *now* to lessen the consequences — but the media and our nation's leaders not only ignore it, Congress has even cut money from the budget that could provide the means to deal with it.

The threat is called electromagnetic pulse (EMP) and it could come about as the result of detonating one well-placed nuclear device high over the United States. In fact, it could happen even without a nuclear attack as a result of a naturally-occurring solar flare from our own sun.

What is EMP?

According to a government website, an EMP is: "The electromagnetic radiation from a nuclear explosion caused by Compton-recoil electrons and photoelectrons from photons scattered in the materials of the nuclear device or in a surrounding medium. *The resulting electric and magnetic fields may couple with electrical/electronic systems to produce damaging current and voltage surges.*"

All you really need to pay attention to is the last sentence. EMP is an electromagnetic surge that would follow the high-altitude detonation of a nuclear bomb. It could turn the United States into a Third World country.

Without going deep into physics, an EMP caused by a nuclear bomb has three components. The first, designated E1, is the result of electrons being stripped from atoms in the upper atmosphere in the aftermath of a high-altitude detonation. As they travel downward through the earth's magnetic field at near-relativistic speeds, they produce a massive, though momentary, electromagnet pulse. You won't feel it, but the electronic equipment all around you will. In the old days of vacuum tubes and relay switches, most equipment would likely have escaped damage from the E1 component of the pulse. But today's microchips and delicate electronic devices, though incredibly convenient and efficient, will be fried by the pulse. Things like modern automobiles and trucks, computers, radios, televisions, cell phones, pacemakers, and anything else dependent on computer chips, whether plugged into the power grid or not, will short out and simply stop working. *Kaput!*

This also includes aircraft in the sky. Unless their avionics are "hardened" (and commercial aircraft and most military aircraft are not hardened against EMP), they will simply cease operation and the thousands that are in the air at any moment are going to simply fly into the ground with everyone onboard. Almost all microelectronic components damaged by the E1 component of an EMP will be *unrepairable*.

The E2 component resembles the surges caused by lightning and are less likely to be damaging to most equipment. But if protective equipment such as surge protectors are damaged by the E1 pulse, it may now allow the E2 pulse to cause further damage.

The E3 component may be the worst. It is caused when a nuclear explosion distorts the earth's magnetic field. As the field distorts, then tries to regain its original shape, it induces currents into long metal conductors — like the power lines and such that crisscross the country. The longer the conductors, the more current will be produced. It is this component of EMP that will overload the nation's power grid and fry *everything* connected to it, from your laptop, which is plugged into the wall recharging, to the transformers at the power stations.

The 370 or so largest transformers connected to nuclear, hydro, and fossil fuel-burning power plants around the country are what make the electricity these plants generate usable, but they will be destroyed by the pulse. Without these transformers, the country will go dark. And they cannot be easily replaced. The size of a building, they are *no longer* produced in the United States and current procurement time is three years.

What will happen?

Without electric power, radio and TV stations and phone services won't work, so there'll be almost no communication. Water systems will cease to function, gas stations won't be able to pump fuel, banking transactions (including ATMs) will fail, and the network for distributing food will collapse. Perishable foods and medications that require refrigeration or freezing will spoil in a day. Emergency services will be unavailable, including those necessary to fight the tens of thousands of fires that will start from short circuits on the grid.

The inability to produce or distribute proper medications would doom many needing cancer treatments or suffering from heart disease, Type I diabetes, and other ailments.

Most farmers won't be able to plant, fertilize, irrigate, or harvest, but even if they could, they won't be able to get their products to market because there will no longer be transportation. What is harvested won't be preserved since there will be no power to run refrigeration and none to run the factories that ordinarily can our food.

Supermarkets typically have just a few days' supply of food and are being resupplied continuously every 1-3 days. Once the power goes out, the supermarkets will quickly be emptied and it could be months before they're resupplied.

Imagine the great metropolitan areas of this country: the corridor from Boston to Washington, DC, which includes the great cities of New York and Philadelphia among them, and has a population of about 50 million people, the Chicago area with its millions, the Los Angeles to San Diego corridor, Seattle, Portland, etc., and suddenly there's no food coming in, the water is turned off, and sewage facilities no longer carry away and treat our daily waste.

In no time at all cities will become quagmires of hungry, thirsty people living amid filth, squalor, and disease.

From an enemy's point of view, a single large device exploded 250 to 300 miles above Iowa would disrupt the entire United States. But getting a missile that far inland could be a problem for them. On the other hand, because the radius of destruction of one high-altitude explosion is very large (as much as 1400 miles), three missiles, launched almost straight up, from freighters off the Pacific, Atlantic, and Gulf coasts, should just about cover the lower 48 states with EMP surges that would all but incapacitate our nation.

Recovery time, if it happened, would take years but more likely a decade or more. In the meantime, deaths in this country would be *at least* in the low millions.

All of this would seem to be the fodder for fiction and, in fact, a scenario involving an EMP attack is played out in a book by William Forstchen titled *One Second After*. Though he's populated the book with rather two-dimensional characters, the events described in the book are credible and thought-provoking and make it worth a read.

The problem with an EMP event is *not* news. We've known about nuclear weapon-induced EMP since 1945. Enrico Fermi anticipated it prior to the detonation of the first atomic bomb, called Gadget, at the Trinity test site in New Mexico. The media and the American people briefly became aware of it after a high-altitude detonation of a hydrogen bomb during the Starfish Prime Test of 1952 when effects of it were felt in Hawaii (900 miles away from the test), where the resulting voltage surges blew out 300 street lights and damaged a microwave link. This was with a weapon that wasn't even designed to maximize EMP and it was detonated back in the day of vacuum tubes when electronic equipment was more robust than today's highly efficient but sensitive computer chips which can be fried by even *modest* current surges.

Solar flares

Even if someone were able to convince me no one would ever launch a nuclear weapon over the United States, I would not rest easy. Nuclear weapons are not the only things that cause an E3 pulse. A giant solar flare caused such a pulse on September 1, 1859. Back then, there was no electronic infrastructure, but telegraph lines acted like antennas and transmitted the energy along their wires, causing shocks to many telegraph operators and, in some cases, causing fires. A large solar flare of this sort is now called a Carrington Event, named after the British astronomer, Richard Carrington, who first described it.

Solar astronomers and many engineers feel that with the United States (and most of the rest of the industrial world) now crisscrossed with power and communication lines, a solar flare with the magnitude of the one that occurred in 1859 would blow out power station transformers and plunge this country and much of the rest of the world into the dark for years. (Imagine trying to build transformers if there's no electricity at all!) It could also cause fires across the continents as circuits overload, overheat, and arc.

The 1859 event is not the only time solar flares have wreaked havoc. It's happened many times since, only on smaller scales because the flares were much smaller. The 1859 solar flare happened at the dawn of the electric age. Had it happened a few decades later when the world was more electrified, we'd probably now take the threat seriously and we'd have been "hardening" the grid to EMP all along. But it didn't, and we haven't.

Solar astronomers are positive it's only a matter of time before there will be another Carrington Event. They just don't know when. However, next year is one of the prime times it may happen. NASA says the solar cycle we're entering now is about the same size as the one that produced the original Carrington Event.

With a major Carrington Event, all the things that could follow a nuclear weapon-induced E3 strike may happen, except it won't be just a local event but one that affects the entire world.

The solution

The lowest estimate I've seen for the projected cost of a recovery for just the solar disruptions is $1 trillion, but most estimates run into the many trillions of dollars.

However, the FBI projects the cost of hardening transformers that service major metropolitan centers at about $200 million. That's 1/5000th of the smallest estimate of the cost of damage. In fact, it's less than 1/2000th of the job package President Obama recently proposed. And hardening the grid wouldn't just make the country more secure, it would provide meaningful jobs, unlike the kinds government spending usually create.

There are voices trying to call attention to the problem. The Heritage Foundation has been calling for a national EMP recognition day to raise awareness of the threat.

An EMP attack will be the most catastrophic event to happen to our nation in its history — more devastating than 9/11, more devastating than Pearl Harbor, in fact, more devastating than all of the wars this country has ever fought.

It's about time for the mass media to talk about it, and for Congress and the President to address it. This is a real-world problem with a relatively inexpensive fix.

— *John Silveira*

"New" Yarn from Old Sweaters

By Margaret Mills

Years ago, when my grandmother learned that some women purchased new fabric to make quilts, she was shocked. She was an "old-school" fiber artist — quilting, crocheting, and sewing to stretch her budget and provide for her family. Quilts were thriftily made of leftover bits of fabric; rugs were woven or braided from worn-out clothing. While the resurgence of these crafts brings some long-overdue respect for the artistry and skill of spinners, weavers, knitters, and seamstresses, the economics of such handwork has shifted. It is difficult these days to make a garment as cheaply as you can buy a similar item from a big box store. Thrift, of course, is not the only factor in the renewed interest in handcrafting fiber items. For many, it may not be a factor at all.

The variety of yarns now available in yarn and fabric shops boggles the mind — as does the price. Not content to stick with the economical and practical (but uninspired) acrylic yarn, I cast around for a means of acquiring wool yarn for less. One option in keeping with grandmother's thrifty mindset is to salvage wool from a knitted or crocheted garment. Such recycling has also experienced a resurgence, so you can find a number of tutorials and articles on the internet detailing the process. A local fiber arts store even offers workshops on recycling yarn from sweaters.

Recycling a free sweater is best, of course, and recycling the yarn from a sweater you already own would be ideal. Not having an old, out-of-style wool sweater lurking in the back of the closet, I began a search in our local thrift shop. While you might pick up a wool sweater at a yard sale for pennies, our thrift shop was sweater savvy: the pure wool sweaters were priced higher than the machine-made acrylic. Still, a wool sweater for under $10 works for this project, and I found a selection.

Look for a sweater that is close to 100% wool. A little nylon or acrylic serves to strengthen wool fibers and prevents breakage when you are unraveling the garment. Beware of felting, where the sweater has been washed in hot water or dried in a dryer. If you cannot differentiate the stitches, it is felted. Also beware of serged seams where the sewn edges of the sweater have been cut. The pieces of the sweater should be sewn or crocheted together. Also check for any moth damage to avoid winding up with little short bits of yarn when you unravel the sweater. Likewise, any fancy knit-in color patterns will result in lots of short bits of yarn.

I finally located a $7 sweater with seams sewn with the same yarn. This sweater was a drab green mixture of mohair and wool with 5% nylon. It was hand-knit in Italy, but it was not particularly fashionable or attractive.

Dismantle

The first step is to dismantle the sections of the sweater. A pair of sewing scissors or sharp-pointed embroidery scissors is good for this. A tapestry needle is useful for picking out those stitches, too. Locate the seams, then clip the knot or backstitch holding the seam together at the end. Remove the thread.

With this sweater, the mohair tended to tangle around itself, and the thread holding the seam was the same green yarn, so it was difficult to see. Still, the sweater was reasonably easy to dismantle. I took the sleeves off first, then removed the front sections from the back section. There were also buttons to remove.

Unravel

Once the sweater is dismantled, begin the unraveling process by finding the end of the work. The knitter will probably have knotted the end after the final stitch, or woven it into the body. Many, but not all, sweaters are knit from the top down, so tug at the bottom corners first. Loosen the first thread and pull. It should unravel. If you find yourself undoing each stitch, you are pulling from the wrong end. Wrap the yarn in a ball as you unravel to prevent it from tangling. Unraveling our Italian hand-knit sweater was pretty straightforward. The mohair tended to tangle and resist pulling, but that only slowed the process slightly. I had several balls of yarn when finished, at least one for each sweater section.

Skein

The yarn will be kinky from the knitting. The next step is to wrap it in hanks. If you wish to measure the amount of yarn you have salvaged, set two chairs back to back, then measure a two-yard piece of string and wrap it around the chair backs, adjusting the chairs to measure exactly two yards. Wrap the salvaged yarn around the chair backs. This creates hanks exactly one yard long. You will be able to determine the amount of yarn you have by counting the strands in each hank. Use this opportunity to combine some of your balls of yarn as well. Just tie the ends together and keep wrapping. Don't make them too thick or they will take too long to dry when washed. I ended up with four hanks of yarn. Tie the hanks in two places with a piece of string or light yarn to hold them in place.

Wash

Fill a pan or sink with lukewarm water. Do not use hot water as you do not want to felt the wool. Add a gentle detergent to the water and submerge the hanks for about three hours. Rinse the hanks of yarn in cool water and gently press out the excess water. Hang them to dry on a clothes rack or over the shower curtain. I left them to dry overnight, but much depends on your humidity, temperature, and the amount and weight of the wool. Some people recommended weighting the hanks to further straighten the yarn, but mine straightened quite well without any additional weight.

Once the wool is dry and straightened to your satisfaction, take it down from the rack and roll it into balls. I ended my experiment with more than 400 yards of green mohair yarn, for several hours' work and a $7 investment. Δ

Reduce your property taxes

By Carolyn Evans-Dean

The recent housing boom caused many properties in the United States to be assessed at higher values, creating higher tax bills for homeowners. Once the market went bust, few municipalities returned to re-evaluate properties, leaving the tax bills a bloated mess. This can be the case anywhere, whether you reside in a big city, small village, or a remote area. Throwing money away on over-inflated property taxes doesn't fit with a frugal, self-sufficient lifestyle and generally tends to tick most folks off. Luckily, most municipalities offer a grievance period once the new tax bills are generated, to allow a homeowner to challenge their property assessment.

Though many homes appear to be picture perfect from the curb, the interiors aren't always in line with what the tax man expects to find.

Having served on the local Tax Assessment Board of Review for several years, I'd like to share what I've learned in the hopes that it might help others to gain some tax relief. Although every area has its own procedure, many places have a system similar to the one that I am going to describe.

First, there's a bit of terminology to learn…

Tax Assessor is the term used to describe the person or people who look at your property from the outside to determine its value. In most areas, these people are trained real estate property appraisers. However, in rural areas, they may be real estate brokers who moonlight as tax assessors or the position may be held by more of a political official than a trained professional. In some instances, a town may actually hire appraisers from outside of the area to determine the assessments.

Tax Assessment is the term used to describe the amount of money that the city, town, village, or county thinks your property is worth. This amount should be close to the amount that you could reasonably expect to sell it for. Most property assessments are considered to be "drive-bys" because an assessor is unlikely to knock on your door and ask to tour the premises. In most areas, the assessors only view about 25% of the properties over the course of a year. This means that they may not have physically made the trek to your property in four years. In many other areas of the country, properties are reassessed even less frequently due to a lack of staffing in the assessment offices. If you live in a particularly remote area, the length of time since their last visit may be considerably more.

Property Tax is the term used to describe your share of the tax bill in your area. Everyone should be billed at the same percentage rate of the property value (aka millage). So if you own a $100,000 home and the rate of taxation is at 75%, then your taxes are based upon a value of $75,000 instead of the larger value.

Comparable is the term that is used to describe a property that sold recently (within the last 18 months to 2 years) that is similar or "comparable" to yours. It should be relatively close in proximity to your structure and be approximately the same size. A really good comparable will even be built in the same architectural style. Three similar properties are usually used to help pinpoint value.

Tax Assessment Board of Review Members are regular citizens who have been sworn into office to hear the grievances. Although they may receive a stipend to compensate them for their time, there is no monetary reward in it for them if they do not reduce the taxes on your home. They are also not the ones who raised the taxes causing you to seek relief in the first place.

Inventory is the general list of amenities and features that the assessment office thinks are installed on your property. This can include bathrooms, bedrooms, paved driveway, number of acres, outbuildings, pond, pool, etc. Many times, the inventory is flawed because the assessment department personnel have never been invited inside your home.

Evidence is the stuff that you bring to your hearing to back up your claim that your house isn't worth what the municipality says it is.

If you must take photos of a roof in the middle of winter, be sure to safely brush the snow away to make sure the problem is immediately visible.

Building your case

So, you received a tax bill that states that your house is worth more than you think it is. As a savvy homeowner, you decide to fight the powers that be and try to get the taxes reduced. If you are frugal, you won't hire any companies or individuals who state that they can grieve your taxes for you in exchange for a fee or a percentage of the savings. Why should you pay them for something that you can do for yourself?

Make sure that you start this process immediately. There is usually a time limit for filing a grievance. Your local tax assessor's office should be the first place that you call. Express your concern in a reasonable and rational manner and ask if there is a process in place to grieve or argue the assessment. That office will be able to provide you with the proper procedure, direct you to any forms that you may need, and provide you with information about any comparable properties that they used to determine your tax liability. If you have any additional information that can be included with the application, it should be stapled or clipped to it.

Take detailed closeups of any property repairs that are needed. Fuzzy photos will not be helpful to your case.

In some municipalities, a duly appointed representative can appear to challenge your tax assessment in your absence. The person can be an attorney, a relative, or some other professional. In most cases, you must provide your written permission for them to represent you.

Incidentally, if you are in the process of purchasing a home and have a signed purchase offer, you may be able to grieve the current assessment. Since a property assessment is supposed to reflect the current market value, there is nothing more current

Carefully scrutinize the assessor's inventory of your property. Assessors often assume that a larger home contains more amenities than a smaller one.

than what the property is about to sell for.

Next, the assessment office will provide you with a date and time to appear before the Tax Assessment Review Board. Ask them to provide you with the comparables that were used to determine the value of your home. Make sure that you've taken time to prepare your evidence. Take photos of the houses that the assessment office has deemed to be comparables. If no comparables have been provided, then you should seek out your own. Be advised, any photos that are submitted as evidence may not be returned to you after the conclusion of the case.

Be respectful and don't traipse across other folk's property on a photographic mission without permission. Make notes about each property and the ways in which the comparables differ from yours. If you notice that a comparable property has a sizable deck or other attribute, while yours does not, then you've just found a logical argument for your taxes to be reduced. The review board is comprised of regular citizens and they will generally listen to logic.

Keep in mind that if you have a 2,000 square foot house, the comparables should be in the same vicinity of your home and of similar construction, size, and style. Just as neighborhoods vary, the property values can fluctuate based upon proximity to a major highway, a waterway, a town, or houses that are flashier than yours. Similarly, negative features like a trash dump or a CAFO (Concentrated Animal Feeding Operation) in the vicinity have a detrimental effect on property values. If the comparable is out of the area, then it isn't a true comparison because it doesn't reflect the actual value of the properties in your neck of the woods.

If you know of a nearby home that is similar to yours that the assessment office neglected to use as a comparable, take a photo of it. Often times, local government offices have searchable online databases, allowing you to find out the assessed value of any home in your area. Verify the tax bill for that property and compare it to yours. If it is currently assessed for less than yours, it should be admissible as evidence.

Take photos of your property, making sure to include shots of any negative features. If your roof is in poor repair, then get a shot of the water-stained ceiling. If your bathroom is old fashioned or downright primitive, by all means, get a really good shot. Most people have never seen a composting toilet before. One of the assumptions made by assessment employees is that a home has a modern, up-to-date bathroom and kitchen. Not having one can reduce the value (and thus the taxes) of your home.

Keep in mind that if you live in a municipality that requires building permits for construction and you erected a porch without the benefit of having one, then you are in violation. The penalty for such an offense may be a stiff fine or you might be forced to apply for a permit after the fact. In some extreme cases, your local Code Enforcement Office may require that you tear down illegal additions. After all, you've just provided them with the evidence to incriminate yourself. There might be a similar penalty for having that composting toilet in certain areas of the country.

Double check the inventory listed by the assessor. You will want to pay careful attention to the square footage and the number of bedrooms, bathrooms, and fireplaces. Make note of any discrepancies.

If you are in the process of a major repair, ask if the property can be given a one-time "unfinished" assessment. This would temporarily reduce your property taxes to reflect that the home is not yet complete. This is a courtesy that is only extended for one year and the property taxes will be raised again the following year.

A special note: if you are not a native speaker of English or feel that you can better express your case in your native tongue, plan to bring someone along to interpret for you. In most cases, interpreters are not available onsite to assist. In one situation, I can recall having to draw from my (lousy and limited) Spanish to assist a man whose house was listed as having an extra 1,000 square feet of living space!

Not everyone has granite countertops and ceramic floors, but if you live in an area where they are common, your home will be presumed to have them, too.

Having your say

On the date of your appointment with the Assessment Review Board, arrive early and make sure that you bring all of the collected evidence and personal identification, such as a driver's license or a passport. You will be sworn in to testify, so make sure that your testimony is wholly factual as it is a matter of public record and will likely be recorded.

The tax assessment office will be asked to provide the review board with the information that they have on your property. You will be asked to present your case after the assessment employee. Do so in a clear and concise manner. When possible, type up your notes beforehand and use them as a guide to make sure that you present all of the evidence you've gathered without rambling.

There are times when a physical tour might clear up any ambiguities with the inventory of your home's amenities. If that is the case, then extend an invitation to the assessment employee to visit the premises. Show off that composting toilet and outdoor solar shower with pride. Again, make sure that you are not inadvertently shooting yourself in the foot by showing off the basement (or attic) that you turned into living space last year!

If there is a hardship or disability involved, make sure that you mention it to the board. It may make them more sympathetic to your plight or it may remind them to mention any special veteran, senior, or disabled citizen tax breaks that may exist in your area. Once you've finished, the board will usually inform you that they will consider the evidence you've provided and will give you a time frame as to when to expect a response via mail. Make sure that you thank them for their time and service to the community.

If all goes well, the next communication that you receive from the assessment department will be a letter indicating that you've won your case. You win some and you lose some, but you won't get any tax relief at all if you don't try. Δ

Lenie in the kitchen

Muffins for breakfast, bread for dinner, and pie for dessert

By Ilene Duffy

I grew up in a family that must be unusual, but I think it's the good kind of unusual. When my mom passed away six years ago, my three sisters and I made sure that we each received items that were sentimental to us. There wasn't a hint of an argument over who got furniture (even though we all loved Great-aunt Belle's antique rocking chair), family heirlooms, jewelry, cookbooks, or kitchen supplies. We made sure to give a little something from my mother's kitchen to each of our cousins, since they loved their Aunt Katty dearly. My youngest sister, Cindy, continued to live in Mom's house for several years, without a word of coaxing from the three of us older sisters that the house should be sold and the proceeds divvied up.

A year after Mom's death, we were all together at her house and had the task of dividing up more of her possessions. Lucky for us, there were four handmade afghans to choose from — older sisters getting to pick theirs first since they hadn't brought home many items yet. If any of us *really* wanted something, we told each other to speak up and "just take it!"

I'm happy to have Mom's super old metal Ovenex muffin pan. They don't make 'em like that anymore. My boys will always remember the pumpkin pies Grandma baked for them. Now I'm so pleased to make good use of one of her Pyrex pie pans in my kitchen. And none of my sisters wanted Mom's bread machine, so when my old, diehard bread machine finally croaked, I was grateful to have Mom's as a back-up.

I love cooking and baking, but when the weather turns colder outside, I especially enjoy tying on my apron and getting a baked item ready for brunch, dinner, or dessert. I must have really been in the mood to bake one day recently, since I started with muffins in the morning, made bread in the afternoon for dinner, and had some peaches that were too ripe for eating, but perfect for a pie. There were no complaints from my Duffy men that day.

Most good cooks have loads of cookbooks, and my mom was no different. When we divvied up the cookbooks, one that I took was her copy of *The New Settlement Cookbook.* The copyright of this printing is 1954, so it must have been a gift to her from a friend in the early years of her marriage. It's a great cookbook, with menus for planning meals and parties, as well as an abundance of old-time recipes. In the quick breads section, I found a banana bread recipe that I thought I could modify in order to use up some zucchini from my garden. I must have modified that recipe even more than I usually do, since that banana bread recipe wound up making some pretty yummy zucchini muffins!

Zucchini muffins

½ cup milk
1 heaping tsp. sour cream
2 cups zucchini, grated
1½ cups flour
½ cup whole wheat flour
2 tsp. baking powder
½ tsp. baking soda
½ tsp. salt
1 tsp. cinnamon
½ tsp. nutmeg
5 Tbsp. butter, softened
½ cup sugar
⅔ cup packed brown sugar
2 eggs

Robby, Dave, and Jacob are happy to test warm zucchini muffins.

Preparations:

Preheat oven to 375° F. Oil and flour a muffin pan.

In a mixing bowl, add the milk and mix in the sour cream. Add the grated zucchini and mix. In a medium bowl, add flour, whole wheat flour, baking powder, baking soda, salt, cinnamon, and nutmeg. Mix thoroughly and set aside. In a large mixing bowl, mix butter and sugars, then add the eggs and mix until thoroughly blended.

Add the milk and zucchini to the butter mixture and blend in. Add the flour mixture and blend just until incorporated. Drop by spoonfuls into prepared muffin pan. Bake for 18-20 minutes until the muffins test done in the center. Cool on a rack for a few minutes before taking muffins out of the pan onto a cooling rack. Makes 12 large muffins. Next time I make these, I might dust the tops of the muffins with a bit of cinnamon sugar before baking. Also, I might like to add some chopped walnuts to the batter.

Egg bread

A traditional Jewish egg bread is known as *challah* and is typically served with the Sabbath meal. It's so good, I like it anytime. To add fiber, I exchanged a bit of the white flour with some whole wheat flour. To add zing, I added a few dried herbs as well, which is not traditional at all, but it sure came out good.

This recipe makes a two-pound loaf, so if you're going to try it using a bread machine, make sure your machine is big enough.

1 cup water
1½ Tbsp. honey
¼ cup canola oil
2 large eggs
3 cups flour
1 cup whole wheat flour
½ tsp. salt
2 tsp. dried parsley
1 tsp. dried oregano
¼ tsp. dried basil
2½ tsp. yeast

Preparations:

In a large measuring cup, add water, honey, and oil. Gently warm in the microwave. Water should be warm, but not hot. In a separate bowl, add the eggs and gently mix, then add to the water and mix. Set aside. In a separate bowl, mix dry ingredients except the yeast. Add the water mixture to the bread machine pan, then gently add the flour mixture on top of the water. Make a small well in the top of the flour mixture. Add the yeast to the well. Place bread pan in the bread machine and start it on the dough cycle.

Oil and flour a large bread pan. I use my favorite long pan that is about 18 inches in length and about 4 inches wide which is big enough to hold this 2-pound loaf. If you don't have a big pan, then you'll need to separate the dough in half and use 2 normal-size bread loaf pans.

When the machine beeps done, place the dough on a lightly floured board and gently squeeze out the gas. Knead gently a few times. If the dough is sticky, rub a bit of olive oil on your hands. Form the dough to fit the prepared pans. Place a lightly dampened towel on the bread and let it rise in a warm place for about an hour. Preheat oven to 350° F. Bake 25 minutes. Cool on a cooling rack for a few minutes before removing the bread from the pans to continue to cool.

Peach blackberry pie

I bought too many peaches the other day and they ripened so quickly that they seemed a bit past their prime for eating. We are so lucky to have loads of blackberries in our yard, so I continued my baking spree to make a peach and blackberry pie for dessert.

Pie filling:

4 peaches
1½ cups blackberries
¾ cup sugar
1 Tbsp. flour
1 Tbsp. cornstarch
1 Tbsp. instant dry tapioca pudding
1 tsp. cinnamon

Pie crust:

2 cups flour, divided
½ cup whole wheat flour, divided
1 tsp. salt, divided
2 pinches of baking powder
¾ cup shortening, divided
2 pats of butter, divided
1 egg
about ¾ cup cold water

Preparations:

Heat water in a sauce pan until boiling. Add peaches to boiling water for one minute. Cool peaches in a bowl until they can be handled. Wash blackberries and drain thoroughly. Skin the peaches and discard the skin. Then cut the peaches into chunks and place in large bowl. Add blackberries. In a small mixing bowl, mix remaining pie filling ingredients. Add to the fruit mixture and gently mix. Set aside. Preheat oven to 350° F.

I like to make pie crusts in individual bowls, so I put two bowls side by side and add ingredients to make each crust separately. In *each* bowl add 1 cup of flour, ¼ cup whole wheat flour, ½ tsp. salt, and a pinch of baking powder. Mix. Divide the shortening in half and add it to each flour mixture along with a pat of butter in each bowl. Use a pastry blender to gently mix in the shortening and butter. Don't overly mix.

In a small bowl mix the egg and then mix in the cold water. With a fork, slowly add and mix in just enough water and egg mixture to one of the bowls of flour until a ball of dough forms. Don't use too much water or the dough will be tough. Repeat with the other bowl of flour.

On a floured board or pastry cloth, place one of the balls of dough and roll it around gently to add a bit of flour to all sides of the dough. With a rolling pin, roll the dough to make a circle about one inch larger than the pie pan. Fold dough in half gently and place in pie pan. Unfold and center dough to fit. Flour the board or cloth again and roll out the top crust. This crust only needs to be a bit bigger than the pie pan.

Use a slotted spoon to gently stir the fruit and then place the fruit on the bottom crust. You don't need to add all the liquid that has collected at the bottom of the bowl or your pie will be runny. Add the top crust and seal the edges. Poke holes in the crust for vents. Bake about one hour. Cool pie until the people you live with can't take it anymore. Δ

Persimmons — the backwoods sugarplum

By Tom Kovach

Persimmons are great-looking trees with drooping leaves that have a kind of bluish tint. They produce fruit that look a bit like tomatoes, but the insides are very sweet, almost honey-like, with a texture of jelly. Persimmons are great for landscapes and will grow best in growing Zones 4 - 10. What also adds to their attraction is the fact that they are low-maintenance trees.

The Oriental persimmon can produce fruits as large as tomatoes, while the fruit of the American persimmons are smaller with a richer flavor and a drier texture. But the American trees themselves grow larger and are more tolerant of cold weather than are the Oriental types.

American persimmons usually need another variety to assure pollination, while the Oriental ones do not. One can harvest and eat the so-called "non-astringent" Oriental persimmons when they are fully colored, yet still firm. But one should not eat the "astringent" Oriental or American persimmons until the fruits are fully colored and very soft or they will have a bitter taste. Astringent varieties have a high tannin content, which accounts for their mouth-puckering taste. Their fruit must be fully ripened and almost jelly-like before they lose their bitter flavor and become sweet. Non-astringent varieties can be eaten much earlier and can be eaten when still firm, but they won't be as sweet and juicy as the fully-ripened astringent types.

(Photo: Charles Sanders)

The branches of this tree bear a heavy crop of persimmons.

When planting, buy bareroot plants of persimmons in spring with healthy roots (black on the outside, white on the inside). Avoid large plants in small or shallow containers as persimmons form a big taproot, which cannot grow properly in a small pot.

If you are transplanting, sever the roots of a healthy sucker the spring before you intend to transplant it. Push the spade into the ground in a one-foot circle. The following spring, prepare a planting hole. Remove soil to a depth and width of about two feet and then rough up the sides and the bottom of the hole. Dig around the sucker near where you cut the previous spring. Dig under the plant and lift it, disturbing the roots as little as possible. Set the tree in the new hole at the level it previously grew. Backfill the soil, working it in around the roots with your fingers or a stick. Water thoroughly. When done with this, protect the trunk from sunscald by painting equal parts with white latex paint and water. If the leaves still wilt, provide temporary shade.

Plant persimmons in full sun or partial shade. Persimmons will grow in shade, but the fruit turns out best when the tree gets at least four hours of sun a day. Persimmons tolerate a wide range of soils as long as the soil provides good drainage for the trees' deep roots. Don't plant persimmons near a walkway, patio, or driveway

Folks say you can forecast the winter by using persimmon seeds. To try this, take some persimmon seeds and carefully split them open. As folklore has it, the shape most of the seeds take on will indicate the type of winter weather you'll have. The knife means there will be a cold, icy winter. The fork means there will be a mild winter, and a spoon shape inside the seeds means there will be lots of snow. — *Charles Sanders* because the dropped fruits can cause a slippery mess where people walk.

In the autumn, pick up and burn or shred twigs dropped from the persimmon trees to destroy diseases and insect girdlers that feed on these twigs. Delay pruning branches that seem dead after a particularly severe winter because such branches sprout new shoots eventually.

In late winter, spread wood chips, straw, or leaves a few inches deep around the tree, as far out as the spread of the branches. Mulch keeps the soil moist and it prevents fallen fruits from splattering as they hit the ground.

In early summer, if the fruits are still crowded after the natural fruit drop, thin to a few inches apart. Thinning yields larger fruits, keeps limbs from breaking, and ensures a good crop for the following year.

Persimmon trees may be affected by black scale. This is caused by insects that look like small, black dots clinging to stems and twigs. They weaken the trees by sucking out plant juices. They can be controlled by spraying the persimmons with dormant oil before trees sprout leaves in the spring.

When ready to eat, astringent types of persimmons are soft and the cap separates easily from the fruit. Non-astringents are fully colored and are crisp. If the fruits are nearly ripe and freezing weather is in the forecast, clip the fruit off and bring them indoors. Place them in a bag with a ripe apple or in a container with some alcohol. The ethylene gas given off by the apple or the alcohol vapor will speed up the ripening process. Nearly ripe fruits will also ripen slowly if they are just placed in an open bowl at room temperature. Contrary to myth, a hard frost is not what ripens the persimmon's fruit. Fruits fully ripen when the growing season has been long enough.

Some of the Oriental persimmons include: *Eureka:* an astringent with medium large, deep-red fruits. They have a great flavor and are cold hardy. *Fuyu:* A non-astringent with large, orange-red fruits with excellent flavor. *Giboshi:* An astringent of medium size, cold hardy, and delicious in flavor. *Hachiya:* An astringent with large, orange-red fruit that is often seedless but with great flavor. *Hanafuyu:* A non-astringent with large, orange-red fruits and great flavor. It is a semi-dwarf tree. *Saijo:* An astringent with small, yellowish-orange fruit. Very sweet, often seedless and hardy. *Tanenashi:* An astringent with large orange fruit, outstanding flavor, and almost always seedless.

Some of the American persimmons include: *Early Golden:* An astringent with medium, yellow fruits with good flavor. They are hardy, freeze well, and may self-pollinate. *Meader:* An astringent with medium, pale-orange fruit. It is very cold hardy, very productive, and may self-pollinate. *Morris Burton:* An astringent with small, tasty, reddish-orange fruits. A bit slow to bear but has a great fall leaf color. *Szukis:* An astringent with small, tasty, orange-gold fruits, very cold hardy, and self-pollinates.

If you are planning to plant persimmon trees, it's best to talk first with an arborist who is familiar with them. You will find persimmons are easy to grow and produce not only great fruit, but also add color and character to a landscape. Δ

Persimmon wood is very hard. Way back, when things were still made of wood, golf club heads were made of the tough, impact-resistant wood. It still makes good spindles and other items requiring a dense, hard wood.

— *Charles Sanders*

Processing and cooking with persimmons

By Charles Sanders

Persimmons are a tasty and versatile fruit that fit into innumerable recipes. But first you must process them. You can do this either by mashing them by hand through a colander or by putting through a food mill.

If you use a colander, first wash the fruit, place a colander atop a catch bowl, pour a few cups of fruit into it, and just begin mashing them through with your hands.

The food mill is a little neater to operate. To use it, again, wash them, then pour the fruit into the mill's pan and begin turning the crank. The angled plate at the bottom of the pan forces the pulp through the colander-like bottom and separates out the seeds. The more you turn the crank, the more pulp goes through and the drier the remaining seeds and skins get. Simply dump out the leavings, refill with more persimmons, and continue cranking. You can find these handy kitchen utensils at flea markets, yard sales, and other outlets.

The persimmon puree can be frozen or canned. To freeze, pour two cups of puree into a ziploc bag, then freeze. (Two cups is enough for a double batch of cookies or a pudding.)

To can persimmon pulp, ladle it into prepared pint jars and process it in a pressure canner at 10 pounds pressure for 10 minutes.

The following are a few of my mother-in-law's great recipes:

Persimmon cookies:

1 cup persimmon pulp
1 cup chopped nuts
1 cup raisins
2 cups flour
1 cup sugar
½ cup shortening
1 tsp. soda
1 egg
½ tsp. each cloves, cinnamon, and nutmeg
dash salt
½ cup flaked coconut
½ cup shredded carrots

Mix all the ingredients together well. Drop the stiff batter by the spoonful onto a greased cookie sheet. Bake for 15-20 minutes at 350° F. Makes 2-3 dozen.

Persimmon bread:

2 cups flour
½ tsp. baking soda
½ tsp. salt
2 tsp. baking powder
1 tsp. cinnamon
½ tsp. nutmeg
1 cup persimmon pulp
½ cup milk
2 eggs
1 cup sugar
¼ cup butter or margarine
1 cup chopped walnuts, (optional)

Sift all the dry ingredients together. Mix the persimmon pulp, milk, eggs, and sugar. Add the flour mixture and the margarine. Mix until it's all well-blended. Stir in the chopped nuts. Pour the batter into a well-greased 9x5x3-inch loaf pan and bake at 350° F for 45 minutes. Tasty!

Persimmon fudge:

4 cups sugar
1 cup evaporated milk
1 stick butter or margarine
⅔ cup persimmon pulp
½ pint marshmallow cream
1 cup chopped nuts
1 tsp. vanilla

Combine the sugar, milk, butter and persimmon pulp in a heavy saucepan. Cook over medium heat, stirring constantly, until the candy reaches the soft ball stage (a bit dropped into a glass of cold water should form a ball).

Remove from heat, then add the marshmallow cream, nuts, and vanilla. Pour into a buttered pan, cool, and cut.

Persimmons in the food mill and pulp in the catch pan

Persimmon pie:

1 cup sugar
1 Tbsp. margarine
3 eggs, well-beaten
1 cup persimmon pulp
¼ tsp. salt
1 tsp. vanilla
1 can (12 oz.) evaporated milk
1 uncooked pie shell

Cream the sugar and margarine, add the eggs and beat until smooth. Add the other ingredients, mixing well. Pour into an unbaked pie shell and bake at 350° F until the crust is brown and a knife comes out clean when inserted in the filling near the edge.

Persimmon and pecan pie:

1 unbaked pie shell
1 cup persimmon pulp
1 cup sugar
3 eggs, slightly beaten
½ tsp. cinnamon
¼ tsp. salt
½ cup dark corn syrup
1 tsp. vanilla
1 cup chopped pecans

Combine the pulp, sugar, eggs, cinnamon, salt, syrup, and vanilla. Pour into the pie shell and top with pecans. Bake at 350° F for about 40 minutes. Chill and serve with whipped cream.

Persimmon pudding:

Here is a very good version of an old country treat.

1 cup persimmon pulp
1 cup milk
1½ cups sugar
1 egg
1 tsp. cinnamon
1 tsp. nutmeg
1 tsp. vanilla
2 Tbsp. melted butter
3 tsp. baking powder
pinch salt
pinch baking soda
⅔ cup flour

Blend ingredients well, pour into a 9x13 pan, and bake at 325° F for about 45 minutes. Cool and serve.

Persimmon pudding #2:

Here is another recipe for this great dessert.

2 cups persimmon pulp
2 cups sugar
2 large eggs
1 tsp. soda
1½ cups buttermilk
1½ cups flour
⅛ tsp. salt
1 tsp. baking powder
2 tsp. cinnamon
½ tsp. cloves
½ tsp. nutmeg
2 Tbsp. butter

Mix the persimmon pulp and sugar. Add the eggs and beat well. Add the soda to the buttermilk; stir until foaming quits. Add to the pulp mixture and stir. Sift the flour and add the salt, baking powder, and spices. Sift into the persimmon mixture; beat well. Put the butter into a 9x13 pan to melt. Pour the melted butter into the batter, leaving just enough to grease the pan. Beat well and pour into the greased pan. Bake at 325° F for about 45 minutes.

Persimmon jam:

3 lbs. persimmons
7 cups sugar
juice of 2 lemons
6 oz. liquid pectin

Wash, peel, and seed the persimmons, then mash them. Place the pulp into a kettle, add the sugar and lemon juice and mix well. Slowly bring to a boil over high heat until the sugar has dissolved, stirring frequently. Boil hard for 1 minute, then remove the kettle from the heat and stir in the liquid pectin. Skim thoroughly with a metal spoon. Pour into hot, sterilized pint jars, seal, and process in a boiling-water bath for 5 minutes.

Persimmon butter:

Here is another good bread spread.

1 lb. crabapples
1 lb. ripe persimmons
2 lbs. sugar
¼ tsp. cinnamon
¼ tsp. cloves
¼ tsp. nutmeg

Cook the unpeeled crabapples and whole persimmons until soft. Put all through a colander to remove seeds and skins.

Add the sugar to the pulp and juice and spices. Mix well. Cook in a 325° F oven for at least 1 hour. Two hours will improve the flavor. Stir often to prevent it from crusting over (and to enjoy the aroma!). Pour into hot, sterilized pint jars, seal, and process in a boiling-water bath for 5 minutes.

Serve with hot biscuits and butter.

Persimmon marmalade:

Here is a treat that goes great when spread on hot, buttered biscuits.

6 cups persimmon pulp
1 cup orange juice
6 cups sugar
chopped nuts (if desired)

To the thick persimmon pulp, add the orange juice and sugar. Add the nuts if desired. Cook until thickened as with jelly or jam. Pour into hot, sterilized pint jars, seal, and process in a boiling-water bath for 5 minutes.

Persimmon cream candy:

2 cups sugar
1 Tbsp. dark corn syrup
1 cup half and half milk
⅛ tsp. salt
2½ Tbsp. persimmon pulp
1 heaping tsp. butter

Mix the sugar, syrup, half and half, and salt. Let it set for about 20 minutes to dissolve the sugar. Place the mixture over high heat and quickly bring it to a boil. Boil to the soft ball stage or about 230° F on a candy thermometer. Remove from heat and stir in the persimmon pulp and butter. Return to heat and boil, stirring constantly until the soft boil stage. Set aside until partially set. Beat until the mixture shows signs of hardening. Pour into a buttered pan. Δ

What to do in case of an UNPLANNED HOMEBIRTH

By Rose Peck

What would you do if you were having a baby and you couldn't get to the hospital? Are you prepared to have your baby at home? Thousands of babies are born unplanned at home every year.

As a doula (childbirth support person), I try to educate people about the physiology of labor and birth, and always go over the signs of early labor with my clients at one of our first meetings. Most women experience many hours of clearly identifiable labor before the birth of their baby, but everybody and every birth experience is different. Some women experience very rapid labors; when a baby is born extremely quickly, with a labor of less than three hours, it is called precipitous birth. It is responsible as expectant parents to learn about what to do in case you end up with an unplanned homebirth, particularly if you live in a remote area, have uncertain transportation, a long commute to your planned birthing place, or may encounter inclement weather.

For this article, I'm addressing unplanned homebirths, or births that occur in unexpected locations (such as your car). There is a group of people who promote the idea of "unassisted childbirth," meaning that only the mother or parents deliver their baby. While some people are comfortable and confident with this, I believe that laboring women can benefit from experienced, knowledgeable birth attendants, and that it is always best to have a professional available to help (licensed or lay midwives, doctors, nurses, or whoever you choose) in case of an emergency or surprises.

However, sometimes birth can go extremely fast, or events may prevent you from reaching your birthing place of choice or prevent your birth attendant from reaching you, such as extreme weather, washed-out roads, or car breakdowns. My midwives shared a story with me of a woman they knew who gave birth at her friend's house, after getting stuck in a snowstorm during some rough winter weather here in the Pacific Northwest a few years ago. So, we should all be prepared for the possibility of an unassisted birth.

There are limited statistics available about unplanned homebirths. The most recent data is from 2006, when only 19 states were using a new birth certificate reporting system that includes a question about whether a homebirth was planned or unplanned. At that time, only 16.8% of homebirths in these 19 states were unplanned. Of the nearly 25,000 homebirths in the U.S. that year, between 3,000 and 5,000 of them may have been unplanned.

The first thing to do is throw out everything you have seen in movies or on T.V., although boiling water and gathering towels are a good place to start in terms of supplies. Please forget about yelling at the mother to push, the mother lying down on her back to deliver the baby, or ever reaching hands or fingers into the mother's vagina, unless you are the laboring woman and you have washed your hands.

In natural labor — which it will always be if you are out of a hospital — and in cases of precipitous labor, most mothers will instinctively get into the best position for them to push out the baby, which may be hands and knees, kneeling, side-lying, squatting, or standing. All of those positions are OK. The best thing for an observer, helper, or partner to do (after calling for help) is to encourage the mother, help her with whatever she asks for, stay with her, and clean up the mess that may ensue. The best thing for the mother to do is to pay attention to her body and how she is feeling (eat and drink as she feels like and use the bathroom often), and to try to stay relaxed.

During labor

If you are at home and your baby is coming more quickly than you can get help, warm the room you are in, and prepare warm blankets (warm in a low oven, wrapped in foil, or in the dryer), get a bowl to catch the placenta, get clean towels for the mother to sit on and absorb amniotic fluid and blood, and wash your hands thoroughly if you might touch the baby.

If you want to try to slow down the birth to allow more time for care providers to arrive, and mom is willing to change positions, try side-lying or knees-to-chest positions for the mom (like on all fours, but with the upper body resting on a pillow).

Let the mother catch her own baby, if she is in a position to do so. Do not tug on the baby or on the cord after the baby is born. If the baby gets stuck at the shoulders and mother's pushing alone is not bringing the baby out further, help the mother turn onto all fours, which may help the baby maneuver out. If that still doesn't work, the mom may try reaching in to grab under the baby's armpit with a finger and help pull the baby out on her own (this is known as the Gaskin maneuver).

After the baby is born

It is perfectly fine (and actually safer, unless you have training) to leave the umbilical cord attached to the baby. While it is still pulsing, it is still delivering vital oxygen and nutrients to the baby. Sterile scissors (boiled for 10 minutes) can be used to cut the cord, and strong embroidery thread can be used to tie off the cord.

Do not try to pull the placenta out by the umbilical cord. Once the placenta is delivered (anywhere from a few minutes to an hour or more after the baby arrives), you can put it in a bowl or a bag. Some people choose to leave the cord and placenta alone until they naturally detach from the baby, which is known as "lotus birth."

The best place for the newly born baby is on the mother's bare chest, covered by warm blankets. If the baby is bluish, gentle but vigorous rubbing of the body can help with circulation. If the baby's airways are clogged, try holding him with the head slightly lower than the body to help it to drain. There may be a white, lotion-like substance on the baby's body, called vernix. Just rub it into the skin. There is no need to bathe the baby unless there is meconium (first bowel movement) on the baby. Note: passing meconium before birth may be a sign that the baby is distressed, so if you haven't already, call your care providers at this point.

To slow the mother's bleeding after birth, strongly massage the uterus through the mother's abdomen. She may do this herself. Also, putting the baby to the breast to suckle can stimulate the uterus to tighten up, helping to limit bleeding from the placental site. The best position for the mother is reclining or lying down after the birth. She should get up to use the bathroom only with someone accompanying her, in case she experiences faintness or an increase in bleeding.

If something seems wrong at any time, call 9-1-1, if you haven't already.

If you are in the car and know you won't make it to your planned birthing location, pull over and call for help, and try to follow the above guidelines. It is a good idea to have towels and a change of clothes in your car if you are planning to drive to a hospital or birth center to give birth, just in case.

This information is just a starting point for informing yourself about what to do in the event of an unplanned homebirth or a precipitous labor. If you think you have a high likelihood of birthing (or being present at a birth) without trained medical assistance or a midwife present, enroll in a childbirth education class, and read as many books as you can about birth to prepare yourself.

Even if you plan to give birth in a hospital, it is only prudent to prepare for the possibility of a homebirth. We all have a responsibility to care for ourselves and our children, and the more knowledge you have about your body and your choices, the better off you'll be. Δ

The physiology of birth

The mother's body

The uterus is the baby's home during pregnancy. Within the uterus, the baby is inside a bag of waters called the amniotic sac. The sac may break at the start of labor or any time during, or the baby may be born within or partially within it, although this is very rare. The waters should be mostly clear and have a salty odor. If the waters are green or brown tinged, the baby may have had the first bowel movement, which may be a sign of distress. The muscles of the uterus contract during labor, pushing the baby down and pulling the cervix open. The cervix is the opening at the base of the uterus, which goes from nearly closed to roughly 10 cm open in the course of labor. The birth canal, or vagina, is between the cervix and the exterior genitalia, or vulva. Women typically feel waves of squeezing as the uterus contracts rhythmically, every couple of minutes. As the baby descends in the mother's body, the mother may feel the urge to go to the bathroom. When the baby's head is crowning (beginning to come out of the mother's body), she may feel burning or stinging, or feel ecstatic. The baby is born and placed in the mother's arms, snuggled onto her abdomen or chest.

The baby's body

A head-down birth is most common. Feet or bottom down is called "breech" and is a riskier way for a baby to be born, as the umbilical cord is more likely to become compressed by the baby's head when the head emerges last. Babies are usually reddish, bluish, or purple when born, and should become more pink (for Caucasian children) as they recover from the squeezing of labor within a few minutes. They may have a white coating of vernix on their skin. The umbilical cord connects the baby to the placenta, which is the source of nourishment from the mother's body. The placenta will be delivered after the baby, usually a few minutes later, but it could be up to an hour or more afterwards.

Horse labor and putting up firewood

By Tom Kovach

It never ceases to amaze me how hard my parents and others worked on farms before the advent of power equipment, power saws, and tractors. The horses did the bulk of the work, that's true, but there was a lot of sweat and toil from every man, woman, or child who worked on a farm prior to modern machinery.

I grew up on a farm in north central Minnesota, and we didn't get electricity until 1950 when I was five years old. My dad worked with horses until he got a tractor in the early 1950s. When they say farmers work from sunup to sundown, that's not exactly true — they actually worked before sunup and after sundown.

There were ten of us children (I was the youngest) and lots of chores — milking, taking care of a huge vegetable garden, putting up hay, etc., — but putting up all the firewood for the winter is what really amazes me.

My father, Joseph Kovach, used horses on our farm until the 1950s.

My dad would go cut wood when all the other chores were done. He'd use dead trees if they were available, otherwise he'd have to cut down live ones and let them dry and season for about a year. He'd use anything, but the best firewood was red or white oak. Ash, pine, and others were also used. All this cutting was done by hand. My dad kept a very sharp double-bladed axe and a hand saw for all of his tree cutting. He bought his first gas-powered chainsaw much later.

My mother, Mary Kovach, stands with two of our farm horses.

Through the years, I've cut a lot of wood with a chainsaw. It makes things much, much easier, but it still involves a lot of work. But then I think, wow! My dad did all of his cutting in those days by hand! He felled those trees with an axe, and then he used the hand saw to cut them into small-enough pieces to fit the wood-burning stove in our house.

Most of the wood wasn't for cash. He'd take it to a general store in town and trade it for things we couldn't grow, like sugar and coffee. He'd also trade some of the wood for shoes or other clothing for us kids. Oftentimes he'd take a load of wood into town on a sled pulled by our work horses. The horses got through drifts where the old vehicles of the day could not make it.

Working in the woods is not only hard work, it's also dangerous. One time a log fell on my dad and broke his leg. He tried to ride one of the horses home but that only made matters worse as the tired horse spooked and kicked his bad foot. Not only was he hurt badly, but he couldn't help around the farm for weeks. Those were the hazards of cutting wood; it's risky business now, but it was downright dangerous back then.

Horses did all the pulling and lifting, but a human hand always had to be there to direct them and give them commands.

To emphasize how important horses were to the wood-cutting operation of those days, I recall a funny story a friend told. He's about ten years older than me, and as a teenager he worked with his dad and the farm horses. He remembers one time his dad hired out his team of horses to a local farmer to skid logs out of the woods. The horses were paid 50 cents an hour, and my friend as a teenager was only paid 25 cents an hour. The value of the horses was never overlooked.

When I think back about how hard my father worked with the horses and his hands to put up firewood, I am truly amazed. I also realize how much things have changed. Wood-cutting and other farm chores are so much easier, quicker, and safer today. I certainly give my father, and many others like him, credit for how hard they worked to keep their families warm and fed in those early years. Δ

Reload your own brass

By Dale Petry

Not long ago a friend called to say he had seen an unusual rifle at the local gun shop. Shortly after that call I found myself in possession of a very nice Marlin M375, which was Marlin's 336 lever action chambered in .375 Winchester. Unfortunately, that shop didn't have any .375 Winchester ammunition. A quick search of the shelves of three other shops revealed that .375 Winchester cartridges are scarce and more than a little expensive. When I finally did locate two dusty and neglected boxes of shells, I was dismayed to find them priced at nearly $44 per box.

Instead of forking over $88 for two boxes of shells, I simply checked a few catalogs, ordered some dies and a few components, and loaded my own ammunition. My total cost per box was $9.26 — a significant savings.

Ammunition has never been cheap, but it has skyrocketed in price over the past few years. For most of us, ammunition priced at $40 or more per box usually means that an otherwise useful firearm ends up standing in a corner to collect dust. It's simply too expensive to shoot such costly ammunition with any real degree of regularity.

One reason ammunition is expensive is the cost of raw materials. The price of copper and lead have gone up, dragging the cost of cartridges skyward with them. What many people don't realize is that the shiny brass case represents a very large portion of the cost of a cartridge. If you pick up that fired case and reload it, you can easily make ammunition for less than half the cost of buying factory-loaded shells. Such reuse is also environmentally friendly.

These two boxes of .375 Winchester shells would cost close to $90 at the local gun shop. The author reloaded both boxes for less than $20 total.

There is another reason why ammunition is expensive: Economies of scale. The large ammunition companies can make cartridges relatively cheaply when they set up a manufacturing line for a common caliber like .30-30 or .308 and then run millions of those cartridges. On the other hand, it is much more expensive for them to stop that line, then spend considerable time retooling and resetting equipment to produce a small batch of cartridges in a rare or obscure chambering such as .218 Bee, .25-35 Winchester, or the like. If you own a firearm chambered for a rare cartridge then you know that such ammunition is usually expensive and often hard to find.

Reloaders can make their own supply of ammunition for far less money. I have been safely and successfully reloading for more than 20 years. Reloading is easy and safe provided you exercise a little care and caution. If you can read a cookbook and follow a recipe, you can reload your own ammunition.

Types of equipment

There are several different types of equipment that can be used to reload. There are progressive reloading machines, capable of reloading 500 or more rounds per hour and frequently costing $500 to $1000. These units are complex and typically not recommended for the novice reloader. On the other end of the spectrum is the Lee Loader. These simple die kits can usually be found for about $30, and they do effectively reload cartridges. Unfortunately, I have found the Lee Loader somewhat slow to use.

The more common reloading setup consists of a single stage press, a set of dies, powder measure, scale, and a few other odds and ends. These machines are simple to set up, easy to use, and are capable of respectable reloading rates. With a little practice and some basic familiarity, it is easy to load 100 rounds in an hour. That hour of work can generate a savings of $100 or more.

Prices for basic, no-frills, single stage reloading kits vary considerably. The Lee Challenger reloading kit costs about $100. This equipment is a little on the rudimentary side, but it works. The Hornady Lock-N-Load Classic kit and the RCBS Rock Chucker Supreme kit both cost more (about $325) but are definitely heavier, better constructed, and built with an eye towards longevity. My own RCBS kit was purchased 21 years ago and has seen extensive service. I fully expect it to serve another two or three decades. Along with a reloading kit, you'll also need to budget around $40 for dies and a shellholder.

Other components

In addition to the equipment, you'll need your fired cases, some bullets, powder, and primers. Your local gun shop is often the best place to buy these components. Primers and powder can be mail ordered, but the extra charge for hazardous materials shipping quickly make mail order more expensive. Most local shops in my area sell primers for about $3.50 per box of 100. A pound of powder usually costs $20 - $25 and will load between 150 and 200 rounds of common deer cartridges. You'll likely pay about $12 per hundred for 50- and 55-grain .22 bullets used for cartridges like .223. Larger 120- to 180-grain soft point bullets in most calibers run about $20 - $24 per hundred. Expect to spend around $50 to buy the primers, powder, and bullets needed to start loading your fired cases.

While we are on the topic of "hazardous materials," let's clear up a common misconception: modern smokeless gunpowder is not explosive. When burned in a confined

These empty cases, new primers, powder, and box of bullets are destined to become low-recoil .260 Remington loads for the author's daughter.

space (like the inside of a rifle barrel) it generates rapidly expanding gases that propel a bullet. It will readily ignite, but outside of a gun barrel, or other pressurized area, modern gunpowder hisses, burns, and makes smoke, but it does not explode. I am far more concerned about the explosive potential of a gallon of gasoline in my shed than I am about a few pounds of gunpowder in my house. Store gunpowder in its original factory container, keep it cool, dry, and away from open flames, and it's relatively benign.

Read the manual

The reloading process is simple. Your first task is to obtain a reputable reloading manual and read it. Read it carefully. Speer publishes an excellent reloading manual and I highly recommend it. It has an excellent section that details the reloading process step-by-step. Each different cartridge has its own section and lists several "recipes" for tried and tested loads. Each recipe or load will detail very specific components. Your job is to follow these tested recipes *exactly*. Reloading is quite safe, provided you follow these tested loads. Substitutions and changes to these loads are *not* recommended!

Reloading

Once you've read the reloading manual and obtained your reloading kit and components, you are ready to begin. The press needs to be securely mounted to a stable surface such as a workbench or sturdy table. If you are reluctant to drill holes in the dining room table, simply mount the press to a scrap piece of 2x6 lumber, and then use C-clamps to secure the lumber to the table.

Setting up and adjusting equipment varies from manufacturer to manufacturer. I've used equipment made by Lee, Lyman, RCBS, Hornady, Redding and others. The basic reloading process is very much the same regardless of the brand of equipment you buy. Simply thread the resizing die into the press and adjust according to the maker's instructions. Lightly lubricate several fired cases with sizing lubricant and place one case on the press ram. Pull the operating handle. The die will simultaneously resize the case and punch out the spent primer.

It is then a simple matter to use a repriming tool to place a new primer in each case. Fill the primer tray with appropriate primers, place a case on the tool, and squeeze the handle. Your resized case is now reprimed and ready to hold the correct amount of an appropriate powder.

Mount the powder dispenser to the bench (or scrap lumber as with the press). Check and re-check your reloading manual. You will have to adjust the dispenser so that it drops exactly the right amount of powder each time you operate the handle. Adjustment is simple and usually requires turning a single knob, dropping a charge of powder, and checking the charge on your scale. With a little trial and error you can have the dispenser adjusted and ready to go in less than a minute. Once the dispenser is correctly adjusted for the specific powder you are using, you can simply place each case under the dispenser and operate the handle. Each case will be filled with the appropriate amount of powder. It is important that you work systematically and carefully. Place one charge in each case and *one charge only!* Visually inspect each case to ensure that each case has an appropriate powder charge.

Now you can install the seating die in the press and adjust it according to the manufacturer's instructions. It may take a few minutes the first time you do this, but with a little practice it is an adjustment that can be made in a minute or less. Place a resized, reprimed, and charged case in the press, carefully place a bullet in the case neck, and pull the operating handle. You have just created a reloaded cartridge!

Potential savings

Buying the equipment and the components can be a considerable investment. Whether or not it's an investment that pays for itself is largely a function of two factors: how often you shoot, and what calibers you shoot. If you shoot infrequently, it would take many years to recoup a $300 investment. If, however, you enjoy shooting, practice regularly, and end up shooting a box or more of ammunition each month, you can pay off the investment and realize considerable savings in a year or two.

There are savings to be had on almost any caliber of centerfire ammunition. .223, .30-30 and .308 are common calibers and are priced somewhat more reasonably than rare calibers, but you can still save about 50% over the cost of factory ammo by reloading them yourself.

Very real savings can be had by loading your own "high performance" loads. Regular soft point factory ammunition in .243, .270, .308 or .30-06 can be found in every gun shop for

A neat, well-organized work space helps keep everything orderly. There is less chance of making a mistake if your workspace is well laid out.

Reloaded cartridges work great! The author took this fine 198-pound Adirondack buck with one reloaded .308 cartridge.

about $20 per box. If you are looking for something using a specialized high performance bullet like the Nosler Partition, you can expect to pay $40 or more per box. Reloaders can create performance ammunition using these premium bullets for far less money.

Perhaps the greatest savings occur when you happen to own and shoot an "oddball" caliber. I've been loading .218 Bee for an old 1940s vintage Winchester Model 43 for many years. These fine little varmint shells cost $78 per box at the gun shop. I load them for about $11. It doesn't take long to recover the cost of a basic reloading kit when you can save close to $67 on a single box of ammunition. In addition to the .218 Bee and .375 Winchester, I have reloaded .32-20, .38/55, .350 Remington Magnum, and a truly antiquated round called the .310 Martini Cadet. The per box savings on all of these cartridges was substantial.

Reloading fired cases definitely saves money. The prudent reloader saves all fired cartridge cases and can often get a half dozen or so firings out of a particular case before it is too old to be reused. At some point it necessary to find more cartridge cases to reload. You can often find them lying about at informal ranges that seem to spring up in abandoned gravel pits. Friends who don't reload are often happy to give you their fired cases (especially if you repay them with the occasional box of reloads). Sometimes it is necessary to buy new, never-fired, empty cases. Most cases cost somewhere between 25 and 50 cents each. Buying cases will make reloading somewhat more expensive, but the savings are still significant. That $8.56 box of .308 Winchester reloads would cost me closer to $10.50 if I had to factor in the cost of buying new brass every once in a while. Even with this added expenditure, the reloads are still half the cost of factory-loaded ammunition.

I know that my investment in reloading equipment has paid itself off in the form of savings many years ago. Any time I buy a new firearm it's a simple matter of buying another set of dies for $30 or so and I'm able to reload this new cartridge as well. It's an investment that provides great savings, great personal satisfaction, and a measure of independence. Δ

Reloading equipment and component suppliers:

Midway USA
www.midwayusa.com
1-800-243-3220

Natchez Shooters Supply
www.natchezss.com
1-800-251-7839

Cabela's
www.cabelas.com
1-800-237-4444

Recycled saw blade knives

By Winston Foster

If you're looking to get further use from an old circular saw blade, try making some recycled knives from it. The one used here was a 10-inch diameter blade, but other sizes could be used.

I drew up a pattern for a curved hunting or skinning knife with a slightly tilted handle. After cutting out paper patterns that suited me, I traced them onto the saw blade. As an afterthought, I traced a couple of ulu blades, too. Curved ulu knives are of Eskimo design and work well on kitchen vegetables as well as meat.

I found a welder who cut out my patterns with an electric plasma cutter, then touched up the edges with a grinder. He also burned a pair of 1/8-inch holes through each handle so I could rivet the leather handles in place (this steel is too hard to drill).

In my design, the handle is slightly narrower than the back of the blade. This way I can slide a brass hilt down the handle, but it won't slip over the blade. I suggest the hilt be just large enough to prevent your hand sliding down the blade, but no larger or it will get in the way of your work. Large hilts are a nuisance unless you're planning a knife fight with a Comanchero.

I cut the brass hilt blank from a piece of scrap brass that was about 1/8-inch thick and was the width of the planned thick leather handles. To make the slot in the hilt, I used a metal drill bit to drill a line of small holes down the center. I cut between the holes with a hacksaw blade, then I carefully enlarged the slot with a tiny file until it fit on the handle.

As a special design on the skinning knives I added a thumb rest on the top of the hilt. This was another piece of

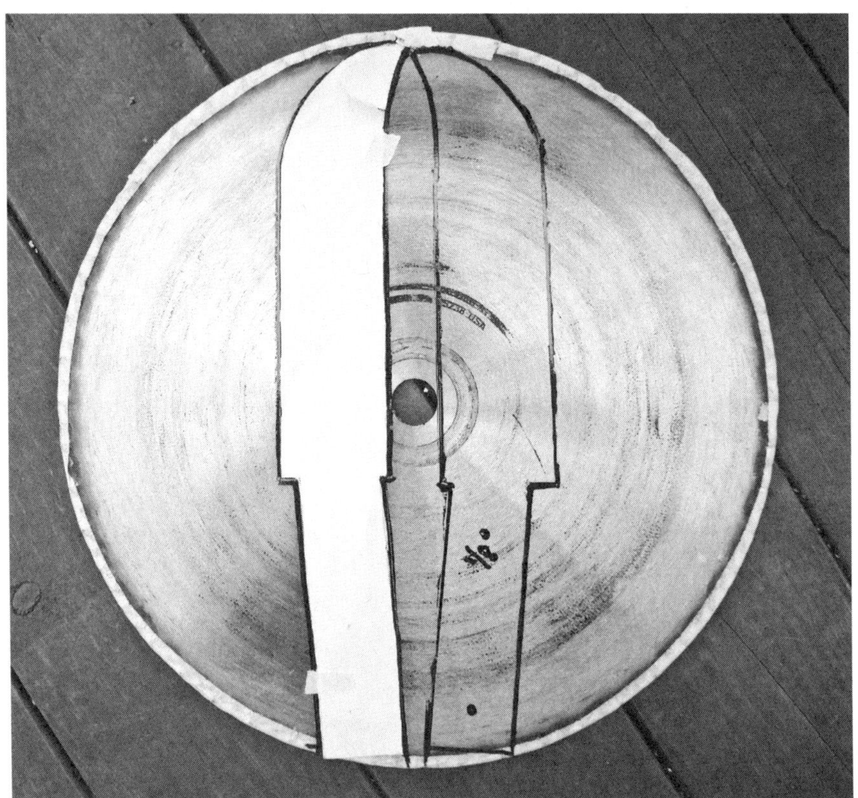

The knife patterns are traced onto the sawblade.

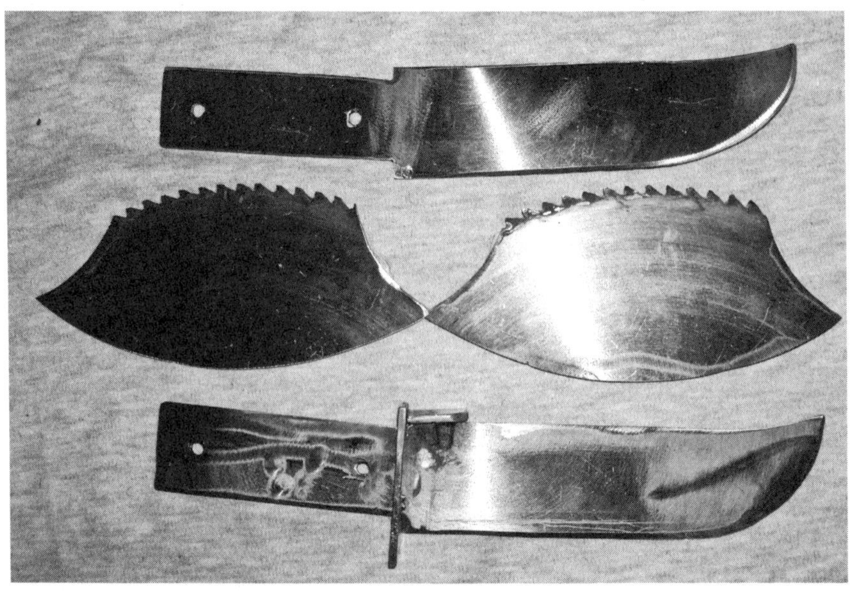

The knife and ulu blanks with a partially-completed knife

The finished skinning knife, ulu, and sheaths

hilt brass with a groove cut partway into the bottom edge to help stabilize it on top of the blade. With some luck and the proper brass, the hilt and thumb rest could possibly be bent using a single piece of brass.

I prepared both the hilt and blade for soldering by pre-tinning both, then reheated them and soldered the brass pieces to the blade.

As I do on any knife I get ahold of, I drilled holes in the hilt just in case I need to attach the knife to a long spear handle.

To attach the thick leather pieces to the handle, I glued one of them on with contact cement tight up against the hilt, then drilled out the rivet holes. The other side was then glued on and drilled from the far side. I pushed copper rivets through the holes, hammered them into place using a ball peen hammer, then used a file to smooth off the riveted side.

The knife cases were made using leather recycled from an old briefcase. The handle-holding strap was riveted to the belt loop with a smaller rivet.

I used a hand saw to cut a tight slot in a scrap of walnut wood to make handles for the ulus. I wiped epoxy glue on the blade and into the slot, carefully centered the blade in the slot, then tapped it in place and let it dry. After that I sharpened and resharpened the blades. Δ

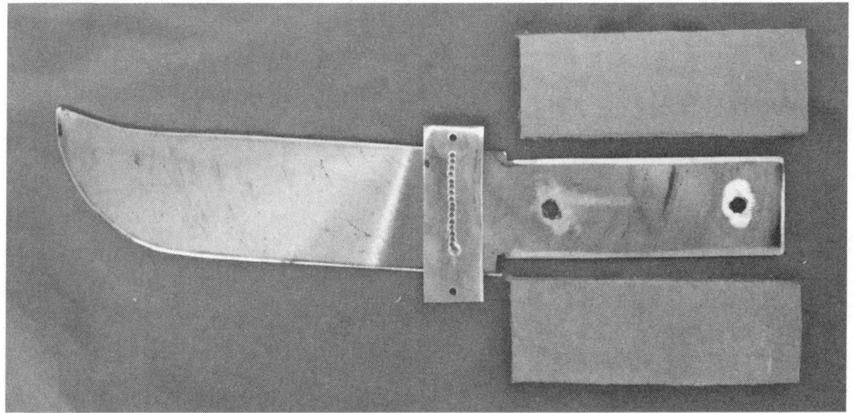

The knife, brass hilt, and leather handle blanks

Other titles available from Backwoods Home Magazine

The Best of the First Two Years
A Backwoods Home Anthology — The Third Year
A Backwoods Home Anthology — The Fourth Year
A Backwoods Home Anthology — The Fifth Year
A Backwoods Home Anthology — The Sixth Year
A Backwoods Home Anthology — The Seventh Year
A Backwoods Home Anthology — The Eighth Year
A Backwoods Home Anthology — The Ninth Year
A Backwoods Home Anthology — The Tenth Year
A Backwoods Home Anthology — The Eleventh Year
A Backwoods Home Anthology — The Twelfth Year
A Backwoods Home Anthology — The Thirteenth Year
A Backwoods Home Anthology — The Fourteenth Year
A Backwoods Home Anthology — The Fifteenth Year
A Backwoods Home Anthology — The Sixteenth Year
A Backwoods Home Anthology — The Seventeenth Year
A Backwoods Home Anthology — The Eighteenth Year
A Backwoods Home Anthology — The Nineteenth Year
A Backwoods Home Anthology — The Twentieth Year
A Backwoods Home Anthology — The Twenty-first Year
A Backwoods Home Anthology — The Twenty-second Year
Emergency Preparedness and Survival Guide
Backwoods Home Cooking
Can America Be Saved From Stupid People
The Coming American Dictatorship — Parts I-XI
Hardyville Tales
Creative Home Improvement
Chickens — a beginner's handbook
Starting Over — Chronicles of a Self-Reliant Woman
Dairy Goats — a beginner's handbook
Self-reliance — Recession-proof your pantry
Making a Living — Creating your own job
Harvesting the Wild: gathering & using food from nature
Growing and Canning Your Own Food
Jackie Clay's Pantry Cookbook
Homesteading Simplified: Living the good life without losing your mind
Ask Jackie: Animals
Ask Jackie: Canning Basics
Ask Jackie: Food Storage
Ask Jackie: Gardening
Ask Jackie: Homestead Cooking
Ask Jackie: Homesteading
Ask Jackie: Pressure Canning
Ask Jackie: Water Bath Canning